keeping archives

3RD EDITION

Editors

Jackie Bettington

Kim Eberhard

Rowena Loo

Clive Smith

AUSTRALIAN SOCIETY *of* ARCHIVISTS Inc.

First published 1987
Second edition 1993
Third edition 2008

Australian Society of Archivists, Inc.
Canberra, ACT, Australia
www.archivists.org.au

Published by the Australian Society of Archivists Inc.

National Library of Australia Cataloguing-in-Publication data

Keeping archives

Bibliography
Includes index
ISBN: 978-0-9803352-4-8

1. Archives – Administration. 2. Archives – Textbooks. 3. Archival resources – Textbooks. I. Bettington, Jackie 1968 – II. Australian Society of Archivists.

025.1714

Design and typesetting by Deborah McLeod of Double Up Productions Pty Ltd
Printed in Australia by Superfine Printing Co Pty Ltd

contents

acknowledgements

Editors

Jackie Bettington, Kim Eberhard, Rowena Loo and Clive Smith.

Authors

Jackie Bettington, Peter Crush, Louise Curham, Lisa Darnell, Kim Eberhard, Cassandra Findlay, Robyn Gamble, Elizabeth Hadlow, Jenni Jeremy, Lyall Kupke, Ted Ling, Rowena Loo, Lyn Milton, Ann Pederson, David Roberts, Maggie Shapley, Steve Stefanopoulos and Enid Woodley.

Reviewers

Adrian Cunningham, Kathryn Dan, James Doag, Robert French, Nola Fulwood, Belinda Hennessy, Ian Gilmour, Sally Golding, Christine Ianna, Lucas Ihlein, Annabel Lloyd, Sigrid McCausland, Colleen McEwen, Lyn Milton, Mick Newnham, Mary Paton, Margaret Pember, Bob Pymm, Catherine Robinson, Maggie Shapley, Peter Shaw and Phil Taylor.

Photographs

Rahnee Alvarez, Kim Eberhard, Sally Golding, Pat Jackson, Lauri Korhonen, Kevin Loo Loredana Napoli, Tim Robinson, Emma Scott, Peter Shaw, Betty Stirton. Abbotsleigh, Aquinas College, Archives New Zealand, Australian Society of Archivists, Bunbury Cathedral Grammar School, Community and Personal Histories (QLD), Knox Grammar School, Library & Archives Canada, Loreto Mandeville Hall, Loreto Province Archives, Meriden, National Archives of Australia, Noel Butlin Archives Centre, North Sydney Boys' High School, Northern Territory Archives Service, Presbyterian Ladies' College Sydney, Public Records Office Victoria, Queensland State Archives, Ravenswood, Roseville College, St Aloysius' College, St Ignatius' College Riverview, St John NSW, State Library of Queensland, State Records New South Wales, State Records Office of Western Australia, University of Sydney and Waverley College.

Cartoons

Michael Burke, Bearfacts.

Drawings

Frank Upward, David McCarthy, Archival Survival and Deborah McLeod.

Design & Layout

Deborah McLeod, Double Up Productions Pty Ltd.

Copy editing

Lynne Cafferky and Ann Mealey, Wordsmart.

Indexing

John Simkin.

Screen shots & Web pages

Australian Society of Archivists, City of Sydney Archives, Collections Australia Network, MoReq, National Archives of Australia, One-2-One, Public Records Office of Victoria, State Records New South Wales, Tabularium, The National Archives (UK), University of Adelaide and University of Melbourne Archives.

Special Thanks

Alison Bell, Debby Cramer, Amanda Daylight, Sr Theresa Elliott, Julie Gleaves, Angela Henrickson, Geoff McIntyre, Sarah O'Neill, Nicki Ottavi, Margaret Paterson, Mary Paton, David Roberts, Steve Stefanopoulos, Kathy Switzer, JoTait, Maianna Tetuira, Diana Tilley-Winyard, Sigrid McCausland, Ann Pederson, Gerard Foley and ASA Council.

about the CD

This book includes a CD-ROM which contains a range of resources for the novice archivist. These include sample forms, examples of policies and procedures, checklists, hints and tips. The material on the CD is arranged according to the chapters of this book, although only some chapters have additional material.

The abstract for each chapter highlights whether there are appendices included on the CD. In addition, the CD includes a table of contents to help you navigate the material.

preface

CLIVE SMITH

The first edition of *Keeping Archives* was published (by the Australian Society of Archivists) in 1987. Edited by Ann Pederson, this was a ground-breaking work, providing a comprehensive manual and textbook covering all key areas of archival work. In eleven chapters, it provided a sound and practical introduction for the novice archivist, often working alone in a challenging environment. It also quickly became a basic textbook for students in many courses in archival theory and practice in Australia and beyond.

The spectacular success of the first edition led to a second edition in 1993. Published by DW Thorpe and edited by Judith Ellis, the second edition included a number of new chapters and revised and updated existing chapters. The new material reflected in particular the then emerging debate about the role of the archival profession in the electronic records environment that was threatening to replace the traditional paper-based recordkeeping systems and early articulation of the records continuum.

Fifteen years have now elapsed since the second edition was published. In that time, developments in electronic communication and transaction systems have transformed our world. Most of us communicate primarily via electronic mail. We get our most up-to-date information via the World Wide Web. Governments, businesses, universities and schools not only transact business electronically, but increasingly rely on electronic recordkeeping systems. Archives have not only embraced the new technologies to manage their existing collections and make them accessible, but have also recognised that they need to ensure that the electronic records of today are managed so that the archives of the future are made in the first place, captured into a recordkeeping system and kept, preserved and remain accessible for as long as they are needed.

During this time there has been a steady, even increasing, demand for a new edition of *Keeping Archives.* While it has been a long time coming, that time has seen a number of significant developments in archival theory and practice (for example: the evolution of the records life cycle concept into the multi-dimensional records continuum model; national and international standards for archival description; and national and international standards for records management). These developments have informed, and are reflected in, this new edition.

At the same time, the authors and editors have been conscious of the multiple roles of *Keeping Archives* – trying to simultaneously serve as a practical manual for the novice archivist, a textbook for students and refresher for the experienced archivist. We see the former (i.e. the practical manual) as the greater need, but we hope that, where space limitations might have forced us to curtail or omit discussion of theoretical principles, the endnotes and reading lists will point the interested student and practitioner! in the right direction.

While archival principles and theories unite the work of many archivists, the diversity of environments in which archivists work result in variations in archival practice. This book is not immune to such variety of views and approaches. As with the previous editions, the authors of this edition come from a wide variety of backgrounds, reflective of the diversity of archival roles and environments in which archivists work. Consequently, the various ways of doing archival work are emphasised differently from time to time throughout the book, and readers may need to select the approach or advice that they think best suits their situation. However, where we think that one approach is preferable we say so.

It is simply not possible to include everything we want to include in this book and keep it to a reasonable size (and price). At the same time, we know that most of our readers have ready access to a computer, so we have included a CD-ROM. The appendices have been moved to the CD, and we have also provided copies of the various forms and other documents that you might find useful. Some of these are in Rich Text Format so that you can adapt them to your situation.

Happy archiving!

Clive Smith

section 1
getting **started**

Undertaking the establishment of an archive may seem to be a straight forward task; perhaps it is?

'Keeping archives' seems to imply simply that – keeping 'stuff' which is important.

This section begins to 'unpack' the implications within those two words – 'keeping' and 'archives'. What are archives? What are archivists? What do they do that makes them different from other 'keepers' or information professionals? How do you 'keep' stuff? Where do you keep it? Who keeps what? Where do I begin?

The chapters in this section will provide you with practical guidance on developing frameworks, both figurative *and* physical, for the establishment of an archive and archival program.

The first chapter of this section introduces the archival endeavour and archives profession to new comers. It explains where archives sit in relation to other information institutions and professions. It also provides an overview of the principles which underpin our professional activities, and why these principles differentiate archival practice from, say, library practice. Professional associations play an important role in supporting professional practice, by providing networks and forums for training and on-going education; the Australian Society of Archivists is the leading association in this field in Australia. Our members engage in professional debate and discourse, and have led the way in the development and refinement of new models and paradigms which in turn inform our practice.

The subsequent chapters deal with practical issues which must be considered when starting an archive:

- the legal or policy framework which will support and validate the archive
- how and where to start when establishing a new archive
- the physical framework of the building which will house the archive and archivist
- the steps required in order to maintain the archive – to preserve it – for as long as necessary.

If you are just starting out, it may seem that there is a lot to take in, a lot to understand and organise before you can actually get to work on 'the stuff'. You might find yourself a little overwhelmed: there's so much to do. It's important to remember to take things one step at a time, and to seek advice from people who have been through a similar experience. All of the authors in this book started out once, and were novice archivists once. Draw on their experiences, their skills, and continue to ask questions. Remember that confidence comes with practice. These chapters are a great place to start.

Remember also that the advice and guidance presented here are just that: there are many ways to tackle a project. You might find that what works for some, isn't appropriate to your situation. It is important to adhere to the principles laid out here, but actual practice might differ to suit the needs of your archive. Setting up an archive and archival program will involve developing frameworks, practices and physical environments according to the resources available, all of which can be improved over time. Continually striving to achieve best practice and the highest standards is a good way to approach any undertaking; be assured that many 'out there' are still trying!

CHAPTER 1

what are **archives** & **archival programs**?

ROWENA LOO, KIM EBERHARD & JACKIE BETTINGTON

CHAPTER ABSTRACT

Archivists manage information. They provide links between disparate records, the context in which they were created, their creators, the original 'business' those records documented, and the potential use they have, after day-to-day administrative use has ceased, to researchers. Archives represent a very small percentage of all records created. Archivists are skilled at determining which records should be kept, in addition to managing and providing access to those records.

This chapter will give you an overview of what archives are and what archivists do. It outlines some basic theory and concepts which underpin contemporary archival practice in Australasia.

In this book, we will frequently refer to 'Australasia', a short way of referring to 'Australia and New Zealand'. Archivists (and archival institutions) in both countries have worked together in developing the standards of practice reflected here.

What are archives?

Organisations and individuals have always kept records of their daily activities. Archives are those records that have been selected for on-going retention. The selection could be for many reasons. Some are selected because they are essential for understanding the history of an organisation or family. Others may prove a person's (or an organisation's) rights or entitlements. Other archives are selected and kept because they provide evidence in a broader sense, as they document the development of a nation or society's economy, culture, natural or built environment or government.

The word 'archives' covers a wide variety of records, including the diary rescued from the attic, the manuscript of a novel, letters, official government documents, and files created by business or government. Archives can also include maps, plans, photographs, sound recording and moving images. As business is increasingly done in electronic ways, archives can also be emails, word-processed documents and other digital content.

... and why do they matter?

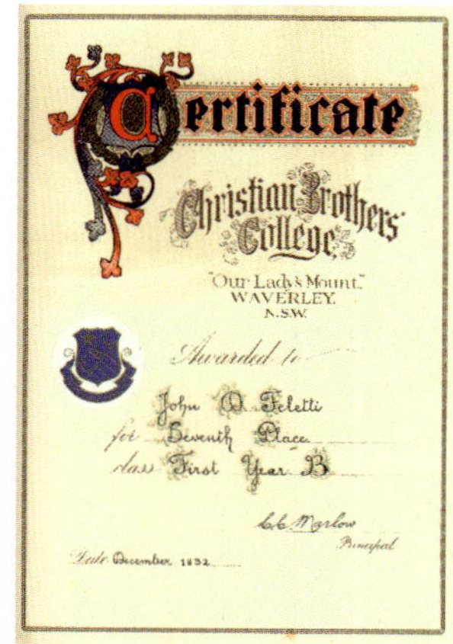

Archives are an asset to an organisation, community, state or nation when they are managed well. Good recordkeeping practices lead to the creation of comprehensive and accurate records, which, by extension, creates good archives. Archives will inform future generations of the actions taken today. Records support accountability and transparency, whether they document the interaction of government and individuals, the management of a golf club, or the administration of a school. Collectively, the records of private corporations, business, community organisations, government agencies, cultural and collecting institutions form the 'story' of a nation, providing evidence of our heritage and cultural identity.

Archives hold much of our personal, corporate and social memory. While they were originally created for a particular business purpose, they are retained and kept for a wide variety of purposes today. They tell our stories, document our identity and have ongoing use for scientific and technical enquiry.

Records of a mine site, abandoned because the yield was too expensive to extract, may be used to show that the mine is worth revisiting with new technology. Weather notes from early colonial settlement may provide raw data for monitoring climate change. Maps, plans and photos can show changing vegetation patterns and architectural drawings can assist in either preserving our built environment, or documenting hazardous materials to protect today's workers.

Records, archives and recordkeeping

Records are 'information, created, received and maintained as evidence and information by an organisation or person in pursuance of legal obligations or the transaction of business' (AS ISO 15489-1 section 3.15). As archives are also records, those records selected for ongoing retention, the terms 'archives' and 'records' are both used in this book.

The term 'recordkeeping' refers to all activities associated with the making and maintaining of complete, accurate and reliable evidence of business transactions (records). This term is used is this book when it is not necessary to distinguish archival functions from traditional records management functions.

Archives and archivists

Records like this – the look, feel and smell – are enough to tempt many into the profession

The value and uses of archives are many and varied. It is the task of the archivist to ensure that archives are selected (or appraised), preserved, arranged and described and made available to researchers so that they can be used, re-used and interpreted for these different purposes. In order to do this, archivists also work to promote archives and archival holdings.

Many archivists also provide advice on the management of records and recordkeeping systems, to ensure that records of current activity are created and maintained, so that archives will be available in the future. With the growth in electronic records, archivists are increasingly becoming involved in the 'front end' of records management. The records continuum model (see below) was developed in light of this integrated view of records and recordkeeping. Increasingly archivists and records managers are seen as part of a single recordkeeping profession.

This book provides practical and theoretical guidance on how to undertake this archival work and manage particular types of records such as photographs, digital records and audio-visual records.

> The Australian and New Zealand Standard Classification of Occupations (ANZSCO) is used for the collection, analysis and reporting of occupational statistics in Australia and New Zealand. Archivists are part of the unit group 'Archivists, Curators and Records Managers' within a broader 'Information and Organisation Professionals' group. The duties of an archivist are described as "Analyses and documents records, and plans and organises systems and procedures for the safekeeping of records and historically valuable documents."
>
> 1220.0 ANZSCO – Australian and New Zealand Standard Classification of Occupations 1st edition, 2006.

Where do archivists work?

Archivists work in a wide variety of places. The Commonwealth and State governments, and some local governments, employ archivists to manage their archival records. Manuscripts libraries and other institutions which collect archives also employ archivists. Business corporations, religious bodies, universities and schools, museums, professional and trade associations, and community organisations are other examples of groups that employ archivists, and some work as private consultants.

A 2004 survey of the Australian Society of Archivists (ASA) membership (Loo 2004) examined where members worked. The table below outlines the responses:

Type of Organisation	Percentage
Government archival institution	27.5
School, church or community archives	25.7
Government agency and statutory authority	20.9
Collecting archive or manuscript library	6.8
Consultant	5.8
Private sector (commercial)	5.5

Other respondents worked for educational institutions or professional organisations.

The professional archivist

The management of archives is based on theoretical principles, which continue to evolve and which are used to guide the practical work of archivists. In recent years, for example, archival theory has focused on how best to achieve proper archival management of electronic records, to ensure they can be preserved and made accessible for the future.

An archivist at work.

In Australia, the recognised professional body to which archivists belong is the Australian Society of Archivists Inc (ASA). Membership of professional bodies such as the ASA, or Archives and Records Association of New Zealand (ARANZ) helps foster professional identity and provides access to networking, support, training and educational opportunities. Professional membership of the ASA requires an Archives Studies qualification from an accredited university plus the equivalent of one year of full-time experience as an archivist (or in closely related work such as records management). Alternatively, a Professional member can have a university degree (in any subject) plus two years of relevant experience.

Professional development is an ongoing commitment, and part of belonging to a recognised profession.

In addition to professional archivists, many people work as voluntary, part-time and honorary archivists, caring for the archives of, for example, schools, community groups and religious bodies. Others combine archives duties with unrelated tasks as part of their responsibilities. Recognising this, the ASA therefore has a category of Associate membership, to which those who work as archivists without qualifications (or who simply support the aims of the Society) are welcomed.

Rows of files or ledgers immediately spring to mind when people first think about records and archives.

Some theory... to underpin the practice

By now you've realised that archives are unique, irreplaceable original 'documents'. Archivists manage records in a physical sense by developing and implementing storage and retrieval systems. They also 'manage' the records in an intellectual sense, by researching and providing details about the provenance and context of the records' creation, i.e. establishing who, why, how, when and where were these records created. Other information is also important: What relationship do the records have with other records? What relationship was there between the agency, or person creating them, with any other agency or person? How do these records fit into a broader social context?

While this book is a practical manual on the 'how' of looking after archives, it is also important to understand some of the theory that explains the 'how'. What are some of the principles archivists adhere to when they 'process' collections?

The work of archivists around the world is unified by adherence to two fundamental and related principles:

- principle of provenance (respect des fonds)
- principle of original order

Applying these two principles together enables archivists to preserve the meaning, integrity and authenticity of records. The following discussion of these principles and other concepts is based on an Australasian perspective of their meaning and use.

Provenance

The principle of provenance is concerned with preserving the relationship between records and those responsible for their creation, management or use. The archival use of the term ' provenance' is similar to its use by museum professionals and art dealers. Art dealers, for example, are concerned with the provenance of art works because the history of ownership of a particular painting may add significant value to what may otherwise be regarded as an ordinary work of art. Provenance in this situation is concerned with understanding the object and connecting it historical significant events, people and places. Paintings and artworks are often made to be sold and frequently change hands. Knowing the history of ownership assists in determining the authenticity and, therefore, their monetary value. Provenance from an archival perspective is also concerned with authenticity, but typically to understand the context of each record and to determine the evidential and informational value of each record.

For archivists the term provenance is concerned with 'administrative' origin and history of a record, record system or collection. It is concerned with identifying, describing and linking administrative relationships between records and those responsible for their creation, management and use over time. Provenance provides essential contextual information for understanding a record. Details about the person, organisation or government department responsible for creating the records provides valuable contextual information such as *why* they were originally created and what relationship a particular series of records may have to others.

Information about provenance proves the origin of documents and records. If records and archives are to provide primary evidence of an act or event, the authenticity of records must be preserved as records move through various hands over time.

Provenance in practice

When receiving transfers of records, it is important to know exactly who created them: Are these records of school attendance from the official roll teachers, or are they a list kept by a prefect with a grudge? Are the minutes of the board meeting the official set signed by the chairperson? Or are they a working version from one of the board members? If the records have passed through several hands – archival repositories, personal ownership etc – the chain of custody must be proven and verified in order to satisfy any doubt about the authenticity of the records. It is essential for an archivist to establish where records originated, and whose hands they have passed through before accepting them into the archives as part of the official record.

Knowing the administrative or social context in which records are created can provide useful background about the how the organisation or individual operated. For this reason, archivists investigate the circumstances surrounding the creation of series of records, not just the content of records. More information about implementing a standardised approach to describing context and relationships can be found in *Describing Archives in Context: A Guide to Australasian Practice.*

Documenting changes in administrative and recordkeeping responsibilities over time also adds to the depth of contextual information; this can also impact on the value of the records. Knowing the administrative or social context in which records are created can provide useful background knowledge about the how the organisation or individual operated. For this reason, archivists investigate the circumstances surrounding the creation of series of records, not just the content of records.

CASE STUDIES ON THE IMPORTANCE OF CONTEXT...

You receive a box of minutes from the OH& S Committee. The more recent minutes are in excellent order, full and complete, whereas the earlier ones are on scraps of paper, and some appear to be missing. Was the OH& S committee established as a routine event, or in response to a major incident? Did the committee exist before the extant minutes indicate? Were minutes not taken? Does this indicate that the organisation did not take safety seriously until something happened?

You are the archivist responsible for the historical records of a group of hospitals in your local area, all of which have since closed or have been incorporated into the local area health service. You find a box of minute books marked 'ladies committee', and at face value, they seem to be minutes of fund raising and charity events, documenting cake stalls, chocolate wheels and two dinner-dances. Some further investigation reveals that the 'ladies committee' was actually an extremely influential group of society women whose fundraising and lobbying efforts in the early 1920s led to the government of the day agreeing to match their fundraising efforts dollar for dollar, with the end result that a hospital was built to the specifications and in the location chosen by the very same women of the 'ladies' committee'. Understanding the social context of the day, and discovering some background information about the ladies in question considerably added to the informational value of the minute books.

A related concept used by early European archivists is *respect des fonds.* 'Fonds' are the entire group or collection of records created by a particular organisation or individual and the 'respect' entailed not mixing the fonds – not mixing records of different provenance. The term 'respect des fonds' also related to preserving the administrative context of records and the relationships between those records. Preserving the relationships between records, for example, may involve documenting that an index relates to a certain series of correspondence or that a register relates to licences issued by a specific government agent. Chapter 8: *Arrangement & Description* provides practical guidance on how archivists apply the Principle of Provenance and Respect des fonds.

Sometimes records are maintained in order, even after administrative use has ceased. This is not always the case.

Original order

Archives are kept in the order in which they were originally created, maintained or used. This is the 'principle of original order'. This principle is applied to enable archivists to preserve the context of the creation and use of records and to maintain the authenticity of those records. This respect, or preservation, of original order is why archives are not rearranged into subject or date order. Such rearrangement would ruin the original context of their creation, thus destroying valuable evidence of the organisation or person who created them.

As outlined above, archives have many potential uses and an archivist cannot know exactly what these uses may be in the future. Rather than rearranging records in a way that might be 'useful' to a particular audience, archivists preserve the original order so that records can be understood in their original context, giving room for users to interpret and analyse the records in a multitude of ways.

If the original order is difficult for users to understand, finding aids (see Chapter 12: *Finding Aids*) may be developed to provide different access points to the records, while still maintaining the original context. Often archivists find it difficult or impossible to identify the original order because those records have been poorly managed, handled or stored. In these situations where observing the principle of original order is not possible archivists will impose a new order based on research and analysis of the administrative history, functions and activities of an organisation. Chapter 8: *Arrangement & Description* provides practical guidance on how archivists create calm and order to a chaotic collection or accumulation of records.

Arranging archives

These two principles of provenance and original order provide the basis for how archivists arrange and describe records. Unlike a book, an archival record cannot be understood on its own as a single item. Meaning comes from its relationships – to other records, and to the organisation/s that created and used it. Archival arrangement and description aims at preserving and documenting these relationships. The emphasis on relationships explains why archivists talk about 'arranging archives' rather than cataloguing individual items.

Early archival practice arranged records in groups, according to the organisation or person that created them (sometimes called the "fonds" or the "record group"). Over time, this has proved to be tricky to maintain, especially if the functions of the organisation or person change over time, it becomes very difficult to keep track of who or what may have been responsible for a particular activity.

Records group? Or records series?

All the records of an inspector are maintained together as one 'record group'. Over time, the responsibilities of the role change – some activities are added; others are divested to other positions within the organisation. How can these changes be tracked if all records are grouped together and described as a single unit? What if the position of the Inspector is abolished, but the function continues to be performed? If you do not know exactly when those changes occurred, or which role assumed responsibility for an activity, how would you find the records of those activities, short of combing through a very large 'group' of records?

A development in Australian practice in the 1960s revolutionised the way records are arranged and described (Scott 1966). Now known as the 'series' system, in practice, it means that the primary unit of arrangement and description is the *record series.* A series is a set of records in the same identifiable sequence or that result from the same function or activity. Record series are then linked to the organisation/s or person/s that created them over time. Thus, if a record series has multiple creators over time, it is included (virtually) in the 'fonds' or 'record group' of each of those creators, and the old problem of having to decide whether to split the series or arbitrarily assign it to one 'fonds' or 'record group' is avoided.

A record series can be comprised of different record formats, or the format can remain the same over long periods of time. Some simple examples of series are:

- minutes of meetings – although minutes of different committees form separate series
- annual reports
- registers of admission
- construction tender ocuments
- architectural plans (for a particular project)
- student files

Where once all of these series had physical entities, such as ledgers, guard files, exercise books, they now all have digital counterparts such as 'Word' documents, web pages or databases. The format may have changed, but the principles involved in managing them have not.

Chapter 8 covers arrangement and description in more detail.

Selecting archives – appraisal

An archivist identifying records of possible long-term value during a hasty office clean-out in 2005.

Not all records are kept forever. As indicated earlier, selecting what records should be retained is a key part of the archivists' role. Selection, known as 'appraisal', is the process of evaluating business activities (or functions) to determine which records need to be captured and how long the records need to be kept in order to meet business needs, the requirements of organisational accountability and community expectations (AS 4390 1996). Researching and analysing the functions of an organisation or person within the broader context of their roles, legal responsibilities, and expectations of the wider community to determine what records should be kept, is a key skill for an archivist.

As with approaches to archival arrangement, approaches to appraisal have also changed over time in response to different ways and means of creating records, and different societal expectations.

A brief history of appraisal....

Archival appraisal emerged in the mid twentieth century in response to the burgeoning growth of paper-based records in government organisations. Early archivists simply accepted whatever records were deposited with them by their creators, and left it to those creators to decide what needed keeping.

In his manual originally published in 1922, English archivist Hilary Jenkinson recognized the necessity for decreasing by selection of some kind the intolerable quantity of documents accumulated by modern administration. However, he did not regard archival appraisal as being the responsibility of archivists. He believed that each record was unique in its context and of equal value and that those involved in the creation and use of records during their active administrative use, were in the best position to determine what should be retained permanently and when it should be transferred to an archive. The archivist's role was primarily to 'preserve' archival records at the end of the active life of those records.

In contrast, US Archivist, T R Schellenberg (1956) advocated that archivists needed to be involved in the selection of records to ensure records of value to researchers were retained. He devised a system of values to assist archivists in making appraisal decisions. He explained that 'public archives have two types of value: a primary value to the originating agency and a secondary value to other agencies and non-government users' (Schellenberg, 1956, p. 28).

Dr Theodore Schellenberg, Director of Archival Management, National Archives (Washington DC) with Robert Sharman of the Archives Office of Tasmania 1954

Schellenberg's 'taxonomy of values' have since become adopted as the appraisal framework throughout the United States and in other English-speaking countries, including Australia.

By the 1970s there emerged increasing criticism of the approaches advocated by Jenkinson and Schellenberg – collectively known as 'traditional approaches to appraisal', 'bottom-up approaches to appraisal' or 'micro-appraisal'. The traditional approaches had worked fairly well in a paper-based world, but the explosive growth in the volumes of records generated in the later decades of the twentieth century, especially in conjunction with the widespread adoption of digital technology, gave rise to a re-examination of these approaches. Critics argued that the traditional approaches involving retrospective file-by-file appraisal could not keep up with the demands of digital recordkeeping and the increasingly dynamic administrative structures, entities and workplaces in which records were generated and used.

In response to these challenges, different approaches to appraisal emerged in the 1990s such as 'macro-appraisal' and 'functional appraisal' (both forms of 'top-down appraisal'). These approaches shifts the focus of appraisal away from individual records or records series to the broader context in which records are created.

Appraisal is covered in more detail in Chapter 5: *Appraisal & Disposal.*

Records Continuum

Traditionally, records management practitioners viewed records as having a 'life cycle', which (despite its name) was a linear progression through a number of defined stages:

- creation
- active use
- intermediate storage
- disposal (either destruction or transfer to archives).

Archivists were involved only at this last stage.

As with changes in appraisal theory, digital recordkeeping also challenged the relevance of this model. The Records Continuum model was developed in the 1990s by Australian academics, and is partially a response to the changes wrought by the digital age.

Unlike the previous 'life cycle' models of records management, the continuum model presents an integrated view of:

> *...the whole extent of a record's existence. Refers to a consistent and coherent regime of management processes from the time of the creation of records (and before creation, in the design of recordkeeping systems), through to the preservation and use of records as archives.* AS4390 pt 1, 4.22

Rather than passing through defined stages, the continuum model sees a record as potentially existing in multiple dimensions:

- **First dimension:** As a 'trace' or record of a particular business activity or transaction
- **Second dimension:** Organised and managed as evidence of that transaction
- **Third dimension:** As part of the entire corporate memory of an organisation
- **Fourth dimension:** 'pluralised' as part of the broader societal memory.

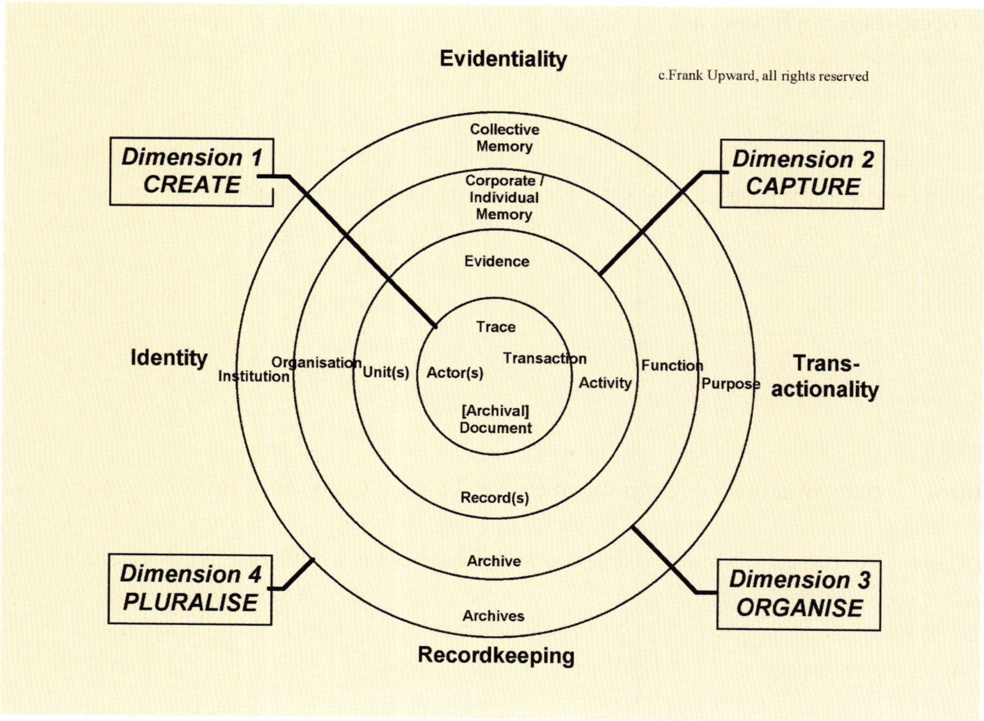

While archives traditionally operate in the third and fourth dimensions, this model recognises that, especially with electronic records, the archivist cannot wait for the records to arrive at the archival doortstep. The archivist must be more proactive in ensuring that appropriate recordkeeping systems, including appropriate policies and practices, are in place so that records are created and maintained.

"By the way, from now on Ed wants to be addressed as, 'Gatekeeper, Protector of the Archives' ..."

It is also useful to recognise that different types of archives (and archivists) usually work in different dimensions. In-house archives generally occupy the third dimension and collecting archives the fourth. Government archives increasingly span the second, third and fourth dimension.

As such, this model is commonly regarded as being more applicable in the government sector where changes to legislation for most archival authorities have given them a stronger role in setting standards and policies for records management. Increasingly however, other archives are becoming involved in the second or third dimensions. For example, in-house archives may find they work more closely with records management staff, and collecting archives may be more proactive in approaching potential donors and explaining what types of records the archives would be interested in retaining (so the famous author does not delete drafts of the great novel, or emails to and from eminent colleagues!).

Professional debates

From the discussion on appraisal and the records continuum, you can see that archival theory and archival practice continue to evolve. This is a symbiotic process, where advances in theory inform practice and practical challenges serve to advance theory.
At any time, there are a number of issues and debates which challenge the profession.
As a practical manual, this book will not go into them in any detail. However, as these debates and challenges can affect the work we do now, and how it may change in the future, some of these current debates are outlined overleaf.

Custodial vs postcustodial archives	Driven by the growth in electronic records, there has been debate as to the extent that archival controls can or should be applied to records left in their original creation environment, as opposed to being brought into the custody of the archive. Post-custodial approaches can also be used to recognise the wishes of creating groups to share control, ownership of or access to, their records.
Proactive vs reactive archival management	Changes in appraisal theory and recordkeeping models have given rise to debate over how proactive archivists should be in the creation and management of records before transfer to an archive. Does proactive involvement undermine the traditional independence or objectivity of an archivist, and was this objectivity only ever illusory anyway?
Memory & heritage vs evidence, business & accountability	The records continuum model has a strong emphasis on records as evidence of business transactions. There is debate on the practice of appraisal as to whether archives should be selected based on the business functions and activities they document, or broader cultural and 'heritage' interests.
Records-centric v macro approaches (functions / society focussed)	Traditionally, appraisal decisions were made by examining the record. As outlined above, there has been a shift to appraising the function rather than the record. There are ongoing debates about the benefits and risks of these approaches.
Power, control and the marginalised in society	It is increasingly being recognised that archives tend to document history from the side of the 'winners'. There is growing interest in how archives can and should document the experiences of the marginalised and dispossessed, and oral rather than written cultures, including, for example, the experiences of Indigenous Australians.

Tensions between privacy and confidentiality vs access	As technology makes it easier to collect and share information, there is also a growing movement to ensure people's privacy is protected. It can be difficult to find an appropriate balance between protecting privacy while providing access to archival records.
A converging vs diverging profession	There is debate as to what extent archivists should remain a stand-alone profession into the future. Who to 'converge' with is a matter of debate – are we 'recordkeeping professionals' with records managers, 'information professionals' with librarians and knowledge managers, or the collections / heritage sector, with libraries, galleries and museums?

Table 1.1: Professional debates

Professional journals, such as *Archives and Manuscripts*, and texts such as *Archives: Recordkeeping in Society* and others listed in Further Reading below, explore these and other debates in more detail.

Professional development ASA Publications

The work of the archivist

In order to professionally manage an archival collection, an archivist needs to be familiar with:

- what records and archives are, and how they have evolved in modern society
- how to collect archives and how to assess the long-term value of records
- how to look after archives
- how to understand legal issues and responsibilities including copyright, confidentiality, privacy and access
- how to arrange and describe archives for management control and to make them available
- how to provide services for those wishing to make use of the archives
- how to encourage people to make use of archives

The sections of this book: *Getting Started, Managing the Archives, Providing Access to Archives,* and *Managing More than Paper,* step you through the basic archival processes and practices common to all archives. While archivists may specialise in certain areas, especially in larger archival organisations, expect to undertake a full range of these activities if you work in a small archives, especially if you work as a 'lone arranger'. A lone arranger is often also conservator, museum curator and perhaps also records manager!

Recordkeeping professionals

As noted earlier, there has been growing convergence between records managers and archivists. The Australian Society of Archivists and Records Management Association of Australasia have developed a joint statement of knowledge for recordkeeping professionals. The statement outlines three common knowledge domains:

1. Purposes and characteristics of records and recordkeeping systems
2. Context
3. Recordkeeping processes and practices.

Table 1.3 Matrix of Knowledge reproduces the matrix from this statement.

Introductory seminars covering the 'basics' of archival practice are regularly offered by the Australian Society of Archivists, as are intensive workshops – Continuing Professional Development – for those with prior education and training.

RECORDKEEPING KNOWLEDGE DOMAINS

TIME: PAST / PRESENT / FUTURE

SPACE / DIMENSION

Knowledge Domain	Knowledge Domain	Knowledge Domain
Purposes & characteristics of records & record-keeping systems	Environmental & recordkeeping context	Recordkeeping processes & practices
Records are: • reliable • authentic • useable • evidential • outcome of social and business activity Systems: • capture, manage and preserve • are compliant • are made up of entities and aggregations • use metadata schemas	Context is about: • expectations of individuals, organisations, communities and society • legislative frameworks • policies and governance • risk • standards • technical frameworks • information management frameworks • stakeholders • culture and language • continuity and change	Practice is about: • documenting context • custody • storage • functional requirements • preservation • care and handling • application of metadata • reference and access • classification • capturing records into systems • business and systems analysis • applying disposal frameworks

Underpinning Knowledge Domain:
Recordkeeping theories & principles

Theory and principles are about:

- systems of control, provenance, original order, classification systems, custody principles
- records continuum theory, life cycle theory, accessibility of records, arrangement & description
- mandate and ownership of business process, risk principles, administrative change, appraisal theories
- ethics and codes of practice, advocacy and education of value of records for memory

DEPTH OF KNOWLEDGE

Figure 1.1: Matrix of Knowledge Domains from Statement of Knowledge for Recordkeeping Professionals.

The matrix illustrates that archivists and records managers, as recordkeeping professionals, share a common body of knowledge, although each group specialises in different areas. The statement ably summarises our common goals:

- recordkeeping professionals support societies, communities and organisations as they try to make meaning out of decisions, actions and memories.
- recordkeeping professionals provide an essential bridge between the past, present and future dimensions in which records and their contexts belong; through understanding the environments that generated the records and the way records act as evidence of those environments.

Conclusion

Archivists are custodians of our social and cultural memory, protecting, preserving and making it available to current and future generations. For those new to the profession, we welcome you to an interesting and rewarding career.

This book will be a useful guide to the many challenges that face the novice (and even the experienced) archivist, whether day to day challenges of engaging with clients or special projects such as arranging microfilming or imaging of certain series of records.

While the book is mainly a practical guide, this chapter has highlighted how theory and principles underpin the work we do and how we do it. With that as background, the next chapter will look at 'Getting Started'.

CHAPTER 2

getting **organised**

KIM EBERHARD

CHAPTER ABSTRACT

For the novice archivist, or even the more experienced one, starting an archives 'from scratch' is a daunting experience. Equally challenging is starting with an archive that may have been poorly managed in the past – and unfortunately this is an all too common experience.

This chapter is your friendly guide to this daunting challenge. It provides advice on the key tools and structures that need to be in place for an archive to effectively operate. It examines the catalyst for establishing the archives, understanding what you already have, so you can develop appropriate policies. It also looks at the who, what and where (staff, resources and facilities) needed for the day to day operation of any archive.

Example policies are included on the accompanying CD.

Some thoughts before you start

You've inherited personal responsibility for an 'archives' – perhaps an overly full filing cabinet, or some 'stuff' collected on the lower shelves of the library stack? Perhaps you've been assigned the role of 'family historian', having rescued a number of shoe boxes full of family papers prior to the sale of an uncle or grandparent's home? Chances are that the bulk of the 'collection' will consist of paper records, ledgers, photos, minute books and a variety of other 'bits' that seem to have no relationship to one another, let alone to the organisation they purport to represent.

You've agreed to 'look after the archives', so where do you start? What is involved? You have little dedicated space, few financial resources, and not much time, at least for now, in which to make things happen.

Establishing an archives program and facility requires careful planning and thought. There are several aspects which need to be considered when getting started.

- the collection and the catalyst – why establish the archives?
- recognition of value, and commitment
- policies to underpin all activities, provide framework and context
- resources – staff, space, budget, materials
- facilities – storage, processing, office and display/exhibition areas

"Ed, I think we need an archivist ..."

It is also important not to let yourself be overwhelmed by the potential magnitude or complexity of the task. Remember to take one step at a time, and be aware that you'll grow more comfortable with your role as you gain experience. The collection itself is obviously the most vital element of all. Strangely, though, dealing with it – *fully* knowing the range, depth, breadth of it, understanding the context of all the disparate parts, and the relationships between them as well as the relationship of the whole archive to the parent organisation and society as a whole – comes *after* the archives are established. While there must be enough realisation of the value of the 'stuff' to instigate the establishment of the archive, true in-depth understanding comes with time.

Ideally, it would be possible to set up an archives – facility and program – by following a series of steps:

- gain an initial level of control of the collection
- create the policy framework
- endorsement of policy – allocation of funds
- design & build facility
- delivery of archival program – all services and processes.

However, the development of an archives rarely follows a linear path. There are several interim steps, and/or deviations along the way. You will need time, dedication, perseverance and energy. Remember that you are not alone, and many have done this before!

In an ideal world, it would be possible to work through an establishment checklist step by step. The reality, however, is usually vastly different. You may find that you are expected to provide a range of services, such as research and displays, in order to strengthen your case for full funding and allocation of necessary resources. This could mean that you and your archival program will need to 'make do' for a period, gradually developing a 'wish' list and/or a facility brief for eventual implementation (with several amendments) while working on policy documents *after* the program has been in operation for a considerable time. All of this is likely to happen *before* you have adequate space in which to carry out all tasks.

Diagram of the steps involved in establishing an archives facility and program

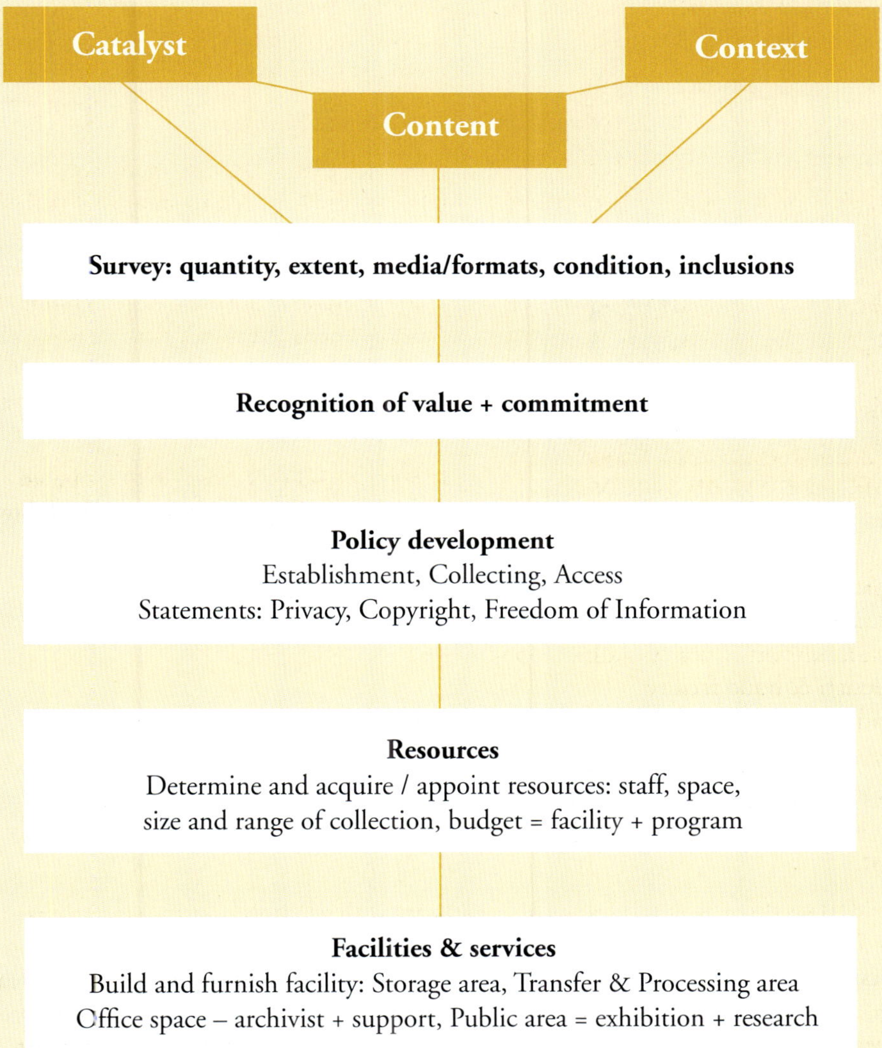

A 'perfect world' step-by-step guide to establishing a new archives program and facility. Reality may mean that some steps occur before others; you will need to revise and review as time passes.

A word of caution: it is possible that you've been lured into accepting responsibility for archives because you have an affinity with 'old' things. It is important to understand that archives have value beyond their *intrinsic* value as 'old' objects. Indeed, many of the records in your archives may be less than 10 years old so are hardly the stuff of popular imagination! Remember that archives are unique, and provide evidence of the actions of an organisation, the development of an area, or the fortunes of a family. Therein lies their true worth.

Arranging a disorganised pile of what looks like worthless junk into a functioning, informative and useful information source is very satisfying. This chapter will guide you through the steps required to make this happen. Taking the first step is the hardest – that involves making decisions about where to start, what to do first, how to find the materials you need, and having confidence in your own ability to make it happen.

The processes involved in establishing a major public archives authority is beyond the scope of this book. Therefore, we will concentrate on the establishment of a small-scale archive that is either a collecting or in-house archive. Both will require very similar organisational commitments, policy frameworks and resources such as staff, facilities and budgets.

The diagram on the facing page outlines the 'big picture' elements involved when establishing an archives program and facility. It will take a significant amount of time to create an archive, a high level of perseverance and energy on the part of the instigator to bring the 'idea' into fruition, and financial resources, preferably available from the outset.

The collection and the catalyst – why are you establishing an archive?

Before you commit to establishing an archive, it is important to assess the motivations behind the idea. It is also important to assess the current 'collection' (if one exists, regardless of its physical condition) as well as the potential or necessity to augment it over time. The thinking and investigations undertaken at this stage will become important later when you are developing the policies and statements which provide the administrative framework for your operations and it is important to keep notes of your findings.

Few archives are established without the prior existence of some form of collected or accumulated material. Gaining an understanding of the type, range and quantity of material is a vital step, as is assessing – in broad terms – its relevance or significance to the organisation, institution, community or society. You need to answer three broad questions:

Catalyst What has prompted the idea of establishing an archive?
Context What and who is the collection for? What are the relationships?
Content What is in the existing collection? Will more need to be found/transferred/bought?

Let's work through these issues one by one.

Catalyst: What has prompted the idea of an archive?

Before...

There are a number of catalysts which result in the establishment of an archives program and facility.

In the public arena, most archives or records authorities exist as a result of a public awareness of the accountability function of recordkeeping. Archives – records of activities, decisions and actions – are the legacy of one generation to the next. The actions of a government affect an entire population and the records of that government form the backbone of the history of that society. Generally speaking, national and state institutions were established throughout the 20th century, although the concept of modern state archives dates from the French Revolution. More recently, especially in third world or former colonial territories such as the Pacific region and throughout Africa, public (government) archives have been established as an indication of independence, and as a counter to corruption and political instability.

A collecting archive may be established where there is a realisation that an area or aspect of society is not being documented elsewhere. Examples of this include the Gay and Lesbian Archive, archives of trade unions and the labour movement, or archives of migrant / ethnic communities.

An in-house archive is usually established in response to an anniversary or event such as the centenary of establishment, new incorporation, a merger or acquisition. It may also come about as the result of one person's dedication over many years, 'keeping' bits of information that they considered too valuable to throw out and in many cases, this turns out to be true! Many organisations have the beginnings of an archive scattered throughout various buildings and storage areas. The impetus for the establishment of a 'proper' archive may come as a result of interest and by way of research queries and requests – from members of the public or former employees and often genealogy will be the main focus of their enquiries.

Whatever the motivation behind the idea of establishing an archive, it is important to ensure that the concept is sustainable, which requires further investigation and thought. You will need to be sure that the collection you intend to manage and use is unique and relevant to the organisation, i.e. you will need to research the context of the collection, and the relationship it has (or does not have) to other existing collections.

Context: Who is this collection for, and what does it relate to?

When making the decision to establish an archive program, it is important to consider what the collection relates to, where it fits within an organisation and its history, as well as the relationships of the collection to collections within other organisations, or held in collecting institutions.

It is important to think about the context of the collection. Where does it fit within the history of the organisation? What does it 'say' about the history of the organisation? Are the records complete, or is there a reason some parts are missing? Are there records of previous or related organisations?

Most in-house archives contain records of activities of the organisation's past, and will limit the collecting activities to the records created *only* by that organisation. However, some also manage the records of predecessor or successor organisations or institutions, for example records of businesses or agencies which have become part of the current organisation through purchase or acquisition. The archives of Westpac Banking Corporation, for example, holds records of several banks which were taken over by the Bank of New South Wales (as Westpac was then known) over time.

Alternatively, the intended archive might also include records of similar organisations, the local area or prominent individuals associated with the organisation. Some archives have a particular subject focus. Melbourne University Archives, for example, actively collects records of business and the Seaborn Foundation at the National Institute of Dramatic Art collects records of performers and performances.

Is there another related institution or organisation which is a more appropriate holder of the collection? If the answer is yes, then the proposal to establish a new archive should be reconsidered.

The range of materials likely to form a small archive

Is there a legal requirement for material to be held or retained, and is that retention a permanent requirement? If yes, then there is an unequivocal reason for the records to be retained. Where, and by whom, is another matter, and should be fully explored before committing resources. It is possible that the records in 'your' care are actually public records (despite, or because of, their age). An example could be records relating to indigenous people, and these may be better placed in the care of specialist keeping places or with state authorities.

Context of the records: is it appropriate to establish an archive with this material?

A group of several hospitals, all once in private or semi private hands, have been amalgamated over approximately 40 years into an area health service administered by a state government. Some hospital campuses are being decommissioned and the land sold. Boxes of records (from at least three formerly independent hospitals) including board records, personnel records and admissions registers, amongst a vast variety and range of other 'bits' are gathered from a building slated for demolition where they have been 'stored' for nearly 20 years. The records are sent to another location, to be sorted, processed and managed as an 'archive'. An area is dedicated for this 'archive' and storage furniture, office equipment and basic supplies are purchased. An archivist is employed to manage the process.

On the surface, there seems to be nothing untoward about this archive. However, some research into the broader context and legal aspects reveals several issues:

Recovery of estrays – removal of significant portions of the collection

Even though much of the material held by this archive is not required, under state legislation, as part of the permanent record of that state, a significant portion is. The state is fully entitled, under an aspect of records legislation in that state, to undertake action to recover 'estrays'. If this action occurs, the archive will be considerably weakened through a loss of material. It will also have committed resources unnecessarily.

Supplementary material exists elsewhere

It was also discovered that another archive was being established at the same time in conjunction with a museum devoted to the nursing profession. Much of the material related to the same hospitals, as they were previously used for teaching and training. The existence of two 'parallel' archives severely limits the resources available to each, and lessens the overall value of each in terms of research and exhibition 'clout'.

Some organisations may have collecting ambits which overlap one another. An example is that of a religious order and school, or chamber of commerce and individual business. Some collecting archives have closely related collecting programs which have had to be refined over time to avoid unnecessary and unhealthy competition. Before you decide to establish an archive, it is advisable to investigate the collecting focus of other institutions. You may find that an archive or collecting institution already exists which has a focus very similar to, or related to, the program you intend to begin.

You will also need to consider the range of existing material, and if necessary, how supplementary material will be collected. Will existing material form the whole collection, or is it possible that more exists elsewhere? What sort of resources will you need to find the 'rest' of the collection? Will material be sought through donations only, by purchase, by targeted approaches to all potential record creators within the chosen field, or through a combination of these approaches? Careful thought will need to be given to each of these methods, as the resource implications of this can be enormous in terms of potential cost (at the very least).

Many archives have been established with an open-door approach to taking in material, in the interests of gaining bulk and therefore 'substance'. This can eventually prove a costly mistake, as the collecting ambit of your archives will definitely have an impact on the resources required to manage the collection, and will later affect, in broad terms, the appraisal practices of the archives. It is essential to deeply consider the implications of a particular collecting focus before you start, as the information you gather now will inform the policies you create later on.

Content: The collection – what's in it?

It is important to gain an overview of the material which will form the archive. The material you initially 'find', or have been given, may not form the entirety of the collection, but could be the foundation of one, and may have been the catalyst for establishment. It is vital to understand, in big picture terms, the quantity, range and breadth of the material, to establish some date ranges and to determine the types of material / media on which the records are stored. It is also important to note the physical condition of the collection – it is unlikely that it will be pristine, free of pests, dirt or damage or deterioration. All of this information will feed directly into the development of your archives facility brief and budget. In some cases, it will be the first level of intellectual control, upon which basic reference and research services may have to rest.

Discovery: the initial survey

An overall survey of the material in question is the first step. This will involve determining the location or locations of the material and gauging the quantity and condition of the material. Allow – in most cases – a day or two to do this. Expect to get dirty, and be prepared to move boxes of all sizes and weights. It may be advisable to have someone with you to assist in this, and to take notes for you, if possible.

You've been shown into a shed/storeroom/attic/ basement in which lies an assortment of boxes, files, containers and objects. This, apparently, is the archive. Chances are that more is stored elsewhere, and you will need to ask questions of relevant staff or people to determine the possible location of more. The best people to ask are long-term office or administrative staff, and the maintenance team.

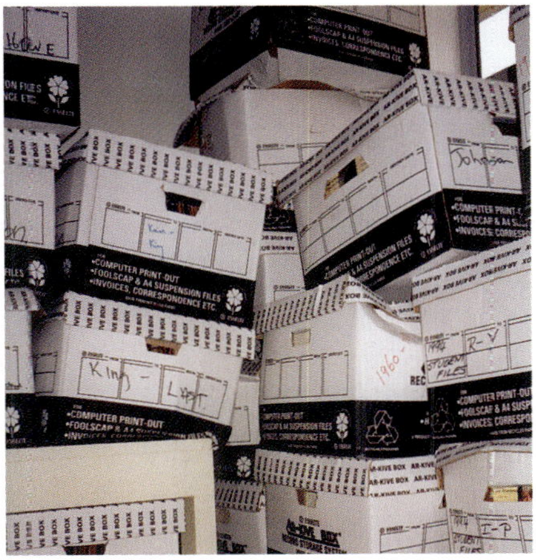

*Getting started – the hardest part is deciding **where** to start!*

Practicalities

Things you'll need to take with you may include paper and pen for taking notes (or a laptop with a long battery life), some sort of overall or coverall for your clothes, possibly a torch and a mobile phone. It is advisable to devise a survey form on which to enter raw data, so that you have quantifiable data upon which to base your reports or findings.

Don't take everything at face value – keep searching

The labels on most boxes of 'stuff' are not accurate, or comprehensive, so don't rely on them! Open a number of boxes, and take a little while to look through them. Try not to get side tracked, remembering that you're after an overview at this stage, not intimate knowledge. That comes later. Paper records will probably form the majority of the material you'll survey, and most contain clues, or metadata, about what it is and where it came from. Take note of file titles and dates on labels. Is the material generic to the main organisation? Or is there an indication that this collection contains 'stuff' from other sources? What is the extent of the collection? Are there administration files? Publications, Minutes, Reports? Is there evidence of a filing system or records schema? You may come across bound volumes, guard files, ledgers, some of which are very heavy and difficult to manoeuvre. These will probably be important. Minutes and reports are generally treated with some respect by an organisation, and they will contain much of the base information you need later to determine an administrative history or 'skeleton' which helps with gaining contextual insights into the overall collection. At the survey stage, however, they will help set time and date frameworks which are vital clues in gauging the extent of the collection. If you've found minute books for 1962–1978, but you know that the organisation existed in the 1920s, chances are that much more material is being stored elsewhere...so you'll need to ask more questions, and keep looking. What types of media are there? Paper records, yes – but what of film, sound recordings, microfilm or fiche, electronic/digital storage media (floppies, CDs, DVDs), photographs (glass negatives, 35mm prints, framed or over-sized images). Are there textiles, trophies, honour boards? Art works? Items which should form part of a museum?

Expect to get dirty

This survey stage is probably when you'll agree with the cliché of 'dusty old archives'. As well as an appreciation of the size of the collection, you will also gain a *feeling* for the condition of the material. Make note of the extent of any damage and if you can read the papers, open the volumes or see the images on the photographs, it's probably not too bad! If there are files which have been eaten through, or volumes/bundles of photographs all stuck together, then you have a problem. Dust, grime, grit, and pest leavings (birds, rodents, and insects) will probably be evident. Other damage will also be apparent – fading from exposure to sunlight, water damage (rising waters from floods, penetration of water from rain, leaks, burst pipes), fire and/or smoke damage. Mould and mildew will be easy to smell as well as see.

While this process turns some people off, it is actually one of the most exciting stages of establishing the archive. This is about discovery and to some extent exploration. By asking questions of people, you begin to form relationships. Your interest in the 'old' stuff is proof that past events and people, are valued. This is the beginning of what archives are all about: forming links between past, present and future.

After the survey is complete, you will have more questions to ask. It is vital that the organisation and the archivist are clear about what will form part of the archive, and what will not. Traditionally, archives and museums are separate institutions, a distinction which may not be clear to those who are commissioning the archive. Information from the survey will help clarify this, and feed into the policy frameworks which form the next step in the process of getting started.

Sometimes a survey is difficult to undertake, even if you know the location of the records.

Value, responsibility and commitment

Collective value

Once you've undertaken the survey, and confirmed that establishing an archives program is the correct way forward, it is important to take stock of what you are about to do. Archives are an asset to an organisation, community, state or nation when they are managed well. Good recordkeeping practices lead to the creation of comprehensive and accurate records, which, by extension, creates good archives that will inform future generations of the actions taken today. Records support accountability and transparency, whether they document the interaction of government and individuals, the management of a golf club, or the administration of a school. Collectively, the records of private corporations, business, community organisations, government agencies, cultural and collecting institutions form the 'story' of a nation. They provide evidence of our heritage and cultural identity. Establishing an archives program is therefore not to be undertaken lightly, given the significance and value of the records in question.

Processed series safely stored in a mobile shelving unit (compactus)

Responsibility and commitment

An archives program should not be established on a whim, or on a temporary basis. Establishing an archives program is tacit acknowledgment of the value of the records to be cared for, and as such requires sufficient long-term resourcing to guarantee its existence. Adequate space, staffing and recurrent funding is required, regardless of the scale and size of the archives. A great deal can be achieved over time with careful long-term planning and a genuine commitment from the parent or host organisation to support the archives. There are a number of possible sources of funding for archives. One-off funding such as a bequest or donation may be the catalyst for the establishment of an archive. Further regular funding will, however, usually need to be found to ensure the on-going survival of the archives. Small amounts of reliable recurrent funding are more valuable in terms of long-term survival than one-off largesse.

Going ahead – what happens next?

Once you've answered questions about context and content, and confirmed that establishing this particular archive is the appropriate action, you are ready to undertake another step in the establishment of an archive. The development of policy creates administrative frameworks for all that you will do.

Policies: Complementary frameworks

Policy – simple, or complex?

It is important to remember that archives and archivists must have a framework in which to operate, as do any other units of an organisation. This takes the form of a policy, or suite of related policies, which determine the type and scope of the archive, the range of services offered, and the position of the archivist.

One of the most important steps in establishing an archives program is the development of an archives policy. This is, in reality, a complex document that should be reviewed regularly. It should cover the establishment and position of the archives within an organisation's wider administrative and/or governance context, and should, either separately or as appendices to the policy which 'establishes' the archive, also include details about the type of collection, reasons for collecting, and conditions under which the collection may be used and/or viewed (which is generally referred to as 'access'). The 'policy' may take the form of a single statement, or it could be made up of several inter-related policy statements.

Legal issues such as copyright, privacy and freedom of information must also be addressed in policy statements, unless the parent organisation has already done so in a manner that will include the archives.

Resource implications

The policies you develop early on will need to be reviewed over time. At the outset, it is important to think through the implications of the 'wish' list because each extra facet to the program will incur a drain on resources: staff, space and finances. While 'thinking big' is commendable, it is also wise to think in practical terms. Perhaps 'keeping it simple' is the best way to start.

The development of specific policies such as a collecting policy, an access policy or an appraisal statement are covered in detail in separate chapters – see chapters 6, 11, and 5 respectively. What follows is an outline of the components of an over-arching archives policy, as well as some pointers for the development of more specific access and collecting policies. Some issues related to privacy, copyright and FOI are also covered.

Components of an archives policy framework:

- Establishment policy
- Collecting policy
- Access policy
- Appraisal statement
- Role description of the archivist
- Retention & Disposal Authority (RDA) or schedule
- Privacy statement
- Copyright statement
- Freedom of Information statement

Establishment Policy

This document is the legal instrument which establishes the archives program as a legitimate business activity of an organisation. In the public sector, this takes the form of archives or recordkeeping legislation, such as the NSW *State Records Act 1998*. It sets the archives within an administrative context, establishes reporting lines, outlines the range of activities the program intends to undertake as well as the range of services on offer, and sets parameters around the content and extent of the archives collection. The adoption of a policy establishes the facility on a professional footing, and clearly states that the archives is an organised and well-managed facility which provides valuable and important information services to the organisation and possibly the wider community.

It can be a deceptively simple document to create. It is recommended that the policy becomes a work in progress, with regular review and revision.

Why is it so important to develop the policy as a first step? A policy is binding once it has been approved by the governing board or council of your organisation. As such, presenting an archives policy to that board for endorsement means that the 'idea' of establishing an archive can become an approved reality. Without this endorsed policy, the entire archives program is on shaky ground. The space required, initial and recurrent funding, the appointment of an archivist, and the subsequent actions of that archivist – including disposal of records – operates without any secure legal or administrative basis.

What is in the Policy?

The policy has a number of components. It should clearly set out the authority of the archives policy, the purpose and objectives of the archives program, the administrative position of the archives within the overall organisation, and its relationship, if any, with related organisations. The authority of the archives and the archivist, which includes the right and responsibility of the archivist to develop and undertake disposal activities should also be included. Finally, the policy should make clear that the archives is the recognised (proper and only) custodian of the archives/collection.

Components of an archives 'establishment' policy

- Authority of the archives policy
- Purpose and objectives of the archives program
- Administrative position of the archives within the overall organisation, and its relationship, if any, with related organisations
- Authority of the archives and the archivist
- Authority of the archivist to develop retention and disposal authority
- Authority of the archives – obligation of staff and other organisational units
- Recognised custodian – successor options

It may be preferable, or it may be a requirement of your organisation, to have the role and responsibilities of the archivist as a separate statement. The policy documents underpinning the collecting parameters of the archives program, and the policy outlining access conditions, may also be separate. However, it must be clear that the various documents *in combination* support the establishment and operation of the archives program. In time, a retention and disposal schedule will also form part of the overall archives policy documents.

The authority of the archives policy

This should clearly state that the policy is a public statement of purpose and objectives for the archives program. The document is the instrument which establishes the framework within which the archives program and its procedures and practices functions. Include an explanation of the process by which the policy has been developed, and which authorising body will or has endorsed it. It is important to note that all amendments must be undertaken through the same process.

The purpose and objectives of the archives program

The policy should explain in *broad* terms the objectives of the archives program, which could be to collect and preserve records, archival and heritage material created by or relating to the organisation. This section should clearly state whether the archives is an in-house program, whether it has a specific collecting brief and focus, or whether it is a combination of both. If the archives program is to have an outreach component, a summary of the range of activities should be included, for example the archives program will facilitate use of this material for reference and educational purposes, and instigate and participate in programs and publications designed to increase awareness of the organisation's heritage. If the archives has a role in supporting the current recordkeeping activities of the organisation, this should also be noted. Similarly, if the archives has a museum component, or operates as, or includes a specialist facility, audiovisual archive, oral history repository, indigenous keeping place or manuscript library this should also be made very clear.

Location within the organisational structure

This section should clearly state where the archives 'sits' in relation to the rest of the organisation, and spelling out its relationship with other administrative units within the organisation. Even if the archives is a stand-alone unit, the archivist will report to someone like the CEO, the council or board, the business manager. This must be made clear. If the archives operates with the assistance and guidance of an advisory body or committee, this relationship should also be made clear. If the archives supports another collecting activity like a gallery, or library, then this should also be made clear. Some archives have special relationships with other organisations. For example, some independent schools have religious affiliations, and the archives of those schools relate in many ways to the archives of the founding religious order or church. Similarly, the archives of an historical association may have a relationship with the archives of a local or regional council. These relationships should be made clear in the policy document.

The authority of the archives and the archivist

It is important to spell out the 'authority' of the archives, to make clear that the archives is more than just a place to store 'old stuff', more than a jumble of papers and objects that no-one else wants. The archives should be a professionally organised and managed facility. Therefore, the archives policy should stipulate that the archives is staffed/headed/managed by a professional archivist (someone with the appropriate level of education and training in archives administration and recordkeeping practices). If this isn't immediately possible, the organisation, by virtue of its archives policy, will be encouraged to support the person appointed to acquire the relevant education and training.

Authority to dispose or destroy

An archivist is properly trained in the process of making disposal and retention decisions. This involves research, analytical skills, experiences, an understanding of the cultural context of the organisation, and where necessary, a knowledge of the legal requirements regarding certain types or classes of records. These skills and expertise mean that the archivist is the right person to be undertaking the appraisal of records and making disposal decisions. This authority should be reflected in, and underpinned by, the archives policy. The policy should state that the archivist will develop and implement a retention and disposal authority (or schedule) for the parent organisation.

Once this schedule has been adopted or endorsed by the highest management or governance body in the organisation, the schedule ('retention and disposal authority' or RDA) should itself form part of the overall archives policy framework.

For further information about appraisal, and the role of the archivist in developing retention and disposal authorities, please refer to Chapter 5: *Appraisal & Disposal.*

Obligations of the organisation

The establishment of relationships with record creators, other departments and donors is one of the most important aspects of an archivist's role. Without appropriate authority, it is almost impossible to instigate routine procedures and practices, such as regular and orderly transfer of records to archives. Nor will it be possible to influence good recordkeeping practices at the point of creation. In the public sphere, all government agencies (local, state and federal) are obliged to create and maintain full and accurate records. Further, they are obliged to comply with standards outlining records management systems, retention and disposal practices and storage requirements. In short, the authority of archivists is mandated under law. Non-government archives, a category into which almost all 'small' or in-house archives fall, operate without the benefit of supporting recordkeeping legislation. One way to overcome this is to outline the responsibilities and obligations of the staff of your organisation in relation to records and archives. This can be achieved by inclusion of a statement in the archives policy. State that staff are required to cooperate with the archivist in relation *inter alia* to the materials required and practices applied in records creation, transfer, and disposal.

Recognised custodian

Finally, this section of the policy statement should state that the archivist is the recognised custodian, and archives the appropriate repository, for the organisation's archives.
A provision for a successor archives should also be included, to guard against the possible eventuality that the current organisation ceases to exist.

Collecting policy

Development of a collecting policy is discussed in greater detail in Chapter 6: *Acquisition*. It is mentioned here in light of the relationship between the overall 'establishment' policy of an archives, and the more specific collecting policy, which sets out the detail of what is, or is not, to form the fabric of the archival collection. The answers to questions asked very early on about the content and context of the collection will now inform the collecting policy. There are practical and resource implications associated with items in a collection which must be thought through at the earliest possible point in the development of the archival program.

Access policy

This policy or statement outlines the conditions under which records within the archives may be accessed and/or used. Access is discussed in greater detail in Chapter 11: *Access & Reference Services*. There are two aspects to access: (a) whether or not records may be viewed and used and (b) how this will take place. It is mentioned here due to the relationship of an access policy to all other policies for the archives. There are also practical and resource implications associated with access which must be thought through at the earliest possible point in the development of the archival program.

Role description

The role description could form a separate statement, or it may be incorporated into the body of the policy document. Regardless, it should contain an overview of the range of duties expected of the archivist, and if not already included elsewhere, make mention of the level of professional skill and expertise required of the person appointed to manage the archives program. It is important to think this through as early as possible in the development of the archival polices as the archivist will be the major resource – and therefore the major recurring cost of the archival program. It may be practical to have only one archivist, as there may be space limitation, or it may be possible to split the role and have a manager supervising specialist staff or a group of volunteers. Understanding the diverse range of activities undertaken by an archivist or team of archivists will also help when (and if!) designing the space required.

The role statement does not need to provide detail on the exact nature of archival duties. However, the full range of activities required to be undertaken should be incorporated. This will reflect the overall nature of the archives program, and will relate directly to the objectives established earlier in the policy. A typical in-house archive undertakes a comprehensive range of activities. A generic role description for an archivist working alone or in a small archives is included on the CD accompanying this book.

Privacy statement

Guarding the privacy of the individual is an ethical as well as a legal issue for archivists, given the nature of the materials under care. In Australia, privacy provisions in the *Privacy Act 1988* (Commonwealth) affecting private sector organisations came into effect on 21 December 2001. Many private organisations choose to abide by ten basic principles laid out in the National Privacy Principles (NPPs), which aim to ensure that information about people which is held by an organisation is handled responsibly. While not all countries have NPPs, they are based on common sense and respect for the privacy of the individual, and as such are worth considering when establishing programs and procedures for your archives.

The 10 NPPs relate to:

- NPP 1 & 10 Collection of information
- NPP 2 Use and disclosure
- NPP 3 Data quality
- NPP 4 Data security
- NPP 5 Openness
- NPP 6 Access & correction
- NPP 7 Identifiers
- NPP8 Anonymity
- NPP9 Trans-border data flow

Some states within Australia have set regulations which must be met when caring for, using or storing documents which may contain information of a personal and therefore private nature. Most organisations, institutions and corporations have developed a privacy statement, which sets out publicly the reasons for collecting information about individuals and how the organisation manages that information.

The standards set therein must be maintained for the life of the records. Privacy issues must be addressed when gathering information, when storing it, and when destroying records.

It is important that the archives develops a privacy statement, if the parent organisation has not already done so. The statement should reflect the ten NPPs at the very least, and also include any specific regulations current in your jurisdiction. Of particular importance to note are the following:

- no private information will be passed by the archives to a third party without permission (NPP2)
- no information of a private or personal nature, i.e. that which is not on the public record, about specific individuals will be used in exhibitions, displays or publications produced by the archives (NPP2)

- all records should be stored in secure, lockable storage units, with access limited to the Archivist and senior staff (NPP4)
- anyone wishing to view or correct records held about them may do so through the archivist (NPP6)

Copyright statement

Copyright subsists in all artistic, musical, and literary works (a letter or an email is a literary work) and is owned by the creator or author (or their employer, if created in the course of employment). The copyright owner has the exclusive right to make copies of the work or to distribute or publish it. Copyright extends to almost everything in an archives collection, including written and printed material, photographs, maps, plans, sound recordings and moving images. Frequently, the copyright in archival material is owned by external people or organisations (for example, copyright in a letter held by the archives is owned by the writer of the letter not by the recipient).

It is important that you, and people seeking to use material in the archives, recognise the need to acknowledge copyright before reproducing any original material held within the collection. Copyright issues may affect the work of the archives: for exhibitions and publications, and may affect researchers.

As the archivist, you need to take necessary steps to seek and secure permission to reproduce any work by third parties held within the archives – for example, photographs taken by commercial photographers, architectural drawings, sketches and plans, works of art or musical items.

Similarly, people wishing to reproduce material held by the archives in which copyright is owned by the archives, a parent organisation or an individual, must seek permission to do so.

A copyright statement should form part of the policy framework for your archives. For more information about copyright, see Chapter 11: *Access & Reference Services.*

Resources: staff, volunteers, and budget

Every facet of the archival program will involve some form of resource. The resources of an archival program (apart from the collection itself!) are the people (staff and volunteers), the space (office, processing area, public area and storage), and money.

In an ideal scenario, it would be possible to plot the number of staff required, the size of the collection (including room for expansion), and the space required for processing, public areas and the archives office and have this dream become a reality! It is more likely that the archivist will be appointed and expected to begin 'work' before any concerted planning is undertaken. The archivist will then have to 'make do' until better planning and resource management allows the development of an appropriate space, complement of staff and recurring budget. Managing the various resource elements will require a significant portion of the time available to an archivist, and it is important to factor this into the size and scope of the role.

Archives resources	
People	Archivist Volunteers Donors/philanthropists
Space	Public areas – displays, research, reading room Work/processing area Office area Storage area
Finances	Annual budget Donations/grants Bequests

It is important to remember that not all responsibilities and activities are practical in all archives. It will be necessary to evaluate the objectives of your intended program to determine the range of activities which will be undertaken. Conversely, available resources also limit the scope of activities, and it will be necessary to think carefully about what is achievable within your existing framework. The archives program should be a work-in-progress, and it should be reviewed regularly to ensure that the full range of services required is matched by the budget, space and facilities available – and vice versa. Long-term planning (using the policy statement as a basis) and budgeting will help the smallest archives bloom into a comprehensive, multi-faceted program.

Staff and volunteers

The archivist is one of the major resources of the archives program. The archivist needs skills in order to manage the program, and to undertake the specific archival duties as outlined in the role description. Basic archival practices such as appraisal, accessioning, arrangement and description, and disposal are described in detail in subsequent chapters in this volume. Expect to undertake a full range of these activities, especially if you work as a 'lone arranger', or do not have the resources to engage extra staff. Management skills will be required in terms of human resources, budget and finances; the archivist will need an ability to work alone, often unsupervised. Time management, project management and goal-setting skills will also be required. It may be possible to split the role of managing the archives from undertaking archival work by employing two (or more) people. This again has resource implications which must be factored into the overall budget, as well as the space requirements for the archives.

Many archives augment their resources by using volunteers to carry out routine (but engaging!) processing work, such as the arrangement and description of photographs, or indexing large registers, etc. Volunteers may be former members of staff, or groups of students, or those with a passion for history just willing to help out. Using volunteers has many benefits: they often have intimate knowledge of a collection or the history of an organisation; volunteer groups form an added aspect to the 'community' or 'friends' of the archives. For archivists working alone, volunteers can be a welcome source of (occasional!) company. However, there are resource implications in this too: extra space to accommodate the volunteers is needed; the archivist will need to invest time in setting up procedures and to train the volunteers; and it may be necessary to supervise the volunteers. It is important to weigh up the benefits and implications of setting up a volunteer program. See also Chapter 14: *Advocacy & Outreach* for advice on working with volunteers.

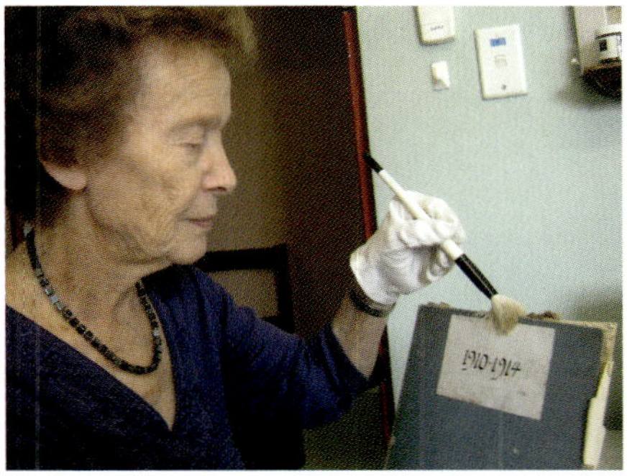

Volunteers can assist in many ways, and are a valuable asset to the archival program.

Occupational Health & Safety

With people comes responsibility. Occupational Health and Safety (also known as workplace health and safety or WHS in some states) issues must be considered when planning or occupying an archives space. Experts in the area of OH&S are available to consult regarding plans, or for renovations of an existing space; most organisations have an OH&S committee who can assist in this area. Some simple issues to consider include: is there enough room for appropriate desks and chairs? Is lighting and ventilation adequate? What height are the storage shelves? Many answers to these questions will come from adequate planning and consultation, regardless of whether you are working with a pre-allocated space, a potential renovation or purpose-built facility.

Budget

It is vital that an annual budget is developed and approved as soon as possible. Without this, there is no grounding for any of the projects you wish or need to undertake. Relying on donations, or through diversion of funds allocated to general administration or another unit of the organisation is not sustainable. The scope and complexity of the budget will depend on the administrative nature and budgeting preferences of the parent organisation. Having a separate budget is another tangible indicator that the archives has standing as a unit of an organisation, and deserves resourcing in the same way as any other unit in the organisation. It is important that you ensure this occurs, just as it is vital that policies are approved by the board or council.

It may be that the parent organisation factors in capital expenditure on an organisation-wide basis. If this is the case, you need to ascertain how to have your requests for extra space, furniture and major pieces of office equipment (computers, scanners, printers etc) incorporated into the overall budget.

If the archives is a stand-alone organisation, you will need to seek professional accounting advice on preparing and administering an annual budget.

The basic budget will need to cover, as a bare minimum, archival supplies and basic stationery and office equipment. You must be clear about whether or not the archivist's salary and other costs for personnel are incorporated into the budget, or are included elsewhere in the accounts. You will also need to factor in the costs of conservation (assessments and treatments) and professional development and/or training for staff. Ideally, you will factor in, over several years, the costs of replacement equipment, extra or replacement storage furniture, and possibly renovations to the existing space.

Basic budget inclusions	
Basic Supplies	Archival folders, file covers, boxes, papers, photographic supplies : albums, sleeves; cleaning and handling materials
Stationery	Paper, pens, pencils (various grades), printer cartridges etc.
Conservation	Costs of assessments/reports; conservation/restoration work
Purchases	Purchase of archival records as part of the collection; reference books, professional texts etc.
Professional development	Annual subscriptions, seminars, workshops, conferences
Capital expenses furniture	Furniture, office equipment, additional/replacement storage

Time management

One of the most critical resources of any endeavour is time. Managing this – getting the most out of the hours you have to devote to the archives – can be a tricky and demanding task in itself. Chances are that you have been allocated 'part-time' hours – perhaps three days per week. It is possible that the people you report to do not understand the complexity of what you are undertaking daily, or forget that you are only working part time: they will still expect a 'full time' service, or evidence of productivity that meets their expectations. It is important that you are clear about what you can or cannot achieve within given time allocations.

Volunteers can assist by processing quantities of material. It is important to establish processes and procedures before they start, which involves an investment of time and effort by the archivist.

You will need to be realistic about what you can achieve in a given time, and to set limits on the range of services you can provide. Avoid the temptation to promise too much, and avoid the temptation to waste time by wandering down 'interesting' paths that may not yield the results you – or your parent organisation – expect. You may need to consider limiting the hours the archives are open to the public, or you may need to ask that researchers or potential donors make appointments before visiting – this is one way to avoid surprises, and to gain control over the time you may spend on such areas of activity. Your organisation may expect several displays or exhibitions, which can be very time-consuming to research, develop and create. Such projects may mean that all other services or activities may have to be temporarily suspended.

Managing your time, and that of your staff, is clearly related to setting overall goals for the archives program; these should be regularly reviewed against available resources.

Goal setting and self-management

Establishing an archives (or any project, for that matter) involves starting with the macro (or 'big picture') level and gradually working through to the final details. To keep yourself on track, it is recommended that you set some realistic goals and time frames, and regularly check your progress against them. This will help you manage your time, and ensure that you can see results for all of your efforts. The goals you set will depend on the focus of your archives program, or the demands of your parent organisation: this should also be refected in the archives policy.

Long-term planning will help you prioritise the tasks at hand, and you will be able to see, at least on paper, how the archives will develop over time into a useful information resource. A plan, or set of goals, will keep your work focussed, and ensure that nothing is left out, or is continually put off because you are reacting to a series of crises. It also ensures that all work is undertaken methodically and systematically, rather than in a chaotic or ad hoc way. This is critical not only for the successful administration of the archives, but also for the overall well-being of the archivist and volunteers on hand.

Sample (simple!) goals for a new archives program	
Initial establishment phase – goals	
• Create a draft suite of policy documents and statements	Created
• Design an archives facility	In progress
• Identify the range, extent and location(s) of archival material	In progress
Second phase – goals	
• Overview of series	
• Overview of photograph holdings	
• Identification of potential donors	
Third Phase – goals	
• 20% of Series fully described	
• 20 % photo collection indexed and described	
• 10% donors contacted, visits arranged	

The Facility

Full technical details of building a new facility or renovating an existing building to suit are given in Chapter 3: *Buildings & Storage.*

The components of an archival facility are outlined below. It is acknowledged that many fledgling archives begin as a filing cabinet, or in a disused office, gradually growing into renovated or purpose-built facilities. Often, one space must be multi-use. More often, lack of space curtails the range of activities and services able to be offered by the archives, which in turn may impact adversely upon its chances of growth into better facilities. Be prepared to be flexible, at least initially, but keep the long term goal of a fully equipped purpose-built or renovated facility at the forefront of your planning. Most importantly, make sure that your parent organisation also remains aware of these needs as a long-term goal.

Areas required

The scope of your archives program will determine what sort of facility you will need.

As a bare minimum, you will ideally have separate spaces for an office, for processing and for storage. If you are able to claim an exhibition space and a reading room, to serve as a space for researchers and visitors, this should be incorporated into the overall design of your archives layout. Further details of what is required for storage and public areas are provided in other chapters of this book.

Components of an archives facility	
Administrative area	Office for the archivist – administrative duties, meetings, phone calls, etc Extra desk space for extra staff or volunteers Reference material
Processing area	Space to receive and process collections – large benches Storage for supplies and tools
Storage area	Shelving (mobile and/or static) to house boxes of various sizes and shapes Separate area for fully described and accessioned material
Public area	Display or exhibition space, desks for research and reading

The administrative area

You will need a desk for general business activities such as communications, for data entry, report writing and general administrative tasks. The papers and records you create as a routine outcome of the activities you undertake will need to be stored, so a filing cabinet, credenza or bookcase will also be needed.

Office space, separate from processing and storage areas

You may need to provide an extra desk or space for your volunteers. If they are responsible for data entry, you will need to consider a separate computer terminal, and preferably network the computers, to ensure data is updated and available to you as it is processed.

A large, dedicated work space for processing material is essential. There should be easy access to material required such as boxes, tissue, acid fee file covers etc.

You will also need bookcases to hold the reference collection which will build up around the collection. A reference 'library' will develop, consisting of a combination of information about your organisation, your location and related organisations. Technical reference material such as archives administration manuals, archival standards, preservation and conservation guides, and the publications of related professions will form part of your reference library.

The processing area

You will need a large flat space – preferably a table raised to standing height – for processing parts of the collection. Ideally, the processing area should be separate from the office area to avoid cross-contamination between archival material and the papers of your routine activities.

Space will also be required for storage of materials and equipment. This could be as simple as a standard metal cupboard, or could be incorporated into a purpose-built processing bench. You will need different sized spaces for flat boxes, acid-free (or archival quality) files, rolls of tissue and Mylar. Knowing what supplies you will require depends on the range of archival materials you will be processing and the likely quantities and sizes of records to be processed.

It is advisable to speak to archivists working with collections of a similar size and range as yours. They will be able to tell you what works (and what doesn't!), and you may be able to visit a facility to see how the processing area has been arranged.

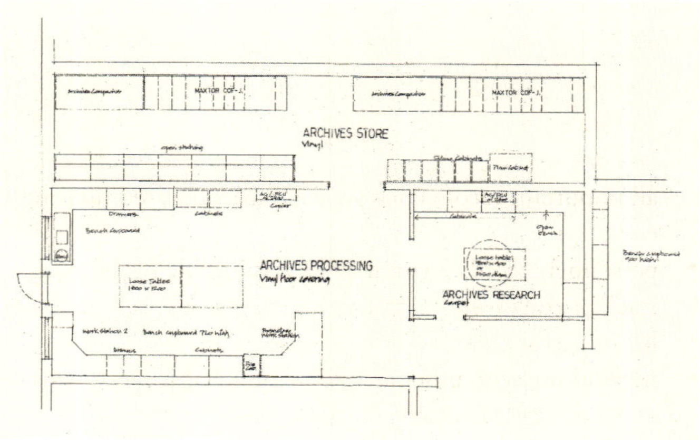

Architectural drawing of a floor plan for a new (small) archive facility. It incorporates separate areas for storage, processing and research or public areas.

Some practicalities

Understand the basic principles

You may choose to manage the administrative aspects of an archival program through a database which has been designed specifically for archives. This is a valid option, implemented in archives of all sizes, from small in-house programs right through to national collections. However, it is important to remember that a database won't help you work out what a series is, nor will it automatically document context, or provide you with appraisal decisions. Understanding the principles which guide archival practice is something to be learned and mastered before you start.

It is vital that you maintain records of everything you undertake regarding the records in your archive, starting with accessioning material as it comes in. It may look 'messy' to an untrained eye, but if the material is properly – although simply – accessioned, it is relatively easy to fully process even after some time has elapsed.

Keep records of what you do

Detailed records about the program and practices that have been implemented in the archives should be created and maintained. The records you create as part of your everyday work practices will include the products of archives administration: accession registers, detailed series lists, series descriptions, indexes to holdings, finding aids etc. You should also consciously document activities and actions such as appraisal and disposal decisions such as why something was retained, or something was destroyed, and also how this happened (e.g. shredding, pulping etc).

Long term and high-level records such as five-year plans, annual goals, policy development and reviews will form the skeleton of the records of the archives program, but other records are also important. Expect to maintain records about the following:

- operating system and database, and any specialist software you have purchased and implemented;
- lists of suppliers, budget forecasts and expenditure – all important records of how you have allocated funding over time
- personnel records – you may be responsible for keeping track of your volunteers, or extra staff
- list of useful contacts
- networking with other archivists, or allied professionals such as conservators, exhibition experts etc

Reference material about the local area, or about the subject of your archival collection, must be accommodated within your overall archive space.

A backlog of material yet to be processed is common. It may be necessary to re-box material as a first step towards gaining control of the material within.

- Professional development – membership of a professional association, conference/seminar/workshop attendance etc

Keeping your own records is particularly important should practices ever change. Records documenting your current practice will assist subsequent archivists to understand what has been done, how it was done and why.

One word of caution: be sure to accession, even in a very basic way, everything that comes into the archives once the program has started. It is tempting to think that you'll remember who brought the box in, where that file came from, when it arrived, and what it relates to. Be assured that quantity will eventually overwhelm you if you don't keep track of it from the start! It is also common for someone to ask for the return of a file, even after only a few weeks. The new archives and the archivist do not look very professional if they cannot quickly lay their hands on something 'given' to the archives only a short time ago. Take the time to make note of all material as it comes in so that you will also avoid becoming overwhelmed by new material even as you are trying to deal with the 'old'.

There is always a backlog

An archive without a backlog is extremely rare. Be prepared to accept the fact that there will always be more that can be done – more accessioning, more series descriptions, more administrative research, better finding aids, more detailed indexes – the list goes on. There will always be new material arriving. You may never quite get around to working through the boxes at the very back of the shed.

It is important to remember the big picture. An archives with a basic grasp of everything in the collection is probably more efficient than one with detailed descriptions of one series, and only a vague understanding of the rest.

You may need to re-box material as it arrives. The boxes could be too large, or falling apart, or simply non-existent. You need to be able to store material efficiently in the space available, even if the material is not fully processed. Re-boxing into standard archival boxes may be an important first step, done at the same time you are accessioning (gaining elemental control of) the material. This may be the *only* step you ever undertake in regard to processing this particular material. Do not worry, as this is common practice. In time, you will be able to see how this material fits with other accessions or series in the collection. You will be able to make informed decisions about the relevance of the material, which will in turn affect your decision about what to do next: if it's important or significant or likely to be in high demand, it will be fully processed and, if not, it may sit as accessioned material or as backlog for many months or even years.

A bookcase which itself is of historic value doubles as storage for reference materials.

Physical control

The administrative context for your archives program has been established through the creation and endorsement of the archives policy. You have space, you have mastered the principles underpinning archival practice and now you're ready to tackle the first box. What supplies will you need? It is your aim to have the collection properly housed in boxes of appropriate size and arranged on shelves which offer the most efficient use of the space available while providing adequate protection for their contents. There is a wide range of products available from commercial suppliers, and the choice of material depends largely on the formats in your collection. In terms of paper records, the following is the most basic list of what you will need.

Basic supplies

Acid-free file covers come in different sizes and shapes – open foolscap or A4-sized folders, four flap folders, and document wallets. Various styles lend themselves to various record formats or it can come down to a matter of personal preference. The idea is to protect the records as well as you can.

White cotton tape: This is approximately 12mm wide, and serves to tie records securely into acid-free files. This provides further support, as well as maintaining the physical integrity of a bundle, series, and section of a series of records together.

Samples of boxes commonly used in archives. They come in a range of sizes, shapes and materials – ideally, you should aim for acid free or buffered

'Type 1' boxes: These are an Australian invention, c. 1960. They are made of one piece of cardboard, and have been designed so that (a) the bottom cannot fall away from the rest of the box, (b) to maintain a reasonable weight per box, to facilitate handling and (c) to ensure proper protection by way of a box with a closing lid. These are available in a number of materials, which vary in price per unit:

- standard (brown) cardboard, not acid free is the cheapest option. These can be used for storage of temporary records and they can also be used for more permanent purposes as long as the contents are adequately protected by acid-free file covers.

- acid-free (usually blue) cardboard: for the storage of permanent records. These are more expensive, but offer a higher level of protection.
- polypropylene (available in a variety of colours), these are the most expensive option. Made of very stable compounds, these acid-free boxes are the most desirable option.

Material which has been processed into acid free file covers which forms a buffer for the acidic box.

Protection for other formats

Acid-free cardboard or polypropylene boxes come in a range of sizes and shapes, with specific ones available for audio/visual formats, textiles (including hats, uniforms, costumes, vestments, banners, etc), index cards, microfilm, maps and plans and photographs. (See Chapter 16: *Plans, Photographs & Objects* for further detail).

What if the budget doesn't cover it?

It is possible to 'make do' with materials which are to hand if the budget doesn't immediately stretch far enough to cover the purchase of archival quality supplies. However, it must be remembered that 'make do' is a temporary approach, and it is vital that steps are taken to gradually increase the available resources so that the collection may be properly housed.

Conclusion

The best way to develop confidence in newly acquired understanding of theory and principle is to put it into practice! Once you've established a draft policy and determined the parameters of what the archives program will include, go ahead and work with the collection. Take a high-level inventory of the collection. Tackle a straightforward series, such as minute books, as a starting point. Do not be afraid to make mistakes as it is always possible to revise a series description or contextual note if necessary. Start gathering information about the context and provenance of the records in the collection by talking to staff, asking questions, reading up, if possible, on the history of the organisation and/or local area. A wonderful support network is available by making contact with archivists in similar situations. They will readily provide advice and encouragement, as well as tips and comments on how best to proceed. Participating in workshops, seminars and professional development events helps to refine and extend knowledge, which translates into better practice.

CASE STUDY

Establishing an archives in a Not-For-Profit (NFP) organisation

A charity organisation has been in existence since the1930s. Its main role has been the provision of care and respite services for children in need, although at one stage it was classed as a home for under-privileged and abused children. In recent years, former clients and their relatives have been contacting the organisation, mainly in pursuit of genealogical information. Staff in administration do not have time to answer these queries – there are too few of them, research is beyond their skills base, and the records themselves are dispersed across the various locations on the property, which covers some 40 acres and has over 10 individual buildings. As the research enquiries steadily increase, there is a growing understanding among senior staff that something must be done to 'sort out the records'. They are also aware of the potential for sensitive information about children falling into the wrong hands. This coincides with a general push to demolish or renovate some of the buildings, and sub-divide and sell off some of the excess land. The resulting funds will be channelled into other services the NFP is now providing in response to changing demands and expectations.

Senior management has taken their concerns about the records to the board of directors. There is an understanding of the uniqueness of the records of this NFP, as well as awareness of the sensitive nature of the contents of the records. A high-level commitment is made to set up a small in-house archives, if they can find a volunteer to run it. They are prepared to set aside a small budget, which can be used to cover establishment costs such as archival boxes, shelving and office equipment. A volunteer is found with the appropriate enthusiasm and time to attend to the 'records' issue. Recognising that she lacks the expertise to develop policies and systems, or to design a storage facility, she persuades senior management to devote some of the set-up budget to engaging a consulting archivist who helps with the initial design, set up and policy development.

The archives program to be developed in this case will be a very streamlined one. The first step undertaken by the volunteer archivist is to find and quantify the records held in various places across the site. She spends several days doing this, and discovers that most of the records are in reasonably good physical condition, although scattered across four buildings. Her rough survey indicates that the date range of the records found covers the whole period of the NFP's existence. In addition to individual files for each child who had attended the facility, she discovers intact administrative records covering a period of 30 years, a time of significant change and development at the site. Included are many photographs, maps and plans, correspondence, minutes, management reports and other material.

Some priorities are set. The first one is to gain complete control of the files of individual children. This involves listing each one into a database to facilitate search and retrieval. At the same time, the files are re-boxed into type 1 archive boxes. Further work will be undertaken to fully arrange and describe, and index all other records about the children, but this will wait until after initial basic control has been gained over the whole collection. Parallel to this work is the development of an access policy, which sets out the conditions under which information may (or may not) be disclosed – to whom, and in what circumstances. The NFP has a general privacy statement, but this needs to be refined to cover the records of an archival/historical nature as well. These three measures are undertaken to enable genealogical enquiries to be answered appropriately and within a reasonable time frame.

The second priority area is to find, and if necessary, renovate a suitable space within the existing buildings to house the newly-boxed collection as it is processed. Second-hand library shelving is purchased. The budget would not stretch to cover mobile shelving (even second hand), but the cost of purchasing a new one, as well as a map cabinet, has been factored into long-term financial planning for the NFP. There are no outreach activities planned, as this demands too many scarce resources.

The establishment of this small in-house archive was in response to a relatively narrow, specific need. It is a work in progress, which has spanned four years. Work is being undertaken with minimal resources, but the results have been gratifying to the volunteer archivist, senior management and, not least, to the people seeking answers to questions about their past association with the NFP. Keeping things simple, setting priorities, and sticking to basics has meant the development of a successful and valued archives.

CHAPTER 3

buildings & storage

TED LING

CHAPTER ABSTRACT

An archive needs a home, to keep the collection safe and protected and to provide a suitable working environment for archivists and archival processes. Good buildings and storage contribute to the effective functioning of an archive. While few of you will have the luxury of purpose-built accommodation, this chapter also provides advice on making the most of what facilities you may have.

This chapter describes some of the features of a typical archival building, large or small, and appropriate storage practices. It examines building fabric, environmental conditions – what they are and why they matter, fire and security protection, lighting, maintenance, pest control, and disaster preparedness. On the storage side, you will also find advice on different types of shelving and packaging materials. Finally, the chapter covers issues involving moving from one building to another.

Introduction

Archive buildings come in a vast array of shapes and sizes. Some are truly massive, such as the National Archives and Records Service facility at College Park in Maryland, USA. Some buildings are quite small. Regardless of their shape or size, they all exist to preserve and protect the records stored within them, and they must also provide a safe and comfortable working environment for the staff who work there, and they will usually include facilities to allow researchers to access the records held there.

Think of it in this way. Regardless of whether your institution is large or small, and regardless of whether you occupy a new building or are adapting an existing one, your goal should be that long after you and all your staff are gone, long after the researchers who consult the records now are gone, and long after the building itself has reached the end of its useful

Old houses are often used for archives. In many ways a good solution as it is relatively simple to separate storage, processing, office and public areas, there are drawbacks, such as security and environmental conditions. Houses were not built to support huge floor loads. Only install compactus or shelving units after obtaining engineering advice.

Old buildings are often converted into archives facilities. This one is used primarily for storage only.

Sheds are often used for archival storage which is usually far from acceptable.

life, the records will still be there and will still be in good condition (Kitching, 2007, p. 31).

Irrespective of the type of building you may have, for example, a dedicated facility built at considerable expense, or a small historic house where you may only occupy one or two rooms, the building has to protect your records from environmental extremes involving temperature and relative humidity, rain, vandalism, and possible pest infestations.

The typical archive building

A typical archive building is generally divided into four parts, that is:

- staffing;
- public areas;
- arrangement and description (processing); and
- storage (or the repository);

Staffing

Your institution may have many staff, or perhaps only one or two. Provision will need to be made – often up to sixteen square metres – for each person. When planning an office layout remember to allow not only for personal space, such as desks, chairs, computers, visitor's chairs, bookcases, filing cabinets, but circulation areas as well. People need to be able to move within their own area, and of course to other areas.

You should take into account noisy machines, such as a photocopier or a printer, and ensure that they are located where they will not interfere with staff and their work.

The ability of your building to provide for the creature comforts of your staff, such as thermal comfort and lighting, should also be considered. Recommended levels are as usually as follows:

• Temperature	23°–26° Celsius (summer)
	20°–24° Celsius (winter)
• Humidity	40%–60%
• Overhead lighting	240 lux–400 lux

It is preferable that any amenities areas are completely separated from the office area, to reduce the risk of food and liquid damage to records, and to avoid the risk of pest infestations. If your facility does not have an amenities area, and you are required to provide one, try and ensure that it is as far away removed from the office area as possible. You can use fabric screens, panels or even imitation pot plants to separate the two areas.

Public areas

The design and layout of your reading room, and display areas if you have them, are most important. These are the public face of your archives. There are a number of issues that need to be addressed. How do researchers find what records they want? Where are the finding aids? Are they clearly labelled? How do researchers access the records, and return them when they have finished?

When designing a reading room it is important to remember that:

- some researchers prefer to work alone; while others prefer to work in groups;
- researchers look at records in a wide variety of formats – paper files, plans, volumes, and photographs – so facilities must be available to accommodate all of these; and
- some researchers will write their notes, others will use laptop computers, and some may want to use a digital camera to photograph what they are researching.

You will also need facilities outside the reading room – lockers in which researchers can store their bags, coats and umbrellas, and possibly an amenities room (as researchers should not be permitted to bring food or drink into the reading room), rest rooms, and possibly a designated smoking area.

An orientation room, or desk, should be included to enable staff to meet with first time researchers coming to grips with your records, finding aids and methods of operation.

Reading room ambience

You should not overlook the general ambience of the public areas of your building. The use of colours, fabrics, materials, and furniture are all important. They should enhance the aesthetic and functional appeal of the area, not detract from it. In this context it is desirable that as much natural light as possible be allocated to the reading room.

Noise levels should be kept to a minimum. Curtains and carpets are a good way to absorb noise. Floors with hard surfaces – slate, or vinyl – are not recommended in reading areas due to the noise factor. Noise can have many sources – researchers distracting each other, staff distracting researchers, external noises – nearby plant rooms or traffic. If the reading room is adjacent to a major road, it may be necessary to double-glaze all windows in the room.

Tables and chairs should be ergonomically based, that is, have adjustable height settings, and be comfortable to sit on and work at.

If you have the space, it is a good idea to have an area set aside for group research – a table that can accommodate several persons – so that people who want to work together, and discuss their research, can do so without disturbing other researchers. Private work areas may be needed for researchers using their own computers and tape recorders. Remember to allow for sufficient power outlets, particularly for laptop computers, and good overhead lighting.

If you have maps, plans and posters in your collection, then a large flat table will be very useful. Researchers using large volumes should not be permitted to simply place them flat on the table as this could damage the binding. Such volumes need additional support; they should be placed on lecterns, or even a padded cushion will do.

Again, noisy machines, such as microfilm readers and photocopiers, should be screened from general areas so as not to create a nuisance for other readers.

The area should be clearly signposted. Similarly, all finding aids should be identified plainly. The area will need supervision; depending on staff numbers it may be necessary to use cameras and possibly mirrors. If a separate room is provided it may be desirable to use glass partitioning when separating them.

Providing for disabled researchers

Provision should also be made for disabled researchers. Doors should be wide enough to allow the passage of wheelchairs. Door handles and light switches should not be too high that they cannot be reached by a person in a wheelchair. Reception counters should not be so high that they are intimidating to persons in wheelchairs. The tables and chairs in the

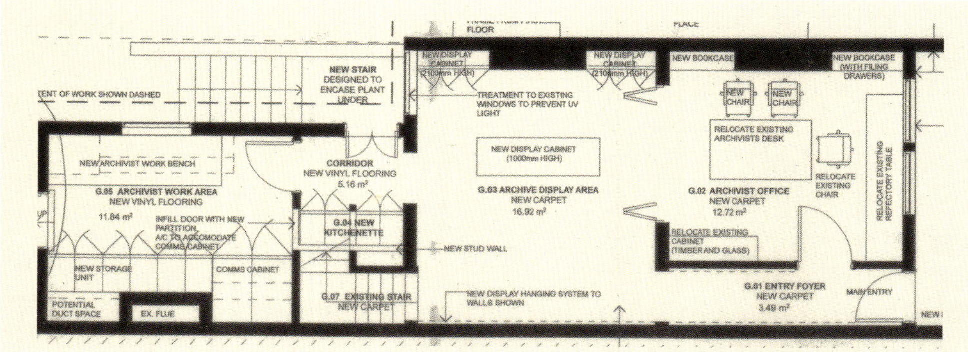

Floor plan for the converted ground floor of an existing terrace house. There is space for the Archivist's office, work space/processing area and an area for permanent displays or exhibitions.

reading room should be able to comfortably accommodate disabled researchers.

It may be necessary to provide a rest room that is fitted out specifically for use by disabled persons.

Hearing or sight impaired persons should also be taken into consideration when designing a reading room layout. They may require the provision of special phones to enable them to communicate, or enlarging equipment to enable them to read documents.

Processing room

When planning the design of your building you need to allow for a designated room or space for records processing, and possible arrangement and description. In this area you can inspect records being transferred into the building to ensure there are no problems with insect pests or mould. Some records may have been affected by water or fire, and you need to have space to in which to rebox them. You can also undertake cleaning, sorting, listing and minor conservation tasks that may be needed.

The area should have a vinyl or tile floor, and be provided with benches and a large table for sorting, and some static shelving to store the records while you are working on them.

A small store room, or at least a cabinet, should be also provided to house empty boxes, as well as office and other supplies.

Storage – Building fabric and structure

In many cases archival institutions must make do with an existing building, rather than a new one, due to financial restraints. When you are assessing the suitability of a building as the home for your archives there are many factors that should be considered.

The most important feature is location. An ideal building should be located on a site that is clear of pollutants, well clear of tracts of water, and close to a main road and public transport. Try and avoid heavily polluted areas as much as possible even if they might mean cheaper purchase costs or rent. A light industrial area or technology park is preferable.

Consider the neighbours; are there signs of neglect or vandalism in the area? Ascertain if there are hotels or garages or any other nuisance establishments near to the site.

Ideally, the area in which materials are processed is separate from the storage area. Where this is not possible due to space constraints, it is still prudent to keep processed records and parts of the collection separate.

An area dedicated to materials storage. This keeps new materials – boxes, file covers, albums and sleeves – clean and separate. It is also easy to do a quick stock take at budget time, or to re-order when stocks get low.

The ready availability of public transport should be noted. This will of course be of interest to both your staff and visitors. Will there be sufficient parking for both staff and visitors?

The building and its surrounds should be considered not only in the context of their present suitability but whether they are likely to remain suitable for your needs for the foreseeable future.

The overall functionality of the building should be considered. The manner in which your storage, staffing and public areas will coexist is vital.

You should make a thorough inspection of that part of the building which is being proposed for the archives. This will give you an impression of the quality of the premises; whether they are clean and have been cared for, or abused and neglected.

Apart from functionality, during the inspection you should look for any signs of possible problems, for example, rising or falling damp, water leaks, stains in the ceiling or floor, streak marks down the walls. There may be musty smells which could indicate rising or falling damp, or mildew. The inspection should not be confined to obvious open areas, but should include corners, store rooms and any other 'out of the way' places.

If the building has been freshly painted this could mean something is being hidden and you should carefully scrutinise such areas.

You need to know if the building contains any environmental hazards such as asbestos, or halon fire suppression systems. Asbestos is dangerous if left in place and costly to have removed.

You should check the building's roof to ensure there are no problems, such as rust or leaks. Ideally, the building should have a good drainage system designed to remove water from the building and the property as quickly as possible.

Does the building have a loading dock? If it does it should not open directly onto the proposed storage area, but neither should it be some distance away meaning that records have to travel through a maze of corridors. Ease of vehicular access to the dock should also be noted, particularly if there is to be frequent movement of records into and out of the facility. This is not so important, however, if the movement of records is minimal.

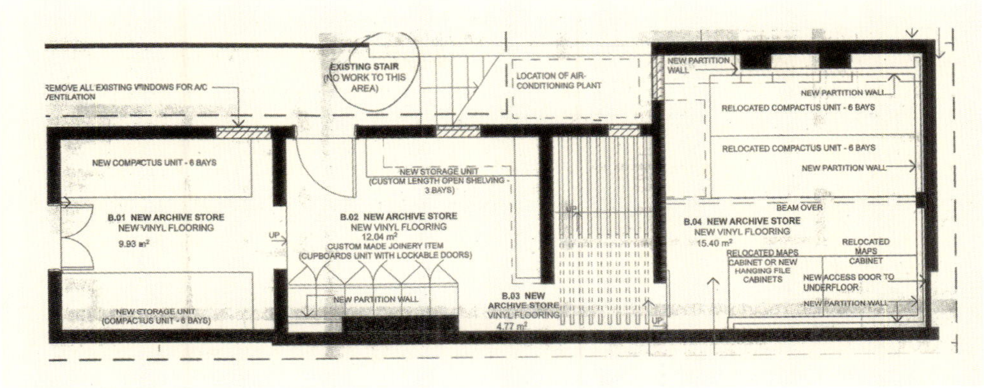

Floor plan for the converted basement area of an existing terrace house. Different types of storage are included, such as compactus units, map cabinets, hanging storage for framed objects, and large open shelving for odd-sized items. Basements are not generally recommended for archives; however, this was a case of having to make the best out of a situation in which a residence was converted to house the archives plus another unit of the organisation.

Look for signs of insect pests – dead bodies or droppings – both inside and outside the building. If traps or baits are prevalent the extent of the pest problem should be ascertained. You may need to obtain a pest report.

In the ideal world you should never store your archives in the basement of a building, especially if there are pipes in the area. If you have to use a basement, then ensure that the records are not located below or near pipes, boilers or other items of plant or equipment. If, however, the shelving must be located below pipes, then have large covers placed across the top to deflect any water should those pipes leak. Keep shelving away from the walls, with at least 50 mm clearance, and ensure that all records are housed in the shelving and not placed on the floor.

Whatever storage area you are using, the structure of that area should form an effective seal to help you maintain strict environmental controls. If the walls are made of brick or concrete the internal sides should be sealed otherwise there is the likelihood that contaminants can be released. Sealing can be achieved with good quality paint, though you should ensure that the vapours from the paint have dissipated before records are brought into the area. Likewise the ceilings should be intact, and any gaps or holes should be patched. You should also check above the ceiling to see if there is any form of insulation, which will help minimise the effects of solar radiation in the storage areas.

You may experience problems with moisture penetration through the walls or floor. A vapour barrier (a form of sealant) may need to be applied. You can usually rectify smaller problems by visiting your hardware store and studying the sealants that are on supply.

Find out what the fire rating of the walls and doors surrounding the proposed storage area are. Fire ratings are basically the level of time it takes before a fire will burn through or the structure collapses; the longer the rating, the better. Ideally you should have a two-hour rating, but at the very least try and aim for a one-hour rating, particularly if your storage area does not have sprinklers.

There should be no windows or skylights in the storage areas. Ultraviolet light from sunlight can damage records, and skylights simply mean another roof penetration with the possible risk of leaks. If windows are already there, it is preferable that they be enclosed with insulation and wood panelling, for example, or with blackout curtains, or similar material.

The extent of your building's airconditioning system should be noted, as should its reliability and its maintenance history. If the building is not airconditioned find out if it has forced ventilation. If there is no airconditioning or ventilation, then ceiling fans will be very useful, especially in locations which have high humidity. It is essential that at the very least the air be kept in motion.

The airconditioning system needs to be running continuously, even in the silent hours. There is no point switching it off at night or on weekends. While you may save on energy, you will also be hastening the degradation of your records.

You should ensure that there are no gaps around the doors leading into the storage areas, or that there is any other possibility that conditioned air may be lost. Any small gaps around the window frames should be sealed. Likewise, gaps around the door frames leading to the storage areas. Leaks and gaps simply deny you the environmental conditions you are trying to achieve. There are a number of commercial sealants and gap fillers available from hardware stores, including silicone. Dust strips can also be used on doors to seal gaps. Tight fitting external doors with good quality draught extrusion fittings should also be fitted. These will help maintain stable environmental conditions inside the building and prevent the entry of dirt and dust.

As a general point, minimise access into the storage areas; the greater the movement of people through these areas the more you are likely to lose the conditions you are trying to achieve.

The floor of the storage area should be checked to ensure it is level, which is particularly important if you are going to use mobile shelving. It is important to find out if the floor can take the weight of fully laden shelving. If there is any doubt you may have to obtain a structural engineer's report. The floor should be covered, preferably with vinyl. Carpet cannot sustain the wear and tear that vinyl can, and also collects dust and small fibres which will simply add to the overall pollution level of the area. Bare concrete floors should be discouraged as they also can give off contaminants which will affect both records and people.

Finally, in assessing the long term suitability of the building to house your archives, the storage capacity should be able to accommodate existing record holdings, as well as anticipated annual growth rates for at least ten years. In calculating capacities, remember to include records held externally that may be coming to your custody at a later stage.

The importance of environmental conditions for long-term record storage

Records are created in many physical formats. Each format usually involves a combination of components, which in some cases occur naturally, and in other cases are manufactured. These components often react differently to environmental extremes. As a result, each record format usually has its own set of preservation requirements.

All materials degrade over time and, in this context heat, moisture and light are all contributing factors. With lower temperature, humidity and light levels, and the absence of dirt and dust, the process of degradation can be slowed.

Temperature and relative humidity

Constant temperature and relative humidity levels can greatly assist records protection, irrespective of their format. Frequent fluctuations in either temperature or humidity will only hasten records degradation. Whatever environmental levels you adopt these conditions should be monitored 24 hours a day, and any deviations should be remedied. If a pattern of drift is established, even within set tolerances, action should be taken to return to stable conditions. The critical factor here is that conditions must be constantly sustained.

Strict controls should apply in all areas where your archives are held – not only the storage areas, but conservation laboratories and other locations, even if the records are only held there on a temporary basis.

For paper, it is suggested that between 18° and 20° Celsius and 50% relative humidity are appropriate. For films, photographs and magnetic media the tolerances are less; the

An existing building converted for archival use may have issues which affect the environment for your collection. Here, a de-humidifyer has been installed in an attempt to ameliorate the effects of constant rising damp and high humidity.

lower the temperature the better. Less than 18° Celsius is desirable, with a relative humidity level between 35% and 45% if possible.

The preservation of colour film requires even more stringent conditions than does black and white film; the reason being the dyes or pigments used in the film which can fade over time. Most institutions simply rely on their black and white film storage area for colour film preservation.

Air quality

The air that passes through the storage area has an important role to play in records preservation. Ideally the building should be airconditioned, so that air is kept in continuous motion day and night, being recirculated to all parts of the facility. The air entering the building can contain contaminants such as dust, sulphur dioxide and carbon monoxide, so it must be filtered. The air inside the building has pollutants too. The records you are trying to protect can release contaminants as they deteriorate, and people using the building can do likewise, for example, body odour. Whatever filtration system you use it should be capable of removing the bulk of these impurities. There should also be a regular intake of fresh air. In areas which are staffed regularly the level would be set at 10%, but in storage areas the level can be less.

Light

The last environmental criteria is ultraviolet light, which is found in natural light, and can also emanate from some light fittings. Ultraviolet light can have a detrimental effect on records, whatever their format.

To guard against the effects of ultraviolet light inside the building you can place filters over each light fitting, or you can use fittings which emit low ultraviolet light. The latter is preferable.

All light fittings should be covered with diffusers. They reduce the glare and help spread the light more evenly.

Monitoring environmental conditions

There are a number of ways you can monitor environmental conditions in your storage area, ranging from very sophisticated and expensive, to simple and inexpensive. The most sophisticated means is with a building management system. With its wide array of sensors it can record conditions on an ongoing basis. Further, when fully integrated with an airconditioning system, it can make adjustments when conditions stray outside designated parameters, or at least alert you that conditions have strayed.

Older style thermohygrographs can also be used but they need to be monitored more closely, recalibrated from time to time, their readings noted, and the graph paper replaced at intervals depending on the speed of the instrument. You can also use sling psychrometers or hand held probes and recorders, which can measure both temperature and relative humidity levels. They can be purchased from conservation supply centres. Portable electronic dataloggers can be used too. In a small repository area only one or two would be needed. They are powered by a lithium battery and can monitor conditions without interruption for over a year. The results can then be downloaded to a computer system. There are a number of different products available, but they are generally expensive. Their advantage is their portability, and the fact that they can fit inside storage boxes, and tell you precisely what environmental conditions you are achieving.

What can you do if you are not achieving the desired conditions? Assuming your storage area is as sealed as you can possibly make it, and there are no gaps in the ceiling, walls, or under the doors, if the temperature levels are outside the optimum range then heaters or fans may help to either raise or lower the levels as necessary. If the humidity levels are too high you use portable dehumidifiers, or moisture absorbing crystals. Dehumidifiers can be purchased or hired. Crystals can be purchased at supermarkets and hardware stores. The latter are cheap and easy to use, though they work best in small rooms and need to be replaced fairly regularly. Ceiling fans can also help too.

Fire protection

Fire protection is all about the safety of people, the preservation of records and other assets and the building itself. Protection should be viewed on a number levels. Obviously, you would like to avoid fires in the first place. But if they do occur the means should exist to detect them at the earliest opportunity, and then they should be rapidly contained and extinguished.

Avoidance and safety

The risk of fire can be minimised with good housekeeping, well trained staff, and up to date emergency procedures. Train your staff on what to do in emergencies. Evacuation procedures should be tested (and drills held if necessary) at least once each year.

Remember that many fires have their origin with faulty electrical equipment.

Appropriately maintained equipment will go a long way towards reducing the risk of a fire.

Fire exits and emergency lighting should conform with local codes and standards. Be sure that all signs and exit lights are clearly visible, particularly if you are using high shelving in your storage areas.

Fire exits should never be locked on the inside, and should be capable of being opened in a single movement, for example, 'crash bar' type. They should never have anything placed in front of them, such as stores or furniture, which would impede a person's escape. You should ensure that exits remain clear on the outside of the building, that is, that there are no stores, garbage bins, or even parked cars which would restrict movement.

Detection

You should be fully aware and familiar with the building's fire detection system. Ideally, the system should have a direct telephone line to the fire brigade. Such a line will ensure the brigade is notified automatically whenever there is an alarm. The building should have a network of smoke and heat detectors. If all of this is beyond your finances, you can install smoke detectors which you can purchase at hardware stores. They are quite cheap, and an electrician is not needed to install them.

Containment and suppression

Having detected the fire you need the means of containing it, then putting it out. Large buildings use either wet pipe sprinklers or gas flood systems, such as Inergen or FM200. Gas systems usually work best in confined spaces, such as small vaults.

If suppression systems are beyond your budget, at least try and ensure that the building has a series of hand held extinguishers. The two most common types are: carbon dioxide, red with a black band, and dry chemical, which are red with a white band. Both are suitable for fires involving paper, or live electrical equipment.

There is a tendency to place extinguishers near electrical machines, for example, photocopiers, but this is not a good move. The best place is near major exits or exit routes so that people can reach them quickly and easily.

Fire blankets can also be used to extinguish very small fires. Again, they can be purchased at hardware and department stores and are quite cheap.

Of course you or your staff should only tackle the smallest of fires. If there is a risk of personal injury the fire should be left to the fire brigade to extinguish.

Security

Regardless of whether you occupy an entire building and you are responsible for security matters, or you are just one tenant, and the building owner is responsible, ideally the building should have an alarm system, with offsite monitoring by a security company. The system should cover all access points to the building, both doors and windows. If this is too costly, at the very least good quality locks to all main doors and windows are essential.

All doors should be of good quality and it is preferable that they be solid, rather than hollow core. Solid doors provide greater security and are more fire resistant. External points of entry, such as the front door and loading bay door, should have double–keyed deadlocks fitted.

One of the best forms of security is the use of neighbours, or other tenants if your premises are rented. If you are sharing with another agency, then each should be encouraged to support the others, creating an informal security network.

There should be good lighting around the foyer areas, loading docks, grounds and parking areas. As far as carparks are concerned there is of course the safety of staff and visitors to consider, particularly at night.

Lighting and energy management

Lighting levels in frequently used staffing and public areas, where concentrated desk type activity is required, should be between 240–400 lux. In the storage areas, where regular access is not required, a level of 80–240 lux is appropriate. Even if your premises are quite small, and staffing and storage areas are colocated, you should attempt as far as possible to have dual light levels.

Overhead lights in the storage area should be positioned to illuminate the spaces between the rows of shelving.

To provide better protection for your records, all light fittings, particularly those in the storage area, should be fitted with low ultraviolet emitting tubes or ultraviolet filters.

Depending on how large your storage area is, it is a good move to have timed lighting installed, though an electrician will be needed to do it. If the area is only small then the main switch should be connected to a timer. It is a good way of saving energy when no–one is in the area.

Occupational health and safety

Many things in a building can represent a hazard to staff and visitors. Some materials, for example, carpets and curtains, give off vapours and other contaminants, and can also be harmful to the records you are trying to protect.

If staff or visitors repeatedly complain of illnesses – sore throats, coughs and colds, running noses – it may be that they are reacting to something in the building. Regular cleaning and maintenance will go a long way towards ensuring the removal of many of these contaminants.

Materials handling equipment

Depending on how large your building is, you will need an array of devices to help your staff retrieve records from the storage area, or move records about the building. These devices can include step stools, ladders and platform ladders.

Retrieving records from high shelving, or plan cabinets stacked on top of each other, requires special attention to ensure the safety of staff and the prevention of damage to the records. This is particularly the case if the records themselves are large or heavy, for example, maps and volumes. Platform ladders are often used. They are made from aluminium and are light and easily manoeuvrable, and have a platform at the top that can accommodate a person, or two persons, allowing them to retrieve the records from the shelving. If you are using this type of ladder ensure that the wheels can be locked in position so that the ladder will not move while someone is on it.

Maintenance

It is assumed that a contractor will undertake most of your maintenance. Irrespective of whether you are responsible for the contract, or it is arranged by another party, the contract should include the following items:

- airconditioning systems;
- fire protection – alarm panels, smoke and heat detectors, extinguishers;
- security – alarm panels, motion detectors, surveillance equipment; and
- electrical systems – switchboards, distribution boards, lighting.

There are, however, a number of things which you can do to assist. Storage areas should be kept clean at all times. Regular dusting and vacuuming will help reduce the build up of dirt and dust.

Periodic walks around the building and simple observation will alert you to potential problems. On the building's exterior look for roof leaks, blocked gutters or drains. Inside, look for any evidence of water marks on the ceilings and walls.

If your storage area only has a domestic–type airconditioner, rather than an entire airconditioning system, it should be serviced periodically and by a reliable company. Pay particular attention to the filters; they should be cleaned or replaced as necessary.

Hand held fire extinguishers and hose reels should be checked from time to time. As a guide, industrial strength extinguishers and reels are inspected every six months.

Smoke detector batteries should be replaced as recommended by the manufacturer.

Door and window locks should also be checked to ensure they are functioning normally.

Integrated pest management

Disasters can come in many forms, but one of the more insidious is attack by insect pests. To reduce the risk of pest infestation it is generally not necessary to fumigate the building and storage areas at regular intervals. There are other steps that can be taken.

Keep the building's surrounds free of organic mulches, or flowerbeds, as they can often attract termites and other insects; inorganic material such as rocks and stones are preferable.

Make regular inspections of the building, both internally and externally. Watch for signs of pest infestations developing, for example, dead insects, droppings, webs or nests. Pay special attention to dark corners. Look for holes or cracks in gutters or walls and any hollows in retaining walls. Note if there are any dripping taps or pools of water. All of these can encourage pest development.

If there are any holes or gaps in the floors or walls, particularly in the storage areas, they should be sealed. If the gaps are small you can use silicone; if they are large there are a number of commercial fillers available at hardware stores that will suffice.

Good housekeeping and common sense measures can go a long way to keeping pest problems to a minimum. Keep the building free of dirt and dust. Thoroughly inspect incoming record transfers to ensure that a pest problem is not being introduced. Confine eating and drinking to the amenities area, and empty rubbish containers regularly.

If necessary, you make use of blunder (or sticky) traps to catch crawling insects such as cockroaches and ants, baits to poison rodents such as rats and mice, and inhibiting growth regulators, a new generation of chemicals which prevent the development of mature insects or ensure that those that do survive are sterile.

Most of these products are readily available, in some cases at the supermarket, and are generally quite cheap. They are easy to use and dispose of when no longer required.

If you do have a problem affecting your records these are some of the basic ways you can treat them.

Freezing – the objects are sealed in polyethylene (bags or heat sealed packages) with as much air removed as possible to ensure that moisture is not removed from the object and that condensation is later avoided on thawing. They are placed in a freezer for at least two weeks, with a temperature of at least -20°C. After two weeks the objects, still enclosed in polyethylene, are removed from the freezer and allowed to reach room temperature. This will kill insect eggs, larvae, pupae and adults.

High temperature – the objects are sealed in black polyethylene (bags or heat sealed packages) to ensure that moisture is not removed from the object, and are heated to at least 55°C for at least three hours. The objects, still enclosed in polyethylene, are removed and returned to room temperature. This will kill insect eggs, larvae, pupae and adults. Several designs exist for more effective enclosures such as tents and boxes.

Oxygen deprivation/low oxygen environments – insects may be killed in low oxygen environments by sealing the objects in oxygen impermeable film packages, and reducing the level of oxygen. The oxygen may be reduced by placing oxygen scavengers in the package, or with a gas such as nitrogen. The amount of oxygen scavenger needed to reduce the oxygen levels in the package varies according to the size of the package. The method will kill insect eggs, larvae, pupae and adults.

Before you use any of these treatments, however, you should seek professional advice to ensure the objects will not be subjected to any further damage.

Full fumigation

If you have a pest infestation which cannot be resolved by any of the above means, you may have to fumigate, however, fumigation should always be a last resort. A licensed contractor should always undertake the work. Before fumigating have the contractor advise you what product will be used and ensure you receive a copy of the *Material Safety Data Sheet* for that product. The sheet will inform you what effects the product has and what safety measures may need to be imposed. Ensure that all staff and visitors are aware that the facility is being fumigated, and that access is restricted at that time.

Disaster preparedness

The most common threats to an archive building and its contents are fire, flood and vandalism. No matter how small your budget, the records you hold are important. For this reason you should develop a disaster preparedness and response plan. Establishing a disaster preparedness plan involves:

- an assessment of possible risks – what are the risks to your collection and how likely is it that these risks might become reality. What can be done to minimise these risks?
- an identification of the most significant records in your collection, those for which salvage would be a priority. In this context some record formats need to be attended to more rapidly than others, for example, computer tapes and colour photographs cannot stand prolonged wetting. Most papers and coated papers (glossies) need prompt treatment, more so than ordinary office bond type papers;
- the establishment of a disaster response team or person with clearly defined responsibilities;

- an identification of key companies who may be able to assist you in an emergency, or other cultural institutions prepared to provide assistance and materials;
- the training of staff so that everyone knows what to do in an emergency, whatever form it may take; and
- and the writing of the plan itself.

Once the plan has been developed you should test it regularly and keep it up to date.

Maintaining a disaster preparedness kit

As part of being prepared for a disaster, you should also assemble an emergency kit. Here is a list of the items that would typically be included in such a kit:

Instruction sheet	Scissors
Perforated paper towels	Torch and batteries
Absorbent cloths	Electrical extension cord
Rubber and cotton gloves	Clipboard
Disposable face masks	Note pad, pens and pencils
Dust coat	Marker pens
Rubbish bags	Sticky labels
Plastic bags	Plastic bucket
Twist ties	Squeegee bucket and mop
Masking tape and dispenser	Pre–cut plastic sheeting
String	Pre–cut archival quality blotting paper
Paper–cutting knife	Disposable camera

Do not use a wheely (garbage) bin to store your disaster preparedness items. They are too tall and to access the contents you have to tip them over and spill everything on the floor. You should use large plastic boxes (with wheels so you can easily move them), that provide ready access to the contents. Ensure that you check the contents periodically so that nothing has gone missing. Items such as torch batteries should be replaced from time to time.

It may also be desirable to purchase a small fire proof safe in which to store key documents, photographic negatives, or accession registers as added protection in an emergency.

State and national archives usually have large purpose-built storage such as this.

Shelving

Your repository should be fitted out with shelving to accommodate your records. Records should never be left uncovered, nor should they be stored on the floor. It is preferable that steel shelving be used, not wooden. The latter can give off contaminants and, unless properly treated, is also susceptible to insect infestation and is more likely to burn than is steel shelving.

If you find that you have insufficient shelving to meet your needs and there seems to be no alternative to using the floor, then some type of blocks or pallets should be used so that record are not located directly on the floor. This can make a very big difference should there be a flood in the area. You should also be aware that some wooden pallets can release contaminants which may be harmful to your records and can, of course, attract insect pests.

Shelving methods of operation

Shelving can be supplied in static or mobile forms.

Static shelving is ideal for small buildings. It is cheaper than mobile shelving, and there are no moving components, so nothing can break down or wear out.

Mobile shelving consists of units mounted onto bases fitted with wheels (sometimes called mobiles or carriages). The bases run on tracks (rails) secured to the floor. Static shelving units, usually fitted at one or both ends of a group of mobile units, are mounted on plinths (bases) secured directly to the floor. Mobile shelving allows you to store far more material than static shelving over a given floor area – often more than double the quantity. Because the shelving moves, only one access aisle is needed. When a document is required, the particular row of shelving is located and an adjacent aisle is created by moving the shelving units apart. Another advantage of mobile shelving is its potential to enhance security – mobile units can be locked to prevent unauthorised access.

Static shelving such as this can immediately increase the capacity of your designated 'archives' space. Of course, it is never enough!

Yet there are a number of issues that you should consider before installing mobile shelving. It requires stronger floor loadings than static shelving, so a structural engineer may be needed to ensure that the floor loadings are sufficient, and because the shelving moves on tracks, an uneven floor can interfere with laying the tracks and the subsequent operation of the shelving.

Tracks can be placed below ground (sunken), or above ground (raised). Above ground tracks are particularly useful if the floor is uneven, or if your property is leased and the shelving has to be removed when the lease expires. If above ground tracks are used, false floors can be installed to cover them, making it easier for staff and trolleys to pass over the tracks, and reducing the risk of accidents.

Large compactus units require mechanical assistance to move – see the handle and wheel arrangement.

Choosing between hand operated or electric mobile shelving

Mobile shelving can be supplied in hand operated or electrically operated forms.

Hand operated – the operator moves a row of shelving by turning a handle, steering wheel or similar device located at the end of the row. The handle is connected, through a series of cogs and chains, to an axle located underneath the shelving. In turn, the axle is connected to wheels that run on the tracks.

Electrically operated – the operator moves the shelving by pushing a button located at the entrance to the row. The button is connected to a motor that drives the shelving. This type of shelving is very easy to use, but it is more expensive to purchase. It also has a number of components that could break down over time, or ultimately become obsolete.

If the cost of new shelving is beyond your reach you can often purchase second hand shelving at government furniture stores. Used shelving should be checked for the presence of rust and thoroughly cleaned prior to use, and it may be necessary to have it resprayed if the original paint has been badly damaged. Polyurethane varnishes are suitable for this purpose. Ensure the varnish is thoroughly dried, preferably for at least one week, before using the shelving.

Boxes and other forms of packaging

All records should be boxed, preferably in archival quality containers. Records should not be stored loose on shelves, or on the floor. They are susceptible to damage from dirt and dust, insects, fire and water. An added advantage of boxes is that they act as a buffer around the surrounding environmental conditions, and the temperature and humidity levels are usually lower inside boxes, than they are outside. Finally, paper boxes will also absorb water should a flood occur.

Boxes

Archival quality containers are now commonly manufactured from fluted board, solid board and polypropylene. They can be purchased commercially, in large and small quantities, and at fairly reasonable prices. They are available in a large array of sizes to cater for most record formats.

Fluted board containers are made from two layers of paper with a piece of corrugated (or fluted) board in between. These containers are lighter, and generally cheaper, than solid board and are usually just as strong. The fluting gives the containers their strength.

Standard files and smaller documents should be stored in boxes. Larger documents and certificates should be stored flat, not folded, and placed inside paper folders or plastic jackets.

Plastic packaging materials

There are many packaging products made from plastics that can be used to store records. Plastic is of course a very general term and can include a number of variations. Some plastics include coatings or plasticisers that can cause chemical degradation of records and these should be avoided. The most widely available plastics are:

- **polypropylene** – a good quality plastic;
- **polyester** – a good quality plastic, but note that there are different types; the most appropriate is uncoated polyester (eg. Mylar–D);
- **polyethylene** – a low cost alternative to both polypropylene and polyester. Only use low density polyethylene (LDPE) resealable storage bags (for example, 'zip' bags), the type you can buy at supermarkets. Polyethylene is, however, weaker and floppier than polyester or polypropylene, so it may not be strong enough for large or heavy items; and
- **polyvinyl chloride (PVC)** – you should not use any packaging materials made from PVC. If the product carries no identification, the easiest way to tell if it contains PVC is if it has a sweetish smell, reminiscent of a new car interior. PVC contains plasticisers which affect the resin binders in photocopiers and laser printer toners, causing them

to flow and adhere to other surfaces. In effect, the image transfers from one surface to another. A way to test for PVC is to place the plastic in direct contact with a photocopied image for a few days and put it in a warm place. If the plastic sticks to the image then you know it is PVC.

Photographs should preferably be stored separately in albums. They should not be kept in bundles nor held in boxes or bags. You can use albums of the 'slip in' variety, the type available at supermarkets and department stores. Higher quality albums made from polypropylene can also be purchased from dedicated suppliers and are ideal. In either case the photographs are held in see through sleeves which protect them and provide ready access to each item. You should not use 'magnetic' photographic albums, where photos are held against the page. These albums use plasticisers, which is how the photos are held in place, and can actually damage the photos rather than preserve them.

Negatives should be held separately and not grouped in bundles, regardless of whether you have individual negatives or strips. They should be stored in jackets.

If you are storing films, such as Super 8 or 16/35 mm, use plastic (polypropylene) canisters rather than metal ones. The same applies to the core, or spool, around which the film is wound. Metal canisters and spools generally rust over time and can accelerate chemical degradation of the films. If you cannot afford polypropylene canisters, wrap each film individually and place them in boxes.

Maps, drawings and other large items should best be stored flat and placed in plan cabinets or racking. If space allocations, or your budget, preclude this they should be rolled and stored in tubes. They should not be folded as they will crack and tear along the folds. Rolled plans should not be held together with rubber bands as the bands corrode over time. Depending on the nature and value of each map or plan, you may want to consider using interleaving paper between each item. This will help prevent abrasion, ink transfer and transfer of adhesives between the items. Try to avoid rolling large numbers of plans together as this simply makes retrieval and use more difficult. If possible, fragile items should be supported by rolling them around an inner core, for extra support.

Audio and videocassettes, and compact discs, can be stored in boxes.

If you are located in the tropics, and you are storing documents inside plastic jackets, you may need to insert a paperboard sheet into the jacket as well to counter the effects of high humidity levels. If you are planning a project to place records into plastic sleeves try to do this on a day when conditions are dry. You can then be confident that you will not be trapping moisture inside the sleeves as you place records into them.

Archival quality containers

You should be aware that the terms 'archival' and 'acid free' are sometimes used fairly liberally. As far as paper is concerned look for terms such as 'permanent', 'wood free', or 'lignin free'. Or ask if it has passed the photographic activity test (PAT) if you intend to use the material for storing photographs. The PAT test is a form of rapid aging whereby materials are assessed for their long–term suitability for photographic storage. If you are using plastics for photographic storage, look for terms such as 'photo safe' or 'copy safe'.

If your budget is such that you cannot afford boxes, then use the cartons in which your photocopy paper is supplied. They are not high quality, but they are sturdy and will provide some protection. Otherwise wrap the records in plain paper, but not newspaper nor coloured paper, as both are highly acidic.

You can also use lidded polystyrene boxes that fruit and vegetables are often packed in. Most supermarkets will give them away, but be sure to clean them before use. They should not be seen as a long–term solution, or used in very large quantities, as they could be a hazard in the event of a fire.

Equipment to facilitate the movement of masses of records is important – it can take the form of large 'crates' such as this, or be something as simple as a hand trolley.

Moving the collection

From time to time you may have to move your entire collection to new premises. These are some of the issues you should take into consideration when planning and carrying out the move.

Appoint a supervisor

Appoint a staff coordinator to oversee the move. This person should have the responsibility and the ability to make decisions, which will often be required 'on the run'.

Planning for the move

When planning for a move, talk to other people who have gone through similar moves, and ask them lots of questions. Look at established shelving installations similar to the one you might be planning to buy to ensure they are suitable for your collection.

Detailed planning and preparation for the move are essential. Develop a plan, but keep it clear and simple. Carefully examine the records to be moved and the space that will accommodate them, and try to anticipate difficulties. However, even well laid plans go awry; so be flexible, be patient, and have an alternative plan for when things do go wrong.

Hiring professionals when moving an archive is recommended.

Well before the move, walk through the new location with the removalist – look for anything that might prove to be a hindrance, for example, narrow door widths, low ceiling heights, access to lifts, lack of parking facilities for removal vans.

You should consider whether to restrict services to the public during the move. If such services are restricted ensure that everyone who needs to know is informed well in advance.

If you have the resources, undertake a complete stocktake of the collection prior to the move, and ensure that all records are appropriately packaged, all are accounted for, and any unwanted records are removed from the collection.

Be sure to number and label all boxes clearly. Shrink–wrapping boxes once they are placed on trolleys is one way to help keep things together and to prevent material from falling off the trolleys during the move.

Moving an archive is an enormous job.

Communication before, during, and after the move

Cooperation and support from all staff are essential. Maintain active communication with all people and departments involved in the move.

All decisions should be in writing and disseminated as widely as possible.

The removalist

Ensure that the moving company has first hand experience in the packaging and transportation of archival materials, particularly when a long distance move is involved.

Interview all potential removalists and only use a company that has demonstrated practical experience with archival collections, or similar materials.

Mass storage – rented space in a commercial warehouse.

After the contract has been let talk to the removalists, and get to know their supervisor.

The removalist should only pack and unpack records under direct supervision by your staff.

The move

A staff member should be with the removalist at all times. Have staff on site at both locations for security, and to monitor any sudden changes.

As almost all moves operate to very strict timeframes, set aside an area in the new location for problems that may arise in order to keep the momentum going, but leave these problems till later.

At the end of the move do a final walk through both buildings with the removalist to ensure that nothing has been left behind in the old building, and everything is accounted for in the new building.

Using commercial storage providers

It may be that your resources preclude you from establishing your own storage facility and you may decide to use a commercial storage provider instead. If you do, the facility that the provider has available must meet all the features that have been outlined in this chapter.

You should undertake a thorough tour of inspection of the facility. Apart from the obvious features, such as the level of airconditioning, fire and security protection, there are other factors to consider. Is the storage area solely dedicated to records, or are other items held there, such as furniture? Does the company have a comprehensive maintenance and cleaning plan in place? How clean are the storage areas? Does the facility provide a search room if needed? Has the company prepared a comprehensive disaster plan? Does the company provide a record retrieval and return service, and at what cost?

Summary checklist

The following is a summary of the basic requirements needed for records preservation as well as providing appropriate conditions for staff and visitors. The list assumes that you have a very minimal budget.

Building fabric

Whatever building is to be provided for records storage the area should be well sealed to assist with the maintenance of stable environmental conditions.

Brick or concrete walls and floors should be sealed to prevent the release of contaminants and to prevent moisture passing through them.

Any gaps around door frames, windows frames and elsewhere should be sealed.

Windows or skylights in the storage areas should be avoided if possible; if they are already there they should be covered.

The building should have a pitched roof and a good drainage system.

The building should be free of environmental hazards such as asbestos and polychlorinated biphenyls.

Environmental conditions

The aim should be to establish a temperature range of 18°–20° Celsius and relative humidity of 50% for paper storage and less than 18° Celsius and 35%–45% relative humidity for black and white film and magnetic media.

Whatever conditions are achieved they should remain constant at all times and should be monitored.

Ceiling fans should be used to keep the air moving if there is no air–conditioning system.

Heaters, fans, dehumidifiers and moisture absorbing crystals should be used whenever conditions stray outside the nominated parameters.

This compactus unit is the sum total of the archive area for this organisation. Although lockable, its location in a busy corridor is far from ideal, and there is an obvious lack of space for processing, or for accessing the materials contained within, short of using the floor.

Lighting

The lighting levels in the staffing and public areas should be between 240 lux and 400 lux. For the storage areas they should be between 80 lux and 240 lux, depending on the level of usage.

Light fittings in the storage areas should be fitted low ultraviolet emitting lights or have ultraviolet filters placed over them.

Fire protection

Whatever fire safety systems are available in the building they should be known and understood by all staff.

All exits should be clearly identified and emergency lighting should be kept in working order.

Your work space should have enough room to spread material as you are processing it

At the very least, storage areas should be fitted with smoke detectors. A supply of hand held extinguishers should be available and staff should know how to use them.

Security

Solid doors with double keyed deadlocks should be used, particularly for the storage areas.

Locks should be placed on all windows.

Records storage

All records should be held in containers, preferably archival containers, and should be stored in shelving, not on the floor. If you cannot afford boxes, use the boxes that your photocopy paper comes in.

Staffing and public areas

These areas should be designed to be functional and to provide for the creature comforts of the people using them.

Maintenance

A program of regular maintenance should be developed. At the very least, the facility should be dusted and cleaned regularly. A program of regular walking inspections, both inside and outside the facility, should be implemented.

Integrated pest management

A program of good housekeeping and cleaning, regular inspections and monitoring for pests should be implemented.

Disaster preparedness

Disaster preparedness and response plans should be developed.

Finally

Remember that you are not alone. If you need information about your building, or its maintenance, or want advice about preservation, you have access to other sources of expertise, including the Internet.

The National Archives of Australia has information about storage and preservation available on its website (www.naa.gov.au).

Other notable Internet reference sources are *Conservation Online* operated by Stanford University (http://palimpsest.stanford.edu/), and the International Council on Archives (www.ica.org).

CHAPTER 4

preservation

ELIZABETH HADLOW

CHAPTER ABSTRACT

Preservation involves the ongoing care of archives so that they survive into the future. It includes surveying collections to recognise issues and problems, preventative preservation, conservation treatments for individual items and disaster preparedness. While preservation may seem daunting and costly, there are practical solutions for different budgets and resources, as well as basic conservation treatments that can be performed with minimal equipment and materials.

This chapter advises you on implementing appropriate preservation programs and practices for your archive. It includes consideration of definitions, discussion of ethics and responsibilities in relation to preservation and conservation, as well as the principles of surveying collections and recognising material and format types. Deterioration mechanisms and issues are covered so that you can recognise when there is a problem, and principles of preventive conservation for different sized archive collections are considered and explained.

Please refer to the accompanying CD for checklists and forms.

Definitions and ethics

Preservation, briefly defined, is the care of records so that they survive and remain accessible for as long as they are required – sometimes this is for as little as ten years, but can be indefinitely. The Australian Institute for the Conservation of Cultural Material (AICCM) defines preservation as:

> *All actions taken to retard deterioration of or prevent damage to cultural material. It involves controlling the environment and conditions of use, and may include treatment in order to maintain an object as nearly as possible in an unchanging state. In the case of archival material, moving image and sound, this may include transfer to another medium.* (AICCM 2002)

The AICCM breaks preservation into sub-groups including:

- **Preventive conservation** – pro-active, macro strategies such as environmental control that provide care to the greatest number of records
- **Conservation treatment** – intervention to repair or stabilise individual records

- **Restoration** – conservation treatments that return an item to as close to original condition as possible. These are usually aesthetic treatments that are time consuming and costly, and not often applied to archival records.

The basic definitions this chapter will use are that *preservation* refers to everything that contributes to the physical well-being of the collections, and *conservation* refers to direct physical intervention with the material and is only one part of preservation (Teygeler 2005).

Like archivists, conservators follow a Code of Ethics that regulates and guides them as a professional group. Conservators work in a wide variety of heritage areas, and so the Code needs to be broad in its definition of preservation and how it should be applied to collections.

The marriage of archive and conservation principles needs to be established in a workable and practical way for the greatest benefit of all records. Archivists and conservators should articulate their needs and principles very early in their working relationships so that the best preservation outcome for the archives can be reached.

Responsibilities

Who is responsible for the preservation of archival materials? The answer is, of course, that everyone who has contact with a record has responsibility for its care. For our purposes here though, it is necessary to recognise specialisations and key areas of responsibility.

Conservators are trained in material science and are technical experts in their chosen specialisation, e.g. paper conservation, metals conservation, photographic conservation, preventive conservation and so on. Generally only the largest archives have conservators on staff and most organisations will only have access to conservation advice through consultants or perhaps from government archives. It is therefore necessary for record managers and archivists to be conversant with key preservation strategies that will ensure the long-term care of their collections.

A preservation lab

Archivists, records managers and indeed all who work in archives are the most important personnel responsible for day to day preservation. They need to be mindful of how their archives are stored and handled; train staff and users in the handling of archives; and educate others on the importance of preserving the archives in perpetuity. Explaining to people the importance of the archives in their care is half the battle – when people understand that their small actions can have a large impact, they will be more willing to undertake the preservation strategies that you implement – they are no longer just a cog in a wheel, they have real responsibilities and can see their place in the whole. Often seemly insignificant things such as not eating or leaving rubbish in storage areas can have the greatest impact on their long term care.

"We have to store these records carefully, so make sure you find a nice, cool place ..."

A key responsibility for all who work in archives is keeping their knowledge current. Staying up to date with new techniques and issues ensures that out-of-date practices that can be detrimental to archive preservation are discontinued and replaced with better strategies. Preservation is an area that requires constant learning to remain current as technologies change and develop. It is important to recognise the limitations of your knowledge so that you know when to ask for advice and when you can manage an issue by yourself. Publications such as this one are very important for providing a grounding to grow from, but it is equally important to read journals and periodicals, as they will provide the most up-to-date information. Growing areas in information sharing are e-newsletters and message boards and there are numerous examples in the preservation area.

Knowing your collection

The best approach to preservation is knowledge. Knowing your collection allows you to plan the best approach to its care and avoid causes of deterioration. Records at risk can be identified and actions can be taken to mitigate the risks. Storage environments and protective packaging can be targeted towards records with specific requirements and those most in need.

Knowing your collection falls into two basic areas – the building and the archives. Chapter 3: *Buildings & Storage* describes in detail how to assess buildings and storage areas for their suitability. I will be focussing here on how knowing your archive enables you to identify risks and helps you make decisions about what strategies to employ.

Accessioning, listing and cataloguing

So when should you start finding out about your collection? The best time is right at the beginning when records are being deposited into your collection. Gathering information about archives at this time can prevent problems (for example, pest infestations from newly transferred records) as well as helping you build up knowledge about your archive right from the start. It doesn't matter if you already have an existing collection that has not been assessed in this way – starting now means less work down the track.

Accessioning, listing and cataloguing your collection correctly goes a long way to providing the information you need to preserve it. When you catalogue your archives, be mindful of media format, materials, and condition, and include this information in your database. This provides the opportunity to survey your collection from your database. If you are not in the position of having your collection completely catalogued then there are other methods that can be applied to gathering this information.

Surveys

Surveys are the most common approach to identifying what you hold in your archive. There are many different types of survey and many different approaches, and the one you decide on will depend on the size of your archive, your resources, and what outcomes you desire. For example, if you have a relatively small archive and many staff members or volunteers willing to help, then you may be able to survey the whole collection. However, this would be the exception rather than the rule. In most cases a strategic approach or a sample survey will be necessary.

Surveys that determine the format and condition of the archival records you hold are the most common, and the most useful, from a preservation perspective. For example, you might determine that your standard paper files held in boxes are in relatively good condition and are in no urgent need of conservation attention. Your large format photographic negatives that smell of vinegar and are beginning to curl are, however, in urgent need of relocation into cool/cold storage and possibly require preservation copying to ensure their long-term survival.

Decide what information you want from your survey before you start. Do you want to know the condition of all the records to develop conservation treatment strategies? Or are you more interested in determining whether your storage conditions are providing a sufficient level of physical safety for your archives? Or do you need to know the condition of a particular part of your archival holdings? Without knowing the answers to these questions you may end up with results that are not very useful.

The following are some simple data headings to use when undertaking a preservation survey:

- **Preliminary information** – date of survey, surveyor
  - The date is particularly important as it enables comparative surveys down the

track – such as comparing the condition of particular items over say a ten year period.

- **Location of archives** – address, description of storage area (type of shelving, environmental conditions, attic, basement, internal cupboard, etc)
  - The more information you have about the storage environment the greater your capacity to make informed improvements.
- **Type of archival record** – format, size, material, date range
  - All of this information is very important for your ability to provide storage that best suits your holdings, as well as separating materials that might adversely affect each other.
- **Condition of archival record** – general appearance, discolouration, tears, creases, dirt, mould, insect damage, fastenings (paper clips, staples)
  - This information will inform your decisions about conservation treatments – whether they are necessary, what they might be, how long they will take, whether storage improvements might be sufficient.
  - This information is also an indicator of the suitability of current storage and handling practices. For example, overfilled boxes of files will often exhibit particular signs of wear – creases, tears, abrasion. Fixing this type of problem is relatively simple but can decrease damage dramatically.
- **Storage containers** – archival/non-archival, folders, boxes, sleeves
  - When you do your assessment, take all things into consideration – the quality of the materials used, how overcrowded the containers are.
- **Future access requirements**
  - Determining the likelihood and amount of access required to your records can help determine what records to prioritise for preservation treatment and/or copying, and what storage containers are best for them.
- **Suggested action** – relocate into air-conditioned storage, re-house, repair, remove from use, no action
  - Some of these actions can be implemented immediately – such as removal from use. This allows time to implement longer term strategies for handling, repair and so on.
- **Priority ranking for action**
  - This is where you get to decide what can be done now and what needs more time, more money, more staff, or all of the above!

Remember that preservation surveys are carried out on a regular basis in all types of organisations, so ask others how they went about their surveys, what software tools they used, how long they took, how many people were required and so on. You will probably be surprised at how helpful people will want to be and how much information they may be able to provide before you start.

Knowing your materials

In Australia, archives have now been collecting for over a century and so the types of material are very varied. In other countries with longer written histories the collections are even more diverse with consequent complexities. Archival holdings now include such materials as paper made from cotton rags, wood pulp or other plant fibres; film negatives made from nitrate, acetate, and polyester; leather or vellum bound books; magnetic tape; compact discs; architectural plans on plastic, paper and fabric; and parchment documents. That is only a sample of the media carrying the information – the information itself might be written in iron gall ink, carbon typewriter ink, silver gelatine emulsion, dyes, and many other materials. The range of shapes and sizes is just as daunting – maps, index cards, microfiche, moving picture film, videocassettes, CD and DVD, diaries, ledgers, letters, wills – the list seems endless. All these materials react with their environment, with each other and to handling in very particular ways. It is important to know how to reduce the causes of their deterioration.

While this chapter focuses on paper-based documents, it will also discuss other materials commonly used to create documentary formats such as still photographic negatives and prints, books and parchment.

Creating new archival records

Archival media should have certain attributes to be considered 'archival'. A high-quality archival record should display the following attributes:

- permanence, or the ability to last as long as possible
- strength and durability, or the ability to withstand use
- inherent stability, or to be relatively chemically inert and not adversely react with other materials
- continued accessibility, or the ability to be readable in future years

You should consider these factors when you are creating new records that will be required as archives, so that you are reducing the preservation burden for future archivists, records managers and conservators.

Deterioration factors

Archives deteriorate due to two main factors: the environment in which they are stored and inherent problems with the material they are made from.
We have control over only one of those factors with historic material – the storage environment, and that is covered in more detail later, both in this chapter and in Chapter 3: *Building & Storage.*

The other factor, inherent instability, can only be fully controlled in new records by choosing archival materials displaying the characteristics described above. Materials used for historic archives may not have been chosen based on their archival properties.

It is an unfortunate fact of life that decisions about materials used to create records are usually a matter of financial and procedural expedience rather than archival requirements. Many of us are dealing with the reality of that fact in our management of historic archives. The most common and worst examples of inherent instability are acidic newsprint paper and 'vinegar syndrome' in acetate film negatives. The deterioration caused by inherent instability cannot be removed but may be lessened by good storage practices.

There is not enough space here to describe all the materials found in archives. We have focussed only on the most common and those that require the most attention.

Weather tight buildings are the first step in providing sound environmental conditions for the long term storage of archives. Torrential rain compromised the guttering and roof of this building, and the records stored within it were severely damaged by water, and later, mould.

Paper

Paper is still the most common format in archives today, and it will remain so for some time to come. Paper will never be completely removed from archives due to its historic predominance over all other media. Paper records can be made from paper, card and board and come in many formats, including standard files, books, photographic media, maps and plans.

Paper is made from cellulose fibres sourced from a variety of plants. The type of plant fibres and the method of manufacture determine, to a large degree, the final characteristics of the paper. The most permanent papers are those made from plant fibres which are high in cellulose, such as cotton. (Heritage Collections Council 2000).

It is an unfortunate fact that technology and industrialisation were not kind to the development of paper. Most paper found in archives today is not made from pure cellulose fibre and does not meet archival requirements – that is it doesn't remain stable over time – this is particularly true in Australia where most of the records were produced after the introduction of wood pulp as the main fibre source in the mid-nineteenth century. Ground wood pulp usually contains deleterious amounts of lignin unless specifically treated to remove it and is generally considered to be too unstable for long term storage. This is reflected in the Australian Standard 4003-1996 (AS4003-1996) on permanent paper which states that lignin content shall be kept to trace levels only.

There is also a major distinction between permanent paper and archival paper. The main difference being that permanent paper only has to comply with specific chemical properties and fibre content, whereas archival paper also has to display certain physical characteristics – the main one being durability. The National Archives of Australia has very clear specifications in this regard and has produced a range of archival quality papers and boards with their own watermark.

In today's world there is a push to use recycled goods wherever possible and paper is one of the most easily recycled products. However, the use of recycled paper in the creation of records for retention periods of greater than 10 years is not recommended. While some recycled papers can claim to comply with AS4003-1996, i.e. they contain only trace amounts of lignin and have alkali reserves greater than 2 percent, they are not considered to be of archival quality because they do not display the necessary durability. This is mostly because each time a paper fibre is recycled it becomes shorter – meaning that the durability of the fibres is reduced (e.g. folding and wear characteristics).

Most state and national archive authorities have very good information on their websites about what papers are recommended for the creation of new records. These are good sources of current information as they are regularly being updated.

Photographic media

Photographic media can loosely be divided into two types – prints and negatives. However, these categories can sometimes get blurred. Photographic media are more common in archives than many of us realise. They appear in operational records (e.g. railways, building maintenance, children's homes, corrective services records) and records of public functions (e.g. public works constructions, state functions). Their myriad uses are also reflected in their myriad formats.

Photographic processes are chemically complex and as a result the preservation issues relating to them are also more complex. Photographs are some of the more sensitive materials held in archives and they require different preservation strategies to those required for paper collections. They have similarities with motion picture film and many of the storage recommendations for film can be applied to other photographic media. The key to looking after photographic prints effectively is to identify them correctly.

The main areas of sensitivity to be aware of with photographic media are:

- **The silver image layer**
  - Silver is particularly sensitive to deterioration caused by contact with the acids and oils in human skin. This means that plastic gloves (Nitrile or surgical gloves are best) need to be worn at all times when handling photographic materials.
  - Silver is also very susceptible to damage from atmospheric pollutants, which is why it is important to house photographic materials in enclosures that have passed the Photographic Activity Test (P.A.T) (ISO 18916 2007) and to ensure that potential contamination from air pollutants is minimised.
  - The silver in photographic materials can migrate to the surface of the image under certain conditions causing what is referred to as 'silver mirroring'. This creates areas where a silver sheen appears over the surface that usually obscures the image. This type of damage is often associated with high relative humidity, allowing the silver to move through the emulsion more easily. The best way of avoiding this problem is by keeping the relative humidity fairly low and stable.
- **Acetate film**
  - Acetate film undergoes an autocatalytic degradation process commonly referred to as 'vinegar syndrome', whereby the acetate breaks down creating acetic acid which then attacks the film in a cyclical way, speeding the deterioration process,
  - i.e. the breakdown of acetate produces the acid that continues the breakdown of the film. This process cannot be stopped, only slowed down by storage in very low temperature and relative humidity environments (see Chapter 18: *Moving Images*).
- **Dye fading and colour shift**
  - Colour dye fading can occur both in the light and in the dark. One of the best ways of delaying the onset of this problem is by low temperature and relative humidity storage. Fading of dyes is usually more problematic in lit conditions (see Chapter 18: *Moving Images*).

Prints or positives

Depending on the age of material in your collection, you may have a large range of photographic media, Table 4.1 has some examples and their periods of common use.

Photographic process	Period of common use
Daguerreotypes (direct positive on silver plate)	1839 – 1860s
Salted paper prints	1839 – 1860s
Albumen	1850 – 1900s
Wet collodion positives on glass (Ambrotypes)	1851 – 1880s
Lantern slides	1851 – 1900s
Tintypes (positive on coated iron sheet)	1852 – 1930s
Carbon prints	1860s – 1930s
Platinum prints	1873 – 1914
Cyanotypes (also known as blue prints in some formats)	1842 – present
Silver gelatine	1880s – present
Opaltype (positive on opaque white glass)	1880s – 1920s
Autochrome (colour positive on glass)	1904 – 1940s
Chromogenic prints or C-type prints and colour transparencies (standard colour prints and slides)	1935 – present
Silver dye bleach (Ilfochrome or Cibachrome)	1960s – present
Digital colour printer technologies	1990s – present

Table 4.1: Photographic positive processes

Most photographic print formats are made up of at least two layers – the print base and the image layer. The print base is commonly paper, coated paper or plastic, but historic processes have also used metals (such as iron or plated silver), and glass. The image layer is usually made up of an emulsion that holds the materials that create the image. The emulsion is commonly gelatine, but can be egg whites (albumen) or cellulose nitrate (collodion). Modern photographic prints also contain a baryta layer made up of white reflective barium salts. Modern digital prints have emulsions made from synthetic media. The materials that create the image are usually silver and silver salts, again with the exception of modern ink-jet or other digital prints.

Negatives

Most photographic negatives are on flexible film bases similar to those used for motion picture film and as this media is covered in Chapter 18: *Moving Images* I will not go into too much detail here. The other common media base for negatives is glass, which is still in use in some applications, for example astronomical photography. Photographic negatives also contain an emulsion layer that holds the materials that create the image.

The main issue to raise here is that photographic negatives are usually the master photographic image and for this reason they are very significant records and should not be overlooked. Table 4.2 contains examples of photographic negative processes.

Photographic process	Dates of common use
Calotypes (very rare negative on paper)	1839 – 1860s
Albumen negative (on glass)	1848 – 1880s
Wet collodion negative (on glass)	1851 – 1880s
Collodion dry plate (on glass)	1854 – 1870s
Gelatine dry plate (on glass)	1870s – present (rare now)
Nitrate cut roll sheet film	1890s – 1950s (mostly replaced by introduction of acetate)
Acetate sheet film	1920s – present
Polyester film	1950s (specialist applications) 1990s – present (common use)

Table 4.2: Photographic negative processes and their period of common use

Books

Books in archive collections come in many shapes, sizes and formats. The type of binding used reflects the age of the book, materials available at the time, the use the book would be put to and the training and competency of the binder. The 19th century saw an increase in turnover which resulted in a lessening of standards, which has inevitably lead to books that deteriorate more quickly and are generally less durable.

Unlike flat documents, books are three-dimensional objects created to open and shut. To do this, they need to be both flexible and be made from materials able to withstand use. Different book structures have been created for different applications. Some are seen as simply decorative and others purely functional. The basic structure of all books entails a cover of some kind and a binding mechanism to hold everything together. The two common types of binding mechanism are sewing and adhesive. Some consider that only sewn books are actually 'bound' – they do not count paper backs or adhesive bindings as true bindings. However, given their inclusion in our archival holdings, it is necessary to discuss them all. Different binding types and structures are outlined in more detail below.

As with all things, the materials the book is made from will greatly influence its durability and rate of deterioration. To withstand heavy use, a book needs to be made from good quality, durable materials.

Materials

Leather is one of the common materials used to cover books. It is made from the tanned skin of animals (usually cow, goat and sheep). As with paper, there are good quality leathers and poor quality leathers. Poor quality leather has often not been tanned properly, or it is thin and lacks durability, or a combination of these and other factors. One of the more common types of deterioration seen in leather covers is 'red rot', which causes the leather surface to become very friable and shed red-coloured powder. It is caused by the action of sulphur-dioxide from the atmosphere or sulphur compounds remaining in the leather after tanning.

Book cloth is another common covering for books and is made from dyed and coated linen or cotton. Modern book cloths are also made from synthetic materials and have included materials such as pyroxylin and cellulose nitrate (gun cotton). Book cloths can be quite susceptible to mould and insect attack, as the coatings and adhesives used are a desirable source of food for these pests. Another problem that can arise with book cloth is the bleeding or transfer of dyes. Dyes used for cloths can be water soluble and will readily bleed or transfer colour. It can take as little as the sweat on your hands for this to happen.

Paper, card and board have also been used to cover books. As with all types of paper, they come in different qualities and you can refer to the section on paper for more details. Some books that appear to have a cloth cover can actually be covered in a textured paper look-alike. These are usually not as durable as their cloth counter-parts.

The **adhesives** traditionally used in book construction have been animal glue, starch paste and polyvinyl acetate (PVA). All three adhesives can become quite inflexible with age. PVA is particularly problematic to remove once set, and more so when aged.

Mould can develop quickly and can cause a great deal of damage.

Printing and writing

There are two major branches in bookbinding, with a definite distinction between the two.

Letterpress binding covers printed books destined for reading. Under this label come fine, edition, library and pamphlet binding. The term evolves from the time when all printing was relief surface letterpress.

Stationery binding encompasses books intended to be written into. There is quite a wide range here and as such they are well represented in archive collections. The most common in archives are the ledger and account books, but also found in this group are duplicate, receipt, and bank books.

Generally speaking, the stationery binder of old was more concerned with the quality of the paper used than that used by letterpress binders. Good-quality hand-made paper was used for high-class account books with the expectation that if machine-made papers were being used, they would be durable and heavily sized with a good writing surface.

The **paper** used to form the text block is a very important part of the book, both from a structural and chemical perspective. The quality of paper for letterpress varies more widely and follows intended purpose, for example paperback books today use extremely poor quality paper as they are not intended for long-term use.

The two types of paper are summed up by Vaughan. The particular qualities required in a paper that is intended for printing are different from those in a paper to be used for writing. Paper used for printing requires a fairly smooth surface and should be opaque. It should not be sized too heavily, as printing ink dries partially by penetration. Writing papers, on the other hand, require a particular surface for a pen and must be fairly heavily sized so the thin ink will penetrate through and spread (Vaughan 1944).

One aspect of paper structure not discussed above that is particularly pertinent to book construction is grain direction. Most machine-made papers have a grain direction caused by the action of the machines on the fibres in the pulp as the paper sheet comes together. Paper is always more flexible along the length that runs with the grain, and thus the grain direction of a book page should run from head to tail. If it doesn't, then the text block will be very inflexible and difficult to open, causing increased stress on the book.

Types of binding

Until the end of the 18th century, almost all books were bound in the **flexible style** (Johnson 1978). This describes a binding where the covering of the book is fully adhered to the spine. The text block is sewn onto cords or tapes that are laced into the cover boards. Ideally, the spine should remain flexible and allow the pages to fall open fully. Sometimes however, the application of too much glue or inflexible spine linings means that these books can be difficult to open.

Case bindings are the most common type of modern binding, their numbers swelling at the introduction of book cloth. Their structure consists of two very distinct and separate parts – the cased cover and the text block. The cover is joined to the text block by the endpapers, which are either sewn into or pasted onto the text block, and then pasted to the cover boards. This type of binding is not very strong and the cover boards readily detach from the text block, especially where only pasted on endpapers were used.

Library style binding was developed in the 19th century, when the increased demand placed on libraries required the development of a more sturdy and durable binding. The text block of library bindings is sewn onto tapes which are then inserted and adhered into slits in the cover boards. The covering of the book is adhered directly to the spine of the text block. French joints or grooves are included between the covers and the spine to provide more flexibility in opening the book and to make the joint more durable.

Hollow-back bindings were developed after the flexible and library styles. The covering material does not adhere directly to the spine but to a hollow or tube along the spine.

Quarter, half and full bindings refer to the covering materials. Full bindings are those where the entire cover is made from the same material, for example, full leather describes a book whose boards are covered entirely with leather. Quarter and half bindings were developed as an economy measure and they have a reduced amount of the more expensive covering material (usually leather), the rest of the covering being made from something cheaper (usually cloth or paper). A half binding is where the spine and a small overlap onto the boards and the corners are covered with one material, and the remainder of the boards are covered with something else. A quarter binding is where only the spine and a small overlap into the boards are covered with one material and the remainder with something else.

Paper back spine structure is made up simply of adhesive. The guillotined edges of the pages are adhered to the spine of the cover using an adhesive such as PVA. They are the least durable of all book structures, and are often not very flexible. Cheap hard-cover versions can also be secured in this manner and may have a cord adhered top and bottom to make them look sewn.

Maps and plans

Large-format records such as maps and plans have very particular needs in terms of storage and handling and so it is useful to describe here some of the more common types of large-format records so that you can develop preservation strategies to meet their needs.

Maps

Maps have been around for as long as humans have travelled and owned property. As we have travelled more, and as land ownership has swelled, greater numbers of maps have needed to be created more quickly. This development is reflected in the types of maps now seen in archive collections. Maps can be hand-drawn using pencil, ink and watercolour, or they can be printed using more modern methods and materials. They can be on paper, linen, plastic or a combination of materials.

Damage to maps tend to be related to their size, and the way they've been stored and handled. Where the map consists of layers, such as paper adhered to linen, damage can be caused from the paper and the linen expanding and contracting at different rates, or the adhesive layer becoming brittle and reducing flexibility, causing cracking in the paper. Rolling or folding maps can also cause damage, as the paper often develops a memory of being rolled or folded and becomes unwieldy to handle. Folding also causes wear along the crease and breaking of paper fibres, resulting in tears and cracking. If the paper is brittle, unrolling can also cause splitting and cracking.

Architectural plans

Industrialisation and technological advancement in building and engineering created a huge demand for the production of technical drawings used to design these structures. To meet this demand, the way these drawings were created had to change. The traditional hand-drawn plan could not be produced quickly enough to meet the demand, and so mechanisation replaced hand-drawing for a large proportion of these records. Photographic technologies were utilised and adapted to fill much of this need. Therefore, architectural plans in archive collections fall into two main categories, hand drawn plans and those that are based in some way on photographic technologies.

Hand-drawn plans are similar to hand drawn maps. They are drawn with pencil, ink and watercolour on paper, linen and plastic, or a combination of these. The other main type of architectural plan is more complex and we will go into this type in more detail.

They are split into two main types, **photo-reproductions** and **photomechanical**. The term photo-reproduction indicates a print that was produced using a photographic process, i.e. the image was manufactured using photosensitive chemicals. The term photomechanical reproduction indicates a print that was produced using a plate, whereby that plate was prepared using photographic processes and the photosensitive chemicals are used to produce the plate, not the print (Kissel & Vigneau 1999).

Photo-reproductions tend to be the less stable of the two processes, as they can often contain chemicals left from the photographic process used to create them. Generally speaking, photomechanical reproductions are more stable and behave more like conventional prints. The photographic and chemical nature of photo-reproductions needs to be taken into consideration when choosing storage environments and enclosures for these records. Good examples of this type are blueprints. Not often associated with photographs, blueprints are chemically exactly the same as cyanotype photographs and they require the same type of storage environment. They are highly reactive to pH and also humidity. The image-creating chemicals do not like alkaline or humid conditions.

Examples of photo-reproductions are Aniline prints, blueprints, diazotypes, ferrogallic prints, Photostat prints, pellet prints, sepia diazo prints, Vandyke prints and wash-off prints. Examples of photomechanical processes are Electrostatic prints, Gel-lithographs and Hectographs (Kissel & Vigneau 1999).

Parchment

The term parchment is usually used generically to describe any animal skin that is treated, stretched and dried to form a writing membrane. The techniques used to treat the skins are too varied to go into in detail here. Sources of skins include calf, sheep, goat, deer, as well as smaller animals such as rabbit. Parchment has been used extensively in the creation of legal, banking, property and heraldic documents. These documents are well represented in archive collections, especially government and banking archives. Parchment can be written on, printed on, painted on, stamped, and embossed – which is why it can be confused by some with paper or fabric. The main points of difference to note is that it will have none of the imprints from papermaking (including laid lines, watermarks or wove patterns) nor the weave pattern of fabric.

Clarkson describes parchment as highly stressed sheet material, relatively inelastic and having a stiff handle. Drying under tension keeps the individual fibres in the network separate and imparts a certain opacity and flexibility to the membrane. As long as the material stays dry, the dermal network cannot revert to its original orientation (Clarkson 1994). And there in lies the problem. Many parchment documents held in archives today have often been subjected to adverse environmental conditions, usually water or heat, and have subsequently started to revert to the skin they originally came from.

Parchment, being a proteinaceous animal skin, is entirely different from the cellulosic chemistry of paper. It must therefore be treated quite differently. It usually has a creamy off-white colour, is opaque and smooth of surface. Whilst robust and stable given the right conditions, parchment documents can often be completely stuck together, extremely brittle, so black they look burned, and highly shrunken making it all but impossible to access the information they contain.

Magnetic and digital media

Section 4 deals with the issues surrounding these media types, so we will not duplicate the information here.

Preventive strategies

Preventive conservation refers to the passive and wholistic strategies used to delay or prevent damage to collections. It is now widely recognised that the most effective way of preserving the largest number of records is not to treat each one individually, but to adopt strategies that provide the basic level of care essential for the safety of the whole collection and to then focus on particularly significant or at-risk items where necessary.

Preventive conservation includes such things as general risk management, providing good storage conditions, integrated pest management (IPM), good handling procedures, disaster preparedness, and developing appropriate exhibition methodologies.

The two biggest risk factors for archival collections are storage environment and access procedures.

CDs and DVDs are not suitable media for permanent storage of records. It is very easy to damage CDs. This one was destroyed by a post-it note.

Environment

All buildings and areas used to store archives need to be assessed for their suitability, and where they are found lacking they need to be improved to the best of our abilities. Chapter 3: *Buildings & Storage* has a detailed account of the factors that need to be assessed and the procedures to implement for the best outcomes.

Temperature and humidity

Baseline environmental conditions in the building should be determined so that appropriate air-conditioning is applied only where necessary. If you are fortunate enough to have a building with high thermal mass (that is, the building is solid enough to respond slowly to changes in the outside environment) or insulation that maintains good temperature and relative humidity ranges, then you may not need to go to the expense of air-conditioning at all. Where air-conditioning is required you must be able to run it 24 hours a day, seven days a week, and it must include humidity control as well as temperature control. Monitoring the system is also crucial. Do not rely only on the air-conditioning system's own internal monitoring. Use your own external monitors. If air-conditioning is not feasible for your organisation, you will need to employ other strategies to manage the environment, or perhaps sort the collection into parts that require very strict environmental conditions and those that can be more relaxed, so that you reduce the burden on air-conditioning.

Guidelines for the environmental conditions for the permanent and long-term retention of records are described in Chapter 3: *Buildings & Storage*. The key factors to consider in storage areas are:

- **stability**: no cycling or dramatic changes in temperature and relative humidity. Cycling is when the temperature and humidity go up and down through a set point on a regular basis, for example, the temperature might vary between 25 and 35 every day.
- **consistent temperature:** < than 25° C

- **consistent humidity:** < 60% relative humidity
- **lighting**: only on when area in use, consider timer switches, illumination levels allowing only enough light to undertake required tasks, covering shelves with curtains or wrapping items to protect from light
- **cleanliness**: good housekeeping to reduce dust is important for IPM

Monitoring your environmental stability conditions is very important. Monitoring provides the following:

- information about whether your air-conditioning is performing as it should
- an early warning system for risk factors such as mould and pests (high humidity and temperatures produce a higher risk)
- information to provide to your facilities or building manager to aid in remedying problems
- the ability to strategically locate your collection, allowing the most at-risk records to be located in the best conditions
- the ability to strategically locate your collection, allowing the most at-risk records to be located in the best conditions.

Light

Light is also an important factor to consider in your storage and access areas. Damage from light exposure is cumulative, i.e. the longer an item is exposed and the higher the exposure levels, the more damage will occur. Generally speaking, given all other parameters are equal, if you double the light level you will double the damage over the same time period. The most damaging types of light are those with high energy, as they cause increases in chemical activity in the materials they hit. Ultra-violet (UV) light has the highest energy, and therefore it is the most damaging. Sunlight is one of the chief sources for UV light and you must therefore ensure that your storage and access areas do not allow sunlight to fall over the shelves or reading desks. Use low ultra-violet emitting light sources or place ultra-violet filters over the lights. Most fluorescent tubes emit some ultra-violet light, but you can get tubes that are nil or low UV output. Filtering sleeves are available for tubes. In storage areas lights should be off whenever the rooms are not in use. This should include corridor lighting where possible.

In storage areas, lights should be turned off whenever the rooms are not in use. This should include corridor lighting where possible.

Users of your reading room obviously need enough light to be able to read the records without causing eye strain. However, you can achieve good results for both your readers and for the records being accessed by keeping in mind the information outlined above.

Copying – either by conventional photography, photocopying or scanning – is the other source of light exposure for your records. All copying processes use some form of additional lighting. The thing to consider is how many times a single record will be copied

– if it is only once the damage caused by light will be negligible. However, if you have some records that are accessed and copied frequently, then consider having these items preservation copied and only supplying the copies to readers. Providing surrogate copies also has benefits in reducing handling. If an archive contains information that is of interest to more than a couple of people, it is probably best copied. For example, the convict records held at State Records NSW are extremely popular with many different researchers and family historians, and for this reason they have been microfilmed, allowing only the copies to be accessed. Exhibiting records is another facet of access, and it is considered in more detail later in the chapter.

Access and handling

In many collecting institutions, collection managers are in the position of being able to restrict public access to simply looking at an object in a glass case. Any increased access to objects in museums and galleries requires special requests and a very high level of supervision.

Access to archives is seen in a very different light. The public expects to be able to handle and copy original material with minimal supervision. This is both a good and a bad thing. It is wonderful that the public have the opportunity to handle such important and significant material, but the cost is that it puts this material at a much greater risk of damage, with the potential that future access could be compromised.

This is why implementing good handling and access guidelines and practices is so important to the preservation of archives. It is important that the procedures be undertaken by everyone who handles archives – from members of the public, to archivists, to retrieval staff and volunteers. Obviously, different levels of training will apply to different people, depending on their level of access and what they use the archives for. Members of the public will need to know how to turn pages, how to recognise weak areas, how to use book supports and so on. Staff who undertake copying will need to know all of that and also be trained in how to remove fastenings (such as staples, pins, etc) and what materials cannot be copied.

Good handling practices begin with respect for and knowledge about the archives. When people understand why they are being asked to do something, they are generally more co-operative and the outcome is usually more positive. It is very important to tell people what they are not allowed to do. This needn't be confrontational, but you must be firm and provide strict guidelines on how your archives are to be handled. Ensure that they understand that their co-operation is absolutely vital to the preservation of the records. As was already stated earlier in the chapter, the responsibility for preservation lies with everyone who handles archives and so handling guidelines are a good place to start a positive culture towards archive care.

Outlined here are basic handling guidelines that will lessen the risk of damage to your archives.

General handling guidelines for all records:

- **Handle archives as little as possible**
  Use secondary supports such as rigid board to support records wherever possible. This removes the need to handle the record directly.
- **Ensure hands are clean**
  Wash your hands with soap and water and dry thoroughly before *and* after handling records. This is for the protection of both the records and your health. Hands must be washed at least once every hour.
- **Examine all records for signs of damage prior to handling**
  Assume that the records are fragile and treat them accordingly.
- **Never use 'post-it' notes or other self-adhesive stickers to mark pages**
  Use a slip of acid-free paper or good quality bond paper. These markers often get mistakenly left in archives for lengthy periods, so it is important to use good materials.
- **Use only pencil when taking notes or writing on marker slips**
  Ink marks are nearly impossible to remove and will cause permanent damage.
- **Use soft, flexible weights to hold pages in place**
  These can be made cheaply from zip-lock bags and lead shot (or any other small, round, heavy substance) (Image 4.1).
- **Do not lick your fingers or use rubber 'thimbles' to turn pages**
  Use a spatula to help separate the pages. This is for both your own health and that

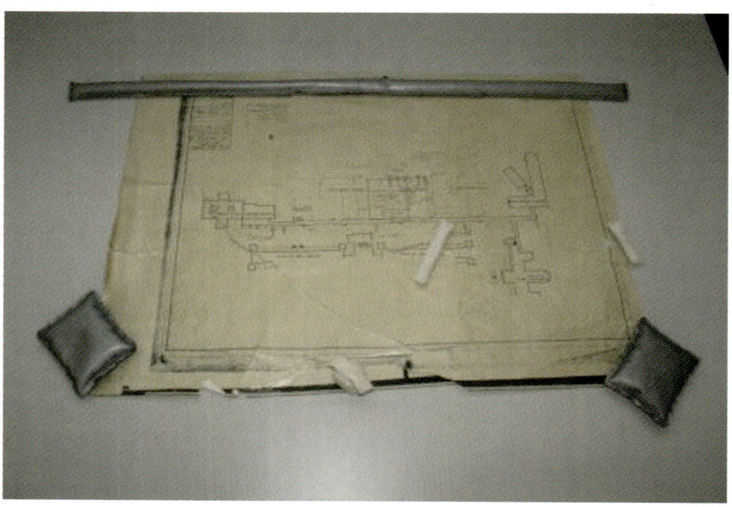

Image 4.1: Soft flexible weight used to hold archives in place

of the archive. Records may have been fumigated, mouldy or stored in questionable conditions in the past and this poses a health threat.

- **Get assistance to carry heavy, awkward or large items**
  Again, this is both for your safety and that of the archive.
- **Prepare a clean, flat work space prior to moving archives**
  Benches should be dusted and then wiped clean with a mix of methylated spirit and water and dried completely. Working on a clean sheet of white paper makes it easier to spot dirt and debris that can cause damage. It also makes it easier to spot any flakes of the document that might dislodge.

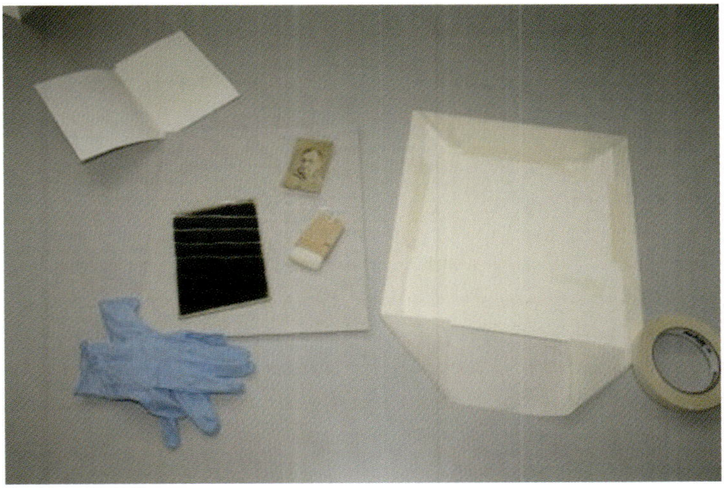

Image 4.2: Glass plates supported by tissue wrapped mount board

Photographic materials

- **Plastic gloves are to be worn at all times**
  Nitrile gloves with a polyethylene coating or clean, close-fitting, non-powdered surgical gloves are preferred. PVC or rubber gloves should be discouraged, as they may react adversely with your photographs. Avoid any gloves containing sulphur.
- **Photographs are more reactive to heat than other records**
  They may curl if handled directly for lengthy periods. This also applies when copying under hot lights or on a photocopier or scanner. Reduce handling and copying to that which is absolutely necessary only.
- **Glass plates**
  - where possible, restrict public access to this material as it is very fragile.
  - place plates on mount board covered with tissue paper (Image 4.2).

- thoroughly inspect plates prior to handling (wherever possible) for signs of cracking, breaks or lifting emulsion
- when handling is necessary, always hold the plate at a low height over a soft workspace, to prevent breakages in case of dropping.
- place the plate emulsion side up (dull side up) to prevent scratches occurring.

Books

- **Always support the spine adequately**
  Use book pillows, foam blocks or other devices to ensure the spine is supported and not over-flexed (Image 4.3).
- **Turn pages from the centre fore edge or top corner if appropriate**
  The bottom fore edge corner is often the weakest part of a page as it is the most frequently used in the life of a book. Use spatulas or plastic letter openers to separate pages where necessary.
- **Do not remove books from shelves by pulling on the top of the spine**
  Grasp the book by the centre of the spine and pull out that way. If necessary, push the books on either side further into the shelf to allow better access.
- **Do not force the spine of a book**
  Open gently from the front or back cover first to determine the strength of the structure, otherwise you could break the back and rupture the sewing structure.
- **Wear gloves when handling books with gold decoration on the covers and fore edges**
- **An overhead photocopier or digital camera should be used when copying**
  Placing a book on a flat bed copier or scanner will over-flex the spine and cause damage.

Image 4.3: Book pillow supporting an open volume

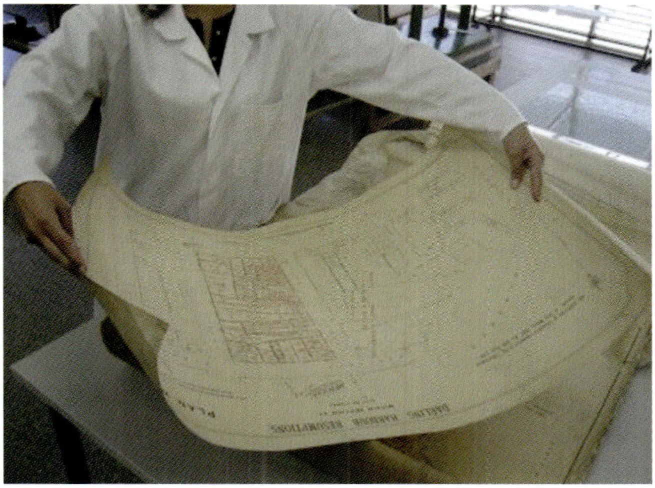

Image 4.4: The correct way to hold a plan if no rigid support is available

Maps and plans

- **Do not hold by the edges or corners**
- **Fully support at all times**
  Polyester sleeves or rigid board can be used to help support large format records.
- **When carrying an item without a support**
  Examine it closely for areas of damage. Hold the item from areas that are not damaged. Use both hands and hold the map at the centre of two facing edges, allowing it to fall into a gentle bow or very shallow u-shape, with no buckles or kinks (Image 4.4).
- **When moving large numbers of maps**
  Use a large flat bed trolley. Do attempt to carry more than one item at a time. This relies on the strength of the plan at the bottom of the pile and will cause damage.

CDs and DVDs

- Only clean with a soft lint-free cloth in motions out from the centre. Do not use circular motions.
- Handle the discs at the edges or from the central hole.

Magnetic media

- Do not place next to any other magnetic or high voltage devices.
- Do not touch the tape. Handle only by the case or the spool.

More detailed information about CDs, DVDs, magnetic and other audiovisual media is covered in Chapters 17 and 18.

Other access considerations

Your reading room and access areas are your public face and the way you present these areas to the public plays a part in how the public will interact with your records. The area needs to be clean, tidy and generally well presented. Consider putting up information about handling practices or providing leaflets about caring for records.

Provide your readers with gloves, book supports, paper place markers, pencils and any other tools you would prefer them to use when handling your records. Plastic gloves are now preferred over cotton gloves. Nitrile gloves with a polyethylene coating or tight fitting surgical gloves provide the best fit giving the user greater dexterity. Cotton allows the accumulation of dirt, the passage of sweat from the user to the archives, and usually do not fit well which compromises dexterity.

Protective packaging

Protective packaging is anything that provides a higher level of protection to the records. This need not necessarily be archival paper or board. Though this is usually the ideal, it is not always possible.

Informal studies at State Records NSW have shown that ordinary corrugated cardboard boxes provide a buffer to fluctuating temperature and relative humidity, as well as the obvious barrier to light and dust, and therefore records stored in boxes are better protected and safer.

If this is the case then why do we need archival enclosures, acid-free papers, alkaline buffering? Well, for the most part the answer lies in the information we've already discussed in the section dealing with paper structure. Some papers contain substances deleterious to records, and some records are especially susceptible to damage.

It has long been observed by conservators, archivists and other collection managers that enclosures made from papers and boards containing ground wood pulp both discolour prematurely themselves and cause discolouration and other effects in records stored in contact with them. Such observable damage includes discolouration, fading, brittleness and foxing (small brown spots). The bulk of research in this area shows that the main component in these papers causing the damage is lignin, though recent studies have indicated that there are usually other substances in the paper associated with lignin that also have an impact (Burge et al. 2002).

So the question still remains, do you need archival enclosures for everything? And the answer is, ideally, yes. They will always offer the best possible protection for your records. But as we do not live in an ideal world, the answer is that we usually have to make compromises and prioritise, based on the best information we have at hand. This is why it is so important to know what is in your collection – you can then decide which records are at most risk if placed in non-archival enclosures, and which records are more robust and less susceptible to damage.

What is an archival enclosure?

For our purposes here, it is an enclosure that presents no physical, chemical or biological risk to the records it stores. Archival enclosures should be as non-reactive as possible with the records they store, and the best examples will actually provide proactive benefits such as acid scavengers. Examples of archival enclosures currently in use in archives include

- non-buffered 100% cellulose fibre paper or board, including 100% cotton, or delignified wood pulp
- alkaline buffered 100% cellulose fibre paper or board, including 100% cotton or delignified wood pulp
- polypropylene plastic
- polyethylene plastic
- polyester plastic

A good rule of thumb is that if the manufacturer claims it has passed the Photographic Activity Test (P.A.T) or it complies with Australian Standard 4003-1996 for Permanent Paper then it will be acceptable for most uses as an archival enclosure. Enclosures for photographic materials should always have passed the P.A.T.

What to consider when choosing protective packaging

The first thing to point out is that protective packaging should always be a secondary consideration to overall improvements in environmental conditions. As was discussed by Burge et al in 2002, lowering temperature and relative humidity in storage areas logically reduces the interaction between poor quality enclosures and records, but it will also slow the general deterioration of the records themselves. They surmise that developing good storage conditions may be the priority over rehousing (Clarkson 1994). While their research was specifically focused on photographic records, the results can be applied elsewhere.

The next thing to decide is what you can afford. Even the largest government archives struggle to house their entire collections in archival enclosures – and the reality is that most are not able to. They therefore have to make decisions similar to small archives – what part of the collection is most in need of good quality enclosures and what can we afford? To put it colloquially, we all want the best bang for our buck.

There are some basic questions to ask when making this decision:

- What part of the collection is most at risk from poor quality enclosures?
- To what degree will the records benefit from the archival enclosures?
- Is there another area where the resources could better be directed?
- Can you make the enclosures yourself and is this the most effective use of your time and resources?

Wrapping material for textiles, photographs etc on hand and ready for use.

The part of your collection most at risk will depend on what records you hold. Generally speaking however, photographic materials are some of the most sensitive records and require the highest level of care. As was stated above, enclosures for photographs should pass the P.A.T. Acetate and nitrate film (including microfiche, microfilm, sheet film negatives, etc), magnetic media, and video are also especially sensitive. Information regarding packaging for these materials is covered in Chapters 17 and 18.

Standard paper records can be made up of many different types of paper. Generally speaking, papers made prior to 1850 are of much better quality than those manufactured in the late 19th and 20th centuries. We must then decide which of our paper records will benefit most from good quality enclosures.

Another rule of thumb is that the lignin and acid content of a full box of records made from ground wood pulp or lignin-containing pulp will cause more damage than that in the enclosure. The benefit of an archival quality enclosure in these circumstances is therefore questionable. However, when considering papers made prior to 1850 from good quality pulp such as cotton or linen, then the answer is quite different. Their inherent problems are negligible and therefore the impact of an enclosure made from ground wood pulp on these papers would be more obvious and detrimental.

Where possible, it is a good idea to isolate all records from poor quality boxes so that no record is in direct contact with the box, e.g. an isolating layer of card or plastic within the box is much cheaper than replacing the whole box. You may also decide for other reasons that files will be placed in individual folders, and in such a case the folders could be made from archival board that will act as an isolating layer from the box.

The question of whether to make enclosures yourself or buy them pre-fabricated will depend on your circumstances. Generally speaking, it is cheaper to buy paper and board and make enclosures yourself. However, if you are a lone archivist or record manager and have even a moderately sized collection, this may be completely out of the question, and you are better off spending a little bit more to have enclosures pre-fabricated. This saves not only time, but also the space required to cut and fold paper and boards. Included here are some examples of all-purpose, easy-to-construct enclosures suited to most applications within an archive (Image 4.5).

Image 4.5: Example of a four flap envelope and the tools to make it

Basic types of enclosures

The most basic types of protective packaging involve very simple wrappers fixed with string or cotton tape. While these are cheap, easy to make and readily at hand, they do not provide the level of protection that other basic enclosures can provide. This is usually because they are not close fitting enough; they are more prone to wear and distortion; and they often have pressure points that generate damage to the records. Where nothing else is available however, they do provide basic protection, particularly from light, dust and to a very small extent provide buffering of temperature and relative humidity.

Some of the most common types of purpose-made enclosures are boxes, folders and envelopes.

Boxes

Standard Type 1 boxes (NAA specification) are the most common boxes you will see in archives around Australia. They are designed to take standard A4 and foolscap files and can be made from cardboard (archival or non-archival) or polypropylene. Their features include a small hole to assist removal from shelves, an attached lid that slots into place and rigid walls. One of the advantages of these boxes is that their size usually prevents the box becoming too heavy, which is an important occupational health and safety concern. These boxes can be adapted to take many different types of records (Image 4.6). When placing records in boxes, it is important not to over-fill or under-fill the box. Over-filling will result in the records sustaining tears, creases and abrasion during removal and replacement, and under-filling will result in the records slumping or moving around. Generally speaking, it is a good idea to leave about two fingers width of space to ensure that records do not slump and to provide adequate access. To improve the protection offered by boxes made from non-archival materials, you can introduce box liners, padding made from archival quality foam and folders made from archival quality paper.

Using interleaving sheets and dividers between groups of records in boxes and folders can provide a number of benefits. Where non-archival quality boxes or folders are being used they offer the opportunity to isolate records from poor quality board. To gain the most benefit, dividers or interleaving folders should be made from archival paper. This means that in all box types the records are only in contact with good quality materials. They also protect records from each other. Sometimes inks and other media can off-set onto adjacent records and interleaving sheets and dividers prevent this sort of damage from occurring. The other important function of dividers and interleaving sheets is to provide better access. In boxes of loose records, individual files are often difficult to identify and remove, and in many cases the entire bundle of records must be removed from the box, sorted through to find the record that you want, and then the rest placed back into the box. Dividers can be used in boxes to separate records into smaller groups providing access to only those records that you are looking for (Image 4.6).

Image 4.6: Improving file storage by including dividers and individual folders

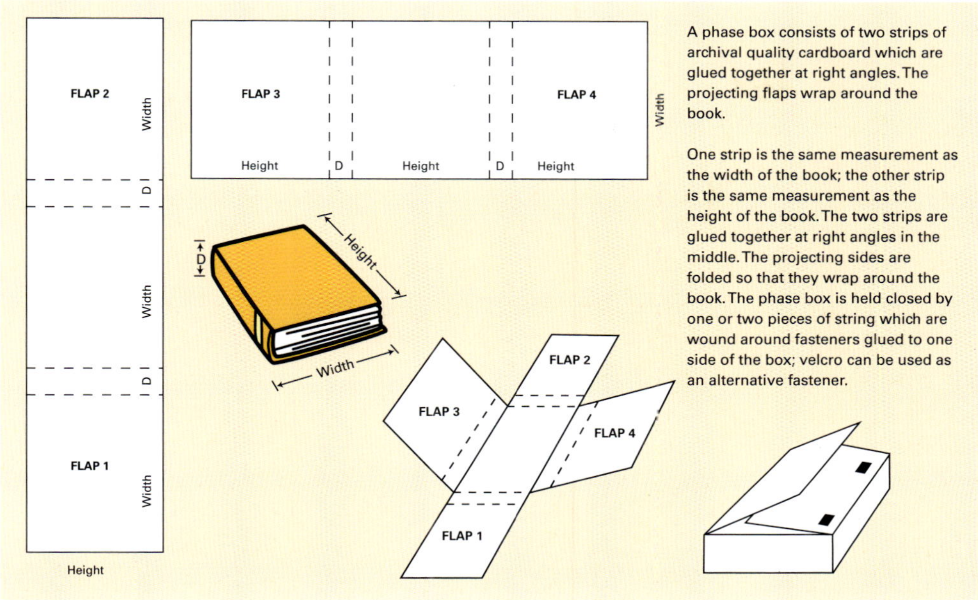

Image 4.7: How to make a phase box

Envelopes can be made from paper, lightweight board and inert plastics, and they can be seamed or un-seamed. The two most common are four-flap envelopes and polyester (or polyethylene) sleeves. It is usually more cost effective to buy pre-fabricated polyester sleeves rather than making them yourself as specialist equipment is required and they can be fiddly to make. Four-flap envelopes made from paper or board are easy to make yourself and require easily available, inexpensive equipment.

Phase boxes were designed by the Library of Congress and are so called because they were a phase in the Library's book conservation program – books requiring conservation but unable to be treated immediately were boxed to prevent further damage. They are a useful style of box because, again, they are relatively simple to make and require minimal equipment. And their uses extend beyond being a phase in a conservation program – they are an effective protective enclosure in themselves and can be the permanent enclosure for the records. The most useful application is for books and other hard-covered files. They are not as useful for loose paper files. Image 4.7 shows how to make a phase box.

Dust jackets

Another useful, inexpensive and quick way of protecting books from dust and light is to make a book jacket or chemise. These are easily formed from a sheet of archival paper or polyester. Tabs are cut in the paper where it folds around the cover of the book – the tabs should extend well into the inside cover of the book and can be folded so that no sticky tape or glue is required.

Large-format enclosures

The best way to store large-format records, such as maps and plans, is flat. Achieving this can be difficult, especially in small archives where space and money are tight. Plan cabinets offer a good solution if you can afford them. They enable the storage of large volumes of large format records in a relatively small floor footprint, and they can also be converted into compactus style mobile shelving to provide even greater space savings. However, these options can be expensive. Small quantities of large-format materials can be stored interleaved between rigid sheets of archival board. For larger collections and where the records are particularly long, you will probably have to consider rolling them. This does not mean simply rolling the plan up and tying it with string or an elastic band. There are two ways to roll large-format records safely – the first is to simply roll the record and place it in a specially designed long plan box, and the other is to use a solid core to roll the plan around. The second offers the best protection for the plan – it will stop crushing, and will prevent the record from being rolled too tightly. Ordinary card tubes can be adapted by covering them with a layer of aluminium foil then an additional layer of archival paper. The record is then rolled around the core and an outer layer of archival wrapping added for protection. The core should be at least 100mm in diameter.

Never roll the following:

- brittle records
- multi-layered records, e.g. paper or photographs adhered to linen
- records on heavy weight paper or card, as these will retain a very strong memory of being rolled.

Integrated Pest Management

Integrated Pest Management (IPM) is used across many industries, including agriculture, food processing and of course, in museums, galleries and archives. It involves strategies aimed at reducing or eliminating the risk from pests using primarily preventive measures, rather than reactive ones. The key to IPM is its focus on making the environments where we store and use records unattractive and hopefully hostile to pests. The strategies range from the simplest of measures, such as good house-keeping practices, to more complex strategies such as isolating and treating records for pests prior to introducing them into our collections. Chapter 3: *Buildings & Storage* reviews some simple and effective measures that can be implemented to reduce the risk of pests.

One of the strategies employed as part of IPM is to undertake perimeter spraying of buildings. Spraying of records is not part of these strategies. Fumigation of records is absolutely a last resort. This is for both the protection of the records and for the health of those accessing them. Fumigants often leave residues on the records which can cause damage to the records and they are often toxic and harmful to human health. IPM has been introduced across archives to remove the need for fumigation and it is a very rare occurrence these days.

Pests are an obvious threat to the long-term preservation of archival material.

Pests common to archives are cockroaches, silverfish, rats, and mice. Less common are termites, wood borer, book lice, moths, birds and possums. The other pest often overlooked in the context of IPM is mould. It is one of the most insidious pests in archives, can be one of the most destructive, and is hazardous to human health. It is important to be conversant with what these pests look like in all stages of their life cycles, to recognise their droppings, and the damage they can cause.

Cockroaches, rats and mice can cause large areas of loss in paper records because of the way they ingest food. The damaged areas will be chewed and often be covered in small black droppings and regurgitated matter. Rats and mice also find paper records good nesting sites, and they will burrow into the paper causing tears and strips. Silverfish on the other hand tend to cause more surface damage as they are grazing insects. They will cause holes, but the holes will result from persistent grazing of the one area. Termites channel into materials and usually create covered tunnels through which to travel. Undetected they can decimate archives, but they usually require a point of access into the building, whereas other insect pests can be brought into the collection in the egg stage on boxes and infested records. Wood borer create small holes in the records. They are more common in books and bore through the text block as they would through a tree. They often congregate near the glue areas of the spine. The holes are often discreet and difficult to find, but there will commonly be frass (paper/wood dust mixed with insect droppings) in the area.

Mould in its early stages can look like a coating of dust, but as it grows it can develop into any number of permutations – myriad colours, fluffy and tall, spider-web like and mildewy. The most common observed in archive collections are the mildew-like growth on book pages, the white, fluffy mould growing on the cloth and leather covers of books, and of course the mould that grows after a major flooding incident. What type of mould you get can depend on the food available (i.e. your collection type), what mould is endemic to your area or the area where the records may have originated, the air quality in your storage areas and how wet the area gets. The best way of dealing with mould is to prevent it altogether through frequent monitoring of your records, ensuring the relative humidity remains below 60 percent (because generally mould won't grow below this percentage) and providing sufficient airflow and ventilation. Mould causes serious damage, but also makes paper more susceptible to other damage, such as physical tears and abrasion, and some claim an increased susceptibility to light damage. The brown foxing spots seen on paper are now commonly thought to be a type of micro fungi (Burge et al. 2002).

Insect eradication

Freezing is generally the preferred method of treatment for pest infestations. It is easy, accessible, cheap and effective. It is also considered to be one of the safest methods of pest eradication. However, there are some records that must never be frozen.

Do not freeze:

- records on glass or containing any glass components
- items of mixed media, e.g. items containing metal and wood together.
- items with painted media, e.g. illuminated manuscripts

Similar rules apply with heat treatment of records. In addition, photographic materials should not be subjected to heat treatment of any kind.

Where freezing and heat cannot be used, then oxygen deprivation is a good option. This treatment should not adversely affect records, however it is more difficult to apply and requires specialist equipment.

Chapter 3: B*uildings & Storage* has some more detail about eradication techniques.

Mould eradication

If you do find mould in the early stages of growth, deal with it immediately:

- **Make the environment hostile to its growth**
  Reduce humidity to dehydrate the mould. If necessary, hire a dehumidifier to reduce the humidity quickly, or move your archives to an area where the humidity is lower and there is more ventilation.
- **Brush surface mould away using a vacuum cleaner fitted with a High Efficiency Particulate Air (HEPA) filter**
  This must be done in a fume hood or a well-ventilated space and staff must wear appropriate masks that are suitable for small particulates and fumes. HEPA filters remove mould spores from the return air of a vacuum cleaner and are therefore the only safe vacuum to use to remove mould.

Ethanol has sometimes been recommended as a sporicidal agent to permanently kill and prevent further mould growth. Studies in recent years (Nitterus 2000) have called this practice into questio, both because of its ineffectiveness and because it is a possible activator to spore germination. Its use is therefore not recommended at this time until further investigation has taken place.

If mould is allowed to take hold in your collection it will be extremely difficult to remove and it can decimate your records. It will cause staining, weakening of paper, and in the worst cases will completely devour it.

A more detailed description of removing mould growth is included in the Conservation Treatment section of this chapter.

Disaster preparedness and salvage

Preparing your organisation for a potential disaster is a very important part of preservation. You do not want to go to all the trouble of putting your records into wonderful air-conditioned premises and archival enclosures only to have them destroyed by fire or flood. Chapter 3: *Buildings & Storage* outlines the basics of developing a disaster plan and what you will need in the early stages of a disaster, so this section is going to focus more on the salvage operation.

One thing you should remember is that a disaster is not defined by its size, but rather by the ability of your organisation to deal with it. A leaking pipe can create just as must damage as a large natural flood. Do not make the mistake of thinking that disasters only come in the shape of large scale natural events or terrorist attacks. The most common are the day-to-day events such as the air-conditioning contractor knocking a fire sprinkler head with his ladder or the toilets backing up. The old scout motto 'be prepared' is your best defence in all instances.

Before going into any detail about the salvage operation, the importance of relevant training cannot be stressed enough. Contact the government archives, libraries, museums or galleries in your State to find out what training might be available. The best courses will provide training both in the development of a disaster plan and in the salvage of records, with the very best providing the opportunity to handle and treat examples of damaged records.

Records salvage

As water damage is one of the most common results of disasters, this section is going to focus on this area. Mould growth is one of the most common kinds of damage in the event of a disaster involving water. Flooded areas and records must be dried out as quickly as possible to prevent mould.

Handling water-damaged records takes some practice, so if you don't have access to a training workshop that provides a salvage simulation, it is advisable to find some material you can wet yourself to see how it reacts and to practice handling, drying, and freezing techniques. It is also important to know how to operate any equipment you will use to respond to a disaster, for example, wet/dry vacuum cleaners, dehumidifiers, water pumps, and so on. It is advisable to wear close-fitting plastic gloves when salvaging water-damaged material, as this will protect the records from damage and also protect you from possible hazards in the water. It is also advisable for your staff to wear masks capable of filtering mould, as mould can grow very quickly in very damp conditions.

In the event of a disaster, consider whether you have a clean, dry, well-ventilated space that is large enough and you have the staff to deal with the quantity of wet records that are damaged. If you do not, then you will need to contact a salvage company to undertake the work for you. It is best to have all the details prepared in advance about who you are going to contact and to have discussed the salvage company's methodology thoroughly so you know what to expect. Ask the company for their resume and be sure that they have experience in disaster salvage of archival records. Do not go with the cheapest option unless you can be sure the company has the relevant experience. If you are unsure about any aspect of the company's methodology, then contact a trained conservator for advice.

Air drying is the most common method for salvaging wet records. Most records can be air dried without sustaining much further damage. Air drying requires good ventilation and air circulation. Fans and dehumidifiers can be used to increase the air circulation and speed the rate of drying by removing humidity more rapidly. Large, flat tables or dry floor spaces can be used to lay out wet records. Cover drying areas with dry blotting paper or some other absorbent material to prevent pools of water forming around your drying records. Change absorbent material regularly to aid in the drying process and to prevent the growth of mould. Some records can be pegged out on washing line to dry (see Table 4.3). Screens made from flyscreen or mesh can be useful to lay out flat paper records – these are useful to include in your disaster store.

Freezing is an option that can be used to buy time for some records; however some records should never be frozen when they are wet as they will sustain permanent damage.

Freezing is an option for:

- records that have already developed mould
- records printed on coated paper
- records with water-soluble inks and dyes
- leather and vellum bound books

For more detailed information about freezing procedures see Table 4.3.

As a general rule, if you cannot dry your records within 48 hours you will need to consider freezing them to prevent mould growth and other problems. Freezing does not dry the records and the records will need to go through other drying processes to recover them fully. Blast freezers are preferred as they cool the records very quickly reducing the growth of ice crystals that can cause damage.

Never freeze the following types of wet records:

- photographs, film, glass plate negatives (including microfiche and microfilm)
- records with painted components
- electronic media
- magnetic media
- vinyl records
- records with mixed media (e.g. wood and metal components together)
- veneered wood (e.g. volumes with decorative wooden covers)

Be very cautious when freezing architectural plans, especially those of mixed format. More modern types of plans such as coated plastics and papers can block (stick together) permanently with other records if frozen together. If freezing is absolutely necessary, ensure that all sheets are interleaved with waxed paper prior to freezing.

Material Type	Procedure
Paper files	Air dry flat. Lay out individually or interleaved with blotter in small piles on a bench covered with absorbent material or on screens. Ensure that documents are kept in order and record all relevant information when removing documents from boxes, hanging files or other binders.
Pamphlets, booklets	Air dry flat or hang over a washing line. Interleave pages with absorbent material. See Image 4.8 pamphlets and photographs air drying
Coated papers	Lay out individually on waxed paper and allow to air dry. Freeze interleaved with waxed paper and then vacuum or freeze dry later
Photographs	Hang to dry by their corners from a washing line using negative clips, pegs or paperclips. Do not allow to touch each other. Or lay them out flat, emulsion side up on absorbent material. If drying is not possible immediately, place in tubs of clean, cold water – they should be left this way for no longer than 48–72 hours and water should be replaced daily. Air dry as above or send immersed in water to a photographic processing laboratory. See Image 4.8

Material Type	Procedure
Books	If strong enough books can be placed on their ends and fanned out until the covers sit at 90 degrees. Interleave every 15 or so pages with absorbent material. Fragile books should be laid flat with absorbent interleaving placed intermittently between pages – replace regularly. Sodden books can be packed spine side down and interleaved with waxed paper into bread crates for freezing and later freeze or vacuum drying. See Image 4.9 – books fanned out.
CDs, DVDs, vinyl records	Hold only by the edges. Wash gently with water and then set to dry vertically. Washing up trays are good for this purpose.
Parchment and vellum	These are very fragile when wet. Always support using a rigid board or tray. Contact a conservator immediately. If you cannot contact a conservator straight away then interleave with waxed paper and freeze immediately.
Film (including microfilm, microfiche, motion picture film)	If wet, immerse in clean, cold water and send packed in the water to a film processing laboratory to be reprocessed and dried within 48 hours.
Sheet film negatives	Can be treated as per photographs or if time constrained as per film.
Glass plate negatives and lantern slides	Air dry immediately laying emulsion side facing up on clean absorbent material or stand vertical in a drying rack. Do not freeze, vacuum dry or freeze dry.
Video and audio tapes	Send to a specialist for cleaning and copying within 24 hours. When the copy is returned, check for readability and discard the original. Do not play the original as it may damage equipment.

Table 4.3: Describes the basic salvage procedures for various types of records.

Image 4.8: Pamphlets and photographs hanging on string lines to dry

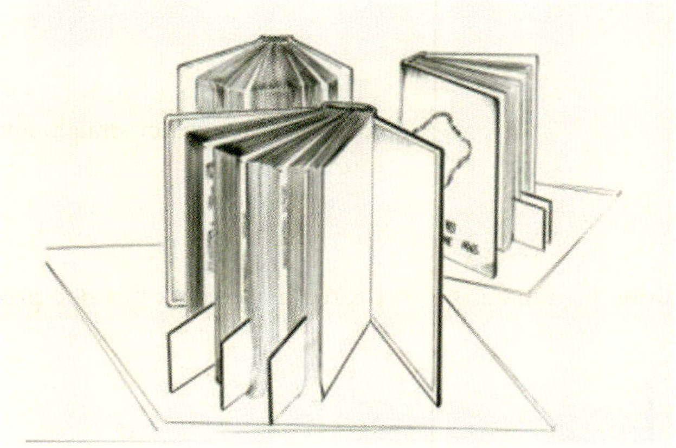

Image 4.9: Diagram showing how to fan books to air dry

Exhibiting archive collections

There are a number of factors to consider before placing archive collections on display. The first is to weigh up the benefits versus the detrimental effects the archives might be exposed to. The key benefits are promotion of your collection and providing greater access to the public. Exhibitions and the resultant promotion can bring other benefits such as donations, funding from government and general awareness of your organisation in the public sphere. Access is of course one of the primary reasons for collecting archives in the first place.

Exhibition conditions can have very significant detrimental effects on archives – and these need to be considered carefully and measures put in place to prevent damage. The main factors that cause damage to items on display are outlined below.

As was mentioned earlier in this chapter, light is a significant agent of deterioration in all organic materials, including paper, leather, adhesives, coatings, some dyes and inks, and gelatine. Illuminance is measured in lux and ultra-violet exposure is measured in microwatts per lumen. For periods of display longer than a couple of days, light levels should be kept to as close to 50 lux as possible for all organic materials and ultra-violet exposure should be removed completely where possible or kept below 75 micro watts per lumen. In practice this means exposing no records to direct sunlight and reducing all other sources of light as much as possible whilst still allowing enough for viewing. Hand-held light meters that measure both lux and ultra-violet exposure are a good investment if you exhibit archives regularly. This will ensure you are not exceeding the exposure levels. If you do not have one of these meters you may be able to utilise the Canadian Conservation Institute method of using an SLR camera to measure your light levels, or you could borrow a meter. If you have little or no control over the lights in your exhibition area, then consider removing every second bulb for ambient lighting. To give you an idea of illuminance levels, standard office lighting is usually between 600 and 1500 lux, so you need to reduce your exhibition lighting by considerable amounts if your records are exhibited for long periods.

Exhibition times for organic materials should be kept fairly short, and records rotated off display and rested in dark storage for at least four times the length of the display period. Most exhibiting institutions display their objects for no longer than three months at a time, and then ensure these items are returned to dark storage for at least nine months before displaying again. This is a protection against over-exposure to light, but it also ensures against physical damage such as book spines being over-stressed and retaining a memory of being open at a particular page. Another method of reducing the light exposure of books and pamphlets is to turn the pages at set periods during the display time. This method also has the advantage of moving the page opening to a different point in the spine.

Conservation treatment

As has been discussed above, conservation treatment involves intervention with an individual record or a small collection of records to effect repairs, stabilisation or restoration. The two general principles followed by conservators when undertaking conservation treatments are reversibility, and to do as little as is necessary for stabilisation, or 'less is best'. Reversibility is sometimes used interchangeably with 'retreat-ability', though this is a misnomer, as retreating an item is far more realistic than reversing a treatment so that an item looks exactly as it used to. To make a conservation treatment retreat-able requires using only materials and methods of the highest quality that can be easily removed and undone. This is one of the key principles that conservators follow, as it is recognised that many treatments can permanently change the fabric and nature of an archive, removing its authenticity and the ability to undertake further research about its manufacture, structure and chemistry. Treatments must not disfigure or endanger archives and must be fully documented so that future archivists and conservators know how to re-treat an archive where necessary. Treatments are therefore undertaken with great circumspection.

The question of who should undertake conservation treatments is a cause of much debate amongst heritage professionals. It is generally recognised that complex treatments should only be undertaken by conservators, as they have the skills required to do materials testing, use specialised equipment and have the requisite experience. There are some more simple treatments that might be undertaken by non-conservators, but before anyone attempts such actions they must be aware of the potential for harm. Archives are unique items that are irreplaceable and even the most well-intentioned actions can have the most dramatically adverse effects. We have all seen the result of the well-intentioned sticky-tape repairs! See Image 4.10

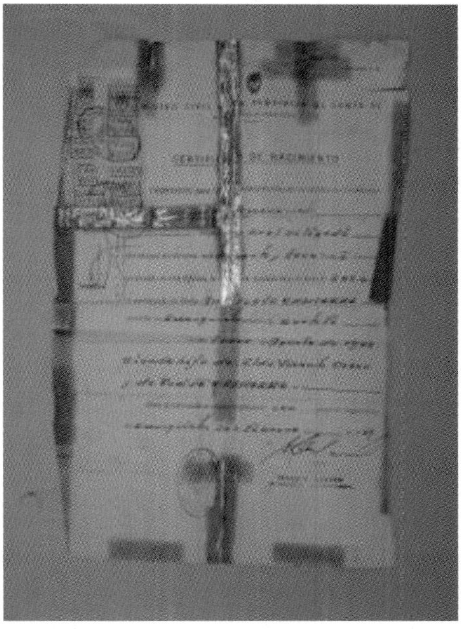

Image 4.10: Example of severely degraded self-adhesive tape

Many also see the requirement for conservation as being a failure in our preservation strategies – if we have well-structured preservation programs in place we should not need to treat any individual records. As Harmut Weber puts it, 'if restoration is necessary, then prevention has failed' (Weber 1999). Conservation treatments are usually time consuming and costly, and so archive managers need to consider such things as the significance of the archives proposed for treatment and whether the resources could better be allocated elsewhere.

Some basic cleaning and repair techniques that can be undertaken with minimal training, materials and equipment are outlined below. If you are unsure about any of the processes described, then do not proceed and seek advice from a professional conservator. The Australian Institute for the Conservation of Cultural Materials (AICCM) provides a list of members in private practice on their website (www.aiccm.org.au). Other similar organisations and websites exist internationally. It is also a good idea to practice on a 'fake' record before you attempt to repair an original. This will provide familiarity with the materials, equipment and techniques and should prevent unnecessary damage being caused to original documents.

An important part of any conservation treatment is to record both the original condition of the archive and to document any treatment that you carry out. This includes very minor interventions such as surface cleaning, as well as the more complex such as washing, lining, repairs and so on. The publication *ReCollections* has easy to follow instructions about how to complete a condition and treatment report.

Preparing your workspace

To safely undertake any treatment on an archive, you must first prepare the space you will work in.

Prepare a clean, flat and un-cluttered surface. Clean the table surface with a mix of methylated spirits and water. Do not use common household cleaners, especially those containing bleach or ammonia, as residues could damage your archives.

Working on butcher's or blotting paper is also a good idea, as it can be replaced regularly when it gets soiled, preventing cross-contamination. This is particularly necessary when dealing with mould and rusty metal fasteners.

Clean your workspace regularly. Brush dirt, eraser and rust residues away and wipe the bench down at the end of each day. It is important to thoroughly clean the table after dealing with metal fasteners as metal debris will easily become embedded in documents causing future damage.

Removing fasteners

Before undertaking any treatment or copying procedure, it is often necessary to remove any fasteners holding pages of documents together. This includes pins, staples, split pins, cloth tapes, etc. Removal of such items may also be necessary if they are corroding.

Before removing such fasteners, consider whether they are contemporary to the document and whether removal is absolutely necessary. This is particularly relevant to the removal of cloth tapes or ribbons as these will often be damaged during removal and cannot be replaced. Cloth ribbons or tapes associated with wax seals should never be removed.

Pins can be removed by gently pushing on the pointed end, and then pulling with tweezers.

To remove staples and split pins you will need a flat spatula, tweezers, and a thin wedge-shaped piece of polyester film or paper. Cut the polyester film to fit between the staple arms. This will be used to protect the document from damage when you lever the arms upwards with the spatula. Slip the plastic film under the arms and then slip the spatula between the film and the staple arm, gently levering the arms to 90 degrees, one at a time. Turning the document over, place the slip of plastic film under the staple bridge and gently lever the staple out of the page. Ensure that the arms come out as straight as possible. The same process is used to remove split pins.

To remove cloth tapes or ribbons that can be thrown away, cut the tape or ribbon as close to the surface of the document as possible. This causes less drag on the paper as the tape is pulled through the hole. If you need to retain the tape or ribbon, then untie the knot and take the ribbon through the hole in small lengths at 90 degrees to the page, trying to avoid dragging on the hole.

Cleaning of paper

Surface cleaning is the most common cleaning technique and involves the removal of loose and partially ingrained dirt from the surface of a record. Soft brushes (such as Hake, shaving or paint brushes) either alone or in combination with a low-suction vacuum cleaner, can be used to remove loose dirt from the surface of paper records and books. Gauze should be fitted over the nozzle of the vacuum cleaner to prevent any part of the record being sucked up or torn (old pantihose is good for this purpose). The nozzle of the vacuum should be held at least three centimetres from the surface and the brush used to lift dirt off the surface. Pages should be firmly held in place with a flat, gloved hand and soft weights. Where there is a concern that the dirt/dust is harmful, appropriate fine particulate or fume masks should be worn (see Image 4.11).

Image 4.11: Surface cleaning with brush and vacuum

Ingrained dirt can be reduced or removed with soft plastic erasers, however this type of cleaning should be approached with caution as it can dramatically change the appearance and nature of the paper surface. Do not clean records with pencil markings or other fragile media, or those printed on coated or overly fibrous paper, as the surface finish will be permanently damaged. Never clean photographic emulsions with this method.

Apply only minimal pressure and use small, circular motions over the surface of the page. Clean edges using gentle motions off the page. Take great care around tears and fragile edges. All eraser shavings must be removed using a soft brush and gentle vacuum suction (see Image 4.12).

Image 4.12: Surface cleaning with an eraser

Removing mould

Removing mould can be a difficult, dirty and time-consuming task. It is important to determine whether the mould is dead or alive before beginning work. If the mould is alive, it indicates that the environmental conditions of the storage areas are unacceptable. After cleaning, items should not return to these conditions, as there is a good chance the mould will return.

There are also health and safety implications to be considered. Certain mould spores (whether they are dead or alive) can have serious health effects. Personal protective equipment (PPE) such as dust coat, plastic gloves and face mask should be worn to ensure that the procedure is safe. A well-ventilated space or fume-hood should be used where possible.

Mould removal procedure

Once thoroughly dry, mouldy records must first be vacuumed with a vacuum cleaner fitted with a HEPA (High Efficiency Particulate Air) filter. The filter ensures that the spores are not re-circulated around the room. Do not use the brush attachment that comes with the vacuum cleaner as it will get dirty and hold the spores. Instead, use a soft brush or paint brush to brush the dust and spores into the cleaner nozzle and clean the brushes with soap and hot water at the end of each day. Personnel must wear a dust mask able to filter very fine particles/fumes whilst working and plastic gloves are also recommended.

Refer to the instructions for vacuuming documents above.

Volumes

Thoroughly vacuum the covers, endpapers, text block edges, turn-ins, and all affected pages. When brushing the head and tail of the text block, brush from the spine to the fore edge so that debris does not collect down hollows or around end bands.

Refer to the instructions for vacuuming documents above.

Files and individual pages

Files and individual pages can be vacuumed with a vacuum cleaner fitted with a HEPA filter (as above). Do not use a solvent treatment (such as 80 percent ethanol/water solution) on paper, as the inks are likely to be sensitive to the solution.

Other considerations

- After cleaning and removing the records, it is important to thoroughly clean the shelves by vacuuming and then wiping with an 80 percent solution of methylated spirits in water before placing other items on them. This will reduce the chances of re-infection.
- When cleaning up mould, try to keep the work area as clean as possible. Butcher's paper can be used to work on to protect surfaces. The paper can be replaced easily when it gets dirty. If possible (and it may not be with space restrictions) have a 'dirty' area and a 'clean' area to separate the mouldy items from the clean items.

Cleaning of photographic prints and sheet film negatives

Clean only with a soft brush, using short and gentle brush strokes – a vacuum cleaner should not be required.

Cleaning of glass plate negatives and lantern slides

Check plates for signs of cracks, breaks and chips prior to handling. Do not handle if they are broken. Seek advice from a conservator. Lay plates or slides emulsion side up (dull side up) on a tissue-wrapped rigid board. This will assist in manoeuvring the plates and minimise handling (see Image 4.2). Clean the emulsion side with a soft brush only. Ensure the board is free of all debris prior to turning the plates emulsion side down. Clean the glass side with a soft brush – do not use a vacuum cleaner. Clean your workspace regularly by replacing the tissue on your board, and vacuuming and wiping the table as described in 'Preparing your workspace'.

The glass side of heavily soiled plates can be cleaned with a small cotton ball or swab dampened with a 50:50 mix of ethanol and deionised water. **Do not get any of the solution on the emulsion side**. If you are unsure which is the emulsion side, do not proceed with any wet cleaning.

Use small, gentle circular motions to swab the glass, replacing swabs when they become soiled. Continue swabbing until no further dirt is seen on the swab. Use a dry cotton ball to dry the plate using small circular motions. Allow to air dry for a further 30 minutes before placing into protective packaging.

Removing self-adhesive tapes

Self-adhesive tapes such as masking tape, sticky tape and packing tape will all degrade, leaving permanent staining and brittleness in the document. If the tape is not already too deteriorated, it can often be removed with the assistance of heat. If the tape is not easily removed using the following method, discontinue immediately. Tape that is too deteriorated may be very brown and brittle. If you have not already sourced the crepe erase described below, do not proceed with this treatment.

Removing self adhesive tape with a hair dryer

Hold the page securely in place with soft weights. Hold a hair-dryer set to warm (not hot) at a distance of about five centimetres to the page and then lift the edge of the tape with tweezers. Cut sections of the tape away as you go, as this will make the process less unwieldy. Remove the adhesive residue that remains on the page with a crepe eraser using small circular motions, removing the balled-up pieces of adhesive regularly. Crepe erasers can be purchased from conservation suppliers.

Repairing paper

Tears are one of the most common types of damage sustained by paper records. And unfortunately tears repaired with unsuitable materials are one of the most common problems faced by conservators. If you do not have appropriate materials or training to undertake repairs, it is better to place the torn page in a paper or polyester envelope and take it to a trained conservator for treatment. If you need to read the document contents then it can be copied through the polyester sleeve and the copy used for access.

Testing for solubility of media

Before commencing any treatment, a conservator will test the solubility of inks, watercolours, paints and other media on an archive. This is to ascertain what treatment can proceed. Before considering a repair, you must carry out solubility tests using any solvent (this includes water) you intend on using during the treatment. As the main component of starch paste is water, all media on a record should be tested in water prior to undertaking any repairs. Wet a double zero watercolour brush with distilled water and place a very small droplet on a discreet are of the media you are testing. Allow the droplet to sit on the ink for at least one minute and then wick up the water with a small triangular sliver of blotting paper or a small cotton swab. Examine the blotting paper with a magnifying glass and, if there is any colour wicked into the swab, the ink is soluble. Repairing around this media cannot proceed without the risk of the inks running.

Materials to use

Conservators use wheat starch paste they prepare themselves as an adhesive to attach repair tissues. Repair tissues are made from the best quality papers available and are matched for their weight, strength and flexibility to the record needing repair. Japanese tissue papers are commonly used, as are handmade European papers. Tengujo tissue is recommended for repairing small tears in most paper records, as it is long-fibred, strong and fine and will not obscure text. Pre-glued or self-adhesive repair tissues are not recommended for use on archives as the adhesives often contain impurities that can damage archives and make the tapes difficult to remove later.

Wheat starch paste is prepared from pure, dry wheat starch powder (which can be purchased from conservation suppliers) and deionised or distilled water (usually available from chemists). Use the method recommended by the manufacturer to form the paste or use the simple recipe described overleaf. Do not use pre-prepared, commercially available wet pastes as they may contain additives harmful to your archives.

Recipe for starch paste

1 part pure starch powder (conservation grade)

4 parts deionised or distilled water

Place the powder and water into a stainless steel saucepan, mix thoroughly and allow to soak for at least one hour – overnight is better.

Place the saucepan over a high heat.

Stir the mixture constantly as the paste will stick otherwise. Continue stirring until the paste gels – it will go through an opaque white phase and then turn a more translucent, opalescent colour. The paste should be stirred for at least 20 minutes – 30-40 is better. When it has been translucent for some minutes and the paste creates peaks it is ready.

Allow the paste to cool in the saucepan. Once cooled, pour over deionised or distilled water – the paste can be stored this way for some time without refrigeration.

Paste needs to be sieved before use to make it smooth. It can then be diluted with distilled water and 'mashed' with a brush until it is smooth and the consistency you are after.

Repair technique

Repair tissues need to have a feathered edge as this provides the best bond and will not form ridges or fractures in the original record. To form a feathered edge, tissues are water cut by running a thin line of water along the surface with a paint brush and then gently separating the paper along the water line. The repair should extend beyond all edges of the tear by a few millimetres.

Paste out the repair tissue so that the fibres fan outwards. Lift the pasted tissue with tweezers or a spatula and lay paste-side down onto the torn page. Smooth the repair tissue with a soft, dry brush and then place Reemay® and blotting paper on either side of the page and weight down until dry. Cut any excess repair tissue from the edge of the record with a scalpel.

Implementing a preservation program

If you have read the rest of this chapter, you will already have a good understanding of the elements that make up a preservation program. The importance of having a preservation program in place lies in its planning and execution. The development of the plan should focus on all areas of your archive so that problems are detected and solutions found. And the execution should involve everyone.

The key elements to a plan are as follows:

- **Knowing your collection**
  - Survey
- **Security**
  - Funding
  - Risk assessment of threats
  - Physical security of records
- **Environmental control**
  - Appropriate to your holdings
  - Stable
  - Storage areas
  - Access areas
- **Maintenance**
  - Integrated pest management
  - General housekeeping
  - Infrastructure management and maintenance
- **Handling**
  - Care
  - Security
  - Education
- **Preservation copying**
  - For access
  - Reformatting to avoid obsolescence
  - Reformatting due to inherent instability
- **Disaster preparedness**
- **Conservation intervention**
- **Education**
  - Public awareness
  - Lobbying for funding

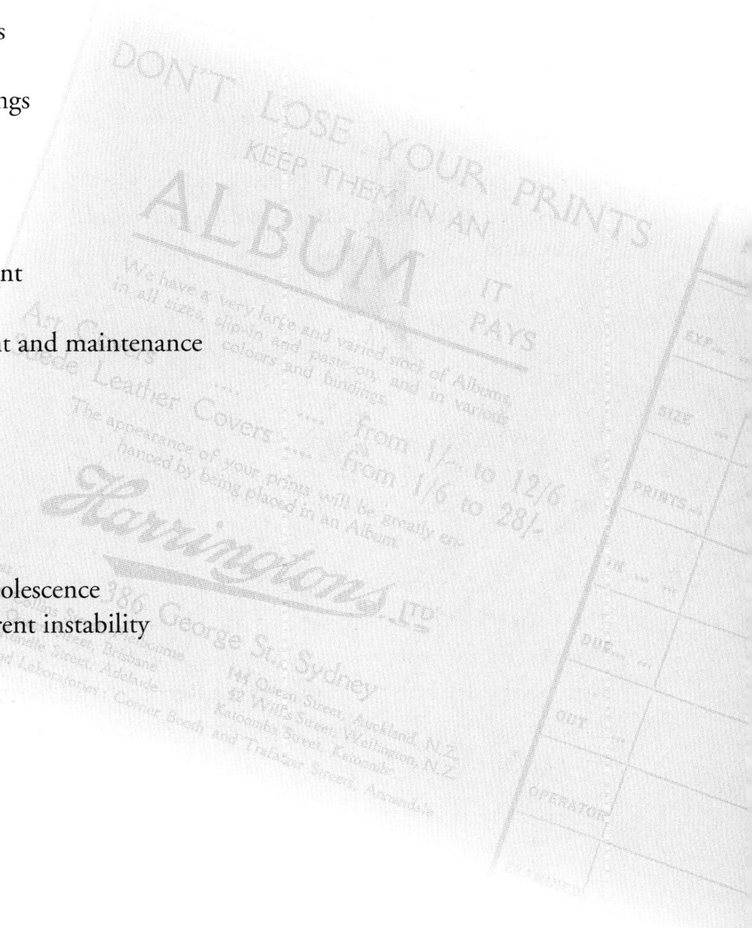

Prioritising the different elements depends on the individual circumstances of your archive. If your archives are stored in good quality enclosures, but the building leaks or has poor air-conditioning, then obviously you will prioritise the building needs in your overall strategy. These questions usually come down to common sense and they cannot be prescribed in a general way.

If you are unsure how to proceed, then seek the advice of a conservator or preservation professional. Your local government archive or library is a good place to start as they will be able to provide advice as well as point you in the direction of consultants in your local area.

Conclusion

As Helen Forde points out:

> *Let us be honest and admit that archival materials are not indestructible, and they were never intended to last indefinitely. We do, however, have to satisfy ourselves that the actions we take now will not accelerate decay, and will not cause our successors greater problems than those posed by the original material itself.*

We have discussed in this chapter some of the reasons why records are not indestructible and ways of lengthening their useful life.

An over-arching preservation strategy embraced by all levels of your organisation and focusing on all levels of archive use and management is crucial. Your staff, volunteers and readers must understand and take an active part in the preservation of your records, and all practices must have undergone a preservation review. It is pointless educating your readers to handle records carefully when your service guarantees necessitate unsafe handling practices by your staff because they are pressed for time.

Key factors to bear in mind for the preservation of records are:

- storage environment
- management of risk factors, such as disasters and pests
- knowledge of your collection
  - condition
  - materials of creation
- storage enclosures
- handling

Conservation intervention should play a small part in the overall preservation management of your archive. Where good preventive measures are in place, conservation will be needed infrequently. This approach has a two-fold benefit: it is the most cost effective to implement and it advantages the greatest number of records.

And always remember, you are not alone. The problems you face have probably been faced by others before you – make use of their knowledge. This will not only make your job easier, it will more than likely prevent mistakes.

section 2

managing the archives

This section, *Managing the Archives*, deals with the 'stuff' of the archival endeavour. At the heart of any archival institution are the archives themselves. It is the collection, whether large or small, whether distributed or all under one roof, that makes the archives.

The first four chapters in this section, of *Appraisal & Disposal*, *Acquisition*, *Accessioning*, and *Arrangement & Description*, follow a logical process. To put it very simply, these chapters cover deciding what you want, negotiating to get it, getting it in the door in an ordered way, and managing it. However, in practice no archivist can calmly walk through these steps. Any archive has a backlog of perhaps unappraised or poorly described material, or there may be a drive to accept material before proper appraisal takes place. These chapters not only outline the principles and best practices of archival work, but also provide hints and tips for the real world.

The first chapter examines appraisal. However, while there are no right or wrong answers, there is definitely 'good' (and therefore also 'bad') appraisal. This chapter provides numerous tools and references to help you on your way.

Fortunately, acquisition, accessioning and arrangement and description are more straightforward, in theory if not always in practice. Acquisition complements appraisal, as an acquisition policy (or collection policy) outlines the vision of what you want your archives to be. This chapter also covers the practical side of acquisition, to ensure you have a clear position with regard to the ownership of items in the collection.

Accessioning and *Arrangement & Description* turns the 'stuff' into a controlled, known and accessible collection of archives. I encourage you to review and reflect on the substantial practical advice in these two chapters.

The final two chapters in this section bring a slight change of pace and look at other ways we build and manage our collections. *Enriching the Record: Documentation Programs* looks at strategies archivists use to address gaps in the collection and complement what we hold.

Finally, *Using Computers*, recognises that archives have very different levels of automation. This chapter covers the basic tasks for which computers can be used right through to collection management systems and the opportunities of Web 2.0.

The chapters in this section contain numerous references to relevant standards and provide advice on best practice. While these may not be achievable in the short term for many small archives, it is important to be aware of them and ensure your efforts are directed towards achieving them in the longer term.

Approaches to archival work can vary, depending on the context of the archives and, as discussed in Chapter 1, what dimensions of the continuum you work in. As a final word of encouragement, keep this in mind as you read the chapters and select those aspects that best suit your needs.

CHAPTER 5

appraisal & disposal

JACKIE BETTINGTON

CHAPTER ABSTRACT

Appraisal is an analytical process that archivists use to determine which records need to be created and captured into a records system and how long the records need to be kept. The disposal or retention of records is the key outcome of appraisal. The results of appraisal and disposal decisions and actions shape the scope, colour and texture of the archives – what is remembered, and what is forgotten. It is a subjective, challenging and risky endeavour that is central to archival practice.

Making decisions on records retention and disposal is not easy and there are often no indisputable right or wrong answers. However, it is critical that archivists provide clear justifications and accountable records of their appraisal and disposal decisions and actions.

This chapter explores these issues from a theoretical and practical perspective. It will give you an overview of the various approaches, methods, instruments and resources available to assist archivists in undertaking 'good' appraisal and disposal. It covers understanding the focus and purpose of appraisal and disposal, who are the primary beneficiaries of appraisal and disposal, when it should occur, how it should be undertaken and when to apply the various approaches, methods, instruments for appraisal and disposal. Additional resources for this chapter are included on the accompanying CD.

> *In a practical sense, appraisal raises many vexing issues for the archivist and it would seem that present theories and methodologies often lag behind some of our daily concerns and challenges. It must be said, however, that no matter how imperfect our theoretical framework, there will never be a simple answer or scientific quick fix to what are often subjective areas in our field (Anthony 2003, p.26).*

What is appraisal?

Appraisal is an analytical process that archivists use to determine which records need to be created and captured into a records system and how long the records need to be kept. The disposal or retention of records is the key outcome of appraisal. In undertaking appraisal archivists typically seeks answers to the following questions:

1. What records need to be created and captured into records systems and the risks associated with not doing so?
2. What records need to be retained?
3. Who should create these records and why?
4. How do these records relate to the creator's business functions or the life of a community, place or person?
5. How do these records relate to the other records?
6. When are or were these records created?
7. How are or were these records used?
8. When are or were they used?
9. How often are they used?
10. Who uses them?
11. Why do they use them?

Interestingly, a formal definition and any explicit references to appraisal have been omitted from the International Standard on records management, *ISO 15489*. This situation reflects the lack of professional consensus on appraisal. The process of capture is explained in *ISO 15489* as being that of 'determining that a record should be made or kept... Decisions about which documents should be captured and which discarded are based on an analysis of the organization's business and accountabilities' (2001, p.14). This is appraisal. Due to the silence of *ISO 15489* on appraisal many archivists, particularly those practising in Australia and New Zealand, continue to refer to the previous *Australian Standard AS 4390: Records Management* for a formal definition and explanation of appraisal.

AS 4390 was developed by the Australian archives and records management community in the mid 1990's. It defines appraisal as:

> *the process of evaluating business activities to determine which records need to be captured and how long the records need to be kept, to meet business needs, the requirements of organizational accountability and community expectations (1996, clause 4.3, p.6).*

In considering the practical challenges appraisal presents the archivist, Piggott (2001) has identified the following 'archival appraisal truisms':

1. Appraisal is not a science
2. Appraisal is not free of bias and subjectivity
3. Appraisal is the primary archival function on which all other functions depend
4. The great trinity mystery – can't keep all, all records have some value, can't predict all future research interest
5. Destruction to protect privacy is not appraisal
6. Disposal does not just mean perpetual preservation or eventual destruction
7. It is easy to justify keeping but not destroying
8. There is a reluctance to copy and destroy records
9. Older records are fewer resulting in fewer to select and being more inclined to keep

Most of these observations of appraisal in the real world are discussed elsewhere in this chapter. However, it is worth noting here simply to convey the message that *appraisal is not easy and there are no right or wrong answers.* The key to successful appraisal is to be conscious of how you and the context in which appraisal occurs impact on it; and how to effectively apply the various methods and instruments; and how to undertake 'good appraisal'.

The power and implications of appraisal

The primary reason why archival appraisal is not easy is because the meaning and implications of appraisal are more complex and far reaching than simply determining what needs to be kept and what does not need to be kept. It is a contingent, subjective and political process that invariably involves an element of risk. It is about 'deciding what will be remembered and what will be forgotten. To ask how we appraise is to also ask for whom, and this is to ask why we keep archives at all' (Wickman 2000, p.65). Often the answers to these questions are found deep within the social norms and the professional and organisational conventions in which archivists live and work.

In recognition of the often hidden complexities that underpin decisions relating to the retention or disposal of records, Harris (2000, p.45) offers a richer and more evocative definition of appraisal:

- Appraisal is the activity whereby archivists identify societal processes they think are worth remembering and the records that will foster such remembering.

- Appraisal is the telling of a story using records systems and the sites of records creation as the primary raw materials.
- Appraisal is a fever characterised by obsessive remembering and forgetting.

The political dimensions of appraisal and disposal are most evident in communities experiencing extreme tension such as war, terror or oppression. Table 5.1 provides an insight into how societal norms and political power operate to distort the documented memory and evidence of the experiences of a nation. It demonstrates the extent to which appraisal and disposal may be intentionally and unintentionally applied to reinforce existing power relations and promote what those in power regard as 'normal' and 'important'.

> *The absorption of apartheid bureaucratic culture and, at a deeper level, of apartheid ideology, shaped (State Archives Service) SAS's functions and left indelible marks on SAS's contribution to social memory. Its archival appraisal program, fashioned in the 1950s, was characterised by incoherence in both theory and methodology (Harris 2002). In practice, appraisers made decisions around one central question: does this record possess actual or anticipated usefulness to researchers? Until the 1970s blossoming of social history and revisionist historiography began to influence the program in the late 1980s, SAS's fashioning of appraisal into a tool for academic researchers, particularly historians, resulted in the experience of apartheid's marginalised and oppressed being poorly reflected in the public records chosen for preservation. The fact that most of SAS's appraisers were taught as undergraduates by establishment-aligned Afrikaner historians was an important contributory factor. Of course the public records chosen for preservation reflected apartheid power relations and carried the reductionist constructions of process typical of any bureaucracy.*
>
> *A more fundamental skewing of social memory is evident in SAS's collections of non-public records. With the exception of the Boer resistance to British imperialism, they documented poorly the struggles against colonialism, segregation, and apartheid. Black experiences were also poorly documented, and in most cases were seen through white eyes. Similarly, the voices of women, the disabled, and other marginalised people were seldom heard. This is partially explained by the difficulty experienced by SAS in securing donations of records from other than establishment-aligned sources. But the heart of the issue was a collecting policy which quite deliberately directed archivists away from grassroots experience towards society's pinnacles, and which eschewed the documentation of orality.*

Table 5.1: The power of remembering and forgetting in Apartheid South Africa

Just as archival appraisal and disposal may determine what is forgotten, it can also be applied to fill gaps and reduce any existing biases in the collective memory of any community or individual. Archival appraisal, disposal, acquisition and documentation programs, for example, may be applied to ensure voices silenced by past decisions on the retention and disposal of records can be heard once again by current and future generations. The work of the various Truth and Reconciliation Commissions around the world is an example of archives and archival documentation programs established specifically to reduce past biases in the memory and evidence of the experiences of various nations. Table 5.2 provides an example of how the Truth and Reconciliation Commission in South Africa has sought to recall voices previously omitted from the National Archives (formerly the State Archives Service).

In the life of any individual, family, community or society, memory is of fundamental importance. It is the fabric of identity. This is something those who devised and imposed apartheid on South Africa knew well. At the heart of every oppressive tool developed by the apartheid regime was a determination to control, distort, weaken, even erase people's memories. For those of us who spent many years in prison, this attack on memory was felt deep within us, actually in our bodies – the physical yearning to touch loved ones, breath in the smells of home, feel the texture of a favourite jersey. The struggle against apartheid can be typified as the pitting of remembering against forgetting. It was our determination to remember our ancestors, our stories, our values and our dreams that we found in comradeship. As has been known and practised in our country for many centuries, the memory of an individual is founded in collective memory, and it is with this ancient wisdom in mind that we inaugaurated the Nelson Mandela Centre of Memory and Commemoration Project. It is the task of the Centre to continue to unravel the many silences imposed by our apartheid and colonial pasts, to find space for the memories suppressed by power.   *We have mandated the Centre to locate and document – and facilitate public access to – the many archives that contain traces of my life and those who have lived it with me.*

Table 5.2: Removing biases of past decisions on the retention and disposal of records

The examples provided in Table 5.1 and Table 5.2 are extreme cases used here to illustrate the implications of making decisions on the retention or disposal of records. Nonetheless, archivists working in any context also risk silencing some voices and privileging others. The content of much of this chapter is concerned with assisting archivists in becoming more aware of the factors that influence the choices they make in retaining or disposing of records. While it is not expected that anyone can make decisions on retention and disposal free of subjectivity or bias, being aware of what influences decisions, undertaking consultation and documenting the appraisal and disposal process are steps that archivists can take in making their decisions more transparent and more broadly understood.

For example, in making decisions to retain 'personnel files' it is convention to retain permanently only those relating to executive managers or individuals who are famous (or infamous) beyond the organisation. This convention reinforces a broader social norm that those with more money and social standing are more significant than those who earn less and are of a lower standing or profile. The latter group constitute the majority of people so applying this norm is creating a documentary bias that silences the majority but gives an enduring voice to the minority.

Another example is the high levels of bureaucratic control placed over indigenous people in Australia and elsewhere. This resulted in the generation of huge volumes of records documenting in great detail the lives of individuals and families within indigenous communities. Many of these records have been retained by archival authorities and provide a rich cultural resource. Consequently, the experiences, good and bad, of many indigenous people are often more thoroughly documented, and therefore remembered on a collective basis, than those of non-indigenous people, much of which was not documented in the first place or, if it was documented, then it has subsequently been forgotten. However, while there are great volumes of 'official records' they tend to represent indigenous people's experiences in a way that reflects the norms of those in power and controlled bureaucracies. Consequently, over the past few decades there are programs and projects for establishing a more balanced and inclusive view of the experience of indigenous people that draws not only on written records, but also oral histories.

The key point is that social norms, organisational practices and power relations can implicitly distort decisions on the retention and disposal of records and therefore, determine what is remembered and what is not. As archivists, we need to be conscious of such subjectivity and biases and recognise the contingent nature of appraisal and disposal.

What is disposal?

Disposal is the key outcome of appraisal. The appraisal process broadly identifies what needs to be kept as records, how long to keep those records and what records are of continuing value as 'archives'. Disposal is concerned with implementing these.

Disposal is defined in AS4390 as being:

> *A range of processes associated with implementing appraisal decisions. These include the retention, deletion or destruction of records in or from recordkeeping systems. They may also include the migration or transmission of records between recordkeeping systems, and the transfer of custody or ownership of records (1996, clause 4.9, p.6).*

Similarly, 'disposal' (or disposition, as it is referred to) is defined in *ISO 15489* as being

> *...the range of processes associated with implementing records retention, destruction or transfer decisions which are documented in disposition authorities or other instruments (Section 3.9, p.3).*

The term disposal encompasses far more than 'throwing out' records. *ISO 15489-1* explains that disposal may include:

> *a) immediate physical destruction, including overwriting and deleting,*
> *b) retention for a further period within the business unit,*
> *c) transfer to an appropriate storage area or medium under organizational control,*
> *d) transfer to another organization that has assumed responsibility for the business activity through restructure, sale or privatization,*
> *e) transfer to a storage area managed on behalf of the organization by an independent provider with whom appropriate contractual arrangements have been established,*
> *f) transfer of responsibility for management to an appropriate authority while physical storage of the record is retained by the creating organization,*
> *g) transfer to an organizational archives authority, or*
> *h) transfer to an external archives authority (Section 9.9, p.16).*

Fundamentally, the terms 'disposition' and 'disposal' are synonymous. The term 'disposition' is used in *ISO 15489*. In developing a standard for the international community, the term 'disposition' was favoured over the term 'disposal', which is typically used in Australasia. As the primary audience for this book is novice archivists in Australasia, the term 'disposal' is used in this book.

From an archival perspective the term 'disposal' encompasses a much broader concept of the 'fate' of records than what is understood by the layperson. This situation often causes conceptual confusion when archivists attempt to communicate what disposal is and what it involves to stakeholders. Additionally, given the vast quantity of poorly structured digital records, many of which are dynamically generated, archivists are often concerned more with identifying what need to be created and captured as records. In this situation archivists may be dealing with records that don't yet exist. So in this situation the focus is on ensuring that the right records are generated and retained with all the necessary characteristics of full and accurate records, rather than selecting archives from an existing collection.

To more accurately reflect what archivists do in the digital environment and to facilitate better communication with stakeholders, archivists and government archival authorities increasingly refer to disposal as 'retention and disposal' or 'decisions on records retention and disposal'.

Following our discussion of definitions, we will now consider the results of appraisal and disposal.

Results of appraisal and disposal

Appraisal and disposal are usually undertaken to achieve one or more of the following outcomes:

- systematic and planned disposal of records
- total reduction in storage space for records
- accountable disposal actions
- an archival collection of full and accurate records that is useful and meaningful for as long they have enduring/continuing value
- more efficient records management as the organisation gains a better understanding of what records it needs to make and keep and what it can discard
- reduced risk of inappropriate or untimely loss or destruction of records and
- longer term cost reduction due to efficient management of information, reduced storage management and reduced exposure to legal and financial liabilities
- selecting or acquiring archives for a collecting program

The tangible products of the appraisal and disposal processes may also include one or more of the following:

- retention and disposal policy
- retention and disposal program and strategy
- retention and disposal guidelines and templates
- an appraisal report
- a records survey report
- a records inventory
- A Retention and Disposal Authority (RDA)

Appraisal and disposal projects do not necessarily generate all these outputs. The reason for this is a mix of resource constraints and the overarching approach adopted for appraisal and disposal. Nonetheless, the ultimate outcome of the appraisal process 'determines the size, shape, colour, texture and content of our archival collections' (Gleaves and O'Neill 2003, p.57). We will discuss this further in the following section.

Understanding your own approach to appraisal and disposal

Archival appraisal and disposal are contingent activities. They are shaped by the context in which decisions and actions on retention and disposal are made. Table 5.1 and Table 5.2 in this chapter illustrate in an extreme way how appraisal and disposal are influenced and determined by the context in which decisions are made and actions undertaken. Although many archivists and archives apply checklists, RDAs and sets of predefined criteria for making retention and disposal decisions, the use of these instruments requires 'interpretation' of general retention and disposal requirements and application of these to specific records or business activities. Likewise the development of retention and disposal instruments is a subjective activity. It requires determining what is significant enough to warrant ongoing retention and what is less significant and not worth ongoing retention.

For example, to comply with laws relating to child protection it may be necessary to keep child protection case files for at least 10 years after the child turns 18 years old. To support longitudinal studies into child protection researchers, may require these case files to be retained longer. But without the letter of the law to determine how much longer these records need to be retained, the decision on the retention of them will be based on the experience, research and opinion of the archivist and others who may be involved in making that decision. Where case files are paper-based files it is generally clear what documentation case managers and the organisation have generated or accumulated to form the documentary record of how a child's case was handled. Retention and disposal decisions may be readily applied to each discrete file or collections of files. However, where case files are part of a broader electronic case management system, it may not be clear what constitutes a 'case file'. Applying retention and disposal requirements in this situation requires the archivist to draw on experience, research and opinion to determine what is 'the record', the trigger for implementing disposal action and how to preserve these records through migration and other methods.

Because appraisal and disposal are subjective and contingent activities it is critical that archivists provide clear justifications and accountable records of the appraisal process and the results of that process. There are various methods and instruments available to assist archivists in ensuring appraisal and disposal are accountable and reasonable. There are also instruments such as the *ASA Appraisal Statement* (see Appendix 5.1) available to assist archivists and others to evaluate whether decisions on retention and disposal are 'good'. However, before considering these, it is important that every archivist consciously understands their own approach and how they may influence the outcomes of appraisal and disposal.

To understand your own approach, is to ask and consider the following points:

1. Why are you undertaking appraisal and disposal? Perhaps it is due to
   - the challenge of ensuring electronic records and archives are created and captured in the first place
   - a need to do something with records once their 'useful' life has finished
   - having too many records, not enough space
   - having too many records, not enough resources
   - technology obsolescence or replacement or
   - the business risks associated with keeping everything?
2. What is the focus of appraisal and disposal? Perhaps it is
   - business activities such as human resources management and product development
   - entities – organisations/people or
   - records?
3. For whom is appraisal and disposal primarily being undertaken? For example it could be
   - organisational or administrative personnel or
   - future researchers?
4. When should appraisal and disposal occur? Should it occur at the
   - end of life cycle or at
   - various points of the continuum?
5. What is the scope of appraisal? Will it be
   - retrospective (for records that already exist)
   - prospective (for records that do not yet exist) or
   - both?
6. How should appraisal be undertaken? Should it be undertaken
   - at a micro level
   - at a macro level
   - or a combination of these?
7. What instruments should be used for appraisal and disposal? Should it include
   - policies
   - appraisal reports
   - lists and
   - RDAs?

We will be exploring these questions further in relation to the various approaches applied by archivists in Australasia. As you read through the relevant sections consider: What is my preferred approach for undertaking appraisal and disposal? You may find it is a single theoretical model or it may borrow components from multiple models. For practising archivists you may also consider whether your preferred approach is the most suitable for your archival context and why you believe this to be the case.

Magda employed strict criteria of Appraisal and Disposal when dealing with Ed's old underwear.

In reading the remainder of this chapter you will discover that there are many variations and options available for undertaking appraisal and disposal. None will be perfect for any or all situations, but some will be more suitable to a collecting archive than, say to an in-house corporate archive. Understanding the various approaches, their conceptual rationales, strengths and weaknesses will enable you to make more professionally informed decisions and better cope with the practical and ethical challenges that are presented to you when making choices about what to keep and what not to keep.

Why undertake appraisal and disposal?

In practice, appraisal and disposal are challenging and often resource-intensive archival processes that require a significant level of research, consultation, negotiation and operational processing.

AS 4390 cites several reasons for undertaking appraisal and disposal (Part 1, p.3). These reasons focus on current recordkeeping in a business environment and include:

- requirements for creating and keeping records are identified and implemented
- risks for not meeting requirements are defined and more readily understood
- adequate records are made and kept
- records required beyond the life of a digital recordkeeping system may be more readily identified for migration to successive systems

- records not required beyond the life of a digital recordkeeping system may be more readily identified for exclusion from any migration process to successive systems
- appropriate and compliant custody and ownership requirements for records are identified and implemented.

For collecting archives appraisal and disposal ensures that only those records that fit within the collection or acquisition policy of the archives and the broader organisation's missions and objectives are accessioned. In its guidelines for creating a Synagogue Archives, the American Jewish Archives explains that:

> *Using a collection policy to select materials for retention and preservation is called appraisal. Archival appraisal is the application of the guidelines and criteria of a collection policy in determining what records an archives will collect. Appraisal is the process archivists use in determining which records should be accessioned (or accepted) into their repository.*
>
> *... appraisal should be recognized as the process whereby the goals of a collection policy are put into action, resulting in the development of a strong and useful collection of records. In using the guidelines of a collection policy a congregational archives will decide if a collection of records--be they minutes of the board, administrative office files, or the papers of a synagogue member--meet the criteria established in the collection policy and are worthy of permanent retention in the archives. Conversely, through appraisal the archives will also decide which materials will not be kept and therefore be targeted for disposal.*[15]

Once temporary records have been identified and removed from collections via appraisal and disposal, then resources may be more efficiently allocated to making records of continuing value more accessible to current and future researchers.

To ensure appraisal and disposal are systematic and accountable activities, *ISO 15489* provides a clearly structured methodology in which appraisal is initiated at the point where a new records or business system is being designed. Known as the 'Designing and Implementing Recordkeeping Systems' (DIRKS) method, it is more effective when dealing with future records in a business context. However, it is difficult to apply to legacy records and when working in a collecting archive. This methodology is discussed in detail in Chapter 15: *Digital Recordkeeping* and to a lesser extent later in this chapter.

For many archivists appraisal and disposal are undertaken to ensure the archival collection is of the best quality and within the scope of their overarching collection policy and resource constraints. There are usually more records available than what any archivist or archive can effectively manage. Typically there are many records of little if any value beyond their immediate purpose. So archivists develop selection criteria to assist them in selecting the best records for ongoing retention, management and use as archives.

Specific triggers for undertaking appraisal may include:

- the quantity of records has outgrown the physical storage space available
- a change of personnel, closure of project, completion of a program or cyclical event such as the end of financial year or school year
- the merger, acquisition or closure of an organisation
- the death or relocation of an individual may trigger a potential donation to a collecting archives
- an office relocation requiring a the reduction in the quantity of records before their transfer to a new site
- embarrassing litigation cases in which the organisation is not able to produce all or adequate evidence
- greater public scrutiny of some organisations and the consequential need to retain of only those records that are necessary and that ensure efficient and effective access mechanisms (e.g. enterprise-wide search tools and finding aids) are in place to reduce the cost and time required to search, retrieve and distribute records.
- review cycles set to revisit past appraisal decisions to validate specific disposal actions or undertake broader reappraisal as discussed later in this chapter.

Are there alternatives to appraisal and disposal?

Increasingly, archivists are challenged with the view that it is not necessary to select archives because technology provides cheap storage options with sophisticated search and retrieval functionality that enables immediate access to all records. Technology may provide these benefits but they typically lack the contextual information and integrity required for ensuring archives remain meaningful and reliable over a long period of time. Keeping everything means that there will also be at a lot of ephemeral or low-value records retained. Many of these records may be duplicates or multiple versions of records. However, there is little if any information about the purpose, difference and authority of each version or copy. Everything that is retained needs to be managed and unless it is contextualised and of value, then over time as the volume of records increases, keeping everything may confuse users and result in frustration as they try and work through long lists to determine what is the best record for their needs.

Appraisal and disposal invariably involves risk. No one can pre-empt the future use and value of all records or consider the expectations and needs of all stakeholders. Deciding not to keep something and removing it, carries the risk that records of significance will be destroyed. Those who are very risk averse may argue that it is necessary to keep everything simply 'just in case' any of those records may be useful to someone at some point. Over time, this creates a significant resource overhead and requires archivists to clearly present a long-term cost-benefit analysis for keeping everything.

Conversely, there is also an increased risk of valuable records being destroyed when records appraisal and disposal occurs in an unplanned or unsystematic way. The time and cost pressure to reduce the physical office space allocated to records or to vacate office premises often results in appraisal and disposal decisions being made in haste and without sufficient documentation of the process. The decision not to save something is usually irreversible – 'once it is gone, it is gone'. This scenario is very common where records creators in the contemporary business environment regard information as having only transitory value to them in undertaking their particular work. To alleviate such risks archivists can educate records creators of the potential risks and broader value of records and provide simple tools and systems to reduce this risk.

Unplanned appraisal often happens in a hurry – in direct competition with the office shredder.

What is the focus of appraisal?

Fundamentally appraisal may focus on one of two things – the records or different contextual facets relating to the records. For an in-house archives or government archives a facet may be a function and activity, an organisational entity or particular level of the organisation. For a collecting archive this may be particular topics or subjects, industry, geographic area, event, demographic attribute or community.

Appraising all records at the item level (file, folio or object) is well beyond the capacity of most individuals and the financial resources of any organisation. With the explosion in the volume of information, a trend that is expected to continue for the foreseeable future, archivists have tended to adopt macro-level or top-down approaches for appraisal and disposal.

Another key problem with item level appraisal is that it tends to fragment the historical record because it considers the record in isolation of its broader context and may result in destroying the evidence of the provenance and original order of the record. It also may mean that the chain of evidence and custody is broken, an important consideration from a legal and authenticity perspective.

For whom is appraisal and disposal being undertaken?

How the purpose of an archive is defined significantly influences the approach adopted for appraisal and disposal. Where the primary purpose of an archive focuses on achieving administrative outcomes such as efficiency and use by the umbrella organisation, then in practice appraisal will probably be a process that defines and eliminates records. Where the primary purpose of the archives is culturally-based, then appraisal will probably be more concerned with selecting and evaluating records so a culturally rich collection is established in conjunction with the associated services for research use such as access and reference services, documentation programs and finding aids. This tends to be the case for collecting archives.

Typically one role is privileged over one, but the balance of power periodically shifts from one to the other (Reed 2003, p.66). This is particularly the case for government archival authorities as the political pendulum swings between celebrating and protecting cultural heritage; and establishing efficient and accountable business practices. While these two purposes can and do co-exist, there is a tendency to favour one constituency over another. Where heritage is of primary interest, then appraisal and disposal tends to be undertaken with the benefit of current and future researchers in mind. However, where administrative and business concerns are of primary interest, then current and future administrators and officials tend to be the primary audience for undertaking appraisal and disposal.

Much of our appraisal theory and methodologies have been derived from the government sector. Determining research value is of lesser concern to archivists operating in the government or corporate archives. It is still an important factor but not the overarching one or key driver. For collecting archives, however, research value is often the primary focus yet it is also the most subjective and ambiguous area to work with. It is often more difficult to determine parameters for appraisal and interpreting the value of records for research purposes. For example, how do you objectively determine what constitutes a 'significant' or 'controversial event', are there levels of 'significance' or 'controversy' and how should changes in be accommodated (e.g. re-appraisal discussed later in this chapter).

When should appraisal and disposal occur?

Appraisal is a core skill and responsibility of many archivists. It is a critical archival process because appraisal decisions shape the historical record. It is a significant responsibility that has been the subject of much debate amongst academics and practitioners. Possibly the most significant debates have occurred in the context of identifying where appraisal and disposal fit within the primary theoretical records models – the life cycle model and the records continuum model. These models are introduced in Chapter 1: *What are Archives & Archival Programs* and discussed further in this chapter specifically in relation to appraisal and disposal.

Records life cycle model

Traditionally appraisal commences once the active administrative use of the records was completed. Appraisal is a process that occurs at the end of the record life cycle and usually involves reviewing the value of a physical record and the physical inspection of those records prior to confirming the appropriate disposal action for those records.

This approach is often labelled as a 'traditional' or 'bottom-up' approach and is used by many archivists, particularly those working in a mostly collecting archives environment. But this situation is changing.

Appraisal using the traditional approach involves identifying 'records' as being worthy of 'permanent retention' and transferring those records to the custody of the relevant archival institution. This approach was articulated by various European and North American archival academics and archival authorities, including Hilary Jenkinson and the Public Records Office of the United Kingdom and T.R. Schellenberg and the National Archives in the United States.

The traditional approach is records-centric and generally works well where the vast majority of records are paper-based records. Such records are static and usually self-contained in terms of content, structure and context. They do not rely on external technology to manage, store and use them and are generally contained in a relatively stable format (thermal paper, etc excluded).

However, by the 1990s computer technology increasingly became the preferred channel for business communication. With this change in communication preferences, the traditional approach to appraisal became problematic. It soon became clear that early intervention was necessary to ensure that actions are actually documented and that the essential information and evidence pertaining to those actions are captured into proper records systems. Unless this occurred, then there would be few archives to manage in the future. The speed at which records could now be generated and distributed via technology also meant that the volumes of records were dramatically increasing. For example, it takes significantly less time to compose and send an email than a paper-based letter or memo.

Additionally, information professionals working in the business environment were challenged by a more fluid workplace in terms of the employment arrangements (e.g. temporary, casual, and contractual arrangements) and frequently changing organisational roles (e.g. changing position descriptions and acting arrangements), structures (e.g. downsizing, re-aligning structures with changes to senior management and revisions of strategic plans), ownership (e.g. mergers and acquisitions) and business models (e.g. joint ventures, strategic alliances, etc).

Records continuum model

From this contextual chaos emerged new approaches to appraisal and recordkeeping generally through the records continuum. Some of these changes are reflected in *ISO 15489*. This standard focuses on the principles and methods for designing and building recordkeeping requirements into business information systems to ensure that when those systems are implemented, full and accurate records are effectively captured and controlled for as long as they are needed. This includes the capture of the relevant metadata and ensuring integrity and accessibility over time. (Refer to Chapter 15: *Digital Recordkeeping*, for further guidance on how to achieve this).

In the continuum view appraisal occurs at a number of points, at various times and at different levels of aggregation (e.g. at document, file or folder, box, series, group or collection levels). In contrast to the records life cycle view, recordkeeping is not a linear process. It is 'iterative and recursive' (Reed 2005, p. 125) and involves evaluating the context of the record rather than the record itself. Consequently, appraisal from a continuum-based approach is a more analytical and abstract activity. It involves asking a variety of appraisal questions at different points of the continuum. Some of these are summarised in Figure 5.1.

Appraisal questions in the continuum model

- Capture of a record into a recordkeeping system – Is this a record?
- Reach – To whom does this record need to be meaningful and usable – just me, my immediate work team or community, my whole organisation, the broader community? Does it need to be meaningful for current and/or future users? Which records need to be contextualised beyond the immediate user group?
- Migration – do I need to continue to keep this record? Does this record need to remain usable and accessible?
- Implementing destruction or retention – should this record be destroyed or retained as previously 'sentenced'.

Figure 5.1: Appraisal questions in the continuum model

Appraisal when viewed from a continuum perspective needs to be integrated with other recordkeeping processes (preservation, access, description, etc) as these operate throughout the life of a record and occur at the four different dimensions or perspectives of the records continuum. These dimensions relate to the creation of documents that results in their existence in the first place; the capture of those documents as 'records' into a recordkeeping system; the organisation of records as part of the individual or corporate archive; and more broadly within the a collective community archive e.g. a government archive, collecting archive or a virtually as a distributed national collection as in the case of the Collections Australia Network (CAN) portal which aims to be the public gateway to collecting institutions, including archives in Australia.

The key thing to note here is that when working electronically, these four actions or perspectives can be designed up front into business information systems (manual, electronic or both) and incorporated into workflows and procedures. They may also occur simultaneously i.e. when an electronic document is created by someone, if the appraisal decisions and disposal actions are built into electronic systems and processes, then they may be simultaneously captured as full and accurate records with the relevant recordkeeping controls and preserved through the generation of archival quality renditions, for example capture into PDF/A as per *ISO 19005-1:2005 Document management – Electronic document file format for long-term preservation – Part 1: Use of PDF 1.4 (PDF/A-1)*, and made accessible within the organisation or beyond via finding aids and other mechanisms.

According to the continuum view, there is no need to 'wait' until administrative use has ceased before managing a record as an archive. Records are appraised and their disposal determined prior to the creation of a record and archival processes may be automated. Sentencing of individual records or groups of records and implementing the relevant disposal action (be it destruction by deletion, transfer or retention as an 'archive') may also be automated. As an exercise in risk management most archivists and organisations prefer to review and confirm the disposal status and action prior to implementation. For example, this is a mandatory requirement set for the New South Wales public offices by State Records NSW.

System design and development needs to include audit trails or other means that ensure any disposal action is documented. These audit trails in turn need to be managed as 'records' in a record system.

Undertaking appraisal during the design of systems and at the point of capturing records into a records system is conceptually sound. However, in practice, few organisations and individuals can actually achieve such a systematic and efficient way to manage archives and undertake appraisal and disposal. This is partly due to the complexity of achieving this outcome on a wide scale; the fact that we are really operating in a hybrid recordkeeping environment of paper, electronic and other record forms; the co-existence of many known and unknown stores of unappraised and poorly controlled 'legacy records'; and the reality of 'exceptions to the rule'. Nonetheless, it may be achievable for specific types of records or business activities that are more structured, routine in operation and appraised as having continuing value, e.g. board agendas and minutes, annual reports and registers.

Advocates of the records continuum model argue that records appraisal should occur as early as possible, preferably when a process or system is being developed. This is generally feasible and achievable in a business setting. However, there are situations where concept does not readily transform into practice. For example, sentencing records at the point of system design or records capture may be difficult where a record relates to activities, issues or topics that span multiple disposal classes in an RDA. In this situation records will need to be reappraised later to ensure that the correct sentence has been linked to the record.

Applying appraisal as early as possible is also a very difficult principle to apply when dealing with personal and community archives. Nonetheless archival work involving advocacy, documentation programs and building communities provide archivists working in the collecting environment with opportunities to educate existing and potential donors on the principles of good recordkeeping to ensure that their documented memories are full, accurate and sustainable.

What is the scope of appraisal?

Consideration also needs to be given to whether appraisal will not only determine future acquisitions (prospective appraisal) but also change the existing holdings of the archives (retrospective appraisal or re-appraisal). This applies for all archives irrespective of whether they are physical or virtual, centralised or distributed. The answer to this depends on the purpose of appraisal, extent of existing resources and the degree of alignment between the existing holdings and contemporary appraisal and disposal decisions. Re-appraisal is considered later in this chapter.

How should appraisal be undertaken?

Because appraisal is a process that is ambiguous and involves a fair degree of risk, determining which approach is best is a subjective and therefore contestable decision. The evolution and development of the different theoretical models and instruments particularly over the past 70 to 80 years reflects the inherent subjectivity of making appraisal decisions and the professional challenges archivists face as technology, regulations, business models and community expectations of archives and archivists change.

Appraisal theories exist to guide archivists in determining what to keep and what to discard but there is no single appropriate solution for all archivists because decisions depend on the context and purpose of the archives. All approaches share the common objective to efficiently and systematically gather and organise information about the 'records universe' of interest, so that archivists have sufficient information to systematically analyse and make decisions about the disposal of records.

Appraisal theories and approaches

There are essentially two approaches to appraisal that have emerged and been applied in Australasia over the past 70 to 80 years. These approaches are bottom-up appraisal and top-down appraisal. They encompass a number of theoretical and practical responses to the ambiguity of appraisal and disposal. This section explores these approaches further and key methods that have been developed for implementing them. The methods discussed include Schellenberg's appraisal criteria, Macro-functional appraisal and the Minnesota Method. Specific instruments such as records surveys and RDAs to enable planned and consistent application of these methods are discussed later in this chapter.

Bottom-up (traditional approach) to appraisal and disposal

The models advocated by Schellenberg and Jenkinson are regarded as bottom-up approaches because they focus on records first and then ask questions about the context and value of those records. These models are not mutually exclusive and are discussed further below. Each model is based on the assumption that the priorities and values of the two distinct user groups (creators and researchers) are different. The Jenkinsonian Model is primarily concerned with the values important to the creators of records. In contrast, Schellenberg's approach to appraisal is primarily concerned with the values important to users. While the interests of each of these user groups can be aligned, they are not always. Appendix 5.2 provides a checklist of questions that may be applied when undertaking micro-level appraisal.

Jenkinsonian Approach

In 1922 Sir Hilary Jenkinson, an archivist at the Public Records Office in Britain developed a *Manual of Archive Administration.* This manual essentially codified archival practice at the Public Record Office and became a de facto standard for managing archives. Jenkinson's approach to archival appraisal was records-centric and driven by the need for an efficient and highly controlled approach to records management. His approach was premised on the role of the archivist as primarily that of advisor, facilitator and preserver of records and the existence of a highly structured civil service and centralised registry that provided standardised services and procedures for an entire agency or department. Archivists played a passive secondary role in appraisal. Records administrators took the primary role in determining what records would be kept as 'archives'.

In Jenkinson's view, it would be a conflict of interest for archivists to be actively involved in the selection of records because their primary role was that of 'preserver' of the record. Jenkinson argued that archives were made and kept as evidence of business undertaken by the organisation and used primarily for business purposes. For appraisal purposes, the subsequent use of records for the value of information they contained was incidental and of little, if any concern.

Jenkinson saw that records appraisal was an activity that should be integrated with the business activities undertaken by business administrator. He believed that if archivists played an active role in the destruction of records or selection of records for permanent retention, this would result in an artificially created historical record or memory. He believed that archives needed to be 'organically accumulated by those who create and receive'. Archivists could provide advice and support to ensure records were meaningful and usable and facilitate the process of transfer to archive, but they should not undertake appraisal or disposal other than as recipient of records when transferred to the archives. Jenkinson's approach directed practice in the PRO UK for many years (Reed 2002, p.201).

Schellenberg's Approach or American Approach of the 1940s – 1950s

T R Schellenberg, an archivist at the National Archives in the United States prepared various works on archival administration for archivists working in 'modern archives'. In contrast to the PRO and other European archives where records spanned from medieval and early European times, the National Archives of the United States and the National Archives of Canada viewed themselves to be 'modern archives' that required a different approach. Schellenberg's approach was also records-centric and encompassed the traditional European archival principles of provenance and original order. However, a key point of difference was how he viewed the role of the archivist in the appraisal and disposal of records and for whom appraisal was being undertaken.

During and following World War II the United States, as did many other countries, experienced a significant increase in administrative growth. This situation resulted in a huge increase in the volume of records and therefore, the volume of potential archives. It prompted Schellenberg to identify a way to efficiently and systematically select and appraise records. He proposed a value framework that considered the value of the content of records for research purposes as well as the value of records as evidence that certain business activities and transactions had occurred. He differentiated records from archives and defined a new set of values for appraising records, primary and secondary values.

Schellenberg developed a set of appraisal criteria that recognised the different types of value records contain. One record may be of significant legal value but of low financial value. Another record may have ongoing operational value as a precedent for specific actions or policies. The primary value of records is related to the purpose for which a record was created to support the business needs and administrative needs of the creating organisation. In this situation primary use is typically considered from the perspective of the creating organisation or person. In considering the primary value of records, archivists consider the attributes of records that demonstrate how the creating organisation conducted its business at all levels of the organisation. Records that have these values provide evidence of how the organisation operated and depended on an understanding of context and provenance. The primary value of records was assessed according to three main criteria:

- operational value
- financial value
- legal value

Decisions to retain documents needed to consider the potential operational, legal and financial uses of records by the creating organisation or person. However, it is not possible or prudent from a resourcing point of view to retain all records just in case they may be useful to somebody in the future. There needs to be a trade-off between the utility of records over time and cost and effort to keep those records.

The secondary value of records relates to those uses beyond which they were initially created. Secondary value encompassed research and other uses by future business administrators or researchers. The secondary value of records typically related to the content of records in terms of the uniqueness, the degree to which information is concentrated (quality) and the importance of the information contained. It is the value of the information content rather than the provenance and function that is important here.

Schellenberg's appraisal criteria are summarised below in Figure 5.1.

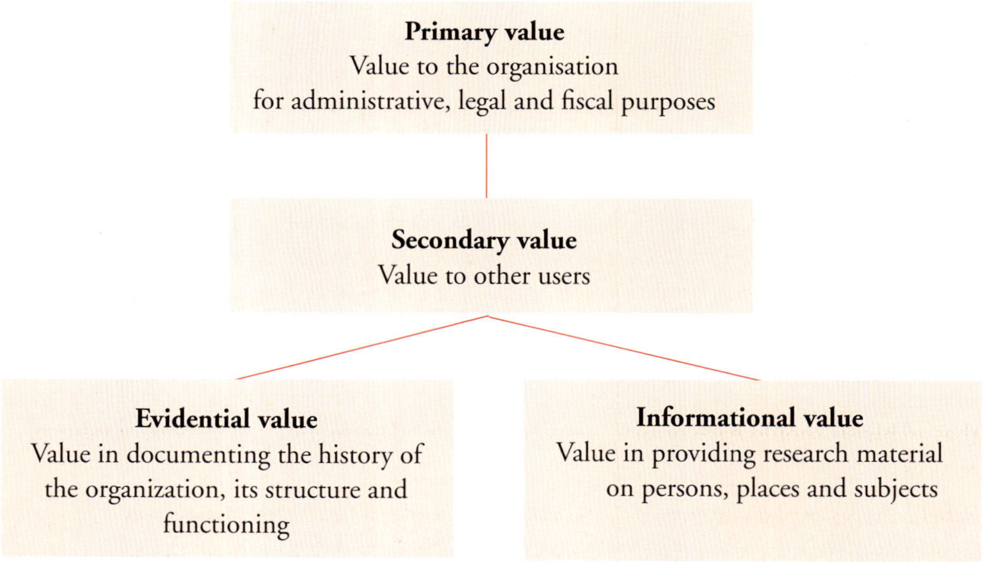

Figure 5.1: Schellenberg's appraisal criteria

From Schellenberg's perspective the value of records needed to be considered in light of their evidential and informational value. Evidential value referred to the role of the record as proof of something, be it a policy decision or position, action, event, procedure or dealings. As 'evidence' the record object, its purpose and the role it played in a 'transaction' are important considerations and attributes. To determine the evidential value of records requires the archivist to have a good understanding of the context and use of the records under consideration.

Informational value is concerned with the utility of the information contained in the record, rather than the 'record' itself. For example, a record may contain brief biographies of board members or a photo of a staff member who later become 'famous'. These records may not be of value for proving a particular matter, but they may provide useful information for organisational staff responsible for ensuring birthdays are celebrated, or preparing obituaries, award citations, or marketing activities. They may also be of value for future historical researchers or biographers external to the organisation.

Schellenberg's appraisal criteria aimed to provide a rational and comprehensive framework for making appraisal decisions. The evidential-informational dichotomy presented by Schellenberg was not intended to be absolute. The dichotomy of values was defined broadly to present different perspectives but they are often misinterpreted as mutually exclusive categories.

In practical terms the value framework provided a more tangible basis for determining retention periods, arrangements for storage (e.g. on-site for records still in use, or off-site in cheaper storage facilities for records referred to occasionally). Schellenberg's approach was records-centric but in practice it required a mix of top-down and bottom-up appraisal. Determining the primary value of records is a top-down approach, whereas determining the secondary value of records tended to be more of a bottom-up approach to appraisal.

Schellenberg's approach was based on the records life cycle model. It was a pragmatic response to information overload and required archivists to undertake a more active role in the appraisal and disposal process and work more closely with agency personnel. He proposed that archivists work with records managers, an emerging profession in Schellenberg's day, and devise better ways to classify and manage records. He believed that agency personnel should be primarily responsible for determining primary value but that archivists should have primary responsibility for determining the secondary value of records.

Schellenberg's explicit attention to the value of records to future researchers was a significant departure from Jenkinson's approach as it shifted the appraisal decision away from the record creator to the archivist as the 'agent for future research interests'.

Applying bottom-up approaches

1. Receive request for appraisal and disposal action on legacy records
2. Research the context of those records, including legal requirements for retention
3. Develop or modify an existing appraisal checklist
4. Inspect and survey the legacy records and interview the custodians of those records
5. Prepare a survey report and inventory
6. Draft a retention and disposal authority
7. Undertake consultation to validate findings and recommendations
8. Finalise the retention and disposal authority
9. Submit the retention and disposal authority for approval
10. Implement the disposal actions

Applying bottom-up approaches to appraisal

Pros and cons of bottom-up approaches

Despite the emergence of new theoretical models and approaches to appraisal, many archivists continue to appraise records by reviewing them directly and applying Schellenberg's appraisal criteria. This approach may be more suitable in small to medium-sized collecting archives or in-house archives that operate using the life cycle model and focus on paper-based legacy records.

Some advantages of applying bottom-up approaches are that:

- they are easy to implement
- they resolve immediate problems
- they may be more closely managed, controlled and directly implemented by the archives and requires minimal involvement of other personnel
- there is a large body of documentation, experience and tools available to anyone implementing these methods

Some disadvantages of applying bottom-up approaches are that:

- they are reactive
- they are usually inefficient in the longer term
- they lack integration with and support other recordkeeping process
- they may result in fragmentation of evidence and memory and consequently, reduce the likelihood of retaining full and accurate records
- they may fail to manage vital records appropriately
- they may fail to manage migration of records, especially electronic records
- they may result in the wrong records being taken by archives to document a function
- decisions are more prone to inconsistency; there is often duplication of effort, limited accountability and higher costs in undertaking and implementing appraisal decisions
- they require the archivist to actively deliver appraisal and disposal activities whereas top-down appraisal tends to be more policy and standards oriented and facilitates appraisal and disposal rather than doing it
- they perpetuates the perception of archives as storage facilities for 'old records'
- it is usually more difficult to apply and manage access to archives using bottom-up approaches.

By the 1970s there emerged increasing criticism of bottom-up approaches on the basis that it concentrated too much on the records at the end of the life cycle and did not adequately consider the purposes and systems involved in creating, controlling and using records. In practice archivists assessing the primary value of records tended to deal with the records manager rather than the records creators, thereby reducing the effectiveness of decisions relating to primary evidence because records managers, like archivists, were not intimately part of the process of creation and use. It soon became apparent that bottom-up approaches simply could not keep up with the demands of digital recordkeeping and the increasingly dynamic administrative structures, entities and workplaces in which records were generated and used. A new approach to appraisal was needed if archivists were to ensure their archival collections were worth preserving and of value.

Top-down approaches to appraisal and disposal

In response to the criticisms of bottom-up appraisal, top-down approaches or macro-appraisal emerged in the 1990s shifting the focus from appraising records to appraising the context in which records are generated. The term 'macro-appraisal' will be used in this chapter. Macro-appraisal provides an alternative approach to the traditional ways articulated by Jenkinson and Schellenberg.

Macro-appraisal is a strategic rather than operational approach. In contrast with bottom-up, which focuses on the individual or file level, macro-appraisal assesses the value of records, agents or business entities. Macro-appraisal is a more holistic perspective and tends to document organisations, individuals and communities from a governance and management perspective, rather than from the routine operational or day-to-day perspective.

Macro-appraisal approaches consider 'why' records were created and used in the first place rather than what they may be used for or who may use them in the future. It considers the purpose, function and mandates of the record creator rather than the specific content and form of a record. In practice the latter needs to be considered, but the emphasis is on the former.

Piggott (2001) defines the goals of macro-appraisal as including:

1. To ensure individual appraisal decisions are informed by a broader perspective and context – fundamental to any archival work
2. To encourage overall coherence and consistency in appraisal decisions – less ad hocery
3. To help manage risk
4. To help make appraisal more cost effective in its use of storage and allocation of resources
5. To reduce the risk of appraisal being distorted by narrow transitory concerns of individuals or groups
6. To minimise the risk of having significant gaps or overlaps in the appraisal regime and collection
7. To provide a transparent and accountable basis for setting priorities and making hard decisions in an environment where typically archives are allocated inadequate resources for their needs.

In an organisational setting, macro-appraisal is based on the premise that understanding the structures and functions of the organisation provides a more comprehensive and efficient framework for making appraisal and disposal decisions. Understanding the organisation and its role and relationships within the broader environment or documentary universe (contextual analysis) is the key activity, whereas identifying, documenting and analysing documents (documentary analysis) is the focus of bottom-up approaches.

ISO15489 advocates a macro-appraisal approach and the need to consider 'community expectations'. However 'community expectations' is not clearly defined or explained in this standard and in practice it is difficult to apply. This is particularly the case when appraisal is applied up front at the point of system design and records creation and tends to be a bias towards the interest of the record creator. In this respect macro-appraisal, particularly macro-functional appraisal shares a common emphasis on the views of the record creator with Jenkinson's approach.

However, this weakness may be addressed through broad and effective community consultation when undertaking appraisal and disposal. As with all approaches to appraisal, a key issue here is to define and agree on whose interests will be included or more specifically the 'community' or 'communities' to be considered during input and decision-making consultation processes. It is also very important to document how you determine the consultation group and why you have selected specific interests to be represented. Consultation techniques are discussed later in this chapter.

Macro-appraisal is a popular approach within the public sector environments in a number of countries including the UK, New Zealand, Australia, Canada and the Netherlands. The development and adoption of this approach was triggered by a combination of:

- frequently changing organisational structures
- increasing emergence of digital records and potential threat of loss of these records if they were not identified as records from the outset
- realisation that micro-appraisal methods requiring records surveys and developing specific RDA are too resource-intensive and inefficient, particularly when only a small portion of records are identified as having archival or continuing value
- the need to establish more efficient ways for dealing the burgeoning volume of paper-based records.

The macro-appraisal model as developed by academics and articulated further by archival authorities and *ISO 15489* is scalable and may be applied at the government-wide level, organisation-wide level and within particular business areas of divisions of an organisation. In practice, using macro-appraisal also means that many records will be destroyed without direct or item-level inspection or review by the archivist.

Macro-functional appraisal

Macro-appraisal using a functions-based approach involves analysing the functions and activities of an organisation and identifying the most significant of those functions. The assumption here is that the most significant business functions and activities produce the most significant records and therefore it is not necessary to review the records or deeply analyse all functions and activities. The significance of business functions and activities (and therefore records) is determined at the organisational level and broader societal or community level. Adopting a functional approach enables the archivist to more strategically understand and document the relationship between the creators of records, the functions and processes that produced and are documented by those records and the stakeholders involved.

Macro-appraisal, particularly macro-functional appraisal:

- requires an analysis of the functions and activities undertaken by an organization and identification of types of records that support those functions and activities
- is proactive rather than reactive
- is more suitable for hybrid and electronic recordkeeping environments
- is the preferred approach of archival authorities in Australia and New Zealand and internationally through *ISO 15489*

Methods for undertaking macro-functional appraisal are extensively documented in guidelines, procedures and templates issued by archival authorities in Australia, New Zealand, Canada and the UK, for example the *Designing and Implementing Recordkeeping Systems (DIRKS) Manual* developed and issued by the National Archives of Australia (2001) and the State Records Authority of NSW (2007).

In practice, macro-appraisal does not replace the need for individual appraisal projects or attempt to predict the future trends in research. Additionally, for as long as legacy records exist and organisations operate in a hybrid information environment encompassing a mix of paper-based and digital records micro-appraisal will remain relevant.

The key tools or instruments used for undertaking macro-appraisal are:

- a Business Classification Scheme
- the DIRKS Manual and
- disposal management software

By the completion of a macro-appraisal the following are developed:

- appraisal report
- Retention and Disposal Authority (RDA)

Applying macro-functional appraisal

1. **Define the scope** (e.g. the health sector).
2. **Identify organisational entities and their role within this scope** (e.g. hospitals provide medical services to the general community).
3. **Identify in general terms the interaction between each of these entities** (e.g. ambulance services provide initial first aid to some patients admitted to hospitals).
4. **Identify the 'ambient functions'** (high level functions such as 'regulation' and 'patient care' that provide context for grouping similar functions) and draft the macro-functional framework. This framework includes a brief description, history and mandates for each of the ambient functions.
5. **Identify the organisations** that primarily implement each function.
6. **Identify a broad range of stakeholders** for consultation.
7. **Consult with stakeholders** to develop criteria for assessing the relative significance of each function.
8. **Confirm with stakeholders the entities responsible** for performing each of these functions.
9. **Use DIRKS steps A – C** (see Chapter 15: *Digital Recordkeeping*) to identify the business functions associated with each ambient function and develop a retention and disposal authority. **Alternatively, use the ambient functions as a framework for prioritising functional appraisal** at the business function level.

Applying macro-functional appraisal

Some advantages offered to archivists and organisations adopting macro-appraisal include:

- establishing a strategic focus for appraisal
- avoiding duplication and redundancy
- reduced labour required to undertake appraisal (in the longer term)
- accommodating digital records and other technology-dependent records
- it is more accountable and systematic
- it is usually easier to apply and manage access to archives using macro-appraisal approaches

Some disadvantages include:

- it may in practice favour or privilege organisational interests over research interests and
- it may be more difficult to apply in the collecting archives
- applying selection decisions based on function for agencies that are still using subject-based classification files

Ultimately, like all appraisal approaches, macro-appraisal is not definitive or conclusive. It is a tool and it is subjective. Consequently, it is contestable and involves risk. The key is to ensure all appraisal decisions:

- are well informed
- give due consideration to the risks involved
- are documented

Documentation strategies

Documentation strategies for appraisal are macro-level proactive and comprehensive appraisal initiatives that aim to ensure that a core set of documentation relating to an area of interest is captured and retained. They are carefully planned and in order to succeed require a significant level of coordination, management and marketing.

Documentation strategies are usually multi-institutional in scope. Across the nominated institutions members or partners seek to fill any existing or potential gaps in the collective memory relating to a particular area of human activity. Documentation strategies recognise that one archive cannot collect and maintain the whole records universe relating to a specific topic, theme, industry or entity and usually requires a collaborative and cooperative method that spans multiple disciplines and organisations. Documentation strategies spread the appraisal and acquisition decision-making process more widely than other methods.

Documentation strategies also recognise that written or text-based records are not the only archival form and that it is often necessary to document experiences using other means and often in conjunction with other professional groups. For example, oral histories and photographic initiatives require the involvement of historians, photographers and audio-visual specialists in the appraisal and disposal process.

Documentation strategies are often used in conjunction with other appraisal methods. An example of a documentation strategy is the Australian Science Archives Project (ASAP) of the 1990s. This project was established to document Australian science and encompassed a cross-organisational view of science in Australian history (Reed 2003, p.75). From May 1999 the academic, research and heritage activities of work of the ASAP was transferred to the Australian Science and Technology Heritage Centre (Austehc) in the Faculty of Arts at the University of Melbourne.

The Minnesota Method is primarily a documentation strategy and is discussed further below.

Documentation strategies

Documentation strategies typically involve the following steps:

1. Choosing and selecting the topic of interest
2. Selecting advisors and establishing the archives
3. Structuring the universe and examining the documents available
4. Selecting and placing the documents with the relevant archival institution

Advantages of documentation strategies may include:

- opportunities for valuable networking, learning and development with other archivists and related professionals
- suitable for collecting archives and records of any form
- reduced competition between collecting archives
- establishing a more comprehensive and richer historical record of a particular topic, theme, etc. than what otherwise may have been achieved

Disadvantages of documentation strategies may include:

- it is often resource intensive to undertake
- the documentary universe may be too ambiguous to define and may be too large to tackle
- each participant has a different perspective and agenda so it may be difficult to align these
- much time, energy and resources may be lost in negotiating approaches etc with other institutions and maintaining good relations (Williams 2006, pp.49–50).

Minnesota Method

The Minnesota Method (MM) was developed the 1990s by the Minnesota Historical Society (MHS) in response to the practical challenges of trying to acquire the totality of the records identified in acquisition policies of the MHS' collecting archives. It was driven by the following challenges, familiar to many collecting archives.

1. MHS's potential acquisitions far exceeded their ability to appraise, accession and process them
2. The types of business collections that had historically been acquired often included material lacking in real substance or value
3. Records of Minnesota business were only one of several collecting areas for which MHS is responsible.

In response to these challenges the MHS developed the MM for the purpose of implementing a more efficient process that enabled the MHS to establish a smaller but richer collection that provided the maximum value to a variety of users. The MM is a mixed model that draws on many appraisal theories and aspects of collection policy, documentation strategy, macro-appraisal and functional analysis. It is flexible and systematic and may be implemented in a variety of settings.

The MHS' goal for the method was to prioritise which business records and the relative quantity of those records within the State of Minnesota the MHS needed to acquire. Prior to the MM the development of the MHS archive was more a matter of chance resulting in many gaps and a skewed collection. It is a macro-appraisal approach that focussed on business records in the State of Minnesota. Fundamentally it involved identifying the collecting universe for business records, an analysis of MHS' collection of business records, consultation with academics in the relevant disciplines and then the micro level appraisal of records and establishing the appropriate levels of documentation required based on a determination of the 'significance' of different categories of records (Hyry and Wiederman 2004).

Applying the Minnesota Method

There are six steps to the MM:

1. Define and analyse a particular collecting area and survey the existing holdings that relate to that area
2. Determine the documentary universe for that collecting area
3. Define the criteria for prioritising and applying these criteria in selecting records from various industry or business sectors, record creators, geographical regions and chronological periods
4. Define the functions most appropriate to the collecting area and the level of documentation required to support those functions.
5. Test the model by applying it to actual appraisal situations.
6. Update the method based on an evaluation of the testing.

Some advantages of the MM include:

- enabling archivists to proactively control archival abundance with minimal resources
- explicit recognition that appraisal is not an objective process
- it is documented and accountable
- explicitly considers the utility of archives

Some disadvantages of the MM include:

- past use is not necessarily the best indicator of what future use may be, so the challenge of ambiguity remains
- may be easily misinterpreted resulting in primary evidence records that are not often used e.g. articles of association, being discarded, when they really should be kept for reasons other than research utility
- may also be easy to misinterpret and discard records that have no or poor finding aids and those records that have time-based access restrictions imposed on them e.g. for privacy etc.
- initially a costly approach in terms of staff time and a time lag between effort and results (Williams 2006, pp.51–2).

In 2001 the University of Melbourne Archives (UMA) established a project to develop a more efficient and effective approach to acquiring records and to re-examine its existing holdings. The UMA applied a modified version of the MM called 'Minnesota Lite'. The UMA adopted the MM firstly, because of the similarity between the collecting mandate and scope of the UMA and the Minnesota Historical Society; and secondly because of the practical challenges experienced in applying reactive collection development practices and being overwhelmed by the level of documentation applied to those records acquired. Figure 5.2 provides a summary of how the UMA implemented Minnesota Lite.

The University of Melbourne's Minnesota Lite

The UMA's Minnesota Lite involved the following steps:

- **Step 1: Analysing existing collections**

  This involved an audit of UMA's current business collection, benchmarking the collection and defining the core records necessary to undertake research into a company's performance and management. The core records identified were 'executive minutes (including supporting papers), executive correspondence, annual financial statements, and production/sales data' However, some flexibility was incorporated to allow different records to be considered where relevant for different industries or company structures (e.g. incorporated companies and unincorporated companies)

- **Step 2: Surveying the broader documentary universe**

  This involved reviewing relevant published sources such as the Business Review Weekly, identifying the collection scope of related organisations such as the National Business Collecting Archives (NBCA), and holding a forum with business historians and archivists from other organisations to better understand research interests and what companies and industries forum participants believed should be targeted. Although consensus could not be reached via the forum it did provide valuable insights relating to the direction in which business research may progress. A report documenting this research was prepared. It identified the sectors and industry for collection priority

- **Step 3: Defining a broader set of criteria for selecting which companies' records to collect**

  The following mission statement was developed to provide focus and to more readily communicate the purpose and scope of UMA's business archives: 'To support The University of Melbourne's teaching, learning, research, and community development agendas, UMA will aim to ensure that records generated by select businesses incorporated in, headquartered in, or operating in Victoria, irrespective of the ultimate location of the business' ownership, will be considered for collection.' A list of criteria for selecting which companies' records it will seek to collect was developed. It was decided not to use weighted criteria as it would reduce flexibility and require more effort to apply. The criteria developed were:
  - economic impact to Victoria
  - australian ownership
  - number of employees
  - longevity of business
  - businesses with unique social, cultural and labour significance

- **Step 4: Determining documentation levels**

  Due to resourcing constraints and potential reluctance of targeted companies to produce extensive documentation of records, the UMA did not adopt the four-level (A-D) approach to documentation within the MM. Instead it was decided to limit documentation to just level A

- **Step 5: Targeting companies and implementing the new strategy**

  This step involves approaching companies targeted and requesting they transfer the core records to the UMA

- **Step 6: Review the list of targeted companies**

  The list of targeted companies will be reviewed regularly, possibly once every five years. Companies that have declined UMA or have agreed to transfer records to UMA will be removed, and where necessary, new companies will be added to the list

Figure 5.2: UMA's application of the Minnesota Method

Applying the MM has enabled the UMA to rationalise its collection and collection development practices in an informed and systematic way that maximises the use of the UMA's limited resources while building a richer, less biased and more comprehensive collection for current and future users. The UMA is now in a good position to target companies within the priority areas identified in step 3. This was found to be the key advantage of the MM and the focus of the UMA's implementation of it. The MM's approach to documentation was less useful, with the UMA instead implementing a simpler singular level of documentation based on a generic retention and disposal authority.

Which method is best?

The answer to this question is simply – it depends. Selecting the best appraisal method depends on many factors relating to the purpose of the archives, past and present appraisal practices and the broader documentary universe. Often it is necessary to adopt a mix of methods. For example, archival records are critical resources for understanding environmental changes and the implications of those changes. In her analysis of appraisal practices and environmental records Woodley (2004) argues that records relating to the environment have largely been overlooked because archivists tend to focus on records relating to human history. Woodley explores the appraisal of environmental records using Algonquin Provincial Park in Ontario as a case study. Her research reveals that a key problem is the lack of an adequate approach or methodology for appraising environmental records.

As a result of her research Woodley recommends macro-appraisal as the best method available for appraising the records created via the official functions and activities of Algonquin Provincial Park. However, because the creation of many records relating to environmental monitoring, assessment and research is undertaken by entities and individuals outside of government, there are many gaps in the official archives of the Park. Consequently, she recommends the adoption of a broader formal strategy for appraising and preserving environmental records that draws on a number of appraisal methodologies including macro-appraisal, the documentation strategy and the MM.

The method or mix of methods will determine the choice of instruments developed and applied to appraisal and disposal activities. The following section explores the various instruments that are widely used by archivists adopting either bottom-up approaches or macro-appraisal approaches. While these instruments cover the majority of situations archivists often face specific challenges that require additional instruments or methods. These challenges include competing stakeholder interests in determining the value of records, dealing with case files and dealing with backlogs. These challenges will be discussed later in this chapter.

What instruments may be used for appraisal and disposal?

Making choices about the instruments for documenting and implementing appraisal and disposal stems from the approach or mixes of approach adopted. This in turn should reflect the archival context in which appraisal and disposal occurs. Common instruments include:

- appraisal and retention and disposal policies
- retention and disposal program and strategy
- retention and disposal guidelines and templates
- appraisal reports
- records survey reports and inventories and
- Retention and Disposal Authorities (RDAs)

Documentation such as RDAs and appraisal reports allow archivists to readily apply precedents, recall or communicate to successors why certain decisions were made (evidence and accountability) and use as a tool for training and knowledge transfer.

If the documentation of appraisal is to serve as an instrument of accountability this information needs to be made available to the relevant constituency. A related question is which channels are the most useful for disseminating appraisal documentation to stakeholders. The World Wide Web is increasingly used to publish appraisal and disposal documentation or to publicise the existence and availability of those reports (Marshall 2006).

Appraisal and retention and disposal policies

Typically the purpose of a policy is to provide a clear and authoritative position on a particular matter or activity. The archives policy and/or recordkeeping policy provides an overarching framework for all archival or recordkeeping decisions and actions. They will usually include a reference to appraisal and disposal. This may provide sufficient 'clout' and direction for undertaking appraisal and disposal. However, there are times when it is better to develop a separate policy on appraisal or retention and disposal. This situation arises where organisations demonstrate a particular weakness in appraisal and disposal and a more dedicated and explicit approach is required. It may also be regarded as necessary simply because of the importance of appraisal and disposal in developing and shaping the memory and evidence of an organisation or community.

In 2007 the Public Records Office of Victoria (PROV) developed a retention and disposal policy because it perceived there was a need to:

- *provide consistency and transparency with regard to appraisal decisions made by Victorian public sector agencies, including PROV*
- *provide the tools necessary to enable Victorian public sector agencies to comply with recordkeeping requirements as set out in legislation and standards*

- *provide guidance regarding appraisal methodology and practices to be used in the Victorian public sector*
- *define appraisal objectives to ensure that appraisal decisions address requirements for legislative and regulatory compliance, business environments, fundamental rights and entitlements, and community expectations.*

An appraisal policy may cover appraisal and disposal or just focus on the process of appraisal. The choice depends on the need for the policy in the first place. Many organisation-level appraisal policies cover both appraisal and disposal. Typically these policies:

- recognise the legal constraints for destroying and transferring records
- identify ownership and custodianship issues and requirements
- assign and authorise individuals or roles for making decisions and implementing disposal
- establish a framework for designing an appraisal and disposal program
- provide a framework for auditing the appraisal and disposal program
- align and link appraisal and disposal to other official statements, standards and legislation

To ensure policies 'carry weight' all policies need to be approved or endorsed at the highest level, preferably at the chief executive or board level. They should conform to the governance and management requirements of the organisation. To support relevance and acceptance, policy development should be done in consultation with key internal, and where relevant, external stakeholders. Where possible, those consulted could include legal expertise, information technologists and business subject matter expertise and community stakeholder representatives. In designing consultation activities it is important to clearly communicate and gain agreement on:

- the role or capacity in which stakeholders participate
- the level, frequency and type of consultation required for each
- expectations on the outcome of the consultation process, including how feedback is handled and communicated.

Once approved or endorsed the policy should have a review period or validity period (usually three to five years) set and implemented at the appropriate point.

The implementation of the policy should include an awareness and training program that is ongoing and the policy requirements should be incorporated into the organisation's monitoring and audit program and business procedures.

Policy versus procedure

- Policies are the working set of parameters that provide a framework for decision-making and desired action in a given situation. They must provide guidance for situations that may not have occurred; thus they must be broad enough to be flexible but not so broad as to be useless.
- Procedures by contrast, provide the mechanism and details needed to implement the policy.
- Therefore, policies allow latitude in decision-making while procedures remain firm and specific.
- The distinction between policy and procedure is best made by those drafting the CMP [Collection Management Policy]
- The ultimate determination of policies is the responsibility of the appropriate administrative entity (e.g. Director, Board of Trustee) with recommendations and discussions with staff.
- However, the procedures for fulfilling the policies will be developed by the staff based on professional expertise, guidelines, and practices.
- Policies and procedures must take into account professional standards and guidelines and mould them into the institutional setting, with a consideration of the institutional mission, objectives and activities.

(Smithsonian Institution Archive 2007)

Guidance on whether policies or procedures should be developed

Retention and disposal program and strategy

Policies provide authority and are rules-based. However, it is also useful to develop a more practical strategy and plan for collecting and analysing information and managing resources used for appraisal so archivists can make 'sound defensible appraisal decisions'. The choices made will depend on the circumstances and needs of a particular archive and the broader organisation and regulatory environment in which it operates. The strategy provides high level direction on how appraisal aligns and supports the strategic business objectives of the organisation and how it will actually ensure the relevant policies are implemented.

Irrespective of the approach or mix of approaches adopted for appraisal and the context in which an archivist works, for effective appraisal to occur it is not possible to work in isolation and take on the full responsibility for all appraisal and disposal decisions and actions. For well-informed and effective appraisal and disposal to occur archivists need management support and a multidisciplinary team to undertake appraisal and disposal. Where possible, the consultation group should consist of legal expertise, information technologists and business subject matter expertise and community stakeholder representatives.

To ensure the policy and strategy is implemented a clearly identifiable, managed and monitored program needs to be developed and implemented. This program does not need a single dedicated person or team, it may incorporate multiple projects, initiatives and existing program areas; it may be decentralised, partially outsourced or shared. The actual structure and delivery of the program depends on the needs, capability and preferences of each organisation. The important thing here is that the program needs to be defined, documented and implemented to ensure the theory of the policy and strategy are transformed into practice.

In developing a retention and disposal program choices should be made in the context of *ISO 15489* and the organisation's governance and management framework and culture.

As shown in Figure 5.3 the components of a retention and disposal program may include:

1. **An understanding of the strategic and operational business drivers for undertaking appraisal and disposal in the organisation**. For example, the strategic need for reduced turn-over time for handling customer interaction may require an appraisal and disposal program focussed on business efficiency and ensuring the timely sentencing and disposal of records to reduce the volume of out of date information available to customer service personnel.
2. **An understanding of the internal and external constraints or controls imposed on the organisation**. For example, an organisation operating in a highly regulated environment may require clear, comprehensive and detailed disposal procedures that are incorporated into business information systems to ensure the management of records complies with internal and external authorities and the relevant business process is highly accountable. An example of an external constraint may be the limited availability of appropriately skilled and experienced personnel resulting in a need to 'outsource' some appraisal and disposal activities.
3. **An improvement and ongoing management strategy for the retention and disposal program** to ensure it is sustainable, meets its purpose and objectives and makes a positive impact. It may include training and development for archival personnel, other staff and volunteers. This contrasts with the monitoring and auditing activities which provide the detail on the progress and success of the program.

4. **The appraisal and disposal process**. This involves the actual appraisal and disposal activities and the development of the relevant instruments for the organisation in question. This may include all or some of the activities shown in Figure 5.3. For example reporting should encompass periodic reports to management and 'for the record' to establish an accountable appraisal and disposal program. Aspects that may be reported on include: what records, functions, etc. have been reviewed; what has been recommended for disposal action; justification for decisions; the quantities and types disposed, ongoing issues and risks; link to legal and regulatory framework; links to corporate governance matters.
5. **Activities to monitor, audit and evaluate the appraisal and disposal program** may include: monitoring the recordkeeping context for changes in retention requirements, monitoring storage, preservation and destruction facilities and equipment; auditing disposal practices against the principles of 'good appraisal' and the corporate appraisal and disposal policy; and evaluating the program and updating it periodically (e.g. once every two to three years or sooner if required).

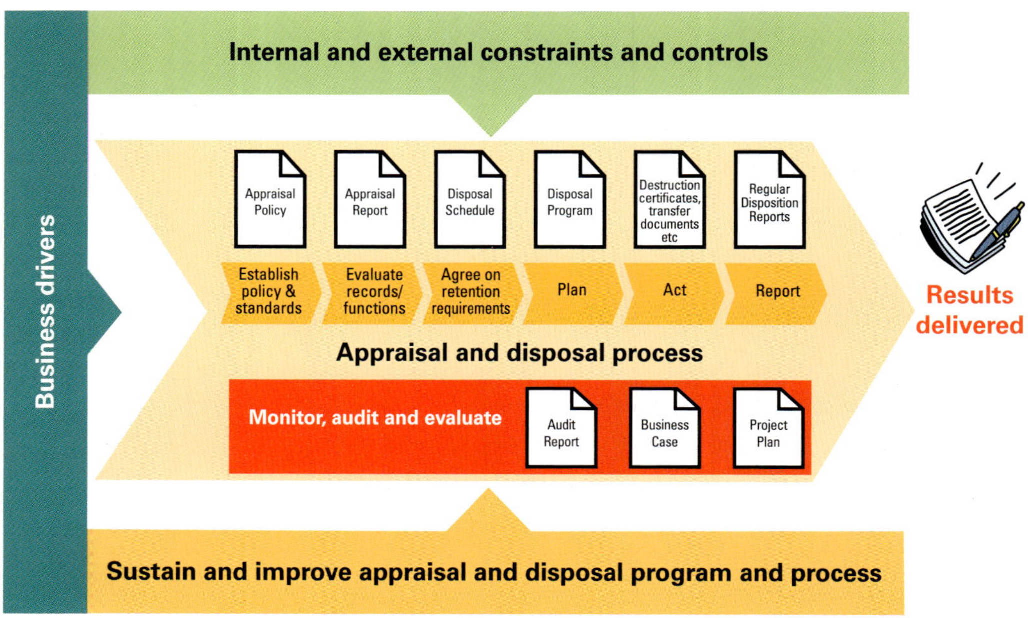

Figure 5.3: Components of a retention and disposal program

When implementing an appraisal and disposal program there are a number of common pitfalls that may be avoided through applying the theory and practices discussed in this chapter and careful management and control. These pitfalls include:

- analysis paralysis
- being to risk adverse
- not being able to accept the subjectivity of it all
- building up the backlog (builds up the risk too)
- presentism: focusing on the NOW without considering the FUTURE value of records
- using a paper-mindset when dealing with electronic systems
- trying to please everyone
- lack of support and recognition with the broader organisation context of competing priorities and interests

Retention and disposal guidelines

Archivists cannot undertake all appraisal and disposal activities and it cannot be assumed the one archivist will 'always' be there. Consequently, even when working as the sole archivist for an organisation it is important to develop and maintain clear procedures and a suite of templates to ensure your appraisal and disposal program supports the policy and strategy.

There are numerous guidelines and templates available free of charge from State and National archival authorities and commercially through private providers. These are useful resources for developing organisation-specific guidelines and templates. For example, the *DIRKS Manual* available from the National Archives of Australia and State Records NSW, the *Continuum Resource Kit* issued by Archives New Zealand and the *Australian Records Retention Manual* published by Information Enterprises Australia (2007).

Guidance on sentencing records and implementing disposal actions are two common areas that usually require non-archives personnel to contribute directly to the appraisal process. These are discussed later in this chapter.

Records surveys and inventories

A records inventory is a summary of the records held by an organisation or part of an organisation. It lists records, usually at the series level, and can assist identifying:

1. the purpose and use of records
2. the location of records
3. the custodian and owner of records
4. the age and frequency of use of records
5. the retrieval system used for each series
6. the form of the record
7. the amount of space used for records series

8. current disposal practices
9. the comparative value of different records series
10. identifying duplications and gaps in records collections
11. security and access requirements

It is a tool widely used in micro-appraisal techniques and where a disorganised collection of records is inherited by the archives or is being appraised prior to transfer to the archives.

As explained in further detail in Appendix 5.3, compiling a records inventory usually involves the following seven steps:

1. determining the purpose of the inventory
2. determining the data to be collected
3. determining the data collection method or mix of methods to be used
4. collecting data
5. analysing data
6. reporting on the recordkeeping issues and actions required
7. maintaining the inventory

Appraisal report

Appraisal Reports document the process of appraisal and serve as an accountability mechanism. Typically they contain sufficient information to justify the appraisal recommendations and decisions contained in a RDA, provide an understanding of the context in which records were made, kept and used and significant recordkeeping issues. They may be developed in conjunction with a RDA, records survey or records inventory.

Archives New Zealand (2005) has recommended the following sections be included in an appraisal report:

- executive summary
- appraisal circumstances
- agency information
- methodology
- relevant precedent
- disposal criteria
- series or class information
- access recommendations
- custodial arrangements
- transfer arrangements

Similarly, State Records NSW (2007) requires agencies to submit an appraisal report containing information about the:

- organisation
- relationships with other organisations and stakeholders
- committees
- records held by the organisation
- retention periods and disposal actions
- any external stakeholder consultation undertaken or reasons for not undertaking external consultation

The Committees referred to above relate to those that the organisation hosts or has established. The committees usually have either an advisory role and may be directly related to the business operations of the organisation. They may also help to identify relevant stakeholders for consultation and the implementation of appraisal decisions.

In the United States appraisal reports typically contain a description of the relevant agency or agencies; a description of the records, based on the archivist's research, examination and discussions with agency personnel; and recommendations for disposal. The aim of the appraisal report is to demonstrate to anyone who reads the appraisal in conjunction with the RDA that NARA has reached a logical and reasonable decision regarding the disposal of a particular group of records.

Library and Archives Canada (LAC) appraisal reports include these aspects, but in line with their macro-functional approach to appraisal, the reports also contain information about the context, agency functions, and the relationship of agency records to those produced by other government agencies. The purpose of these reports is to identify all agency functions and to make recommendations on whether the records generated by the relevant agency represent the best source of documentation for those functions within the Canadian government. A summary of how all findings and recommendations have been validated via research and consultation and the results of these activities is also included.

Appraisal reports should be brief but informative. Take care not to fall into the trap of generating excessive levels of documentation. LAC recommends that agencies limit their reports to 20 pages in length. Appraisal reports also allow archivists to readily apply precedents, recall or communicate to successors why certain decisions were made (evidence and accountability) and as a tool for training and knowledge transfer (Marshall 2006, pp.188–9).

Retention and Disposal Authorities (RDAs)

Retention and Disposal Authorities (RDAs) are key instruments and control mechanisms used in recordkeeping. RDAs enable organisations and archivists to standardise decision-making, ensure consistency and to apply precedents. ISO 15489-Part 2, section 4.2.4 explains that a RDA (referred to as 'disposition authorities' in the Standard) is a ...formally approved schedule of classes of records, retention periods and appropriate disposition actions that is submitted for approval by an external authority.

RDAs should be approved by the CEO, board or external authority. ISO 15489 also advises that the determination about capture and retention of digital records needs to be considered in the system design stage and implemented in accordance with the RDA.

RDAs:

- identify the records to be kept
- identify the minimum period the records need to be kept
- authorise disposal action
- identify the point in time or the business process at which disposal action or actions are to occur

There are two main types of RDA.

1. **Specific Schedules**. These schedules are developed for a specific organisation, function or collection of records, for example an RDA issued for accounting records within an organisation or an organisation-wide RDA for a specific bank or government agency or a list of specific records e.g. list of existing records within a local government.
2. **General Schedules**. These are developed and used across a broader sector comprised of various organisations and functions. Examples include industry-based schedules such as the ASA's schools RDA or government schedules issued for a specific sector or function e.g. the University schedule or Energy sector schedule in Queensland, and General Deposal Authority for Administrative Records issued by the State Records Authority of NSW.

RDAs may also be categorised as 'administrative' and core or 'functional'. The former encompasses functions, activities and records related to common administrative functions such as human resources management and governance. These functions are supporting business activities that are generally undertaken by any organisation. The latter relates to the core business or unique functions of the organisation. For example for a school this could include student management.

The choice of method used for developing schedules, depends on the overarching appraisal approach or mix of approaches adopted.

Developing RDAs using a micro-appraisal or records-centric approach

Those undertaking micro-appraisal may consider the following methodology:

1. Undertake background historical and administrative research on the individual, organisation or community relating to the records. Include a review of legislation (including the relevant Statutes of Limitations), regulations, policies and procedures to identify any specific retention requirements or expectations.
2. Undertake a collection level survey of the records and determine the areas of priority often based on consideration of ownership, risk and level of current use.
3. Survey the records at record group or series level in accordance to the priority assigned in step 2. For further information on the records survey process refer to the relevant section in this chapter.
4. Appraise the records surveyed using the relevant values framework e.g. Schellenberg's or the appraisal checklist referred to earlier in this chapter and document in an appraisal report.
5. Undertake any additional research required to support the administrative, legal, historical and financial requirements for the records under consideration.
6. Develop an RDA that includes the title of the records class or series, a brief description of the records, where relevant the date range and format, a references to sources and reasons for retaining records (e.g. Reference to a particular Act or internal policy) any specific storage and preservation requirements, the disposal status (permanent or temporary), the disposal sentence and disposal trigger. Each entry should be assigned a unique identifier for easy reference in electronic and manual sentencing and disposal management systems.
7. Undertake consultation with key stakeholders to confirm the appropriateness of the recommended disposal actions and to ensure all records have been included. Ensure all feedback and responses to the feedback are documented in appraisal report.
8. Finalise the RDA and prepare a covering memo or letter explaining the purpose of the authority, how it was developed, who was consulted and the costs and benefits of implementing the authority.
9. Submit the authority and covering memo or letter for approval and endorsement.

Developing RDAs using the DIRKS methodology

Those adopting a macro-appraisal approach may consider applying Steps A to D of the DIRKS methodology. The DIRKS methodology is particularly suitable for developing RDAs for in-house archives and recordkeeping programs. However, it may be readily adapted for application in a collecting archives setting. For example, the political archives collection at the John Oxley Library (Anthony 2003).

The DIRKS methodology is primarily a cost-efficiency method that is driven by the needs and interests of records managers. For those following the DIRKS methodology, the business classification scheme provides the structure of the RDA. To undertake appraisal and develop a RDA using the DIRKS method it is necessary to complete steps A to D.

- **Step A: Preliminary investigation:** context defined, understood and documented in a contextual analysis document.
- **Step B: Analysis of business activity:** business classification scheme developed and validated
- **Step C: Identify recordkeeping requirements:** retention and disposal requirements identified and risk analysis conducted
- **Step D: Assessment of existing systems**: identify and analyse existing systems noting any gaps between the requirements identified in step C and the capacity of systems to function as records systems and ensure records are of sufficient quality

Completing steps A to D enables the archivist to gather and document all the contextual information required for developing a RDA and make informed decisions on the retention and disposal of records. RDAs may be developed using the following method:

1. Develop disposal classes for each function and activity identified in the business classification scheme developed during step B
2. Briefly describe the records in each class
3. Identify the date range for each class (where relevant e.g. inclusion of examples of legacy records)
4. Determine appropriate disposal actions and triggers based on the findings of steps C and D
5. Validate disposal classes with your research findings from step A – C
6. Consult with stakeholders
7. Finalise and submit for approval by the highest level possible (e.g. CEO, Board and, for those operating in a government context, the State, Provincial or National Archivist where relevant)

More information and templates are available in the *DIRKS Manual* and Chapter 15: *Digital Recordkeeping*.

General advice for developing and implementing RDAs

Irrespective of the method and type of schedule or schedules developed it is critical that:

1. All appraisal and disposal decisions and actions are documented, justified and traceable
2. Key stakeholders are consulted in the development of RDA and are given a reasonable opportunity to review and comment of RDA or the relevant part of a schedule
3. Stakeholder feedback and responses are documented and communicated to them

4. RDA are approved and their use authorised by senior management and/or the governing body of the organisation
5. RDAs have a validity period and are reviewed and updated before the expiry of that period
6. RDAs are published and accompanied by a training and awareness program
7. A master schedule is kept by the archivist or records manager and a duplicate used to mark up any changes
8. Disposal activity is monitored and audited
9. Recordkeeping requirements and associated disposal requirements are proactively monitored, updated and RDA re-issued accordingly

Additional guidance for packing boxes when transferring or destroying records is provided in Appendix 5.4 of this chapter.

Paper files

Sector-specific RDAs and requirements

Public sector

For archivists working in public sector organisations the archival authority within the relevant jurisdiction is legally mandated as the lead agency for appraisal and disposal. Consequently, there is a plethora of policies, standards, guidelines, templates and RDAs available, usually via the relevant archival authority's website. The development of RDAs and the submission of those authorities to the State or National Archivist for approval are usually mandated in legislation with some additional requirements mandated via regulations, policies and standards. Although the advice and resources issued by archival authorities are designed primarily for use by public sector agencies within their jurisdiction, much of it provides a valuable basis or framework for adaptation elsewhere. However, it is critical that when adapting these resources for use elsewhere that sector and organisation specific research, analysis and consultation are undertaken to ensure the final appraisal and disposal decisions are relevant, appropriate and in accordance with the legal and other requirements of the particular sector or organisation.

Private schools

The Records Retention Schedule for Non-Government Schools provides a practical guide for archivists working in non-government schools in Australia. The *Schedule* is functions-based and was developed using the initial steps of the DIRKS methodology as outlined in *ISO 15489 Records Management*. The functions covered by the *Schedule* are:

- governance
- compliance
- administration
- support groups
- student services
- student management
- student activities
- education
- communications
- alumni activities

Each of these functions is defined and then divided into activities or aspects of that function. For example under the term 'Governance' the activities of strategic planning and senior management have been identified. Within each activity categories of records or sub-activities are listed, described and supplemented with examples of records. The retention status is identified with a recommended disposal action.

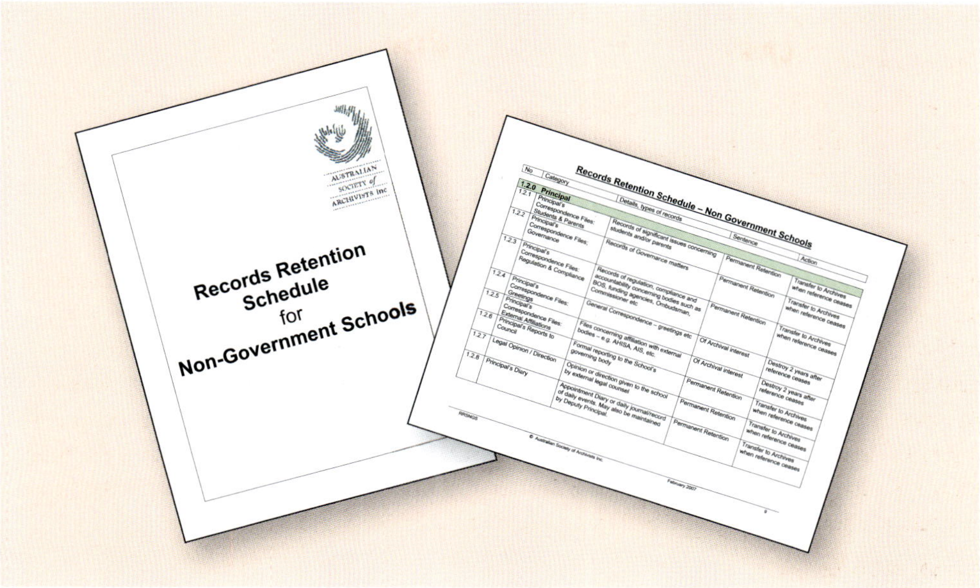

The Records Retention Schedule for Non-Government Schools

The *Schedule* does not differentiate between physical and electronic records and touches on the importance of taking care in migrating any records deemed to be vital or of continuing value. A brief and pragmatic procedure for the destruction of records is also included in the *Schedule*.

Like all recordkeeping tools and processes, the application of the *Schedule* needs to be sensitive to the requirements of each school and jurisdiction. It provides a standard for school archivists to adapt to their specific context and requires authorisation by the highest governing body of the school.

The research and analysis undertaken in developing the *Schedule* ensures that as far as a 'generic' schedule can, it conforms to the law and records management codes of best practice and supports accountable and transparent decision-making. It also supports the ASA Code of Ethics principle '3.1.1 Archivists ensure that the principles which govern the selection of records for preservation are themselves recorded'.

By providing a common platform for non-government schools to develop and implement their own context-specific appraisal and disposal program, the *Schedule* also promotes consistent or standardised archival practice within this sector.

Other private sector organisations

There are only a small number of RDAs for private sector organisations are available from various commercial providers and professional associations. These RDAs tend to be industry specific. The *Australian Records Retention Manual* (ARRM) (Information Enterprises Australia 2007) is an example of a general resource that may be used by private sector organisations in Australia as a basis for developing retention and disposal instruments such as an RDA. Reference to the ARRM does not constitute endorsement of the product by the author, editor or the Australian Society of Archivists Inc. It is used here as an example of a resource and approach to establishing a framework for making decisions on the retention and disposal of records in the private sector. Specifically, it illustrates aspects of legislation that may be relevant in making decisions on the legislative requirements for making, keeping, using and preserving records.

The ARRM aims to assist organisations with developing develop their own RDAs. It provides: guidance on undertaking appraisal and disposal; an RDA for common administrative records and functions; some management guidance on a selection of record groups (e.g. board and committee minutes, leases and superannuation records); an overview of the laws of evidence and statutes of limitations; and a list of nearly 2000 Australian laws and regulations that contain recordkeeping requirements.

The framework used for the 'schedules' (i.e. RDAs) in the ARRM is a mix of function, subject and record type and includes:

- ephemeral records
- administrative and management
- archival (historical interest)
- building, construction and maintenance
- corporate and secretarial
- electronic data processing
- finance
- health, safety and environment
- legal
- manufacturing
- marketing, public relations and sales
- personnel
- product development
- purchasing
- quality control
- scientific and technical
- stores

The list of laws covers all jurisdictions within Australia. While the list is comprehensive, it is simply a starting point. Anyone using the ARRM should supplement this with their own research. The laws include only those that apply to the private or business sector. The entry for each law or regulation contains the following elements:

- Businesses affected (a)
- Records affected (b)
- Retention period (c)
- Penalty (d)

An example of an entry from the list of laws contained in ARRM is shown in Figure 5.4.

1 (Fed) AGED CARE ACT 1997, Sections 88.1-88.2, 89.1:

(a) (A), (B) and (C) Approved providers; (D) Former approved providers

(b) (A) Records that verify claims for payments of subsidy (s.88.1); (B) Records that enable proper assessments to be made of whether the provider has complied with its responsibilities as set out in Chapter 4 (the Act - sections 53 to 68) (s.88.1); (C) Records of the kind specified in the Records Principles which may include: care recipient assessment and classification records; care plans for care recipients; medical records, progress notes and other clinical records; schedules of fees and charges (including accommodation bonds) for past and current care recipients; agreements with the care recipient; accounts of care recipients; records of accommodation bonds (including payments) or accommodation charges; and records of each recipient's entry, discharge and leave arrangements (including death certificates) (s.88.2); (D) Records kept when an approved provider must be retained (s.89.1) Note: Records may be in written or electronic form

(c) (A) and (B) 3 years after the 30 June of the year in which the record was made; (C) Not indicated; (D) 3 years after ceasing to be an approved provider (d) (A) & (B) Up to 30 PU; (C) Not indicated; (D) 30 PU

Figure 5.4: Excerpt of legal recordkeeping requirements from ARRM's list of laws

Documenting appraisal and disposal using technology

To assist archivists with establishing efficient and accountable practices for developing and maintaining RDAs, a number of taxonomy and disposal management products are commercially available. These products enable archivists to develop, maintain and publish taxonomies or business classification schemes that provide the conceptual framework (e.g. functions and activities for macro-functional approaches to appraisal as advocated by *ISO 15489*) RDAs. These products also enable the development, maintenance and publication of RDAs. Typically these products conform to the requirements of State and National archives in Australia and New Zealand and *ISO 15489.*

Currently there are two key products available in the Australasian market: aka and one-2-one. Some screenshots and reports from these products are provided below to illustrate the application of technology to the appraisal and disposal methods discussed in this chapter.

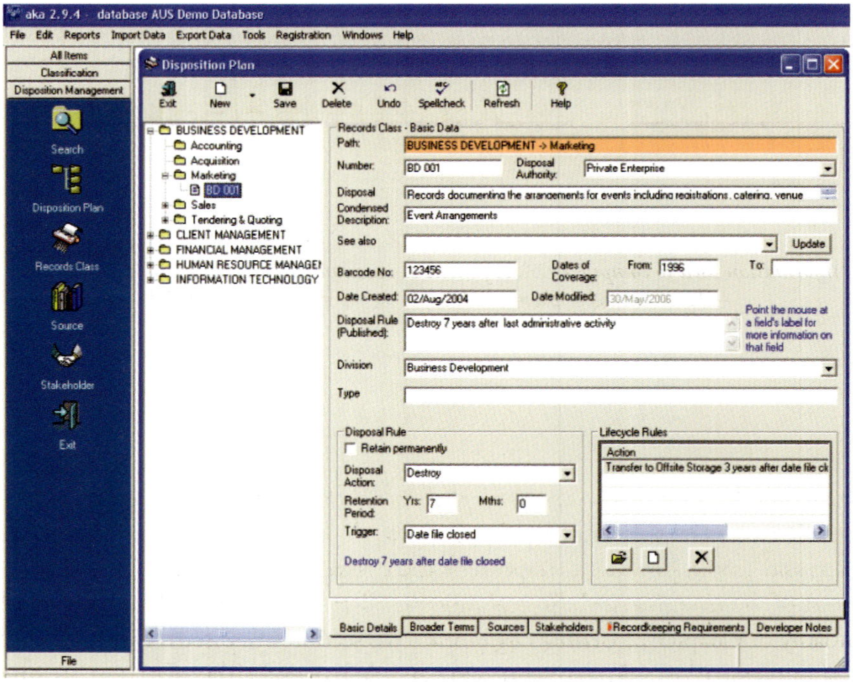

Main disposal management screen in aka used to enter and maintain information used to compile RDA. A functions-based heirarchical business classification scheme is used as the underlying conceptual basis for the RDA.

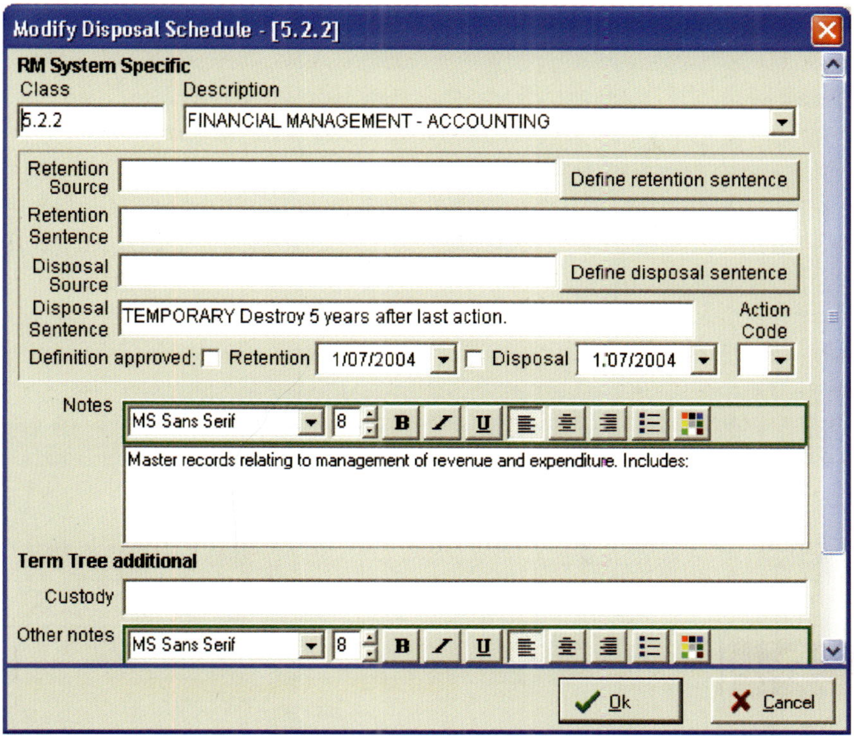

Main disposal management screen in one-2-one for entering and maintaining information used to compile RDA. A functions-based heirarchical business classification scheme is used as the underlying conceptual basis for the RDA.

Implementing RDAs

The design, development and authorisation of the RDA are just the beginning. Implementing an RDA will require archivists to work proactively with records creators, custodians and service providers. Implementation activities should be undertaken within the context of the retention and disposal program discussed earlier in this chapter and more broadly in Chapter 2: *Getting Organised.* This section will discuss two fundamental aspects of implementing a RDA – sentencing and destruction. Transfer issues are discussed in the Chapter 6: *Acquisition* and Chapter 7: *Accessioning.*

Sentencing

State Records NSW (2007) defines sentencing as the:

> *... process of identifying and classifying records according to a RDA, recording/registering the appropriate disposal decision and action for the records, and applying the disposal action specified in the RDA.*

In its *Sentencing* guidelines the National Archives of Australia (2007) explains that the:

> *... difference between sentencing and appraisal is that appraisal makes generalised decisions about groups of records, while sentencing applies these decisions to individual records. Together, appraisal and sentencing help you identify how long records should be retained, and ensure the process of disposing of records is completed in an authorised and managed way.*

Determining when sentencing should occur depends on the overarching records model adopted by an organisation. Where a life cycle approach has been adopted, then sentencing is a retrospective activity that occurs after the day-to-day administrative use of records has been completed. Where a continuum approach has been adopted and the DIRKS methodology implemented in accordance with *ISO 15489*, then the intellectual effort of assigning a sentence is applied up front during system design or when a record is created (in accordance with the authorised RDA and often using automated processes). Once the sentence is near expiry, the sentence is confirmed and usually either deferred (with a reason for the change documented) or implemented.

Rows of legacy records awaiting sentencing

The following steps are typically followed when sentencing records:

1. Identify the context and purpose of records and the organisation, individual or community to which the records relate.
2. Determine from the record what is being documented and why.
3. Identify the appropriate disposal class in the RDA. If there is not one, then you will need to undertake appraisal and incorporate this requirement into a future release of the RDA and/or gain authorisation for including it as an 'addendum'.
4. Identify the disposal and any other action required in the relevant RDA.
5. If the trigger event for disposal has already occurred (such as action is completed), confirm and implement the disposal action. If the trigger event has not yet occurred (e.g. the record is still in active use), set a review date for the future.

6. Determine the various dates on which certain records are to be destroyed and ensure that it is documented and authorised. Where secure destruction or transfer is required, then the relevant certificates will need to be issued.
7. Check to ensure all systems (manual and digital) are updated and correctly reflect the disposal actions and status of records.

Sentencing and implementing disposal involves risk. In recognition of this risk State Records NSW Standard on appraisal and disposal of public records requires public offices to confirm that disposal decisions are current and accurate and are authorised prior to the disposal action occurring. For archivists working in any archival environment, to provide an additional level of quality and risk control, it may be prudent to ask the following series of questions:

If these records are destroyed or lost because of poor disposal controls:

1. Will any client or user suffer loss of rights or be significantly inconvenienced?
2. What is the cost of reconstructing these records?
3. How long will reconstruction take? Minutes, hours, days, months, years!
4. Can these records be replaced from another source?
5. If so, then is this other source on a format that is easily used and cheap to access?

While there are no definitive generic answers to these questions, answering them and any others relevant to a particular situation will help archivists justify their decisions and feel confident they have made the best decision given the information and resources available at the time of sentencing and implementing disposal actions.

Destruction

Destruction of records in a timely and appropriately managed way can reduce storage costs, allow archivists and organisations to focus on higher priority records and save time in searching and retrieving records. Any destruction should be in accordance with a valid and approved RDA. However, it is also necessary to consult with the relevant personnel to ensure the records are not needed for legal, business or other purposes (e.g. records subject to pending freedom of information requests or anticipated litigation or investigations).

Any destruction process should be:

- authorised
- irreversible
- secure
- documented
- appropriate for the media and sensitivity of the records and
- as environmentally sound as possible.

Methods of destruction

For paper:

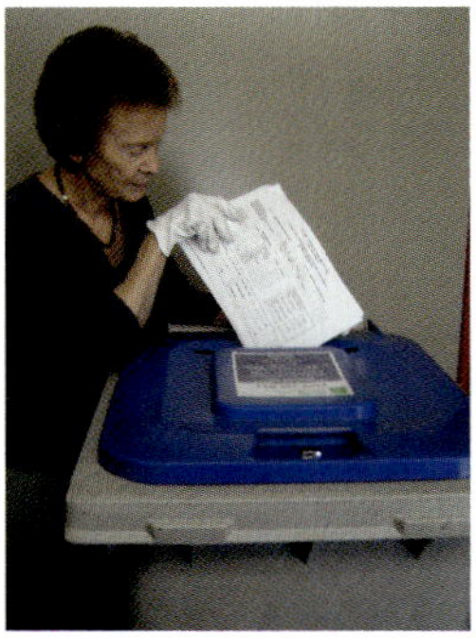

1. *Shredding* reduces paper to fine ribbons and may be used for most documents, but is not suitable for very sensitive information.
2. *Pulping* reduces paper to pulp and is often used in recycling. It is appropriate for highly sensitive records.
3. *Burning*, in an enclosed incinerator or in a secure facility, is also suitable for sensitive records.
4. *Dry maceration* reduces most materials to fine particles. This is appropriate for highly secure material.

For other media:

1. *Cutting, crushing, shredding or chemical recycling* can be used for magnetic and optical media, videos, film and microform.
2. *Reformatting* can be used on most electronic media including computer hard-drives, but it is not suitable for secure data. For further information on dealing with secure information on electronic media, see the NZ Government Information Technology Security Manual at www.gcsb.govt.nz.

Burying or dumping are inappropriate destruction methods because paper and other material takes time to compost and may be uncovered at any time.

(Archives New Zealand 2006)

Some methods for destroying records

For accountability purposes a record of what has been destroyed needs to be made and kept as part of the organisation's or archives records system. This may take the form of a 'destruction log' and should include the following information:

- records that were destroyed: title, date range, format, brief description and quantity
- what destruction action was taken: shredding, pulping, etc?
- the relevant disposal class reference and rda relating to the destruction
- when destruction was undertaken
- who took the action
- reference to the authorisation or contract number for external authorisation and
- certificates of destruction

Any records systems, registers and finding aids should be updated to show the records were destroyed, when they were destroyed and the relevant references in the RDA.

Practical challenges in appraisal and disposal

While theory and methods provide frameworks and instruments for undertaking appraisal and disposal, they do not provide much support for dealing with some of the practical challenges faced by many practicing archivists. These challenges are include dealing with:

- competing stakeholder interests
- digital records
- audio-visual records
- appraisal, disposal and risk management
- backlogs and legacy collections
- mixed and poorly organised collections
- case files via sampling techniques: also referred to as 'selective appraisal'
- records of very short-term value via 'normal administrative practice'

Further discussion of the challenges relating to the appraisal and disposal of digital records and audio-visual records and ways to deal with them is provided in the Chapter 15: *Digital Recordkeeping*, Chapter 17: *Sound Recordings* and Chapter 18: *Moving Images*. The remaining challenges are discussed below.

Competing stakeholder interests

Competing interests will often emerge when considering the value of records from the perspective of different stakeholders, For example, case histories of children who are subject to abuse, may only have limited value to the responsible government agency with a retention period that expires within 10 years of the child's 18th birthday at which point the child is regarded as an adult.

- Solicitors and risk managers may argue that if it is only necessary to keep records for the period identified in legislation, then retaining them for longer increases the risk and associated costs of unnecessarily having to produce those records as evidence should a discovery order or freedom of information access request be received by the agency.
- The child involved may regard the case history as their personal history that should be retained permanently and preferably transferred to them once the legally required period of retention has passed.
- Academic researchers and public policy analysts may also argue that these records should be retained for at least 30 years to enable trend analysis and other research to help understand the circumstances in which abuse occur and to develop new methods for reducing child abuse.
- Given the sensitive information contained in these records to meet legal compliance requirements it may also be required to close them for 100 years. This long period

of restricted access may prompt a finance manager to challenge the cost of retaining an extensive collection of records that cannot be readily accessed. From a finance and resource perspective a shorter retention period that aligns with the minimum period for legal compliance may be preferred.

To help establish priorities and make decisions a risk assessment may be used balance competing interests. Shepherd and Yeo (2003, p.161) explain:

> *...A key question is: what level of risk will the organization accept? To assess risk, the possible consequences of the absence of records should be identified and their severity matched against the likelihood of their occurrence. The consequences could be financial (fines, damages arising from inability to initiate or defend legal action, disruption or loss of business) but could also be measured in terms of less of opportunity, amenity, reputation, prestige or goodwill. A risk assessment seeks to judge how far the absence of particular records would be likely to incur such consequences, and how serious their impact would be. The highest risks are those where both impact and probability are greatest...*
>
> *The risks of destroying records must be set against the costs of maintaining them. Costs include accommodation, equipment and the services of records staff or contractors ... risks attached to retention and costs of destruction may also be taken into account.*
>
> *A further factor is the organization's attitude to the interests of external users. Most internal business needs are ephemeral and will expire at some point. However, especially in the public sector, the political or social benefit of retaining records may determine longer retention periods. The need to protect the interests of citizens may justify higher costs, although the balance between costs and benefits of retention after organizational needs have been met must still be weighed.*

Further guidance on incorporating risk management into appraisal and disposal is provided in the *DIRKS Manual* and more broadly in *AS4360: Risk Management* and its associated handbooks.

Stakeholder consultation is another way to balance competing interests.

Stakeholder consultation can be undertaken to initially determine what records need to be retained, for how long and by whom. It may also be undertaken to validate the research and analysis undertaken by the archivist in developing instruments such as RDAs. As applied in the MM and Minnesota Lite at the UMA, stakeholder consultation may form a core plank in undertaking transparent and informed re-appraisals of existing collections and developing new strategies for reducing, selecting or evaluating records.

Given that stakeholder views will probably vary, undertaking consultation also introduces the problem of prioritising different voices, ensuring all have equal access to the consultation process and the risk of making compromises that do not fully satisfy any stakeholders but are reluctantly accepted by the group.

To be effective stakeholder consultation needs to be inclusive, planned and well managed. Documenting the consultation method, process and content is important for transparency and accountability.

Identification and selection of a representative group of people without that grouping becoming unwieldy to manage is central to successful consultation. It may be useful and efficient to assess the value of drawing on some existing 'groups' used by the organisation or broader community for other purposes e.g. professional groups, advocacy groups, committees or networks. The selection of participants could be demonstrated through a set of selection criteria and explanation of how each person meets those criteria.

The selection of different types of consultation methods will be determined by the purpose of the consultation and degree of participation. For example, for a consultation process aimed at simply keeping stakeholders informed, then there is a low level of participation required and much of it will involve activities such as briefings, reporting and using other means to communicate the purpose, reason and benefits of appraisal and disposal. This form of one-way communication is probably more effective for educating stakeholders and generating interest, but less effective in reducing the bias and subjectivity involved in making appraisal and disposal decisions.

Input consultation involves seeking input from individuals and groups in making decisions about the retention and disposal of records. This may involve surveys, focus groups, and advisory committees. The goal in this case is to improve the quality and acceptability of appraisal and disposal decisions by considering the comments and interests of those likely to be affected by them.

In some cases, particularly where the ownership and control of records or business activities is shared by two or more organisations, a partnership approach is usually more effective. This involves sharing the decision-making and implementation with the partner organisations. More formal and ongoing mechanisms such as advisory committees are more effective in ways to implement this form of consultation.

Apart from the means and methods identified above, consultation may also involve publishing notices and articles in relevant newsletters, websites available on the internet or organisation's intranet, using email discussion groups or forums and postings to relevant mailing lists. Whatever is used it is critical to ensure openness about why people are being consulted, how they will be consulted, the level of participation expected and how much influence stakeholders will have in making decisions about the retention and disposal of records. Participants need to be provided with relevant, comprehensive, balanced and accurate information and any feedback, positive or negative, handled fairly.

In reflecting on his many years as an appraisal archivist in Government archives, Tony Newton suggested appraisal is an activity best shared by many stakeholders and one that should be proactively discussed within the archives or broader organisational setting. He identified a lack of consultation with records users in the appraisal decision-making process as a key area of concern and weakness in making decisions about the retention and disposal of records. He explains that reasons put forward by archivists for not consulting are many and include:

> *A lack of representation of the wider community by specialised interest groups such as historians; unwieldy administrative burdens resulting in appraisal projects not being finished or dragging on due to ongoing input and conflicting feedback; and that archivists are the people professionally trained to make such decisions (Newton 2001, p.90).*

Newton challenges the validity of these claims and draws on the successful consultation experiences of Stare Records New South Wales in developing a general disposal authority and thesaurus for Local Government in NSW. He explains the consultation process as follows:

> *The project was large, difficult and complex and involved very widespread and throughout consultation with also most 200 councils and approximately 30 stakeholder groups who were associated with or had a stake in Local Government records.' (p.90)... [Consultation was undertaken] across the State to 'promote discussion and gather as much feedback as possible. All significant drafts of the authority were placed on State Records' website for comment and input, and the draft was sent to community history stakeholder groups such as the History Councils, the Historian for the City of Sydney, the Royal Australian Historical Society, the Society of Australian Genealogists, and the Sydney City Council Archives (Newton 2001, p.90).*

In Newton's view the consultation process was a great success. The project kept to its planned timeframe and the community history groups provided valuable feedback that resulted the revision of many classes of records and a more balanced view some areas, particularly in relation to regional, local or specialised programs. In his overall assessment of the development of the disposal authority and thesaurus, Newton believes it is possible to 'invite planned and well-managed input to the appraisal process from stakeholders and gain some real benefits that might just result in a better final product' (Newton 2001, pp. 90–1).

While consultation processes for many archives does not need to be as complex and comprehensive as the one conducted for the Local Government thesaurus and disposal authority, it is an important activity for ensuring appraisal decisions are well informed, comprehensive in consideration, consistent and relevant. The consultation process itself enables appraisal to be open and accountable and promotes a greater understanding of recordkeeping and the value the work of the archivist brings to the organisation.

Consultation also provides opportunity for underlying assumptions to be challenged, justifications to be tested, resulting in more balanced and robust decisions on the retention and disposal of records. From an implementation perspective, consultation also provides an insight into the areas needing greater support (e.g. training and education requirements can be targeted) and more encouragement to adopt and implement appraisal decisions (e.g. when planning implementation it may be necessary to incorporate more incentives and support mechanisms for those within the organisation who were not interested in participating in the consultation process or appear determined to de-rail it).

Dealing with backlogs

Archives typically have backlogs of unappraised or inadequately appraised material. They are a fact of life and a legacy of many many decades of paper-based records management practices and inadequate resourcing levels for managing archives. This material is often poorly documented, poorly organised, fragmented and mixed up. Dealing with this usually requires micro-level appraisal to be undertaken. But even in this situation it is important to ensure appraisal is still undertaken systematically and that the approach is carefully planned and documented. Understanding the context of the records before appraising them is still necessary. This may mean undertaking a survey of what's there to determine provenance, series etc as discussed previously in this chapter. You may also note the

"To keep, or not to keep: That is the question, T.R. ..."

physical condition and any issues that require immediate action – for example, records infested with lice may need to be isolated and fumigated before any further inspection of them is undertaken.

Techniques for sorting records of unknown or mixed origin are provided in Chapter 7: *Accessioning* and Chapter 8: *Arrangement & Description.* Techniques for determining preservation and storage needs are covered, respectively, in the Chapter 3: *Buildings & Storage* and Chapter 4: *Preservation.*

Normal Administrative Practice (NAP)

Not all records are worth keeping for any notable length of time. These records are usually of short term or once-off value and may include (but not always) working drafts, back-up copies and 'sticky notes'. To deal with these in a pragmatic and efficient way archivists apply 'Normal Administrative Practice (NAP) to allow them to be destroyed without formal authorisation or documentation. NAP is essentially a common sense approach that recognises that such records are often routinely destroyed in the normal course of business because their value is very transient and it is not worth controlling them.

NSW State Records (2007) defines normal administrative records as those that:

> *...are ephemeral, facilitative or duplicate in nature (and not of continuing value to the organisation) may not need to be placed within recordkeeping systems and may be required for only a few hours or days. The destruction of these types of records is acceptable as a part of normal administrative practice for a public office.*

In applying NAP within Commonwealth Government agencies, National Archives of Australia warns that:

> - *what is a normal administrative practice for one agency may not be a normal practice for another.*
> - *deciding what records to destroy using NAP should be done with an understanding of the business context of the records and risks associated with that business.*

Items that are often destroyed under NAP include those of:

- facilitative, transitory or other items of short term value or interest
- rough working documents and/or calculations
- drafts not intended for any further use or reference
- copies of material retained for reference purposes only (e.g. convenience, local or reference duplicates of records)
- published items that are not an integral part of an agency's record

National Archives of Australia's NAP checklist

The NAP checklist is a practical tool that can be used to develop your agency's procedures on NAP. It provides guidance on specific questions you can ask about a record to help identify if it has any agency business, accountability or cultural value.

Any decision to destroy a record as NAP should be made after considering the context of the business activity that it supports. With this in mind, ask yourself the following questions about the record:

Is the record covered by a specific law or a Records Authority issued by the National Archives?

If not, is the record:

- needed to clarify, support or give context to an existing record?
- needed to show how the agency business was carried out?
- needed to show how a decision was made?
- needed to show when or where an event happened?
- needed because it indicates who made the decision or gave the advice?
- needed because it contains information on the rights or obligations of government or private individuals?
- a formal draft of a Cabinet submission?
- a draft of an agreement or legal document?
- likely to form part of a record that will be needed to support legal proceedings?

If the answer to all these questions is no, then you can consider destroying the record as a normal administrative practice. If the answer to any question is yes, the record should be retained so that appropriate coverage under a Records Authority can be developed.

(National Archives of Australia n.d.)

Guidelines for applying Normal Administrative Practice (NAP)
<http://www.naa.gov.au/records-management/keep-destroy-transfer/NAP/NAP-detail.aspx#section4

Sampling case files

Sampling is a form of appraisal which is used where a large series of records cannot be retained. It is also known as 'selective appraisal'. Sampling aims to establish a representative sample of the quantity, quality and content of the population of records. To ensure rationale selection occurs and to enable accountable decision-making it is important to determine and document a technique for sampling.

Sampling is an option when:

- the information content of each record is relatively thin
- the volume of records is great
- the records are relatively uniform in terms of form and partly in terms of the content

Provided the sampling methods are appropriate most researchers can rely on samples of between 5 – 20% and the archives avoids the cost of managing, preserving and storing the whole series.

But again the key problem is choice. Before undertaking sampling it is imperative to determine whether sampling appropriate for the situation and, if so, what is the most appropriate technique and optimal size of the sample to guarantee sufficient representativeness to accommodate many research possibilities.

Sampling methods include:

- systematic or numeric
- chronological
- topography
- quality
- alphabetical
- random
- birthday or event-based

It is possible to use more than one method at a time. However, no single method can serve all possible purposes. Whatever method or methods are selected, it is advisable to: test the method of methods of selection prior to full implementation; to document the reasons for adopting the approach taken; and clearly explain the sampling method so it may be readily understood by most people.

Reappraisal of records and archives

This chapter has emphasised that making choices about the retention and disposal of records is a contingent and subjective activity that involves risk. The selection of approaches, methods and instruments applied to appraisal and disposal is shaped by the context in which appraisal occurs and the outlook of archivists and others involved in appraisal and disposal. The application of specific methods and instruments assists in rationalising appraisal and disposal decisions and addressing risks associated with retention and disposal. However, the contingent nature of appraisal and disposal and changes in archival thought and practice also mean that revisiting appraisal decisions of the past to confirm or modify may be necessary.

Reappraisal is the systematic process of revisiting past appraisal decisions. It is defined by State Records NSW as 'the process of re-evaluating the holdings of an archives or manuscript repository to determine which holdings should be retained and which should be de-accessioned'.

Reappraisal is a vexed and contentious issue. Each generation will have different views and priorities on what to keep as archives and what to destroy. A key issue is whether contemporary views and priorities should be applied to past appraisal decisions. The selections of the past give insight into what past generations viewed as worth remembering and can, therefore, implicitly tell us much about the past.

Many archives undertake reappraisal projects because gaps in the collective memory have been identified. Often questions about past appraisal decisions and practices involve a revision of appraisal methods. For example the Algonquin Provincial Park and environmental records discussed earlier in this chapter and in Post-apartheid South Africa as discussed in Table 5.3.

Reappraising appraisal in post-Apartheid South Africa

... questions have permeated discussion of those two core "shaping" functions of public archives, appraisal and collecting. With the former, the focus has been on appraisal as an institutional process: who should be responsible for appraisal? To whom should appraisers be accountable? How transparent should the process be? How reliable are the appraisals done during the apartheid era? These questions are rooted in an intense distrust of SAS's appraisal practice, which was characterised by an unrelenting opacity. Some have gone so far as to recommend that the appraisal function be taken from public archives and given to independent boards comprising academics and other "stakeholders". The intensity of this distrust was illustrated in November 1995, when South Africa's National Cabinet imposed a moratorium on the destruction of all public records – irrespective of whether or not they had been appraised by SAS – until the completion of the TRC's work. By 1995, however, debate had yielded substantial agreement that appraisal is an archival function and archivists should be responsible for it. Nevertheless, democratic imperatives demand that levels of transparency be high, that public account of appraisal decisions be given, and that there should be some measure of public participation in

the decision-making. These positions are reflected in the National Archives of South Africa Act, which charges the National Archives with the appraisal of public records, subject to the approval of its overarching appraisal policy and monitoring of the policy's implementation by the National Archives Commission. Debate around the theoretical and methodological underpinnings of appraisal practice has been less widespread, but equally vigorous. Located mainly within SAS (later National Archives) structures, the debate has pitted defenders of SAS's established practice against advocates of macro-appraisal.[58] *... Macro-appraisal, they argue, provides an explanation of archival value which is rooted in the archival bedrock of provenance, which, unlike the idea of usefulness, secures a workable yardstick and meshes with a methodology appropriate to modern records environments. Moreover, it displaces the notion of the appraiser as a neutral handmaid to users of archivesand replaces it with the view of the appraiser as an active documenter of societal processes. In 1996 SAS formally embarked on a macro-appraisal inspired overhaul of its appraisal programme, which has now been inherited and developed by the National Archives.*

(Harris 2002, pp.73–4).

Table 5.3: Reappraising appraisal in post-Apartheid South Africa

Another common reason for reappraisal is the challenge of dealing with what is later viewed as poor appraisal decisions or practices of the past, often a symptom of little or no formal appraisal being undertaken.

Typically past appraisal decisions have not been adequately documented making it very difficult for archivists to retrace the decision-making process and the provenance and original order of records donated many years before. In the collecting archives context this is particularly problematic because there is a disconnection between the archives and donor. In the case of a government archive or corporate archive the context of records can be more readily and confidently recreated simply because of the stronger administrative and historical relationship between the archives and the organisation of which it is part and the availability of published resources such as establishing legislation, Government Gazettes, Government Directories, Hansard and Agency Annual Reports.

Reappraisal may also require archivists to revisits and renegotiate with donors or their heirs. This may be a sensitive matter and needs to be managed with diplomacy. Sometimes it is difficult just working out who the donor may have been and what were the terms and conditions of the donation, simply because the process was not documented or only partially documented.

Sometimes reappraisal projects are triggered by cost-cutting strategies of the umbrella organisation. This is particularly the case where the practical concerns of space and resource constraints drive the need for reappraisal.

Irrespective of the trigger for appraisal the goal remains the same – to analyse the records or business processes to determine the value of records and consequently their disposal status – 'is it needed?' is the key question not how much will it cost to keep and store? It is also critical to document appraisal and reappraisal decisions from both a corporate memory and accountability perspective and to establish a means for professional accountability.

A key aspect of reappraisal is determining whether past decisions on the retention and disposal of records were 'good'. However, evaluating the appraisal and disposal process is an important activity when conducting either appraisal or reappraisal. Determining what 'good' appraisal is is difficult but can be facilitated by the application of various professional standards. The following section introduces some of these standards.

Conducting 'good' appraisal and disposal

> *Good appraisal ensures that the destruction of records is a deliberate and well-considered process rather than a result of carelessness or by accident*
>
> ASA Statement of Appraisal

It is difficult to define and implement performance indicators and measures to determine whether appraisal and disposal is effective and meeting its purposes. However, it is fair to say that in an organisational context effective appraisal and disposal relies on having an effective records management program in place that is managed by professional and experienced personnel.

Archivists advise, facilitate and undertake good appraisal through reference and application of the following:

1. **Standards and Codes**, such as the *Australian Society of Archivists Appraisal Statement, Australian Society of Archivists Code of Ethics, ICA Code of Ethics, State Records NSW Standard on Appraisal, ISO 15489* and Organisational Code of Conduct.
2. **Professional Methods**, such as the micro-appraisal and macro-appraisal approaches discussed previously in this chapter.
3. **Standardised and systematic processes**, based on professional standards etc. Such as the *DIRKS Manual* which is based on ISO 15489 and is widely used for undertaking a range of recordkeeping activities, including appraisal and disposal.
4. **Instruments**, such as the appraisal checklist, RDAs, appraisal policies, appraisal reports and destruction logs.

5. **Systems**, such as disposal management software and records systems that conform with *ISO 15489* and certification or endorsement schemes implemented by archival authorities.

To support professional appraisal practices in Australia the Australian Society of Archivists issued the '*ASA Appraisal Statement*' (the Statement), which may be found at <www.archivists.org.au> and Appendix 5.1 of this chapter. The purpose of the statement is to establish a common '...basis for the development and implementation of appraisal methodologies and practices by recordkeeping practitioners and organisations, and serve as a benchmark for judging appraisal practices.'

According to the Statement 'good appraisal' occurs when it:

1. Conforms to Law
2. Supports Accountability and Transparency
3. Complies with Standards and Codes
4. Responsive to Needs of Others

The Statement also identifies the following practices for enabling good appraisal:

1. Planned process
2. Well justified
3. Comprehensive consideration
4. Informed
5. Consistent
6. Documented and Transparent
7. Reported and Audited
8. Mandated
9. Risk management
10. Current
11. Circumstantial

An alternative view of what constitutes 'good appraisal' is provided by State Records NSW in its *Standard on the Appraisal and Disposal of State Records* (2007). Developed specifically for use in the NSW public sector, this standard requires that appraisal and disposal is:

- analytical
- comprehensive
- authorised
- accountable
- implemented

See Appendix 5.5 for a set of compliance requirements developed by State Records NSW for applying its Appraisal Policy.

Summary and conclusion

Appraisal is an analytical process that archivists use to determine the value of records. Disposal is the key outcome of appraisal. It is concerned with the specific action to be taken as a result of appraisal. In practice, appraisal and disposal are challenging and often resource-intensive archival processes that require a significant level of research, consultation, negotiation and operational processing. It is also a contingent and subjective activity that invariably involves risks that need to be identified and managed. A common aim for all approaches to archival appraisal and disposal is to make them as routine and systematic as possible so they become embedded in the routine way of working.

Traditionally appraisal is a process that occurs at the end of the record life cycle and usually involves reviewing the value of a physical record and the physical inspection of those records prior to confirming the appropriate disposal action for those records. The traditional approach is records-centric and generally works well where the vast majority of records are paper-based text records. This approach is often labelled as a 'bottom-up' approach or micro-appraisal and is used by many archivists, particularly those working in most collecting archives environments.

The models advocated by Schellenberg and Jenkinson are regarded as bottom-up approaches because they focus on the records and then ask questions about the context and value of those records. The models are not mutually exclusive and focus on identifying, documenting and analysing documents (documentary analysis).

During the 1970s it emerged that bottom-up approaches simply could not keep up with the demands of digital recordkeeping and the increasingly dynamic administrative structures, entities and workplaces in which records were generated and used. A new approach to appraisal was needed if archivists were to ensure their archival collections were worth preserving and of any value.

By the mid 1990s the continuum view was articulated. It rejected the linear perspective of the life cycle mode and presented an iterative approach in which appraisal occurs at a number of points, at various times and at different levels of aggregation. Appraisal involves evaluating the context of the record rather than the record itself and is a more analytical and abstract activity.

Making choices about the instruments for documenting and implementing appraisal and disposal stems from the approach or mixes of approach adopted. This in turn should reflect the archival context in which appraisal and disposal occurs. Common instruments discussed in this chapter were:

- appraisal and retention and disposal policies
- retention and disposal program and strategy
- retention and disposal guidelines and templates

- appraisal reports
- records surveys and inventory
- Retention and Disposal Authorities (RDAs)

To assist archivists with establishing efficient and accountable practices for developing and maintaining RDAs a number of taxonomy and disposal management products are commercially available. These products also enable the development, maintenance and publication of RDAs. Typically these products conform to the requirements of state and national archives in Australia and New Zealand and *ISO 15489*.

It is difficult to define and implement performance indicators and measures to determine whether appraisal and disposal is effective and meeting its purposes. Archivists advise, facilitate and undertake good appraisal through reference and application of standards and codes, professional methods, standardised and systematic processes, instruments such as RDAs and systems.

Many archives revisit their appraisal decisions. Sometimes reappraisal projects are triggered by cost-cutting strategies of the umbrella organisation. Reappraisal is the systematic process of revisiting past appraisal decisions. It is a vexed and contentious practice. A key issue is whether we should impose contemporary views and priorities on the past, as the selections of the past give insight into what past generations viewed as worth remembering. Past appraisal decisions can implicitly tell us much about the past.

Where appraisal decisions have been clearly documented in terms of reasons, requirements and the decision-making process (i.e. 'good appraisals'), reappraisal may be more confidently undertaken. However, in practice, such documentation is not always available to the extent necessary to make fully informed reappraisal decisions.

This chapter has defined, discussed and analysed key approaches and challenges associated with archival appraisal and disposal. Appraisal and disposal is a central archival process that determines what is remembered and what is not. It also determines what records pass the archival threshold – the subject of the following chapter.

CHAPTER 6

acquisition

PETER J CRUSH

CHAPTER ABSTRACT

Acquisition is the processes associated with acquiring records that are relevant to your archives. For many archives, it may be argued that the acquisition process is the point at which archival activity begins – in theory. In reality, it is often an accumulation of records and other old material that provides the impetus to establish an archive. In these cases this initial accumulation, and the individuals or organisation that collected or merely received or stored them, influences future acquisitions so that the process evolves. In these latter cases, it is that initial accumulation and the individuals or organisation that collected or merely received or stored them, that so influence future acquisitions. The process then evolves rather than being the conscious product of careful consideration of all of the factors involved.

This chapter identifies the factors that influence the acquisition process. Your archives will operate more effectively, with fewer headaches, if you analyse these factors as early as possible and document, in an acquisition policy, the stance the archives will adopt on each point. An acquisition policy will be different for each archives because the circumstances of each factor will be unique to each. Further resources are included on the accompanying CD.

What is the acquisition process?

Acquiring archival records can be a complicated business. The degree of complication depends largely on the type of archives making the acquisition. The simplest acquisition process is the transfer of inactive archival records from the business unit that created and maintained them, to the in-house archives of that same organisation. With in-house archives, ownership of the archives does not change at the time of acquisition, custody does. For the collecting archives, the acquisition process is considerably more complex. Decisions need to be made about whose records to collect, how to go about collecting them, who will own the records and how their access to researchers will be managed.

But first let us look at the basic steps in the acquisition process:

- identify and list the organisations, families and individuals whose records fit within the scope of your holdings
- establish relationships with other archives whose collecting scope overlap with your own and negotiate cooperative agreements
- approach potential donors to develop their interest in your objectives
- advance your relationship with interested donors by explaining your collection scope and the conditions that would apply to any donation
- negotiate and sign the Deed of Gift
- collaborate with your accessioning officer to make arrangements for the preparation of the records for transfer, and for the actual transfer.

These basic steps are influenced by the following factors selected for investigation:

- the legal status of the archives
- how the archives will be governed and managed
- the scope/boundaries/limitations of the holdings
- should we accept all that is offered?
- ownership of items/holdings
- methods of acquisition
- documentation of acquisitions
- de-accessioning policy and process.

The prudent archives documents its response to these factors in either a specific acquisition policy or a broader archives policy (see also Chapter 2: *Getting Organised*).

Developing an acquisition policy

The holdings of any archives are, by definition, judged worthy of on-going preservation for periods of time measured in centuries rather than decades. The managers of the holdings will inevitably change during the life of the archives, rendering it important that there exists a succinct body of authoritative information that summarises the fundamentals on which the archival holdings are based. The acquisition policy (which is sometimes referred to as a collection policy), is that succinct body of information. An example of an acquisition policy is provided in Appendix 6.1.

For those who are planning to establish an archives, the opportunity exists for them to analyse the above factors and decide precisely their stance on each to meet the unique projected needs and aspirations. The policy will then guide the efficient development of the collection, avoiding as many potential pitfalls and diversions as possible.

Creating such a policy after the archival collection is in existence, enables the archivist to reflect on past experience and to assess whether circumstances particular to the collection require inclusion. For example, it may be desirable for an archives that accepts records from a range of ethnic groups within Australia to have the title of foreign language items translated into English, and for the translation to be included with such items before they are accepted.

When the governing body of the archives adopts the acquisition policy it confirms its commitment to the archives and to the fundamental acquisition policy, principles and practices that it will apply. This provides a firm foundation, but with room to move and grow. Each position taken within the policy will have implications for the institution's future. The most useful and effective policies are those that are realistic, taking into account the limits imposed by the governance and the resources of the body that is ultimately responsible for the archives and its holdings.

Factors influencing acquisition

Before examining the factors influencing the acquisition process, let us reflect on the motives and activities underlying the establishment of an archives. Who provided the inspiration to establish the archives, what was it intended to preserve and why did they wish to establish it? This reflection will surely provide invaluable background information, identify helpful stakeholders and alternative views, and hint at promising strategies to be pursued in advancing the objectives of the archives. These three factors – who, what and why – plus the amount of resources to be committed to it, strongly influence the future of the archives.

The **who** might be an individual, a family, a community group, a not-for-profit organisation, a company, a government organisation or any other entity that can be identified and defined.

The **what** might be 'any of that old stuff worth keeping', the historical records of the church, as much published, unpublished and three dimensional stuff as possible that tells the story of our region/armed services/industry, historical material we can use for displays in our public spaces, and as much other material as your imagination can envisage.

The **why** could be 'to clean up that mess and make the most of it', 'to preserve evidence of the church's beliefs, principles, governance, property, rights, responsibilities, obligations, congregation, activities, services for legal, administrative and informational purposes', 'to keep alive the memory and preserve and make accessible to the public information about the development and life of our region/armed services/industry', 'for the education and enjoyment of the public', 'to stimulate interest in our activities to grow our customer base' and so on.

Clarifying the *what* and the *why* may help the who decide not to proceed, but may also result in refining the *what* and the *why*, and is most likely to help the *who* to establish whether the collection will be one of archives, or of other material, or a combination of several specialised collections such as archives, library, museum and art gallery.

We will now look at these in more detail.

The legal status of the archival institution

Confirming or establishing the legal status of an archives helps identify the limits of its authority to act and, more importantly, its expected longevity and stability.

- Is it completely autonomous and subject only to the rules it makes to govern its own activities – consistent, of course, with the laws of the community in which it is located?
- Is it a part of one of Australia's levels of government – Local, State or Commonwealth?
- Is it part of a parent organisation and therefore subject to the authority, policies and procedures of that parent body?

The status of the archives or archival unit within a parent organisation, or within society at large, will establish the parameters in which the collection must operate. These parameters will exert a strong influence on the nature and purpose of the collection. They will influence such things as:

- the archives they will acquire
- governance arrangements
- financial requirements
- financial sources and any limits on funds
- legal rights and obligations
- the sector/s of society they serve
- the risks that the collection might face
- the ultimate fate of the holdings

The legal status of the archives will influence which of the following categories of archives they fall into – government, in-house, collecting, combined, clearing house or commercial. These categories have been identified as having the following specific characteristics that indicate how they are likely to operate.

Government archives: A government agency usually with legislative responsibility for providing a centralised archival service for agencies within that government structure. (Local government archives may be governed by State government legislation)

In-house archives: That part of an institution or organisation maintained for the purpose of keeping the archives of that institution or organisation. An in-house archives usually restricts its acquisition to records generated by its parent institution or organisation, or by other closely associated bodies or people. Also referred to as corporate archives, dedicated archives or institutional archives.

Collecting archives: An organisation or part of an organisation that has as its principal function the collection of the records of a variety of organisations, families and individuals. Collecting archives are often referred to as manuscript libraries or manuscript repositories (Acland 1993).

Combined archives: An archival program responsible for both the archives of its parent body, and for collecting archives that relate to the responsibilities of the parent body. This type embraces the Canadian concept of 'total archives' (Cook 1993).

Clearing house archival program: Exemplified by the Australian Science Archives Project, which maintains a register of information about the archives of science in Australia and acts as an archival broker, e.g. arranging the deposit of the archives of individual scientists in suitable collecting institutions.

Commercial archival operations: Offering consultancy services ranging from archival processing and documentation of records and their contexts to storage and preservation (McKemmish 1993).

Table 6.1 Types of archives

The legal status of an archives is the strongest indicator of the probable future security of its holdings. Non-government organisations, businesses, families or individuals are much more vulnerable to market conditions and economic fluctuations than are government agencies. This vulnerability puts any archival holdings held by non-government archives at a greater risk than holdings within a government archives or a large, well-endowed collecting institution such as a State library or a major university.

How the archival institution will be governed and managed

The definitions of types of archives in Table 6.1 indicates where to begin any search for detailed information about the governance of any archives. When you think about the acquisition of government archives, it is clear that both the archives, and the agencies that create the archival materials, are part of the larger government organisation. In this sense government archives arguably fall within the in-house archives category. It seems that the main differences between these categories are governance and scale.

Government archives in Australia have specific publicly accessible legislation that defines their role and responsibilities. Some have advisory councils (e.g. National Archives of Australia) or councils with executive authority (e.g. State Records Council of South Australia) or Commissions (e.g. State Records Office of Western Australia) to which they must relate and which influence the performance of their responsibilities. But fundamentally, government archives are the managers of archival materials created by other arms of the same government. They need to be concerned more with the identification and documentation of archives to be preserved, than with whether the archives meet your scope criteria, or whether the donors are agreeable to your conditions about change of ownership, access and intellectual property issues.

In the government sphere, issues can be dealt with at the whole-of-government level and expressed in subordinate legislation or other regulatory form, leaving it for the government archives to administer and monitor the regulations. The scale of government archives activities is such that they are generally semi-autonomous agencies that have a tangible, separate identity.

Perspectives of recordkeeping illuminated by the records continuum model are increasingly being adopted. This renders recordkeeping practices more of a partnership between managers of current records and archivists than they once were. Acquisition and accessioning processes now tend to see archivists assisting records creators prepare archives for transfer in a more controlled and informed fashion, with records creators being more aware of the continuing life of materials in archival custody.

The scale and geographical jurisdiction of government archives has led to such innovations (informed by North American experience) as the State Records Authority of New South Wales' Regional Repositories network. It provides an example of communities of interesting acquisition practices that result in more regional public archives finding their way into State Government archival custody while still being locally accessible (Doubleday 2006, Logan & Boadle 2006).

In-house archives are also able to establish a corporate-wide archives acquisition policy that may be implemented in a fashion similar to that followed by most Government archives. The efficacy of the policy will depend on who approved it and on managerial will, influenced by the corporate value as perceived by a majority of the leaders within the wider organisation.

Riley (1997) proposes that integrating archival programs into the core business of independent schools presents strong evidence that such a process of integration would broaden the archives role within the eyes of all staff, both teaching and administrative. This integration would have a strong impact on a schools acquisition policy and practice, as well as on the way in which it fitted into the school's management structures.

Collecting archives differ widely from government and in-house archives in that they serve stakeholders outside of their institutional context. They do not usually acquire archival records from the body in which they operate. They establish the subject scope of their archival holdings in consultation with their sponsoring body, and they solicit records that match the scope of their collection. Their acquisition processes include:

- advertising their existence and services
- responding to organisations and individuals who would like the archive to accept their records into archival custody
- identifying record creators whose archives match their collection scope
- establishing contact with potential transferors to raise interest
- negotiating and documenting a gift or a purchase or possibly a loan of targeted archives.

Collecting archives are frequently part of cultural organisations that collect materials other than archives as their core business and in these instances often share technical services and managerial infrastructure. Collecting archives, as a group, include a significant proportion that exist with limited resources and are operated largely by volunteers.

A new type of collecting archives that prompts a review or re-interpretation of archival principles is the community archives. An example of a community archives is the indigenous archives characterised by efforts to draw together, among other records, copies of records that were produced by government and non-government agencies in the course of influencing the lives of aboriginal people. These collections tend to be based on specific language groups and have an objective of using technology to make the archives accessible to all members of the group in their daily lives so that they can add to, and interact with, the total archive (Huebner & Cooper 2007).

Scope, boundaries and limitations of the holdings

The scope of an archives will often be indicated by the function of the organisation that manages the holdings, as described in Table 6.1.

Although we expect that all holdings will be archives, or authentic records worthy of on-going preservation, descriptions of the holdings of some archives suggest that, on occasion, a wider definition than this, or an evolved practice, has been used. Such a wider definition or evolved practice has allowed the inclusion of, for example, publications and records where an unbroken chain of legitimate custody has not or cannot be established. Perhaps the acquisition policies of such archives provide information about these apparent anomalies. The description of the intended scope of holdings appearing in the acquisition policy should, in all cases, be as detailed as possible.

Government and in-house archives usually formalise the scope of their holdings by developing records disposal authorities that are based on the formal appraisal of the records or functions and activities of their parent bodies (see Chapter 5: *Appraisal & Disposal*).

In the hypothetical example provided below of the Nirvana District Council, the main limitations on scope are the geographical boundaries of the Council as they have been drawn during its history, and that the archives be non-government. This latter limitation indicates that the archives is a collecting archives sustained by a local government body, not a government archives. Collecting archives usually define their scope in terms of the general societal fields of activity that they wish to have represented in their holdings.

An example of scope for collecting personal records and notice of an extension to that scope appeared in the *2005/06 Annual Report of the National Archives of Australia Advisory Council:*

> *The archives' collection policy for personal records is to acquire the papers of a target group of people who have been closely associated with the Australian government in an official capacity.*
>
> *In November 2005, the Council approved the broadening of the target group of people from governors-general, prime ministers, deputy prime ministers, cabinet and other ministers, parliamentary secretaries, presidents of the Senate and House of Representatives to include ministers assisting, leaders and deputy leaders of the Opposition, leaders and deputy leaders of political parties, leaders of the Government and the Opposition in the Senate, Federal and High Court judges, and other persons who have made a significant contribution to the democratic leadership of the nation or otherwise have a close association with the Australian Government.*
>
> *This will ensure that valuable official records, as well as related private material that may complement the official record, are retained by the archives* (p.124).

This extension confirms this particular government archives as a combined archives, that is, an archives that acquires not only government archives but also private or personal archives using the same basic methods that a collecting archives does. Records produced by the same person will be identified as either official or personal and each category will be acquired using different processes and will be described in ways that reveal those differences.

School archives provide examples of archives that may start as in-house, taking only the school's administrative records into custody. They may then become combined archives when they fill the gaps in the in-house archival record by acquiring from old scholars or other members of the school community, gifts of private records that relate to the school and its activities. Gleaves and O'Neill (2003) provide a lively discussion of this process. They conclude by saying:

> *We are not dealing with just the evidential record, the non-personal, we are dealing with the history of education, of a community, of children. By conjoining the archives with the museum, and the administrative record with tangible evidence of students' lives, we are creating a living archives – the indefinable art of appraisal has a role here, not a hard and fast collection policy (*p.60).

A collecting archives is sometimes constrained in the breadth of its collecting by available resources. For this and other reasons, archivists find that in framing their acquisition policy, 'they are building social structures of remembering and forgetting' (McKemmish et al. 2005). That is, our acquisition policies determine what we will collect and therefore remember, and what we will not collect, and therefore forget. For whatever reasons, holdings will be representative and each collecting archives will consider the fields of activity from which to draw examples. It would be to the benefit of each to maintain an awareness of the holdings of other collections and, wherever possible, establish a 'community of practice' with them to, among other things, minimise any overlap in holdings and thus make the most of the overall available resources (McKemmish et al. 2005). Samuels (1992) has described this approach since 1986 as a documentation strategy:

> *The key elements of [which] … are an analysis of the universe to be documented, an understanding of the inherent documentary problems, and the formulation of a plan to ensure the adequate documentation of an ongoing issue or activity or geographic area. The strategy is designed, promoted and implemented by records creators, administrators (including archivists) and users. It is an ongoing cooperative effort by many institutions and individuals to ensure the archival retention of appropriate documentation through the application of redefined archival collecting policies, and the development of sufficient resources* (p.125–6).

Cunningham (1998) has been a long time advocate for the establishment of an Australian national documentation strategy. Examples of the application of both 'communities of practice' and 'documentation strategies' in the particular context of building collective memory archives are provided by Piggott (2005) when he reports that:

> *[c]ollecting institutions have reasonable understandings of each other's strengths and intents, and some have loose bilateral agreements. There is some evidence too that government archives are using 'place of deposit' powers to redistribute custody of series to more appropriate community settings …* (p.75).

The opposite of these collaborative approaches is the undesirable practice of archives competing with each other for the same material.

The fundamental principle for the acquisition policy is to include a clear statement of the subject, function and activity areas and any other salient characteristics of the records that the archives is to acquire.

Should we accept all that is offered?

The holdings of the archives are generally limited by the category that the archive falls within (government, in-house, collecting, combined, clearing-house or commercial) and by the subject scope of the holdings. There may be reasons other than these that militate against what material is to be accepted.

For example, are we going to accept or acquire three-dimensional material? If so, should we limit the size of individual items? Do we accept electronic archives? What about duplicates? Do we accept publications? How should we deal with extremely fragile or damaged or pest infested material? Are we going to impose any limits on the total quantity of our holdings? Will donor-imposed limits on granting access to the records they created, affect our decision to accept them?

Most of the questions reveal potentially expensive commitments that do not provide a benefit commensurate with the cost. The acquisition process is simplified when the archives has established policies to guide responses to such situations when they arise.

Let us consider a hypothetical collecting archives and see how the questions affect its acquisition policy.

A 1938 Australian cricket blazer, cap and tie are given to the archives of a school. The implications are many, despite a clear provenance and connection to the school. What about storage, cleaning, display and insurance?

CASE STUDY

The collecting archives is part of the Nirvana District Local History Collection, which is, in turn, part of a regional library run by the Nirvana District Council. The archives acquires the records that possess on-going value of non-government organisations, families and individuals – but not of the Council itself – and that are, or have been, located in, or associated with, the Council in activities within the boundaries of the Council. The Council has signed memoranda of understanding with all adjacent councils agreeing to discuss with them any negotiations they enter into with prospective entities who were located, lived or worked within localities that at some time in the past fell within the boundaries of the Nirvana District Council or its predecessor council/s.

Are we going to accept or acquire three-dimensional material? If so, should we limit the size of individual items?

We define a three-dimensional object as any object with a depth exceeding 10 centimetres. The archives will only acquire three-dimensional objects that are essential to the explanation and interpretation of other archival material being sought or already in custody, and such explanation or interpretation could not be adequately conveyed by photographs, or other visual recordings of the object's properties. Any such visual recordings will be produced by the archives at its expense on archival quality materials and documented and preserved in a way that ensures their authenticity and linkages to the archives to which they refer. The archives will suggest preferred possible custodians of excluded three-dimensional objects.

The hypothetical Nirvana District Council collecting archives, if it did exist, might well be influenced in making this policy by noting the practice of the University of Melbourne Archives that:

> *No archives ought to collect "related" non-archival material lightly. Indeed our own policy guidelines on this point states "we are an archive, not a library or museum (although we operate a support library), only in very exceptional circumstances will we take in non-archival material." [For example] the 1990s ... saw the archives hand over eight huge trade union banners to a better home at Melbourne museum, but where they continue to complement our extensive labour collection* (Piggott 2007).

Do we accept electronic archives?

The archives will accept electronic archives wherever possible on the understanding that:

- they will be adequately documented prior to acceptance (name/s of creator, date range of the archives, list of operating system/s, list of creating program applications, certification that any and all password or encryption protection has been removed, and a intelligible representation of the top two levels of any directory folders in which files have been saved)

- that the Council will check them for viruses (rejecting those that are infected)
- the Council will download them onto the Nirvana District Council's computer network archives server
- at some time in the future, who will convert them to the agreed digital archives format once that has been determined

The original medium and equipment (if included in the acquisition) on which the archive was stored will be preserved within the archives (notwithstanding the definition of three-dimensional objects) for as long as it is viable given the expenditure of no more than $500. When it is no longer viable the medium and or equipment will be disposed of in the most environmentally sustainable and cost efficient fashion that is practicable.

What about duplicates?

Check to ensure that what appears to be a duplicate is in fact one, because circumstances such as:

- copies of the same document placed in different contexts, or
- copies forming part of another document to which they are attached, or
- the inclusion of annotations on a copy may render each unique and therefore deserving of retention.

If these types of circumstances are not present, then only accept duplicates on the clear understanding that they will be sold with the proceeds going to the archives.

Do we accept publications?

Publications will be accepted only when they are:

- a product of the business of the creator of the records being transferred (and then only one clean copy of each)
- rare
- have been annotated to the degree that they constitute a record falling within the scope of the archives

A list of the publications owned or collected by the creator of the archives being donated, transferred or sold should be accepted.

Publications such as these may be included in an archival collection if they are rare, or have been annotated. These belonged to a school principal and were used as teaching aids; hence they contain many annotations about teaching practice, and pupils.

How should we deal with extremely fragile or damaged or infested material?

Fragile, damaged or infested material will be examined sufficiently to determine the significance of its contribution to the total body of archives held for that creator. A record will be made of the assessment and examination, and the items judged to be sufficiently whole and significant will be accepted and sent to the library's conservation laboratory for treatment. The assessment report will be referred to the achivist who will make the final decision as to what proportion of the residue will be returned to the creator.

Material which has accumulated prior to the development of a clear acquisition policy can include anything and everything.

Are we going to impose any limits on the total quantity of our holdings?

The holdings of the archives are limited only by the selection criteria and other related definitions and procedures detailed in its acquisition policy. The selection criteria and related definitions and procedures will be reviewed from time-to-time, but the results of any review will not be applied to material previously identified as archives. Council is committed to ensure that archival quality facilities will be provided for all archival materials acquired in accordance with its acquisition policy.

Can people have access to the holdings, and if so, under what conditions?

Archives will not be accepted if general public access is to be withheld for more than 50 years from date of acquisition. Access to the holdings will be granted in accordance with documented conditions agreed with whoever negotiated the acquisition with the archives. An acquisition agreement or Deed of Gift formalises the acquisition. See Appendix 6.2 and Appendix 6.3 for examples.

You should consider the questions raised in the case study in order to develop a clear policy on what will and will not be acquired by your archives. Best practice and current standards should also be consulted, for example standards and guidelines issued by State and National archives.

Ownership of items or holdings

The question of ownership is an issue for all archives, including in-house archives. Ownership status should be made clear from the outset and recorded.

There are some instances where individuals believe they own the intellectual property inherent in the records of their activities, even though they were employees of the parent body at the time the intellectual property was created. Such a situation may arise in the case of academic researchers working within universities. This example becomes even more complex if yet another party has provided funding for the research undertaken. It provides even more justification for any archives to have clearly documented policies about the ownership of archives that it will acquire, even when they appear to unquestionably be the property of the parent body.

The case of a collecting archives is different. It may have the custody of archives not only that it has purchased, but also that it holds on the basis of a gift or a short or long-term loan. Whatever the basis of the custody, it is essential that the receiving archives ensure that it is acquiring archives from the legitimate owner, or custodian, of those archives. The on-going authenticity of the archives is dependent upon preserving an unbroken chain of legitimate custody since the record was created, and evidence of this fact must be obtained, recorded and preserved.

The archives should clearly determine the legal ownership of records, as well as the ownership of any copyright or other rights inherent in the records. Additional rights are being recognised associated with records of, or about, indigenous people. Dr. Michael Ames, former Director of the University of British Columbia Museum of Anthropology, noted:

> *People are the artists or creators of their own histories and cultures and therefore also have, in essence, and should be granted in practice, exhibition and moral rights to their cultural representations. This "cultural copyright" or creative control should be recognised even though the photographer, filmmaker or archives may have legal possession of the images.*
>
> *Archivists handling ethnographic archival material must respect this cultural copyright and the meanings and values that aboriginal groups attach to these records* (Laszlo 2006, p.301)

Archives of all types are generally reluctant to accept material on loan (except possibly short-term loans for exhibition or similar purposes) because of matters such as:

- security
- valuation
- insurance
- the potential for disputes with the creators or their relatives or business partners at any time in the future ensuring that it does not expend scarce resources preserving archives that are ultimately reclaimed without reimbursement

If material is accepted on loan, the loan arrangements should be fully documented to safeguard all parties and the material.

Records of outsourced activities

The outsourcing of activities to a separate organisation, by an organisation that has ultimate responsibility for the outcome of those activities, presents a situation where the outsourcer needs to be very clear about the ownership, custody and use of any transactional records received or created by the contracted organisation in the course of providing the contracted service. Conditions concerning the ownership and custody of such records, must be included in any contract to protect the interests of the outsourcer and any of the clients of the outsourced service once the contract has been completed. All conditions applying to such an arrangement need to be known by any archives that may consider acquiring the records.

These many different aspects of 'ownership' must be clearly documented and signed by all interested parties with all parties retaining a copy of the documentation as discussed later in this chapter.

Methods of acquisition

Archives are either acquired by gift, bequest, purchase or loan in the case of collecting archives, or transferred from a current working environment into an in-house archives or a government archives.

The acquirer should have a very clear idea of the intended scope, boundaries and limitations of the archives. These factors contribute to the development of an acquisition program with targets for a given period. To fill any gaps in the holdings a strategy should be in place using the following:

- advertising
- exhibitions
- an attractive website
- cultural gifts programs
- fund-raising events
- friends organisations

It is important that the archives keep copies of all publicity and advertising calling for gifts as this material gives the donors their first impression of the arrangements applying to making a gift. It may be necessary, at some time in the future, for the archivist to modify false impressions and this can be done more easily when access to the original notice is available.

Not all transfers of material to archives involves this level of ceremony; recognition of the cultural significance of archives should not be taken lightly.

Even more targeted activities may be pursued, with particular regions, organisations and individuals being visited to inform them of the benefits of donating their archives to the collecting archives.

Such an approach requires substantial resourcing and may be pursued as a start-up activity only by smaller archives. Those archives with fewer resources may use newsletter articles to report on new acquisitions or publish short histories based on material acquired. They may establish a relationship with a local journalist who is willing to include articles in the media and they may offer to speak to interested or less obvious groups. They should also be aware of the role the World Wide Web can play in providing them access to people of interest. It is, however, important to manage expectations and ensure that prospective donors are aware of conditions that may apply to any gift that they may wish to make.

High quality, simple and attractive brochures are a minimal requirement for any acquisition program.

The in-house archives must ensure that all staff of the parent organisation are aware of their responsibilities when records are no longer needed for current business. This suggests that a regular training program be in place, and that it is important to communicate to staff how useful the archives has been to them and that the recordkeeping process is a continuum.

Documentation of acquisitions

This aspect of the acquisitions process is the most sensitive. It involves the relationship between you, the archivist, and the donor, or transferor. Completion of the Deed of Gift, or transfer documentation, will be achieved smoothly if you have developed a relationship of trust. You will have explained clearly all of the conditions that apply to the donation and all of their implications. You will have answered all questions openly and honestly. You will have alerted the donor to the cultural gifts program and to other archives that might be more appropriate as custodians of the archives. You are the archives as far as the donor or transferor is concerned, and future relationships between that person and the archives will be coloured by the relationship you have established. You will be assisted in this aspect of the acquisition process by being thoroughly familiar with the Code of Ethics of the Australian Society of Archivists (ASA 1993).

Whatever the method of acquisition, it is of paramount importance that full and complete records of each acquisition are created. These records contribute to the authenticity of the archives, and to the archives power to manage them as it sees fit. This power includes the right to dispose of holdings.

An example of the contents of a Deed of Gift can be seen in Appendix 6.2 and a copy of the template used by the State Library of South Australia is in Appendix 6.3.

It is important to note that records of each acquisition will be quite deficient if they do not include details of:

- the donor
- the records to be donated or transferred
- the transfer of ownership or licensing to the archives of any intellectual property and moral rights inherent in the archives
- any conditions that may apply to the use of, or accessibility to, the material

Both the donor and representative of the archives must sign the Deed as close to the time of the transaction as possible.

Every archives must maintain an acquisitions register that includes the date of transaction, a concise description sufficient to identify the consignment, and details of its source. Much of this data will be included in the accession register as the archives are incorporated into the system of control. The accessioning process is discussed in the next chapter.

De-accessioning policy and process

Essential to the acquisition policy are details of arrangements for disposing of, or de-accessioning, items from the holdings.

Collecting archives sometimes take material into custody before thorough examination. It is only following a thorough examination that material can be assessed as having met the criteria. In those cases where the criteria is not met, the archivist will offer the former owner or donor of the material an opportunity to take back any such material. If they decline to do so, the material may be destroyed or offered to another collecting organisation – these are options that may be included in the de-accessioning policy.

You will remember that the District Council of Nirvana's collecting archives had a policy for dealing with duplicate material that might be applied more generally. This policy stated, 'do not accept duplicates unless they are accepted on the clear understanding that they will be sold with the proceeds going to the archives.'

Some archives provide storage services for records that are not archival. For example, some records need to be kept for a number years to meet legal requirements but may be destroyed at a future date. The retention of these records should not be part of the de-accessioning process. It should be part of your appraisal and disposal program. Refer to Chapter 5: *Appraisal & Disposal* and Chapter 7: *Accessioning*.

Instances may also arise when an archives changes the scope of its acquisition policy. Its de-accessioning policy must enable it to negotiate the transfer of part of its holdings to another archives or collecting institution, or make some other arrangement.

Every archives must be extremely prudent when developing its de-accessioning policy for the obvious reason that few prospective donors are likely to trust their valued archives to an organisation that gives itself a very wide escape clause when it comes to fulfilling its prime responsibilities of preservation and use. It has been known for users of, and donors to, archives to become proprietorial about the holdings and for the donors and users to have much to say if they hear of any intentions to de-accession items. Providing details of the arrangements for de-accessioning, particularly at the time material is donated, should anticipate and mitigate any difficulties that may arise.

Review of holdings can be particularly difficult if items proposed for disposal have already been cited as sources in scholarly or published works and there is the likelihood that they may not be able to be located in the future. This is a reminder that the records of all de-accessioning must be kept because they also contribute to the provenance of any item.

Summary

This examination of factors that affect the acquisition process has demonstrated how they are each specific to any one archives and how they inter-relate to such a degree that acquisition policies for any two archives will never be the same.

The first basic step of identifying potential donors is influenced by what type of archives we are, and by the scope, boundaries and limitations of our holdings.

Establishing relationships with other archives will be affected by the intended scope of our holdings, the type of archives we are, any limitations that we put on the nature of archives that we will accept, how our archives is managed and possibly even our de-accessioning practices.

The process of approaching potential donors or exciting their interest is about promoting our services, objectives and the benefits our existence can contribute to a community and is influenced by the methods we decide to adopt in acquiring archives.

Advancing your relationship with a potential donor is perhaps the most demanding. It is influenced by all of the factors we have investigated, and our individual ability to establish a good working relationship with the donor. Above all, the donor must trust you and your archives. Knowing that you have a clear policy on all the influences that affect your archives, and therefore their records, will give them confidence in donating or transferring their records to you.

When you obtain a signed Deed of Gift you possess tangible evidence that you have achieved your goal. It remains only to work with your accessioning officer and the donor to finalise the agreed arrangements for the preparation of the archives for transfer, and for their actual movement to the archives.

Conclusion

When managed well the acquisition process contributes to:

- raising the profile of the archives among those who may contribute to its holdings
- achieving the intended scope of holdings of the archives in a balanced fashion
- establishing and maintaining a good relationship with donors or transferors of material
- cordial and mutually beneficial arrangements with other archival or collecting organisations that have mutual interests
- the accessioning process by providing good quality information about the former owner and creator of the archives and of the archives themselves
- the archives reference and access services by having a clear record of any limitations on the access and use of the archives
- minimising the volume of unwanted material being taken into custody

Good management of the acquisition process is built on creating and applying an acquisition policy, or collection development policy, that incorporates the factors examined in this chapter.

All staff should be familiar with the policy. It should also be widely available as it makes expectations and outcomes clear for all parties.

CHAPTER 7

accessioning

MAGGIE SHAPLEY

CHAPTER ABSTRACT

The process of gaining control over material which has been transferred to your archives is known as accessioning. Material that has previously been held by another person, organisation or institution, by part of your own organisation, or even by another archives, is now in your custody and is your responsibility. You need to control it, both intellectually and physically, to effectively manage its preservation and use. Accessioning involves surveying what has been received, entering information into an accession register and providing storage for the new accession. Accessioning procedures will vary for in-house and collecting archives and for particular formats. Records may also need to be de-accessioned.

This chapter gives you an overview of the nature and purpose of accessioning and details the information you should capture during the accessioning process. Some of the variations in practice suitable for different types of archives are also introduced. Sample forms are included on the accompanying CD.

What is accessioning?

Accessioning is the process of controlling records in your custody by gathering and recording information about them. You should accession all archives that are in your custody, whether you now own them or they are on deposit or long-term loan to your archives. The process of acquisition is the subject of Chapter 6, and relates to both the legal transfer of ownership and the custody of the material. Accessioning only takes place once acquisition has been completed and the records are in your custody.

Accessioning should be done as soon as possible after the transfer of custody, preferably on the same day. If left until a later date, there is the risk that the material will become intermingled with later transfers, or the records will be overlooked if some unexpected event occurs.

You will also want to assure the person transferring the records of your care for the material by confirming its arrival and raising any issues, such as missing files, promptly. This is part of a mutual obligation of archiving: you have received something of value, and have agreed to accept custody and to commit resources to its preservation and to making it accessible to researchers.

The basic steps involved in accessioning are:

- to conduct a preliminary survey of what has been received
- to record information about the material in a register
- to provide suitable storage for the material.

These steps may vary depending on the scale of the operations of the archives, the format of the material transferred and whether you are an in-house or collecting archives, but the documentation you produce in relation to the material will be basically the same. It will include:

- the allocation of a numbering system that you will use to link information about the records to the records themselves
- information about the provenance, content, format, date and condition of the records
- information about conditions of transfer, for example about access or disposal, particularly if verbal agreement has been reached which is not covered by a formal deed of gift
- information about the circumstances of the transfer: who was involved and when did it take place?

Accessioning is a necessary precursor to arrangement and description (see Chapter 8) and preservation (see Chapter 4) work. By gathering information at the time of accessioning, you are in a better position to prioritise arrangement and description and preservation work, so that resources are directed at those records most in need. Because both arrangement and description and preservation work require professional skills, and can be time-consuming activities, it is important to have this overview, which assists with resource allocation, based on the information the accessioning process provides. If you were to launch straight into arrangement and description work as transfers arrived, you would soon be overwhelmed by new transfers, and find yourself with a backlog of transfers without any basic information about what records were now in your custody.

Transfer procedures

Having step-by-step transfer procedures readily available, for instance on your website, makes your expectations known to potential depositors. You could specify that:

- you wish to survey the records in situ beforehand, where possible
- you wish to see a list of the material before agreeing to accept the transfer
- records be appraised using agreed disposal authorities
- records be packed in archives boxes
- records be provided in a particular electronic format or on a specific medium.

You may also want to indicate if you will supply the boxes, and whether you will arrange pick-up of the records or expect the depositor to engage a commercial transport company.

You may request the list as an electronic document so that you can reorganise it or amend it more easily.

As a result of articulating your expectations, you are more likely to receive organised, boxed and listed records, which will make the accessioning task much easier. There will, of course, be exceptional circumstances, when it will not be possible for a depositor to comply with your requirements. You may, for example, be dealing with an organisation which effectively no longer exists, or with a deceased estate. In this circumstance, you may need to be flexible about your transfer expectations.

Preliminary survey

'The most common fault is haste in dealing with archives, due to anxiety to make them available for use,' advised Sir Hilary Jenkinson (1965, p.84) and his advice is still valid.

When you first receive a transfer of records, it is tempting to dip into every box and rummage around to see what is there. This is the case particularly when you are receiving the records of someone famous, or infamous. If you do not have a list of what is to be transferred, you may just be curious to see what is there and whether it is likely to be valuable for research purposes.

The best survey method is to work systemically: start by checking that the number of boxes you have received corresponds to what was sent, using either the transport company receipt or the list the depositor has compiled. It is much easier to find a missing box while the trail is still warm, another reason to start as soon as you receive the records.

Is the transfer an addition to an existing accession? Have you received records from the depositor before? If so, you will need to check the documentation for that accession so that you can assess whether the records are related. You may, for instance, have now received minute books for later years that are part of the same series as those already in your custody.

You should start your survey with the first box and look in every box. You should not unpack all the boxes at once, but work on one box at a time, keeping the contents of each box together. Always resist the urge to reorganise records into what may appear to be their proper order until you have at least surveyed every box. You will then have gathered the information you need, and the list or information which makes sense of it all may well be in the last box. In fact, it is always worth checking the last box for the list, as the depositor may have checked the contents box by box and, when finished, put the list in the last box.

If you have a list compiled by the depositor, keep the original on your file and use a copy to mark off the records received. Take notes as you go through the contents of the boxes. You will be looking for labels and markings on boxes, file covers and other containers.

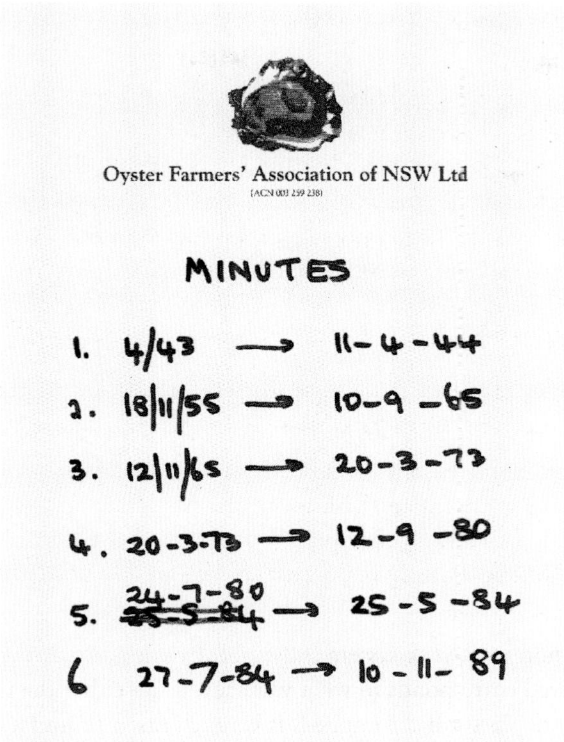
Oyster Farmers' Association of NSW Ltd
(ACN 003 259 238)

MINUTES

1. 4/43 → 11-4-44
2. 18/11/55 → 10-9-65
3. 12/11/65 → 20-3-73
4. 20-3-73 → 12-9-80
5. ~~25-5-84~~ 24-7-80 → 25-5-84
6 27-7-84 → 10-11-89

A basic list compiled by the depositor will help you to complete the Accession Register but you should check it first against the records.

The main things you need to confirm from your survey are the:

- provenance, that is, who created the records
- format and condition of the material
- date range of the material

You will need to use your judgement about how much time to spend on the survey. For a large well-organised collection, you may spend less than an hour if it is literally a matter of checking off files against an existing list. If files are missing (or there are additional files not on the list), you need to amend the list and alert the depositor. When requests are received in the future, it should be clear which files were never received, rather than it being suspected that you have lost them.

Surveying a large disorganised collection will take longer, as you will be gathering information with a future arrangement and description project in mind.. For small accessions, the survey may only take a few minutes, but you may choose to spend longer in order to complete the arrangement and description of the collection at the same time. See Chapter 8: *Arrangement & Description* for information on the process of arrangement and description.

You would expect to complete the survey on the same day you receive the records so that within 24 hours of receiving records, you have enough information to complete the accession register and can organise and record the location of the records.

> It is important to assign an accession number and create at least minimal accession documentation the day the records are received. Despite the best of intentions, you don't know what might happen to prevent you getting back to complete the job – and the last thing your successor wants is to have to try and find out what this 'stuff' is when the trail has gone cold. This is true of the largest and smallest deposits.

Provenance

Determining the provenance, or who created the records, is an important step. Whatever the person transferring the records to you may say, you should confirm the provenance from the records themselves. It is easy to assume that the records from someone's office or transferred by a particular company or organisation are created by them, but they may not be, and the person transferring them may not actually know whose records they are.

The creator of the records is the person or organisation who made the records, either by writing them or receiving them, and who has gathered them together into a system, such as receiving correspondence and placing it on a file. Within 'their' files, there will be letters written by other people that they have received and filed, as well as drafts or copies of letters they have written and sent to others.

The person transferring the records, the depositor, is not necessarily the creator of the records, but could just have temporary custody of them. For instance, the depositor may be the spouse or child of the creator. In an institution, the depositor may be the records section, but the creator may be another section. Alternatively, the depositor may be the organisation which has succeeded the creating organisation.

The provenance of records should not be confused with what the records are about. Records may be referred to as, for instance, the 'Florey Archives' but actually be records *about* Florey rather than records created *by* him.

Important clues as to who created the records are:

- if there are original letters or emails in the records, who are they addressed to?
- whose signature block appears on copies of letters or emails sent?
- if there is a distribution list on a document, whose name is ticked or underlined?
- whose handwriting appears as notes on reports or correspondence?

The creator of the records will not necessarily sign the copies they retain of the letters they have sent, or identify themselves in their personal diary. Remember too that records can be 'inherited', by people in the same family, by people doing the same job and by successor organisations and companies.

You need to check labels on files, boxes, suitcases or any other packaging, and also note the date of the material – you may need to do some basic research to find out who the secretary was at the time or the name of a predecessor organisation.

If the records are of mixed provenance, it is preferable, if possible, to accession the records of each provenance separately, that is, to physically separate the records and allocate separate accession numbers. If the records are too disorganised to do this easily, then note the separate provenances and the need to do this work later.

Format and condition

Simple terms like 'Papers' or 'Records' can cover a number of formats, so it is more useful to refer to formats such as 'minute books, subject files, and cassette tapes'. Until the collection is arranged and described, this level of information will help someone wanting to locate a set of photo albums (not included) or a recording of a conference (possibly included). It will also highlight where special storage may be needed, and help when prioritising arrangement and description jobs.

You should record any observations that will assist in quantifying future arrangement and description required, such as 'material in box 1 appears to be same series as boxes 7 to 9' or 'photographs in boxes 4 and 5 unsorted and uncaptioned' or 'file register included in last box'.

You should also record notes about any conservation concerns or possible disposal action. You might decide to rebox the collection if the present containers were falling apart or awkward to lift. Before you dispose of any original packaging material, such as boxes or wrapping paper, record any information such as any attached labels or lists, either by transcribing the information or taking a photocopy.

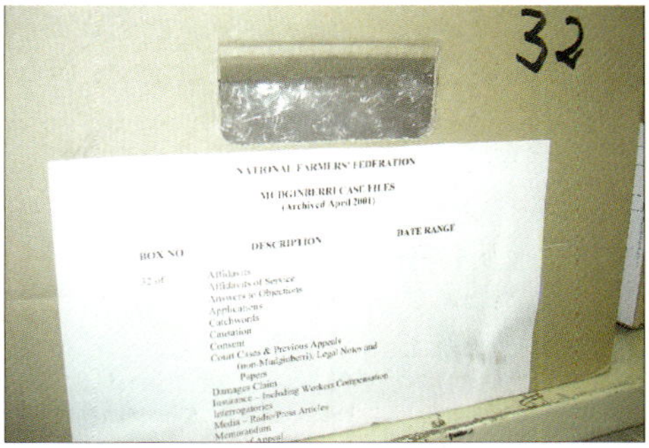

Record any information on the original boxes before discarding them.

If it is within the conditions agreed with the depositor, you might immediately dispose of duplicate copies of publications or isolate material which would contaminate other records (such as records that are affected by active mould) for separate storage or disposal, depending on its value.

Date range

At this stage, you may only be able to record an estimated date range based on your brief survey of the records. If the date range seems to contradict the provenance (from what you know about the organisation's history or the person's career), consider the possibility of 'inherited' records. Technically, an individual or organisation cannot create records after they have ceased to exist, so you may find that part of the collection has a different provenance.

Some records are hard to date, such as subject files and index cards, but any date range is better than none at all. Even a range of decades will help others, who do not have ready access to the records themselves, in the future. Even if you are only able to ascertain that records date from the 1950s to the 1990s, this will assist someone wanting records from the 1920s because they can save themselves a fruitless search.

The depositor, the Maritime Union of Australia, has provided a basic box list for records of the Newcastle Branch:

Box 1: Minutes

Box 2: Minutes and conference papers

When you look through the first box, you find a run of minute books clearly labelled 'Minutes of the Executive Committee' and another set labelled 'Annual General Meetings' so you note the format as minute books (to distinguish them from loose copies of minutes) and that there are separate series recording the two different types of meetings. You see from the headings to each set of minutes that they are meetings of a predecessor to the Maritime Union, the Seaman's Union. You check the front of each volume to find the earliest date for each set, and then the last entry of the most recent volumes to record the end dates, and note that these dates predate the existence of the Maritime Union so both sets can be attributed to the Seaman's Union..

In the second box you find more minute books, labelled 'Annual General Meetings' and assume they are the same as those you saw in the first box. However, you resist the urge to organise the records into what seems to be their obvious order. You check the headings in the minute books and find that they are, in fact, minutes of meetings of the Waterside Workers Federation, another predecessor union to the Maritime Union.

One minute book does not record the name of the Waterside Workers Federation but its placement with the others, fitting into a chronological run, and the fact that some of the office bearers are the same as in the previous book, confirm that it is part of the same series.

Also in the second box are some files which all have titles beginning 'Annual Conference'. You ascertain from a spot check that they all date from the 1980s and the carbon copies of letters on file have the signature block: 'Organising Committee, WWF (Newcastle)'. There are three cassette tapes, labelled '1985 Future Directions Conference' and you check back to the file titles to see that several files are labelled in the same way.

Following the survey you now have enough information to accession the records and a box list which provides improved information about the contents of the boxes:

Box 1

Seaman's Union, Newcastle Branch, Minute books of the Executive Committee, 1961–1985

Seaman's Union, Newcastle Branch, Minute books of Annual General Meetings, 1970–1985

Box 2

Waterside Workers Federation, Newcastle Branch, Minute books of Annual General Meetings, 1982–1990

Waterside Workers Federation, Newcastle Branch, Correspondence files of organising committee for annual conferences, 1980s

Waterside Workers Federation, Newcastle Branch, Cassette tapes of Future Directions conference, 1985

On the basis of this information you are able to complete two separate accession records in the Accession Register, noting that each box was received from the Maritime Union but recording the correct provenance, the predecessor union, for each one.

Figure 7.1: A typical survey

Accession register

An accession register is an essential component of the process, whether you are an in-house or collecting archives, or whether you are a large institution or a one-man band. The accession register is where you record:

- details of the transfer process
- information you have gathered from your survey
- plans for subsequent action on the records.

The entries in an accession register will be chronological in a numerical sequence. In other words, as records are received you will record the date of receipt (and other information) against the next available accession number.

The accession register can be hard-copy, such as sturdy book or binder (hard cover is best – it will be handled on a regular basis) or an online database or spreadsheet. Whatever format it is, it will be a 'vital record' of the archives and should be copied and backed up regularly. The back-up copy should be held in another building.

If you have a hard-copy register, it is preferable to have pre-printed blank forms or columns rather than a completely blank book, so that you are prompted to provide particular information. It is also preferable to allocate accession numbers to the blank pages before they are filled in so that the possibility of allocating the same number twice is eliminated.

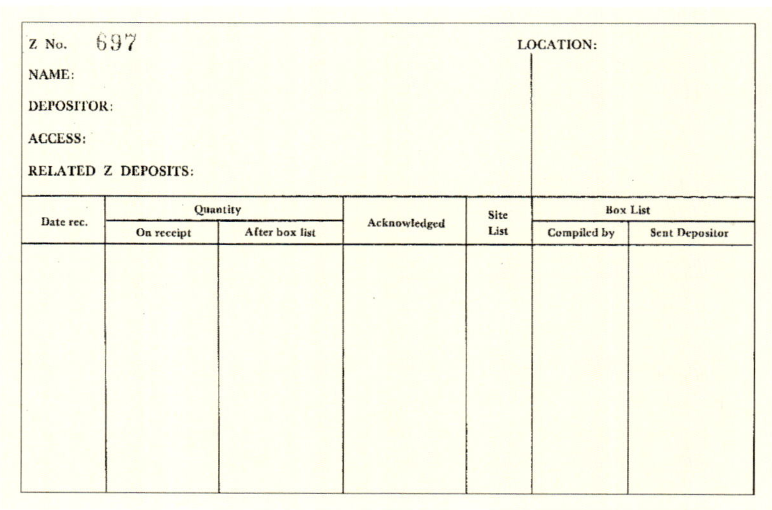

Z No. 697

LOCATION:

NAME:

DEPOSITOR:

ACCESS:

RELATED Z DEPOSITS:

Date rec.	Quantity		Acknowledged	Site List	Box List	
	On receipt	After box list			Compiled by	Sent Depositor

In a hard-copy accession register use pre-printed forms to prompt for the information needed.

The rule is then that you must complete the blank form in order to 'take' the number for the material. The practice of reserving numbers for future transfers should be discouraged – the allocation of a number should depend on the transfer having actually taken place and the accession register being completed with all relevant information.

If your accession register is an online spreadsheet, you can set up columns with inbuilt formatting to record the information in standard ways, such as dates in the format dd/mm/yyyy or dropdown menus to restrict entries to 'Yes' or 'No'.

If the accession register is part of a database, you can verify entries against established business rules (for instance, 'entry must be numeric') and also specify mandatory fields to make sure important information is recorded. There should be a number of mandatory fields which must be completed in order to be allocated the accession number.

Whether hard-copy or online, it is important that the accession register gives a complete history of the accessioning process. Subsequent additions should not replace the original entries (you may need to take steps to ensure that, in an online system, superseded data is not deleted but is moved to a separate field or record, so that you keep the history of the documentation). For instance, if a collection is de-accessioned in the future, the original entry should remain and a note be added to record whether the accession was destroyed, returned or transferred elsewhere, rather than the whole entry deleted. In the future, the question may arise as to whether you have a particular collection (it may have been cited in a publication) and your accession register entry will verify its whereabouts.

Similarly, if the quantity received either increases or decreases when reboxed (the boxes may be less tightly packed or records may be disposed of), the information that 10 boxes were originally received should not be deleted, but a note added to indicate that, after reboxing, there are now 9 or 11 boxes.

The printed forms, online spreadsheet columns or database fields should include the following headings which are explained in detail below:

- accession number
- date of receipt
- depositor
- creator
- format or description
- date range of records
- related records
- quantity on receipt
- conditions of access or disposal
- location
- name of archivist recording information
- date information recorded.

To record subsequent action, you may have a series of check boxes or have the following headings against which the archivist may note the date tasks are completed, or select 'Yes' or 'Completed':

- transfer acknowledged
- new or amended list sent
- recommendations for arrangement and description, disposal, conservation
- action taken on arrangement and description, disposal, conservation
- quantity after reboxing
- updating list of holdings and other finding aids
- updating location register
- promoting collection.

Accession number

An accession number is allocated to a consignment of records received at the same time and with the same provenance. In some archives, the accession number becomes the archival control number – the number which appears on the boxes, on the items, and in finding aids. In other archives, particularly those dealing with many large transfers, it is an

Accession number	Date of receipt	Depositor	Creator	Format	Date range
2008/1	04/01/2008	Sue Smith, Maritime Union of Australia, 9677 4333	Seaman's Union, Newcastle Branch	Minute books	1961-1985
2008/2	04/01/2008	Sue Smith, Maritime Union of Australia, 9677 4333	Waterside Workers Federation, Newcastle Branch	Minute books, conference files and cassette tapes	1982-1990
2008/3	06/01/2008	Helen Johnson, Dieticians Australia, 6352 5889	Dieticians Australia	Master set of publications	1920-2005
2008/4					
2008/5					
2008/6					
2008/7					

Table 7.1: Accession register

interim control and only used on the boxes for location purposes until the collection has been arranged and described, and the series within the accession have been identified and allocated formal series numbers.

What sort of numbers should be used? A common option where accession numbers are used for interim control is to use an annual single number: the first accession for 2008 would be 2008/1. This has the advantage of revealing which year the accessioning took place and the single number will not get too long to remember, as it will start again for the next year.

Another option, particularly if your accession number will become the archival control number, is to allocate single numbers with an alphabetical prefix identifying your archives, for example, NUA 58 to indicate the 58th accession of the National University Archives.

An alternative is to have a distinctive alphabetical prefix for particular parts of your archives. For example, all accessions in the HIV/AIDS collection at the Noel Butlin Archives Centre have an H prefix. If you operate this system you will need separate accession registers for each part.

A word of warning: if you allocate alphabetical prefixes based on names that could change over time, you may be faced with renumbering your boxes or always explaining that 'H'

Related records	Qty (m)	Qty (box)	Conditions of transfer	Location	Archivist	Date recorded
None	0.2	1	Access must be requested	A278/3/1	MS	05/01/2008
None	0.2	1	Access must be requested	Processing shelf 4	MS	05/01/2008
2001/20, Annual reports, 1950-66	1.2	4	Open access, may dispose of duplicates	Processing shelf 5	MA	06/01/2008

stands for 'Headmaster' so the records of the Principal (who is now known as the Chief Executive Officer) are all H accessions. Alphabetical prefixes do not have to stand for a particular word. The National Archives series prefixes, for example, indicate the State Office that first registered the series: where A=ACT, B=Victoria, C=New South Wales etc. (this system was set up before centralised online registration was possible).

Control numbers will be cited by researchers in publications, so you will not want to change them once the records have been used and cited. Some archives use temporary accession numbers in the expectation that by the time the records are available for public access (for example, if they allow access to records after 30 years), the records will have been arranged and described and new series numbers allocated, and these will be the numbers cited by researchers.

Date of receipt

Record the actual date the records were received.

Depositor

Record the name of the person organising the transfer, their position or affiliation within an organisation and contact details such as email address and phone number.

Creator

As discussed above, this is the provenance of the records. It will be the person or body which accumulated the records. It may or may not be the same as the depositor. For instance, the depositor may be a particular person who works in an organisation, and

Accession number	Transfer acknowledged	New list sent	Processing required	Processing completed
2008/1	09/01/2008	09/01/2008	None	09/01/2008
2008/2	09/01/2008	09/01/2008	List files and tapes, copy tapes	
2008/3	06/01/2008	No	Identify duplicates, including annual reports in 2001/20, compile new list	
2008/4				
2008/5				
2008/6				
2008/7				

Table 7.2: Accession register (continued)

the creator is the organisation itself, or the depositor may be the surviving spouse or child of the person who created the records. For in-house archives, it is better to identify the particular department or division as the creator, rather than just the institution or company.

If the records are of mixed provenance, and too disorganised to separate easily, then note all creators identified and note the need to do this work in 'recommendations for arrangement and description'.

Format or description

Record here the information collected in your survey about format and content, including the identification of formats requiring special storage such as photographs and audiovisual material.

Date range of records

Also discussed above, you will be estimating a date range (years only).

Related records

It is useful to note any previous accessions that may contain similar material. This may also be a trigger to arrange and describe this accession together with an earlier accession.

Quantity on receipt

Two components are advisable – a count of boxes or other containers (e.g. 'two cartons, one suitcase and a large hatbox') and the amount of shelving that is taken up (e.g. 'two

New qty (m)	New qty (box)	List of holdings updated	RAAM	Location register	Archives news
0.2	1	12/01/2008		12/01/2008	

shelf metres'). The first measure helps to confirm what was received, in case a container is lost in transit, and the second gives a more accurate measure for management purposes, such as allocating space or arrangement and description work. If the collection is reboxed in the accessioning process this should be recorded ('two cartons, one suitcase and a large hatbox, reboxed to 10 archives boxes').

Conditions of access or disposal

There may be legislation or a formal legal instrument, such as a Deed of Gift governing the transfer of custody and ownership, which you should record here. You may also have noted that the accession includes personnel files which contain private information, or that there are photographs of indigenous people which may need to be restricted. The depositor may have indicated a particularly sensitive issue, suggesting a restriction to public access for a period of time. You may wish to record the applicable disposal authority or class that has been used to sentence the records, or record that the depositor has agreed that duplicates may be destroyed.

Location

Record the repository location for the accession, including any separate or special storage. You should record the location as soon as the material arrives, even if it is temporary (such as 'holding shelf 4'). It is very easy to lose material in an archives repository if it is in an anonymous archives box. You should record its final repository location by row, bay and shelf number or description (such as 'Repository B, Row 302, Bay 3, Shelf 2', or 'Map Cabinet 6, Drawer 3, or Processing Shelves, Bays 1 – 2').

Name of archivist recording information

It is good practice to identify who is completing the register, either through automatic capture of the login code of the archivist entering the information, entering a name, or by staff initialling entries if the register is in hard copy. The information recorded in the accession register will be relied on well into the future, and it is sometimes pertinent to know who recorded the information.

Date information recorded

This may be implicit in other entries or automatically captured in a database but it is worth recording separately if you are accessioning a backlog of uncontrolled records. It indicates if there has been a significant time delay between receipt and accessioning and that the person completing the register may not have been personally involved in the transfer.

Date transfer acknowledged

Record the date when you confirmed to the depositor that you received the material and identified any missing or additional material.

Date new or amended list sent

Record the date you sent the depositor an amended or new list. This may be at the same time as the acknowledgement was sent, or later when all arrangement and description is completed.

Recommendations for arrangement and description, disposal, conservation

You will have gathered this information in your survey and it will assist in the prioritising of the arrangement and description of this accession against others.

Action taken on arrangement and description, disposal, conservation

This may simply be recorded as 'completed' or may indicate progress, such as particular items undergoing conservation treatment or separate storage arranged for vulnerable material.

Quantity after reboxing

Recording the quantity after reboxing will clarify any discrepancies between what was received and what you now have. The quantity disposed of may also be recorded. Recording both the number of metres and the number of boxes is advisable.

Updating list of holdings

This is a trigger, if needed, to ensure that the new accession appears in your online list of holdings. This may be automatic in a database or it may require a deliberate action after ensuring that the information about the records can be made available to the public. You may also need to update online or hard-copy subject guides.

If your archives contributes to other finding aids, such as the Register of Australian Archives and Manuscripts (www.nla.gov.au/raam), or the Australian Trade Union Archives website (www.atua.org.au), you may need additional prompts for these. In a database, the identification of photographs or pictorial material as a format may trigger a prompt to consider the potential of the material for inclusion in Picture Australia (www.pictureaustralia.org) or other online image collections.

Updating location register

This is likely to be automatic in a database, but if you maintain a separate location register or other space control system, you will need to update it to indicate that empty shelves are now inhabited by the new accession.

Promoting collection

This is a reminder to advertise the new accession in your online or email newsletter, on your website, directly to relevant user groups, or to the archival community (for example, in News Notes in *Archives and Manuscripts*).

Providing suitable storage

Having completed as much as you can in the accession register, you now need to provide suitable storage for the accession. Records are more vulnerable to damage and loss if they are left on a pallet, on the floor or on a spare desk. The term 'suitable storage' refers to every layer of protection between the records and the elements, and should be appropriate to the format and condition of the records. These may include:

- folders, wallets or boxes to protect and contain loose material
- archives boxes, preferably acid-free, to replace unsuitable boxes (if they are too heavy to lift safely, falling apart, made of unsuitable material or previously used for food storage)
- shelving, map cabinets, or racks
- secure, climate-controlled repository space.

See Chapter 3: *Buildings & Storage* for more information about appropriate storage.

At this stage, you may have recorded recommendations for improved storage (such as 'all tapes to be rewound' or 'maps to be flattened and placed in map cabinets') or you may take action immediately if the condition of the material is such that urgent action is required.

The accession number should be recorded on every box: either written, stamped or printed on box labels. For the security of the records, it is preferable not to add other information to the box, such as the name of the creator, the contents and particularly not the access status. This information is available in the accession register for those authorised to see it, and the accession number provides the link to this information.

Archives can arrive in a variety of boxes – replace any boxes which have been used for food as they will attract insects and rodents.

A new accession ready to be located in the repository

Some archives also stamp or write the accession number in pencil on each item in a consistent place, such as on the back of the file cover in the top left-hand corner. If the accession number is a temporary control, pencil is preferable. If it is likely that arrangement and description work will be completed before the records will be available for public access, you may prefer to annotate items with their final archival control number at a later date.

Having documented the records, placed them in boxes bearing their new accession number, and located them in an appropriate space, there is a vital final step – recording the location in the accession register. Without this information the records will be effectively 'lost in space'. Even temporary locations should be recorded on the basis that this may become longer than planned.

> It's a good idea to develop a standard location naming system that is flexible, extensible and brief. You can start by assigning a number (or a letter) to each of your storage rooms or repositories (e.g. A, B, C... or 1, 2, 3...). Then, within each room or repository, assign a number to each row of shelving. If a row is double-sided, i.e. back-to-back, treat each side as a separate row (e.g. 1, 2, 3... numbers are recommended, as you may have more than 26 rows). You can combine the room number and the row number, if you like, simply by numbering the rows in one room as 101, 102, 103... and the rows in the next room as 201, 201, 203...

Accessioning for in-house versus collecting archives

Where the archives and the depositor are part of the same organisation, transfers can be planned. A regular, perhaps annual, cycle of transfer can be set up for records that are produced regularly, such as board minutes. An in-house archives is also likely to know when sections of the organisation are restructured or are planning to move premises, and can be proactive in organising transfers. Archives staff can survey records in situ, and gather information about the records from the staff who create and manage them, before they are transferred. Staff members may be asked to apply disposal schedules and only transfer records of continuing value to the archives. Archives storage boxes can be supplied and forms or electronic templates provided so that the transfer is accompanied by the information required for accessioning. The list can be extracted from the records management system, to which both the depositor and the archives have access.

In short, accessioning should be a routine process for an in-house archives, but there can also be unexpected transfers which arrive from branch offices, and unplanned events which result in unplanned accessioning. If there is a records management area separate from the archives, the in-house archivist would be well advised to establish good relations with the records management staff so that the archives becomes an integral part of the records management process.

No matter how well defined your collecting policy may be, it will be impossible for a collecting archives to plan accessioning activity in the same way that an in-house archives can, because of the range of circumstances that can trigger an offer of material to your archives. It may be a death in the family, a retirement, a sea-change or downsizing, a company takeover, a bankruptcy or just a spring-clean.

This is all the more reason to have an organised process where all relevant information can be collected and the transfer can take place quickly and efficiently. It is important that your collection policy is readily available, preferably on your website, as well as your transfer procedures, so that depositors know your expectations. For collecting archives, the provenance is more likely to be unclear, the material more likely to arrive in non-standard boxes and the records not be listed. The survey may therefore also act to confirm that the accession does fall within your collecting policy and may also be used to identify the extent of appraisal which needs to take place.

Dealing with an accessioning backlog

If you accession material as it comes in, a backlog will not develop, but you may have inherited a backlog if you are the first archivist appointed to an organisation or if the archives has not been staffed for a period of time. Getting basic control over the material will be one of your priority tasks if you have a quantity of material which has never been accessioned. While it remains unaccessioned, it will not be evident in finding aids and will be effectively hidden from view in the management of the archives (though physically may be quite obvious). Once the backlog is accessioned, you will have data on record creators and the quantity of material that requires arrangement, and description work to argue a case for additional resources or to schedule the work over a period of time.

When dealing with pallets or shelves (or even piles) of unaccessioned material, you will be undertaking the same accessioning steps outlined above, except that as part of the survey you will be trying to identify which records were transferred at the same time; that is, the separate accessions that make up the total backlog. You will be noting if there are similar boxes bearing similar markings and labels which indicate this, and physically separating the material on this basis. You will also be seeking out any accompanying paperwork which may indicate the number of boxes in any particular transfer. You should then register each accession separately, using any information recorded on packing slips or labels to determine the date of transfer. If a date of transfer cannot be assigned, record the date in relation to the current date; for example, 'before 2008' rather than 'unknown'. You should record the date you are recording the information so that it is clear you are accessioning retrospectively, and not at the time of transfer.

Accessioning for small archives

As a small archives, you need to be realistic about the likelihood of further arrangement and description work once the material is accessioned. Particularly if you are a one-man band, you need to assess whether you can realistically expect to tackle an arrangement and description backlog if you are already fully occupied with reference enquiries and taking in new accessions.

Consider whether you need the interim control of an accession number. If you will only have this one opportunity to document the collection as it comes in (and no prospect of further arrangement and description work in the future), you may prefer to allocate series numbers straight away, based on an initial assessment of provenance, and undertake arrangement and description work and reboxing at the time of accessioning.

It is better to have basic control over all of your collection through accessioning than to have complete item lists for a fraction of your collection and no control over the rest. If you have limited resources, accessioning is not an optional extra, but you will be trying to get the best value possible out of the limited time you can devote to it by collecting and recording as much information as possible about the records from your preliminary survey.

As a small collecting archives, you should consider whether there are formats which would be too time-consuming or resource-intensive for you to collect. You may for instance choose not to accession electronic archives or audiovisual records on economic grounds because of the technical infrastructure needed to manage these formats over time.

Accessioning different formats

Electronic archives

In a well-designed electronic recordkeeping system, the information needed for accessioning, such as provenance, will already be recorded as metadata and will be accessible before transfer. A list of records for transfer to the archives, based on the disposal sentence 'Retain as archives', for instance, can be generated and the transfer of custody from the creator to the archives may take place automatically at an agreed time, with the 'accession register' entries being automatically generated by the metadata attached to the records. At this stage, only in-house archives are likely to receive electronic archives in this way.

For most archives, transfers of electronic archives are still exceptional, with most transfers being hard-copy records. In practice, this means adapting accessioning procedures developed for hard-copy records to accommodate electronic archives.

The intangible nature of electronic records means that you need to pay extra attention to gathering all the information you need at the time of accessioning. This is particularly the case where you are using a third party to store and manage the material in a digital repository until it is available for access. With hard-copy records, you can always easily check again if you have forgotten to record a date or other information, but you may not have ready access to your electronic accessions.

Surveying electronic records can be simplified if you are able to manipulate files, such as sort a collection of email by date sent or received to record the date range. Similarly, you can easily record the names of correspondents by sorting on 'sender'. Electronic records can provide less opportunity for browsing when undertaking your preliminary survey so you need to consciously open files to browse and collect the information you need about their content.

When recording quantity, it should be meaningful for both researchers (the number of files or documents) and for data storage requirements (the number of megabytes). You may need to record additional information about format, software and media in your accession register. Directories of data file formats and software can be used to identify the application used to create a record and assess its stability, for example, PRONOM at the UK National Archives. If electronic records have been converted to a standard format for transfer, then this should be noted in the accession register, recording the original format and detailing what checks have been undertaken to ensure that all data has been successfully converted.

If you receive electronic documents on unstable formats such as CDs or USBs, then you need to firstly appraise the records for retention. It is not uncommon for the contents of the electronic copy to be already printed out in hard copy and included in the same transfer of records. You will then need to assess whether there is an advantage in maintaining the records in electronic format over the hard-copy format. You may decide that the hard copy is sufficient and the electronic copy can be discarded. But if you decide that there is benefit in keeping an electronic copy, then it will be part of your recommendations for storage that the information is transferred from the electronic media to a digital repository.

In the same way that you record physical location for hard-copy records, you need to record the location of your electronic accession in the accession register. If electronic archives are to be stored on a central server or digital repository maintained by the information technology area, it is advisable to develop a quarantined directory structure for the electronic archives, and file-naming conventions, so that the archives can be easily identified and retrieved when needed for access by researchers.

Maps

If maps are tightly rolled, you will need to humidify them to flatten them, so that you can collect information about them. There is little point accessioning rolled-up maps without any information about what places they record, when they were made, and whether they are originals or printed copies. Leaving them rolled up makes them vulnerable to damage if members of staff, having already checked the uninformative accession record, attempt to unroll them in uncontrolled conditions to find out what they are.

Maps should be flattened under controlled conditions to allow accessioning and prevent future damage.

Audiovisual material

Accessioning audiovisual material involves immediate action to ensure their preservation by storing them correctly. For example, tape reels should be stored upright rather than flat and away from magnetic fields. The existence of audiovisual material should always be noted under 'format', so that arrangement and description can be prioritised.

Photographs

If photographs are stored inappropriately, such as in sticky, so-called magnetic, albums, note this on the accession record so that they can be rehoused promptly. It will be beneficial to maintain contact with the depositor or long-serving staff member, who may be able to assist with identifying uncaptioned photographs.

Textiles

Textiles, in the form of trade samples, banners, and uniforms, are often found in archives. Because of the possibility of insect infestation, it is wise to segregate textiles and have them professionally cleaned before adding them to your collection.

Objects

When accessioning objects, or indeed any non-standard format, you might consider whether the object is in fact a record and whether your archives is the appropriate repository for it. It may be that there are museums which collect similar objects (or no longer collect them because they are commonplace) or that the object will require special conservation treatment, which you are unable to provide. Often, 'historical' objects are sent to the archives as a last resort, but you need to consider whether they are within your responsibility, that is, identified in your collecting policy.

The decision to accession objects may be a political rather than an archival one if you are an in-house archives and there is no other option. You may also consider the display value of objects, or their role in explaining recordkeeping processes, such as a letterpress or a company seal.

De-accessioning

De-accessioning is the process of removing material from your archives and can be the result of:

- changes in your collecting policy or the recommended disposal action for particular types of records
- reappraisal of the collection against the existing collection policy or disposal schedules be (see Chapter 5: *Appraisal & Disposal* for advice on appraisal)
- disposal of records whose condition makes them unusable, such as magnetic tapes or floppy disks which are unreadable
- return of misappropriated material or long-term loans
- closure of the archives.

Before de-accessioning material, you need to ensure that you have the authority to do so. Refer to your collection policy, which may define the circumstances under which material may be de-accessioned and the manner in which it may be done (for example, by destruction, transfer to another archives or by sale). You need to also check the conditions of the original transfer for that particular accession, as it may have been agreed at that time that the archives would offer the material back to the depositor or, if the material was received under the cultural gifts program, you may need to report your intended action. Your organisation's policy on disposal of assets may also apply and require you to value the material and dispose of it in a particular manner.

De-accessioning should be documented in the original accession register, but changes should be made without removing the original entry. In a manual register, you might strike through the whole entry so that it can still be read and annotate it to show the new custodian, or indicate that the records have been destroyed or returned. It should still be clear from the accession register which records were at one time held under that accession number. To prevent confusion in the future, the number should not be reused.

You will need to find and remove all references to the accession number in your finding aids, and internal management systems, such as the location register. You will also need to update any websites where the accession is referred to, both on your own and on any collaborative sites, such as the Register of Australian Archives and Manuscripts. It is also worthwhile doing a general internet search, as the material may be referred to on websites of historical and genealogical societies. If the material is going to another archives, you or the receiving archives may wish to alert users and other archives to the transfer, through relevant newsletters and listservs.

If the material is being transferred to another archives, it is good practice to provide copies of all documentation relating to the accession to the new custodian; for example, copies of correspondence with the original depositor, and series and item documentation. The receiving archives should also provide a cross-reference to the previous custodian, with the original accession number in its documentation.

After accessioning

When accessioning is completed, you are ready to write to the depositor to acknowledge and confirm that the transfer of custody has taken place. While it is common to correspond with depositors by email (and this is certainly the best course for an in-house archives), if the depositor is outside your organisation, it is advisable to send the acknowledgement of a transfer on hard-copy letterhead.

It is an important legal document to indicate your taking responsibility for the future management and preservation of the accession. You should take care that the letter reflects the written and verbal agreements made about custody, access and disposal. If, for instance, the material has been deposited but is still owned by the depositor, then you will be acknowledging the 'transfer' rather than the 'donation'. If you spell out your understanding of the conditions of custody, access and disposal, then this gives an opportunity for the depositor to clear up any misunderstandings.

It is also good public relations to formally thank the depositor for the accession and indicate how important it will be for future research. Letting the depositor know the accession number will not only facilitate their own future access, but will inspire a sense of confidence that the records are properly controlled in the system and available for others to research in the future.

For the family of the depositor or the organisation which they represent, this letter is often the only clue they have that a transfer of records has taken place. If the depositor dies, or leaves the organisation or institution, there may be additional records that you wish to acquire and your letter may facilitate this.

You should include a list of the material if you have one at this stage as it may be the depositor's original list, amended to show what was actually received, or a basic box list compiled during accessioning. This step may seem redundant if the depositor has just supplied the list and there are no changes, and perhaps is not necessary for an in-house archives, but is definitely advised for a depositor from outside your organisation, as it will facilitate the depositor's own use of the records in the future.

Once material is accessioned, you will want to let your researchers, other depositors and other archives know about the new additions to your archives. Your website, if you have one, is the obvious place for such news. New accessions are also commonly reported in News Notes in the Australian Society of Archivists journal *Archives and Manuscripts,* or you may have your own newsletter. If the records are to be restricted for a number of years, you may prefer to publicise them closer to their release date.

While the records may not yet be fully processed (still requiring arrangement and description work and full listing), the knowledge that you have particular records will be of interest to potential researchers and you may attract some willing volunteers to assist with the arrangement and description. For instance, photographic collections may relate to a particular community and members of that community may volunteer to help identify people and places. Other archivists will be interested to know of your new accessions so that they can direct relevant reference enquiries your way in the future.

Apart from the accession register, quite a lot of documentation can be generated by the accessioning process. You will have the notes taken during the preliminary survey, the original list supplied by the depositor, the amended list and a copy of the letter acknowledging the transfer. It is advisable to incorporate this documentation into a recordkeeping system so that it can be located in the future – hard-copy or electronic 'depositor files', one for each depositor, where all the paperwork is filed are recommended. If you are using a keyword thesaurus, your files will be titled 'Information Management – Records Transfer – [name of depositor]' or similar. The original list should be retained as well as the amended list, but the various drafts in between can usually be discarded. Because lists can be bulky, if you are using a hard-copy filing system, you may maintain these separately with a cross-reference to the main depositor file.

> Dear [depositor]
>
> This letter is to acknowledge your donation of the papers of [creator] to the [name of your archives]. These papers are a valuable addition to the Archives as a record of [the career or work of creator etc].
>
> The papers have been accessioned as [accession number] and reboxed into acid-free boxes. I have attached a copy of your original list with amendments due to [reboxing/additional items transferred].
>
> As we discussed, the papers will be made available to researchers except Box 2, which contains personal correspondence and is not to be released before 2010. If during processing we identify material of temporary value, we will dispose of it without further reference to you, as agreed.
>
> Thank you for enriching our collection with your donation which will be appreciated by many researchers in the future.

Figure 7.2: Sample acknowledgement letter

Summary and conclusion

At the end of the accessioning process, you should have established both intellectual and physical control and gathered some basic information about the material which has been transferred to your custody. You will have confirmed:

- its provenance and date range
- the type and format of the material
- that it fits your collecting policy or belongs in your in-house archives
- any conditions of transfer, particularly regarding access and disposal

The archives will have:

- some basic descriptive information for your finding aids (though not necessarily a list of every item)
- information that will allow you to prioritise its arrangement and description and preservation
- an accession number that you can use internally to locate the material and use externally in your finding aids.

The depositor will have:

- a written acknowledgement of the transfer
- an accession number
- some basic information about what has been transferred to your custody
- if a list was provided, any amendments to that list.

"We've gotta get these records in fast ... Okay, archive everything on this side as, ummm ... 'stuff' ..."

CHAPTER 8

arrangement & description

LYN MILTON

CHAPTER ABSTRACT

Arrangement and description are the terms archivists give to the processes involved in putting archives in order, in accordance with archival principles, and recording information about the nature and provenance of the records. It serves to ensure that archives are managed and accessible.

This chapter addresses the nature and principles of arrangement of archives – provenance and original order – and gives guidance for restoring the original arrangement if this has been disturbed. The practicalities of slotting arrangement and description into an archives program, and the basic requirements of an area where these tasks are carried out are addressed. The chapter then turns to the description of archives, discussing the various kinds of systems for containing these descriptions – the 'record group' system and the 'series' system and focuses on the series system as the preferred Australasian approach. The accompanying CD contains examples and templates to complement this chapter.

Introduction

In this chapter we will examine the activities that archivists undertake to document the material that is in the archives – the archival equivalent of library cataloguing. However, as we will see, these techniques are quite different. We will:

- briefly discuss the concepts that underlie arrangement
- suggest how you might identify the original arrangement when dealing with a disorganised set of records
- discuss the nature of archival description including the main approaches and kinds of systems for containing the descriptions
- survey the information content of descriptions
- broadly cover the considerations for choosing an electronic system and implementing system change
- indicate the records that an archivist should maintain in relation to the arrangement and description tasks.

Some basic principles and concepts

The purpose of arrangement and description is:

- to create an accurate record of the contents of the archives for management, evidential and accountability purposes
- to assist users in identifying material relevant to their research.

Before we embark upon a discussion of the processes involved, we need to explain the underlying principles and some archival terms that will serve to help you through archival literature and discussions with colleagues. The two underlying principles are generally referred to as the *principle of respect for provenance* and *the principle of respect for original order.*

Provenance

The principle of provenance dictates that the archives of one provenance shall not be mixed with the archives of another provenance. 'Provenance' refers to the corporate (or personal) entity that originally created, accumulated or used the records in the course of its business (or personal activities). For most corporate archives, provenance will refer to the various business units that created records within the corporate body (most archivists refer to such business units within organisations as 'agencies') and examples might include 'Economic Department', 'Building Committee', 'General Manager's Office' or 'John Smith'. A person is the provenance only if the records are private, therefore if John Smith created the records in his role as general manager, the records would be those of his office. However, you may be the custodian of records that John Smith created outside his official role, when 'John Smith' would be the provenance. The provenance is also sometimes known as the 'context' of creation. Identifying and describing provenance is discussed in more detail in this chapter.

Original order

The principle of original order dictates that archives should be maintained in the original order in which the records were kept when active – that is, the order in which they were placed when they were created, maintained and used. The order may be alphabetical, numerical, chronological, or according to some other system devised by the creators, but sometimes the original order cannot be determined even when it is clear the records belong together because no classification number or title has survived on the records. Original order is often not the same order in which the records were kept in secondary storage (where users may not have returned them to their correct places or may have handled them carelessly, or where the position of the records may have been determined by space management considerations rather than intellectual ones).

Applying these two principles, it becomes obvious that, if a specific group of records is in its original order, then those records must have the same provenance. Identifying original order is described in more detail in this chapter.

Record series

A basic concept in arrangement and description is that of the 'record series'. Often known simply as a 'series', a record series consists of the records that have the same provenance and that are part of a discernable filing system (identified because of its arrangement or physical appearance); that are kept together because they result from the same activity; or that are of the same format and document the same function. Examples of series include 'Staff Cards', 'Board Minutes', 'Subject Files', 'General Ledgers', 'Share Registers' and 'Building Plans'. Identifying and describing record series is discussed in more detail in this chapter.

Metadata is information about information. When you describe archives, you are creating metadata (descriptions) about the information (archives). In this chapter, we will be introducing you to the various metadata elements (equivalent to fields in a database or columns in a spreadsheet) that you will use to describe the archives you have arranged.

Planning for arrangement and description

Like all other archival operations, arrangement and description needs to be planned. If you have more than one staff member, you should determine who will undertake the various roles in arrangement and description and how this will fit in with their other responsibilities. You need to make some policy decisions including the kind of system that you will use, whether it will be supported by a collection management system (discussed in more detail in Chapter 10: *Using Computers*), a simple system based on word processing documents or a handwritten one. It is also important to make some general rules for the work, for example how much detail you will use, how much time you should devote to a typical task, how you will allocate responsibilities for work checking and problem solving, and how you will set targets for projects. These decisions will require revisiting on a regular basis, as a variety of internal and external factors can influence them, including special projects, staffing levels and organisational change. You also need to set priorities for the order in which the records will receive attention. The following may be amongst the highest priority:

- constitutional records such as certificates of incorporation, articles of association
- the records of your board or other governing authority
- records in high or anticipated research demand
- any records of commercial value
- senior executive's records.

However, you also need to ensure that the remainder of the records are slotted into a program. You should aim for a quiet, secure place where interruptions are minimal. If possible this should be a clean, environmentally controlled area. You will require a large desk or bench suitable for sorting, shelves for material awaiting attention; supplies of archives boxes, basic conservation materials, archival tape for tying, archival wrapping materials and enclosures, cotton gloves for handling delicate items, stationery items, any forms that you may require, including pencils for use when dealing with original records, and your computer. You may choose to locate some of the source materials for context research here unless they are required more often or urgently elsewhere.

Captain A & D.

Electronic records

An increasing number of archives are created electronically, and it is important that your arrangement and description program does not overlook these records. Electronic records may be created in several formats including:

- documents (e.g. Word documents, Kword, Google docs)
- spreadsheets (e.g. Excel, Open Document Spreadsheet)
- presentations (e.g. Powerpoint, Open Document Presentation)
- images (JPEG, TIFF or PNG)
- audio (BWF, FLAC)
- video (mpeg4)
- possibly others unique to your own organisation.

These records are stored on various systems that include personal computers, networks, Electronic Document and Records Management Systems (eDRMS), and other special systems devised or used by your own organisation.

Earlier theory for the mangement of electronic records involved the transfer of the records in their original format with the intention of retaining the programs and the equipment used to create and use them when they were active records. It is now realised that maintaining the software and hardware would be impossible. Current advice is that your client areas should provide you with exports from the systems (reports and recordkeeping metadata), rather than from the records themselves. If you simply receive floppy disks or CDs and arrange and describe these in the same way that you would describe archives in traditional formats (such as paper files), box them and put them away, it is highly unlikely that the technology (either hardware or software) to read them will still be available once they are available for access as archives, and it is entirely probable that the disks or CDs may have deteriorated.

It is essential to the arrangement and description of electronic records that you obtain as much information as you can from the users about the system that created the records. For example, the name, role and purpose of the system, who created records, who had permission to use it, when it was used and technical information about it.

Arrangement

Introduction

As mentioned previously, two major principles underlie arrangement. These are:

- respect for provenance
- respect for the 'original order' of the records

Determining the provenance of the records and establishing the original order are carried out simultaneously, for the most part. Think about it: If a group of records are established as being part of the same system of original order, then logically they must share the same provenance. And, as part of this process, you will identify the various record series that the records comprise, or of which they may be part.

Because an understanding of provenance is so vital to the work of arrangement and description, you should prepare for these tasks by gaining some knowledge of the history and structure, functions and activities of the organisations, and the biography and positions held by the persons whose records you are to arrange. You should acquire source materials to assist you with this and if possible have these close to the area where you work on arrangement and description. Any information about the recordkeeping systems and structure that you can acquire from the staff of your organisation, your predecessor or the depositor will assist you with this task.

Provenance

Archives derive much of their meaning from the body or person that created them. Indeed, their authenticity and reliability depend upon their creator being identified accurately. They can derive further meaning from the system in which they were arranged, accumulated and used. Archives have a greater relationship to other records in the same record series and other series within the same recordkeeping system, than they do to other records on the same subject created by another body within the same or a different organisation. This is because they document the same process whatever the subject matter.

Irreparable damage has been done to collections when attempts have been made to arrange archives into subjects, as the information required to reassemble them in their correct order has been lost. While it is true that some researchers wish to locate and use all of the records on a given subject, place or person, this is the role of 'finding aids'. For more information see Chapter 12: *Finding Aids.* In the present information environment, web search tools that some archives develop can assist in drawing this information together without destroying essential material about creators of the records.

Example

If we were to bring together all of the records about Parramatta, there would be records about city planning, cleanliness, schools, gaols, children's homes, traffic, conservation, public health and many other subjects. The records would be unrelated to each other because they would have been created by a variety of provenances, including various levels of government, companies and individuals. Records provide information about the agency or person that created them, and under a re-arrangement by subject this information is lost. In addition, such a system would detract from the light that these records would cast on the other records about city planning, cleanliness, schools and so on (including policy, investigations and programs, and similar records relating to these same activities in other places). The records would be difficult and confusing to use because each unit (file, volume, card, photograph, film) would have been created for a different purpose by different body, contain different information and possibly be in a different format and have a different date range.

The persons who transfer or donate archives may provide information about the creators, use and arrangement of the records received by the archives. However, often records will come to the archives in a haphazard fashion, including single items or fragments of series, records inherited from a defunct agency, or amalgamated body, or those that belonged to a deceased family member. Perhaps you may be responsible for establishing order into a disorganised records store, and the archivist will need to use professional skill to determine the provenance.

If there are no external markings of the provenance on the records (e.g. the officer's designation on the spine of a volume or the cover of a file), this calls for careful examination of the contents. When the records consist of correspondence, letter books, and similar file-like material, the addressees of incoming letters and the designations and signatures on copies of outgoing letters should indicate provenance. As we shall see later, provenance may change over the duration of a series and it is necessary to check through the whole series in order to trace any succession of provenance.

Some records give little or no evidence of provenance – their creators did not perceive a time when the records would be of significance outside the walls of the office where they were used. This is common in ledgers and registers where there was no necessity for any identification in the front of the books and the officer did not need to sign transactions. Check the contents of these records for any hint of provenance: officers' names, client names, account names and similar. Sometimes, chance rough workings, letters, memoranda, notes or other documents that are loose within a volume can help you to determine the provenance! If you still have no certainty about the creators, you will need to analyse the contents of the record, therefore determining the activity that it documents, and your knowledge of the structures and functions of the organisation might be the only provenance material available.

When identifying provenance, you need to be particularly careful if your archives contains the records of more than one organisation, including amalgamated or subsidiary companies and other related bodies. You should never treat the series created or maintained by two or more organisations as though they were the same series because this is contrary to the principle of provenance. It is easy to confuse the records of two companies within the same industry. They often produce similar series because they are covered by the same legislation and/or other industry regulations and standards, and carry out similar functions. So when trying to identify provenance, never lose sight of the existence of these distinct bodies. Therefore, as you are working, constantly check signatures on outgoing mail and note that if minutes or ledgers overlap, they are probably the records of another agency or committee.

Example

An archivist found several share registers for the period 1920–1930 in the storeroom. There was considerable confusion because there was some overlap in the date range of the various volumes. The archivist was able to identify two separate series by the physical appearance and by following various shareholders' accounts brought forward into subsequent volumes. The archivist then turned to the sources for the administrative history of the companies involved (printed annual reports in this case) and was able to identify, from the names of major shareholders, that one series belonged to S. Bennett Ltd and the other to Sun Newspapers Limited.

Even if you have only the records of a single organisation, you may find that some series were created by the union representative in that role, or are the records of a professional body, industry body, committee or otherwise related body and are not part of the recordkeeping systems of your organisation. If your collection policy is to keep these records, they form one or more separate series and will require unique provenance documentation.

Identifying the series

After the determination of provenance, you turn to identifying the series. This is facilitated if the records are transferred immediately to the archives by the creators or users of the records or their immediate successors. The transferor can assist with information such as any records system procedures or instructions that may have been used, the name by which the various series were known, their purpose and use, the internal arrangement of the records within them, any control records that are used to identify items within the series, and relationships to other series. These transferors can sometimes advise on the location of other items or series and much of the information that will be required when the series is being described in its context.

However, often the agency that created the series no longer exists and the creators have moved on, the series may be inherited or the records found in 'the cupboard under the stairs' and the archivist has little other equipment other than that contained in the records and their own knowledge of the functions and structure of the organisation or person who created the records. The archivist needs to return to the definition of a series and to determine whether the records belong to the same series, because they are in an identifiable alphabetical, numerical, chronological or other sequence, are in the same format, document the same function or have similar contents.

The following can assist in identifying the series and placing like items together:

- **labels** e.g. general ledger
- a **numerical or alphabetical** system of item titling
- **similarity of contents** e.g. each file contains an application for employment, details of appointments, letters relating to salary rises, grievances and resignation or retirement
- **physical similarity** e.g. volumes that contain customers' addresses, occupations and signatures; cards with a place name on the top and details of gazettals below; files of the same type labelled with client names; same colour file covers; tabs with the same handwriting; photographs of buildings; architectural drawings of a particular building
- the records that clearly document a similar *function*, such as preparing annual returns, designing a building, or the records of a particular project.

CASE STUDY 1

An archivist has become responsible for arranging and describing many records that were transferred to storage without transfer documentation. They find in one location some books that show procedures for taking classified advertisements. They are labelled 'Instructions for taking classified advertisements'. They consist of a typescript procedure that has been much altered. There is evidence that they were circulated within that department for guidance by the staff. In another location, there are some printed books of a later date that are labelled 'Classified advertising manual' and 'Telephone ad. room manual'. They are internally arranged according to the same system, cover the same material as the 'instructions' and document the same activity. The differences they show relate to the available technology. They are the same series.

CASE STUDY 2

A box is labelled Mr X's Files. Mr X was a former managing director. On examination, you find that some of the records are personal and relate to his own interests and private affairs, while the remainder of the records are identified as being created by the secretary of the organisation, identified by the designation of the sender and recipient of correspondence. These records comprise at least two separate series.

You may also find that some of the files predate Mr X's term as managing director or secretary. It often happens that an officer will inherit the records from another part of the organisation, and label them as 'their' files for storage purposes although they in fact have a different provenance. If you do find inherited records, you will need to identify the provenance and series and return them to their proper place, although in the series description you should mention that they were found with the records of Mr X, as this may provide information both about the use of the series and the role of Mr X.

As you identify the series, you may either physically place the records of a similar series together or, if you are less confident about your identification initially map out the various series on paper. Because of the importance of original order, it is advisable that the records are not disturbed until a full examination has been made. Related to this task is determining any relationships between the series. For example, if you suspect that one series is an index to another, look up a few entries to test that this is so.

Original order

Having identified the series, you will endeavour to place them in the order in which they were retained while active. The original order is simple to identify if the records have similar unique symbols such as:

- file numbers and/ or names
- classification systems
- date or alphabetical ranges
- names of people, places, or objects

You might find that a series has been 'top numbered', that is the previous system identifiers have been crossed through and a new system has been adopted, and that the newly created items after top numbering follow this new arrangement. The general rule for these instances is that the new system is the one to use as the archival arrangement, as the users have consciously re-numbered the series, and any control records would use these new numbers. Despite adopting the new notation system the series often continues as a single unit.

Where there is no indication of the original arrangement, you might discuss the order with the users or transferors if the series has been in recent use. If this is not possible or not fruitful, often the order in which the records were transferred is the safest solution. Alternatively, the archivist should make the best judgement possible and then document the reason for this decision when describing the series, for example you might find remnants of an alphabetical arrangement that has been disturbed when the records were boxed and impose this on the rest of the series.

Note that the archivist should not mistake the order in which a custodial agency or storage facility held the records for the one used by the original users or creators if there is evidence to the contrary. For example, files may have been retrospectively bar-coded in no particular order for retrieval purposes.

Some recordkeeping practices can cause confusion when dating the items within a series that would appear to be chronological. For example:

- In handwritten volumes, sometimes the information that is still current when a new volume is commenced will be transcribed from the former into the new volume. This can usually be identified by obviously being written in the same hand at the same time, despite the date range being dispersed.
- In loose-leaf registers sometimes the pages containing current entries are transferred into the new volume.

Also note that, while identifying order, you may find items that are clearly in the wrong series, incidental papers, photographs and plans that might appear to be misplaced and similar occurrences. You should leave these where they were found as they may provide information about the creators and users of the records. However, if you subsequently decide to remove them in order to complete the series to which they belong, you should create a 'separation sheet'. This should give details of the item you have removed and indicate the series and item number to which it has been relocated and record the name of the archivist and the date. You should place this sheet in the location where the stray item was found and also cover this information in the description of the series to which the item is transferred.

Artificial series

Archivists often need to create 'artificial series'. These may be series identified because they conform to the definition by consisting of items that document the same function or have similar content, but for which the original order is unknown. Archivists also create artificial series comprising records in special formats, for example photographs, photograph albums, architectural drawings, published material, trophies and certificates, that were probably created singly and in some cases comprise collected or include donated items. The archivist may gather these together into a series. The descriptive note should always indicate that the archivist has assembled the series and provide information about why this was done. However, any records in these same formats for which the original order is known should remain in their relevant series in accordance with the principles of provenance and original order.

Example

Photographs of the various premises, staff, and work processes were found in cabinets. They are not originals and were probably acquired for publications or exhibitions. It was decided to create several artificial series – photographs of staff, photographs of buildings, etc. However other photographs were created for the Sesquicentenary, unveiling of plaques, visits of the governor, overseas study tours and similar purposes. These belong to, and must not be removed, from the relevant series that also contain other items in different formats (such as reports, visitors' books), so that the context material remains intact.

Once the arrangement has been determined, the records may be put into containers and if possible placed in a controlled environment ready for the initial stages of documentation.

An arrangement & description exercise led by ASA Education Officer Dr Sigrid McCausland

Arrangement will be simpler and more accurate if the records are transferred in the order in which they were created and used. If your organisation employs a designated records manager you should have well-organised storage facilities for the semi-active records with records arranged into series, internally appropriately arranged and labelled including the date for transfer to archives. If you do not have a records manager, you should strive to have a more organised system of transfer to the archives and you will reap benefits from training the staff in understanding series and the importance of original order, identifying the material that will become archives and possibly even obtain their assistance in boxing and perhaps listing records transferred to archives.

Description

Introduction

Description means the tasks involved in documenting or recording information about the records contained in your archives. We often refer to series being described 'in their context'. When describing archives, therefore, we need to pay attention not only to the series and items we identified when arranging, but to the agencies and persons that created them, (and sometimes) the organisations and families that contained these creators and the functions and activities that they document.

International standards for archival description

A number of standards for arrangement and description have been developed with input from the international archives community, including representatives from Australia. The standards identify the metadata elements that should be included in a satisfactory description. These standards are intended to be used by individual archives in conjunction with any national standards. Their purpose is to promote uniformity in descriptions. With an increasing number of archives making their descriptive material available on the World Wide Web, their importance is even more imperative and their existence will therefore contribute to shared archival holdings initiatives. When a system has been developed by an individual archives, these standards are a useful gauge for the comprehensiveness of the system. The major standards are as follows:

- *International Standard for Archival Description (General)* ISAD (G)

  The second edition of this standard was published in 2000. This standard essentially addresses description at series level. The standard may be viewed or downloaded at <http://www.ica.org/sites/default/files/isad_g_2e.pdf>

- *International Standard Archival Authority Record for Corporate Bodies, Persons and Families* – ISAAR (CPF)

  The second edition of this standard was published in 2004. This standard addresses the context entities – agency, person and family – in further detail. This standard may be viewed or downloaded at <http://www.ica.org/sites/default/files/ISAAR2EN.pdf>

These standards identify each element that should be included in the description, discuss the purpose for its inclusion, provide rules for the methods of recording the information and give some examples. Each standard concludes with diagrams of models for archival description.

Systems for archival description

'Top-down' systems

Traditionally, archives were described in top-down systems that first described the 'fonds' or 'record group' (See Chapter 1: *What are Archives & Archival Programs?* for a definition and description of the terms the 'fonds' or 'record group'). For our current purposes, these terms are interchangeable and generally mean the entire body of records created by a particular entity, in practice a description of that entity. The 'fonds' or 'record group' may be broken down into 'sous-fonds' or 'sub-groups' (probably corresponding to particular functions or divisions of the whole entity), and these would be followed by descriptions of the record series created by that agency, thus respecting the principle of provenance. However, under this type of system, in attempting to respect the principle of original order and not break up long-lived record series that had been created by a succession of entities, such series were usually assigned, *in toto*, to the last entity responsible for their creation. These top-down systems are still used in many archives, and quite suitable for documenting stable administrative environments or small archival collections from defunct agencies and persons. There is a wide variety of practice, but generally an agency or person (record group) that created records is identified and given a distinctive symbol, title and some description that would include its history and activities. The series that were created are listed and described following the record group often using symbols that identify the relationship between the creator and the series.

The following examples illustrate this method of description. The first example (Figure 8.1) is of a simple organisation and includes brief descriptive entries. The second example is of a more complex organisation, which could be broken down further (descriptions have been omitted from this example).

Record Group LGSC

Lake George Surf Club, 1930-1962

In the years after the establishment of Canberra as the national capital, Lake George became a popular recreational area during summer. Following a drowning in 1929, a number of regulars formed the Lake George Surf Club to provide a system of organised supervision on weekends during the summer months. In addition to monitoring swimming and boating activities at the most popular location on the lake shore, the Club also provided swimming lessons and courses in water safety and resuscitation. The Club was managed by a small committee and funded by membership fees and occasional donations from local landowners. The use of Lake George for recreation ceased after Lake Burley-Griffin was formed in Canberra. Lake George itself dried up due to prolonged drought, and the Club ceased to exist. The records were donated to the archives by the last secretary/treasurer, Hilary Jenkinson, in 1981 (Accession No 1981/99). No restrictions were placed on access.

Series No	Series Title/Description	Date Range
LGSC1	Minute Books (Contains minutes of Committee meetings and Annual General Meetings. Copies of annual financial statements are sometimes pasted in.)	1930-1962
LGSC2	Patrol Log Books (Exercise books containing brief summaries of weekend patrols, i.e. monitoring of swimming and boating activities, with occasional trenchant comments on members and visitors. At least one book appears to be missing.)	1930-1949 1953-1961
LGSC3	General ledgers	1930-1962
LGSC4	Water Safety Register (Exercise book containing lists of list of classes held, names of participants, certificates issued and signatures of instructors)	1931-1960

Figure 8.1: Record group Lake George Surf Club

Record Group L1 Lake Innes Shire Council		
Sub-Group L1-1 Town Clerk's Office		
Series No	**Series Title/Description**	**Date Range**
L1-1-1	Minutes of Council Meetings	1868-1930
L1-1-2	General Correspondence Files	1868-1930
Sub-Group L1-2 Engineer's Department		
Series No	**Series Title/Description**	**Date Range**
L1-2-1	Road Plans and Specifications	1893-1930
L1-2-2	Water Supply Plans	1925-1930

Figure 8.2: Record group Lake Innes Shire Council

However, such systems are unsatisfactory for describing archives produced by larger organisations that undergo periodic (sometimes frequent) administrative re-organisations, mergers, and the like. While the activities that create records, and the recordkeeping systems themselves, carry on, their administrative context (i.e. provenance) fluctuates, and this is difficult to document in such top-down descriptive systems. It becomes even more difficult if the recordkeeping systems themselves are subject to splits and mergers. To cope with such fluctuations in these top-down descriptive systems, the options may be:

- to disregard that the change had taken place and use either the original or the latest title
- when a small number of changes have occurred, the record group can show both changes in its title e.g. Department of Sport and Recreation (1976–1982), Department of Leisure Sport and Tourism (1982–1985). But this is hardly a solution when there are multiple changes
- to create a new provenance after each restructure and re-register the series that were continued across the administrative change

None of these solutions is satisfactory. At best, a cumbersome system will result but, particularly if the third solution is adopted, the system does not express the reality that some series indeed continued through the administrative change.

Series-based systems

In the 1960s, the Commonwealth Archives Office (now the National Archives of Australia) addressed the problems indicated above. Its solution was the 'series system', which has been adopted by most major and many smaller Australian archives and in several other places throughout the world. In this system, the description of *context* entities (organisations, agencies, families, persons, functions, activities) is separated from the description of *content* entities (record series, items, documents). Describing each entity and then describing the links between the entities results in a full description and shows the records in their administrative and functional context throughout time. Administrative change is carefully monitored and recorded. Series can have more than one creating agency over time (or even simultaneously if that reflects the actuality of creation). These links are outlined in the following diagram.

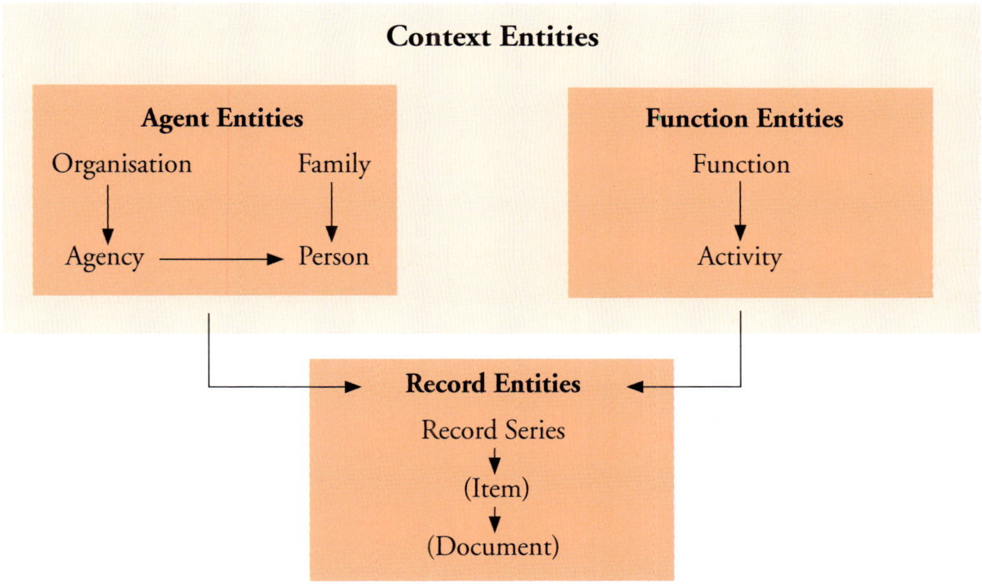

Figure 8.3: Context entities and their relationships

We recommend that newly established archives and those contemplating new systems implement the series system. While the major reason for this is the solutions to the problems of intellectual control that the series system offers, in addition its widespread application in the Australian context also enhances your ability to cooperate with shared data projects and the resulting descriptions will be familiar to experienced users. The 'top-down' systems described above might seem adequate for a small archives dealing with small collections; but the series system can serve these too (and it will only need one more complex collection to establish a need for the degree of flexibility offered by the series system. You don't want to try to operate two systems!). The series system satisfies various national and international standards for archival description and the Australian Society of Archivists Inc has developed *Describing archives in Context: A guide to Australian Practice* to enhance our understanding of the system and the various implementations of it in Australia.

The series system can be implemented in any archives regardless of size or jurisdiction. While the system appears complex, as few as two entities may be used in an application of the system (one context entity and one records entity, e.g. agency and series). Outside this requirement, there are no rules about which entities are used. In deciding which entities you will use, you need to consider the type of archives you are managing, scope of your records, the nature of your organisation and the size of your collection and its anticipated growth. While there are many 'metadata elements' in each form, very few are mandatory. In the series description, for example, you can record as little as the series number, title, date range, quantity, archivist's name and date of registration. The descriptions themselves should be appropriate to the type, size and resources of your archives, your accountability requirements and the needs of the users. A schema for small archives is found in Appendix 8.1.

The various entities envisaged by the system are identified in Table 8.4.

Context entities	**Content (or record) entities**
Organisation Agency Family Person Function Activity	Record series Item (e.g. a file) Document

Figure 8.4: Various entities envisaged by the series system

At least one context entity and at least one content entity are required for a description, but the system is scalable.

As described in Figure 8.3 above, there are hierarchical relationships between the various entities. For example, agencies are part of organisations which belong to families, activities are part of functions, record items belong to series, agencies create series, etc. But there are also relationships or links between entities of the same type.

Link type	Usually known as	Detail
Succession	Preceding or succeeding	The entity (e.g. organisation, agency, function, series) that carried out the same task before or after the one currently being described
Control	Superior or subordinate (controlling or controlled)	The entity to which the current entity is responsible or of which it forms a part
Relationship	Related	Normally only used in the entity series to link two that are interdependent and the knowledge of one series is significant when using the other.

Table 8.1: Common links in series system entities

At its most complete, the system consists of up to nine different levels of description. The information about each entity has a place in the system and there should not be repetition of this information in two or more entities. For example, information about the history of the agency should not be repeated in the description of the series.

Entity type	Examples entities			
Ambient entity	Organisation	Family	Function	
Provenance entity	Agency	Person	Family	Activity
Recordkeeping entity	Record Series			
Contents entity	Record Item	Document		

Table 8.2: Entities in the series system

Ambient entities

Ambient entities are simply entities that place your provenance entities into a broader context. For example, the agencies 'Board of Directors', 'Editorial', 'Marketing' and 'Information Services' form part of the organisation known as Fairfax Media. The organisation does not create the records directly but draws together several records, creating bodies or 'agencies'. In the same way 'family' may not create records but several individual members of a family can be drawn together and placed into context by this entity. The family 'Fairfax' comprises John Fairfax, John Reading Fairfax, Warwick Oswald Fairfax and others.

Organisation

According to Archives Investigator (http://investigator.records.nsw.gov.au), the definition of an organisation is '...a whole government, municipal council, incorporated company, church or other body that is generally regarded as independent and autonomous in the performance of its normal functions'.

If your archive is an in-house archives, you will probably want to use the organisation entity to describe the parent organisation as a whole. If your parent organisation has amalgamated, or merged with others or has or otherwise acquired archives that are beyond the scope of your organisation as it is currently constituted, these would be described as separate organisations. However, many archives, especially collecting archives dealing in small collections, would not require this entity.

Family

According to the Australian Society of Archivists (2008), a family may be described as 'a group of related persons'. It is advisable to use this entity if you have records of families that are a significant feature of your records, as the entity family draws together the records that were created by the various family members. Many archives would not require this entity.

Metadata elements for an organisation or family registration

Note that only the metadata elements shown in bold are mandatory.

Element	Organisation	Family
Unique identifier	A unique registration number for this organisation	A unique registration number for this family
Title/ Name	The official title for this organisation	Family name
Start date	The date the organisation was established or commenced business	The earliest date that the family had significance to your records
End date	The date the organisation was abolished or ceased business	The latest date that the family had significance to your records

Element	Organisation	Family
Mandate	The legislation; proclamation, charter; legal instrument that established this organisation and identified its role and functions	
Location	The physical location of this organisation	
Description	A brief note that identifies the instrument that created the organisation, describes its powers and responsibilities, internal structure and the circumstances of its abolition if relevant. The description should not duplicate information contained in any other entity	Include some general genealogical information about the family that clearly distinguishes it from other families of the same name and its importance to your organisation and its records
Functions performed	List or link to any registered function.	

Table 8.3: Metadata elements for an organisation or family registration

The organisation/family description should link to the following descriptions to express relationships:

Entity	Relationship type	Note
Organisation	Superior, subordinate, preceding, succeeding, organisation	The link should express the period of the relationship and allow for any brief note; or the date of succession.
Agencies	Subordinate to the organisation	
Function	Performed by the organisation	
Persons	Belonging to the family	

Table 8.4: Links that may be made to organisation or family entities

Provenance entities

Provenance entities are those that create records. It is recommended that, if possible, you register the major record-creating agencies of your organisation prior to beginning series registration, i.e. those you know you have records of. The advantages of this are that you will begin to gain some familiarity with the organisation, that you will have some experience in using your system whether on paper or electronic and that you will be able to commence registration of your series as soon as they are identified rather than stop this process to register the context entities.

Agency

An agency is a distinct and recognisable part of an organisation that usually has its own recordkeeping system (Australian Society of Archivists 2008).

For in-house archives, agencies might be departments, sections, units, or committees. The policies, recordkeeping practices and structure of your organisation will determine the sections of your organisation that constitute agencies. For collecting archives, the agency will probably simply be the organisation that created the records, though if it's a large collection from a complex organisation, you will probably need to describe a number of agencies.

Agency registration can be a stimulating and challenging task. In many organisations, source materials can be difficult to locate, as there may not be a constitutional requirement to make a formal annual report containing the structure of the organisation. You will be fortunate if you can identify an area in your organisation that is responsible for organisational structure and can provide this information historically, but you are more likely to be searching for records such as:

- official company documentation, such as memoranda and articles of association; charters; legislation and proclamations
- organisational charts
- internal regular reporting to senior executive
- regular memoranda or emails to senior staff
- the records of a senior executive or planning agency probably include files relating to the structure and functions of the various subordinate agencies
- procedure manuals
- internal directories at least attest to the dates that agencies were in existence, although they might not be useful in showing hierarchies of agencies
- media releases announcing the creation of new units or units closing down, appointment of new council members, directors, etc.

Secondary source materials might include published histories or staff publications.

If in your various duties as archivist you come across sources of materials for administrative history, make a record of these and create a descriptive document or database that can be shared with your contemporary colleagues or successors.

One of the most challenging aspects of agency registration is determining 'agency boundaries', that is, determining the agencies that need to be registered, the commencement dates of agencies, and whether the changes within an agency history, such as change of title or status and addition or subtraction of functions, constitute the continuation of the agency or the creation of a new one; and the abolition dates. Many archives will not have, within their own resources, the material to complete perfect descriptions of all of their agencies. Depending on the size and complexity of your agency, registrations require constant vigilance, as organisational change is a constant phenomenon.

The role of agency registration is to provide context for the series, not to write a full history. If you identify a good published history of the agency, you may make a note of it in your description or provide a hypertext link. However, remember that web addresses change and you need to keep them up to date.

Unless your archives comprise only personal records it is likely that you will need to register at least one agency. An example of a completed agency registration is shown in Appendix 8.3.

Person

Some record series may be created by a person rather than an agency. These are not official records that have been created by the person in the course of duties, but records that have been created outside the recordkeeping system. The creators of these records may be board members or senior staff members. These personal record series may provide a wider context for the records of the organisation in addition to providing some insight into the major characters that influenced the organisation. Collections that are primarily manuscript collections may have a higher proportion of series created by persons than by agencies.

The role of person registration is to provide context for the series, not to write a full biography. If you identify a good published biography you may make a note of it in your description or provide a hypertext link. However, remember that web addresses change and you need to keep them up to date.

Source materials for well-known persons include biographical sources such as published biographies, *The Australian Dictionary of Biography, Who's Who in Australia, Debrett's Peerage* and directories specific to the person's occupation or interests may be used in addition to the results of internet searches. For those less known, staff records, the series created by the person or similar internal sources may be all that is available.

Metadata elements for agency or person registration

Note that only the metadata elements shown in bold are mandatory.

Element	Agency	Person
Identifier	A unique agency registration number	A unique registration number for this person
Title/or Name	The official title by which the agency is known	Full name
Start date (birth date)	The date that the agency commenced or was constituted.	Birth date
End date (death date)	The date that the agency was abolished or ceased business.	Death Date
Mandate	The legislation, proclamation, legal or other document that established the agency or the decision that resulted in its creation.	n/a
Location	The physical or virtual location of the agency	
Description/ Biographical note	This should be a brief description covering the establishment and functions of the agency and if available the internal structure; and other data determined by the size and purpose of the agency. The reason or circumstances of creation and abolition if relevant and tease out whether any change in the history of the agency constitutes the creation of a new agency. Any general comment about the records of the agency may be made here e.g. any known destruction or location elsewhere, but comments specific to individual series should be in the relevant series description.	Brief biographical details concentrating on the person's role with your organisation and its records. Identify any external positions held that might contribute to the person's role in the relevant industry or profession
Function	List (or link if you have an electronic system) the major functions carried out by the agency or person	

Table 8.5: Metadata links for agency or person registrations

The agency or person form should link to the following records to express relationships:

Entity	Relationship type	Note
Organisation	Containing the agency	The link should express the period of the relationship or the date of succession and allow for any brief note
Agency	Preceding, succeeding, superior, subordinate/the agency to which a person relates	
Functions	Exercised by the agency or person	
Families or person	Families to which the person belongs or person who had a relationship with the agency	
Series	Created or controlled by the agency or person	

Table 8.6: Links that may be made to agency or person registrations

Functional provenance

Over the last decade, archival systems have increasingly implemented functional provenance to supplement structural provenance (the agency, person or family that created the series). The fact that records document functions rather than subjects has been recognised and developed in recordkeeping system methodologies, and it seemed logical to expand this concept into archival control systems. Further, organisations have become increasingly complex, as have been the records they create. Functions are more stable than structural provenance and, while a long-standing series may have a succession of creating agencies, the functions will not change. Most users will not be expert in the administrative history of the organisations whose records they need to use, and a functional approach assists users in identification of records required for their research often more effectively than following the links from agencies.

Various archives have levels of functions that link to organisation, agencies, persons, series or items. Often the two or more levels of functions are known as functions and activities. The practice of archival institutions varies in relation to recording functional provenance, but we recommend registering functions as entities almost parallel to structural provenance. The advantage of registering functions as entities is that because you research them in the same way that you research structural provenance, issues such as whether the function continues through a name change (e.g. Pollution and Environmental Control) or conversely changes in scope despite continuance of name, are addressed. While you will find that full registration of functions is a time-consuming task that can be particularly challenging on the resources of a small and/or new archive, the advantages it will provide you and your clients will justify the effort. However, if your organisation is small, your archives is small and has a stable structure, where the functions are virtually identical with the business units of the agency, it is not necessary to use functions.

The source materials for the identification of functions and activities will often be the same as those for structural provenance. However, for the initial identification of functions and activities, you should aim to identify any previous attempt to identify the functions of your organisations, any business analysis that has been undertaken, classification schemes and similar documentation and decide whether this is a suitable analysis for your purposes.

Metadata elements for function or activity registration.

Note that only the metadata elements shown in bold are mandatory.

Element	Contents	Note
Number	A unique number for function or activity	
Title	Title you have selected for this function or activity	e.g. the latest name by which it has been known
Start date	The exact date if known	The start and end dates of functions are often more difficult to identify than of structures as they are less often officially documented.
End date	The exact date if known	
Mandate	Any instrument that established and controlled the function or activity	
Location	The physical or virtual location where the function or activity was performed	
Description	Include the circumstances of commencement; the definition and follow the development of the function and its abolition.	

Table 8.7: Metadata elements for function or activity registrations

The function or activity form should link to the following records to express relationships:

Entity	Relationship type	Note
Agencies	Performing the function/activity	The link should express the period of the relationship or the date of succession and allow for any brief note
Persons	Performing the function/activity	
Families	Performing the function/activity	
Function	Previous, subsequent, preceding and succeeding	
Series	That document the function/activity	

Table 8.8: Links that may be made to function and activity registrations

Records entities

In archival finding aids, there should normally be at least two levels of records entities – series and items.

Series is the central entity to the system and it is therefore particularly important to document them. The series description includes information about access to and disposal of the series and the items that comprise it, also information about the physical format of the series, advice on using the series and related material that will assist the user. Much of this information is not obvious from the item list. If you are responsible for a small archives, the series entity is the place where you should concentrate your effort.

Appendix 8.2 is an example of a completed series.

Describing Archives In Context: A Guide to Australasian Practice *provides further advice on the Series system. Available from the Australian Society of Archivists.*

Metadata elements for series description

Note that only the metadata elements shown in bold are mandatory.

Element	Contents	Note
Identifier	A unique number within this entity	
Title	Use the title that was in use when the records were active	If the title does not survive the archivist needs to construct a title based on the function; format and purpose of the series, e.g. 'Files Relating to Reconstruction'; If this is necessary reference should be made to the status of the title in the descriptive note below.
Series start date	The date that the series commenced (not necessarily the same date as the earliest contents)	The dates in this section should be the dates that the series (as distinct from its contents) commenced and ended. There may be documentation that creates the series e.g. board minutes and any series of legal significance, but the date range of many series may be difficult to determine. The date range may be apparent from control records or from an annual single number system.
Series end date	The date that the series ceased (not necessarily the same date as the latest contents)	
Contents start date	Exact date of the earliest contents	
Contents end date	Exact date of the latest contents covered by this description	
Function or keywords	List (or link if you have an electronic system) the function that this series documents and the date range	
Quantity	The size of the series e.g. in shelf metres	

Element	Contents	Note
Physical characteristics and technical requirements	Describe the physical format of the records e.g. files, cards, photographs, electronic records; any type of equipment that is required to use the series; the physical condition of the records particularly if they are withdrawn from access or preservation copies are to be used.	If possible select a few descriptors for the format and use them consistently.
Description	The following may be included in the description if relevant: • any *documentation* that establishes the series • the *content* of the series • how it is *arranged* • whether it is *indexed* • *any change* over time including changes to system of arrangement or format • identify any known parts of the series that have been *destroyed or kept elsewhere* • provide *advice* on using the series • the location of any *finding aids* to its contents • comments relating to its *physical condition* • any details about gaining *access* to the parts of the series not yet transferred to the archives • details of its *abolition* • any series that succeeded it. If the series is electronic and consists of exports from the system your series description needs to include a description of the orginal format of the records, the type and name of system that created them, who were the original creators and users, how they used the system and the date range for which the system was current.	

Element	Contents	Note
Disposal status and history	The name and/or number of the disposal authority and the section that relates to the series. Provide any information about parts of this series that have been destroyed	
Accruals	Indicate the growth rate of the series	
Archival history	Provide details about the source of the records.	Was it transferred immediately from the creating agency, another custodial agency, or storage facility? Indicate the name of the donor if outside your organisation, and the date received into the archives and accessioned.
System of Arrangement	Brief description e.g. chronological, alphabetical	A series may continue despite changes of arrangement.
Range of control symbols	The range of numbers or other identifiers of this series held by the archives	e.g. A1– A2000
Access status	Identify whether the series is available for access and any period for which the series is closed for public access	Available for public access 30 years after creation.
Copyright and reproduction	Identify any restrictions that apply to reproduction of the series	The period for which restricted by copyright; the details of whom to contact for application for reproduction.
Language		
Finding aids	Identify any of your own or external publications that assist with the understanding or the use of the series	
Location	Where the series is held and/or URL address if a digital version of the series is available	
Copies	Indicate the type of copy e.g. digitised, microfilm, photocopy and the web site or physical location of the copy or copies.	

Table 8.9: Metadata elements for series description

The series form should link to the following records to express relationships:

Entity	Relationship type	Note
Series	Controlling; controlled, preceding, succeeding, related series	The link should express the period of the relationship and allow for any brief note.
Agency	Creating or controlling agency	
Person	Creating	
Function	Documented by the series	

Table 8.10: Links that may be made to registrations in the series entity

Items

Items are the physical units into which the series is divided, e.g. files, volumes, albums, bundles. In order to register items, the series must first be registered. As we have seen, archives should be arranged in the order in which they were kept when active. If the original identifiers have survived, these should be used as the archives 'item numbers'. Not only does this reinforce the principle of original order, but also enables identification of items using controlling series or other finding aids. If there is no evidence of the original system, the archivist can assign numbers for the items to facilitate order, e.g. a single number system such as 1,2,3. The original title for each item should likewise be retained and if this is lost a title should be constructed by the archivist. In constructing a title the archivist should combine elements such as the activity documented, and the physical format of the item.

Some items will come from electronic systems. Many electronic document systems enable the individual documents to be placed into containers and the end result resemble files. Each of these virtual files may be an item. Similarly, a workgroup or individual officer's directory structure may be organised functionally and the documents essentially perfom as a file therefore an item.

The disorganised way in which some electronic records are often received may involve some form of re-organisation of documents into folders by the archivist. Careful records need to be manintained to document this process of allocating documents to 'folders'. Archivist's time can be saved by having clerical staff, or the transferors, listing the items following careful instructions if this is an option.

Metadata for item lists

Note that only the metadata elements shown in bold are mandatory. There are a number of fields on the lists below that are also found on the series form such as location, and physical characteristics. You only need to enter them on the item list if the information is unique to the particular item.

Element	Contents
Series number	Enter the series number
Item number	If possible employ the same number by which the item was known when active
Title	Use the original title of the item if known
Start date	Use the exact earliest date of the creation of this item
End date	Use the exact latest date of the creation of this item
Function /keywords	List (or link if you have an electronic system) the function that this item documents and the date range
Quantity	The size of the item
Physical characteristics and technical requirements	Indicate the format and any implication for the long-term management of the item
Description	Enter a brief description that complements the title if required but that does not duplicate material included in any other entity
Disposal status and history	Indicate whether the item is archival or temporary
Disposal class number	Identify the disposal authority and class or function that covers this item.
Access status	Indicate whether the item is available for public access and for how long restricted
Copyright and reproduction	Indicate any copyright conditions relating to the reproduction of this item
Language	The major language of the item
Finding aids	Identify your own publications or any published sources that assist with the use or understanding of the item

Element	Contents
Location	Enter the location where the item is located. This may include any building name storage area and run, bay or shelf number. The number should be of a kind that is immediately recognisable by all staff with permission to locate items and all registrars should enter it uniformly to facilitate location reporting.
Location of copies	Indicate the type of copy e.g. digitised, microfilm, photocopy and the web site or physical location of the copy.
Availability	Identify any factor that will affect the availability of the item such as fragility, receiving conservation treatment or on loan

Table 8.11: Metadata elements for item registration

The item form should link to the following records to express relationships.

Entity	Relationship type
Series	Series of which the item is a component

Table 8.12: Link that must be made for item registrations

Control data

Every description in every entity should include essential information about when and by whom it was prepared, and provide space for the registrar to make a note that affects the completeness of the registration, e.g. regarding information that could not be found, to indicate whether further work is required or any other comment that they feel is relevant. This information included in this section identifies the registration as an authoritative one and enables the supervisor to provide feedback if required. It is recommended that the following be shown on each description form whether electronic or manually handled.

Note that only the metadata elements shown in bold are mandatory.

Element	Contents
Registered by	Enter the name of the person who registered the series
Date registered	Enter the date the entity was registered
Sources used	
Registration status	You might adopt a range of these to be used in your organisation 'draft', 'approved' and 'cancelled' are often used as status by archives in Australia
Archivist's note	This enables the archivist to record any difficulty in locating sources, time or other restraints on the completion of a description and further work to be done at a later time
Security codes	Indicate whether the record is available for public or other inspection
Amendment date	Enter the date of the most recent amendment
Amendment	Briefly describe the sections of the registration that have been amended followed by the archivist's name

Table 8.13: Metadata elements for control

After description

Recordkeeping for arrangement and description

Registration files

Archivists should be good recordkeepers, just as they expect their transferring agencies to be! It is recommended that a set of files is created for each of the entities you register, and that you create a file (virtual or physical) for each entity you register. Your records management software might be capable of modification to enable the files to duplicate the registration numbers.

For example: Agency File No 1 = the agency that is registered No. 1 in your control system.

Series File No. 1 = the series that is registered No. 1 in your system.

The following may assist you with the contents and management of these records.

Manual system

1. Set up agency and series files for staff use (i.e. each entity you use except items) to keep versions of the registration over time, copies of sources used. Lists of items for series
2. Public set for search room
3. Backup set in another building
4. Repository set if in a separate location (this could double as the back-up set)
5. Keep latest version electronically if possible for ease of updating.

Electronic ystem

1. Staff access to all data in system, both office and repository areas (note: need to specify that the system will track changes over time, or else print out old version for paper file before amending)
2. Public access (this copy will suppress some details such as the specific location; files titles withheld for privacy purposes; information about the acquisition or the control data)

Registration status

You should maintain a control record showing the status of your registrations and identifying records that need more work. You might be able to modify reports already available so that as little as possible needs to be entered manually. This record needs to be kept up to date and can be the basis of progress reports to management and business cases for additional staff or other resources.

For example:

Series No	Status	Comment	Urgency
1	Draft	Archivist still working on this series	High. This is a major series in constant use for inquiries from senior management
2	Draft	The administrative history note needs updating	Medium
3	Approved		
4	Draft	Archivist still working on this series	

Table 8.14: Status of registrations: series entity

Summary reports for various entities

If you have an electronic system, you also need to consider any reports that your system might make for management and/or access purposes, e.g. a simple system showing the registration number, title and date range for each entity is a useful management tool.

Series No	Series title	Start date	End date
1	Semi-official papers of Mr G.A. Robinson, Chief Protector of Aborigines	1 Jan 1822	1 Jan 1849
2	Minute books (Aborigines Welfare Board)	25 Sep 1890	29 Apr 1969
3	Index to minutes of meetings of the Aborigines Welfare Board	21 May 1946	29 Apr 1969
4	Printed copies of acts and regulations srelating to the protection of aborigines	1 Jan 1915	31 Dec 1918
5	Copies of letters sent	1 Jan 1914	31 Dec 1927
6	Circular book (Aborigines Welfare Board)	12 Nov 1952	3 Oct 1957

Table 8.15: Example of a simple report

Inter-entity reports

There are a number of inter-entity reports that are desirable. These may include:

- organisations and the agencies that form part of them together with the date ranges
- series that are created by agency
- series that are created by person or family
- functions and the activities they contain.
- functions/activities and the agencies or series that exercise them.

These may be simple lists that form separate reports.

For example:

Agencies by organisation

Organisation: No. 2 State of New South Wales, 1901–

Agency number	Agency name	Start date	End date
1	Department of Prisons (1874-1970) Department of Corrective Services (1970-)	1 Jan 1901	
2	Department of Main Roads	19 Nov 1932	1 Jan 1989
4	Traffic Authority of New South Wales	1 Jun 1976	16 Jan 1989

Table 8.16: Example of a report 'Agencies by organisation'

Or the same list could be appended to the full organisation details report under the heading 'Agencies that form part of this organisation'.

Physical control

It is recommended that each item is marked with the series and item number as part of the registration process. This will ensure its return to the correct location when removed for use, and facilitate correct citation when used by your clients for submissions or publications. The series number should be placed in a prominent place on the item, such as on the back of a volume or the front of a file cover. An imposed item number (when the original item numbering has not survived) should be written in pencil on the file cover.

Apart from large volumes and sturdier loose-leaf binders whose covers provide considerable protection for their contents, most archives should be placed in archives boxes. This provides protection from dust, pests and light. The National Archives 'type 1' box is widely available from manufacturers in Australia. These are suitable for files to foolscap size, bundles of papers, and small volumes. The advantages of these boxes are:

- their **dimensions** are such that a box is rarely heavy
- they promote **efficient storage**, as five boxes fit exactly to a standard 90cm shelf
- the finger hole at the front not only assists in placing and removing the boxes on the shelf but also provides some **air circulation** to the contents
- the cardboard absorbs water when there is a flood or fire sprinkler activation, protecting the contents from saturation

There are also special boxes available for particular formats including cards, discs and photographs. Acid-free boxes can be used for items of special value and construction. Boxes should be comfortably packed. That is, there should be room for a hand to pack and remove items without damage to either.

Many commercially available boxes are not only larger and heavier when full but also have openings at the bottom and frequently collapse when full with consequences to the order and preservation (and sometimes cleanliness) of the contents and the bodies of the carriers.

When working with the items, minor conservation measures should be undertaken such as replacing rusting clips and straightening crumpled pages, tying items that may otherwise fall apart, substituting new or additional folders if the original ones are unable to hold the contents, using archival tape to repair broken bindings or providing folders or wallets to enclose loose papers. You should develop a conservation report form to record work that requires specialist attention.

These should be retained in series order and may form the basis of submissions for conservation funding.

Location systems

The location system is an essential tool for collection management processes such as stocktaking, as well as the retrieval and return of items. It is a vital record without which the archives could not function. If destroyed, it would be difficult and time-consuming, if not impossible, to reconstruct. It needs to be kept secure and only available to staff, in order to prevent unauthorised access to records. It needs to be backed up, or if in hard copy kept in a separate building.

If you are using a database system, you should be able to design a report showing the locations that you have recorded in the series and item forms. If your system cannot provide this for you, or if some of your archives are described in a separate system (some of your archives may still be controlled in a previous system or you may have a special system for specialised formats), you may need to create a separate location system. Preferably, you should be able to view or print the index in series and item (or other descriptive unit) or location order.

You should develop a uniform system of notation for locations that could include any of the following: building name; storage area; storage equipment type and number; run; bay and shelf number. You will find a brief discussion on location systems in the previous chapter.

Software for archives control

A full discussion about information technology for archives is available in Chapter 10: *Using Computers.* Here we may briefly consider the criteria for selecting electronic systems for arrangement and description. Archival systems need to be relational, that is, there needs to be methodology for linking records and context entities, and items to the relevant series as outlined above. They should enable the registration of functional as well as structural provenance. For each entity, they should contain the fields indicated in the tables above. The system should be capable of producing the reports that you require, and they should be flexible enough to be modified for your unique circumstances if required.

Developing your own system is a time consuming project and for all but the largest archives, or those with highly specialised needs, you should consider the systems that are available either as shareware or for purchase.

There is also the potential for user groups when ready-developed software is acquired. Your information technology staff will have standards and preferences that may influence your selection. Evaluate these systems to determine whether they suit your needs. Prior to selecting 'off the shelf' software, you should read any reports about it and discuss its performance with archives that already use it, particularly similar-sized archives or those in a similar jurisdiction to your own. It should support multiple concurrent users if there is more than one staff member, and should facilitate use in more than one location if required. It should allow for various levels of access if users apart from registrars have access to the system. Software should come with adequate instructions and be user-friendly, that is, the screens should be clearly set out and easy to use, legible, and navigation within the system should be simple.

Introducing a new system

If you identify the need to update your system for archival description, for example the system was a record group system, the data entered manually or devised by a non-archivist, it is recommended that you plan for this as soon as possible. The longer you wait to implement a new system, the more data you will have to transfer. However, you will need to allow time for evaluating the options available to you, which might involve discussions with colleagues in similar archives as well as various people in your own organisation; budgeting for the purchase of equipment and other resources; and presenting a business case to your manager. If the data cannot be transferred automatically, you will need to plan for the conversion of the data from the previous system. If possible, use your former identifiers so that physical re-numbering is not required and users can relocate and cite archives previously used. However, if the system is radically different and you need to change the series numbers, you will need to create a table or similar tool that indicates the old and new numbers for the various series and other entities whose numbers are altered.

Look upon the introduction of a new system as an opportunity to improve the data in the existing documentation, owing to developments of standards in the archival community. For example, introduce functional provenance or add some of the fields in the various forms. Depending upon your resources, you might enhance as you convert your various records or create a further plan that identifies records that need more work and rate the urgency in each case. If you are continuing to add to some of the series already registered, these series can be transferred across to your new system as accruals are received. Inevitably, there will be series that have ceased and you should investigate the possibility of training clerical staff to transfer your data in records where this is relatively straightforward if this is an option.

Procedures documentation for arrangement and description

In addition to recording the reason for individual decisions when describing the various context or records entities in your archives, it is recommended that you develop a policy or procedure manual for your archives arrangement and description processes (or a chapter in your archives administration manual). This should help to ensure some consistency of the work between colleagues and their successors and give some guidance about using the electronic system, as well as form part of the disaster recovery program. The manual should also indicate the levels of access to the system, indicating who can add new entries, amend existing ones and who may view without update rights. While the information technology staff will have technical data about the system, most archivists appreciate a more accessible summary of the practicalities of using it. The manual should indicate the importance of the various fields – those which are mandatory for system purposes or required in your organisation for adequate intellectual control.

This manual is a living document that will be developed over time and will therefore be under constant review as new issues are encountered. Usually you would not begin a draft of this document until you have some familiarity with the records of your organisation and have undertaken some quantity of the descriptive work. However, from the outset you should begin to make notes about areas in which consistency needs to be defined, making rules or guidelines and documenting them.

The manual may include some or all of the following:

- definitions of the entities and the fields within them
- reasons for including each field in your system
- guidance about the contents of each field, e.g. rules regarding the measurement of shelf metres (how precise does it need to be?), how to express the number and type of boxes; the format of dates, the qualifiers that may be used when an exact date is unknown (such as' ?', 'by', 'year of', 'decade of'; use of abbreviations; coping with agencies with exact titles; identify any style manuals that are used for written work in your organisation
- decisions relating to problems encountered
- rules for a minimal description
- data types
- examples from entities already entered
- recommendations for sources of information

It is also advisable to include the field types and sizes at some place in your document. You might feel that this is most appropriate in a separate table where all of the like information is stored together and the section can be located quickly. You could also include this information in the section devoted to each field.

When you are preparing your manual, you may wish to contact the major archives institutions, some of who have their manuals available on their web sites. Colleagues in similar-sized archives would also be willing to assist.

Conclusion

In this chapter we have considered the principles of arrangement – provenance and original order – and have surveyed the description of archives, especially the requirements of the series system. We have also considered some ancillary tasks, such as the records that need to be made in conjunction with these activities. These tasks are challenging for the newcomer to the archival profession and demanding upon resources. Every archival collection is different and you will need to make decisions that best suit your archives, your resources and your anticipated growth rate. See Further Reading for material that might assist you with further study in this area, and it is also recommended that you 'network' with colleagues in similar archives and avail yourself of the activities of the Australian Society of Archivists Inc.

CHAPTER 9

enriching the record: documentation programs

ANN PEDERSON

CHAPTER ABSTRACT

Documentation programs are activities to create or collect resources that complement, enrich and fill gaps in the archival record. In this, documentation programs are a close relative of both reference and outreach activities, in that all three foster and depend on the archives and its constituents sharing responsibility for the historical records.

This chapter outlines the types of documentation programs and introduces issues you need to consider in planning and undertaking such programs. Examples of documentation projects include photographic surveys, recording the remembered past (oral and video history) and copying inaccessible records, images and inscriptions in private hands for deposit in archival repositories where they are organised and managed for public research. Example forms and checklists are included on the accompanying CD.

What are documentation programs?

Documentation programs take archivists out into their communities to assemble documents or to capture information of historical interest for future research. In fact, it is the archival quest to amass representative and complete documentation that motivates undertakings to create, copy or transcribe and organise previously inaccessible sources. Many of these research materials, such as oral or video histories, have been especially designed and created to fill gaps in the written records. Other documentary sources, such as photographs in private hands or gravestones, already exist, but are so scattered and isolated that they are useless for research unless copied and organised.

The family of activities we are calling 'documentation programs' has three basic branches. The first, *created* documentation, comprises projects that set out to make specialised recordings. Some of these proactively document present surroundings and activities, while others seek to recover unexpressed memories of phenomena or experiences. While oral history and video recordings are the best known forms of these, we also include contemporary projects to photograph towns and institutions at regular or critical phases in their ongoing development.

The second major branch of documentation activity comprises efforts to re-record or make *facsimile copies* of existing records and images that are not otherwise available for research. In short, such projects copy individual collections of photographs and documents in order to preserve the copies at the archives for access and use by the public. Examples of this work include the copying, via electrostatic, photographic or digital means, of selected official or personal papers (particularly diaries, minutes and letters) and images held privately in distant or scattered locations.

A third category, though closely related to the first two, is one comprising projects to *transcribe* and *compile* information recorded on gravestones, buildings, caves and other structures in relatively obscure locations into forms more useful to researchers. Projects in this category often require the sending out of teams of people to obscure locations to write out inscriptions and/or to photograph the structures bearing them for later compilation and subsequent use by researchers. These projects are generally more involved with capturing and organising the selected information than they are in facsimile reproduction, unless they are documenting materials where physical characteristics are integral to understanding.

This chapter on documentation programs will have a generalist approach, focussing on the issues to consider when undertaking oral history, video recording, and heritage photography projects, rather than on giving step-by-step instructions.

The reasons for choosing an overview model, as opposed to detailed discussion, are fourfold. Firstly, the archives can undertake an enormous variety of activities under these headings and to attempt to treat even the major types in detail would require several

These items are facsimile copies of records which are not available for research purposes in their original state due to age, rarity and fragility.

books. Secondly, several of the activities highlighted, such as oral history or documentary photography, already have a considerable body of how-to literature available that can be perused. Thirdly, any specific recommendations for equipment and techniques are sure to be outmoded, given the pace of developments in digital technology. Finally, it is rather more important to see these programs as enrichments to and extensions of existing core functions, to be considered only after the overall archival program is progressing well.

The need for planning and commitment

The first questions an archivist or organisation considering documentation activities should ask are: 'what resources are required for such programs?' and 'how will they relate to the other commitments and priorities of the archives and of the organisation as a whole?' If your institution is currently struggling to find the staff, space and equipment to manage its existing collections, it may not be wise to stretch resources further with an outreach venture that depends heavily on having specialist expertise, equipment and money to ensure a quality product.

All successful documentation programs require a certain standard of technical and historical excellence. Unlike written materials, which are easily created in readily accessible (eye-readable) forms, most documentation projects depend entirely on complex, 'machine-readable' only technologies for recording and use. Poor-quality recorders, tapes, discs or photographic/imaging tools can result in totally wasted efforts because the recordings produced are so inferior.

Over and above materials, it is equally important to have expertise, policies and procedures to ensure that the process of selecting and recording the material will create high-quality researchable materials.

However, creating the best documentary products using proper materials and techniques is only the first step. Many archivists do these things well, yet end up with poor programs because they did not plan carefully for the final and most important phase of the project – the facilities and staff to maintain and reference the collections over the years.

Of primary importance is ensuring the ongoing integrity and usability of the original recordings, a task complicated by rapid technological change and limited standardisation. Whatever its method or media, an original recording must be preserved in a secure, usable state for the long term. In the past, recordings on film or magnetic media were stored completely out of use, except to make a duplicating master which itself was accessed only occasionally to make a duplicating master that in turn was used to create additional copies for reference. The expense of proper storage for the original and of producing the recommended copies (the preservation/security original, the master duplicate, and a reference copy) for each individual recording was considerable but essential. Sadly, time and technological obsolescence degrade all equipment and recordings, even the best. In response, the archives community has established specialist facilities and staff, such as the National Film and Sound Archive in Canberra, to maintain and 'refresh' ageing media artefacts and then to 'migrate' them onto trustworthy new formats.

"Gee, now that your mother's diaries have been documented, I can see why she never liked me."

Today, most new recordings still rely on established methods and media, but are quickly converted into digital objects to be protected via deposit into the trusted digital repositories of leading state and national archival authorities. These comprehensive institutions readily offer support to quality local documentation initiatives, providing them with advice, studios, storage, equipment and/or grant support on a cooperative basis at minimal cost.

Because digital objects are infinitely 'clonable' without degradation or damage, making them widely accessible is now much easier than with older media. A few clicks and a recording can be viewable and listenable anywhere in the world, provided standardised technology is employed and the appropriate conditions governing access have been met. However, access to advanced technology and expertise, while costly (less so if shared with larger institutional partners or donated by sponsors), is only one component of the project's full cost.

Whether recordings are made via traditional or digital methods using 'old' or new technologies and media, there are considerable and ongoing expenses involved with identifying its multimedia content, letting researchers know it is available and making (and keeping) it accessible and useable, via the creation of transcripts, indexes, finding aids and electronic interfaces.

The preparation of access tools is more expensive because multiple types of information (images, sound, emotions, text, movements, colours) might be held within a single recording and cannot be easily summarised. It is quite impossible to convey the essence of a multimedia sequence via a text description. Time and content log sheets serve as make-shift 'indexes' to recordings, and transcripts document spoken content, but to fully comprehend its information, one really must experience the entire recording. Creating these finding aids involves time, media literacy and insightfulness, as well as accuracy and concentration. Again, staff members with the necessary combination of qualities for multimedia work do not come cheap.

Even with all the audiovisual expertise and money in the world, a documentation project can founder. A major underlying, though undeclared, goal of all documentation programming is achieving community interest and ongoing support for the archives and its work. There is an all-important social psychology aspect of documentation programs that must be well addressed if projects are to succeed. More than other types of archival activities, such efforts bring archivists into close contact with their communities. Participants are asked to entrust their personal memories and documentation to archival care, where they may become publicly accessible for the first time ever. Some materials may never have been shown before, even to other family members, and are touchstones for primal and personal feelings. Thus, archivists responsible for the conduct of projects and the processes involved – selection, reproduction, preservation and, ultimately, use – must anticipate raising expectations and worries alike and arrange to deal with them wisely.

An experienced archivist will have seen hundreds of photographs, letters and souvenir items and developed a discerning eye, but must never forget that each participant's material is unique and important to him or her. Often, members of the public don't understand what 'making material available to the public' could involve and need examples. One donor was upset when, several months after permitting the archives to copy family images, he found a reproduction of one of them decorating the walls of a fast food outlet. He found that use of his material inappropriate, whereas the proprietor and other members of the community felt that the historic scenes promoted appreciation of the town's colourful past. Everything ended well in the end, but awareness, wisdom and preparation are needed when negotiating the minefields of community and family politics.

Irrespective of such glitches, documentation projects are very exciting and many people will want to participate. All project participants, be they staff, sponsors, interview candidates, donors or volunteers, will require considerable education, guidance and support if one hopes to produce materials of research quality. The key is to arrange for them to do so via well-organised and meaningful experiences, and to show them commensurate appreciation for their efforts.

Considering and weighing all of the factors we have discussed – resources, prior commitments, technical quality, good procedures, time, and a desire and capacity to be intimately involved with people – will help ensure that your documentation activities are well designed to achieve satisfying, quality results for all involved.

Created documentation programs

The search for a way to capture actual events, meetings, performances and encounters so that they can be readily re-experienced has been underway for many years. The challenge has always been how to replicate the sights, sounds, feelings, and movements of life-in-process in a long-lasting record. Since most archives operate under a wide directive 'to collect and preserve their host community's valuable historical resources', a number of them have undertaken special activities to *create* records capturing the present and recent past. Known as oral history, modern heritage projects, local history programs, or historical photography, all created documentation programs select persons, places and events in their communities and set about creating public 'memories' of them via analogue and digital recorders and cameras. The resulting products of such recording sessions are photographic negatives and prints, magnetic and digital 'patterns' on tapes, and discs of various types that the archivist brings under archival control for indefinite preservation and ongoing research.

Special characteristics of created documentation

What makes these materials different from those described in earlier chapters is the way they *come into being*. Most archival holdings start life as ordinary records, created and used to facilitate the business or life activities of individuals or groups. Accumulations of such records evolve over time into 'archives', attaining such status within a recordkeeping regime or being deemed worthy for deposit by an archivist. With created documentation, the archivist, with or without third parties, is the primary maker of unique recordings that would never have been created under normal circumstances – snapshots and/or summaries of experiences, in some cases many years after they occurred.

Whereas all records are intentionally created, these types are more 'self-conscious' and therefore require more caution in their use than others. Oral history summaries of experiences recalled from memory by selected participants are not 'true records' because they are not contemporaneous recordings of unfolding events. But then how many people use a recording device to conduct their business? 'A Day in a Life'-style documentary photographs do not capture the ebb and flow of places and activities, they only freeze a moment in a particular place and time. Yet the answer to the question 'should we bother with such materials at all?' is always a resounding 'yes!'

When used along with a range of contemporaneous materials, including actual records, created documentation such as oral history adds incomparable insights and richness. Locating and acquiring letters, diaries, papers and photographs of the events or persons under study provides the all-important reference points from which to test the authority and reliability of the interviews.

For example, using oral history recordings interactively with those audio and video tapes or discs, and photos that are 'natural' products of ongoing work activity, promotes better historical outcomes. The regular audio recording of meetings of the city council captures discussions during the normal course of business and, therefore, the recordings are primary records of council affairs. However, if the recordings are later interviews with key aldermen giving their recollections and opinions about what happened in the meeting, they have less reliability as evidence. This diminished authority reflects the fact that the interviews were influenced by the personal viewpoints of the aldermen and of the interviewer, particularly if they were recorded much later or if they focus on a specific issue which evolved slowly over time. Such tapes are selected and filtered accounts especially designed to capture definite information and therefore must be used for research with those factors in mind. While audiovisual materials are especially vulnerable to subjective influences, the same filtering is present in paper records. For example, the tape recordings of meetings may be summarised into written minutes that delete emotional exchanges, points of discussion and other information important to understanding how a particular problem might have been solved. Actual decisions are documented, but the all-important questions of HOW and WHY they were arrived at, are not.

Additionally, there are special aspects of sound, video and film media which archivists must appreciate and plan to accommodate. The first is to recognise that these materials capture *actual events in progress* and therefore intrinsically convey several types of information that written records do not like sound, movement, time and emotion. Because of these additional dimensions, such records cannot be summarised, edited or transcribed without distorting the experiences they were created to preserve. Thus, special care must be taken to maintain the *integrity of these experiences* as they were originally recorded, though they will, in future, be migrated/transferred to newer technologies and transcripts, and summaries of their informational contents may be created to facilitate reference use.

A second fact to remember is that there is always more than one person involved in creating audiovisual records. With written materials, the writer both creates the document and determines its content. However, with audiovisual media, there may be several people involved: the subject; the interviewer who may or may not be operating the recording equipment; and perhaps others such as researchers, project directors, artists, musicians or technicians. Having multiple creators means that several interpretations and viewpoints can influence the record. It may present the subject or event as interviewed and/or photographed by another person, and this fact should always be recorded and noted when audiovisual materials are used as historical evidence.

A third concern is the overweening dominance of and dependence upon technology in created documentation programs. Quality electronic devices and storage systems are needed to make, re-experience and preserve and migrate recordings. The recordings themselves are unintelligible if the media, hardware or software is flawed or unavailable. Improving digital technologies are bringing the Holy Grail of 'one-byte-fits-all' management within our grasp, but at the cost of new and greater risks. While by converting to digital technologies allows archives to farewell their 'museums' of past audiovisual forms and equipment, it is still not the perfect solution. The absence of sufficient standards, and the ease with which undetectable alteration, cloning, cannibalisation, deletion or theft can take place, raises huge concerns. In the language of the digital world, the foundation archival concept of a unique, reliable, authentic, actual 'original' translates into a unique, reliable, authentic, logical 'meta-data encapsulated object' to be created, maintained, used and migrated to a new technology before obsolescence occurs.

Keeping one's program and recordings abreast of technological change is a concern for all archivists. While the technology tail truly wags our documentation dog today and for the foreseeable future, all is not doom and gloom. Heritage institutions around the world are actively researching solutions to mitigate the problem, and regularly post their recommendations on the internet. Smaller archives may employ their recommended 'tried and true' technologies with confidence, knowing that their recordings will be suitable for technological upgrade in the future.

A final area of concern requires specialist advice. Because audiovisual recordings, particularly reminiscences, are complex literary works that make assertions and express personal opinions about actual events and people, laws regulating multiple copyrights, privacy and defamation must be accommodated. While there is no need for alarm, caution and prevention are advised. A legal expert should examine copying and recording project contracts, agreements and related records so that any potential risks and liabilities can be identified and minimised.

Regardless of the issues or debate surrounding created documentation, one thing is certain:

> *We live in an audiovisual world where sound, image and motion reign supreme over the written word.*

More and more institutions and people are becoming involved in created documentation programs. They are recording oral reminiscences of the community, making videos of local events, drawing or photographing town landmarks, to name only a few such activities. Not only are people involved with creating records, they are also generating excitement and interest in history as a result of doing so. By taking a leadership role, the professional archival community can join in to promote good documentation program practices and discourage those that are unwise or unsound. Working together ensures that institutions undertaking such activities use their scarce resources wisely, and that everyone working with them can be confident of a worthwhile outcome.

Iconic structures such as this are obvious subjects for documentation. Still images taken of the construction of the Sydney Harbour Bridge in the 1920s show development, progress and change. 'Ordinary' subjects are just as worthy of such documentation.

Re-development and construction works are an obvious catalyst for a documentation program. However, images taken at regular intervals of the same street-scapes or grounds add, over time, to our documentary heritage.

Types of created documentation: Photography

Programs centred on photography and historical photographs appeal to many audiences and afford excellent opportunities for involving the public in archival collecting efforts. Photographic documentation projects are of two major types – current or retrospective. The first is discussed in this section as it is a form of created documentation. The second, retrospective heritage photography or projects to re-photograph (traditionally or digitally) existing images from the past, is discussed later in this chapter. The website of the Visual Materials Section of the Society of American Archivists is an excellent source of contacts, advice and examples of forms for all sorts of documentary photography projects. (See Further Reading)

Modern heritage photography usually involves a regular program of taking and obtaining high-quality photographs of events, persons, places and activities occurring within the geographic area served by the archives. Such a program offers a number of advantages. Firstly, it generates regular increments of significant, technically competent images for the collections. Secondly, many professional and amateur photographers welcome an invitation to perform such a service in their communities. Thirdly, there are good prospects for arranging sponsorships within the imaging industry and partnerships with community organisations such as art schools, camera clubs, or local press associations. Finally, most of the images can be accessioned and used without confusion about ownership, copyright and personal privacy issues because they were taken with permission on behalf of the archives or donated by the photographers.

Well in advance of taking the first shot, documentary photography planners should produce a descriptive brief that carefully explains the project's documentary and artistic goals, contractual obligations, procedures and standards. In addition, planners recommend using a Request for Quotation (RFQ) or Proposal (RFP) to invite prospective photographers and other personnel to tender their services. We will discuss the issues and arrangements for this later when assessing the option of outsourcing. A Provision of Services Agreement should be signed between the archives and each 'outside' person working with the project, whether paid or volunteer, to document the transfer or sharing of ownership of the image and/or of related rights, as indicated in the sample in Table 9.1. When taking photographs that include recognisable persons, photographers should ask each individual to sign a release, consenting to being photographed and granting unrestricted use of the images in which he or she appears. Project documentation should be drafted and/or reviewed by a legal professional for validity and to ensure that the images produced or acquired by the project can be used without complication or risk.

The success of these programs depends heavily on the ability of staff members to make the photographers aware of the kinds of images that are most useful for historical purposes. For example, the project could focus on local organisations in an effort to create a visual record of key work activities of representative institutions – economic, social, political and cultural – that shape the character of everyday life. Another approach is to document the buildings, streets, and neighbourhoods that form the physical fabric of the community. As part of this effort, photographers should be asked to submit logs containing all pertinent information about their images (dates, names, locations, activities and other details) so that the original negatives/in-camera digital files and subsequent prints/copies can be properly labelled and catalogued. These records should be maintained on deposit at the archives as part of the project file.

Because such projects involve continuing photographic activity, the staff should work with the photographers in devising a plan for photographing sites, landmarks, events and similar subjects at regular intervals, perhaps every three to five years. During the rest of the year, project personnel should try to document major events and gatherings by working with local print media personnel or arranging to dispatch a member of the project team to cover selected occasions.

Types of created documentation: Oral history

Oral history is, perhaps, the best known and most widely practised type of documentation program. A concept difficult to define concisely, oral history is essentially an information-gathering technique whereby sound recording equipment is used systematically to capture 'verbatim accounts or opinions of persons who are or were witnesses to or participants in events likely to be of interest to future scholars' (Moss 1974). Aural or sound materials lend a colour and dimension that extends information beyond the written page into an involving experience. With sound, we know not only what is said, but how. The nuance of the tone and timbre of voice, the urgency and cadence of speaking helps us tune in on the emotional wavelength of the speaker and thereby to come closer to his or her experience.

Transcribing the inscriptions on foundation stones or head stones is one way of enriching the records you already have. It may also be the start of a new project which results in a publication or exhibition.

For many years, aural documentation was primarily a tool for scholars of anthropology, music, history and literature. Today, it is used far more widely. Many governments, law and health professionals regularly produce and consume such materials in their decision making, using them as raw material for reports, judgements and recommendations. Around the world, recording reminiscences plays a vital role in documenting and reconciling the tumultuous events of our recent past, especially in settings where natural and human disasters have decimated holdings of written records. National and state/provincial research library and archival authorities are generally the best sources of expertise for beginners. The National Library of Australia, the Australian War Memorial, the National Film and Sound Archive, and the Australian Institute of Aboriginal and Torres Strait Islander Studies (AIATSIS), as well as major state and university libraries, host vibrant oral history programs and solicit cohesive aural collections from research professionals who have used it in their own scholarly investigations.

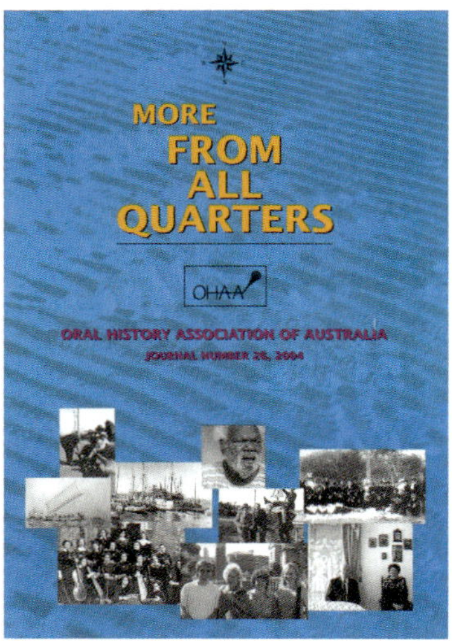

The Oral History Association of Australia provides resources to assist those wishing to undertake an Oral History project.

Australians with an active interest in oral history have formed the Oral History Association of Australia, a highly professional and welcoming body with superb publications and activities. The increasing number of institutions and professional bodies involved with aural documentation underscores its stature as a valuable discipline to enhance and fill gaps in traditional archival collections.

Good oral history is seldom the child of spontaneity. A successful project requires careful research and preparation at many levels: in selecting the focus of the effort; in choosing the persons to be interviewed; in designing the questions to be asked; in mastering the art of being a good interviewer; and in preparing the materials for long-term preservation and use. The following are some suggestions for achieving quality in all five areas:

- design the subject and scope of the project with a clear sense of what can be accomplished in terms of information, quality and the potential value of the project for future research investigations
- be sure to consider the expense and technical problems involved in the preparation, use and long-term maintenance of the 'original' recording manifest on either a physical medium (disc or tape) or virtually on a computer drive or mass storage system
- select and train personnel for the project so that all interviewers are skilled interpersonal communicators who are also well versed in the subject matter to be covered
- select good quality, reliable and manageable recording equipment and media. If you have volunteer workers conducting the interviews, you should have kits of equipment and blank tapes/discs suitable for them to use. Even with the best equipment, you will also need back-ups in case of mechanical difficulties or tape snarls. Use a high quality microphone and invest in special filters to block out extraneous noises. Larger archival repositories with established programs or local broadcasters may be willing to recommend, or even lend, equipment to meet your needs
- do your archival and legal homework so that your effort yields long-lasting, high quality recordings accessible for research and quotation. Have a legal professional vet contracts and agreements and draft guidelines to avoid defamation. Carefully document the purpose and design of the project, the conditions under which the interviews were conducted and any factors that might have affected the objectivity of the interviewee's comments
- ensure that all participants understand and support your project from the beginning. Send a letter of invitation (see Appendix 9.2), introducing the project and explaining in general terms what participation will involve and especially how the material may be used in future. It is especially important that participants understand and agree that portions of their interviews could be used in exhibitions (traditional and website) or in documentary films/videos and publications that may be broadcast or sold. Most participants readily permit research and exhibition use, but many want the option to approve publication or broadcast requests on a case-by-case basis. If further permissions will be required, be sure to have forms and procedures available to facilitate obtaining them. For example, get the participant's agreement to be contacted directly by prospective publishers/documentary makers. Request forms should be in

writing, describe the proposed publication/documentary and copies with signatures given to all parties

- have each interviewer (even if an employee of the archives) and interviewee sign a series of documents agreeing to participate in the project, to donate their interviews and copyrights to the archives and to permit full use of the recordings, transcripts and related materials as outlined above. Examples of such agreements appear in Appendices 9.3 and 9.4.
- keep the project moving with training, direction, regular progress reports and encouragement. Appendices 9.5 and 9.6 outline key procedures and insights to be followed by all new project personnel
- ask interviewees to contribute images and written records to the archives (see Table 9.1 for ideas). If possible, photograph or video informants at the time they are interviewed
- publicise the project during the phases of its development: conception, planning, progress and results as the materials become available for research
- protect original recordings immediately through proper labelling and storage and do not play them except to produce a duplicating master from which additional copies will be made for indexing work or for later reference use
- to transcribe or not to transcribe, that is the question. Because of the expense of transcription and the loss of information that can be conveyed only by sound, it is recommended that archivists not transcribe, but rather prepare notes describing the sequence of topics discussed keyed to the numerical counter of the recorder /player. These notes then serve as a rough index to the recordings
- be sure to thank personnel connected with the recording and, if funding permits, enclose a duplicate copy of the recorded interview as a memento of appreciation
- consider using excerpts from copies of project recordings on web pages, in audiovisual presentations or public service segments for radio and television. Few things add more impact to messages than recordings from 'real life'.

The State Records NSW exhibition 'In living memory' is a clear example of how a created documentation program enhanced a major exhibition on the records of the NSW Aborigines Protection/Welfare Board. The project brought archivists into contact with aboriginal families affected by the board over more than a century and uncovered many fascinating stories. Family members contributed new photos to complement the government photographs and other records and the whole experience was extremely positive, enriching the record and the lives of everyone involved.

Don't forget documents and photos!

The person whose recollections you are recording may also have either valuable documentary material in family albums, in suitcases, in boxes in the attic or in other places. This material can assist during the interview by stirring memories. It is also a valuable asset for an archival collection, and in any presentation of a community's and/or an individual's history.

The following list has been devised by an organisation concerned with documenting the experiences of immigrants and identifies desirable types of documents which might be found among a migrant's personal effects:

Personal records:

- diaries, journals, memoirs
- documentary ephemera (e.g. school memorabilia, naturalisation certificates, passports, employment records, trade union and political party tickets, club/society membership cards, travel brochures, posters, tickets, souvenir ephemera etc)
- letters to and from family, friends
- photographs
- scrapbooks

Government publications and records related to immigration:

From country of origin

- information about emigration (e.g. pamphlets, newsletters, etc)
- exit and travel documentation – copies of completed applications and stamped copies of approvals (e.g. of government agencies, regulations, procedures, etc)

From country of destination

- publicity pamphlets and posters about new country, directed at migrants
- guides for new immigrants, citizenship booklets
- letters to and from new country government authorities about the possibility of immigration; grievances, disputes
- entry and settlement documentation – copies of completed applications and stamped copies of approvals (e.g. of government agencies, regulations, procedures, etc)

Local newsletters, newspapers and journals (in English and other languages): including *ad hoc* publications produced on board the ship on the way to new country, or in holding centres; or by ethnic communities in new country or elsewhere.

Records of social clubs, welfare associations, political organisations, religious groups, and so on that support new immigrants:

- minutes of meetings, statement of objectives, membership lists, correspondence
- photographs of activities and events
- commemorative programs, posters, publicity releases and news cuttings
- reports of office-bearers and events planners

Adapted from Wilton, Janis and Bollard, Angela, *Balancing the books; Oral history for the community,* Ethnic Affairs Commission of NSW, Sydney, 1983.

Table 9.1: Don't forget documents and photos!

Types of created documentation: Video

Television has been an integral and increasingly important part of life in industrialised societies for nearly 60 years, and serves as the major point of contact that most people have with events beyond their immediate experience. This powerful electronic window has been praised and criticised on many levels, but few can deny its unique capacity to capture and present events that would, in former times, never have been recorded, much less viewed, in the intimacy of one's home. Rapid advances in technology, lower costs and a growing interest in re-experiencing moments in one's own life have made personal digital video recording even more popular than home movies were several decades ago. In fact, electronic multimedia equipment and expertise are becoming integrated into our business and personal lives, so much so that the video recording of events and experiences is joining audio recording as a major medium for created historical documentation, and may even replace it as multimedia production and storage technologies standardise and costs fall.

Video: The pluses and minuses

If we are then to consider undertaking video as well as audio history projects, what are the benefits and drawbacks of such an effort?

On the plus side, video recordings undeniably capture human activity far more completely than most other forms of records, except for motion pictures. Colour, movement, sound and perspective are a powerful sensory combination for documenting life in progress. Video technology is also becoming cheaper, more portable and easier to use than its film equivalent. Because video recording is an electronic rather than a photographic process, it also offers the benefit of instant replay, making it possible for users to view the quality of their recording on the spot and re-record portions that are deemed faulty. The quality of immediacy also creates in the beholder a greater sense of involvement with actions and

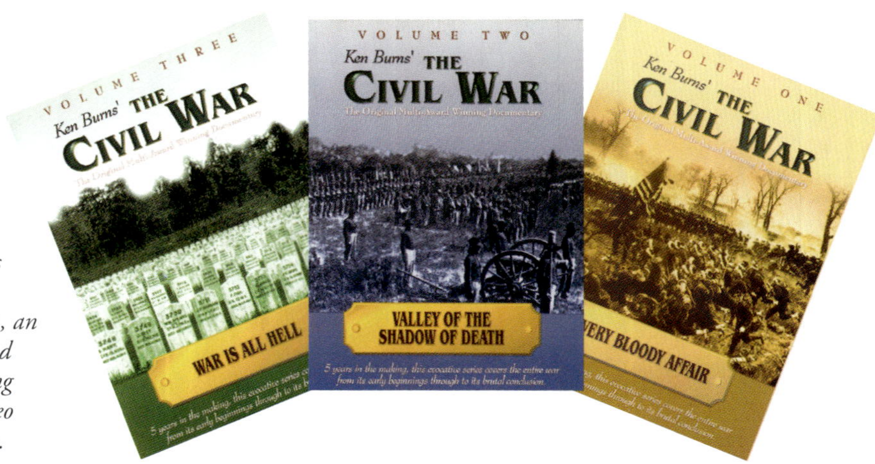

The Ken Burns documentary, The Civil War, *an outstanding and ground breaking example of video documentation.*

events because he or she is watching them as they unfold. A final benefit of video is its popularity. It is literally a household fixture that reaches out to the world and, since surveys have shown that most people use television as their major source of information and entertainment, it follows that people are potentially more receptive to events and messages presented through this medium.

Archival sources are enjoying peak popularity via television documentaries, using techniques that bring historical images and documents 'to life', pioneered by American Ken Burns in his mesmerising series *The Civil War* (1990). Personalising the detail of photographs with voice-over quotes from contemporaneous letters and diaries reanimated the past as never before. Viewers were thrilled and 'The Ken Burns effect' was born. Decades later and after a plethora of archives-centric films by Burns and others, historical materials and archives still bask in well-deserved glory.

The negative side of video documentation is also impressive, particularly the fragility and instability of magnetic media for long-term retention, that is for archives. Traditionally, video and audio records transform dark, light and/or sound into electronic pulses that record their message magnetically by rearranging particles of a metal oxide layer supported by a plastic backing. The resulting recording is delicate and easily altered or damaged physically by scratching and by exposure to other sources of magnetism. Furthermore, the metal oxide coating can degrade and the plastic backing can stretch or grow brittle with age. All of these factors make magnetic media a questionable choice for maintaining information which needs to be kept permanently.

Digital encoding on optical media, or flash memory, is replacing magnetic technology, but standards are still fluid. Nonetheless, projects to 'digitise' recordings on earlier media and manage them in virtual environments are well underway. The general premise is that it is better to transfer now, using the most widely accepted digital technologies and standards, understanding that migration to newer technology platforms will be necessary in the future.

A second feature of video technology that is undesirable for archival documentation is the ease with which it can be purposefully manipulated, edited or recorded without a trace. Archival records must have integrity as evidence of reality, meaning that video cannot be used for recording information which must stand alone as legal evidence, unless very stringent controls and conditions are met, such as those for building surveillance systems.

However difficult these problems of stability and archival integrity are, there is hope that they may be resolved in the near future. Digital disc technology, which uses lasers to incise digitised information on a high-density storage medium, is a promising alternative. Readily available in the entertainment world as pre-recorded compact discs (CDs), mini-discs (MDs) and digital video discs (DVDs), this technology is very popular but, though the recording process is becoming cheaper and more available, the technology is still too 'immature' to be entrusted with the archival record. Most archives are digitising 'archival originals' in order to produce reference copies and/or prepare segments of their holdings for publication or exhibition via the archives' websites. Best archival practice still requires archives to preserve their 'originals' in their 'birth' technology.

Caution is vital when outsourcing any sort of digitisation work to commercial vendors. Requests for Quotation/Proposal or tender documents must specify the technical and managerial standards and processes vendors must follow.

Archivists also have a duty of care to advise their communities on this topic. Many people believe that digitisation will miraculously bring order and permanence to their 'archaeological dig' of personal photographs and documents. Vendors offering to scan vintage home movies and/or personal 'snaps' onto video or DVD 'to preserve them' are everywhere, including the internet. While vendors and the public both desire a quality outcome at a reasonable cost, only a few have the expertise, facilities and equipment necessary to achieve near 'archival' results. And even fewer realise that the digital surrogates require careful storage and management to remain useful and usable into the future.

Neither video nor DVD offer a safe substitute for film, and many people have regretted not having consulted an archival expert and retaining their original images. If you have films in your collections (or videos for that matter) that you want to preserve, contact the national institution responsible for historical film and/or sound collections in your country for advice. In Australia, the National Film and Sound Archive in Canberra, or the preservation department of your state library or archival authority, are important resources. Though they may be obliged to charge a fee for assistance, their advice will be safe and authoritative.

Once digitisation costs come down and standards and portability increase, larger archives may gradually convert their magnetic video and audio recordings into digital objects within mass storage devices. But it is still very uncertain when or if any new or emerging technology will succeed the 'tried and true' photographic and magnetic recording systems.

The third major area of disadvantage of video for archival documentation relates to the production facilities required. Few archives are equipped for quality video recording, largely because such work could only ever comprise a tiny part of our overall mission and because the technological facilities and expertise have, until very recently, been far too costly.

As sophisticated consumers of professionally produced television programs, we aspire to the same level of quality for our own archival audio and video outputs, forgetting that most professional productions are just that – productions – with actors, scripts, direction, lights, cameras and multiple 'takes'. Not at all the 'real life' archival video attempts to capture. In contrast then, archival video may appear long, monotonous, rambling, with poor or uneven illumination and amateurish camerawork when compared with commercial products. The 'talking heads' approach makes even the most engaging participant appear dull. However, the staff, equipment and planning needed to excite jaded viewing palates (i.e. lights, multiple camera angles, cues, re-takes and interruptions to insert photos or documents) can very easily overwhelm continuity of thought and the relaxed atmosphere necessary for genuine rapport. Care and balance are needed to engender interest without sacrificing documentary purpose.

Be part of the multimedia revolution

Today, the world is experiencing a revolution in personal electronic empowerment. Individuals can now purchase hardware and software for video-making that would have cost many thousands of dollars just a few years ago. Increasingly, inexpensive cameras, audio devices, editing and special effects software linked to increasingly powerful personal computers have transformed what we view and download. Websites such as YouTube and MySpace offer a free showcase for home-made video clips, catering to all tastes and interests. Many of these have 'documentary' properties in that they record events or phenomena as they unfold. Production values associated with studio-based work no longer reign supreme. Viewers are accustomed to hand-held cameras, fluctuating focus and now associate them with 'actuality', rather than stage-managed scenarios. What makes these materials so watchable is their subject matter, timeliness, compactness and dynamism. Most are short – the video equivalent of a snapshot. Longer sequences that aim to cover periods of time do require more polish to achieve a level of 'viewability'.

Leading news broadcasters such as ABC, BBC and CNN all encourage viewers to capture and upload mobile phone images and video clips of events for inclusion in breaking news broadcasts. Memorable early examples include survivor coverage of the Bali bombing and SE Asian tsunami. Footage contributed by members of the public is now commonplace in news broadcasts. Some, however, have had such impact that they are forever embedded in public memory as reliable 'witnesses' to the events they portray. Think of the home movie footage of the 1963 Dallas Kennedy motorcade, the Challenger space shuttle explosion, the Rwanda massacres, among others that come immediately to mind.

It is hugely important for today's archives that archival professionals reach out to work cooperatively with these influential sites and each other to ensure that significant documentaries are identified, appraised and offered protection in a managed virtual archives space. Together, industry and archives must build heritage appreciation and empower the individual-as-archivist with sound professional guidelines to digitise and/or upload his/her own born digital 'archives' for potential preservation. A vision of such a project is outlined in Appendix 9.7. Affiliating and familiarising yourself with the work of consortia involved in website archiving via the National Library of Australia's PADI (Preserving Access to Digital Information) initiative will get you off to a great start.

Uses of video for archives

Having assessed the pluses and minuses of video technology as a medium for capturing archival information, let us turn now to some of the uses it can have for archives. Most of these uses stem from the advantages video possesses, that is, its capacity to make a multi-sensory record of events in process and its suitability for reaching a wide audience.

Documentation: Despite its technical limitations, video is still a very effective and attractive way to record community personalities, activities or events. Video interviews are competing with oral history as a popular choice for documenting local identities. Like audio recording, video is now highly portable and brings the additional dimensions of vision and colour to the project. Not only can the person be seen and heard, but aspects of his or her surroundings and related photographs, letters and artworks can also be included. Recordings from multiple cameras and viewing angles allow technical specialists to 'cut and paste' raw footage into a satisfying viewing experience. Skilful use of such post-production editing to explore the speaker's expressions and detailed images of people and events under discussion truly brings an interview subject to life.

Video is also useful to record community or institutional events or to do 'slice-of-life' documentation. Commemorative events such as centenaries offer re-enactments and parades. Festivals present opportunities to document current public taste and interest in art, music, food and entertainment. 'Slice-of-life' projects choose a person or occupation and record their activities over time. Titles might include 'A Day in the Life of a ________' or 'Understanding __________'.

Documentary video is also useful for archival management. Video cameras and viewing sets are often important features of a building security system, particularly the reading rooms, though most often these are monitored live by a security guard and only recorded when that officer is away from his or her post. Video can also be used for special problem-solving studies, such as documenting the traffic or workflow patterns of visitors, researchers and staff for later analysis and use in the planning of facilities and services.

Interpretation/Education: One of the most important and effective uses of video for archives is education, both in teaching research skills and in acquainting users with archival resources and services. Because archival materials are unique and do not circulate like library materials, researchers must generally visit the archives in person to gain access to original records. A video explaining how to use archival sources and services made available on the archives website and at local libraries and educational institutions can be a great help to prospective users, enabling them to learn their way around and achieve results in minimal time. A second and related type of video is the how-to program, which provides instruction on research techniques for specialised interests such as family history or historic photographs. Such videos make use of the archives' holdings and reference staff to explain the use of archival sources and various approaches and methods for solving popular or unusual research problems.

Infotainment: The third type of video is one primarily designed to inform and entertain, with the secondary purpose of raising the level of community interest and appreciation for the archives, its work and holdings. Such programs are the video equivalents of tours, exhibits and publications, and they enable the archives to contact and interest potential users where they live and work. This capability can be very important for archives, such as those of the State or Commonwealth, which must serve a large geographical area. Some sample titles of videos which might be undertaken include: *Know your archives; Treasures of the Aachives; My town/school/club: Then and now* (comparing historic photographs with shots of the present day). Almost any topic that is suitable for a book or exhibit can be videoed and in fact it is a good idea to produce a video version of an exhibit or illustrated publication. The video can live on usefully, carrying the information to a wide audience long after the exhibit has been dismantled and the book has gone out of print. Infotainment projects are especially attractive prospects for sponsorship and joint ventures with media companies or filmmakers and producers. Invite staff members to brainstorm possible subjects and partners, so that a 'wish list' is at hand when opportunity knocks. The possibilities are only limited by the richness of the archives' holdings, the imagination of staff members and, of course, its resources.

Getting into video

As with any other area dependent on technology, video program development requires careful planning, substantial resources and, most of all, expertise. While it is beyond the scope of this chapter to set out a detailed step-by-step list of what to buy and how to produce quality video results, there are activities that you will have to plan to undertake and options available for incorporating video into your archives program.

In developing a video production capability for the archives, you will be planning and managing resources (staff, equipment, facilities) to support a number of distinct work activities, the most important of which are as follows:

- planning/administering the video program, including choosing appropriate technology for the long term and devising a manageable access regime that recognises and respects the rights of participants
- identifying/designing video projects
- selecting and educating staff and participants

- making the video recordings:
  - setting up for the recording session (booking/preparing the site/studio; obtaining/producing titles and other graphic illustrations; deploying/checking the recording and lighting equipment; writing/editing narrative; planning/rehearsing content and sequences; obtaining permissions to use materials covered by copyrights)
  - recording the video
  - editing the video
  - inspecting and packaging the completed video
- documenting/cataloguing/indexing the videos (preservation original, duplicating master and reference copy) for future retrieval and use.
- managing and protecting the video resources:
  - making copies of the original: a duplicating master and a copy for reference use
  - storing the video original and duplicating master
  - monitoring the stability/integrity of originals and migrating them to new technologies as required
- determining terms and conditions of accessibility and use, including establishing regimes for promotion, marketing and distribution
- managing the accessibility regime:
  - arranging viewings of the reference video
  - facilitating/administering permissions for further use
  - arranging for copies of all or portions thereof as required
  - administering fee and/or royalty schemes.
- evaluating/monitoring the video program's benefits and effectiveness

As you would imagine, most of these areas require technical expertise well beyond that provided by archival training. Thus, it is essential to work in concert with one or more audiovisual technology professionals.

Participation in created documentation programs: The options

Whether one is planning a video, oral history or photographic documentation program, or all three, the options available for incorporating such activities within the archives operation remain the same. The archives can set up its own facility, equipment and staff to undertake such work. However, this option is rarely economically feasible for most archives.

An alternative is to contract these activities out to professional firms or consultants who undertake the work on a project-by-project basis, or a 'stand-by/retainer' contract, to provide specialist services as needed. A well run 'outsourcing' regime helps ensure that each project has access to the best available expertise and standards without the ongoing investment in specialist facilities, equipment and staff. Table 9.9 identifies issues to be considered in outsourcing. Related services such as historical interpretation, audiovisual production, exhibition and website design, publication, marketing, distribution and preservation are also candidates for outsource tendering.

A third choice is to participate in joint ventures involving other archives and historical agencies such as museums. Because such efforts have a larger scale, they may attract the participation of professional photographers, researcher/writers and radio/television companies as well as outside funding from government or corporate sources. Also, the larger, more comprehensively equipped institutions with such a consortium might be able to host a centralised technical support and storage facility and permit smaller archives to protect their master recordings on a fee-for-service basis.

If documentary production capability seems beyond the resources of your operation (and it is for most small archives), but you would like to include such material in your holdings or use the occasional video as an educational tool, consider the final option – providing reference to copies of recordings made and archived by others. This 'library style' role limits your technical investment to providing replay-only facilities as your archive owns neither the original recordings nor the right to reproduce them.

Transcribing the inscriptions on foundation stones or head stones is one way of enriching the records you already have. It may also be the start of a new project which results in a publication or exhibition.

Types of activities

Generally suitable for outsourcing	Generally unsuitable for outsourcing
• audiovisual production • data entry • database design • equipment provision and maintenance • indexing • interpretative research for exhibition, broadcast, publication • interviewing • photography • preservation of master/duplicating master recordings and images • production of reference copies and excerpts • specific project management • quality assurance testing • technical support during recording • thesaurus and metadata design • transcription	• liaison with client/community • overall program responsibility • liaison with key vendors • quality and performance monitoring

Outsourcing preparation and considerations

Successful outsourcing requires thorough preparation. Ensure that you:

- validate the proposed program in relation to the needs and constraints of the archives
- identify and prioritise the goals of the specific project
- identify and quantify the appropriate specifications and performance measures to ensure a high quality outcome
- conduct a cost-benefit analysis of the internal and external alternatives
- select a vendor that is competent and understands archival values and requirements

Reasons to use *external* resources	Reasons to use *internal* resources
• to have access to technology, skills, and knowledge not internally available • to improve business processes and enable organisational change • to provide needed short-term services without adding to ongoing operational costs • to focus internal resources on core strategic plans and programs	• to retain skilled personnel who are able to respond directly to the archives particular needs • to obtain needed services at lower overall costs • to take advantage of employees' unique insight into a project or the archival goals • to have ownership and control over resource and personnel assets

Cost of using *external* resources	Costs of using *internal* resources
• contract management costs to the archives • effectiveness costs from lack of understanding of project objectives or sensitivities • higher project costs as organisations may experience greater overall project costs in order to access necessary skills and expertise that are unavailable internally • higher costs from inadequately defined requirements	• opportunity costs of staff time • ongoing costs for additional or re-deploying full time equivalent (FTE) employees or work not being done • unpredictable costs as overtime occurs and as employees spend varying amounts of time month-to-month working on the project • effectiveness costs if in-house resources are not sufficient or skilled enough for the project

Contracts

Have a clear, well-set out contract or agreement that includes the following components:

- clear definition of scope of responsibilities and services (Statement of Work)
- price
- deliverables (delivery schedule and due dates)
- performance standards /guarantees / penalties
- flexibility (business volume, pricing)
- personnel provisions including use of sub-contractors
- ownership of data/ images/recordings
- intellectual property rights
- warranties
- limitation of liability
- confidentiality and disclosure
- right to renegotiate
- changes clause
- force majeure
- dispute resolution
- termination (addresses different termination scenarios, assistance provisions, costs)

The Bottom Line

The decision whether to use internal or external resources on a project is determined by a mixture of both the hard dollar and the soft dollar – the more intangible needs, risks, and benefits – costs. One option may be more expensive in strict dollar terms, but offer by far the best value in overall terms.

Properly managed, outsourcing will enable the archives to diversify and enrich its core programs and activities in cost-effective manner. Critical to success is a clear understanding that the process will need careful planning and management. Clear goals, defined outcomes and quality control are vital. Above all, have agreed-upon safeguards in place, especially a provision not to pay *bills* until the product or service provided is independently established to be satisfactory.

Compiling documentary sources

So far in this chapter we have concentrated on programs which aim to create information that would not otherwise exist, using audio, video and photographic technology. This section explores a different aspect of documentation – projects to compile widely scattered or obscure existing documents into more convenient and accessible forms. Popular examples of this work include the copying of photographs held in private hands and the transcribing of tombstone inscriptions in local cemeteries. The focus of interest may vary, but all such projects share a common approach and purpose in that teams of dedicated staff and volunteers search out, copy and cross-reference valuable but previously inaccessible information to unlock its potential for research.

Compiling or re-photographing historic images

Programs designed to solicit the donation of original photographs or to copy privately held images for research use can also prove fruitful, particularly when they are done in collaboration with newspapers, local photography studios, or organisations of professional photographers. Yet, regardless of whether you are seeking a large collection or a small one, the means of obtaining it will come through contacts with individuals who must somehow be persuaded to join your cause.

Resting beneath the rainbow:
A publication which uses material gathered from headstones as the basis for biographical sketches of people significant to this organisation.

As in other forms of field work, success depends on the ability to inspire confidence in one's self and one's institution. The first step is to provide the public with accurate information about the types of images that the archives wants and does not want, along with guidelines on formats and quality. Most people will understand a need to be selective, but few will be impressed if you invite any and all donations, and then reject many as 'unsuitable'.

Frequently, one donation leads to another. Encourage project participants to suggest the names of other area residents who might be willing to share their images with the archives. And be sure to ask donors if they have written records that might be contributed to the archives as companion pieces to the images. Because the public becomes heavily involved with projects of this type, public relations and careful advance planning for copying project sites are essential. It is vital to document the names and addresses of local sponsors and volunteers and to ensure that you have mailed or personally presented sufficient information in the locality to attract an enthusiastic response.

A retrospective documentation project which copies images that will continue to be held by their owners presents certain legal problems for the sponsoring archives. The institution is receiving not a gift, but rather an opportunity to make copies (usually film negatives or scanned digital facsimiles) of unique materials for preservation and future research use. But what exactly can the archives do with its copies? The announced purpose of making these images accessible for research certainly implies intent to make further reproductions of them, either as viewing prints for the reading room or as copies sold to researchers for private study. And there is a reasonable certainty that reproductions of some images will be in demand for publication. Can the archives legally take such actions and charge fees for services without consulting the owner of the original, who may or may not also own the copyright to that image?

These are cloudy issues indeed, and the last place you want to find your archives is in court. The best protection available at present is an agreement between the archives and the owner of the originals detailing the ways any images copied or acquired can be used.

By the same token, it is vitally important for project field workers to elicit all pertinent details about the image at the time it is offered for copying, as it facilitates image management and can be difficult to acquire later. As a minimum, try to document physical and copyright ownership, date the image, its technology, its location and the subject or the occasion shown. It is also important for image owners to indicate whether or not they wish their names and addresses to be confidential. Some people may not welcome the prospect of being contacted by researchers or photography collectors seeking the originals.

Whether the photo project is current or retrospective, a schedule must be set up for processing and preserving the images and for describing them for use by the public. Great care must be taken to ensure the quality and longevity of the copied images, for they now comprise the public archival record. Most projects recommend creating two archival image 'sets', a preservation master (usually the in-camera image) for separate security storage and a duplicating master to use in making reference prints, each with own preservation and access regimes.

Making the collection of images fully accessible to researchers is an involving but essential process. Each image should be uniquely numbered, then fully described and indexed. Ideally, a view-only print of each image should appear beside any written text so that researchers have all the information they need to 'browse' and select appropriate images with ease. Some projects provide access to their text-and-image database online via their website and/or send it out on CD/DVD to 1ocal historical societies or libraries in the areas where the images were obtained. The distribution of such resources does much to make the local heritage available locally, and the resulting goodwill facilitates both the ongoing work of such projects and a good relationship between localities and centralised archival authorities.

Whether your images are copied or donated, do not neglect to share this bounty with the public. For example, the staff could prepare an 'Historic Image of the Week' series in the local newspaper (accompanied by a short caption and credit line mentioning the archives and, with his or her permission, the name of the donor). A public exhibit of photographic prints drawn from the project files can also be very effective in generating community support. Preparing an electronic version of the exhibition for the archives website extends the benefits exponentially for very modest extra effort.

Other compilation projects

Turning our attention to other types of documentary sources suitable for compilation, we find the numbers of possibilities are unlimited. Scattered sources with research potential for transcribing or copying as text or images include inscriptions on building cornerstones and dedication plates, historical markers, gravestones, the contents of 'time capsules' from significant commemorations, plaques on monuments and business logos or advertising symbols.

Having identified the resources you wish to make more accessible, it is important to think through very carefully the results you hope to achieve and exactly how you will realise them. Many a project has foundered because participants rushed into them without considering such matters as:

- Is there sufficient interest in and need for the proposed compilation project and its products to justify the projected cost and effort?
- Have others undertaken similar projects and products? If so, what aspects were successful and what pitfalls occurred that could be avoided? Is there a 'template' we can adapt to save time/effort and minimise error?
- What physical, technical and intellectual structures and features will maximise the usefulness of the compiled information and make it easy to update and publish?
- What forms of publication (hard-copy or electronic or both) should be planned and how will each be funded and distributed?

New information technologies, properly applied, can combine text and images in well-designed databases that can be easily indexed, updated and published both in hard copy and electronically via the internet or on CD/DVD.

Projects to re-record information may not always utilise sophisticated technology, but they do require specialist advice, careful planning and management to yield optimum results. The following are some of the aspects which must be considered:

- planning/administering the overall project and its outcomes
- selecting/designing the project processes and outputs to optimise quality, accessibility and manageability
- planning the specific project activities:
  - choosing the site/sites to be included
  - breaking the project up into manageable segments (half or full days in sequence)
  - designing the database, its structure, data fields and values
- selecting the information to be recorded: full text or specific portions
- designing the format, sequence, and content of individual entries
- designing the format and content of the final compilation and its indexes.
  - recruiting/training the project personnel (usually volunteers)
  - arranging for transport, supplies, and amenities for project personnel.
- conducting the project:
  - transporting project personnel
  - distributing supplies
  - monitoring/guiding progress
  - deploying/maintaining amenities
  - collecting completed data sheets.
- analysing and processing the data sheets into the final compiled product, usually a database finding aid publication
- distributing the compiled product via the archives website and/or separately as an electronic or traditional publication
- monitoring/evaluating project, product and program success.

These projects have lasting value for the archives, both in terms of making remote or scattered information available to researchers in a compact form and as a way of involving the wider community in heritage activities. Well-planned compilation projects are rewarding and fun as they bring people together in a clearly defined, worthwhile activity that has been organised into manageable segments. Remember that, although the end product is the ultimate goal, the process of achieving it must always be through a well-organised sequence of small, satisfying steps for the participants, whether staff or volunteers or both.

In closing, it is desirable to summarise the common benefits and cautions surrounding documentation programs for archives. Oral history, video and photographic surveys do supplement and render more human the records of our present and recent past. The sensory dimensions of such materials bring our lives back to life in ways ink or paper cannot. But it is precisely because these personal documents have such emotional power that the programs to create them must be carefully planned and executed. Moreover, documents created 'for the record' and especially those relying on memory, raise legal, historical and ethical issues that affect the relationships among the persons recorded, researchers and the archives' staff. Properly structured and funded documentation programs can become major assets that not only enrich the collections, but also raise community awareness and support for the archives as a whole.

CHAPTER 10

using **computers**

DAVID ROBERTS

CHAPTER ABSTRACT

Computers and other forms of information and communications technology (ICT) are essential tools for archives work today – whether you just want to be able to work as efficiently as you can by using the kind of productivity software seen in every office and in many homes, or you want to harness the power of a collection management system or promote your archives and provide services via the World Wide Web.

While ICT can contribute to all aspects of archives work, this chapter will in particular give you an understanding of how it can benefit archival documentation and finding aids, reference services and the distribution and publication of information, including Web 2.0 technologies.

Purchasing computers

Computers are such a normal part of the life of any modern organisation, whether large or small, private or public, that it is easy simply to assume the need for an archives operation to have a computer or computer network.

Despite continued improvements in the capacity and value of personal computers and peripheral equipment, their purchase remains a significant investment when funds are limited, for example in a small archive without the support of a larger 'parent' organisation. This is particularly so when the cost of software and software upgrades, consumables, maintenance, support, and training (altogether called the 'total cost of ownership') is taken into account.

This means that it is worthwhile to consider carefully what you want to achieve by using computer technology and to make informed choices that will help you to meet these goals at the least cost.

Software on a budget

Where the budget is limited, there are a number of ways in which significant savings can be made on the cost of software.

New personal computers often come bundled with office productivity software. Alternatively, retailers often offer deals where this software can be purchased much more cheaply with a new computer than if bought separately. In addition, some kinds of organisations may qualify for special pricing on software purchases. Microsoft, for example, offers discount pricing to certain kinds of community organisations.

Where the budget is limited, it is also worth considering 'open-source' or otherwise free or low-cost office productivity suites and programs as an alternative to the commercial products such as the Microsoft Office and Corel WordPerfect Office suites. Products such as OpenOffice.org and NeoOffice (for Macintosh) are well featured and readily available.

Common tasks

Office productivity software, often supplied as 'Office'-type suites of programs or 'Works'-type integrated products, support a wide range of common tasks. These products can include:

- **word processing:** for preparing correspondence (including standard form letters), reports, forms and other documents
- **spreadsheet:** for keeping track of a budget, managing statistics and manipulating a range of other information in tabular form
- **presentation:** for preparing presentations and talks for clients and stakeholders
- **desktop publishing:** for producing guides, newsletters and publicity materials
- **database:** for keeping and updating contact and mailing lists and other information about clients, and for managing assets, supplies and events
- **email and personal information management:** for email communication and managing personal appointments and contacts and other information.

Depending on its needs, an archives operation may also require accounting, business graphics, project management, website design and management and other specialised application software.

Utilities required in the online environment include anti-virus, anti-spyware and anti-spam software, a firewall and other internet security software.

Collection management systems

In the context of keeping archives, collection management systems are software products designed specifically for managing archives collections and/or collections of other materials that include archives.

Collection management systems can help the archivist to manage the archives in a number of ways. One of their primary roles is to capture descriptive information about the archives – both their intellectual content and their physical attributes – and about the context of the archives' creation and use. In this respect, an archival collection management system can be regarded as akin to a library's catalogue system, with the important difference that an archival system must respect and support the fundamental principles governing the arrangement of archives (described in Chapter 8: *Arrangement & Description*) and accepted methods and standards for describing archives and their context.

Archival collection management systems can also support a range of archival management functions and processes, including accessioning, arrangement and description, documentation of creation and functional context, appraisal and disposal, preservation, repository management, location control and movement tracking, the preparation of finding aids, access and reference services, and digitisation.

"Y'know, it'd be a lot easier to archive these if someone would invent the computer ..."

Why use collection management systems?

Most of the functionality of collection management systems replaces information and information systems in other forms. These may be manual systems, such as accession registers and inventories, or electronic, such as word processed forms and lists. Often these older systems are disparate, having been developed at different times in the past, are poorly integrated, and contain extensively duplicated information. Even manual systems that are well designed and maintained can be cumbersome to use and require significant effort in copying and filing multiple copies of documentation.

Collection management systems have a number of advantages over manual systems and documentation:

- information is entered once, but is used in many ways and combinations through queries and outputs
- updating information is often far less time-consuming, because it does not have to be changed in multiple places
- duplication of information is minimised, promoting data integrity
- information can be easily exported to other programs, e.g. to a word processing or desktop publishing program to produce guides and other publications
- finding aids are easily produced in electronic form for the internet and other means of electronic distribution

- the quality of the information may be enhanced, since collection management systems often impose useful disciplines or require higher standards, providing an incentive for improving documentation and other practices
- collection management systems generally support accepted standards for the description of archives, providing a ready means of adopting these standards and, in turn, promoting the sharing of descriptive information across archival networks
- disaster preparedness may also be improved, since it is easier to maintain a back-up copy of a collection management system offsite than cumbersome paper-based documentation.

An alternative to using a collection management system is to computerise existing forms and other documentation. This can provide at least some of the above benefits. Moreover, information can be found easily through free-text searching, whether the basic text searching offered in, for example, Microsoft's Windows operating systems, or using a fully featured enterprise search product.

This approach, however, has major drawbacks compared with using a collection management system:

- the information is not structured and, consequently, cannot be manipulated and recombined easily. This also limits the archivist's ability to export the information to other programs or formats.
- archival collection management systems, being designed specifically to support archival functions and processes, contain a range of useful functionality that is not available with word-processed documentation.

Types of collection management systems

A range of collection management systems for archives is available. In addition, systems designed for managing other kinds of collections may be used, to varying extents, for archival materials.

Archival collection management systems

There are three main archival collection management systems available that have been developed in Australia. Of these, one, Archives Manager (developed by Teigo Pty Ltd), is a commercial product; the Heritage Documentation Management System (HDMS, developed by Austehc) is available under licence at no cost for non-commercial, heritage and public good purposes; and Tabularium (developed by the author of this chapter) is available as freeware. All are fully featured products supporting the range of archival functions and processes noted above, and reflect accepted Australian archival practices, although each has its particular strengths and emphases. Archives Manager is a stand-alone product, while HDMS and Tabularium require Microsoft Access.

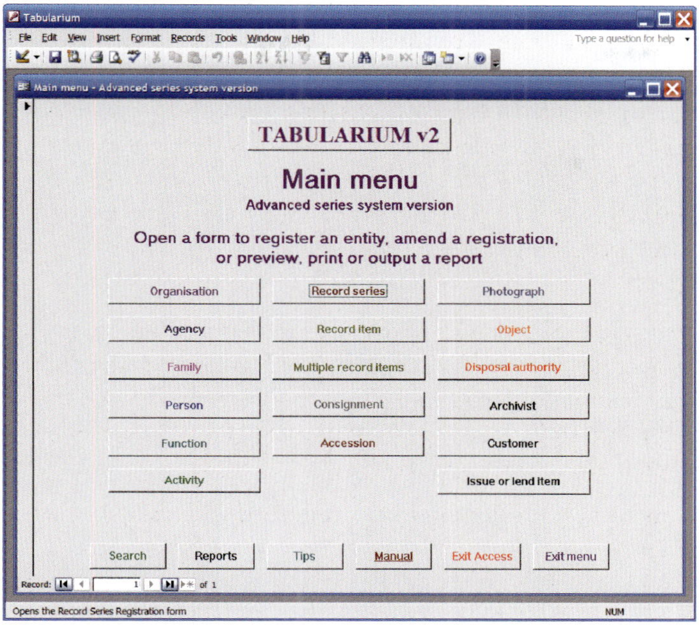

Figure 10.1: The Tabularium main menu shows the range of records, context and other entities that can be documented

In addition to these products, two of the collection management systems developed for state archives institutions are available for purchase. These are Archives One, developed by Technology One for the Queensland State Archives, and the Business Operations System/Archives Investigator combination, developed by PK Information Systems for the State Records Authority of New South Wales.

A number of overseas products are also available. These include CAIRS Archive Management System (CAIRS-ARC); ADLIB Archive; and Minisis M2A.

The *Market survey of commercially available off-the-shelf archival management software,* released by the International Council on Archives' Committee on Information Technology in January 2003, provides a useful summary of available products.

Collection management systems for libraries and museums

Many archives collections are managed in conjunction with, or as part of, collections of library and/or museum materials. In these cases, an option to consider is to use the same collection management system for this range of material, especially where a library or museum system is already in use.

The major benefit of doing this is to improve access to the whole collection through an integrated set of descriptions. This may be particularly beneficial where there are close relationships between the different kinds of materials, such as having the same provenance.

The major drawback of this approach is that descriptive practices and standards for archives differ from those for library materials, which in turn differ from those for museum materials. These practices and standards stem from the fundamental natures of these materials. Trying to describe, for example, an archival series and its context using data elements designed for a published work or a museum object is generally unsatisfactory. Consequently, a collection management system designed for one type of material is likely to fall short in meeting the needs of other types.

A number of options exist for overcoming this problem. One is to choose a library, museum or integrated collections system that provides specifically for documenting archives. Products in this category include Vernon Systems' Collection software, Collections Mosaic Plus, PastPerfect Museum Software and Visual Re:discovery.

Where a library or museum system is already in use, it may be possible to customise it to meet at least the most important descriptive and management needs of the archives. Another approach is to customise a generic database product for documenting archives and other materials. A number of small archives in Australia follow this approach with Inmagic's DB/TextWorks, a highly customisable combination database-management and text-retrieval system. This product has the further attraction that library, museum and archives modules are available, such as Archives Online, developed by Andornot Consulting Inc.

A further option, where appropriate, is to use an archival collection management system that is well adapted to documenting and managing the other types of materials required. Tabularium, for example, provides for cataloguing objects and photographs according to the recommendations of the *Small museums cataloguing manual* published by Museums Australia (Victorian Branch) in 1996.

Finally, products designed for particular record formats may be worth considering, depending on the emphasis of one's collection. For example, Perfect Pictures, developed by Search Tech for pictorial collections generally, has been used successfully for managing archival photograph collections.

Records management systems

These are software products designed for managing an organisation's current, and sometimes semi-current, records. Records management systems are not collection management systems, in the sense we have been using the term above, but, for convenience, we will briefly discuss them here.

Archives, of course, are records: current records do not magically transform into something else when kept as archives. Where an organisation operates an in-house archives, it is desirable that its archives are managed, along with all its records, through an integrated continuum-based approach.

In these circumstances, a further option is to use the organisation's records management system for documenting and managing the archives. One major benefit of this approach is that much of the descriptive information ('metadata'), particularly at the item and document level, required for archival purposes is likely to exist already as the result of current records' registration and filing. Where the capture and management of digital records and/or digitised images of paper records is implemented with the records management system, this record content is also available for archival management.

While a number of records management software products on the market provide for aspects of archives management, the extent of this functionality is generally limited compared with purpose-designed archives collection management systems. At this stage, there are no products on the market designed from the start to meet the full needs of current records management and archives management in an integrated continuum-based fashion.

Choosing a collection management system

Every archives operation is different and, consequently, there is no single collection management system that can be recommended as the best for every archives. When choosing a collection management system for your archives, the chance of a successful outcome, however, will be maximised by taking a systematic and objective approach.

Functional requirements

The key to such an approach is to determine the requirements that the system must meet (its 'functional requirements') and to assess the extent to which each option to be considered meets those requirements. The way in which these requirements are documented may range from a fully fledged 'functional specification' (which may be required by your organisation for technology acquisitions in any case) to a simple but meaningful list of 'must-haves'.

The following list outlines the main areas that need to be covered by functional requirements:

- **descriptive standards:** using a system that complies with descriptive standards for archives *(ISAD(G), ISAAR(CPF)* and, in Australia, *Describing archives in context: A guide to Australasian practice* – see Chapter 8: *Arrangement & Description*) helps ensure that descriptions follow accepted practice, that descriptive information can be shared or exchanged, and that users of the archives can search finding aids where descriptions are consistent internally and with those of other archives.

- **customisable to meet local needs:** at the very least, it should be possible to create additional queries and reports to those supplied as standard.
- **outputs for the Web:** an increasingly important capacity, discussed further in the next section, is to enable descriptive information to be published and searched on the World Wide Web
- **environment and outputs for archives users:** whether or not there is an environment designed for archives users, and the ease of use of this and of any outputs intended for archives users, may affect how useful the system is for people other than the archivist
- **range of records:** the system should be able to document all forms of records and in all types of media likely to form part of the collection
- **context entities and relationships:** the system's capacity to document the creators of the archives and their details of the relationships with the records and with each other will determine how well the system supports the principle of provenance. The capacity to document functional context will enable the archivist to take advantage of this increasingly important aspect of the archives' context
- **materials other than archives:** as discussed earlier, the capacity to document and manage materials other than archives may be important, depending on the nature of the collection.
- **exporting data:** if sharing or exchanging descriptive data is important, the system has to support the export of this data to other systems in standard formats, e.g. as EAD and EAC records in XML, or for contributing to Collections Australia Network, PictureAustralia or other portal sites
- **link to external sources:** it can be valuable to cite sources of information outside the system, such as guides, that relate to an entity documented in the system, particularly if a link can also be made as a hyperlink
- **importing data:** the capacity to import data from external systems, such as item lists prepared in word processing documents, can save a great deal of time by avoiding the need to re-key the information
- **supporting archival functions and processes:** you may need to specify a considerable range of requirements relating to the specific archival functions and processes (listed at the start of this section) that the collection management system is intended to support
- **technological environment:** your archives' or larger organisation's existing technological environment may limit the range of products that can be implemented, regardless of other factors
- **user manual and online help:** the quality and clarity of the user manual and any online help may have a significant practical impact when using the system
- **ease of learning and use:** this may be particularly important if people other than the archivist, such as volunteers, are to use the system or if there is turnover of staff.

Not all functional requirements are of equal importance. It is helpful to prioritise or 'weight' your list, e.g. into essential and desirable requirements. You may find that none of the products being assessed meet all your requirements. In this case, the objective will be to identify the best 'fit'. Weighting the requirements may be particularly useful here.

Cost

This may be a significant factor in choosing a collection management system, particularly where the archivist's budget is severely limited. It is important to identify the full cost of the products being assessed. With the freeware products, HDMS and Tabularium, for example, a licensed copy of Microsoft Access is required, which may involve expenditure but provides a fully supported relational database system and the tools needed to customise the product. If a particular collection management system choice would require you to upgrade existing hardware or software, this additional cost should be considered. Non-cash costs, notably the time required to learn the system and to convert or input existing data, should also be identified and considered, as should the level and quality of after-sales support available from the developer or reseller.

Sources of information and advice

Choosing a collection management system can be a daunting prospect, particularly for the 'lone arranger'. The process can be made easier by:

- identifying reference sites, where a particular product has been implemented
- drawing on the experience of colleagues, especially those operating in a similar archival environment

Building your own system

An alternative to acquiring an existing collection management system is to develop your own, using such user-friendly generic desktop database software as Microsoft Access and Filemaker Pro. There is not room here to discuss this further, but we should at least note that there is nothing to stop the adventurous archivist from building on existing experience and exploring new ways to represent information about archives in a collection management system.

Archival functions

In a sense, archives work is all about creating, managing and providing access to information. So it is not surprising that computers are useful for many archival functions. We have already discussed dedicated software for collection management. In this section, we will look quickly at some of the simpler or more obvious uses of computers for other archival functions.

Preparing documentation and finding aids

The ability to set standardised layouts, templates and styles for different types of documentation used by your archives helps to provide consistency, making it easier for readers to find their way around the publication and promoting your archives' identity. The table below outlines some of these uses.

Document type	Details
Forms	These can be created with word processing or desktop publishing software. Advanced features in products like Microsoft Word enable electronic forms to be created for the archivist or other users to fill in onscreen, with text fields, check boxes and drop-down lists. The data can then be imported into database or spreadsheet programs if required. The CD-ROM accompanying this book contains a selection of sample forms for archival functions.
Guides, finding aids and publications	Producing guides and other textual findings aids and publications is discussed in detail in Chapter 12: *Finding Aids* and Chapter 14: *Advocacy & Outreach.* Preparing large documents, in particular, can be assisted by using such features as outlining (defining a structure for the document based on different levels of headings), automatic creation of a table of contents, and support for creating an index to the publication. Finding aids can also be produced using outputs from collection management systems, which can then be formatted and published or integrated into guides, using word processing, desktop publishing or HTML editing software. This is discussed later in this chapter. Where the archivist wishes to revise a publication that currently exists only in hard copy, or to republish it in electronic form (see below), it may be possible to avoid re-keying it by using a scanner and optical character recognition (OCR) software. A range of fully featured OCR software is available on the market, while most new scanners are supplied with basic OCR and other imaging software.

Document type	Details
Indexes	As a specialised form of finding aid, indexes are discussed in detail in Chapter 12: *Finding Aids.* Indexes can be created using a variety of software, depending on the source of the information, its complexity and the means by which the index will be made available. Simple indexes can be created using tables in a word processing program, with the information sorted on one or more columns. Spreadsheet and database programs provide additional features that can be useful for more complex indexing tasks. Specialised indexing software is also available as stand-alone products or as part of library cataloguing software. Many indexes will benefit from using an 'authority file', prescribing standardised ways of entering names and other indexing terms. One advantage of using a database program for preparing indexes is that one or more authority files can be set up as tables in the database, enabling the authority headings to be available for insertion into the index from drop-down lists. This is also an advantage of using specialised indexing software.
Charts	Organisation charts, administrative history charts and family trees, providing a convenient way of presenting complex information, can be created with business graphics software or charting features in full-featured word processing or presentation programs.

Table 10.1: Preparing documentation

Reference services

Email enquiries

Email is now so ubiquitous in the community that archival researchers expect even the smallest archives operation to have an email address to which they may send enquiries.

The archivist may regard these enquiries as akin to those received by post and apply the same policies to responses to all mail enquiries, as discussed in Chapter 11: *Access & Reference Services.* It is worth noting, however, that email engenders client expectations of faster responses than postal mail. Having a policy of responding quickly to email enquiries, if only with a standard holding reply, is a useful way of meeting these expectations and reassuring the client that the enquiry has been received and will be answered.

A separate email address for reference enquiries can be established. This allows all staff to access the enquiries, even when other staff members are on leave, and setting the account to generate an automatic, standard response to every enquiry.

Providing a computer for client use

Where you have resources in electronic form that you wish your clients to be able to use in conjunction with paper-based resources and the archives themselves, an option is to provide a personal computer for clients to use in your reading room or equivalent area. A number of issues need to be considered regarding how this computer will be used. These are outlined in the table below.

Decision	Considerations
Choosing the electronic resources	The nature of the electronic resources to be made available to clients via the archives' computer will have an impact on how you provide access to them. You may choose to limit these electronic resources to those produced by your archives, or you may include resources from other sources, just as many archives make a library of reference and other supporting materials available for use by their clients. This is discussed further in Chapter 11: *Access & Reference Services.*
Stand-alone or networked	You will need to decide whether the computer is to 'stand alone' or will be connected to your archives' network. A stand-alone machine avoids a security risk to your network, but may limit the range of resources to which you can provide your clients with access. With properly set up network security, limiting access to specific resources, the risk may be minimised. Placing the computer where the screen can be seen by the archivist will also minimise the chance of misuse.
Removable media	A related issue is how to provide access to electronic resources on removable media, such as CD/DVD-ROMs. If you are concerned about possible theft or damage, you may require that the archivist loads and removes media or provide access via a remote network CD/DVD-ROM drive. If you are comfortable with providing the media to the client, you can retain a degree of control by recording their issue and return.

Decision	Considerations
Website and internet	If you want to provide access to your archives' website, you must either provide the computer with access to the internet or provide a copy of the website on the personal computer or a closed network. There are many issues associated with giving clients internet access, so you may prefer to avoid this option. One way of doing so, however, is to use Web-filtering software to restrict client access to certain websites. Providing access to a local copy of the archives' website, without internet access, on the other hand, requires that it be kept up to date. If your website includes hyperlinks to other websites, your clients will not be able to follow these.
Printing	You will need to decide whether you want to provide clients using the computer with the ability to print. If so, you must decide whether the printer will be near the computer, which is most convenient for the client, or in a 'staff only' area, which provides the archivist with greater control, particularly if charging a fee for printouts. Whether you charge for printing or not, you will need to decide what limits you will place on printing by clients.
Other uses	If you decide to provide a computer for client use, you must decide whether the client will be permitted to use it to make notes when using the archives, or if you will limit use of the computer to your resources. One significant drawback of the former is that it is likely to tie up the computer for long periods of time. Letting clients use their own removable media, such as USBs, for taking their notes away with them, opens up the risk of introducing computer viruses. You will need to decide your policy on this. Finally, if there proves to be strong demand for use of the personal computer, you will need to decide how to manage it. You may need to consider a booking system and/or time limits.
Security	If you permit the use of removable media or access to the internet, protection from viruses is an important concern.

Table 10.2: Considerations when providing a computer for client use

Many users of archives prefer to make notes with a personal computer when using the archives, rather than making notes longhand. If you permit this in your archives, you must at least provide convenient access to a power outlet to enable a client to use a notebook computer. It is prudent to stipulate in your reading room rules that clients may use their notebooks only for purposes related to their archival research and that sounds must be disabled and any other offensive or annoying features avoided.

Electronic distribution and publishing

If you provide photocopies or other hard copies of archives, finding aids and other resources on demand to clients, possibly for a fee, you may need to consider also providing copies in electronic form on suitable media. You may decide to provide this service to clients in your reading room and/or to remote clients. As with providing hard copies, you will need to determine the limits and standards of service, such as turnaround times for orders. You should make these clear to clients, to ensure that their expectations are reasonable.

When setting charges for electronic copies, you may wish, in addition to the cost of media such as blank CD/DVDs, to build in a charge for staff time, since making an electronic copy can take more time than a photocopy. This can add up over time to a significant additional burden for the archivist.

An alternative to providing electronic copies on media to remote clients is to provide the copies online. Smaller files can be emailed to the client. Larger files can be placed in a password-protected part of your archives' website for the client to download at their convenience. Many clients value the relative immediacy of this kind of option compared with sending copies by post.

Copyright is a significant issue for this kind of service. Providing material in electronic form makes it easier to re-use, placing your archives' intellectual property at higher risk. This makes it important to ensure that clients are aware of their rights and of copyright restrictions.

Another issue here is security. Most archives providing electronic copies to clients do not allow them to provide their own media, since this exposes your personal computer or network to the introduction of computer viruses. You also have an obligation to ensure that you do not inadvertently pass on viruses to clients through this kind of service. This is a further reason for using good anti-virus software and keeping it up to date. Part of the copying process should be to scan the media before providing it to the client. You should also protect the archives legally with a suitable disclaimer on the order form and media.

Media for electronic distribution

The CD has been the staple medium for the distribution of software and data for many years. However, at the time of writing, most new personal computers now come with a combined drive that can read both DVDs and CDs. Some of these drives may only be able to 'burn' DVDs, rather than CDs. With a colour printer, also now very cheap, CD or DVD cover inserts and labels can be used to give locally produced CDs and DVDs a professional look. While this is the situation for new computers, many users may have older computers which only have CD drives. USBs ('flash drives', 'thumb drives', 'USB sticks', 'memory keys') are also becoming ubiquitous, but are more costly than blank DVDs or CDs.

The CD remains a highly practical medium for electronic distribution and publication of guides and other materials by even very small archives operations. It is also increasingly used for providing digitised copies of archives to users, particularly photographs, as an alternative to photocopies or prints. However, as CDs are rapidly becoming 'old technology', small archives in particular should be careful not to over-invest in this approach.

Designing for electronic distribution

While electronic media can be used to distribute or publish existing materials in electronic form, they also provide the opportunity to produce new or enhanced materials incorporating features that are not available in hard-copy products, such as hyperlinks, the ability to search the text, and multimedia content.

The file format chosen for text-based materials will be influenced by your primary purpose in undertaking electronic distribution. If you wish to provide materials suitable for the user to print and use in hard copy, a format like Adobe's PDF (Portable Document Format), which preserves page layout and formatting exactly, or word processing formats like Microsoft Word's 'doc', RTF (Rich Text Format) or ODF (Open Document Format) will be preferable. If you wish to provide materials for use onscreen, particularly if you wish to use the kinds of features noted earlier, HTML is likely to be most useful.

In this case, as a further step, guides and other materials may be designed from the start for onscreen use. With the assistance of professional designers and/or software, these can become fully fledged multi-media products. Even if kept much simpler, with an emphasis on navigation and usability, a guide designed from the start for use onscreen can provide the user with a much richer experience than that of using a traditional hard-copy guide. However, it may require more expertise to produce.

We examine this topic further in relation to designing materials for the World Wide Web.

The World Wide Web

The World Wide Web presents great opportunities for archivists to make the archives in their care, and the associated services that they offer, far more widely known and accessible than was possible before.

The Web is a subset of the larger internet. We have already discussed email as a part of the services that the archivist can provide to clients. Other growing business uses of the internet include internet telephony, to replace normal telephone services, and videoconferencing. In this chapter, however, our focus is on the Web.

We should also note that much of what follows is equally applicable to intranets, networks internal to an organisation that use internet technologies. Most organisations of any size operate an intranet, of which internal websites are usually a major component. For in-house archives, this can be an important way of providing archival services to the organisation's employees.

Finally we should note that there is a vast amount of information on all the practical and technical aspects of establishing and maintaining a Web presence, which there is no room to address here. In this chapter, we will focus mainly on what is specific to an archives operation.

Why use the Web?

The main benefits of using the Web to provide information and services are that:

- you can reach a wide audience from all over the world
- visitors get quick and convenient access to the information and services that you offer
- the costs of providing much of the information and services is greatly reduced, both for the archives and for the client, compared with traditional methods.

Beyond these benefits of having a Web presence are the imperatives arising from the fact that so many archives, large and small, around the world are doing it. This means that your archives will increasingly be relatively hidden from potential users compared to the rest of the archival world if you do not have a website. Researchers, contending with limited time and budgets, rely increasingly on Web-based resources and services – at least as a starting point for research – and, inevitably, give less priority to searching for archives and other research sources that must be pursued entirely using traditional means.

The major downside is that there remain significant parts of society, even in the developed world, without ready access to the internet. This is particularly so for members of disadvantaged socio-economic groups and for people living in remote locations with poor or unreliable telecommunications services. This 'digital divide' is an issue for larger social policy and should not be a reason for failing to establish a Web presence. It is a significant consideration, however, in determining how the Web fits with your archives' other services.

This highlights a further important point: that a Web presence should complement other archival services, but is unlikely to replace them. Part of planning for a Web presence, therefore, is to determine what part it will play in the archives' overall service mix.

What do you want to do?

The Web presents a range of opportunities for extending and expanding archival services. Having identified the benefits that you may wish to obtain from a Web presence, the next major step is to decide specifically, in service terms, what you want to do with it. A starting point is to make basic information about the archives, such as location, opening hours and a summary description of the scope of the collection, accessible online. This can be achieved with a single Web page or a simple website. Earlier in the spread of the Web, this 'online brochure' approach was often enough of a Web presence for archives and for many other kinds of organisations.

Conceptually, there are three broad categories of services to consider:

- publishing information about the archives and other matters
- providing access to the content of the archives, mainly through digitised copies
- providing transaction-based services.

We will discuss each of these in turn. We should note, however, that, in practice, these kinds of services are likely to be closely integrated in an archival website. If your archive does not have the resources to develop and maintain its own web presence, other options are outlined below.

Publishing information online

A website can be used to publish any of the types of materials that an archives might publish in traditional ways. The major type for most archives will be finding aids, to which we will return shortly.

How these materials should be designed and presented online, however, is affected by the different reading, browsing and searching habits that people adopt online, compared to using hard-copy materials. Generally people browse and scan online, rather than reading whole slabs of text. This affects a website's 'usability' and related issues, which we will discuss in relation to website design later in this section.

We should note here that information published as web pages should be brief and carefully constructed, to enable the user to take in the information on the page quickly and to determine where to go next. This means that existing materials written for hard-copy publication may well to be unsuitable for the Web, and may have to be extensively redesigned or their content developed afresh.

This also means that longer materials that you want visitors to your website to be able to read, rather than browse, should be made available in a form suitable for downloading and printing. This may be an HTML page designed for this purpose, or a PDF, Word or plain text file.

Publishing finding aids online

As in hard copy, finding aids published online may take a variety of forms. The fundamental distinction here is between guides and other finding aids, published as recognisable documents (either as one or more web pages or as downloadable files, as just noted), on the one hand, and online front-ends for searching databases containing descriptive information, on the other.

The issues raised by people's online habits noted above apply as much to online guides as to any other materials published online. We discussed the preparation of guides and finding aids using computers earlier in the chapter.

Dynamic database searching makes the contents of a database containing archival descriptive information, typically a collection management system database, accessible on the Web. The online user enters search criteria, such as a word or date, into a web page functioning as an online query form. The result of the query is returned to the user as a structured web page.

There are two major benefits of providing dynamic database searching of descriptive information on your website:

- all the information (or all that you want to make public) is made accessible and searchable without the need to produce separate comprehensive guides to the collection
- online users have access to all the richness, particularly in the relationships between the records and their context, built into the data structure of good archival collection management systems. This means that, if properly designed and implemented, the online front-end enables the user not only to conduct searches, but also to navigate through the descriptive information by following hyperlinks that reflect those relationships. For example, the description of a records-creating entity links to a description of a record series created by it, linking in turn to a succeeding series, linking in turn to the description of a relevant activity, linking to another series resulting from the same activity but created by a later entity, and so on.

Examples of archival database front-ends providing this functionality include State Records NSW's and the City of Sydney's Archives Investigator, Queensland State Archives' ArchivesSearch and the National Archives of Australia's RecordSearch.

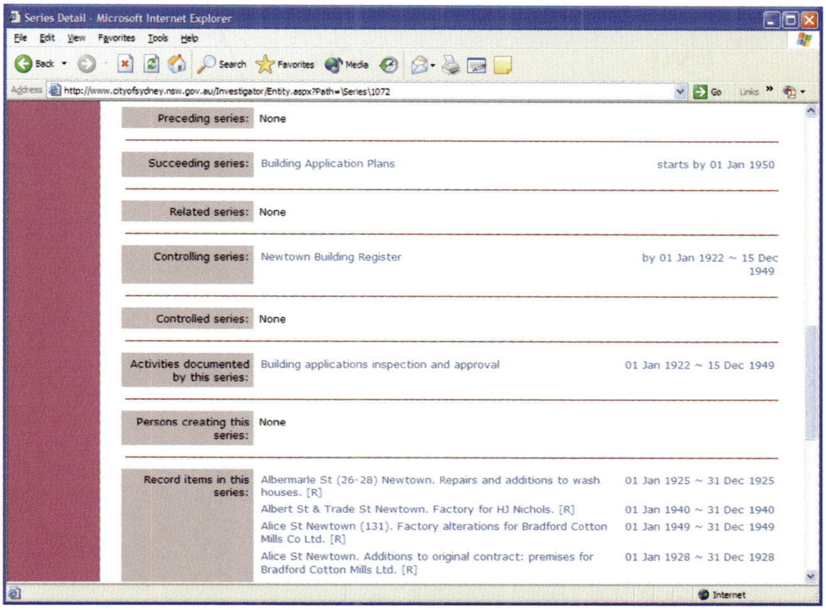

Figure 10.2: Relationship hyperlinks in the City of Sydney Archives' version of Archives Investigator

The same approach can be applied to making smaller or special-purpose archival databases searchable online. Examples can include indexes to specific series or collections and databases of photographs in archival collections.

Developing and implementing an online front-end to an archival database can be a major and costly undertaking. There are no solutions available 'out of the box', one of the reasons being that the design of a solution depends heavily both on the structure of the underlying database and on the technology used in the organisation's website.

An alternative is to produce finding aids in HTML format as outputs from a database of archival descriptive information and place these on your website. The HTML pages can contain hyperlinks to enable the user to navigate through relationships as described above. Both HDMS and Tabularium provide facilities for producing such finding aids. HDMS can also create EAD-compliant finding aids in XML format. At the time of writing, the Collections Australia Network (CAN) (discussed further below) is working with the archives community to enable detailed descriptive information about small archives collections to be accessible and searchable through the CAN website.

Whatever methods you use, the fundamental purpose of publishing archival finding aids online is the same as the purpose of providing traditional finding aids: to help archives users to find records relevant to their research. Being able to conduct much of their preliminary research using online finding aids enables the researcher to prepare better for a (physical) visit to the archives and to make the most of their time there.

While online finding aids are a boon for users, they can also be a frustration, because the user frequently hits a virtual dead-end. Where descriptive information is available at, say, the record series level, item information will be even more useful. Where descriptive information is available online right down to item level, the user must still visit the archives physically to view the records themselves. Online service can be taken a step further if the contents of at least some of the archives, as well as descriptive information, is accessible online.

Providing online access to archives content

The main way of making the contents of archives accessible online is to digitise them. We will discuss the process of digitising in another chapter. For now, we will focus on making digitised images of archives accessible online. We will also briefly discuss text-based content extracted from archives as an alternative or supplement to digital images. We will use the term 'archives content' to mean either or both.

From the perspective of online archival services, there are two ways of providing access to archives content:

- linking archives content to online finding aids
- packaging archives content into online exhibitions, galleries, multimedia and other interpretive products.

Linking archives content to online finding aids

This approach is intended to parallel the reading room process in the online environment: having found a desired record in the finding aids, the user downloads the content, via a hyperlink built into the finding aid, and reads it, instead of requesting the original, physical record from the archivist. This approach is possible with any type of finding aid, but is particularly suitable for the front-end of a collection management system database as discussed above, where a data store of digitised images of archives can be linked to, or integrated with, the underlying database.

This approach can require a deeper level of description of the archives than is normal. A digitised version of an archival record consists of individual images of as many folios (single pieces of paper), or single sides of folios where there is information on both sides, as comprise the record. Where a record item comprises a number of documents, which in turn comprise a number of folios, the documents need to be listed, in addition to the item itself, if the user is to know which digitised images to download. Consequently, the online finding aid often has to be able to display document lists within items, as well as item lists.

Packaging archives content into online products

Archives content can be made accessible through a variety of types of online products, such as online galleries, exhibitions, virtual tours, kits and publications, where the archives content, along with a range of interpretive and background materials, is presented as a 'packaged' whole. These products present opportunities to provide the online visitor (the change from 'user' to 'visitor' here is deliberate) with a far richer and more exciting online experience than is possible with conventional online finding aids. As terms like 'exhibition' and 'kit' suggest, these value-added products are often seen as part of an archives' outreach activities, rather than its reference services.

The finding aid, too, can be given a new lease of life – and the distinction between it and these other kinds of products blurs – when it is designed from the start as an online product incorporating archives content, interpretive material and an imaginative approach to the design of the user's experience.

Photographs and other image-based materials

Photographs are an ideal form of archival material to make accessible in digitised form online. They tend to have a wider, more general appeal than most text-based archival materials, so that they may be more likely to be used frequently and by casual users.

While it is important that the archival description of photographs should place them in their context and relate them to surrounding records, as should the description of any archives, there can also be value for the user in providing common points of access for photographs from across the collection and from a range of series and contexts. Photographs are amenable to standardised forms of indexing, like names, places and subjects, providing an additional basis for online searching. These indexes should preferably be incorporated into a collection management system, or linked to it. A facility for searching the indexes then needs to be built into the archives' website, either as a separate search tool or integrated with others.

Almost uniquely among archival formats, photographs are ideal for online browsing. The most common way of providing for this is to display multiple images together on the screen as 'thumbnails' (small, very low-resolution images). For a record series comprising photographs, a set of thumbnails, combined with appropriate descriptive information, is far more useful than an item list.

Thumbnails can also be combined with online search tools by being made part of the search results, along with summary descriptive information about the photograph, making the search results more immediately useful.

Protecting intellectual property

Photographs can be among the most valuable parts of an archival collection, in terms of intellectual property. Making the photographs freely downloadable risks losing control of this property. Many archives address this by making their photographs accessible online at a relatively low resolution that is adequate for reference purposes. For the user wanting to reproduce the photograph, for example in a publication, high-resolution images can then be ordered, usually for a fee. This may include a reproduction fee, allowing for the user to then be notified of the terms and conditions required for reproducing the image. As an additional protection, the low-resolution image may incorporate a digital watermark.

There are many good examples of online facilities in the archives, library and museum sectors for searching, browsing and ordering archival photographs online. Australian examples include the National Archives of Australia's *PhotoSearch,* the City of Sydney's *ArchivePix,* State Records NSW's *Photo Investigator,* and the State Library of NSW's *PICMAN.* Many of the off-the-shelf archival collection management system products include facilities for publishing HTML pages containing descriptions and digitised images of archival photographs.

Much of the above discussion about making photographs accessible online applies also to other graphical forms of archives, such as maps, plans and drawings. These materials are often physically much larger than photographs. As a result, a digitised image can be much more difficult for the online user to use. The ability to navigate easily around the image and, particularly to zoom in and out, can overcome this problem and enhance the user's experience. Specialised software is available to provide this kind of facility. An example of its use may be seen in the NSW Department of Lands' Parish Maps Project (<http://www.lands.nsw.gov.au/survey_maps/maps_and_imagery/parish_maps>).

A way of reaching a new audience is to digitise some clips of moving image material and post them on a video sharing website (one of the Web 2.0 technologies discussed below) such as YouTube. You can also make links to the clips from your own website.

Text as online archives content

Some text-based archives, particularly some 19th century manuscript materials, are inherently difficult to read. There may be little point providing online users with access to digitised images of archives that they cannot then read. Providing a transcript in addition to, or instead of, a digitised image solves this problem.

Transcripts can be provided online in any text file format, such as HTML, plain text (ASCII), PDF or a word processing file format. HTML tends to be preferred because it downloads quickly, provides reasonable scope for formatting the layout of the text to reflect that of the original, and can have a look and feel consistent with the rest of the website.

Transcribing archives is very labour-intensive. Consequently, it is likely to be worthwhile only in very limited circumstances, e.g. for particularly important or iconic documents. It may be more likely to be a viable option where a lot of other effort is already being expended on the records, as in a packaged product of the types just discussed.

Optical character recognition

Some archival digitisation projects involve the use of optical character recognition (OCR) technology to extract the text content of the digitised records and make it available in electronic form. While the digitised copy may in this case be perfectly legible, there can be other benefits in this approach.

The major benefit from making text content, whether via transcription or OCR, available online is that the text can be made searchable, providing a valuable research tool for online users. Some limitations of OCR are that it works best with typed or printed material in modern fonts, and any output will still require manual checking and correction.

Providing services online

Much of what we have discussed so far about the World Wide Web – publishing information and providing archival content online – involves providing online users with services in the broad sense. An archives' website can also be used to provide specific transaction-based services.

These may include:

- purchasing publications and other products
- ordering copies of archival materials (whether digitised or not)
- requesting archives for issue ahead of a visit
- posting reference and other enquiries

These kinds of online services can be provided in different ways with varying degrees of technological sophistication. Online forms can be easily implemented in a website, enabling the online user to enter and submit a request or order. Where payment is involved, e-commerce facilities can provide for secure payments online. A range of off-the-shelf e-commerce products is available, while many content management systems also contain e-commerce modules.

Archives institutions are now beginning to integrate some of these kinds of services with the online front-ends to their collection management systems. This enables the user, for example, to search the institution's holdings and then order and pay for a copy of a record, within the same online system.

Establishing a Web presence

This chapter cannot attempt to cover the technical and practical aspects of planning, designing and implementing a website. Many sources are readily available for people with any level of expertise and experience. Rather, we will briefly note some of the key issues involved in establishing a Web presence for an archives.

Usability

This can be a critical factor to the success or otherwise of any website, but it is particularly important for archives, where complex information and unfamiliar concepts must often be imparted to the user. Web users who become frustrated with complex or confusing navigation paths, opaque or too much information, or unreasonably slow downloads will leave your website quickly and will be unlikely to return.

Some key points include:

- design the structure of the website first and foremost from the user's perspective
- minimise the number of clicks through navigation paths needed to reach useful content
- write in short, concise bites of text: communicating effectively on a website is very different from writing for hard-copy publication or distribution
- avoid unnecessary graphics that slow download times
- implement the World Wide Web Consortium ('W3C') accessibility standards, so that users with visual impairment or other disabilities can use the website effectively
- avoid surprises for the user, making it clear what happens or where the user is taken when a button is pushed or a hyperlink is clicked

The designer of a website always has a different perspective from the user. It is always valuable to include user testing in the development process.

Search facilities

We have already discussed providing dynamic database searching of descriptive information on your website. It is also valuable to provide a facility for searching text across the website, if there is a substantial quantity of text (such as conventional finding aids converted to HTML). Simple search facilities are available with some Web server and content management system products, while more sophisticated stand-alone products are also available. The search engine Google offers a service whereby a search dialogue is placed on your website, enabling the user to search the website using the Google search engine (more information at <www.google.com>).

Whatever kinds of searching you provide, users find it particularly valuable to be able to save, print or download the results of their searches.

Making your Web presence discoverable online

If people are going to visit your website, they need to know about it first. Beyond promoting the website and its URL as part of the promotion of the archives and its services, there are three main ways for online users to find your site and its content. One is via online search engines, such as Google and Yahoo. Another is to have your site listed in one or more appropriate 'portal' sites, which are discussed further below. Finally, linking your website to and from other suitable sites enables online users to identify additional potential sources of information about archives relevant to their research.

Benchmarking

More than anything else, what works well in a website is a matter of human experience. One of the most effective ways of determining how you want your site to look and work is to visit plenty of other sites and decide what you like and do not like there.

Alternatives to your own website

It may be possible to do some of the things that we have been discussing without setting up your own website. The Directory of Archives in Australia, accessible through the Australian Society of Archivists' website (<www.archivists.org.au>), and the Collections Australia Network (CAN) (<www.collectionsaustralia.net>) enable an archives repository to make basic information about its collection, along with contact details, accessible online, if this is all the World Wide Web presence you require. In the case of CAN, visitors can also see current information about a participating repository, including exhibitions, events and news.

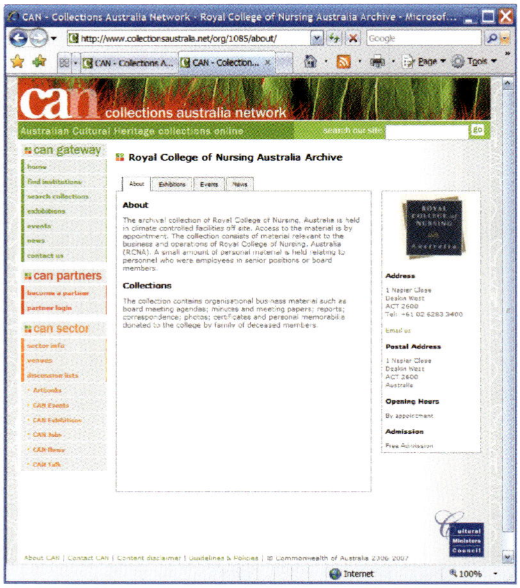

Figure 10.3: Basic information about an archives repository on CAN

The Collections Australia Network and the National Library of Australia's Register of Australian Archives and Manuscripts (RAAM) (<http://www.nla.gov.au/raam/>) go significantly further, by enabling participating organisations to contribute descriptive information about their holdings at the collection level or in more detail.

In both cases, of course, participating can be a useful way of making your archives more visible online, in addition to your own Web presence.

Picture Australia

An option to consider for making archival photographs more accessible online is to contribute to the National Library of Australia's Picture Australia service (<www.pictureaustralia.org>). Participating organisations contribute descriptive information about digitised photographs and other pictorial materials in a standardised (Dublin Core) format. Visitors to the Picture Australia website can search across all the collections thus contributed. The search results include a thumbnail from the participating organisation's website and a hyperlink to a page on that site containing the image. Participating in Picture Australia can make a collection of archival photographs more 'visible' online by being part of a well-known, centralised national database and online search facility.

Web 2.0

In addition to the more traditional uses of the web outlined above, there is also growing interest in how archives can make use of 'Web 2.0' technologies. 'Web 2.0' refers to the growing emphasis on interactivity in the web, through such technologies as blogs, wikis, RSS feeds, podcasts and others.

While there is limited space to discuss these, the table below provides examples of how Web 2.0 can be used by archives.

Technology	Explanation	Archival use
Blog	Short for web-log. An online 'diary' where the 'blogger' makes regular posts, and readers can add their own comments.	Used to generate community. Is a relatively easy way to post news and updates.
Wiki	A wiki is a collaborative environment where all users can edit and amend content. The most well-known example is Wikipedia (<www.wikipedia.org>).	While archives can establish their own community, a more common (and sustainable) approach is to edit entries on Wikipedia which are relevant to your collection strengths, to draw users to your archives.
RSS	Stands for 'Rich Site Summary' or 'Really Simple Syndication'. RSS is an automated process that allows users to 'subscribe' or sign up for an RSS 'feed' on a website, to be notified when the site is updated.	Particularly relevant for archival websites that are frequently updated.
Podcasts	Short audio recordings of speeches, lectures, events, etc. Called 'podcasts' as they can be downloaded and listened to on an iPod®	If your archive arranges talks or presentations, recording and making them available as podcasts opens them to a wider audience.

Table 10.3: Web 2.0 technologies

This is not an exhaustive list (other Web 2.0 technologies include social networking sites such as MySpace and Facebook, and tagging sites such as Flikr and del.icio.us) and there is not space to describe these in detail. While the use of Web 2.0 technologies are not yet mainstream within archives, it is useful to be aware of them and consider where they may be useful.

Conclusion

While computers and the World Wide Web are becoming ubiquitous in how we work, we all have different levels of expertise in technology. This chapter has provided an overview of how we can turn these tools to our use, whether through common computer software, dedicated archival collection management systems or making use of portal sites that are already established for the archival community.

A final message is that using technology is not 'all or nothing'. While some archives may have dedicated collection management systems and a fully interactive website with online services, a simple start can be made by a presence on Collections Australia Network and Directory of Archives in Australia, an email address, and using templates and layouts to give a common organisational 'look' to your finding aids and other publications.

section 3

promoting the archives

Now that you have established your archives, acquired loads of good 'stuff', and documented it all properly, it is time to guide you through the processes of making it available – after all, this is why you have gone to all this trouble. We have called this section *Promoting the archives* because it's not just a case of 'build it and they will come' – you have to let people know what wonders you have in your custody.

In the first chapter in the section, *Access & Reference Services,* we start with a cautionary note – you might not be able to make everything available. We discuss what public access means and touch on reasons why some material might have to be withheld from access for valid reasons of security, privacy, confidentiality or cultural sensitivity. We go on to discuss what sort of reference services you might be prepared to offer, including reproduction services. That brings us to the thorny question of copyright, so we outline what copyright means to an archives, and how it might affect how you make material available. The chapter ends with a discussion of some of the issues in providing reference services and the value of studying the use made of your collection.

The next chapter, *Finding Aids*, builds on the previous chapter. If you want people to come and use your collection, you have to provide them with easy ways of finding what they are looking for – remember, your customers haven't been trained to think about archival material the way you do. All they know is what they want. In this chapter, we discuss what sort of finding aids you can create to make it easier for your users (and less work for you!). We outline some of the different kinds of finding aids you can create, and how many of them can be built from the work you have already done when arranging and describing your holdings.

Of course, one way of making material more easily accessible is by making copies. This not only allows you to give multiple users simultaneous access, but it also allows you to make the material accessible to remote users. So the next chapter in the section is about *Digitisation & Imaging*. For many years archivists have made microfilm copies of some of their collections not only to give access to more than one user at a time but also to save the original from wear and tear. Now, scanners and digital technology can also do this – and make the images available over the World Wide Web. This chapter takes you through the necessary steps and discusses the issues in using these technologies (microfilm still has its uses!).

The last chapter in this section, *Advocacy & Outreach,* takes you beyond just making your collections available. This chapter highlights that your archives (regardless of size) is not an island – it is part of a multi-faceted community, comprising parent organisations, managers, funding bodies, donors, depositors, users, professionals, staff, volunteers, students and people who are just interested. To survive, you need the support (active or passive, but active is better!) of all parts of your community, and this chapter discusses a number of ways of getting people interested and involved – public relations, publicity, publications, seminars, exhibitions, working with volunteers and friends groups, funding, and reporting. Your success in this area will ensure that your collection will endure.

CHAPTER 11

access & reference services

JENNI JEREMY, ENID WOODLEY & LYALL KUPKE

CHAPTER ABSTRACT

The provision of access and reference services are key components of ensuring the successful use of archives by researchers and all that use them. These services are central to the overall functionality of the archives and intersect with many other archival operations including appraisal, arrangement and description, creating finding aids, preservation, digitisation and the dissemination of public programs.

Building on earlier chapters, this chapter outlines the principles and requirements that should inform the development of your access policy, and the elements of a reference service. It also canvasses some of the dilemmas and challenges facing the reference archivist.

Introduction

The term 'access' refers to the terms and conditions of availability of records, documents or information maintained or held by an archive for evaluation or consultation by its users. Managing access to archives involves staff establishing procedures which will ensure that legislative requirements and donor agreements are adhered to, and that the records are protected from rearrangement, theft and mutilation.

'Reference services' is an umbrella term given to the facilities and services afforded to researchers and users of the archives and its records once access to them has been approved. The archivist is crucial, not only in helping users to identify, select and understand the records, but also in the provision of a suitable environment for research, answering telephone and email enquiries and providing suitable reproduction services in order to make available copies of records should copyright legislation or donor permission allow.

Group visits to archives

The level of access and the range of reference services offered will vary from archives to archives and will be dependent upon the nature of the records held, the purpose of individual archives and the resources afforded to each collection. Each archive must decide the framework that its reference services will operate on before it can embark upon such a service provision, identifying which records are available for research, under what conditions they may be accessed and who may see them. For example, will the records be available to everyone or only to approved researchers or identified staff within an organisation? Are there donor restrictions or legislative requirements to be adhered to? These considerations are fundamental to the implementation of any rules and regulations, and careful planning and administration will be required in order to not only assist researchers and users to locate information but also to provide effective services to those requiring original records. Therefore, an access policy must be developed and approved, and then regulations and guidelines drawn up to support the broad intent of the policy.

Access

Access to archives is administered in many different ways, and is dependent upon the type of archives and its holdings and the specific archives legislation and donor restrictions that may need to be enforced. For example, Section 33 of the *Archives Act 1983* indicates that Commonwealth records are generally available for public access 30 years after their year of creation. The legislation also provides for categories of documents that may be withheld even longer than the 30-year specified time period. For some government archives, the decision to release information must be referred to the department or authority currently responsible for the function involved.

Access directions generally fall into three categories: open, restricted and closed. For many archives across the corporate and public environments, access policies will be linked to the organisation's own policies and regulations on access to information and records, for example, student records or personal files. In other archives, closed records would include personnel records and documents containing sensitive personal information. Archives that hold records of indigenous peoples (which might include secret or sacred material) must ensure such material is restricted. Access restrictions may also apply when records have not been processed or appraised, if they contain unseparated personal or confidential information, or if they are in fragile condition.

In collecting archives, policies on access will usually be collection-specific, that is there will be specific policies for the various collections held. For example, each of the businesses or trade unions depositing records with the Noel Butlin Archives Centre at the Australian National University would specify the policy to be applied to its records. Similarly, families and individuals depositing records with the various Prime Ministerial Collections would stipulate the access conditions. The availability of records for research in collecting archives will largely depend on the agreement made between the donor and the archives at the time of transfer of the records into archival custody, or established perhaps with a memorandum of understanding between the two parties.

Most archives will hold material of interest to the staff of their parent organisation, the general public and the media. In order to ensure the ongoing efficient and effective operation of the archives, it is necessary to provide the appropriate level of access to these records while still maintaining a suitable level of confidentiality and security. An access policy may provide different conditions of access for staff, the public and the media, and indeed might even differentiate between parts of the parent organisation (for example, legal department records might be available only to members of that department). It should also be remembered that the archives might also contain records that fall within the public domain, such as publications and press releases, and the access conditions for these records may well have their own separate guidelines. In some cases, the depositor may have stipulated that that their permission is required before each individual researcher can be given access to all or part of the collection they have deposited.

"Right, that's all our gold, diamonds, bonds, and cash all safely locked away ... Er, you brought out the key, right?"

It is imperative therefore that each archive should have a written access policy in order to protect the records from misuse, outline the nature of the information contained within the collection, and the purpose and resources of each individual archive. A carefully constructed access policy will establish the framework within which the archivist and support staff can administer the access to records to be used by researchers and the general public. It should be drafted to meet the requirements of each archive and be sanctioned by the authorities that govern the collection. The access policy provides a full understanding of the resources available in the archive and those required to administer it correctly, thus becoming an effective instrument of authority for the archivist and her staff. Where there are no legislative provisions (especially in non-government archives), the archivist will need to consult within the parent organisation in formulating an access policy if it is to become an effective instrument of authority for the archives.

It should also be noted that the term 'access' may also refer to the opening hours of the archives to its users. It may also refer to the level of use afforded to an archive, such as researcher access only or where a refereed application is required to access the records for research purposes only.

Freedom of Information

Freedom of Information (FOI) legislation in Australia grants members of the public the right to access information which is held by government departments, organisations and ministers, subject to specified exceptions and exemptions. The federal *Freedom of Information Act 1982* came into effect in December 1982, and since then each of the states and territories has enacted similar legislation. FOI aims to encourage transparency of government information that is of general public interest and to provide individuals with a right to request access to, and correction of, personal information about themselves.

FOI and archives legislation are usually complementary. In general, however, FOI is concerned with the granting of access to an individual (even if the individual disseminates the information more widely) while archival legislation is concerned with access to the general public. While FOI is mostly intended to apply to records still in the custody of their creators (and therefore not yet available to the public as archives), in some cases it might be used to provide access to archival records that are restricted (for example, former employees may apply to see their personnel files).

Local government archives and university archives may also be subject to the FOI laws applying to their State or Territory government, and may receive applications from the public requesting access to material in their holdings under this legislation. Such applications may include requests for access to administrative records, such as personal data collected about researchers, like their contact details and reference enquiries.

Formulating an access policy

An access policy is collection- or archive-specific, designed to suit the needs of the organisation and taking into account a range of factors that are dependent on the context in which the archives is operating. Archives whose access provisions are prescribed by statute may need to develop specific procedures in order to administer the principles of that legislation, while other archives may need to consider the following criteria.

Legislation

It is critical that organisations attached to federal, state or local government agencies should be fully conversant with all Acts, ordinances and regulations that apply to the records they create and maintain. As mentioned earlier, access to some records in archives may fall under the FOI legislation and archives staff must be familiar with their obligation to carry out such requests.

Sensitive or confidential records

Organisations and individuals create records that contain information relating to their personal or business affairs, which could cause embarrassment or financial loss if made available to researchers. It is critical then that records of this nature be considered when drafting an access policy or when agreeing access conditions with the depositor. Such records could include personal and health information, fraud or security procedures, or defamatory or libellous information that, if made public, may obstruct or hinder business transactions or impede legal dealings.

In particular, you need to consider whether your collection includes material relating to, or collected from, indigenous people. The collection may contain material that would be offensive to indigenous people. It may contain material that indigenous people would consider secret or sacred. It may also contain material that would be useful to indigenous people in reconnecting with their people. Probably the best guidance for handling this material, and developing an appropriate access policy, are protocols such as those developed by the Aboriginal and Torres Strait Islander Library and Information Resources Network (see Further Reading).

Privacy

Under the National Privacy Principles, an individual's personal information should not be released to a researcher unless permission has been obtained from the inividual. Information from records, however, may be accessible for statistical purposes, providing the individual names or any identifiable information is protected (see also Chapter 2: *Getting Organised*, for a discussion on the National Privacy Principles).

Donor restrictions

When records are offered by a depositor to a collecting archive, the archivist is required to establish or clarify any access restrictions. In doing so, the archivist must consider the implications and the management of any such restrictions upon the records prior to accepting and accessioning them into the collection (see Chapter 6: *Acquisition* and Chapter 7: *Accessioning*). If restrictions are placed on records, or if the archives has a policy of referring requests for access to the depositors before researchers can use them, then this practice must be clearly stated in the archives' access policy and all publicity information about the archives and its services. Information on access restrictions should also be noted in finding aids, print and electronic, as this policy can have a significant impact on users of the records, particularly researchers, who may have travelled some distance to view them.

Users

Policy documents should define the clientele or level of user that the archives will service. The range of users will be determined by the purpose of the archives, the constitution and the resources available. In the case of public archives, users may be prescribed by legislation and will include government bodies and members of the public within an area of political authority. In-house archives responsible for the records of businesses or private institutions may only provide access to its employees or under contract to the organisation. Casual researchers may be required to register for a reader's ticket or pay a special fee to cover services provided.

Equity

Equality of access to records is an important principle intended to ensure that the archives provides reference services without favour or prejudice to its defined users.

Levels of access

The archivist must decide the level of access a researcher or user will have to, and within, the archives. Access levels may range from general admission to the reading or search room through to granting permission to reproduce or publish specific documents. An access policy then should review conditions of access for:

- the reading or search room and finding aids
- collections or categories of archives
- individual series or documents within a series
- copying of individual documents or photographs for personal research
- reproduction or publication of documents, photographs and other archival material

Control

The extent to which materials are physically available for research depends on the records being arranged and described by the archivist so that the appropriate documents may be requested and retrieved. Some types of records require more extensive controls than others, for example a box of loose documents may require control numbers for each, while pages in a bound volume may not. Generally, archives' finding aids will indicate what types of records are housed in a particular box, but not what specific documents or information might be present.

Access policies should explain that researchers will be provided with finding aids and instructions for how to use them, but they will be required to select their own records and do their own research work with no guarantee that they will find what they are seeking. An access policy should also state that records which have not been brought under control through arrangement and description will not be available. This should lessen the likelihood of researchers' dissatisfaction with the results of a search, or with the archivist for not being able to immediately locate a particular document.

Providing reference & access services can be of benefit to a researcher and the archives: here an archivist discusses artwork created by the father of the man looking on.

Physical condition

If the records are in a poor physical condition or have been physically damaged, the archivist should consider restricting access to them until they can be restored by a conservator. Other options for the archivist to consider for providing access to researchers are to offer a duplicate copy of the record, for example a photocopy, microfilm copy or a digital reproduction. Each of these alternatives can be initiated very effectively for frequently used records, where restricting or providing no access would be highly inconvenient to many researchers. Should the majority of records in a collection be in poor physical condition, access to the entire collection might be restricted until reproductive or restoration work is completed. It is vital that records should not be made available to researchers if ongoing handling will accelerate their deterioration.

Security

Archives consist of records of enduring value. They are unique, and many have significance as legal or financial evidence. Access provisions as provided by the archivist, and subsequently the organisation responsible for the records, must protect the material from loss, damage, misfiling or mutilation while they are in storage, as well as during research use. It is good practice to ensure that all users, no matter where they may originate from, do not have access to the records storage areas. Retrieval and return of material should be limited to one or, at most, a few authorised and trained staff members. This practice minimises the risk of misfiling and identifies accountability for any loss or damage.

To request records, a standard request form should be used, and a copy of the request retained until the records have been returned, checked and refiled in their proper location. Staff must be employed to supervise records during use, and security measures established to protect the material, to detect breaches and to apprehend the person responsible. See the Security Measures checklist for recommended precautions.

Service charges

The access policy document should include a statement of the archives' policies and practices in relation to fees or charges that might be incurred by a researcher for the use of the facilities or services, including any reproductions such as photocopying.

The policy should also outline the basis for the charges and explain the philosophy or administrative regulations behind the costs, for example if these maybe imposed due to organisational administration or institutional cost-recovery objectives. If fees and charges change annually, then it is advisable to publish a separate fact sheet of fees, which can be inserted into archives' promotional literature, access policy and other general policy documentation.

In considering the above list of essential criteria for an access policy, the issues outlined will assist the archivist in planning and designing a specific access policy customised to the needs and requirements of the parent or funding organisation relevant to the archives. It is essential that archives staff be aware of, and conversant with, the consequences and implications in the provision of an access service to the public, and the effect it will have on the parent body or funding organisation and the allocation of archival resources, particularly in relation to staff, time and money.

Access management

Once the access policy has been documented and approved, the next step in the process is to prepare the administrative procedures which support the policy. The key element is the design of an 'access application form' to be signed by both the researcher and the archivist to indicate that both parties are aware of their responsibilities in handling and dealing with access to archival material. An access application form records basic details concerning the researcher and their research interests, conditions of access and the archivist's approval.

Included in the applicant's personal details will be their name, address, contact details, and if relevant the applicant's home institution. Some archives may require proof of identity, such as a driver's licence or the name and contact details of a referee, supervisor or academic from a parent organisation. The applicant should be required to date and sign the access application form to signify compliance with the conditions outlined. It may also be useful to signify a stated time period on the access application form, for example one or two years, for a specific research project or for each return visit. Examples of application forms can be easily located and many are now available in electronic format. An example (from the Bob Hawke Prime Ministerial Library) is included at Appendix 11.1.

The access application form is critical documentation if applicants are to be held accountable for what they do to the records or if they publish from them. Formalising access to the archives denotes that the archives can take action against researchers if they violate the access conditions. Information provided by the researcher on the access application form may also be used by the archivist as a source for identifying trends concerning the use of the archives and using this data to plan for other programs, such as digitisation of potentially high-use records.

A common procedure for obtaining access to original records in an archive may include the issue of an annual reader's ticket, or some other written form of permission, to each approved applicant. In this instance, the archivist should maintain these records carefully in order that the information concerning the applicant can be checked for future reference.

Another matter for procedural consideration in the use of archives is citation practice. All references to archival materials should carry an approved form of citation, properly identifying the records and acknowledging the archives. The citation should include the name of the organisation holding the record, the creator of the record, information relating to the record's specific reference or archives number and title, date of the item and/or unique identification of the entry within the item. It is useful to prepare a simple handout containing examples of the archives' preferred method of recording references to its holdings, including full and brief citations. Some major archives such as the National Archives of Australia provide specific brochures on citation of their records.

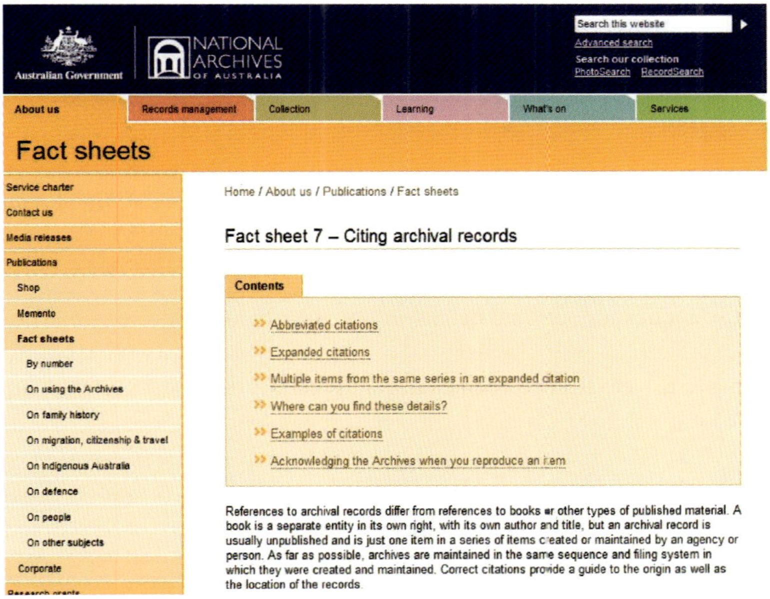

Figure 11.1: An example of a fact sheet

Two relatively complex areas of responsibility for an archivist to consider when crafting policies, rules and regulations for its users include copyright and reproduction. Both can contribute significantly to the workload of staff whether it is a small or large institution and both require individual examination and consideration. These areas are discussed in more detail later in this chapter.

Factors that should be considered for ensuring the security of records are shown in the following table. While this checklist reflects the ideal, smaller archives may not always be able to meet all these suggestions and will need to make adaptations to best suit their environment.

Requirement	Implementation
Restrict entry	Limit access of staff, visitors and tradespeople to the building or archives area by using designated doors and entrance ways.
Identification	All visitors and staff should show identification before being admitted to the archives or search room.
Registration	All visitors should be required to register their name, address, nature of business and time of entry each day upon arrival and when exiting.
Non-public areas	All visitors in non-public areas should be issued with a visitors badge or card and be accompanied by a staff member at all times. Cards or badges should be returned upon departure.
No baggage	Researchers to store coats, bags, briefcases in a cloakroom or designated area until their work each day is completed. Ideally when researchers leave the archive their research materials should be searched.
Requests	Record request forms should be completed for all original records. Users should be limited to three containers, or equivalent in unboxed materials, at any one time. Original records should be used under direct supervision.
Reshelving/refiling	Researchers should not be permitted to reshelve or refile records. To reduce the risk of mishandling or misfiling this should be the work of the archivist.
Copying	Copying to be done by staff members in order to ensure careful handling of the records.
Written rules	Provide a concise set of written regulations to each researcher and ensure these are understood and respected.

Requirement	Implementation
Evacuation procedures	Develop clear procedures for handling physically and emotionally unwell or suspicious persons and establish building evacuation in case of disaster, emergency or threat.
Disaster management	Establish a disaster management procedure and ensure facilities for the preparedness of an internal disaster such as flood are in place and visible.
Storage areas	Limit access to storage areas to staff only and the number of staff involved in retrieving records to a minimum. For additional security ensure storage areas are kept locked at all times.

Table 11.1: Security checklist

Designing reference services

The term 'reference services' denotes the actions involved in assisting people to use the archives. If an archives is to have any value, it must be available for people to do research in. Researchers then are a vital purpose for the archives' existence, so it is important to plan carefully the services that are offered to them. Of course, the resources of the archives limit what can be provided.

Brochure

An archives should produce a brochure which will provide the researcher with basic information about the archives collection and the services that are provided. Items of information that should be included are: street address, website address, contact details, opening hours, nature of the collection, types of records held, access policy, special features or conditions, and any research fees.

For some archives, a small map may be useful to help people find it. Details of how to get there by public transport can also be helpful. If the archives prefers the researchers to give advance notice of their visit, this should also be stated. Look at brochures produced by other archives for ideas.

Contents of the brochure

- ❑ Name of archives
- ❑ Street address
- ❑ Website address
- ❑ Contact details (telephone, fax, email)
- ❑ Name of contact person(s)
- ❑ Opening hours
- ❑ Nature of the collection
- ❑ Types of records held
- ❑ Access policy
- ❑ Advance notice needed?
- ❑ Special features or conditions
- ❑ Research fees
- ❑ Map
- ❑ Public transport information

Table 11.2 Checklist for brochure preparation

Where the collection in an archives has an appeal to people of a different ethnic background, it may be valuable to print your brochure also in the language of that group, particularly if the records are predominantly in that language. Include this same information on your website, as today's researchers are increasingly seeking useful sources of information on the internet.

The brochure is an important means of advertising and it is useful to have it available in many places where people can pick it up. Libraries, other archives, historical groups, genealogical societies etc are generally willing and interested to display such brochures.

Reference interview

When a researcher arrives at the archives, the first task is to establish what they are looking for and how the archives can help them. It is important that the archivist takes some time to discuss their project with them.

Asking questions of the archivist is often the first step for researchers.

The archivist needs to ask the researcher to outline their research topic and then list their specific requests for that visit. The archivist will then explain what records or finding aids they hold which may help the researcher. Some indication of the likely success of their requests can be given at this early stage. The researcher needs to fill out a form with their name, address, date and research topic. The form could also have provision for the archivist later to list the items used by the researcher.

Research room

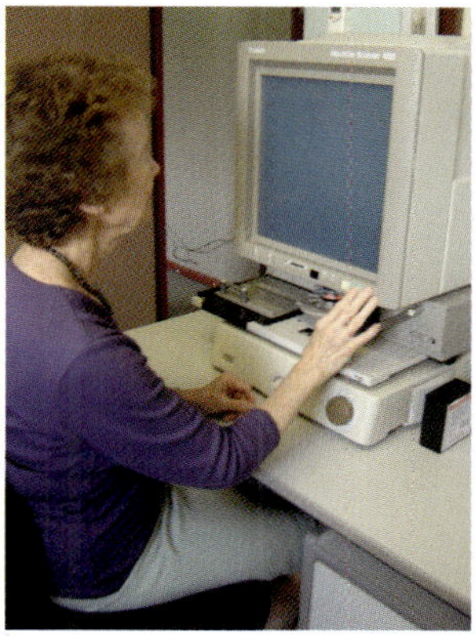

Microfilm readers – one form of equipment researchers use reading rooms.

A separate area or room should be provided for researchers to work in at the archives. The researcher will need to have sufficient table space to place their own note-taking materials on as well as the items from the archives. A larger table to cope with larger items like maps and architectural drawings will also need to be available.

Attention must be given to lighting, soundproofing, heating, cooling and ventilation. Wheelchair access is also important.

The room should contain the reference books and finding aids that researchers will want to refer to. Equipment that is provided for researchers to use, such as computers and microfilm and microfiche readers, needs to be readily available. The position of power points will need to be carefully planned, especially as researchers are increasingly bringing their own laptop computers into the research room.

The archives needs to be aware of the new technology that is being used. Many archives are even providing, or considering providing, computers for researchers to use (see discussion of this point in Chapter 10: *Using Computers*).

The archivist should be situated nearby so that they can readily answer questions, retrieve records and generally supervise the researchers.

Finding aids

The archives should endeavour to prepare guides or finding aids to their collection. These will be valuable in guiding the researcher to the appropriate records for their research. It can be useful to have guides or fact sheets on certain topics or types of records, particularly for those topics that are frequently studied or records that are frequently requested. Indexes to certain records can also be useful to help locate the relevant records quickly. Computer databases are very helpful in this regard. See Chapter 12: *Finding Aids* for further advice on finding aids.

Reference library

The archives will also have a collection of reference books which can assist in the research of a topic. These can range from histories of organisations and local districts to biographies, published guides, directories etc. It is important to realise that these are secondary source material and not primary or archival sources, but that they may be useful in guiding the researcher to request specific archival material.

Requests for records

Once the researcher has discussed their research topic with the archivist and checked the available finding aids and guides, they will request that certain records be brought from the repository for them to examine. It is vitally important that a record is kept of the exact records requested. If the archives does not have an automated retrieval system, a useful method is to make three copies of any request. One copy is attached to the records; the second copy is placed in the box or shelf from which the records were removed; and the third copy is retained by the archives in a file. Having the second copy mark the location of the records should ensure that the records are later returned to the correct place (it also alerts other potential users to the fact that the item is currently in the reading room).

The archives' copy of the requests can be used for statistical purposes at a later date if required. Information can be obtained about various matters, such as the types of research undertaken, and the frequency of use of particular records. Records which are found to be used most frequently may need to be photocopied, digitised or microfilmed to ensure that the originals are protected from damage and are preserved.

Reproduction

Researchers will ask for photocopies of some records. This should be undertaken only by the archivist as original records are involved. It may not be wise to copy some records which could be damaged through copying. Researchers should be informed in advance of the cost of photocopies. (See comments on copyright and reproduction later in this chapter).

Access and Reference using records in the National Archives' Adelaide reading room.

Photographic prints of photographs may also be requested. This may require the service of a professional photographer, otherwise a digital scanner can be readily used. A scale of fees will need to be established for all these services.

Some researchers may ask whether they can use their own digital camera to copy records. The archives will need to establish a policy about this. This issue has been, and will no doubt continue to be, a matter of debate among archivists. Whatever the decision, the fundamental point for consideration is the protection of the records. Excessive light can be detrimental to fragile and delicate records, so if using a camera it is preferable to switch off the flash mode and simply use the available light in the room. Because photocopying also exposes the records to extreme light, using a digital camera without the flash as the alternate way of reproducing the record is likely to be less harmful. There is also a saving of paper by the archives. However, it may be advisable to supervise this to ensure that the records are not damaged in any way.

Enquiries by mail, email or telephone

It is not always possible for researchers to visit the archives. Distance or work commitments are the most likely barriers. Requests frequently come by mail, email and telephone. The archivist needs to establish a method for handling these requests. A careful record needs to be made of each request as it comes. It is important to give the enquirer some indication of the time that they may have to wait for a response. It is also important to indicate at the start if there are any fees for this research.

An archives can develop a set of standard replies to many enquiries which should then be promptly sent. They would indicate how long the researcher may have to wait for a full response; they should include the scale of any fees that are charged; they can also suggest possible alternative sources of information (if any); or they can provide links to your website where FAQs may answer some of their questions.

Over time, an archives will discover that certain questions re-occur. It is helpful to develop a set of answers to FAQs so that time is not wasted by repeating the work. Answering requests can take a large amount of an archivist's time. An archivist may need to apply a time limit to each request. If the request is particularly complex, it may be necessary to suggest that the person engage a professional researcher to visit the archives for them.

Photocopies or digital copies will be made of some records and posted or emailed to the enquirer. The archives is entitled to ask for payment for these copies. As well, if the archives has a policy of charging for research, then the appropriate fee will need to be calculated and an invoice sent. Requesting payment in advance is a wise practice to ensure full payment for the service rendered.

Problem: To do research or not?

There can be a difficulty for the archivist in balancing the desire to assist researchers on the one hand with the need to require researchers to do their own research. The role of the archivist is merely to guide and support the researcher. However, in a small archives the researcher often depends on the archivist's familiarity with the records in the archives to know how to proceed. The archivist should be aware that the willing provision of assistance gives good publicity for the archives. Further discussion of this point can be found later in this chapter under the heading 'Demands, pressures and dilemmas'.

Copyright

Material subject to copyright includes literary, artistic, dramatic and musical works, sound recordings, films, videos and DVDs, and radio and television broadcasts. This means almost everything in an archival collection, whether it has been published or not, may be protected by copyright. Journal articles, letters, reports, diaries, newspaper cuttings, poems, computer databases and even song lyrics are all considered 'literary works', and the term 'artistic works' includes photographs, maps, drawings and architectural plans.

The *Copyright Act 1968* covers works made by a resident or citizen of Australia, or made or first published in Australia. Australia is also signatory to a number of international copyright treaties, which provide copyright protection in Australia for works produced overseas.

While it is not necessary to be thoroughly conversant with the complexities of copyright law, those who work in the reference and access area of archives do need a basic knowledge of what copyright entails and how it applies to the use of material in their collection. The following information about copyright is therefore intended as a guide only, and we recommend that you refer to the sources listed at end of this section for more prescriptive legal advice.

Keeping copyright front-of-mind can be difficult for busy reference archivists, especially when their main aim is to make records publicly available in line with the access conditions of their own institutions. Reference archivists in Australia also need to make researchers aware of their responsibilities and rights under copyright legislation to minimise potential infringements.

What is copyright?

Copyright gives the creators of material certain rights and legal protection. Copyright does not protect the information or ideas within this material but it does protect the economic interests of the creators by giving them the exclusive rights to copy, publish, communicate (which includes making it available online) and publicly perform the material. Anyone wanting to use copyright material in a way that is covered by one of these rights has to obtain the permission of the owner.

Copyright applies automatically from the time that the material is first created – the creators are not required to register their work, to pay any fees or to include the copyright symbol ©.

Copyright also supports the moral rights of the creator, like the right to be attributed as the author.

Who owns copyright and how long does it last?

The first owner of copyright is usually the person who created the work, and upon their death copyright ownership passes to their heirs and so on, until copyright expires. However, if an employee made the work as part of their job, then their employer generally owns copyright. So for in-house archives, such as those within private schools and companies, their own organisation should hold copyright on any work created by its staff and can usually grant permission for copying and publication by researchers.

Those archives that hold records principally created by Commonwealth, State or Territory governments and their departments will find that copyright for much of the collection is owned by the government (crown copyright). Archivists in charge of such collections will need to be familiar with procedures for dealing with requests for use of crown copyright material.

In some cases, specific contractual arrangements may assign copyright to the creator of the work rather than to the employer or government, and it is wise to keep a record of any such arrangements to ensure copyright agreements are honoured.

No matter what type of archive they work for, reference archivists need to be aware that there may often be more than one copyright owner for items in their collection. Correspondence files frequently include letters written by private individuals (who therefore own copyright) as well as those from employees of an organisation. Archival files may also include quotations and commercial brochures from private enterprise, clippings from newspapers and magazines, photographs and perhaps even blueprints or architectural plans.

There may also be more than one copyright owner for an individual work. For example, a photograph of an artwork or sculpture, or a musical work which was composed by one or more people, its lyrics written by others, and its cover illustration drawn by someone different again.

Copyright ownership can be sold or transferred – something else to keep in mind, especially if you work for a collecting archive and would like these rights to be signed over with the purchase or donation of records. It is important however to be aware of any third-party material within donated collections, as only copyright in works created by the donor will be covered in a transfer of this nature.

Material that has been published, broadcast or performed has a fixed time limit, after which copyright expires and it becomes part of the public domain and can be used more freely. The general rule is that copyright for published material lasts for the life of the creator plus 70 years, or in some cases for 70 years after it was first published. So, for an author who died in 1950, copyright would lapse in 2020. As it was the free trade agreement between Australia and the United States that extended this copyright duration from 50 to 70 years, the 70 years only applies to material that was still in copyright on 1 January 2005. Another exception to this rule is material published by the government and covered under crown copyright. Copyright lapses in this work 50 years after the year it was first published or made.

Any unpublished work usually remains in copyright until it is published, which means copyright for the vast majority of material in archival collections can continue indefinitely.

What can an archivist copy for researchers?

In general, material in an archives' collection that is not out of copyright cannot be copied for a researcher without the consent of the copyright owner, unless:

1. It is an unpublished, literary, dramatic, musical or artistic work, its creator died more than 50 years ago, and it is publicly accessible under the archives' own access regulations. (See Section 51 of the *Copyright Act* for more detail).
2. It is a 'reasonable portion' of a published literary, dramatic, musical or artistic work that has been requested in writing by a client for the purpose of research or study. (See Section 49 of the *Copyright Act* for more detail).

Reference archivists copying records for researchers most commonly use the first of these two exceptions as it deals with unpublished works. But because archives hold many 'orphaned' unpublished works (records for which it is virtually impossible to identify or trace the creators and their date of death) the provision of copies under this section can be hampered.

The second exception has a number of provisos attached to it. Archivists need to ensure they are copying only the proportion allowed under the Copyright Act, that they have received the required documentation from the researcher and keep this documentation for four years, and that the copies they provide are marked with the date they were made and the name of the archives. In addition, if the copy is supplied electronically (sent via email, fax or made available online), the archivist must attach a copyright warning notice and must also destroy any electronic copies that were made during the process of providing the copy.

Archivists can provide one-on-one advice. Provision of copies of material must be carefully thought out.

Reference archivists can only provide copies of their holdings for researchers to publish if the material is out of copyright, if the copyright owners have given their permission, or if the material is an old unpublished literary, dramatic or musical work whose author has been dead for more than 50 years.

What can researchers copy?

Most archives do not allow researchers to photocopy archival items themselves, in order to protect the original records from damage and to lessen the potential for copyright infringements. However, photocopying is not the only means of copying available to researchers who visit an archives in person or even online. Researchers may have the opportunity to print copies from digitised or microform versions of archival records, to make handwritten or typed transcriptions, to take digital photographs or to make audio recordings of archival material.

A researcher is usually permitted to reproduce copyright material in any of these ways for the purpose of research or study, so long as the copy is only a 'reasonable portion' of the work under the 'fair dealing' terms defined in Sections 40 and 103C of the Copyright Act. For most published material a 'reasonable portion' amounts to 10% of the work, but for unpublished material there is no 'reasonable portion' defined. Instead, the determination of fair use depends on a number of factors listed in Section 40 (2).

If researchers want to reproduce a copyright work in its entirety or to publish it, then the onus of tracing the copyright owners and seeking their permission rests with them and not the archivist.

While it is clearly difficult for reference archivists to check that researchers are not infringing the copyright vested in archival records, the potential for infringements can be reduced. Placing prescribed warning notices about copyright on or near photocopiers, computers and other equipment that can be used for reproducing material is one way of alerting researchers, and also minimises the liability of the archives. These warning notices are included in Schedules 3 and 9 of the *Copyright Amendment Regulations 1969* which are available online through the ComLaw website at <http://www.comlaw.gov.au/>.

To raise researchers' awareness of copyright legislation, it is advisable to include information about copyright in any brochures about public access to the archives, on the archives' website, and possibly even provide detailed copyright information sheets. Examples include Source Sheet 6 produced by the Adelaide City Council Archives and available through their website at <http://www.adelaidecitycouncil.com> or the National Archives of Australia's Fact Sheet 8 (<http://www.naa.gov.au/about-us/publications/fact-sheets/>).

Many archives also incorporate statements on copyright responsibility into the forms that they ask researchers to complete for access to the archives or when requesting copies, as well as on the cover sheet for archival records that have been copied for a researcher.

Can an archivist copy material for use by their own organisation?

Archivists who wish to publish material from their collection are bound by the same copyright laws as other users of the collection. This includes making material available on the archives' own website. The *Copyright Act 1968* does contain some 'special purposes' provisions for archives but these generally relate to copying for the administrative purposes of the archive.

Where to go for more information

Although it does not give legal advice on specific copyright matters to members of the public, the Attorney General's Department (<http://www.ag.gov.au/>) does provide general copyright information, electronic versions of the legislation and updates on changes in copyright law.

The Australian Copyright Council (<www.copyright.org.au>) is an independent non-profit organisation that aims to assist copyright owners and people working in institutions like archives that deal with copyright issues. The Council may be able to provide legal advice. It also has a very useful range of information sheets and other publications, and runs regular seminars explaining the practical applications of copyright law.

You may also need to consult with the legal advisor to your parent organisation.

Reproduction of records

Due to the increasing pace of life and community reliance on technology, researchers frequently have high expectations for the speed of delivery of copies of archival records. There is also a growing tendency to request copies rather than spending time viewing the originals, and a requirement that these copies can be accessed at a time and place and in a format most convenient for the researcher. Balancing these expectations with the practicalities of providing a copying service that does not overburden our often-limited staff resources can be challenging.

There are of course benefits in providing researchers with reproductions of archival records. Popular original records can be protected from deterioration due to excessive handling if surrogate copies are produced and used for reference purposes. In the case of digital or microform copies, records can be used by a number of researchers in a number of locations at any one time, multiplying the accessibility of the archival collection. The provision of high-quality copies for publication or exhibition (in accordance with copyright legislation) can also promote the archives and its holdings to new audiences and result in increased reference use.

Setting up a reproduction service

When setting up a reproduction service, it is important to first consider the individual circumstances of your archive, especially its purpose, resources, holdings and users. Having a clear understanding of what is both desirable and possible will lead to the establishment of an effective service. Examples of some questions that should be asked when planning a reproduction service are included in Table 11.3.

If you are unfamiliar with the more technical aspects of different reproduction formats, we recommend that you also refer to other relevant chapters in this text. Chapter 13: *Digitisation & Imaging* covers digitising and micrographics. See also Chapter 16: *Plans, Photographs & Objects*, Chapter 17: *Sound Recordings* and Chapter 18: *Moving Images.*

Aspects of a reproduction service	**Questions to consider**
Aims	Why are you offering this service? Who is it principally designed for?
Format	What formats will you offer? • Photocopies: black and white, colour, A4, A3, A2, foolscap? • Prints from digital or microform images? • Photographs: digital, prints, standard sizes? • Digital copies: low resolution for web delivery, high resolution for publication, JPEG, TIFF, PDF, OCR? • Microforms: microfilms, aperture cards, microfiche? • Maps, plans, and blueprints: to scale, colour, digital? • Audiovisual and sound recordings: films, videos, DVDs, CDs, tapes, podcasts?
Limitations	What legal limitations are there? Copyright legislation, donor agreements, access and charging regulations?
Finances	How are you going to fund the service and what should you charge? Will your budget allow it to be provided free of charge or at a reduced rate or will you need to charge on a cost recovery basis? What payment facilities will you offer? Are you able to guarantee secure online payment? Will you provide invoices and receipts?
Resources	What resources will you need? Equipment, staff, physical space, copying supplies, access to power, the internet and equipment service companies?
Operations	How will you operate the service? Will it be in-house, through a specialist service provider or a combination of the two? Will it be self-service or will there be dedicated staff working within scheduled times? Will there be limits on the amount of copies that can be requested at one time/by one person? Will there be prescribed turnaround times for the provision of copies?
Delivery	How will you deliver the copies? Mail, email, online, for collection in person?

Table 11.3: Reproduction service planning checklist

Choosing reproduction equipment

There is a wide variety of reproduction equipment available, many of which combine a number of functions such as photocopying, scanning and printing. Choosing equipment that is most suitable for your needs is essential.

Consideration should be given to the ease and speed of copying, the quality of copies produced, and how true colours are in comparison with originals. When copying from large volumes, it's handy if copiers have removable lids or lids that open to more than a 90-degree angle. Determining whether the equipment caters for the predominant size of material in your collection (for example, will it copy foolscap pages without having to reduce the size of the copies) is also important, and the estimated cost of supplies and maintenance together with the length and conditions of the warranty should definitely be taken into account. It is useful if the equipment is relatively mobile and has the facility to count copies for statistical purposes. Another convenient feature is the ability to add automatic text to copies citing your archives.

Requesting reproductions

Having order forms for the supply of reproductions to researchers can save time and avoids confusion. The forms should specify what is available from the archives, such as the range of formats, sizes, costs, payment and delivery options and turnaround times. They should prescribe the researcher's requirements, identifying and describing the item they want copied (giving the series and item details, title, and specific page/s), the type and number of copies they need, their name and contact details, delivery instructions, their chosen payment method and the date they are submitting their order.

Large ledgers such as this can be difficult to copy, and present challenges to archivists wishing to provide access to the information held within.

Order forms can also be used to make researchers aware of the conditions under which the archives will provide them with copies. These stated conditions might include reminders about copyright responsibilities, restrictions on certain donated collections and the archives' right to refuse copying that may damage the records.

Making reproductions

Most archives do not allow researchers to photocopy archival records themselves. Staff members who are trained in handling original records are less likely to damage or misfile material that they copy.

Self-service copying by researchers is more common, however, when printing from microform or digital copies where damage to the record is not such an issue. Situating the printer, though, so staff can keep a check on the number of copies printed and monitor any possible copyright infringements by researchers is recommended.

With the proliferation of digital cameras, some archives are also permitting researchers to copy archival records themselves in reading rooms. Researchers who wish to use their cameras must usually request permission in writing, and comply with copyright and any other conditions, such as not using photographic flashes, damaging records or disturbing others.

The wonders of modern technology can also allow the manipulation of digital images. Generally archives should aim at providing faithful reproductions of archival records but in some instances, like reproductions for publication, it may be acceptable to use digital means to repair scratches or correct colour.

When your own archive is unable to provide copies of particular formats of records, it may be necessary to engage the services of specialists. It is important to select reputable service providers who preferably have experience in dealing with historical records and will handle the items carefully. Security of any records that are taken off-site for copying is also an issue and materials must be well packaged.

Charging for reproductions

Most archives charge for reproductions, but the charges can vary significantly. The scale of fees may be regulated by legislation in some cases. For example, Section 49 (3) of the *Copyright Act 1968* has a bearing on what archives can charge users when providing copies of portions of published works, limiting charges to cost recovery only.

Cost recovery is a common charging regime for archives and one that supports the ideal of equitable access to archival collections. In determining charges to recover costs only, you will need to calculate the amount spent on servicing the copying equipment, purchasing supplies and the cost of labour and divide the total cost by the number of copies made to come up with a single copy price.

The scale of fees you set for your copying services should factor in postage and handling costs if applicable and cater for international users by deducting a portion for GST (the Australian Goods and Services Tax). If you are using service providers to copy records, you may also need to pass on the full charges of the specialists you engage directly to researchers. It is recommended that prepayment be an automatic requirement for archives that charge for reproduction services to avoid wasting resources copying records for which no payment is forthcoming.

Larger institutions with material that is frequently used by the media and in publications may also charge reproduction fees, but these can be difficult to collect. Alternatively, some organisations like the Mitchell Library in the State Library of NSW offer a scale of fees according to the use to which the copy is to put, and the potential financial profit to be gained from this use.

The end product

When reproducing archival records, it should be common practice to label the copy with the name of the archives, the date it was copied and, where possible, to cite details of the record item. This makes it easier for others to trace the original and discourages the infringement of copyright. One of the simplest ways of achieving this labelling is to include the relevant details on an overlay on the platen of the copier.

Increasingly, copies of archival records are required as legal evidence and archivists are asked to provide 'certified copies'. Certification of a copy does not mean that you are guaranteeing that the information in the record is correct, simply that it is a true copy of a record held in your archive.

Issues in reference services

For many years in some large archives, the reference and access function of archives was considered of lesser importance than the custodial role. As a result, there is a relative paucity of professional literature addressing reference and access issues and little formal training designed specifically for reference archivists. Yet much is expected of those who work in the reference and access area. As the public face of the archives, they act as mediators between researchers, archival systems and the records, a crucial role that requires a range of skills.

Developing reference and management skills

Reference archivists need a high standard of communication and time management skills, as well as technical abilities and a comprehensive knowledge of their organisation and archival collection, its provenance and accessibility. While on-the-job training and experience is often the principal means of developing these skills and should not be underrated, it is important to be aware of other professional development opportunities.

There are many courses available dealing with customer relations, improving communication, time management and making the most of specific computer software programs. Hooking into training offered by other archives and professional organisations, work shadowing and joining the ASA mentoring scheme are also invaluable, especially for the lone archivist. Networking is very useful, not only with other archivists, librarians and records managers but also with bodies that represent the core users of the collection, such as professional historians, genealogists and tertiary institutions. Learning more about users' search methods and research needs can be most beneficial when designing effective reference services, particularly those aimed at encouraging researcher self-help.

Although building knowledge of an archival collection and its attendant intricacies can take considerable time, cultivating and successfully employing customer relation skills can often prove more challenging. Reference archivists need to be able to deal with researchers from a wide range of backgrounds with a variety of abilities and interests. Researchers may not be able to speak or read English, may have a physical disability or may be distressed by information they find within a record. They may be academics experienced in using archival material or people who have no knowledge of what an archives is, let alone how to use one. This myriad of variations means that learning how to identify what a researcher is actually seeking and how to tailor explanations of search strategies, control systems and records to best suit the researcher and their purposes is not always straightforward.

Most reading rooms are as serene as this one at Archives New Zealand Wellington office. Providing reference services requires a balance between potentially conflicting interests, demands and pressures.

In archives where more than one person may be responsible for reference and access services, it is vital to document common practices. This promotes consistency and can assist with future training of reference staff. Where practicable in larger archives, it is useful to rotate new staff through the different specialist areas, including reference and access, to encourage wider understanding of the interdependence of archival functions.

Demands, pressures and dilemmas

On occasion, reference archivists may find that they have to temper their natural inclination to help researchers and remind themselves of how much assistance it is appropriate or possible to perform. Drawing this line can be difficult when researchers are remote, unfamiliar with archives or particularly demanding. Archivists should not interpret records for researchers but rather provide them with the skills to locate, select and understand the records for themselves. They should also remain impartial, polite and not reveal the research interests of one user to another, all of which may be hard to achieve in certain circumstances.

Reference archivists may also have difficulty managing their workload, given that many of their duties are reactive in nature and peaks in reference requests cannot be easily predicted. Coping with competing and fluctuating demands can be even more complicated for the lone archivist. Some may choose to try to limit the amount of reference queries they receive by imposing a research fee, by recommending the use of a research agent, or by reducing the opening hours of the archives. Rostering regular breaks from dealing face-to-face with researchers, using the message bank facilities on telephones and encouraging researchers to use self-service information can also provide welcome breathing space for busy reference archivists. Prioritising and regularly revising these priorities in line with changing demands can help to control workloads and meet deadlines.

Many people equate archives with libraries and this can give rise to a number of misconceptions and potential barriers for reference archivists to overcome. The majority of Australians have been taught in their formative years to access information through books in libraries, and more recently through the internet, and are therefore most familiar with locating information arranged by subject. Conversely, the general population does not automatically think of archives when seeking information and novice researchers are likely to become confused when trying to find primary source material within activity-based archival systems. To address some of these issues, archives often provide more descriptive finding aids. They may also specially design public interfaces for their collection management systems that reflect those most commonly used in libraries and by search mechanisms on the internet.

Unlike library items that are generally self-contained and self-evident, archival records need context to be fully understood. When researchers interact directly with a reference archivist, they can be made aware of this context. But with non-traditional forms of access, such as the provision of information about the collection or digital images of the records themselves on the World Wide Web, there is no guarantee that the user will make these important connections. Devising ways in which contextual information can be incorporated is one of the many challenges archivists face when adopting new technologies.

In an era when the provision of information is becoming increasingly competitive, archives both large and small frequently feel the need to establish an online presence to be seen as relevant in contemporary society. Having information available on the internet certainly means that far larger numbers can be reached and that the range of people using the archives will be much broader and will include many non-traditional users. However, a significant number of these users are likely to have happened upon the archives website when 'surfing' or 'googling', and will have no academic, historical or other training to prepare them for the complexities of archival research.

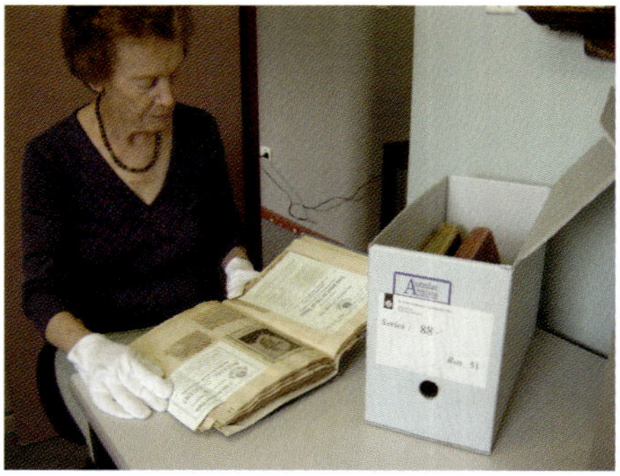

Using archives for research purposes

An online presence will almost inevitably result in different pressures on reference services, and many archives with online services notice a corresponding decrease in the number of researchers physically visiting their premises. Balancing the provision of traditional and non-traditional reference services to best fit the archives, its resources and its users is very important.

The immediacy and convenience of the internet and email means that remote researchers often expect almost instant responses to their requests. These demands may make offering a remote reference service unfeasible, especially for lone archivists. If archives do choose to provide an email address on their website, it is advisable to set up a standard automated response that makes the sender aware of the extent of reference services the archives provides and includes response times. Frequently asked questions (FAQ) pages on the site may also help reduce the number of repetitive enquiries an archive receives, just as having this information available in the form of leaflets can help reference archivists when dealing with visiting researchers or responding to letters.

Having a website for your archives may also lead to requests for additional online content and services. Users may desire access to the archives' catalogues and databases, secure e-commerce ordering, digitised images of archival records in formats that can be 'googled', speedier downloads and so on. Any potential new services need to be fully investigated to ensure that they are workable, economically viable, not too resource-intensive or solely dependent on the skills and knowledge of one staff member, and operate within the bounds of the access conditions and legislative requirements of the archives.

The possibility that information contained within archival records could be used for illegal purposes increases when these records are more freely available. Reference archivists need to think through the implications of providing online access to digital copies of archival records, and in some cases there can even be reasons to limit access to the titles and descriptions of archival items. For example, financial institutions sometimes use the date of birth and maiden name of their clients' mothers for verification of clients' identities. Therefore, including these details in the description of an archival item, while helping researchers to identify the correct record, may also serve those wishing to commit identity theft. Confidential information provided by researchers to archives also needs to be protected, especially if it has been submitted via electronic means and is stored on a database.

Studying the use of archives

Collecting and analysing reference statistics is critical for reporting and effective planning. Documenting the number of researchers who visit the archives in person each day and for how long can help to determine the most appropriate opening hours for your research room. Hits to your website, and particularly its reference and access components, can yield valuable information about what online finding aids are used most. Analysing records of all items requested by researchers can target popular material for future digitisation or exhibition. Surveying users can highlight needs for alternative services.

Databases compiled detailing remote reference enquiries can identify research subject trends and direct the production of source guides and standard responses to frequently asked questions. High copy counts from photocopiers can be significant in lobbying for the purchase of new equipment.

There is huge potential for the use of statistics derived from reference and access services. While accumulating and analysing data may take time, those who persevere will be rewarded with information that they can use to make their archives effective, visible and highly valued by their users, organisations and communities.

Conclusion

Archives are kept so they can be used, and archivists who provide access and reference services have a crucial part to play in making this aim a reality. Archives must design policies and procedures that encourage research and cater for the needs of users, while at the same time ensuring the archival holdings are not compromised in any way. It is important to formulate a relevant access policy that is clearly explained and properly regulated. Reference services must support any legislative requirements and the archives' goals, and be designed with due consideration of both the archives' resources and researchers' needs.

As the public face of archives, reference archivists must always strive to deliver appropriate assistance fairly and efficiently to all users. Reference archivists are the mediators between researchers, archival systems and the records and need a high standard of communication skills as well as a comprehensive knowledge of their archival collection, its provenance and accessibility. Archivists must be aware of changing patterns of research use and adapt accordingly. This can include embracing new technologies where appropriate. Documenting access and reference services, evaluating them regularly and adjusting them when necessary will enable the archivist to carry out this important archival function effectively and professionally.

CHAPTER 12

finding aids

LISA DARNELL

CHAPTER ABSTRACT

Finding aids lead users to the information they are seeking from or about archives. Finding aids come in many forms, such as guides and indexes. The increasing online presence of archives also presents wonderful opportunities to reach out and offer services to users from across the globe, and enable archives to not merely offer traditional paper-based finding aids in electronic format, but to present users with new ways of locating, interacting with and sharing information about archival material. As such, the concept of what is a finding aid continues to evolve.

This chapter introduces the purpose and types of finding aids in both traditional and electronic environments. It gives you tips on planning and preparing findings aids and also explores the relationship between arrangement and description and finding aids.

What are finding aids?

Finding aids are guides produced to assist users to access archival collections. Users come to archives looking for information on something specific – a subject, an event, a person. Finding aids work by allowing users to connect their specific queries to archival collections arranged according to provenance.

Descriptive information captured during the archival description process provides the stuff of which finding aids are made. This contextual information, such as major creating agencies, series they recorded and the relationships between series, shows how and why the records were created, and how they are related to other records produced by that administration or individual.

A wide variety of finding aids can be generated from this one set of information, and the archivist is not limited to particular content and formats. Finding aids may consist of databases, pamphlets, digital or in-house exhibitions, microfilms, loose-leaf folders, CDs, card indexes, research kits, podcasts and newsletters. The scope of the finding aids may range from a general overview of the archives entire holdings; to descriptions of individual series; to specific items of interest within series. They may embrace a number of series, or parts of a number of series. They may form part of a network of global finding aids or be entirely local in purpose, distribution and access.

Most customer enquiries start with a name of a person or organisation, a particular date, a geographical area, particular format (photograph, map, plan, diary), building, event and any combination in between rather than to the administrative framework of the records. The recognition of this gap should inform the structure, presentation and general form of the finding aids.

Archivists prepare ancillary aids such as indexes, special lists, source analyses and subject guides to help the researcher link the topic of their enquiry to the creating agencies whose functions might relate to that topic. It becomes possible to retrieve particular records or information by using a range of reference points, such as format, date, function, name and format.

In the example opposite, the PROVGuide55 describes the types of record held by the Public Records Office Victoria that relate to Land Records, and points the user to specific series that are commonly used in land enquiries.

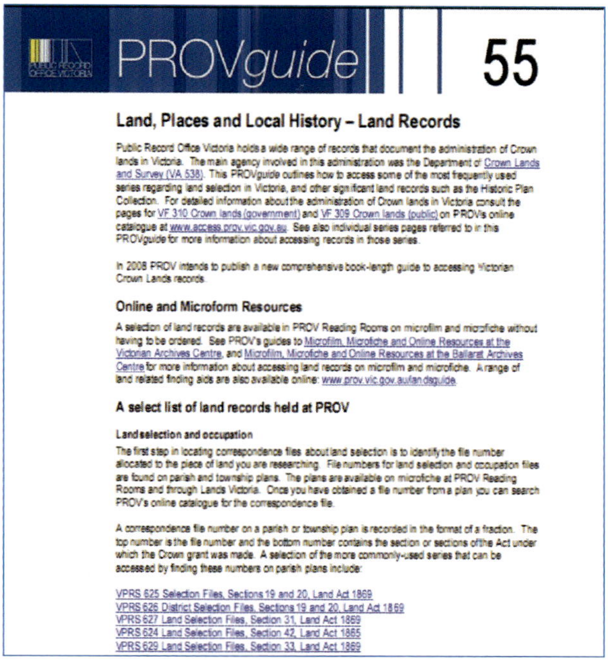

PUBLIC RECORD OFFICE VICTORIA PROVguide 55

Land, Places and Local History – Land Records

Public Record Office Victoria holds a wide range of records that document the administration of Crown lands in Victoria. The main agency involved in this administration was the Department of Crown Lands and Survey (VA 538). This PROVguide outlines how to access some of the most frequently used series regarding land selection in Victoria, and other significant land records such as the Historic Plan Collection. For detailed information about the administration of Crown lands in Victoria consult the pages for VF 310 Crown lands (government) and VF 309 Crown lands (public) on PROV's online catalogue at www.access.prov.vic.gov.au. See also individual series pages referred to in this PROVguide for more information about accessing records in those series.

In 2008 PROV intends to publish a new comprehensive book-length guide to accessing Victorian Crown Lands records.

Online and Microform Resources

A selection of land records are available in PROV Reading Rooms on microfilm and microfiche without having to be ordered. See PROV's guides to Microfilm, Microfiche and Online Resources at the Victorian Archives Centre, and Microfilm, Microfiche and Online Resources at the Ballarat Archives Centre for more information about accessing land records on microfilm and microfiche. A range of land related finding aids are also available online: www.prov.vic.gov.au/landsguide.

A select list of land records held at PROV

Land selection and occupation

The first step in locating correspondence files about land selection is to identify the file number allocated to the piece of land you are researching. File numbers for land selection and occupation files are found on parish and township plans. The plans are available on microfiche at PROV Reading Rooms and through Lands Victoria. Once you have obtained a file number from a plan you can search PROV's online catalogue for the correspondence file.

A correspondence file number on a parish or township plan is recorded in the format of a fraction. The top number is the file number and the bottom number contains the section or sections of the Act under which the Crown grant was made. A selection of the more commonly-used series that can be accessed by finding these numbers on parish plans include:

VPRS 625 Selection Files, Sections 19 and 20, Land Act 1869
VPRS 626 District Selection Files, Sections 19 and 20, Land Act 1869
VPRS 627 Land Selection Files, Section 31, Land Act 1869
VPRS 624 Land Selection Files, Section 42, Land Act 1865
VPRS 629 Land Selection Files, Section 33, Land Act 1869

Figure 12.1: PROVguide 55 Land, Places and Local History – Land Records

In this instance, users are unlikely to be familiar with the agencies that created the records they seek, let alone being familiar with changes in these agencies over time. This guide allows the user to find the records they seek without having to rely on specialist knowledge.

Increasingly, archives are making finding aids available online. The internet environment allows the structured representation of provenance, with the ability to identify preceding/succeeding agencies, functions etc. via layers of hyperlinks. Free-text search across metadata entries based on function or activity indexes can open up new and related topics. The scope of these online finding aids may range from 'meta hubs' providing an overview of national and international archival holdings in a certain area, to an overview of holdings nationally, a general overview of an archives holdings and descriptions of individual series, to exhibitions highlighting individual items of interest within a series. (More information about using computers can be found in Chapter 10: *Using Computers*).

The archivist has an obligation to maintain a view of the records in the context in which they were created (see Chapter 8: *Arrangement & Description*). This is necessary because the demands which will be made on the records for information cannot be predicted. For example, a corporation might use its archives to check a previous policy, to provide evidence for a court case or to produce an advertising campaign. Outside researchers might require information about the corporation's history, its buildings, an uncle who worked there, or its relations with employees. Finding aids which reveal the original structure and function of the records aim to ensure maximum flexibility for future users through their reconstruction of the original recordkeeping systems, rather than by presenting the archivists interpretation of the records.

It is vital that an archives system of finding aids is user-friendly, intuitive and easily accessible. Inadequate finding aids can undermine all the effort expended on arrangement and description. Users may be deterred by a disjointed collection of lists and descriptions, or an unintuitive search interface. They may tire of waiting for assistance because they need intensive help from a reference archivist. If they persist alone, they may simply fail to locate information that is actually there.

A clear, well-planned system of finding aids, which helps users to progress independently, alleviates these problems. Having these resources available in as many forms as possible means less assistance is required from a reference archivist. If the finding aids are online, initial searches and results may be obtained from home or office; researchers may peruse online finding aids, search across collections of indexes, query the archives databases, and (increasingly, as more archival material is put online) retrieve the information they require in digital copy, immediately.

The variety of finding aids

Resources and user needs will determine the number and form of the finding aids an organisation may produce. There is no set number or format required by organisations of certain types. While most archives would create an inventory of record-creating agencies and series, each institution may produce additional indexes, subject guides, special listings and supplementary finding aids specific to its own holdings and dependent on the needs of its own users. For example, a local government archives might add a list of past mayors and an index for council minutes. The need for such supplementary finding aids might, of course, be reduced if the archives is using a fully searchable electronic collection management system and can make that system accessible to users.

Rigidly describing the elements and format of specific findings aids is pointless, due to the many and varied forms they may take, and the increasing availability of finding aids electronically further blurs these distinctions. However, if their purpose, scope and major elements are considered, most finding aids fall into one of seven major types, as shown in Table 12.1.

The finding aids of an organisation should form a network, with common elements such as series titles or record-creating agency to link them. There are no hard and fast rules about which elements are contained in each type.

Major categories of finding aids

The distinctions will frequently be blurred, but most archival institutions produce finding aids in several types. See Table 12.1 for general descriptions.

Type	Scope	Content
General guides	Multiple archival institutions–often arranged by geographical area such as state, country or international region	Standardised summary of information about holdings, sometimes by subject
Guide to finding aids	Single institution	List of finding aids and how to use
Summary guides	Holdings of a single institution	Overview of holdings: administrative history, agencies and series
Inventories	Section of holdings of a single institution, sometimes a single agency within an institution	Descriptions of record: producing agencies, series and items plus background indexes, lists and supplementary finding aids
Control records, produced by creating agencies	Record-creating agency or institution	Registers, indexes and other retrieval aids for the creators
Indexes and special lists	Ancillary aids to any of the other categories or to selected records	Subject, title, function, format , medium and date entries with references leading to specific aids or records
Supplementary finding aids	Subject areas for which there is high demand	Subject guides, background information

Table 12.1: Major categories of finding aids

General guides

The purpose of these guides, which include directories of archives and reports of holdings, is to publicise summary information about different archives and their collections. They can include archives at a regional, state or international level. Some give an overview of holdings and services while some are topic based. Topic-based guides are directories of material relating to a certain topic, such as convicts or mining. Others report information on individual collections held by contributing institutions.

Generally, an entry for an institution will provide the following basic information:

- **basic contact information:** address, phone numbers, e-mail addresses, opening hours, website address
- **brief description of holdings**, ranging from a statement of collecting areas to the names of major creating agencies or individuals and the titles of selected significant and/or frequently used series
- **access conditions**.

The *Directory of Archives* produced by the Australian Society of Archivists is one example of this kind (<http://www.archivists.org.au/directory-of-archives>). Archival institutions are listed, along with contact details, access arrangements and a brief description of collection holdings.

Figure 12.2: Australian Society of Archivists, Directory of Archives

Guides to finding aids

These guides introduce the user to the particular institution and its finding aids. These guides list the finding aids and show the user how to progress from one to another within the system. It often outlines the nature of the holdings and the system of arrangement and description and can also include tips and guides to searching the institutions databases. This information should be as simple and clear as possible, as it is often the novice researchers' first point of contact with the individual institution. These guides may take the form of a tour/orientation session, recorded presentation, pamphlets or posters/wall charts.

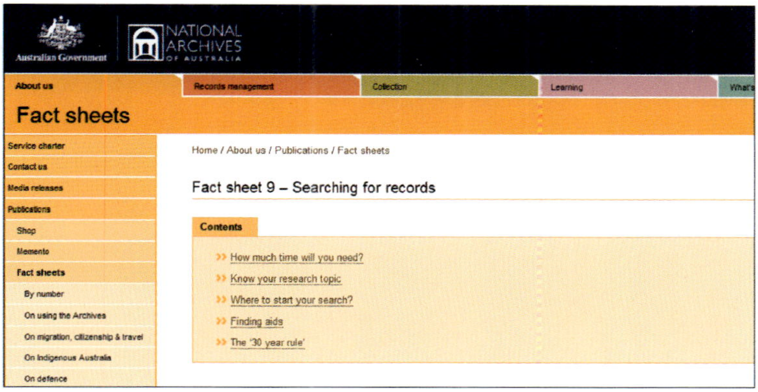

Figure 12.3: The National Archives of Australia website provides a fact sheet that covers tips on searching, a guide to the finding aids which in turn link to more detailed information about specific topics.

Summary guides

A summary guide as a finding aid is often produced when the collection has grown in size and complexity. A need then emerges for an overview of the collection. A summary guide introduces the reader to the holdings of an institution – acquisition policy, scope of the holdings or how the whole collection came about, inventories of creating agencies and usually series titles and date ranges, how to use the records and what finding aids exist. It illustrates not only the creating agencies or individuals but also any connections between them and the record series attached to each. Connections between series are shown. The guide also gives an overall map of the collection.

An institution's summary guide includes the elements useful for approaching its particular holdings, taking into account the other finding aids which have been prepared.

Figure 12.4: The University of Melbourne Archives provide an overview of its collection, information about how to search for this information and a list of subject guides to aid the user.

Inventories

Inventories are basically lists that result from arrangement and description (see Chapter 8: *Arrangement & Description*). They provide the links between the descriptions of the different entities (agency, series, item, etc.). The most common forms of inventories are:

• Inventory of agencies	• a list of agencies subordinate to each organisation • a list of agencies responsible for a particular function or activity over time
• Inventory of series	• a list of series created by each agency or person • a list of series resulting from a particular function or activity
• Inventory of items	• a list of items belonging to each series.

Inventories always contain basic information about the entities inventoried (such as name or title, date range, control number) and might also include a brief description.

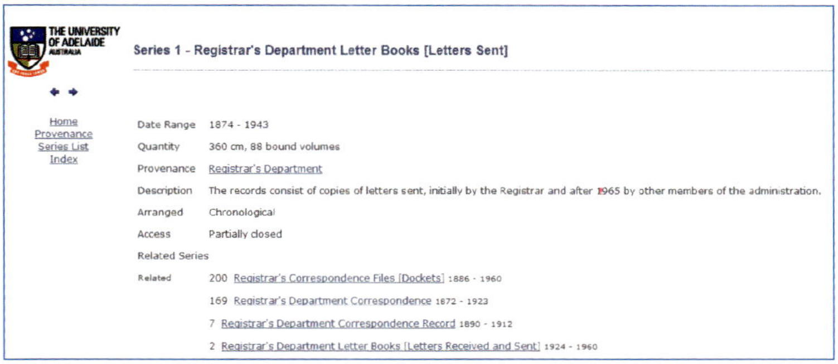

THE UNIVERSITY OF ADELAIDE AUSTRALIA

Series 1 - Registrar's Department Letter Books [Letters Sent]

Home
Provenance
Series List
Index

Date Range	1874 - 1943
Quantity	360 cm, 88 bound volumes
Provenance	Registrar's Department
Description	The records consist of copies of letters sent, initially by the Registrar and after 1965 by other members of the administration.
Arranged	Chronological
Access	Partially closed
Related Series	
Related	200 Registrar's Correspondence Files [Dockets] 1886 - 1960
	169 Registrar's Department Correspondence 1872 - 1923
	7 Registrar's Department Correspondence Record 1890 - 1912
	2 Registrar's Department Letter Books [Letters Received and Sent] 1924 - 1960

Figure 12.5: The University of Adelaide's Series Inventory is available on its website and provides information about individual series including title, date, provenance, and related series.

In a paper-based system, users would use the entries in an inventory to look up the more detailed description of the relevant entry, which may lead them a further inventory or to other related descriptions. For example, a user finding a series listed on an inventory could look up the description of that series and find an inventory of the items in that series, and this may lead the user to find the item that will satisfy his or her needs. In an electronic system, the user would use hyperlinks within the system to scroll through inventories and 'jump' from description to description.

In an archives using an automated collection management system, the production of inventories would be automatic – indeed the production of inventories would only be needed for external use such as publication or to fill a special need (for example, an archivist might print a specific inventory for mailing to a researcher).

A published finding aid – this one for the Benevolent Society of New South Wales. This covers material held by the Mitchell Library.

If preparing an inventory for publication, while your descriptions (of agencies, series, etc.) would provide the basis, you would probably want to add some additional elements, such as:

- **Title page:** This contains the title of the finding aid incorporating the proper name and citation or group of archives, the name of the individual or office responsible for producing the finding aid, the name of the archival repository and the date of completion of the aid.
- **Table of contents**

- **Preparer's note:** This sets out the major decisions made in producing the finding aid, including the influence of original classification systems and recordkeeping systems. There are instructions for using the inventory, lists of symbols or abbreviations, an explanation of control symbols used, the proper form for citations and any acknowledgements.
- **Introduction to the records:** This contains the history of the records, why they are important (in their own time and in retrospect) and how they came to the archives. Gaps are explained where appropriate. Anything unusual about how the records were created or accumulated is explained, particularly for personal records.
- **Administrative history:** This gives brief highlights (1500 words or fewer) of the individual's career and life, or the organisation's foundation, development and major programs. Special lists and supplementary finding aids such as organisation charts, timelines and lists of chief officials can be included here.
- **Series descriptions:** The series descriptions should be presented in context to show their relationships. If the inventory is for a record group, the series descriptions will be grouped in categories which usually reflect provenance, i.e. the hierarchy of an organisation, the key divisions in an individual's work or life or the functions the records supported (e.g. accounting, policy or teaching). Arrangement of categories usually follows a hierarchy of importance or date. For each category there will be:
  - information about the particular activities of the office or individual(s) who created the records
  - the series descriptions for that category. This might simply consist of abbreviated series registrations, omitting such information as donors' personal details which would be inappropriate in a public finding aid. There should also be information about relevant control records prepared by the records creators, item lists, conditions of use and other related finding aids and records.
- **Indexes and other listings:** There might be separate indexes of series titles, subject and names, or any of these might be combined. If the inventory is for an organisation, the functions performed by various sub-sections of the organisation might be included.
- **Bibliography:** The published and unpublished works used to prepare the inventory will assist researchers who require further background.

Control records produced by the creators of records

In addition to the finding aids produced by archivists, there are control records produced by the creating institution during the earlier, active life of the records. These can be incorporated into archival finding aids systems.

They include indexes and registers created to assist in the control and retrieval of records. When the records are transferred to archives, wherever possible these aids should accompany them. The creating agency often prepares useful documentation when transferring records to archives, relocating records, or moving them to off-site storage. These control records can save a great deal of processing time and help to show how the creator used the records. They are themselves archival records, but they can also be used as finding aids.

Control records will probably not stand alone as aids to the user. The archivist may need to produce contextual notes to show how these records formed part of a recordkeeping system which can be used to gain access to other records created within the system. This will all be incorporated into the finding aid system, possibly as part of a descriptive inventory or in the series description of the control record or by links to related series. Some commonly produced control records which users will encounter in an archives are listed in the table overleaf.

Federation: A Guide to the Records *was published by National Archives of Australia to celebrate the nation's centenary of federation in 2001.*

A finding aid published by the Loreto Province Archives.

Control records prepared by records creators

Registers are used to record information about documents or files received or dispatched by an office, or created in an office. For correspondence this would include date, author, summary of contents and a file reference, arranged chronologically. If the register was for controlling files created in an office, it would record the date, file number and title. If the register was created to maintain intellectual control of records stored off-site, it would record date, file number title and barcode, or other unique storage reference.

Indexes also control documents and files, but do so by creating another point of access to the system. The file titles and contents of the documents are arranged alphabetically by name or subject. They may be in the form of card files or a spreadsheet.

Filing system descriptions supply filing classification lists and key codes and outlines of filing systems, explaining the alphabetical, numerical or other codes and symbols used. These indicate how a filing system operated when it was in current use in a business or office.

Procedures manuals for business processes can reveal the original structure of the records and assist in retrieval in the same way as filing system descriptions.

List of authorised terms describe terms used to classify file titles in filing systems. They are sometimes called thesauruses when highly structured.

Electronic recordkeeping metadata is the data used to manage records in an electronic database that illustrates the data's structure, titles, use, dates, creators. It should be associated with the records themselves, but may be available as a report.

Table 12.2: Control records prepared by records creators

It is important to acquire these aids or copies of them. Archivists and record-managers should co-operate with staff to encourage the retention of these records. It is not very useful to retain a register of boxes in off-site storage if the contents are unknown.

Indexes, special lists and subject guides

Indexes, special lists and subject guides are the elements of the system which help the researcher to match up a subject query with the structurally based inventories produced by archivists when arranging and describing archives. The main types are:

- indexes
- chronological listings
- media/format guides

The agency and series descriptions in inventories can be used for information retrieval. Collection titles and series titles can be scanned for general information. However, in many cases these will not yield the information which reference queries require. For example, a structural finding aid gives an overview of a particular corporation's sections and their functions over time. It would be quite simple to locate the records relating to a particular building because the corporation would probably have had a property section. It may be much harder to find records on the treatment of women in the corporation's workforce. It is unlikely that this area would have been handled by a special officer or department until fairly recent times, so that earlier relevant material would be widely scattered.

Indexes can indicate the content of record series much better than just the titles would do by providing extra access points such as subject, name, medium and form.

Indexes

Indexes may be created from the original records or from other finding aids. In some cases, indexing the finding aids may be easier and still extremely useful – for example, if there is a comprehensive inventory of case files, but it is not in alphabetical order, producing a name index from the inventory would benefit users. On the other hand, a series of files might contain a good deal of information about people whose names are not reflected in the file titles. In this case, creating a name index from the contents of the files would be useful.

Sometimes an archivist will decide that it is necessary to index the content of a particular series. This is especially useful for personal papers and general correspondence when other finding aids simply do not provide sufficient access. It might be done for a series which is often requested, but frustrating for researchers, or for series which are currently under-utilised. Census, convict and land records are all examples of high-use collections which benefit from being indexed. The State Records Office of Western Australia provides a host of special indexes relating to popular areas of research, such as the Dead Name Index, Index to Land Records and Colonial Secretary's Office (CSO) Indexes just to name a few.

Finding Aids: a traditional card index

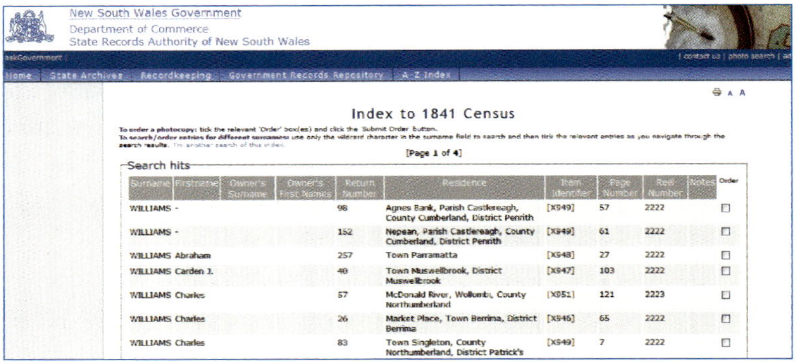

Figure 12.6: An index to census records on the State Records of New South Wales website.

Index entries are taken from the names of the record's creators, the titles of collections, series and items, the series descriptions, the administrative histories and biographies. Sometimes subject descriptors are added. The entries are usually arranged alphabetically, with references to their occurrences in the larger work. If possible, the index entries would also refer users to the relevant sections of a structural finding aid, such as a descriptive inventory, as well as directly to the item required. This ensures that the items are seen in context in the series of collection, which may enhance interpretation of this item or lead to further relevant items.

Since indexing the content of the actual records generally has a low priority for the archivist, and because it is time-consuming, this is the sort of project in which digitisation can be of great utility. However, digitisation is not cheap and your resources will determine whether to 'go digital' is viable, or to opt for manual indexing. Indexing is a task for which the services of volunteers are invaluable, however organisations can also engage contractors for this purpose if resources permit. It must be stressed that the apparently straightforward task of indexing can be disastrous unless house rules are carefully laid down and maintained.

There are nearly as many sets of rules for compiling an index as there are indexes. These rules cover things like alphabetical order, word-by-word or letter-by-letter; the treatment of apostrophes and abbreviations; the order of dates and other numerical items; the format of personal and institutional names and the structure and type of cross references.

Indexing names on correspondence series is a relatively routine task which illustrates the need for these house rules. Typical questions which need to be considered include the following:

- Are family name and initials to be used, or full given names?

- Which names are the family names (i.e. when the countries of origin are unfamiliar to the indexer)?
- Are nicknames and familiar names to be indexed as main entries or cross references?
- Are all names to be indexed, however brief the reference, or only important ones? Which ones are important?
- Will the index distinguish between the names of those who have letters addressed to them and those who are just mentioned in the course of a letter?

It is not the intention of this section to elaborate on indexing rules. Be prepared to spend time on establishing conventions, standardising terminology and assisting the indexers with these.

An index of functions/activities may be useful to supplement an inventory of agencies by function

Chronological list

Since many researchers limit their research to a particular time frame, a useful aid is a time line organised by five- or ten-year date segments, listing alphabetically the names of creators (persons and agencies) active within each segment. It ties the names of creating bodies or individuals to the dates of their operation.

Media/format guides

Frequently, records in a particular medium such as photographs, plans, maps, magnetic tapes and gramophone records make up a significant proportion of the holdings or are very heavily used. Special media guides are useful for these. Users might be looking for records in a particular medium, for example, if they were researching movies or photographic techniques.

If the system is online, no separate guide is needed. Users may query the system for 'all entries before 1930 which contain "photograph" and "automobile"'. Other automated systems might simply produce a hard copy printout of the titles of series containing cassette tapes or plans.

The context of the items should be retained in the same way as for written records. This will depend on the type of aid being produced. If it is simply an index which leads the user to the series descriptions, then context information will be available in those descriptions. If the guide is more detailed, some context information should be provided. The entries should also lead users to related and background material on other formats. These items rarely exist in isolation.

Figure 12.7: The National Archives of Australia provides its PhotoSearch database to allow users to search specifically for photographs it holds as part of their collection.

Supplementary finding aids

These finding aids are usually created to cover popular research topics in a particular institution. They include special lists of background information, subject files and source analyses. Some of these aids supply information which does not require reference to the archival documents. Supplementary finding aids are compiled from the existing finding aids systems and from secondary source material. Selected secondary sources are sometimes made available as well, alongside the archival finding aids.

Special lists of background information

These lists contain quickly retrievable summaries of important facts about an organisation, locality or individual. Such lists are often prepared as an aid to writing administrative history and can be appendices to relevant descriptive inventories. Some examples include lists of chief executive officers, mayors, school principals, committees, public buildings or churches together with relevant dates. They are often arranged chronologically. A timetable of key events may be prepared, however do not include too many items, but restrict its subject area or compile several different lists on different subjects. Otherwise, too much time will be spent searching for the relevant event.

Source analyses

A file of research enquiries can be useful for producing subject guides to popular topics, which then saves the reference archivist time in assisting users. Guides are often prepared for particular types of users such as family historians. Products of this type of initiative may include research kits or research pathways. This information may also be useful when identifying collections, or sections of collections they may be targeted for digitisation.

Information from previous enquiries must however be treated with discretion. There is no problem with making available the lists of records which have been found useful for common enquiries. However, ethical problems may arise when considering how much detail should be revealed about an individual researcher's discoveries. Generally speaking, all researchers should have equal access to records which are open, but the results of one researcher's work should not be disclosed to another without consultation.

In the electronic environment, an archives may be able to take advantage of software that has the ability to store and suggest previous searches, rank current searches in terms of previous searches, and suggest results on this basis. This can be augmented by allowing users to recommend records for certain enquiries and to rank them.

Electronic indexing and searching

Indexes can be in the form of card files, printed lists, printouts or computer output microform or electronic documents. If inventories have been created on computer, several kinds of retrieval are possible. With online finding aids, users are not aware of a separate item called the index. They simply search the indexes via an interface, using certain words or date ranges, perhaps in certain fields such as series titles or dates.

Many systems use free text searching, where all entries are searched for a particular word or string of letters. Other systems just search an inverted file, which is an index created using selected terms from the metadata entries. Authorised terms and thesauri can assist in locating related terms.

Simple but useful finding aids can be created without elaborate programs and databases. The most basic word processing programs contain facilities for indexing and putting lists into alphabetical order. A small archives may also find that a listing of series titles, descriptors and dates in a word processor file with a limited word-searching facility can be a useful addition to the finding aids.

A user consults the State Records Office of Western Australia's indexes.

Data elements used in electronic series descriptions must be useful in generating the required indexes. For example, family names should be entered before initials so that a useful alphabetical list can be generated from that field. Towns and states can go into separate fields so that entries can be listed by state, i.e. geographical area.

Many archival institutions are scanning parts of their collections, so that records are available on demand for users electronically. Scanned records reduce the need for manual data entry or indexing as it is possible to carry out free text searching across scanned documents themselves with the right combinations of formats and software. (See Chapter 13: *Digitisation & Imaging*).

Planning finding aids

The number and type of finding aids is informed by an archives resources and the types of queries received by the archives. An analysis of enquiry types is an important step in the development of finding aids for an archives.

Planning of finding aids is not undertaken in isolation from planning for other archival functions. The archives' overall priorities must be taken into account when goals for the finding aids programs are set. The ability to effectively retrieve information is a major aim of the process of gaining control of archives. This must be considered at every stage of designing records systems and processing records, and all stages should contribute to an integrated approach to retrieval.

The service philosophy of the institution should be considered. In order to encourage self-help, the conditions where self-help is possible must be provided, and the necessary time and money must be spent on creating finding aids which facilitate this. Better finding aids should allow greater user autonomy. Archives are now increasingly using their web presence for the delivery of records, bypassing the need to visit a physical archive. In this arena, it is vital that online aids are effective, and the provision of these services should not be implemented as an afterthought. (See also Chapter 10: *Using Computers*).

Who are the users?

A corporate archives will mainly serve internal customers, from legal departments to human resources. Public archives were once only used extensively by academic historians, but now attract many other users. Genealogists and family historians form a large user group, as do academics from many disciplines other than history. People from vastly different social, educational and cultural backgrounds are now using archives.

It is important to take into account the wide-ranging research experience and interests of the major user groups when designing finding aids and deciding which types will be useful. If, for example, archival holdings consist mainly of scientific research records, and users are generally other scientists, this should be reflected in the finding aids; resources would be concentrated on the access requirements of the trained scientist rather than on those of the lay user. A large government archive that attracts many first-time users of archives may require a more comprehensive suite of finding aids.

Resources

Some important factors to consider are:

- number and skills of staff
- financial resources available
- the time available for production of finding aids
- the cost of production
- IT infrastructure
- cost/benefits – future savings in staff time

Comprehensive and user-friendly web design and maintenance is neither cheap nor quick to produce, and may require more resources than paper-based records to create and host. However, once in existence, they can be easily updated, re-used and manipulated for many different purposes. These considerations will also influence the types and the depth of finding aids produced. Less detailed finding aids might be chosen because of a lack of time, a similarity of item content, cost, or the expectation of limited use. In other cases, detailed item-level description in finding aids or digitisation might be justified to provide access where none exists, produce an inventory as security against theft, prevent unnecessary handling and compensate for lack of staff.

Privacy and organisational confidentiality

Occasionally, it might not be possible to include some material in public finding aids due to privacy or confidentiality concerns, particularly in online systems. Similarly the cultural sensitivities of Indigenous people needs to be considered. A good rule to follow would be that if the information would not be available for public access, don't include it in the finding aids! (See Chapter 11: *Access & Reference Services* for a discussion on access issues). Where privacy or cultural sensitivities would preclude making a name index public, that need not be used as a reason not to produce the index. Access to the index can be restricted to the archives staff, who can then easily make appropriate information available to the relevant person.

These restrictions can sometimes present issues that may be overcome by finding aids. The *Bringing them home: Report of the national inquiry into the separation of Aboriginal and Torres Strait Islander children from their families* recognises the importance of records in assisting Indigenous Australians of the stolen generation to reconnect with their past, by locating records relating to their childhood held in Commonwealth and state archives. To this end, state archives across the country have produced finding aids in the form of summary guides and indexes to assist in this endeavour, as well as allowing special access conditions in appropriate circumstances. Guides such as *Finding your story: A resource manual of the records of the Stolen Generations in Victoria, Tracking Family: A guide to Aboriginal records relating to the Northern Territory* and *My heart is breaking: A joint guide to records about Aboriginal people in the Public Record Office of Victoria and the Australian Archives, Victorian regional office* are all examples of this.

For in-house or corporate archives, there might be descriptions of material relating to business dealings and commercial trade secrets which the management does not want made public, but which the series description has to make explicit. Remember, however, that there is still a difference between a description of the document contents and the actual documents.

Standardisation

There are two aspects to standardisation which relate to finding aids. One is the international pressure to exchange information about holdings electronically in a standardised form. The other is the benefit to be gained from standardising procedures within an institution.

International moves towards standardisation

Initiatives to standardise archival description initially focussed on improving finding aids. It was recognised that in order to be able to share data about collections across multiple archival institutions, there is a need for standardised metadata and archival descriptive standards.

The development of the Encoded Archival Description (EAD) is a response to this issue. EAD is essentially a non-proprietary encoding standard for machine-readable finding aids. Its purpose is to present information in finding aids in a consistent manner and to enable searching across finding aids with consistent results. The strengths of this approach include the ability to represent hierarchical data, and inherited descriptive information, as well as supporting element specific indexing and retrieval. Several institutions in Australia, including the Australian War Memorial and National Library of Australia have begun to use this standard. EAD is based on XML (Extensible Markup Language) and a number of collection management systems can output finding aids in EAD.

Standards for archival description, such as ISAD(G) (see Chapter 8: *Arrangement & Description*), ultimately assist with standardising finding aids, at least as far as standardising metadata. The wider push for standardised metadata will continue to grow. Collaborative collection, use and re-use of metadata and its potential for application beyond manual description, with its inherent biases, is not here yet. However, Evans et al. (2005) summarise the need for this:

> *If archival systems of the future are to provide for emerging concepts of parallel provenance and communities of records, and manage shared ownership, joint heritage and multiple access paths, the capture and implementation of metadata which can describe multiple contexts of creation, management and use in and through time will be essential.*
>
> *A key challenge is to develop systems, processes and tools that will enable metadata to be created once, then used and re-used many times for multiple purposes in different contexts in and through time* (pp.17–42).

Finding aids rely on this information to provide the most access points possible for the widest range of enquiries into the collection.

Standardisation within the institution

It is useful to standardise data elements and terminology within an institution in the areas of function, form and authorised terms. Archival processing is made easier and researchers are helped by knowing what to expect when certain terms are used. This has already been mentioned in relation to the function of agencies and the preparation of indexes.

In fact, most of this standardisation should already have taken place, before the finding aids are produced, at the arrangement and description stage. The ultimate production of finding aids must be considered during all stages of the documentation process. International standards, such as those discussed above, should be used for general guidance.

Format of finding aids

Finding aids form an important part of a user's visit to the archives. They should be highly visible and accessible to users, whether in the form of hard copy folders or via PCs. The technology that enables the conversion of hard or analogue originals to digital formats has enabled the provision of access and opportunities to greatly expanded audiences and in new ways via internet technology.

If the archives has a manual system, the format must be considered in terms of binders, pamphlets, volumes, cards and microform. Makes sure the aids are set out attractively and take care that they are easy for users to follow. Loose-leaf format is ideal for anything likely to be updated, such as series sheets with accompanying items lists, when new consignments arrive.

Many institutions across the globe are beginning to manage more of their finding aids and, in turn, collections online, and presenting them in a way that is both intuitive and aesthetic. The *Edmund Barton* and *Documenting a Democracy* pages of the National Archives of Australia are just two examples.

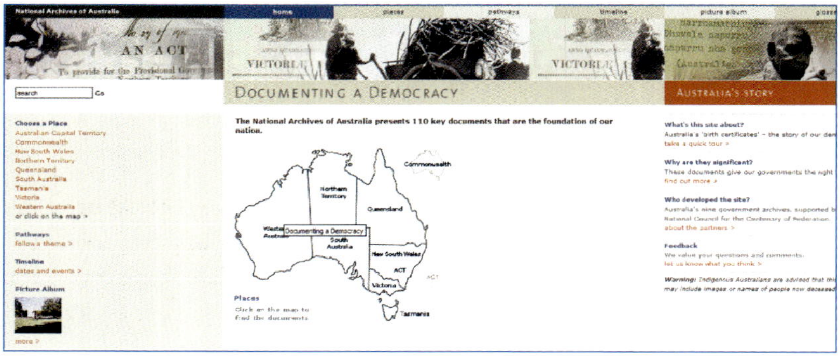

Figure 12.8: The National Archives of Australia 'Documenting a Democracy' online exhibition

Emerging forms of finding aids, such as interactive online exhibitions, podcasts and wikis present archival holdings in a new way, in some cases blurring the line between research, reference and entertainment. Web 2.0 technologies are beginning to be recognised as potential tools in archives. A pilot project undertaken by the University of Michigan has tested the use of social recommendation software and collaborative filtering in what they term a new generation finding aid. This site allows users to create a search profile, discuss issues with other users, leave messages and recommend sources (<http://polarbears.si.umich.edu/>).

Along similar lines, the UK Archives hosts an online community of records users, *Your Archives.* This wiki encourages communication amongst users of the collections and provides space to allow users to contribute their knowledge of archival sources held by both the National Archives and throughout the UK. Users can submit articles about people and series, and are encouraged to update out-of-date finding aids.

The increasing prevalence of these Web 2.0 online collaborative technologies, such as filtering and recommendation systems and user created description, has the potential to revolutionise the way users interact with archival institutions.

Some institutions publish finding aids. As it is an expensive undertaking, it would be wise to consider the following points before proceeding:

- Is your aim to produce up-to-date information, or publicity? Publishing promotes the collection in a way that is impossible for in-house card catalogues and inventories, and increases the collection's potential for users.
- It is useful for people to have something they can take away to plan research and annotate.
- The information is inevitably superseded due to new acquisitions. It can only be a snapshot in time. Reviews invariably criticise this aspect of archives' published information.
- It is difficult to add new material, although the use of desktop publishing means previous versions can be amended and added to, rather than being re-created each time an update is required.

Conclusion

The creation of a well-planned system of user-friendly finding aids should be an important objective for any archival institution. There is little point in carefully preserving or digitising archival items, and then meticulously arranging and describing them, if the finding aids produced are not adequate for a user to identify the records of interest to them.

Users increasingly regard archives as another one of the suite of information services that should be accessible via the Web. The opportunity exists for these expectations to be met and exceeded if archives embrace the evolving online environment, and the technologies it enables. Online finding aids are maturing and moving beyond traditional definitions to inform, entertain and promote, as well as providing instant access to information. An ever-expanding and diversifying population of post-custodial researchers the world over can locate a collection, query it and use the information it contains without leaving their homes.

Despite changes in format and medium, finding aids retain their role of providing the crucial link between the record and the user, and remain vital for the success of any archives program – as well as facilitating the right of every citizen to access the recorded history of their country.

CHAPTER 13

digitisation & imaging

DAVID ROBERTS

CHAPTER ABSTRACT

Archives are unique, literally as well as figuratively. Archivists make copies of archives to preserve the original records, to make the records more accessible and for security in the event of loss or disaster. Micrographics technology has been used for these purposes for many years and remains a valuable approach for many archival programs and projects. Digitising, as the more recent alternative, offers a range of benefits, including integration with other uses of information and communications technology as discussed in an earlier chapter.

This chapter examines both digitising and micrographics and encourages you to consider what you want to achieve, not only for making a range of technological choices, but also for determining the viability of a project in the first place, for deciding which archives to copy and other project parameters, and for integrating the imaging and its results with other operations and services.

Imaging technologies

In this chapter we will examine the two major imaging technologies used in archives work: digitising and micrographics. Before looking at these technologies in turn, we will consider the main issues that are common to both.

Why undertake imaging?

Archival imaging involves making copies of archives and other materials. These copies are often referred to as 'surrogates' because they take the place of the original records, mainly for access purposes. This points to the main reasons why archivists undertake imaging:

- **to preserve the original records:** imaging enables the archivist to provide readers with digital or microform surrogates, protecting the original records from inevitable (if minor) deterioration resulting from use and from removing them from storage environments, and the risk of more serious damage

- **to make the records more accessible:** while an original record is unique and can be used in only one place at a given time, multiple microform copies can be made available in different locations; digital surrogates can be accessed via computer networks, including the internet
- **as security in the event of loss:** should the original records be destroyed or irreparably damaged, microform or digital copies can at least preserve their content, enabling them to continue to be used; if the originals are stolen, copies can be used to identify them when recovered.

While an imaging project or program may be undertaken specifically for one of these purposes, many are undertaken to obtain the benefits of two or all three.

Unlike some applications of imaging in records management, archivists do not use imaging to save storage space by enabling the original records to be destroyed. It may, however, enable high-cost accommodation to be reduced, by storing the original records off-site.

Limitations

For some materials, the benefits of imaging may be limited. There may be little improvement in the accessibility of manuscript materials, for example, if the script is difficult to read in the first place. In such cases, capturing the text of the documents may be more useful. This, however, is highly labour-intensive and is likely to be justifiable only in very limited cases.

Some types of records are difficult or unsuitable for imaging. Records in large formats, such as maps or architectural drawings, can only be copied properly using equipment designed to handle oversized materials, which may not be readily accessible. There are often problems inherent in the records which make them unsuitable for copying onto microfilm, e.g. where the writing is faint or in inks of various colours, it may not be legible when imaged.

Imaging is not a panacea for an archives' problems. It will not improve access to poorly organised and described records and, indeed, may make them even less accessible, since it can be harder to browse or skim through digitised copies or microforms than through the hard copy originals.

Choosing the technology

A fundamental question facing the archivist who is considering undertaking imaging is which of the two major technologies to use. While digitisation has received far more attention in recent years, the answer is by no means simple. Each technology has strengths and weaknesses, which affect their respective values for the purpose or purposes of the archivist.

	Strengths	Weaknesses
Digitisation	• **Accessibility**: Digitised copies of archives can be made widely, conveniently and cheaply accessible to archives users through the World Wide Web and other networks. • **Cost of hardware and software**: Similarly, if you wish to undertake digitisation in-house, the cost of hardware and software required, at least for routine copying of records in common formats, continues to fall with the cost of such tools for the general business and domestic market. • **Security**: Digital copies can be 'backed up' (copied for security and disaster preparedness and stored elsewhere) easily and cheaply. • **Other uses**: Once a document is digitised, its image can be used in interpretive products such as online exhibitions, galleries, multimedia products, etc.	• **Longevity of digital media**: The longevity of digital storage media, both magnetic and optical, remains uncertain and problematic. This means that, as with 'born-digital' records, the archivist must adopt strategies for monitoring the integrity of the media over time and 'refreshing' (copying the contents to new media) when necessary. • **Dependence**: Maintaining and using digital copies is totally dependent on electronic systems. Thus, for example, a serious communications failure in the archives' network can render the copies inaccessible. • **Cost of maintaining copies**: While the cost of storing digital copies continues to fall with the cost of storage media and devices for data generally, the costs for creating, storing and 'refreshing' digital copies over time must not be overlooked.
Micrographics	• **Confidence**: It is a long-established and proven technology. • **Longevity**: Microfilm is known to survive for long periods of time when processed to archival standards and stored in appropriate conditions.	• **Cost of copies**: Each additional copy (for reference, security etc.) made of a given set of images involves extra cost.

Table 13.1: Strengths and weaknesses of digitisation and micrographics

	Strengths	Weaknesses
Micrographics ***(continued)***	• **Lack of dependence**: Use of microform copies is not dependent on electronic systems. At a pinch, the contents of a reel or fiche can even be read using a strong magnifying glass.	• **Multiple locations**: Since microfilms and fiche, like the original archives of which they are surrogates, can be in only one place at a time, a separate copy being required at each location where you wish to provide access. • **Storage for preservation**: The facilities required to provide the necessary storage conditions for the long-term preservation of master microfilm, particularly colour, are very costly. These may be beyond the resources of all but the largest archives institutions.

The hybrid approach

Many archives and libraries have opted for a combination of the two technologies, making archival quality microfilm copies for preservation and security purposes, while making digitised copies for the purpose of improving the accessibility of the archives.

This may be done by filming and digitising separately, both from the original documents, by digitising from the microfilm, or creating the microfilm from the digital image, which is becoming increasingly common. The combined approaches are usually more cost-effective.

Digitising from existing microfilm

Where archival materials have already been microfilmed, a variation on the hybrid approach is to use the microfilm copies as the source for digitisation. While this may enhance preservation and security, the purpose of adopting this option is likely to be improved accessibility.

There are two main benefits in this option. Firstly, because the original records are not used, the risk of loss or damage in the digitisation process is eliminated (or, more accurately, the risk has already been run). Secondly, scanning the microfilm is likely to be quicker, and therefore cheaper, than scanning the original documents (although not as cost-effective as simultaneously filming and digitising, if you have to do both).

The quality of the results is heavily dependent on the quality of the original microfilming job and of the copy used as the source for digitising. The best results will be obtained with high- contrast images and low reduction ratios. Skewed images in the microfilm will require additional effort to correct. Undertaking a test run of a sample, enabling you to assess the quality of the results, is particularly valuable for this kind of project.

The master negative microfilm should not be used, due to the risk of damage. A duplicate negative or even a good quality reference copy should be used.

Recording copies in archival documentation

Whatever form taken by copies of archives – and this extends beyond digitised and microform copies to photocopies kept as reference sets – it is important to record the existence of copies in archival documentation, such as collection management systems and finding aids.

A collection management system should provide one or more fields for doing this at the relevant level (fonds, series, item etc.). The relevant international standard, ISAD(G), specifies 'Existence and location of copies' as an element of archival description.

Finding aids should indicate where reference copies are available, whether they are on open access or must be requested, and any special identifiers, such as microfilm reel number. In online finding aids, this information can include a hyperlink to the digital copy, if available.

Integrating imaging into programs and services

Imaging should not be undertaken as a separate activity, divorced from the rest of the work of the archives. Rather, it should be integrated into the programs and services relevant to the purpose or purposes for which you are undertaking it.

Undertaking imaging as part of a preservation program is discussed in more detail in Chapter 4: *Preservation.*

There are two fundamental approaches to imaging for reference purposes:

- determining and following a forward program
- copying on request

A forward program normally aims to copy the most heavily used and/or the most valuable archives. In such cases, there is an overlap between copying for reference and for preservation purposes. It may be equally valid to use imaging to promote use of little known or newly accessioned archives, where preservation may not be a significant factor.

Providing digitised images to archives users on request may be seen as akin to providing photocopies or other copying services. The archivist must deal with the same questions that arise in relation to conventional copying services, including the setting of charges and standards of service.

There are some important differences, however, between conventional copying services and digitising on request. Firstly, the digital copy can be delivered to the user more quickly and cheaply. Provided the file size is not excessive, the copy can be emailed to the user. Alternatively, it can be made available for download from an FTP ('file transfer protocol') site or the archives' website.

Secondly, unlike conventional copying, digital copying on request results in a copy also being kept by the archives. This enables the archivist to build up a stock of digitised copies of archives that can be made available to all users in the future, whether online or otherwise. Some archives, notably the National Archives of Australia, have used their digitising-on-request service to add significantly to the quantity of digitised archives accessible online. Since copies of the most popular archives tend to be requested multiple times, demand for future copies is determined in pragmatic fashion by users' initial requests, while future copying workload is reduced by making a digitised copy of a given archive only once.

Finally, digitising on request requires certain technical decisions not necessary for conventional copying such as photocopying. These are discussed further in the next section.

Copyright

Making digitised or micrographic copies of archival materials that are subject to copyright, and making those copies available to the public, are acts governed by the provisions of the Commonwealth *Copyright Act of 1968* (as amended). The Act is complex and the period of protection varies with different kinds of materials, so it is wise to examine this question in detail at the planning stage of a microfilming project. Copyright protection belongs to the person who created the material (it can also be assigned by that person to someone else, or inherited like other forms of property), and it is not uncommon for custody of material to be legally transferred without conveying the copyright to the new owner. For example, to digitise or microfilm the letters written to Sir Robert Menzies by a number of different people, the copyright in each of those letters belongs prima facie to its writer. Sometimes it requires considerable detective work to determine the current owner of the copyright.

Consequently, it is important to determine whether the imaging of particular archives is affected by the rights of copyright holders. Copyright is discussed in more detail in Chapter 11: *Access & Reference Services.*

We will now discuss the two major imaging technologies used in archives work, digitising and micrographics.

Digitising

By 'digitising', we mean the making of digital images of hard copy textual or graphical materials. It can include the use of optical character recognition technology (OCR) to capture the content (i.e. the words) of a paper document into electronic form.

The digitising of hard-copy archives should be clearly distinguished from the capture and management of 'born digital' records as archives. Digital records are discussed in Chapter 15: *Digital Recordkeeping.*

What digitising involves

The main activities involved in a digitisation project or program

1. Defining your purpose
2. Deciding what to digitise
3. Specifying technical requirements
4. Planning and management decisions
5. Preparing the documents
6. Image capture
7. Metadata capture
8. Quality control
9. Storage and preservation of digital images and metadata
10. Access and use

It should be noted that the arrangement of these activities does not necessarily reflect a linear process. If you are establishing an ongoing program that will involve a succession of projects, some decisions may be taken once, while other activities will recur repeatedly, within a given project.

In the following sections, we will examine each of these activities in turn.

Defining your purpose

When considering undertaking a digitisation project or program, it is fundamentally important to have a clear understanding of the benefits that you wish to gain. This will help you to:

- determine whether the benefits will justify the investment
- seek funding
- establish criteria for measuring success
- identify which archives to digitise

In the previous section, we identified three purposes for undertaking imaging, whether through digitisation or micrographics:

- to preserve the original records
- to make the records more accessible
- as security in case of loss

Deciding what to digitise

It is a common misconception outside the archives community that whole archival collections can be, or should be, digitised. The reality is very different: the resources required to undertake a digitisation project, particularly the preparatory stages, mean that most archives cannot hope to digitise more than a fraction of their collections. Inevitably, therefore, a selection must be made.

Where the purpose is to **preserve the original records**, priority should be given to the following types of records, to minimise damage or deterioration through use:

- records that are fragile or in poor physical condition
- records in physical formats which make use of the originals awkward or risky
- records that are frequently requested and used

It should be noted that a record's physical nature or condition may equally make it unsuitable for copying or require different methods.

Where the purpose is to **make the records more accessible**, the following types of records are likely to be of higher priority:

- the most popular series or groups of records
- photographs and other pictorial materials, which tend to have wide appeal and interest and vary less in format than textual materials
- records to be included in interpretive products (online exhibitions, galleries, multimedia products etc.), as noted earlier in the chapter
- discrete groups, collections, or fonds which, most likely in conjunction with other factors, represent a neat basis for a project

Where the purpose is **security in the event of loss**, priority is likely to be given to records of great iconic value to the archives or organisation, and to records that have a high monetary value or are highly collectible (e.g. those containing rare stamps or signatures).

Specifying technical requirements

Undertaking a digitisation project or program requires the archivist to make decisions on a range of technical issues. Central to these issues are the technical requirements that are to be satisfied in the digitisation process. Without identifying these requirements, you cannot know whether the results of digitisation meet your and your users' needs.

While the scope and nature of these issues and requirements may seem daunting, there is now, fortunately, a wealth of published advice and experience from the library and archives communities nationally and internationally on which to draw. The following is a brief summary of the key technical issues and commonly accepted practice associated with digitising archives. The reader is referred to the sources listed in Further Reading for key texts which explore these issues in much further detail.

A useful tool for identifying the technical requirements is 'digital benchmarking'. This involves assessing the attributes of the documents to be digitised to determine requirements in relation to image file format, resolution, pixel depth and compression (these are discussed further shortly) and scanning and inspecting a sample of the documents to ensure that the desired results are achieved (see Kenney & Reiger 2000).

It may be possible to undertake some of this benchmarking by reference to the experience of other archivists and archival institutions in digitising similar materials.

Digital formats and their uses

A preservation master image is commonly made as a high-resolution, uncompressed TIFF (Tagged Image Format File) file. TIFF is a *de facto* standard which meets the main requirements for preserving the attributes of the image (resolution, bit depth, colour support and basic metadata). A resolution of 300 dpi (dots per inch) is normally considered the minimum for master-image files, though very large documents, such as maps and plans, may be able to be digitised at a lower resolution to reduce excessive image file sizes. For exhibition purposes, however, 600 dpi may be required.

In addition to uncompressed TIFF, PNG (Portable Network Graphic) and uncompressed GIF (Graphics Interchange Format) are the most common formats for digitisation.

Generally, the preservation master should not be digitally enhanced in any way. Any use of digital enhancement, for example de-skewing, should be in accordance with a documented policy, and the use of any enhancement documented in the metadata for the image. Any 'tidying up', such as removing spots or enhancing colours, should not be used.

The master file is used to create the other copies ('derivative' copies), primarily for access. Copies for access are commonly made as compressed, lower resolution (commonly 72, 90 or 120 dpi) JPEG (Joint Photographic Experts Group) or GIF files.

The resolution used for access copies depends on the nature of the original material. A relatively high resolution image will be slow to download and may be awkward for the end user to use onscreen because of its size. A lower resolution image may lose essential detail.

A common approach, particularly with photographic images, is to make lower resolution images accessible online, with higher resolution, publication-quality versions available separately on request, often for a fee. This can also be a practical way of protecting the intellectual property in archival images, while still enhancing their accessibility.

Small, low-resolution images may also be made to serve as 'thumbnails', which give a rough graphic representation of the image and are commonly 'clickable', providing a hyperlink to the access copy. These are normally made as GIF or JPEG files.

Colour and pixel depth

An important issue is whether to digitise in black and white or in colour mode. Within black and white there are two further options: *bitonal* and *greyscale.* In bitonal images, every pixel is either black or white. Bitonal scanning tends to be suitable for digitising clean typescript or printed documents or line drawings. Its main advantage is that bitonal image files, having a 'pixel depth' (also known as 'bit depth') of one bit, are small and, therefore, cheap to store and quick to process or transfer.

Greyscale scanning (assuming colour, discussed shortly, is not needed) is more suitable for most other types of archival materials, including manuscript and carbon copies of typescript, photographs and other graphical materials. This is because greyscale scanning picks up low contrast detail and tonal variations in graphical elements and even in the paper itself. Greyscale scanning is normally done with an 8-bit pixel depth, meaning that each pixel may be of one of eight possible shades between white and black.

Much archival material is so mixed in format that there is little point trying to separate the documents suitable for bitonal scanning. Consequently, many archives use greyscale scanning as a matter of course.

Colour scanning is needed, of course, where colour is an important element that must be captured in the digitised image. Obvious examples are colour photographs, maps, plans, drawings, posters and art works. In some other materials, judgement may be needed to determine whether, say, annotations in a different coloured ink, are significant enough to the meaning of the record to require a colour image.

Scanning in colour is typically done with a 24-bit pixel depth. As a result, colour image files are much larger than greyscale files of the same resolution.

Optical character recognition

If the project is to include optical character recognition (OCR), further technical requirements must be specified, primarily concerned with the level of accuracy (the number of errors in the total number of characters) of text capture.

OCR involves capturing the text from the image of a digitised document into a form that can be searched, edited, manipulated and published. It is normally suitable only for clear printed, or perhaps typescript, pages without annotations. This has severely limited its use in archival digitisation. Even with these materials, errors rates have often been unacceptably high for library or archives projects, because of the additional cost in proof-reading and manual correction. OCR technology continues to improve and its use is becoming more common in archival digitisation projects, depending on the type of originals. However, for smaller projects involving handwritten materials, manual keying of the text may remain a feasible alternative if an easy-to-read, searchable version is required.

Benchmarking

In the context of a digitisation project, benchmarking involves making and documenting decisions about the technical specifications for the project. Not only must these decisions be made before the project can proceed but, as the name implies, they provide the technical benchmarks against which the quality of the digitisation work can be assessed later. Thus benchmarking is an important part of the quality control for a digitisation project or program.

Benchmarking is particularly important if the digitisation work is to be outsourced, since it provides clear performance requirements for the service contract. It is also important when the work is to be done in-house, because it provides a measure for continuing improvement as the project proceeds.

Planning and management

Digitisation projects and programs require careful planning at the management level and involve making and implementing a range of management decisions. The rules common to the planning and management of any project are applicable here. Let us note, however, a couple of specific issues.

Who does it?

A central management issue is who will undertake the digitisation work. Options include:

- doing it in-house
- outsourcing at least some of the activities
- collaborating with other archives

Undertaking the digitisation work in-house requires that you acquire the necessary hardware, software and skills. Training is especially important here, since working with inadequate training will cause poor results and increased costs, regardless of the quality of hardware, software and preparation. For organisations that can justify the investment, undertaking digitisation in-house provides great control over the project and flexibility in making use of staff and other resources.

Image capture is the activity where outsourcing is most likely to bring benefits, because service providers are likely to possess the necessary equipment, skills and experience already. Outsourcing also provides an opportunity to undertake smaller initial projects, without too much of a commitment. Outsourcing requires particular attention to be paid to specifying technical requirements and the results expected clearly in request for proposal/quotation documentation (see Online Computer Library Center site at <www.oclc.org>).

Collaboration with other bodies may be considered simply as a means of sharing costs, equipment and expertise. It may also be a means for a number of archives to build a virtual collection of thematically related materials.

Identifying and monitoring costs

Any digitisation project or program involves significant costs. These include set-up costs, the costs of digitisation activities and the costs associated with preserving and providing access to digitised materials over time. A realistic appraisal of cost is necessary to judge whether the benefits of the digitisation effort will justify the commitment involved. In some environments, providing a robust cost analysis is required as part of the process of seeking funding. Monitoring costs is important for similar reasons, particularly if reporting is required.

The major area of cost is likely to be in staffing. This needs to include the preparation of the materials, digitisation production/processing, the creation and capture of metadata, inspection and quality control, and a component for project management.

The costs associated with equipment and software need to include purchase or leasing costs, depreciation, installation, maintenance and consumables. The proportion of overheads, such as rent, electricity and data communication costs, attributable to the digitisation project or program also needs to be calculated. A number of the sources listed in Further Reading include useful guidance on how to estimate costs in digitisation projects.

Preparing archives for digitising

Preparing archival materials for digitising is an important step in a project. The aim is to ensure a smooth and efficient process once digitisation starts, as far as possible anticipating problems and dealing with them before they risk holding up the project's schedule.

Preparation may include any of the following:

- conservation treatment, ranging from wholesale cleaning and re-housing to tape and staple removal and repairs of individual documents
- ensuring that the records are in correct order and identifying any missing items
- identifying fragile items whose condition may prevent digitising or require special treatment
- identifying records in different formats from the rest of the project, or records with other features needing attention, such as information on both sides of a page or fold-out pages
- ensuring that any special equipment required, such as cradles or support pillows for volumes, is available
- preparing instructions for staff or contractors relating to any special requirements

- moving the records safely and securely to where the digitising will be done (this will include packaging and other protection, if digitising off-site)
- setting up a suitable space for storing the records during the digitisation process
- preparing any targets or rulers that will be used to indicate the size and clarity of the item
- establishing a file-naming structure or protocol for the image files to be created in the project
- counting the number of images that should be created, to enable you to check later that none have been missed

In addition to these 'physical' preparations, it is also important to ensure that the items are correctly arranged and described. Without this, digitisation will do little to improve access to the records.

Image capture

Equipment for image capture

The two main types of equipment used for capturing digital images from source documents are scanners and digital cameras. There is a range of categories within these broad types, the characteristics of which affect how suitable they are for different archival digitisation jobs.

Flatbed scanners require a source document to be placed face down on a glass plate for scanning. They are primarily suitable for scanning archives that are, or can be, separated into single sheets of paper. Because they involve contact between the document and the glass plate, they may be unsuitable for fragile documents.

Increasingly sophisticated flatbed scanners, capable of scanning at relatively high resolutions, are widely available as part of the office/home PC market. These are generally limited to A4-sized documents, but may meet a significant proportion of the archivist's needs. Scanners for larger documents, starting at A3, are also available, though at much higher prices.

Some mass-market scanners are equipped with transparency adaptors, which enable photographic transparencies ('slides') to be scanned. Most come bundled with basic image capture and processing software. The capacity of a scanner to capture images in the desired format, such as TIFF (most mass-market scanners use JPEG), is particularly important.

As the name implies, sheet-feeder scanners differ from flatbed scanners in that they feed a sheet of paper through the machine. For this reason, the fragility of the document is an even more important consideration.

There are several varieties of sheet-feeder scanners. Firstly, there are sheet-feeder attachments for flatbed scanners, as opposed to scanners with the sheet-feeding mechanism built in. Among the latter, one of the main types is designed to feed large numbers of loose sheets automatically, scanning them in the process. These are mainly intended for business document management use, but may be suitable for some archival digitisation projects. The other major type is used for large-scale documents, such as engineering drawings.

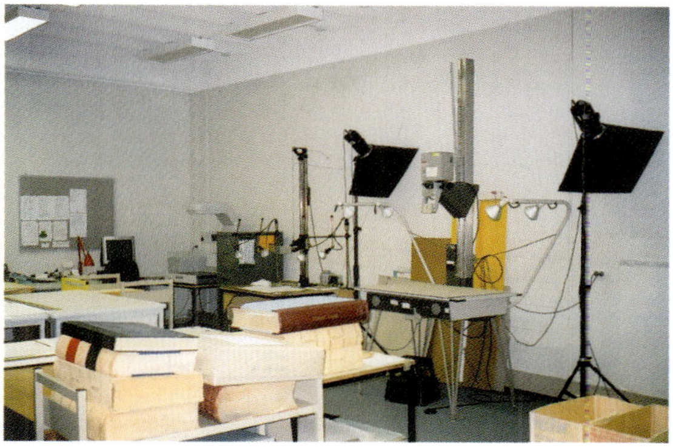

A space set up for digitisation: images are taken of items using a camera

More specialised forms of scanners include those dedicated to scanning from such specific source materials as photographic transparencies, microfilm reels, microfiche and aperture cards. Because of their specialised purposes, purchasing these kinds of scanners is likely to be cost-effective only in projects involving a large quantity of material in that format. Otherwise, a better choice is likely to be to use such equipment in another institution or a service bureau.

Digital cameras differ from scanners in requiring no contact with the source document. Consequently they may represent the only practical means of digitising particularly fragile or valuable documents, or material that is otherwise unsuitable for scanning, such as bound volumes that cannot be fully opened without endangering the binding.

As with scanners, there are increasingly capable digital cameras available for the mass market which can be suitable for some basic archival digitisation jobs. A more sophisticated camera, combining high resolution, a wide range of digital zoom, and the capacity to capture in TIFF format, is likely to be needed for many projects.

Depending on the project, associated equipment may include a v-shaped cradle or support pillows to hold volumes that cannot be fully opened and an overhead stand to hold the camera, similar to the stands commonly used in microfilming.

Again, digital cameras are often supplied with at least basic image capture and processing software. More specialised software, for example, to compensate for the curvature in pages in bound volumes, may also be required, depending on the project.

Image capture and processing software

We have noted already that much of this equipment often comes bundled with basic imaging software. Generally this will be sufficient to support the capture of the image into a PC.

For post-capture processing, such as adjusting colour balance, more specialised software may also be required. Depending on requirements, this can range from widely available products like Adobe Photoshop and Jasc Paint Shop Pro to highly specialised task-specific software.

If optical character recognition (OCR), discussed earlier in this section, is to be part of the digitisation process, suitable software will be required. Basic OCR software is often included in software bundled with scanning equipment. More sophisticated stand-alone OCR products are also available.

We will discuss image management software – for managing and retrieving digital images of archives – later in this chapter.

Metadata capture

As we have noted in Chapter 8: *Arrangement & Description,* that metadata is structured information about other information – in this context, it is about archives – which supports its management and use.

Purposes

Capturing and maintaining appropriate metadata is an essential part of a digitisation program or project. As in other aspects of archives management, metadata serves two main functions in a digitisation project:

1. To help users of the archives to find and use the records needed for their research (in this case, digitised records)
2. To support and document archives management processes.

For the first purpose, descriptive metadata about the records being digitised may exist already or it may need to be created as an arrangement and description project preparatory to digitisation.

Where the records are already described, digitisation may require additional information, e.g. document-level information where the records are already described at the series and item levels; or the assignment of indexing or other descriptors to improve online searching. An example of the latter would be adding Dublin Core-compliant name, place and subject terms to descriptive information about digitised photographs for submission to Picture Australia (as discussed in Chapter 10: *Using Computers*) or to include in HTML page headers, rendering them visible to Google-type searching. Information about rights in the digitised material, such as copyright, is particularly important if it is to be made available online.

Crucial among the metadata for the second purpose are:

- the essential technical details about the digitised image, such as file format, resolution, the size of the image in pixels, its mode (bitonal, greyscale, colour), pixel depth, compression, etc.
- information about the master and derivative copies of the digitised image

Unlike archival description, there are no widely accepted standards for technical imaging metadata. A range of models suitable for different types of digitising projects and materials, archival and otherwise, however, can be found in the literature and adapted for use.

Internal metadata

Some metadata, such as technical information about the image, can be kept as header information in the image file itself. This has the benefit that the metadata cannot be accidentally separated from the image, but the amount and scope of metadata that can usefully be captured and kept in this way is limited.

External metadata systems

Most information about digitised records needs to be held as external metadata. At its most basic, this can include adopting a systematic scheme for naming digital image files and directories, which can be used to identify such information as the source document (series, item, document and folio numbers) and the image type (master, reference, thumbnail). This approach has drawbacks, however, notably the limited scope of the information that can be captured this way and the manual effort required to name each image file according to the scheme during image capture.

"I'm guessing this is the first time you've made a copy of your computer files ..."

External metadata may be recorded in a database set up specifically for imaging metadata or in an existing collection management system. A common approach is a combination of both, with information specific to the image and the imaging process captured in an imaging database (perhaps including the images themselves), plus links to descriptive information about the source document in the collection management system.

Information from both these sources can be combined in online finding aids and image delivery systems. We will discuss these further later in this section.

Quality assurance and inspection

Quality assurance, as the term implies, is concerned with ensuring that the quality of all aspects of image and metadata capture meet the requirements set for the project. As such, it is an essential part of the project's quality control arrangements.

At its simplest, quality assurance involves inspecting the digitised images to ensure that the results meet the required standards of clarity and accurate representation of the source documents. With digitised images, this inspection requires the use of a computer, so it is important that the computer and monitor settings be properly set up for the purpose.

As with microfilming, inspection also involves checking that no documents have been accidentally missed and finding any serious problems with placement of the source documents, such as a skewed image or parts of a document left outside the image.

Quality assurance should start early in the project, with assessment of test samples of digitisation. Once production starts, inspections should be undertaken at regular points in the project. It is sensible to start the project by checking all of a batch until you are confident of the overall quality of the work, when it may be possible to move to a sampling approach.

It is important to assess the digitised images of a range of different types of source materials, since different decisions are likely to have been made for these materials in relation to resolution, colour balance or contrast.

Where the project involves OCR, this aspect of the work should also be covered by quality assurance, to ensure that error rates are kept to an acceptable minimum.

The need for quality assurance applies also to metadata, since metadata capture can represent a significant proportion of the total investment in a digitisation project. The overall value of the project can depend heavily on the quality of metadata: a mis-keyed filename or other identifying metadata may mean that the image will not be found.

The quality assurance process should be systematic, and it is important to document the results of inspections. Quality control worksheets can provide both a checklist of things to look for and a consistent way of recording the results.

Managing digitised archives

Once captured, digitised images of archives must be stored and retrieved. For this, systems are required for storing and retrieving the images and their metadata, while strategies must also be adopted for ensuring that the images and metadata remain useable over time.

Image management systems

This is a generic term for a wide of range of solutions for storing and retrieving images and associated metadata. In the context of archival digitisation, an image management system needs to:

- provide facilities for recording and retrieving technical information about digitised images of archives
- provide for documenting the processes involved in the management of the images subsequent to digitisation
- either provide facilities for recording and retrieving descriptive information about the digitised archives, or provide links to that information held elsewhere and the capacity to retrieve it
- either provide facilities for ingesting and retrieving the images themselves (plus text, where the project involves OCR), or provide links to image (and/or text) files held in a separate digital store
- either provide facilities for archives users to search for and retrieve images of the digitised archives and descriptive metadata, or enable outputting the data necessary for a separate search and delivery system (discussed further below)

Like collection management systems for archives, there is a wide range of approaches available for acquiring an image management system, but few specifically designed for the archival context. Choices include:

- generic systems for managing collections of photographs or scanned images for home or small business use: while widely available, these are very limiting for archival digitisation
- off-the-shelf image management systems (or systems with image management capabilities) designed for libraries, museums and art galleries, media houses, or records management: these can be highly sophisticated and powerful, but also expensive and difficult to adapt to some of the specific needs of archival digitisation
- building your own system: user-friendly generic desktop database software make this a possibility, but it requires a major investment in effort and skill
- incorporating an image management module into an existing collection management system: this offers the benefit of close integration of digitisation-specific information with descriptive metadata about the source materials but, again, requires a significant investment. It is worth noting that some archival collection management systems already contain a limited capability for managing digitised images of archives, which may be adequate for some projects.

Because image management systems are essentially metadata systems, a further problem is the lack of widely accepted standards for the metadata of archival digitisation.

The choice of the most suitable solution depends on a range of factors, including:

- the size and resourcing of your archives operation (and parent organisation, if relevant)
- your current hardware and software environment
- any existing investment in a collection management system and/or other relevant information systems
- the specific functions that you want the system to perform.

Storage requirements

Regardless of the approach adopted for an image management system, an archival digitisation project or program will result in the creation of a large number of digital images that must be stored and retrieved.

Master images, particularly of large documents, in colour and/or at high resolutions, can result in file sizes of hundreds of megabytes. Consequently, digitisation projects require serious quantities of storage. While digital storage media are becoming cheaper all the time, it is still important to estimate the storage requirements resulting from the project in its planning and specification stage.

The size of image files also means that it is more common to maintain them in a separate digital store than as binary objects within an image management system.

Storing such quantities of image data makes systematic backing up an absolute necessity. As extra insurance, offsite storage of backups is a wise precaution. While the image format, as noted above, should not use compression, especially for the master image, it is also important to ensure that the storage system used for master images does not compress them.

Long term integrity of digital images

As with 'born digital' records, digital copies of archives are dependent on inherently unstable media and are susceptible to the effects of technological change. If the digital copies are to remain useable beyond the short term, especially when they are being made as a preservation measure, it is important to adopt strategies for meeting these two challenges.

The strategies – periodic refreshing of digital storage media, the adoption of standards for image files and metadata, migration to new systems when necessary, etc. – are essentially the same as for digital records (discussed in Chapter 15: *Digital Recordkeeping*) and will not be discussed further here.

Making digitised archives accessible

We have noted already the need for an image management system to be able to retrieve and display digital images of archives when required. This can provide the types of access required by the archivist.

In Chapter 10: *Using Computers*, we discussed ways of making archives content – digital images of archives and text extracted from archives, plus descriptive metadata – accessible and searchable to archives users online.

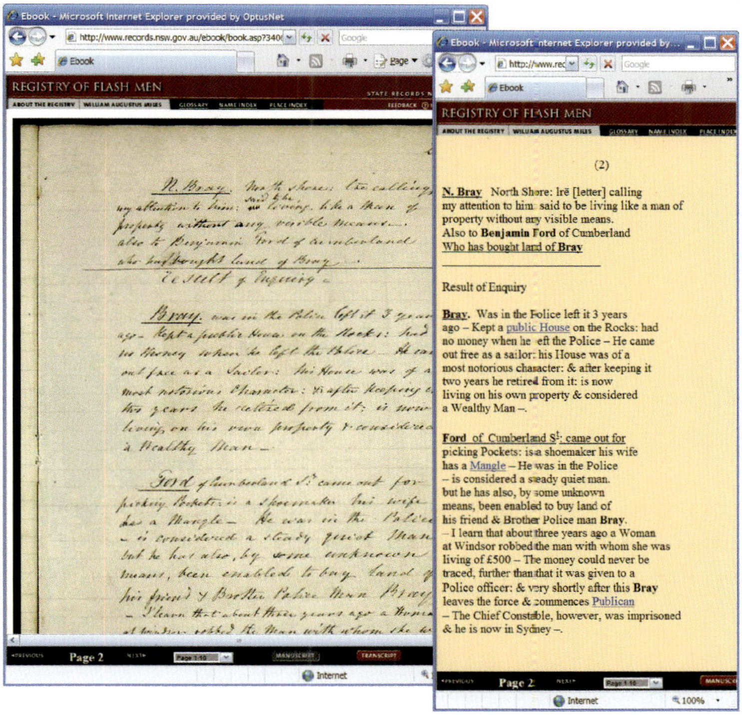

Figure 13.1: Digitised document and transcribed text in State Records NSW's Registry of Flash Men

Similar techniques are suitable where the digitised material is to be made available through offline or stand-alone systems, or through the distribution of CDs or DVDs. One of the advantages of these forms of delivery is that images with higher resolution and much larger file sizes may be made available than those for online distribution, making the digital image a better substitute for the original record.

Let us finish this section by noting that, in addition to providing access to a whole digitised collection, you may wish to provide copies of digitised archives in a variety of forms on request. These may include paper printouts or electronic copies delivered by email or on CD or DVD. This kind of service is best integrated with the archives' other copying services and pricing policies.

Micrographics

By 'micrographics', we mean the use of photographic processes to produce reduced-size images of textual or graphical material on film. This requires some modification, since the development of computer output microfilm means that images can be directly transferred to film from a computer without an intermediate or hard copy.

Modern microfilm readers can be connected to a computer, allowing the reader to enlarge or zoom in on the microfilm image, and to save the image electronically to a disk or USB drive.

Options for microfilming

The archivist is faced with three main options: a contract with a firm which microfilms records for a fee, the development of an in-house microfilming centre, or a mixture of both.

The use of a commercial microfilming bureau has the advantage that equipment costs are limited to the acquisition of reading (and possibly printing) equipment and to the provision of storage facilities for microfilm. Further, there is no need to acquire or hire the skilled personnel to operate microfilming equipment which is essential to ensure a professional and legally recognised product. The commercial bureau is also a source of expert advice.

There are several precautions to take when using a commercial bureau for archival microfilming. First, the bulk of the filming is likely to be done for short-term business use and does not require archival standards of processing. Hence, it is essential that the required archival standards are stated and understood when drawing up the contract for services. Since the records will leave the archives to be filmed on the premises of the commercial bureau, the archivist should have a detailed list of items sent and be sure that sufficient care is taken for their safety. Some archives send a member of their own staff along with the material to supervise and assist with the filming.

Microfilm is a very popular format.

The acquisition of all the equipment and personnel required for a microfilming operation is an undertaking beyond the means of all but the largest archives. To consider this option, the archivist needs to take a number of factors into account. The camera, lights, tables, and related equipment and space needed for microfilming work are very expensive and specialised.

While the actual photography may appear to be a simple matter of snapping a shutter, obtaining archival-quality exposures requires great attention to technical procedures. For example, various colours of paper require light adjustments; the material must be absolutely flat and properly positioned; faded or damaged material may require special filters to render them legible; and the list goes on.

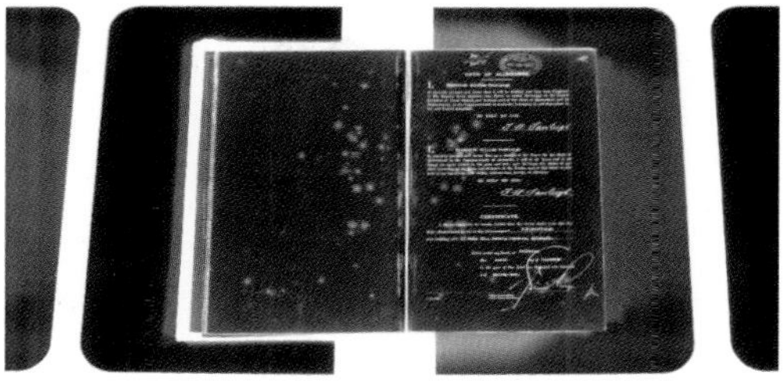

Microfilm as it would look through a microfilm reader.

What microfilming involves

Like digitisation, a microfilming program requires careful evaluation and planning, covering the following steps.

> **The main activities involved in a microfilming project or program**
>
> 1. Defining your purpose
> 2. Deciding what to copy
> 3. Selecting the microfilm format
> 4. Determining the film quality and the number of copies
> 5. Assessing the feasibility and cost of the microfilming project
> 6. Arranging contract with a filming service provider
> 7. Preparing the records for filming
> 8. Final check of the microfilm and the original records

This sequence assumes the use of a commercial microfilming service. For information about the establishment of an in-house microfilming operation, see the Further Reading.

Defining your purpose

As with digitisation, it is fundamentally important to have a clear understanding of the benefits that you wish to gain from microfilming. The considerations discussed earlier in the chapter apply equally here.

Deciding what to copy

Conservation, wider access and security were discussed above as some of the reasons why archivists digitise records. Again, the considerations discussed earlier in the chapter apply equally to microfilming.

Whatever the purpose of establishing a microfilming program, there are likely to be more records which could usefully be copied than resources will allow. A priority listing of collections or record series which accomplish one or more of these purposes should be drawn up to ensure that the most important work is done.

Detailed descriptions of the material should be included to help with estimating the size and cost of the program. Once the list is prepared, it may be worthwhile to contact other archives and libraries to see if any of the materials, especially any published materials, have already been preserved or copied.

Selecting the microfilm format

The choice among roll film, microfiche, aperture cards or other formats will depend on the purpose of the microfilming program, the types of records being copied and the availability of viewing equipment. Microfiche and roll film, for example, are particularly suitable for reference copies because they are popular and easy to use. Fiche, in particular, is inexpensive to duplicate. Aperture cards are most commonly used to copy large single items, such as maps and architectural drawings, because a one-to-one relationship can be maintained between the original items and the microform copies. When making a choice among the more common formats, such as 35mm roll film or microfiche, there is the additional advantage of having established standards of quality and a wide range of viewing equipment.

An older form of micrographics: an aperture card.

Format	Description
16 and 35 mm roll film	35mm roll film remains the most common format for archival microfilming and is normally kept on open reels. Some proprietary systems, particularly those designed for records management application, use roll film in cartridges or cassettes. Jackets comprising transparent sleeves containing strips of roll film are another alternative to open reels.
35mm aperture cards	A single frame of 35mm microfilm is inserted into an aperture or window in a card the size and shape of a traditional computer punch card. Information printed on the card enables the image to be identified without the use of special viewing equipment and allows the item to be handled without touching the image.
35mm slides	Not commonly thought of as a microform, these have some applications in the micrographics industry, such as the reproduction of coloured pictures, maps, or works of art.
Microfiche	This consists of a sheet of film about 105 x 149mm on which a large number of images, normally 60 or 98, have been exposed in a regular pattern of rows and columns. Updateable microfiche also exists but, due to the relative transience of the images produced, it has few archival applications.

Table 13.2: The most common micrographic formats

Microfiche has a number of advantages over roll microfilm:

- a microfiche sheet can be duplicated quickly and inexpensively
- a particular image can be found more efficiently with less effort
- more images can be stored in the same space
- microfiche readers are cheap and easy to maintain
- the individual sheets can be stored in ways that provide more convenient access than roll film, e.g. in holders resembling books.

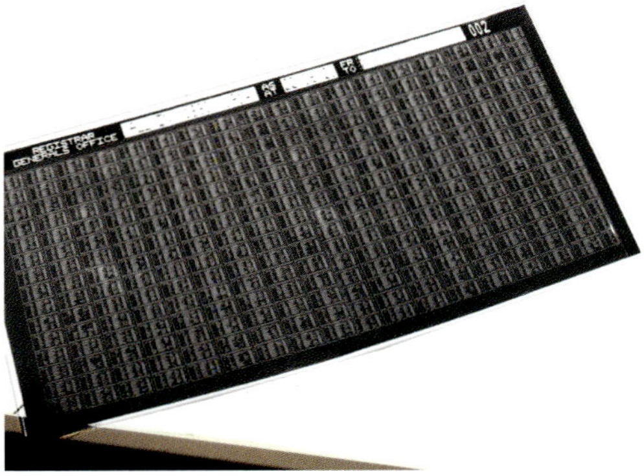

Microfiche

On the other hand, an error in filming onto microfiche cannot be corrected by splicing in a new frame, as is possible with roll film, requiring the whole fiche to be refilmed. In use, microfiche are easier to misfile, lose or have stolen.

Most publications reproduced in microform appear in the fiche format, while most archival microfilming uses roll film.

As outlined in the digitisation section above, microfilm can also be produced directly from images or other computer-based data. This is known as computer output microfilm (COM), which comprises computer-based data produced directly onto microfilm without an intermediate paper format. COM refers more to the process rather than format, as COM can be produced as either roll microfilm or fiche.

Determining the film quality and the number of copies

Because archival records and manuscripts are unique and often fragile, there may be only one opportunity to film them and it is essential that the microfilm product be of the highest quality. This standard of excellence is known as 'archival standard' microfilming. When records are filmed to archival standard, it means that:

- the original records have been arranged and described as accurately and thoroughly as possible, and that any irregularities or flaws in them have been noted
- the film used has a silver halide emulsion on a chemically inert polyester base
- the image of the original record reproduced on the film is a complete, true and faithful copy and has been produced to meet the highest technical standards
- the exposed film has been properly processed and all residues have been removed by an especially thorough washing
- the exposed film has been tested and has met the standards for archival quality both technically and as a true copy of the records it duplicates

It is normal archival practice to produce a minimum of three microfilm copies of each original item. These copies include:

- a security or preservation negative on silver halide film
- a negative copy for further duplication, known as a duplicating master
- a reference copy

Use of microfilm, either for reference or for making a further copy, inevitably results in damage which can become extensive over time. For this reason, the security or preservation negative should be used to produce only the duplicating master and thereafter should be kept undisturbed in the best storage environment, as security against loss of the original records or of the duplicating master. The duplicating master is used only for making further reference copies and is also stored carefully. The reference copies are for everyday use by researchers and staff.

For the security or preservation negative, the most acceptable medium is black and white silver halide film. This is the only type of film for which archival quality standards exist and which is sufficiently stable, given proper processing and storage conditions, to last for long periods of time. For the duplicating master and for the reference copies, one may use the less expensive, easier-to-copy diazo or vesicular films, which are also more scratch-resistant than silver halide. Diazo and vesicular films use different development processes, but are used for similar purposes.

Finally, a choice must be made between a positive or negative image for the copies. Duplicating masters are normally negative; reference copies can be either negative or positive. One advantage of having negative reference copies is that it is easier on the eyes to look at white text on a black background.

Assessing the feasibility and cost of the microfilming project

A microfilming project must be assessed and weighed against the proposed benefits of the filming. The expenses of equipment should be included as well as the labour of preparing and checking the records before and after filming. An outline, such as the following, listing the types of expenses which must be anticipated in a microfilming project is helpful in estimating costs.

Type of expense	What to count
Quantity of records to be microfilmed	Shelf metres of records Number of frames (allow 80–100 frames per cm of paper thickness)
Preparation of records	Preservation work required Removal of pins, staples, folds Final checking of page order Additional arrangement and description, if required
Preparation of identification sheets, targets and notes	Archivist's design time (i.e. the time to design the different types of targets needed) Archivist's fill-in time (i.e. the time needed to fill in all the template-based identification targets) to prepare on PC or by hand and print Stationery costs
Filming	Supervisor's time Operator's time Equipment time Cost of x metres of film at $y per metre length Cost of any protective treatment or coating required
Examination of master	Checking time Cost of residual chemical testing
Filming of retakes and additions	As for preparation, filming and examination above
Reassembly of records	Replacement of pins, etc. Checking of order
Transportation	Of records Of staff
Copying	Cost of copy negative Cost of copy positive x number of copies required Cost of residual chemical testing

Table 13.3: Summary of expenses to consider

Arranging contract with a filming service provider

Choosing a service provider to undertake the photography, processing and duplicating of microfilms should be done with great care. It is advisable to seek written quotes from firms with proven skills and to speak to others who have used the service, before entering into a formal contract. An essential part of a contract is the specification, which describes the records to be filmed and the quality standards of microfilming to be met.

A typical specification should cover the following items:

Documents to be microfilmed

Identify record series, format(s), quantity, approximate size of pages/folios, approximate number of frames, colour of documents (and therefore whether colour testing is required).

Camera

Specify a planetary camera, not a rotary camera.

Film

Specify type of film, no splicing, leaders and trailers; the film to be surrendered on spools and to be boxed and clearly labelled and identified; before any copies are made, the master negative to be surrendered for checking of image placement, etc, and residual chemicals.

Indicators

All identification sheets, targets and notes to be provided by the client.

Image placement

Specify 'comic' or horizontal mode (i.e. with the top and bottom edges of the images parallel to the edges of the film), rather than 'cinefilm' or vertical mode, and placed in accordance with international standards.

Reduction ratio

Typically 11x for documents or 20x for larger materials.

Archival standard

The film to be processed in accordance with international standards for archival materials.

Conditions of microfilming

The documents to be filmed on the supplier's premises in the presence of a member of the client's staff; transportation of the documents to and from the supplier's premises to be undertaken by the client; the documents to remain at all times in the supplier's custody.

Microfilm copies

Master negative 35mm; copy negative (to be quoted for separately); X copy positives (to be quoted for separately).

The Further Reading section lists current relevant international standards. However, these are updated frequently, so check relevant standards websites for current versions before signing an agreement. The *Guidelines for best practice microfilming of public records* by Queensland State Archives also provides practical advice on the contents of microfilm, including informational and identification targets.

In addition to stating the quality standards that must be met, a contract should make clear how errors in the filming, processing or duplication will be detected, what actions will be taken to correct them and who will pay for them.

Preparing the records for filming

Before they can be filmed, the records to be copied must be adequately prepared. This preparation involves:

Arranging and describing the records accurately and completely

Complete arrangement and description of the records minimises the risk of records being out of order or missing. Also, the records will be temporarily passing out of your custody, which introduces the possibilities of externally caused disturbance, damage or loss of the records. Arrangement and description provides an inventory of records sent to the commercial service's premises, which can be used to ensure that they are later returned complete and in good order.

Preparatory conservation work

Records may require cleaning and flattening before they can be filmed effectively. This kind of preparation can also include the simple but necessary task of removing pins, staples and clips.

Preparing and inserting targets and explanatory notes to be filmed along with the records

Targets provide identifying and technical information and are inserted in the sequence of records prior to filming. Targets indicating the start of the reel, the reel number, the series and item number and title of the records being filmed, the end of the reel and continuation of the series to or from another reel should appear on every reel. These identifying targets should be legible with the naked eye.

Specialised targets may also be needed to indicate missing pages, information on the records obscured by the original binding or other problems. Technical targets, such as test charts and information about the reduction ratio used to film the records, may also be prepared.

When preparing records for filming, you should remember that researchers using the microfilm will not have the originals to compare with the film, nor will they necessarily have an archivist with particular knowledge of those records at hand to explain any inconsistencies or legibility problems with the material. You should try to anticipate these needs and provide explanatory notes where necessary to make sure the researcher is fully informed of any factors which might have affected the quality or completeness of the image on the film. Notes may also provide additional descriptive information about the records and a copyright warning.

Preparing instructions for the operator

Remember that the microfilm camera operator is only responsible for producing a technically suitable microphotograph of the records. It is the archivist's responsibility to decide what is to be photographed, to communicate these decisions to the photographer and to prepare the material for placement under the camera. The archivist must provide instructional notes on such matters as what to do with runs of blank pages, when to film covers of volumes or files, and in what circumstances to contact the archives for advice.

Packaging the records and preparing them for transport

The records should be carefully packaged so that the risk of damage in transit is minimised. It may be worthwhile to accompany the records to the service provider's premises and even to be present when the filming is done.

You also need to consider the mode of transport to be used. In particular, extremes of heat and temperature need to be avoided, since damage may be caused by the resultant changes in dimension and moisture in the film. Similarly, care must be taken during the return of the original material and the microfilm copies.

Final check of the microfilm and the original records

Once returned, the original material and the microfilm copies should be checked carefully before paying the bill. To determine technical quality, it may be useful to have the microfilm tested independently by an institutional or commercial lab to ensure that the stipulated standards of processing have been adhered to. If necessary, insist on rewashing, or even refilming, with the refilmed frames properly spliced in. Check the microfilm against the originals to ensure that it is complete and in order. Also check the order and condition of the originals before returning them to the shelves.

When handling the master negative microfilm, exercise great care and wear lint-free cotton gloves. Other basic equipment which is useful for a visual inspection of the microfilm includes a light bench, hand operated film winders, and a magnifying glass.

Storage of microfilm

There is no point in ensuring that microfilm is made to archival standards if the film is then kept in poor storage conditions. Appropriate storage conditions for film-based materials are discussed in more detail in Chapter 3: *Buildings & Storage*. At this point, it is useful to note the most important factors which determine the suitability of a storage environment for master archival film are:

Temperature

A low temperature (ideally 10° C, but certainly below 21° C, for black and white film; 0° C for colour) prolongs the life of the microfilm image by reducing the rate at which the chemical changes that result in deterioration take place. Changes in temperature, such as the cyclical changes of office air-conditioning, should also be avoided.

Humidity

A low level of humidity prevents the growth of moulds which eat the emulsion of the film. However, if the humidity is too low, the film base can dry out and become brittle. Around 30–40%RH is a suitable balance. Good air circulation is also a means of preventing mould.

Shelving

Purpose-designed shelving and drawers should be used for storing microfilm. Alternatively, existing equipment may be adapted.

Hazards to avoid

Microfilm should be kept away from such hazards as heat, light, and water, which could cause damage. For this reason, attics and below-ground storage should generally be avoided.

If storage meeting these conditions is not available to the archives, larger archives may be able to help by storing the security or preservation negatives.

Equally, high-quality storage is of little value if the film is damaged by sudden changes when taking items in or out of storage. 'Conditioning' is the process of allowing the film to warm or cool slowly, and adjust to the humidity level, to prevent condensation building up on the film and damaging it.

As well as a suitable storage environment, the containers used for the storage of microfilm are important. Master negative microfilm should be stored on chemically stable plastic or similar reels or cores. Boxes for individual reels should also be made of stable materials, such as polypropylene. Containers should be clearly labelled with identifying information. Colour coding on containers can help underline the status of a particular copy. A growing standard in Australia uses red for master negatives, green for duplicating copies and blue for reference copies.

It is important to monitor the condition of master microfilm so that corrective measures can be taken if it deteriorates noticeably. A random inspection of a small proportion should be made annually.

This strict environment is not required for reference copies. Here emphasis should be placed on proper handling, care in loading and removing from microfilm readers, and keeping reading and printing equipment clean and working well.

Microfilm readers

A wide range of microfilm viewers or readers is available, new models are introduced regularly and, given the cost of these machines, it is worthwhile to seek expert advice before making a choice. Colleagues and staff of other archives are a good source of advice on the use of equipment in archival operations.

You may want to consider leasing rather than purchasing equipment at first, to gauge user demand and satisfaction before making a major investment.

Some of the desirable features to seek include:

- versatility in terms of the formats of microfilm which the equipment can accommodate (many readers are easily converted between roll film and fiche, or can change lenses for different levels of magnification)
- capacity to adjust the screen's angle and brightness, to suit the needs of different users or changes in location
- quietness and ease of operation, including loading and removing film
- economy of operation, including easy maintenance and reliable, fast repairs

If a reader/printer is to be chosen, the quality of the hardcopy, the speed of the printing process and the ease or otherwise of routine maintenance, such as the addition of toner, should be investigated. A reader/printer which uses plain paper rather than thermal paper is desirable. Newer reader-printers may also include a USB, where users can save the image to their own USB drive, 'memory stick' or 'thumb drive' rather than printing to paper. Security measures to prevent unauthorised printing and a coin-operated printing operation may also be necessary.

You should establish a regular cleaning and maintenance routine for the machine, following the supplier's specifications, and protect it from dust with a dust cover.

Having chosen a reader or reader/printer, you must decide where to locate it. Background glare should be avoided, as should light reflected from the screen. A darkened location with down-lighting to enable users to make notes or consult printed materials is ideal. The intermittent noise caused by the operation of a microfilm reader may be distracting both to staff and to other researchers and, therefore, it may be desirable to isolate it if possible. Equally, users should be able to seek assistance easily. The table or bench on which the reader is located should have enough additional work space for a user to take notes. The height of the bench should be chosen to maximise the comfort of the user, depending on the height of the reader's screen. An adjustable chair should also be provided.

While physical access by researchers to archival materials must be strictly controlled, it is possible to be more flexible with microform copies. For example, reference copies may be made available on open access, removing the need to issue them formally. This has the disadvantages that the level of use of microfilmed materials can no longer be accurately monitored and reels may not be returned to their correct places. These problems can be largely overcome by requiring researchers to hand in reels when they have finished with them, to be put back by archives staff, who can also document their use.

CHAPTER 14

advocacy & outreach

ANN PEDERSON

CHAPTER ABSTRACT

Advocacy and outreach cover a range of activities that aim to positively influence the destiny of host organisations, own collections and even our own professional careers. Successful advocacy and outreach activities are essential for raising the profile of, and building support for, an archive among its stakeholders.

This chapter explains the importance of advocacy and community-building infrastructure and gives you tips for ensuring that the activities or approaches that you may choose to implement, such as website, publicity, training/education, exhibitions and fundraising, provide maximum benefits for the archive and its wider community.

Further information on some of the issues and ideas raised in this chapter are included on the accompanying CD.

Archives and advocacy

Many archives programs struggle or fail to fulfil their responsibilities because they do not understand advocacy – that arsenal of expertise which positively influences the destiny of our host organisations, our own collections, even our own professional careers. Advocacy is a state-of-mind and 'set' of infrastructure tools that support an array of outreach programs and activities. As a framework, it supplies the attitudes, knowledge and techniques that are *prerequisite* to undertaking individual outreach/public program activities and projects. Advocacy mechanisms, like recordkeeping, are a 'background' function; that is, they cannot themselves be seen, rather they become apparent as they are *applied*, in activities such as workshops, press releases, exhibits, newsletters and special events which are held to benefit an organisation or particular programs within it. However, the framework for advocacy work must not be transparent. Too important to be left to chance, it must be articulated into formal, planned components embedded within the managing structure and mission functions of the recordkeeping regime.

Advocacy is clearly about relationships with people, with influencing people to change their attitudes and behaviours. But what does that have to do with records and archives? *Everything*! Without human endeavour, there would be no need for records. Think carefully about recordkeeping work. Behind every record sits a person with a problem or need, as Appendix 14.1 will attest. Record and archive keeping is, above all, a function 'of the people, by the people and for the people' and entirely dependent upon their goodwill and cooperation.

Furthermore, we as records and archives specialists manage the *means of production* and the *products* of recordkeeping activity, all of which depend upon our ability *to communicate with* and thereby to *persuade* others:

- to embrace *our mission* of ensuring essential evidence
- to accept *our vision and management regime* for realising the mission

But aren't there laws and regulations that force people to keep records? Yes, of course, but such are only effective when developed and applied cooperatively to guide (rather than to compel) compliance. We have all experienced compliance/implementation being ignored or delayed and even the firmest laws being changed, when influential people object strongly enough to them. To ensure archival effectiveness, we must build active and productive partnerships with influential cohorts within our service communities.

Because advocacy is about winning confidence, not battles, 'people skills' and issues are paramount. Thus the surge of interest in advocacy in recent years may at last reveal the secret to meeting the recordkeeping challenge. In the past, archivists lavished their attention upon their records, ignoring the people and the work activities behind them. In the new world of strategic management, understanding how people feel and behave, *their* roles in organised activity and what they need in terms of documentation, is vital.

The key to success in dealing with people has always been a capacity to understand and master the art of communicating. In his 1994 book, *Why don't people listen?*, prominent Australian communications researcher Hugh Mackay shares his insights into human communication gleaned from a lifetime of research. Mackay asserts that most people fail to communicate because they focus solely on 'injecting' curative messages into those other people who have, or are causing, the problem. Not only does this strategy fail, it torpedoes any prospect of building the genuine relationship required to transcend differences and minimise disputes. The real cure, Mackay contends, lies in building trust through shared understanding, and he suggests adopting his Ten Laws of Human Communications shown in Appendix 14.2 as a way forward.

The success of recordkeeping advocacy depends heavily on the profession having members, particularly leaders, with the positive attitudes and knowledge needed to establish an advocacy regime. However acquired, advocacy expertise must first build a solid base of clear understanding and commitment within the archives/records profession. Valuable time, energy and credibility are lost when one's efforts are undermined by internal lethargy or nay-saying. Applying advocacy techniques to convert and energise one's own colleagues and influential superiors before tackling the outside world will prove a sound investment. The who, what, when, where, why and how of designing a campaign will depend upon the answers to the following serious questions about your own professional community and host organisation:

- Is the prevailing archives/records professional culture receptive to advocacy?
- Does the archives/records community in general understand, possess, value or seek to acquire 'people skills'?
- Do the archives/records community leaders and educators seek out skilled 'people people', cultivate them and/or encourage them to serve as partners and 'champions' in support of recordkeeping effectiveness?

Hopefully, your answers to all of these are resoundingly positive, but if not, you now know where to begin your efforts. Unless advocacy has a strong support 'at home among the converted', it is doubly hard to apply it in the workplace and wider community.

For our profession and for the future of civil societies, we must also recruit people into the recordkeeping profession who have the personal attributes to master people skills. Individually and as a profession, when we master and apply advocacy knowledge and skills, we discover and create opportunities to maximise the benefits our archives and records programs can bring to their communities.

Building community

The key concept in community building is involvement. Activities that attract people to and involve people with the archives and its work transform those faceless members of the general public, as well as our own higher administration, into personal clients of our services i.e. researchers, donors, volunteers and active supporters of the archival enterprise. Community- building programs are engaging vehicles which bring people face-to-face with archival materials, generating an initial interest and enthusiasm which, properly nurtured, will develop into a continuing relationship of mutual appreciation.

For instance, in one notable case, the patriarch of an influential family was invited to lend some photographs to an exhibit for the town centenary. This man had never entered the doors of the local historical society until the day he came in to discuss the loan, but became so interested that he not only came to the exhibit opening, but subsequently joined the society and donated his family papers to its archives. Furthermore, through his influence, several leading businesses made donations of money and services to the society. Examples of such conversions abound, ranging from the workshop attendee who becomes a committed volunteer to a philanthropist collector like David Scott Mitchell of Sydney, Australia whose bequest established the superb research library of Australiana that bears his name.

Community-building programs, then, must be developed as tools that naturally extend from and enhance other archival work such as research, preservation, and acquisition. They can be very rewarding, both for planners and participants.

Many of the community-building activities serve a dual purpose. Designed to inform and instruct the clients of the archives, they are equally useful for orienting and educating new members of staff and prospective volunteers. In addition the research and analysis involved in these activities often improves the overall standard of archival services. In a material sense, they foster appreciation for the value of historical records and help ensure support for those who care for them.

Perhaps, most important of all, they encourage greater communication between the keepers of archives and the various institutional, social, and professional communities to which they belong. Archivists who plan and take part in community building activities develop perceptions that help them to do a better job of serving the needs of their clients. Correspondingly, members of the community who are introduced to archival work through such projects may come to appreciate the legal and financial as well as the cultural benefits of well-managed modern record services, and use these insights to economic advantage in their personal and business enterprises.

A planning approach to building community

Given resources and imagination, there is a smorgasbord of community-building activities and projects that may be offered. Some of the better known include websites, publications, workshops and seminars, exhibitions and special events such as open days or commemorative celebrations. However, it is essential to select from this banquet with care, choosing projects which complement and strengthen the archives effort overall, rather than those which, though exciting, actually divert staff energies and resources for little lasting benefit.

Careful planning is needed to select those best suited to the purpose, resources and clientele of your institution as a whole. Most people underestimate the amount of work and coordination required in undertaking such projects. Involving the wider community in activities at the archives or using archival materials requires special care. Public interest, enthusiasm and contact with original sources is to be encouraged, but not at the peril of the records. For example, you must ensure the security of the archival items involved without making those enjoying them feel uncomfortable. All users and visitors should be courteously informed, preferably in advance, of protective measures that must be taken to reduce the possibility of misunderstandings.

One cannot absolutely predict public response to a community-building initiative; they can love it or leave it for a dozen reasons that have little to do with the event's worthiness.

One can only research the undertaking well, seek and accept professional advice, plan for reasonable contingencies, and go. Above all, keep good records (you are keeping your own archives too, remember!) and evaluate the project thoughtfully. Thorough documentation of all phases of work will be invaluable in planning future activities.

Pathways *is a brochure developed by the Indigenous Issues Special Interest Group of the Australian Society of Archivists. This is an example of community-building with a twist: the brochure is aimed at encouraging indigenous people to take up formal qualifications in Archives and Records Management.*

Identifying your focus and clientele

At this point, the need to plan is clear, but what exactly should one consider in developing a program of appropriate and beneficial activities? To create an effective project portfolio, archivists should follow four basic steps. Firstly, understand the purpose and operational goals of your institution. Secondly, determine the nature and needs of your audience. Thirdly, locate and obtain the necessary resources. Fourthly, select and plan an appropriate program to suit them.

All community-building activity must harmonise with and enhance the purpose and responsibility of your institution. Study the documents which established your archives and any subsequent records modifying them. Legislation, corporate charters and policy statements establishing your archives define the scope and focus of your work. These same documents will also help you identify your major clientele.

Regular magazines such as Memento *(National Archives of Australia) and* ProActive *(Public Records Office of Victoria) are exemplary publications aimed at a wide audience. If this is beyond the scope of your archives, a short paragraph in the weekly newsletter, or a web page showcasing some of your latest acquisitions could be a place to start your community-building activities.*

Find out who your target audiences are and what is needed to improve their relationships with the archives. Some may not be obvious, because you know them in another capacity or never thought about their capacity to benefit your operation. They may be managers or advisors of your own host organisation, or visitors, researchers or donors to your facility. More significantly, they may be *potential* clients, i.e. people you are mandated to serve, but whom you have never contacted.

Identifying important client groups is a simple matter of knowing where to look. The archives own records are full of information about them and are very readily at hand. For example, the contact details and interests of the archives' current researchers are well-documented in the reader's ticket applications; daily registrations of visitors/ researchers and lists of participants in workshops are also valuable. People, offices or organisations who deposit their records with the archives comprise another important client group – one that uses the archives' facilities and services as extensions of their own information systems. Acquisition and accession records and record request forms (call slips) document their contributions and their patterns of use. The administrators, managers, and advisers of the host organisation are particularly important internal clients because their work effectiveness depends upon archival care of vital organisational records and their decisions impact heavily on archival operations. Records such as in-house correspondence, reports and budget papers will help the archives align itself with management priorities and concerns.

Another important group, often overlooked until their services are needed, comprises information officers and media representatives. These professionals should be sent, at least selectively, special event invitations and externally focused communications such as calendars and newsletters. Maintaining regular contact and encouraging participation in archival activities is a long-term investment that will yield dividends, including that all-important media coverage when the archives really needs it.

Knowing one's clientele and the records documenting them enables the archives to establish a comprehensive user and usage database. One of the first things you will want to do is create a series of mailing lists to facilitate communication between the archives and its key client groups, including new individuals and organisations with untapped potential. This aspect will be discussed in more detail later in the chapter.

Setting priorities

In setting priorities for community building, the rule of thumb is to first improve the quality and delivery of existing services. For example, in the past, obtaining access to archival resources involved an in-person visit, arranged during working hours via fact-finding telephone calls and letters. Services for users living far from the archives facility were poor or non-existent. Today, a wealth of archival information and materials can be made accessible globally 24/7 via the internet. While examining archival originals remains a largely in-person activity, online indexes identifying key records and information explaining how best to use them has increased productivity and reduced costs. Thus one of the first community-building measures your archives should investigate is setting up an internet interface – a website with search, document delivery and email facilities.

Another priority is improving the delivery of frequently requested information. For example, new researchers visit the archives daily. All first-timers, regardless of their previous experience with archives, require orientation and usually ask the same basic questions as they learn their way around. What educational tools could be developed to streamline this process? A basic leaflet about the archives, its location, its holdings and services could be posted on the archives website and/or sent to enquirers in advance of their visit. Attractive, welcoming and easy-to-read signs will orientate newcomers quickly to the facilities. A simple plan of the public areas showing major features and explaining rules for using them should be distributed on arrival. A self-service library of interactive learning tools on selected topics may ease researchers into their work with more confidence. Any or all of these suggestions will facilitate the transformation from new client to productive researcher, making reference services more satisfying and efficient for all. Similar improvements can be made in other archival services, such as negotiating new acquisitions or arranging transfers of records from offices.

After you have improved the delivery of existing services to established clients, target groups with the potential to help your program the most. Your overall strategy must be gradual – building outwards from a solid core of support and avoiding the twin dangers of too many activities and disparate user groups.

Identifying resources

No community-building effort can function without a commitment of resources of various kinds. Facilities, equipment, and supplies come most easily to mind, but these need not be your first consideration, as many such items can be hired, borrowed or donated. Your most important resource will be the time and talents of your staff, their knowledge of the archives and their continuing involvement and commitment before, during and after the project.

Bring your staff together and ask what kinds of projects would interest them and find out as much as possible about their skills and hobbies. You may have a good photographer, writer, designer or speaker among the crew. Others may have special subject knowledge that could be used in creating exhibits or publications. When considering a new idea, ask the staff from a variety of work areas for their views before plans advance too far, and give all interested staff an opportunity to be involved in all stages of the project, especially in the evaluation of its success.

Establishing a firm foundation

In deciding where to start your community building, begin with what you know best. Choose projects that will enhance the services, collections and audiences most important to your archives. Ask staff members for suggestions of educational aids that would make work in their areas of responsibility easier. For example, a one-page handout could explain how to fill out a request for documents from the collections or how to order a copy. Frequently asked questions provide clues to areas where such aids or special small group training sessions could streamline reference service. Likewise, persons contacting the archives by mail often have similar questions, presenting the opportunity to design special information sheets or brochures to satisfy common types of requests.

While these ideas focus upon improving reference services, similar measures are helpful in other areas of archival work. Table 14.1 summarises ideas for community-building initiatives to facilitate a number of archival functions.

Archival function	Audiences		
	Individuals	**Small groups**	**Wider community**
Access and reference	Orientation interview. Basic brochure on holdings, facilities and terms of access. Simple handouts (reading room rules, how to request records, obtain copies, special access). Reading room audio self-tour and/or video with interactive activities	Letter inviting groups to use (universities, genealogical societies, etc). Mini-classes for beginning researchers. Illustrated talks (slides, overheads, powerpoint) about using the archives or starting research. Training for volunteer reading room assistants.	Audiovisuals encouraging use of the archives. Loan/ sales of microforms and CDs of selected records. Seminars on popular research topics.
Finding aids	Leaflet guide to major holdings. In-house finding aids.	Comprehensive guide to holdings. Training for volunteers to index and/ or convert finding aids to Electronic Archival Description (EAD) formats suitable for electronic publication.	Individual guides to records of particular creators (colonial secretary) or on special subjects (gold, convicts, indigenous peoples). Sale of microfilms and CDs of databases, finding aids or indexes.

	Individuals	Small groups	Wider community
Acquisition, appraisal and disposal	Personal contacts with prospective depositors (persons, organisations). Leaflet on donating material to archives. Rotating exhibitions of new acquisitions.	Illustrated talks (slides, overheads, powerpoint) on identifying archival materials and donating to archives. Workshop on identifying materials of historic value or disposal scheduling training for volunteer fieldworkers and/or client agency staff	Field projects to survey and record potential acquisitions or to copy records in private custody. Audiovisual about archives field work. Conference on appraisal.
Arrangement and description		Audiovisual or illustrated talks (slides, overheads, powerpoint) explaining arrangement and description. Training for volunteers.	Work placements or intensive courses for students, volunteers or other professions.
Conservation	Leaflet on handling of various record media. Simple exhibitions (before and after types of damage, particular problems).	Illustrated talks (slides, overheads, powerpoint) on damaging agents, preventative measures, disaster minimisation. Workshops on basic maintenance, preventative and restorative techniques. Training for volunteers.	Audiovisuals on various aspects of conservation. Conferences on conservation issues.
User education and publications	Tours of the archives. Feature articles and news releases on major holdings, collecting efforts, new acquisitions, and research projects. Simple displays on facets of archives work or background of the archives program.	Tours of the archives. Seminars on archival work or research methods for students. Illustrated talks (slides, overheads, powerpoint) about various aspects of archives work on research projects undertaken at the archives by staff or researchers.	Website Downloadable technical advice and publications Newsletter Open days Conferences Major exhibitions Friends of archives events Press and public relations

Table 14.1: Overview of community-building activities for archives

Whichever types you choose, whether designed for individual, group or community-wide application, remember your goal: a coordinated and complementary effort, rather than an array of disparate bits and pieces pulling in many directions. One effort should lead or extend logically to another, either in content or scope or both.

Look into ways that the effort and expense of one project can be used to advantage in related or spin-off activities. Design an audiovisual presentation with sections that can be tailored to different audiences or edit your basic brochure information for web page presentation or into dialogue for a video about the archives (Chapter 9: *Enriching the Record*).

Similarly, the visuals and text of an exhibit might be redesigned for the internet and/or developed into a video which can be shown to audiences long after the original exhibit has been dismantled.

There is also an advantage in clustering activities around a major event or point in time. A local centenary, holiday or festival presents a good opportunity for the archives to attract wider publicity and a larger audience than usual for tours, workshops or exhibits featuring the special theme. Often, institutions sponsoring conferences will plan exhibitions to complement them or vice versa so that the interest generated by one activity encourages participation in the other. Such an approach is useful because it gives participants an opportunity to explore more facets of a subject once their interest has been captured.

Learn from the experiences of other institutions. Many archives, libraries, museums and historical societies have undertaken similar projects and may be willing to discuss their experiences. The internet and email make discovering useful examples and making contact with sponsoring institutions fast and relatively simple processes. Collect examples of well-produced brochures, web pages and video presentations. Ask to study detailed plans for workshops and exhibitions. If possible, obtain permission to examine copies of actual working papers such as proposals, budgets, plans, reports and related documentation from successful projects.

When seeking advice or negotiating access to others resources, remember these colleagues and their institutions have limited time and assisting you requires extra effort for little return. They 'own' their ideas and information; respect their literary property rights and comply with them fully when copying or adapting materials by others. Don't assume they will send you copies of material or publications for free; you should offer to pay the purchase price and shipping and let them be magnanimous if they have that option.

Consider joint ventures with neighbouring and/or related institutions. The benefits of shared projects are numerous. Pooled resources can lead to larger and more professional activities as well as to improved relations with colleagues in related professions.

Community-building activities are as numerous and varied as the archival institutions that sponsor them. However, all successful ones are characterised by the following qualities: a clear purpose, well-defined scope and content, and appealing presentation. Materials and projects for clients, whether internal or public, must be attractive and evoke interest and participation.

The following text focuses upon selected types of activities and is intended to provide general guidelines for development rather than explicit how-to instructions. (For more detailed information, consult the works cited under Further Reading or use the internet to identify examples and explore the electronic literature).

Public relations

Designing a program of archival services without paying specific attention to public relations is like planning a party without inviting the guests. As previously explained, regular interaction with client groups is as important as any purely archival activity, maybe more so. Certainly, effective communication with our constituent host organisations and larger communities is *critical* if we are to obtain the resources necessary to meet our increasing responsibilities. Client relations, public relations or publicity, as this work is variously termed, is a *positive consciousness* that should initially infuse one's work and then later be formalised into publicity, publications (including via your internet website), interviews, speeches and other community-building endeavours.

Maximising that first exposure

Few people can recall their first encounter with archival material because an enjoyable browse of one's old photos, school reports, letters and cards seldom registers as such despite being the most usual 'first' (and all too often, the only) experience. Thus the initial focus for community building should be to maximise those points of interface where the archives first engages its prospective clientele. Ask yourself the following questions:

- How and where are people most likely to come in contact with my archives?
- What are the main conduits of contact at present and whom do they generally reach?
- Which important client groups are not in contact with or being served by the archives and how are these best reached?
- What additional or more effective means of contact should the archives develop?
- Once contact is made, how can the archives encourage further contact and relationship building in a resource efficient manner?

The answers to these questions will identify where and how to maximise your community-building initiative.

It is important to apply client-centred thinking when evaluating archival services, policies and procedures for improvement. Again, answers to questions provide the key:

- How satisfying and efficient is the service and its delivery mechanism for both archives and client?
- How can the outcome and interaction among service, staff and client be improved?

- What questions will clients expect accompanying documentation to answer?
  - Is the language used in such documents appropriate and clear?
  - What examples and illustrations are needed enhance the effectiveness of text?

Scrutinise each archival function for ways to improve outcomes and communication with those doing or explaining the work. A checklist of steps to complete during acquisition should include acknowledging each gift and placing the donor's name on the archives' mailing list. The reference staff could give departing researchers a self-mailing form, soliciting their ideas for improvement. Visitors and researchers should be included when invitations are sent out for workshops or exhibits. Staff members, whether speaking to groups or meeting individuals, should always have a supply of business cards and basic information about contacting the archives. While it may not be appropriate to hand out leaflets in the street, be prepared when casual contact sparks a genuine interest that can be followed up.

Publicity

Publicity is getting a message across to an audience in an accurate, well-presented and timely manner. There are two basic ways of communicating with an audience: the direct method, which uses the mail, the internet or a specialised distribution system; and the indirect approach, which works through an intermediary, usually an affiliated professional association or a radio, television or newspaper journalist. See Appendix 14.3 for hints on managing a mailing list.

With the direct approach, the archivist, singly or working with an in-house publicist, prepares and packages the message which is then sent directly to known recipients and/or posted on the archives website. This method has several advantages. The archivist knows that the message sent is exactly what has been designed and that the timing suits the program's needs. The archivist has also selected the recipients as persons or agencies worth cultivating.

However, there are also disadvantages to direct contact. The archives may not have the resources to produce materials to a professional standard, to maintain an up-to-date website or to bear the expense of regular mailing to a wide audience. Errors in timing can also result from lack of marketing experience or knowledge of competing activities.

Items posted on internet mailing lists (sometimes referred to as 'listservs') hosted by professional associations reach a very wide audience in minimal time. However, you must ensure that your message complies with each mailing list's standards for posting. For example, many mailing lists refuse items that are overly self-promotional or mere advertising.

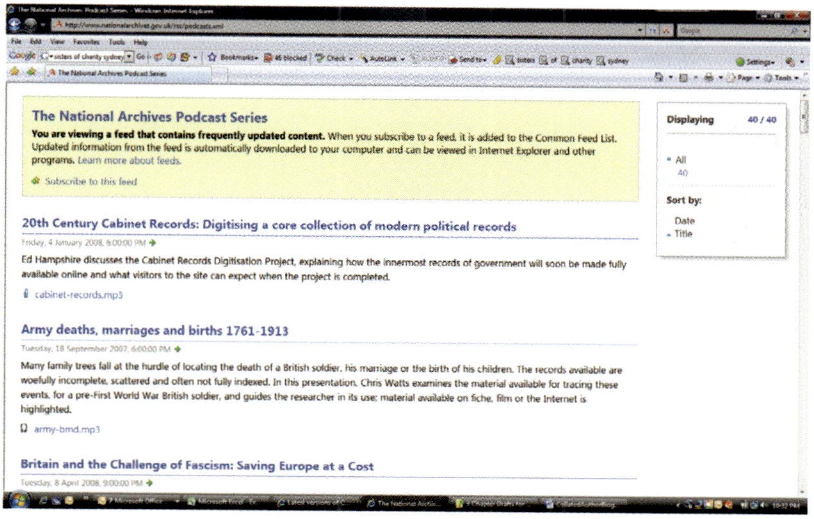

One way of generating publicity, and connecting with on-line users, is to use podcasts of news, events and discussions. The National Archives (UK) has established a feature on their website to facilitate this. While such a move may be beyond a small archives in the short term, it is an avenue worth bearing in mind for the future.

Working through the media, the archivist is able to minimise costs, obtain wider coverage and deliver more professionally packaged messages, but not without certain risks. The message and the timing may undergo changes to meet media programming demands. Each media team attempts to package and present the best material from what is available at any given time. The competition among news and feature items for space or air time is heightened by the additional pressures of deadlines, audience ratings and those all-important sponsorship dollars. Thus, working within the dynamic environment of media requires archival publicists to be both flexible and persistent in their efforts to exploit media resources.

Perhaps the best idea is to plan publicity efforts that combine self-distributed information with selected media exposure, relying more on the former than the latter. Using this approach, one can always be assured that the message will reach a primary audience and may be magnified and multiplied if media coverage is obtained.

Whatever approach used, one of the best ways to increase the chances of success in obtaining appropriate publicity is to cultivate good relationships with writers, editors and program-makers, both in-house and outside, who work in the field. Journalists are greedy for interesting material and most archives hold plenty of it. It is a matter of matching these interests and people on a regular basis. Including appropriate media representatives and publicists in the archives' mailing list will ensure that they are reliably informed of approaching activities and invited to special events.

Create a 'feature stories' file and fill it with ideas and visual materials for feature stories about the archives and its collections. Invite researchers, volunteers and staff members to brainstorm ideas and encourage them to give interviews regarding their work or knowledge. Later in this chapter, ideas for traditional and World Wide Web exhibitions will be discussed, many of which are equally suitable raw material for news items, feature articles or documentaries.

Whatever the topic, care should be taken to ensure that all materials posted on the website, or provided to journalists and editors, are accurate, concise, well written and presented in an interesting way. Beginning the piece with an arresting opener, closely followed by the who, what, where, why and when information is a well-accepted formula. Be sure to include a name and telephone number of the person to contact for more information.

Help with publicity initiatives may be more available and forthcoming than you think. Many people with publicity skills and experience are willing to help a worthy cause. Students learning the trade may be invited to design websites or plan publicity programs as an academic project. Retired members of the media and public relations community have a wealth of experience and contacts and may welcome the opportunity to use them on your behalf. Keep in mind, however, that help is just that. The archives must always accept its responsibility to provide the resources to complete the work.

Publicity is an art that calls for several levels of effort. All archives, large and small, must keep their clients informed about the archives' work and activities. This basic effort involves discussing 'publicity' during major planning meetings. Staff can then report recent accomplishments and develop a calendar of coming events. Assign responsibility for compiling these items into publishable form with deadlines, and monitor their quality and timely completion. These articles should be displayed in the reading room, posted on the archives website and sent to professional newsletters and journals. This information forms a base that the archivist can use to prepare and distribute an authoritative annual report to the archives' primary clientele. As the publicity program grows, archives staff or volunteers can expand on the core material by preparing brief articles describing research projects, notable visitors, accomplishments or materials from the collections for inclusion on the webpage or in an electronic or traditional newsletter.

The second level of publicity involves designing special publicity for specific activities or events sponsored by the archives. Although these are also announced and reported as part of the basic publicity program, they usually require specialised promotion tailored to the needs of each occasion. The effort required to produce customised publicity can be minimised by including the category 'publicity' in a checklist for planning special programs and activities. Attention can then be given in a systematic way to designing the message to be delivered, defining the audience to receive it, identifying the methods most appropriate and to establishing the time frames, personnel and services needed.

Up to this point, the emphasis has been on preparing publicity materials for internet posting and traditional distribution, either directly or indirectly through the media, and on establishing and maintaining a good rapport with professional communicators. But do not overlook the most important public relations assets of all – you and your staff. Opportunities to promote the archives present themselves many times daily in formal and informal ways, within and outside of the workplace. The key to success in this area is to exhibit a genuinely helpful and positive attitude in all interpersonal dealings, be they with staff, clients or the public. Professional expertise, shared with courtesy and good humour, contributes to a pleasant working environment and clearly conveys the message that archives are rewarding as well as worthwhile enterprises.

As a natural extension of this outward-looking mentality, set aside time in the working week to call on or meet with persons or groups whose interest you wish to cultivate. There is a danger here, particularly if you have an outgoing personality, of spending too much time on outreach to the detriment of less exciting but equally important archival tasks. Your time and energy, like your collections, must be protected as well as made available for access and use.

Inevitably, and delightfully, these contacts will lead to invitations to speak before groups or be interviewed on radio or television programs. Anticipating such eventualities, you would be wise to learn a bit about public speaking. Take some images of work at the archives and materials from the collections to accompany your talk. Projected as slide shows, illustrations will add dimensions and increase the impact of your enthusiastic words. It is also useful to look to your staff and to long-time researchers and volunteers for candidates with the potential to share the limelight.

Publicity for the archives is a challenging task requiring flexibility, tact, persistence and a sense of humour. The archival publicist must temper his or her enthusiasm and skills for promotion with the knowledge that creating too much demand without the resources to handle the response can overwhelm or threaten the existence of the very materials and programs he or she hopes to strengthen. However, properly managed, a regular and balanced program of publicity can be an invaluable asset for any archives.

Publications

Publications are close relatives of publicity and are valuable tools for educating the community about the archives, its holdings and services. Also, their impact is longer term and more easily measured since they are produced as discrete items for study and reviewed in professional journals. However, publishing commitments also require considerable investment of resources. Much time and energy, usually of senior staff, go into their preparation, and production costs can be substantial, particularly if multiple colours, illustrations and traditional printing methods are used. The advice on publishing undertakings is as before: proceed with caution and build on established strengths. This message cannot be over-emphasised because failed publications are not only costly, traditional hard copy ones can continue to embarrass by occupying the shelves for a long, long time.

The term 'publication' can be used to describe a wide variety of productions, ranging from a single article to an elaborately illustrated book, to interactive multimedia. Publications today take many forms: traditional print, microform and a variety of electronic outputs including 'live' online downloads. The characteristic common to all is that they convey information to users of archival records and services in a consistent and discrete 'packages' that can be kept and referred to as needed.

Basic publishing

Every archives will find it needs publications to accomplish its work in three major areas: repository services, reference and community education. Whenever possible and appropriate, create traditional print and electronic versions of publications. Publications that can be viewed online and subsequently acquired via download from the archives website can reduce and even eliminate substantial printing, order processing and shipping costs.

Manual-style booklets can facilitate repository services such as depositing or transferring records into the archives by outlining the procedures and documents clients must use to accomplish these tasks. Used in conjunction with personal contact and special training programs, such publications enhance the archives' relationships with clients regularly transferring records under disposal schedules or continuing deposit agreements.

In reference work, publications can enhance existing services in a number of ways. For example, brief answers to frequently asked questions about the archives' purpose, location, holdings, services, hours and conditions of access are useful for everyone. Similarly, how-to information sheets on using the finding aids, requesting records or ordering copies can help researchers learn procedures more quickly and confidently. Descriptive inventories to individual collections can be produced in multiple copies and distributed to libraries and other archives with related research interests. (see Chapter 12: *Finding Aids*).

Checklists outlining the steps and sources for popular research topics such as family or local history are also valuable, as are sheets referring researchers to other institutions whose holdings complement those of the archives. This practice helps to promote the use of the archives collections more widely and enables out-of-area researchers to make more informed inquiries through the mail. Whether traditional print or electronic, all of these publications are simple and effective ways to inform users and help to minimise the strain on resources caused by having to prepare individual responses to repetitive inquiries. And the good news is that most of these are best made available on demand to users via live download from your website. Preparing online publications to download and print forms that are standard, attractive and easy to use, bind and store is essential. No one will want material that presents as a mass of poorly formatted and difficult to manage loose pages.

Additional publications

It is through regular and selective publishing that the archives establishes its wider reputation as a research institution. New additions to the publications family should reflect and reinforce the natural growth of the archives program, rather than be products of momentary inspiration. The archives may begin by publishing an overall guide to its holdings which abstracts basic information, from the descriptive inventories of individual collections, and presents it in a summarised form. A basis for the guide may be established by compiling the individual collection reports which the archives may have submitted to journals or to national guides such as the *Guide to collections of manuscripts relating to Australia.* Such comprehensive work may be further complemented by developing guides to sources suitable for major types of research such as family, local or business history. However, specialised guides should be undertaken with caution as records are often useful for a number of fields and a good index to the comprehensive guide can serve these research interests just as well at less expense.

As mentioned earlier, many archives find it beneficial to combine their publicity and publishing initiatives in a newsletter, announcing and reporting archives activities to the community. The newsletter need not be elaborate – a single page with a distinctive heading will serve. It is more important to concentrate on producing accurate, well-written articles and to publish the newsletter at regular quarterly or half-yearly intervals. Categories for articles may include newly processed collections, program achievements, interesting documents or photographs, a calendar of coming events, special projects and activities, research in progress, notable visitors and staff news.

Regular newsletters packed with images, stories and news of recent or up-coming events will raise the profile of the archives.

The archives will also produce occasional publications inviting clients and members of the community to participate in activities sponsored by the archives, such as exhibitions, workshops, classes and special events such as open days. These pieces serve both as announcements and as forms enabling prospective participants to pre-register for the occasion.

The need for a basic or additional publication is easy to identify. Staff liaising with depositors can report issues or problems that occur in the course of their work. Reference staff can keep track of frequently asked questions and of common research problems and topics. A list of these can then become the basis for ideas for training sessions and workshops, as well as for publications. Having selected those questions and problems that can be handled effectively with a publication, the archivist can then concentrate on the specific information to be conveyed and the best way to present it. To save effort and money, related issues or topics may be grouped into a single publication, provided that the proposed combinations are compatible and the information will not require frequent changes. It is wasteful to put volatile information into a publication that might otherwise be reprinted without change. All publications should be assigned a unique number that embodies their date of production. This number should be altered when the piece is revised, but not if it is simply reprinted. Be sure you create offline archival backups when you post and update your electronic publications and save two copies of each traditional publication as part of your own program's archives.

Good design: A wise investment

Each publication, regardless of how modest, should be designed to attract readers. Appropriate, readable typefaces combined with simple graphics and a pleasing balance between text and white space will enhance the message to be conveyed. Coloured inks and papers can also be effective, but these should be used selectively with the advice of an experienced designer to avoid aesthetic blunders and/or costly mistakes. It is a good idea to think of each of your published pieces, including your letterhead, as family members that share a visual identity. Standard page sizes, typefaces, image specifications and cover formats will help establish continuity of image and still allow each item to have individual distinction. Having a person with professional design credentials or experience create an overall graphic image and framework of standards to be observed in the various components of your program is a worthwhile investment.

Souvenir items

Many cultural institutions, archives among them, offer a selection of souvenir items for sale to researchers and visitors to promote the institution and raise funds. Souvenir publications include postal and greeting cards, notepaper, art prints and posters reproducing graphic items from the collections. More complex examples are diaries or calendars, exhibit catalogues and sets of facsimile documents. Souvenir objects such as carry bags, tea towels, ties, t-shirts, scarves and insignia jewellery are less common in archives than in museums, but many larger institutions do have shops, often operated by volunteers or members of a Friends group, offering such items. This type of publishing is truly an option rather than a necessity. It is expensive because demand is too small and many items fail to recover costs. Furthermore, it can expose the archives' program to criticism from those who view souvenir items as trivial gimmicks. That said, having a small number of attractive souvenir items available can be very beneficial.

Opportunities for the production of souvenir items are frequent, but all should be scrutinised carefully to identify pitfalls and unfavourable consequences. As a general rule, such projects should be undertaken and financed by sources/ sponsors outside the archives and should not be endorsed or condoned by the archives unless they meet stringent quality standards. This policy avoids most of the problems such as high expense and unsold stock that can accompany poorly planned souvenir publishing.

Large-scale publishing

Publications in this category are usually undertaken by archives with comprehensive, well-established programs or by a group of cooperating institutions often working in conjunction with a professional publisher. Examples include publishing the full text of collections of diaries, letters, literary manuscripts or other of personal papers; publishing business/ corporate records; or republishing runs of rare journals, gazettes and newspapers. Other prospects in this category include illustrated publications such as exhibition catalogues and those featuring collections of historic photographs or documentary art. A number of questions must be answered before undertaking such projects:

- What is the need for the publication? Is it compelling intellectually and economically?
- Will all the records be published or only a selection? If the latter, what criteria will be used to select those to be included? Who will make those judgments?

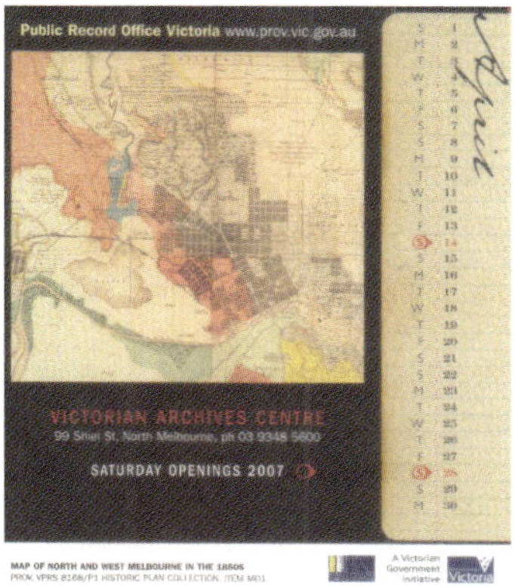

Calendars such as these were developed by the Public Records Office of Victoria (PROV) and Library and Archives Canada (LAC). They are a series of cards designed to fit into an enclosure similar to a CD case. Both showcase special parts of their respective collections using a novel and eye catching format.

- Will the publication be traditional print, microform, CD/DVD technology and/or electronically online?
- Who will own the intellectual property rights, such as copyrights or licenses, and how will these be protected?
- What is the anticipated market for the publication? By whom and how will the publication be marketed and distributed? Is the market large, eager and easily reached?
- What staff, equipment and supplies are needed to prepare the records, the text and the illustrations for publication? By whom and how will these expenses be met?
- Does the archives have the resources and the will, both financial and human, to self-publish and market a quality product successfully?

Unfortunately, the answers to these questions usually discourage self-publishing, but worthwhile projects may still be realised. The answer lies in shifting the initiative and the financial burden of producing the publication to resources outside the archives. Two main possibilities should be investigated. First, the material the archives seeks to publish may be part of a larger body of documentation held by several institutions. This is particularly true with collections of rare journals, gazettes and newspapers. By joining forces with other libraries and archives, the project may be able to attract special funding and produce a more authoritative and significant work than if it were undertaken by a single institution.

Second, the archives should approach established scholars and publishers who specialise in documentary works. These experienced professionals will investigate the proposed project and make recommendations regarding its feasibility. Keep in mind that working with professional publishers requires flexibility and an understanding of the realities of a competitive trade. These outsiders are, in essence, no different from other researchers working on publication projects. The archives is only the source of the raw material; and, beyond the normal obligations to protect materials from loss, damage or legal infringement, it will have no control or responsibility for the quality of the product.

An exception to this situation is one in which the archives develops a formal partnership with a publisher to jointly produce a work. In such cases the archives staff may be responsible for most or all of the work of preparing the records for publication, often to 'camera-ready' level i.e. complete to the point where the publisher has minor adjustments before printing. The publisher usually assigns his or her own editor, designer and publicist to work with the archives to maximise the prospects of marketing success, but will still expect the archives to provide mailing lists and strategies for reaching the largely non-commercial purchasing market. Archival sources are of increasing interest to electronic publishers and vendors seeking to package and showcase culturally specific material. Learn as much as you can about how to maximise the potential of these opportunities and obtain fair returns for appropriate uses. Again, each partner will view the project from a different

Archives Matter! is a publication designed to showcase archives and archivists to the wider public, and to those responsible for archives, be they national or state authorities, or small in-house programs. The publication is the result of a joint project between the Australian Society of Archivists and the Council of Australasian Archives and Records Authorities. As such, it is an example of two bodies with common aims working together to promote, raise awareness of and explain the value of archives. It is highly recommended as a tool for advocacy purposes.

> *Archives have an astonishingly wide variety of uses, from education to employment to entertainment. They help to ensure that the institutions driving our complex modern society are efficient and accountable. They ground our democracy and culture, as well as our communal and personal identities.*
>
> *Australian archivists have responded pragmatically and innovatively to the economic, social and technological challenges of the past thirty years. New technology enables connections with archives users around Australia and the world; archivists have embraced the potential of the Internet to make their resources better-known and easier to use.*

The publication explains what archivists do, what archives are, the variety of valuable, interesting and useful information held within archives, and outlines the resources required to maintain them and to enable the on-going viability of archival programs. *Archives Matter!* can be used by your organisation, or can provide inspiration for you to design your own 'advocacy' tool. Contact the ASA for further information.

perspective, and a successful working relationship will involve compromises, most often in favour of the partner paying the bills.

Whatever level of publication you choose for your archives, the effort should be one that supports the work of the archives as a whole and is reflective of the quality you wish to have associated with your institution.

Exhibitions

Exhibitions will showcase material and attract visitors.

Exhibitions for archives display and interpret archival material to inform or educate the viewer. Exhibitions provide a vehicle for the archives to show off its collections and help fulfil the archives wider mission of encouraging public respect and appreciation for past achievements. Although difficult to measure, the effects of a well-designed exhibition program are undeniably beneficial. Exhibitions inspire interest and involvement which can result in donations of records, funds, services or personal time to the archives. An archives need not be large or wealthy to mount a good exhibition program. Since most archives have very modest facilities and resources, archivists will be relieved to know that research on exhibition effectiveness affirms that viewers respond best to small, well-presented exhibitions. It is the subject matter of the exhibition, its placement and its design, rather than its size or complexity, that determine its appeal.

All exhibitions, however small, require commitments of money and of that even scarcer commodity, staff time and skill. They also present conservation and security problems and are, by nature, temporary in duration. For these reasons, and in light of other priorities and commitments, archivists must not embark on a series of exhibitions simply because it is expected or because other institutions have done so. Rather, the decision to exhibit should be a positive and considered one, made to achieve genuine benefits for the archives.

Planning an exhibit

Once the archives has committed itself to an exhibition program, the first step is to decide the focus the exhibition will have. Below are some questions that will facilitate this process. Is the aim mainly:

- to show off materials from the collection?
- to inform viewers about the nature of archival materials, archival work and/or your archives?
- to educate them on a point of history?
- to interest, intrigue or inspire them?

Ideally the exhibition program will be structured to accomplish all four of these purposes, either simultaneously or sequentially.

After the exhibition goals have been identified, planners must then determine the location, structure and audience for the exhibition. Decisions here are more difficult because they must be reached by weighing many variables, such as resources, facilities, available equipment and existing work commitments, to come up with a workable plan. Sometimes key factors like conservation and security will limit possibilities for the location and presentation of the exhibition. Some venues, though popular, are not sufficiently secure. For example, it would be unwise to place an exhibit case of original archival treasures in the central railway station or a very busy shopping mall.

Small scale exhibitions such as this can be very effective, and relatively inexpensive to develop.

Many archives must mount their exhibitions in donated cases, often obtained from shops which have closed down. While these gifts are most welcome, they were not designed for the display of irreplaceable documents and impose limits on the kinds of records that may be displayed to maximum advantage. Exhibition planners then must determine which of the variables affecting the exhibition are most critical and adjust their choices accordingly to come up with a workable compromise.

If conservation and security considerations seem to be cramping your plans for exhibits, consider using skilful facsimiles or duplicates of printed items instead of unique originals. Reasonable facsimile reproductions can be made by photocopying the originals on to paper of the same age, taken from the blank pages of an old non-archival volume; even better results can be obtained by a skilled photographer. It can often be more appealing to copy and enlarge only the key passage in a document since viewers are not likely to be enthused enough to read many lines of difficult handwriting. The selective use of photographic panels or murals is also effective. All copies of documents and photographs should clearly be labelled as such and identified by the full citation and size of the original.

Once the logistical factors of the exhibition have been defined, planners can turn their attention to content. Choices here revolve around three factors: appropriateness for the proposed audience; the availability of suitable records, photographs and objects; and the exhibitor's knowledge, skill and imagination. You know what you have in your collection that might make an interesting exhibition, but we offer you some ideas for exhibitions related to archives work in Appendix 14.4.

Identifying material suitable for exhibition can be facilitated by keeping exhibition potential in mind as records are appraised, arranged and described or used in the reading room. Staff with these archival responsibilities are often a fruitful source of ideas and knowledge, and exhibition planners in search of ideas and material should make a beeline for them. In fact, it. is highly desirable for archives staff to work closely with public information officers and exhibit designers as a team to produce educational materials and, exhibitions. In this way, the expert knowledge of all is pooled and the resulting project will generate internal enthusiasm and pride.

Different products to consider developing to promote archives: here, a series of bookmarks were developed to promote online biographies about individuals featured in various records of the National Archives of Australia.

Correspondingly, the occasion of an exhibition can provide opportunities for direct communication between the archives and the managers and administrators of its host organisation. Often the direction to prepare an exhibition for an important anniversary or event comes from above. The easiest course is to rush around, prepare the exhibition and present the finished product for applause. But, in so doing, the archivist has missed a valuable chance to acquaint his or her supervisors with the work and resources of the archives. Build upon the initial interest which inspired the directive by discussing exhibition ideas and content with management representatives at key points. Better yet, encourage management to assign a staff member to work with the exhibition team. The exposure to archives resources and the communication developed during the project is an investment that will yield long-term benefits.

Exhibition guidelines

Exhibition planning and design is a specialised field with a rich literature of its own, which archivists are urged to consult, and the sources recommended in Further Reading comprise an archivally relevant introduction. Although unable to offer detailed explanation of the steps involved in mounting an exhibition, this segment will certainly assist those planning exhibitions with and for archives. Of particular value are the summary suggestions embodied in Appendix 14.5.

Exhibition production can be a challenging and exacting task. Supplies for constructing exhibits are expensive, and it is important to measure dimensions and arrange materials accurately to minimise wasteful errors. Be sure to allow space for labels, text blocks and the supports known as *case furniture* that will hold the records safely in position. Many designers prefer to do an inexpensive paper and cardboard model of the exhibition, using copies of the records pasted on sheets cut to size. Mounting the test exhibitions into the case allows the preparer to assess the overall effect and double check all measurements before cutting into the expensive matte board, fabric or Perspex.

Exhibition planners should also consider optional accompaniments such as web page versions, videos, posters, or catalogues to extend the impact of the exhibit over a longer term. For small exhibits, a simple, but attractive publicity poster will suffice. Catalogues, in particular, complement an exhibit, but do not substitute for it. Their main value lies in allowing for more explanation and scholarly discussion than the exhibit panels permit. Videos and coffee table publications are generally reserved for more complex exhibits with substantial outside funding, as high-quality productions can be quite expensive. Web page versions of exhibitions are well within reach of most archives and provide a cost-effective means of sharing the exhibit with wider, more dispersed audiences.

As the exhibition nears the final stages of preparation, arrangements for its promotion should be well advanced. All new exhibits, however modest, should be announced with appropriate publicity. The types and extent of promotion will naturally reflect the magnitude and importance of the exhibit and its proposed audience. A single-case exhibit in the reading room might warrant a poster in the foyer, mention on the webpage and a short piece in the archives newsletter. Having an exhibition opening provides an occasion to bring people into the archives. Even the small exhibit mentioned above could be formally opened and celebrated with refreshments on a day when the reading room is likely to be crowded.

Whatever the scope of your exhibition program, the archives and its staff will benefit most from a balanced approach that is thoroughly in tune with the institution's aims and resources. The community, too, will be enriched from the additional opportunity to explore the archival sources of its heritage and grow in its appreciation of the valuable and important work of archives.

User education: Classes, seminars and workshops

For many archivists, the term 'user education' is synonymous with classes, seminars and workshops. Indeed, these activities are among the most rewarding of all user-education programs, for they are usually enjoyed by both staff and participants and measurably increase awareness of the archives within the larger community. These training activities also benefit the archives in less obvious ways. Staff members involved in teaching gain confidence and renewed enthusiasm for their work when they see that it is interesting to others. Slide shows and videos produced as training aids may be adapted for wider audiences. Teaching research methods often leads to more effective reference procedures and improved finding aids, and many useful publications have their origins in handouts for workshops.

Training for in-house users

As with other user education programs, teaching activities should directly support and facilitate the use of archival holdings and services within the organisation before developing a wider community orientation. Acquisition and reference come to mind as natural areas where regular training sessions can improve the delivery of services to in-house users, such as officers who will be transferring material or using their own records housed in the archives. The purpose of the training is to equip new staff and client representatives to fulfil their responsibilities in such areas as:

- understanding the functions of archives within the organisation
- handling records and archives appropriately
- conducting surveys of archival functions for needs and effectiveness
- developing and implementing disposal schedules
- donating historical materials to the archives
- transferring records to the repository
- recycling or destroying obsolete records
- requesting records or information from the archives

'Introducing the archives': Members of the Wanganui Maori Land Court visiting the local repository to gain an overview of records which may be helpful to them.

An understanding of the nature of the archives' work, its procedures and documentation can contribute greatly to the smooth operation of these important functions where clients interact directly with archives staff.

Volunteers are another important audience for in-house training. A general introduction to the purpose and overall operation of the archives program is as important for prospective volunteers as it is for new staff, and an orientation session could profitably include individuals from both groups. However, it is important for instructors to remember that volunteers do not have the same accountability as paid staff and to understand that all training sessions which include volunteers must explain and maintain that distinction in a tactful and friendly way. Overall, there is a benefit in training staff and volunteers together, as both groups then have a better understanding of the working relationship they will enjoy in future. Some examples of training sessions which could be suitable for volunteers include:

- replacing fasteners, folders and containers
- flattening and cleaning records and other works on paper
- encapsulating materials
- indexing
- conducting oral/video history interviews
- transcribing/indexing interview recordings
- assisting reference staff
- photocopying and/or scanning rare or unique materials
- preparing and updating bibliographies and special lists
- conducting tours for visitors
- giving talks about archives work and using archival sources
- writing newsletter articles

Volunteers are an important asset for the archives and should be well informed about the program and its operations. More information about recruiting and managing volunteers will be presented later in this chapter.

Volunteers can assist in a variety of ways, such as cleaning archival material or encapsulating documents once they have been given appropriate instructions.

Educating members of the community

As a complement to and extension of in-house training, the archives should also develop educational activities for outsiders, whether they be members of the public or individuals from a specialised client group. As mentioned earlier, few people have had any opportunity to learn about archives work or original records in the normal course of growing up; therefore, it is in the archives' own interest to plan programs to bridge this gap of experience and to minimise it in the future. Naturally, the type and content of educational offerings will vary according to the purpose of your archives, its scope and its clientele; smaller institutions may work informally, while large ones may have a calendar full of scheduled events. The main point is that an appropriate level of outreach is necessary so that the archives can develop a base of community support from which to grow.

Mini-classes

The first priority of archival trainers must be to convert first-time users of any service into confident, competent ones as quickly as possible. While this process always requires the archivist to spend some individual time with learners, the amount of that time and the extent of information conveyed can be modified by using group instruction and independent learning aids. A number of archives have instituted programs of mini-classes, half-hour sessions with practical exercises scheduled at regular intervals or when the need arises. Sessions conducted at the point of service enable participants to familiarise themselves with the area and its facilities. Most classes combine talks and exercises to present basic information on the following topics:

- introduction to the reading room
- using archival sources general and various types such as newspapers and photographs
- research techniques and/or sources for popular fields such as family history
- conducting needs assessments and surveys of various types
- drafting disposal schedules

After a few presentations, the staff will know what works best and can develop basic outlines and handouts for regular use. Instructors can include experienced clients and volunteers as well as staff to provide a variety of viewpoints and expertise. In this way, the classes reflect the needs of the users, build upon the strengths of the staff and resources and involve everyone in the excitement of learning.

An individualised alternative or supplement to the mini-classes is to develop a packaged audio tour to orient newcomers to the reading room. Modelled on the museum self-tour devices, these instructional aids employ a portable audio player with headphones that the new reader carries to numbered sites in the reading room. The narrative then explains the sources and how to use them, incorporating tasks for the researcher to do to improve their understanding before moving on.

Seminars and workshops

Extending beyond the immediate need to orient and instruct researchers and staff, the archives can also benefit from sponsoring workshops and seminars that provide a more thorough coverage of archival subjects. In a pure sense, seminars differ from workshops in that they are usually directed discussions of issues and ideas, whereas workshops are practical, hands-on occasions where participants develop skills and techniques to solve problems. Both of these programs are most effective with groups of up to 20 people.

Possible topics for workshops and seminars are as varied as the range of materials within the archives multiplied by the interests of the intended audience. In other words, the choice is vast. However, first ventures should be designed to explore established strengths, both of the collections and of available expertise. A modest half- or full-day program, executed with confidence, will provide a base of success and enthusiasm on which to expand and diversify. Appendix 14.6 provides some suggestions for mini-classes, workshops and seminars on popular themes. It also gives tips on scheduling, promotion and administration which are at least as important to the success of the effort as having a good topic.

Conferences

Conferences are more comprehensive undertakings than seminars and workshops, both in content and in numbers. A program is usually organised around a theme, featuring one or more large general or plenary sessions followed by smaller, more focussed presentations that are offered in concurrent, as well as sequential, sessions to allow participants more choice.

A show of local hospitality is an important complement to a good program, and the larger audience may include out-of-area participants who will need food and accommodation. Special tours, social events and/or entertainments add zest and contribute to the overall quality of experience. However, all of these ingredients content, venue, and hospitality must be measured and combined carefully to ensure a balanced result. Too much or too little of any one of them can spoil the overall effect.

Planning a successful conference can involve a considerable commitment of time. The effort is manageable if the work is shared, and good delegation skills are essential for conference coordinators. Most meetings involve planning in two main areas (program content and local arrangements) and it is wise to select a responsible person to coordinate each of these. Appendix 14.7 provides a schedule and checklist of activities for basic conference planning.

Workshops provide invaluable opportunities for attendees to learn new concepts, and for you to showcase the archives.

Students learn about primary sources, caring for archival materials, and develop a great sense of belonging when included in the archives program. Some students also work in the archives as volunteers.

Conference planners must also decide in advance whether or not to publish the proceedings and make the necessary agreements with authors and printers. Several cautions are worthy of note. Editing verbal presentations into written form is difficult, as is working with multiple authors; persistence and skill are needed to produce proceedings in a timely manner. Conference papers also vary considerably in quality, so it may be best to encourage selected authors to submit a written version for publication by a refereed journal, noting that the paper was first presented at the conference. In this way, the work is published, the conference credited and someone else does the editing and foots the bill.

Activities for students

Students are among the most important client groups, particularly for school and local community archives. In the writer's, view all students above age 10 should have some exposure to the riches of contemporary and original sources as part of their general education. Otherwise, a critical, perhaps unique, opportunity to acquaint them with archives and archival work is lost and the level of community ignorance perpetuated. Few archives are equipped to manage mass onslaughts of researchers, particularly inexperienced ones, and they should not be expected to do so. After all, research is an individual or, at most, a small group activity, and there are ways, in addition to on-site visits, to have students interact with original sources.

Facsimiles of archival materials can be electronically downloaded from the archives website and taken into classrooms where students can examine them and learn to evaluate evidence or pursue a line of research appropriate for their age and level of experience. Projects focussed on local and family history provide excellent laboratories for both exploring and for creating documentary sources. Whatever the proposed project, archivists must recognise that their responsibility is to encourage and support the educational effort, not to design or conduct it; the latter is the domain of the professional educator. Supporting and encouraging activities may include the following:

- Developing policies, plans and procedures to:
  - establish and nurture an appropriate level and scope of interaction between the archives and the education establishment
  - promote and facilitate the use of archival sources and services by educators and students
- Giving presentations to groups of educators to make them aware of the archives and its holdings and to:
  - identify archival materials related to course curricula
  - explain the terms under which such materials can be made available

- suggest ways teachers and students can make effective use of primary source materials

- Collaborating with educators to expand the use of archival materials for learning.
- Working with educators to:
  - identify local structures, sites, events or individuals on which the archives holds documentation sufficient to support a local history research project
  - design ongoing school projects to document community life using a combination of photography, oral/video history and archival research

Policy and planning work is particularly important because it establishes a framework for an ongoing relationship and enables the archives to respond selectively and appropriately to requests for student activities without being overwhelmed. Some questions that archival policy-makers should ask include:

- At what grade level should students:
  - be introduced to primary sources in a classroom setting?
  - become engaged in solving research problems using archival resources?
  - be permitted to do individual or group research at the archives and under what conditions?
- What types of experiences are appropriate for the archives to provide for students and how should they be managed? What facilities and staff would be required?
- How will the products of student work, particularly those of high quality, be recognised and used?

The answers to these questions will provide a sound basis for discussion with educators and enable you to determine a level of involvement in student activities that is suitable for your program and resources. Remember, there is no requirement for the archives to cater to every interest group or demand. It is better to do a few things well. Some suggestions for activities that could involve, and benefit, students are given in Appendix 14.8.

Community support systems

'He who has a thousand friends has not a friend to spare...' is the opening line of a famous couplet by Ali Ben Abu Talab, and one that archivists are well advised to take to heart. While it is true that ongoing, responsible enterprises must plan their programs within the bounds of the recurrent financial support they receive from their own budgetary authorities, a gift of special funding and assistance from outside community sources is always welcomed and appreciated. The ability to attract and utilise extra equipment, services, personnel and funding is an acquired skill and one which can, with practice, become an important asset for a developing archives. However, before hitting the solicitation trail, you must do your homework and adhere to a few basic rules:

- Outside support must always be considered as an extra. It should not be viewed as a requirement for the success of any venture.

- Outside support should only be sought for specific projects of limited duration. Few benefactors are willing to give to general ongoing programs and they prefer to see the results and the gratitude quickly, certainly within the same budget year.
- Develop and maintain a wish list of defined projects, items or areas where special funding or help can be used to maximum effect. The list should describe the commitment required in terms of time equipment, services and funds and should outline the benefits the gift will bring to prospective benefactors and to the archives.
- Before seeking outside support, determine your objectives, themes or messages and requirements (e.g. security and conservation) that the project must meet. While flexibility and room for compromise are integral to project planning, these are the points you must explain and stand firm on when negotiating with prospective donors.
- Prospective donors, whether of time, money, equipment, facilities or services, all hope to gain some benefit which is meaningful to them. Altruism is a nice idea in the abstract, but in the real world donors want a clear benefit in return for their help. Your job is to find out what they want and build it into the project proposal.
- Philanthropy is a very competitive business. Most donors have limited funds and many requests for them. You must find out what their funding cycle is and get your request in early to ensure consideration. The proposal must be well prepared, succinct and specific.
- Develop and maintain a 'hit list' of funding and support prospects. See that key representatives of these groups/agencies are on the mailing list to receive the archives newsletter, calendar of activities, and invitations to special events such as exhibit openings.
- Seek a variety of types of support. Money is only one among many possibilities. The archives may benefit equally from a special piece of equipment, a gift of flowers or refreshments, the use of a meeting or conference venue, free publicity or a complimentary brochure. Services which could be donated include graphic design, typesetting, printing, photocopying, word processing, audio or video recording, consultancy (automation, exhibits, fundraising), photography, music, compere or public speaking duties and interviewing.
- Allow plenty of time for the donor to deliver the gift. Many businesses are willing to contribute equipment, facilities or services during their slack periods. If you allow donors to set their own schedule, you will improve your chances of success.
- If at first you do not succeed, do not be discouraged. Seek advice on how you can improve your proposal and/or its timing in the future and identify other sources of support. Potential donors who cannot help you themselves may be prepared to suggest other prospects and may even offer to use their influence to help you on your way.
- Donors or contributors who have given once are fertile ground for additional aid.

However, you must proceed with caution as you do not want to over-exploit your friends. On the other hand, those who have helped you in the past may want to continue the special relationship and may be offended if they are not asked to do so.

- Show your appreciation in ways which are both appropriate to your institution and meaningful to your benefactors.
- Managing community support and participation well is a demanding task. Designate a capable senior person to manage/handle this important work.

Exploring sources of support within the archives service area is a gradual process. Most archivists begin by asking for specific help or funding for a well-defined project or activity, such as refreshments for an exhibit opening, folders for a seminar or workshop, or guides for an open day tour. The most difficult part of getting started is making that first appeal. Once you have asked and been successful, the task gets easier and your credibility as a worthy cause grows. Offers of assistance may come spontaneously. Attendees at a workshop seeking further involvement with archival sources may offer themselves as prospective volunteers. Community businesses may volunteer their services, facilities and/ or equipment for future projects, particularly if they see their competitors gaining valuable publicity for similar contributions.

Once the ball is rolling, it will gain momentum and it will be necessary to establish regular and formal structures to manage the support to the archives' best advantage. Possibilities include a volunteer program, a Friends group and a special funding body. These may be separate entities or they may be combined under the overall umbrella of a community relations program. If your archives is part of a larger organisation, there may already be programs for personnel to handle these tasks for you. Many educational institutions, for example, have strong, well-organised alumni groups and may also operate a special trust fund or foundation to manage special grants, gifts and/or income generated by educational and special activities. Research institutions, particularly universities, form development offices or special corporations to seek and manage funds for the benefit of the institution. Your first step then is to investigate the potential use of any existing structures for the benefit of the archives. Tapping these important resources can begin with a meeting to explain your program and present a shopping

You may need to get out and about to develop community support networks. Here an archivist speaks to a group of people about archives during Heritage Week.

list of your needs. You need not feel that you are an indigent seeking a handout; rather, you are offering these public relations experts another vehicle for receiving and managing community support. Those without access to in-house support management and will need to set up their own. This task, while essential, is complex and will require considerable time and effort from senior staff.

Volunteers

Volunteer 'gifts of services' are the lifeblood of many archives, particularly small ones. In fact, most would not exist and could not continue without the dedicated efforts of their honorary archivists. The work performed by volunteers covers all archival functions and activities, but experience indicates that the types of assistance outlined in Table 14.2 are useful, easily managed and enjoyable for participants. (The success of each of these activities depends upon the archives having clear and authoritative policies, standards and procedures for each type of work. These guidelines must be user-friendly and meet all the requirements for administrative effectiveness, legal accountability and archival principles).

Function	Activities
Preservation	Replacing fasteners, folders and boxes; flattening and cleaning documents; encapsulating materials; checking temperature and humidity readings; photocopying and/or scanning records/images
Arrangement and description	Indexing finding aids, minutes, newspapers, annual reports, yearbooks, newsletters, oral/video history interviews; preparing/updating special lists and bibliographies
Reference	Assisting reference staff in supervising use of records; photocopying; registering, orienting new readers; explaining finding aids; restacking information leaflets, reference supplies, tools
Acquisition and disposal	Packing and listing records for transfer (to archives or to security destruction facility)
Educating and public relations	Conducting tours of facilities and exhibitions; writing feature and news articles; giving talks about services, collections and research methods; updating mailing lists; helping with mail-outs and special events; staffing special events; proofreading publications; maintaining website
General administrative support	Providing clerical assistance (telephone, photocopying, mailing, typing/word processing/data entry/encoding material for website); administrative arrangements

Table 14.2: Activities that can be performed effectively by volunteers

Volunteer labour, though freely given, is not without cost to the archives. Recruiting, training, scheduling and supervising of volunteers is essential and must be a significant job duty assigned to a reliable staff member. Management must deploy volunteer help responsibly, to augment, rather than to replace, work by paid staff. Volunteers also do not have the same accountability as paid staff, and solving problems such as low productivity, poor quality of work and absenteeism must depend more or less exclusively on persuasion and tact. Many problems can be minimised, if not avoided, by setting standards of qualification and performance for volunteers, along with clear policies and procedures for each type of work they will perform. The status of volunteer should be a distinction that is earned and maintained. Therefore, it is important for the archives to formulate policies and guidelines for recruiting, managing and terminating persons volunteering to work on its behalf. Some matters to address include:

- a formal application process
- a clear explanation of the commitment expected from volunteers, including training, standards of performance and attendance
- sets of procedures and quality standards for each type of work proposed for volunteers
- a system for establishing accountability for volunteers, including procedures for evaluating work performance, for assessing suggestions of suitable projects and duties and for resolving problems and disputes
- a clear understanding that all products, resources and funds generated by volunteer labour are the property of the archives to be managed and administered according to its requirements
- an objective and tactful process for terminating volunteers
- an advisory body composed of staff, volunteers, managers to assist with the management of the volunteer program, including evaluating ideas for new projects and duties

Working with volunteers can be very rewarding both in terms of productivity and in the development of management and interpersonal skills. Particularly in a small archives, where one archivist may be responsible for everything, a committed corps of volunteers can be an essential resource, supplying labour but also insights, ideas, community contacts and feedback.

Friends groups

Given nurturing and good management, enthusiastic volunteers may organise, evolve into or lead the effort to develop formal bodies known generically as Friends groups. While volunteer programs operate within the archives program and are directly accountable to it, Friends groups are separate benevolent entities whose purpose is to rally and focus community support for the archives. Because they are independent, Friends groups can engage in activities that the archives may not be able to undertake, such as raising and retaining money and political lobbying to promote archival courses. At the same time, Friends groups can be a powerful platform vulnerable to domination by those seeking to change the policies and/or programs, even the personnel, of the archives. Therefore, every care must be taken when the organisation of a Friends group for the archives is proposed. Several measures can help to ensure that the Friends group remains friendly to the archives:

- Archives staff should work closely with Friends group organisers to:
  - embed goals and purposes that fully serve the archives with the basic organisational documents
  - limit the terms of service of office bearers and ensure a ratio of new (1/3) to continuing (2/3) members in each executive.
- Archives staff should be encouraged to become active members of the Friends group, but should avoid a disproportionate representation, particularly as office bearers.
- The archives' administration should be welcoming and supportive of the Friends group, but mindful of the limits required to maintain the group's independent legal status. For example, would provision of office space and/or administrative support for the Friends compromise their status?
- The archives should maintain regular official communication with the Friends group, both to inform them of activities and needs and to acknowledge and report on the use of their contributions. Individual members of the Friends should be added to the archives mailing list.
- Show special appreciation for your Friends group by having some Friends-only occasions.

A well-managed, effective Friends group is a great asset to its beneficiary as the extensive literature in the subject attests. Some of the more popular achievements of Friends groups include:

- fundraising for new facilities, renovations and additions
- purchases of major or specialised equipment
- development and/ or operation of programs for volunteers
- sponsorship of publications, exhibits, seminars/workshops and special events (films, tours, lectures and parties)

Friends groups provide a direct means for people of many backgrounds to share their enthusiasm and appreciation for archives and to contribute tangibly to the growth of your institution.

Funding arrangements

Funding for community building is a complex area. Part of the complexity lies in weighing the cost associated with such activities against such difficult-to-measure benefits like community awareness, appreciation and cultural enrichment. Responsible planners must always develop budgets for their work and keep good records of their expenditures. Community building requires significant investment of staff time and this cost should be monitored. Estimates should include internal expenses such as hours of time, mileage, photocopying, postage and equipment maintenance. A carefully devised budget based upon a reasoned estimate of costs will enable planners to make accurate funding requests.

Meeting the costs of community building can be done in various ways. A portion of recurrent funds should be set aside for this work, but supplementary sources (grants, sponsorships) should be investigated as well.

Fees

Charging participants reasonable fees or asking for donations may offset some costs. Fees are particularly appropriate for publications, workshops/ seminars, conferences and other activities offering services above and beyond the normal level. Setting a fee for an event is difficult and requires one to balance a number of factors, including the actual costs per participant, what the market will bear, what related institutions are charging and your community service obligations.

Institutions with regular income from fees and the sale of publications should establish a special account or fund to receive and re-apply them to further community building. Again, this is a specialist area and will require expert advice. While the existence of special fund does enable the program to be more flexible and responsive to unforeseen opportunities, it also has definite disadvantages. It does imply that community building must pay its own way, which is not often the case. Lastly, advisors and accountants must oversee and regularly audit the fund to ensure it is used responsibly and complies with relevant taxation laws.

Special funding

Identifying discreet community-building opportunities among ongoing archival services is also challenging, but doing so is essential to open the way for special funding. To be eligible for special funding from community-based entities such as a granting agency, foundation or private/corporate benefactor, an activity must be well-defined and limited in duration. While seeking special funding is more common among archival agencies in anglophone countries outside Australia, it is a skill of increasing importance and a few tips on how to succeed are presented in Appendix 14.9. Although these suggestions were formulated for developing proposals for external funding, they are just as valid for preparing requests for support from internal sources. All financial analysts, regardless of selling, will be impressed with a well-prepared and well-researched request.

Documentation and evaluation

If greater understanding and appreciation of archives are our goals, we must document these aspirations and measure our progress towards achieving them. Accurate records and reports will identify successful outcomes worth repeating or expanding, and enable us to devise future plans and budgets to maximise benefits and avoid mistakes.

Abstracting information from the records provides a storehouse of statistical data that is invaluable for justifying expenditure and improving forward planning. Selecting what to measure is important as indicators must represent the time and effort involved in accomplishing the work. Accurate use and user statistical indicators are provided in Table 14.3.

- number of contacts made with prospective depositors (individual and organisational)
- number of new gifts/accessions
- number of visitors/researchers
- number of readers tickets/researcher cards issued
- list of research topics
- number of records retrieved/refiled
- list of titles of record series used and nature of use
- list of record services used and frequency of use
- number of copies provided
- number of letters sent
- number of publications produced
- number of events/workshops held
- number of participants in events/ workshops
- number of hours of training and advice provided

Table 14.3: User statistical indicators

It is especially important to document the ultimate benefits (cultural, operational and financial) that users attained as a result of their interaction with archival holdings, services, expertise or facilities. A brief *Register of benefits* explaining the money saved, skills/ knowledge acquired, disasters avoided, community and organisational benefits gained or visibility achieved demonstrates the value of archival work in terms guaranteed to impress even the most critical manager.

That said, each archives must adjust the level and range of client use statistics it keeps according to its own resources and needs. Over-documentation is almost as bad as no documentation, and compiling unused statistics wastes valuable time.

Sometimes it is difficult to rally the energy and/or reserve the time for post-event assessment. One way to ensure that proper reviews are conducted is to select appropriate reporting and evaluation mechanisms and build them into the schedule of activities when the event is first planned. Appendix 14.10 suggests some useful steps.

Communicating your effectiveness to management and the community

As professionals, we can identify four main outputs or resources that our programs offer for use by our various clienteles. They are:

1. Holdings (the bodies of records and information contained therein)
2. Services (storage, preservation, reference, disposal activities and facilities equipment)
3. Expertise (technical consultancy, training, advice and assistance)
4. Experiences (learning to use sources, equipment, facilities to solve problems or perform tasks and thereby gaining new benefits, knowledge, insights and enjoyment)

How we acquire, prepare and present these resources for use, and the benefits/impacts which result from their use, must be documented through statistics and other measurable indicators of the extent to which we have achieved our planning goals. In designing these effectiveness measures, always remember to select indicators that:

- accurately reflect/document the work you are doing in both time and effort
- can be gathered accurately and easily (preferably automatically in an electronically useable form) in the course of normal work activities
- are expressed in terms that are readily understandable and meaningful, particularly to those who *fund and supervise* your program.

Reporting your achievements *regularly* to superiors and 'significant others' inside and outside the organisation must be seen as a very high priority. Keep them informed, with evidence documenting the great value of your work. Particularly helpful is an easily scanned list of accomplishments, each with a brief explanation of the benefits or impact achieved in terms of:

- **worth gained** – in dollar value (actual or percentage of increase) of such commodities as: new users/members; donated services, products, equipment, records; volunteer or student labour, publicity in value of column inches, number of people reached; contacts made, output/productivity increased; knowledge/skill/expertise gained; impact/outcomes achieved
- **savings attained** – actual savings in costs, time and/or effort; expenses avoided by having the essential records, equipment, expertise or services meant that the organisation did not have to pay for
- **risks minimised** – penalties and embarrassment curtailed or avoided by having the essential documentation, equipment, expertise or services and/or not repeating mistakes/failures of past
- some other **indicator** or measurement that is understandable and precious to your management

It will be helpful if you always ask your users to explain how the records have helped them in their tasks/projects, preferably in writing and in quantitative measures (how much money was saved, what costs were avoided, how much time/productive space was saved or reclaimed, etc.) Do this immediately when their gratitude is fresh!

Whatever the context or the nature of your archives/records program, success is best measured in terms of impacts that are positive and meaningful to the host enterprise that pays the bills. Recordkeepers must demonstrate that archives/records played a role in enabling the organisation to make/save money, improve business, win acclaim, attract customers and/or other tangible benefits.

Good documentation and evaluation systems are important for the continued success of all archival programs. Without them, managers and planners lack objective information on which to base future decisions and the means to determine whether or not their efforts have been *worthwhile.* And it is that last word, worthwhile, that evokes a parting thought.

We who labour in and with archives know our work is worthwhile, but unless we inspire the major client groups within our communities to share our enthusiasm, we will be undervalued, even ignored. Involving yourself in advocacy, education and public relations is essential to archival success and effectiveness. Opportunities abound; seize them today.

"We need to get the community excited about archives ..."

section 4

managing more than **paper**!

This book has so far looked at how to establish an archival program and how to manage and promote archival collections. As such, preceding chapters have focused on the general principles and approaches to archival work. Many of these principles and approaches were developed to support the selection, management and use of text-based paper volumes, files and documents. Typically, these records form the majority of records within archival collections. Many archivists, however, will also need to deal with other records such as plans, photographs, digital records and films. These records have the potential to bring the written record to life and provide a much stronger connection and understanding of the past than can be conveyed through words alone. They also capture and present evidence and information that cannot be captured in written form and present a wealth of material for promoting the archives and capturing the interest of the parent organisation and potential donors.

In practice, however, these records present archivists with additional challenges and may require different approaches to their management, care and use. They may also require archivists to work directly with conservators, information technology professionals and archivists working in specialist fields such as 'audio-visual archives.

This section focuses on how to manage this 'other stuff' within the archives. It provides guidance on applying archival principles, processes and services to digital records, maps and plans, photographs, objects and audio-visual records. Each chapter in this section outlines why these records warrant additional care and the technology or production processes behind them. Inherent risks and ongoing costs and effort associated with managing these archival records are also discussed.

While these issues are serious, and the management of these records is often undertaken by specialists in larger organisations, a little knowledge and guidance can produce great results. This section encourages archivists to implement a range of simple, practical and affordable solutions to common challenges. It demystifies the many technical standards and tools that apply to these records and provides ideas for making sure these valuable records don't just languish on the shelf.

The first chapter in this section, Chapter 15, covers digital records. In practice most of us work in a 'hybrid' environment where paper and digital records co-exist. On face value it may seem easier to preserve the printed version of digital records, but this is generally not the case. Chapter 15 encourages archivists to take a more proactive approach based on the records continuum and introduces the emerging framework of standards and approaches for preserving digital records and establishing digital archives.

Beyond the virtual world of digital records, archivists often need to care for physical objects, maps, plans and photographs. Because of their physical size, shape or composition these records require additional management. Chapter 16 considers the key issues associated with these records and how to address them without breaking the budget.

Similarly, moving images and sound recordings add texture and life to the words contained in the written archival records. Collectively referred to as 'audiovisual' records, much attention needs to be given to their storage, handling and use. Chapter 17 covers sound recordings and also introduces the specialist strand of the archival profession known as 'Audiovisual archiving'. Chapter 18 focuses on moving images as both cultural resources and sources of evidence and information (records). It also notes importance of not just preserving the moving image record itself but also the related records such as scripts.

While some records need extra special care and effort a lot may be done without busting the budget. Following the advice and guidance provided by the authors will enable you to bring your archival records to life and provide a much richer experience for your users.

CHAPTER 15

digital recordkeeping

CASSANDRA FINDLAY

CHAPTER ABSTRACT

As organisations and individuals increasingly transact business electronically, records – the archives of tomorrow – are being made and kept in electronic form. Digital media is fragile and hardware and software becomes rapidly obsolete, presenting challenges to the archivist and requiring more proactive intervention in the lift of the record and the systems that generate them.

This chapter explores the nature of the modern work environment and the records it generates. You will find advice on how to build recordkeeping systems that keep reliable digital records, how to use recordkeeping metadata to manage digital records, and ways to ensure that the records we create today will remain authentic and be accessible for use in ten or one hundred years' time as archives.

Introduction

We are all digital record-keepers. Whether in a private company, a school, council or government department or at home, tools like email applications, word processors and databases help us to create and process information. Some of that digital information will need to be kept as evidence or memory of your activities, whether those activities are in support of business, the administration of government or the documentation of personal endeavour. While there are usually ways of keeping that information for immediate reference and use within the application used to create it, these applications are generally not designed with the kinds of functionalities that protect and manage records. Nor do they come with ready-made rules and procedures to help us to know which information must be kept as a record, and how that record should be managed. For this reason, organisations, and sometimes individuals, need to build systems that keep and manage digital records. Archivists and other recordkeeping professionals are equipped with knowledge, skills and techniques to design and implement these systems or to advise on their design and implementation. Digital recordkeeping systems, properly designed, support the work processes that we perform by ensuring that good evidence of that work is made, retained and made available in the way we need it to be. The information that we keep with and about records, recordkeeping metadata, is equally important. Much of what we know about digital recordkeeping is equally relevant for keeping records in any format;

however, there are also certain techniques in digital recordkeeping that we apply to the special challenges which digital records pose, such as technological obsolescence.

The digital recordkeeping environment

The working environment of today has been totally transformed as a result of the information age. Where the bureaucracy of organisations was once a regimented world of forms in triplicate, file registries and typing pools, the typical worker now controls both the means to create information, and the tools to manage it, at their desktop.

The people and organisations whose records have traditionally formed the core of collecting archives and manuscript collections now usually create content using computing tools. This shift has paralleled the rise of the internet as the primary mode of communication for business as well as personal purposes, with official use of email and internet transactions now supported by an international legal framework that facilitates the digital striking of contracts and keeping of evidence of those contracts. The law has also evolved to support the acceptance of digital information as evidence in the courts and for other purposes.

The proliferation of tools for generating digital information has seen the emergence of the idea that one day we may all be working in 'paperless' offices. While there is still no sign of a reduction in the mountains of paper that our work generates, there can be no doubt that the exponential growth in the quantity and variety of digital information forms will continue for the foreseeable future.

The internet is, for many organisations, the primary means by which they conduct business, whether we are talking about a school which is emailing parents or a bank offering online transactions. Laws introduced internationally have served to support the confidence that business and individuals have in conducting business electronically. The *Electronic Transactions Act 2000*, which exists in the Commonwealth and all States and Territories of Australia, provides for equivalence of contracts and other agreements, struck using digital means, with the old paper forms for these kinds of agreements. What this means is that, where a law requires an undertaking or contract 'in writing', or requires a 'signature', these can be achieved using electronic means without the legal validity of the transaction being called into question. The Act also, however, requires that an organisation keeping digital records of such transactions ensures that the method used to generate the records supports the maintenance of the integrity of the records, and that the records remain readily accessible for all future uses.

Increasingly, evidence laws in Australia also reflect the move to the equal reliance on electronic and paper forms. Legislation such as the *Commonwealth Evidence Act 1995* abolished the 'best evidence' rule, meaning that copies of records from electronic systems may be provided as evidence in courts of law. There is still, however, need for the public office providing the records to ensure that there will not be any opportunity for the opposing side to question their integrity. This Act is mirrored in many other Australian jurisdictions.

Challenges

In the latter part of the 20th century, the shift into digital modes of doing business had a profound impact on archivists' approaches to their work. It soon became apparent to the profession, as electronic or 'machine-readable' records emerged, that old ways of identifying and managing them were becoming less effective. An archivist who would once receive transfers of orderly files would be confronted with reams of almost meaningless computer print-outs or, worse, nothing at all. The legacy of a great writer's career being evaluated for a collecting archive was perhaps not left in the form of a collection of papers but rather on a series of near-obsolete disks.

The problems that were identified as electronic records became more prevalent were:

- lack of clarity about where the records were being made, or if they were being made at all
- the decentralisation of information and records management to the user, meaning a loss of corporate control
- poor quality records being kept, lacking in contextual information that was once easily apparent on documents and files
- challenges to the authenticity of records kept in inadequate recordkeeping systems.

Proactive approach

These challenges clearly indicated that a more proactive approach was required. It was no longer possible for the archivist to remain the passive recipient of records at the end of their 'life'. As noted by recordkeeping theorist David Bearman, in his 1994 book *Electronic Evidence*:

> *...the challenge to archivists, records managers, auditors, legal counsel, freedom of information and privacy personnel, and every program manager in an organization is to ensure that electronic data is captured in a way that makes it an electronic record and to address how this can be done...the challenge has become to focus on 'recordness', something we were hardly even conscious of during the reign of paper, and to build on a methodology for ensuring that this ephemeral attribute of collectivities of data is captured and kept.*

A fundamental rethink of the nature of records and recordkeeping was needed, for both the management of records in the context of their creation and use, and for their identification and management as archives.

Principles of digital recordkeeping

Much of digital recordkeeping theory and practice is based in an understanding of information processes known as the 'records continuum model'.

The records continuum model

The records continuum model was developed by Frank Upward and others in the 1990s as a way of explaining the impacts of time and purpose of records on their management and use. Rather than taking a linear view of a record's existence, from creation through to a period of inactivity and finally archiving or destruction, the model presupposes an existence influenced by four dimensions: creation, capture, organisation and pluralisation. In each of these, influencing factors such as evidentiality, transactionality, identity and aggregation, or recordkeeping containers, result in specific recordkeeping activities. Underpinning all of these are space and time, also imparting different uses, custodial arrangements and meanings for records. The model gives us a more complete picture of the complexities and contingencies of recordkeeping, and offers a framework from which archivists are better equipped to influence recordkeeping behaviours in all parts of the continuum.

Driven by a 'records continuum' view, there are certain principles which underpin contemporary approaches to digital recordkeeping:

- the emphasis of the role and purpose of a record as giving it its 'recordness', over and above its documentary form
- the importance of the recordkeeping system as the means to define, capture and keep records
- the need for systematic making and keeping of contextual information that is vital for understanding and using records
- the need to preserve digital records so they do not lose authenticity or accessibility

The nature of digital records

In the digital world, records are constructs or entities that appear as a result of the manipulation of data using hardware and software at a particular point in time. This contrasts with paper records, which are fixed in form and presentation, with their content apparent to anyone viewing them. Some digital records may appear in a different way to different users, for example, a web page viewed using a different browser. Much of the contextual information about digital records, for example, transmission details of an email, may be hidden from the user, or stored in a separate repository from the information in the record itself. Sometimes digital records take documentary form, sometimes they don't. All of this complexity brings to light the importance of precisely identifying a record in the digital environment and distinguishing it from other information, using a consistently applied standard.

The Australian Standard AS4390 – 1996 *Records Management* defines records as: 'Information created, received, and maintained as evidence and information by an organisation or person, in pursuance of legal obligations or in the transaction of business'.

(AS ISO 15489, Part 1, clause 3.15).

There are several important things to note about this definition:

- to be a record, information must have taken part in some sort of business transaction – remembering that this 'business' may be performed by a private individual or a corporate body
- the record must also be retained by the organisation or person involved in the business as evidence that can be relied upon 'down the track'

This definition highlights the fact that, to implement successful digital recordkeeping, there must be a conscious effort to firstly create transaction evidence in record form, and to then keep that evidence in an appropriate way. For an institutional or government archive, influencing these activities means it is influencing the creation and protection of archives. Even in the context of a collecting archive, there is a need to consider tactics such as engaging with potential donors to implement some simple strategies to capture and protect their works for the long term, such as retaining, not overwriting draft versions or using open standards for document formats.

The importance of recordkeeping systems

Central to contemporary approaches to digital recordkeeping is the recordkeeping system. The Australian Standard AS4390 – 1996 *Records Management* defines recordkeeping systems as:

'...business information systems capable of:

- capturing
- maintaining and
- providing access

to records over time'.

(Note: This standard was superseded by AS ISO 15489-2002 *Records Management.* However, both standards still contain relevant and useful information on records, records management and recordkeeping systems).

Recordkeeping systems come in all shapes and sizes. Some are dedicated systems designed solely for keeping records. Some business applications with a different purpose are designed so that they can keep records. Some recordkeeping systems contain digital records only. Some contain all formats.

For example, records management software applications are commonly implemented in organisations to control and provide access to paper-based and digital records. These tools are deployed to desktops of staff members, providing them with the capability to register, classify and retrieve records themselves. Importantly, such tools cannot be implemented without associated business rules, guides to classification and appropriate user rights and permissions. Those implementing such systems must research the recordkeeping requirements of their organisations and ensure that the chosen system, and the actions of the staff, meets those requirements.

This example of a typical recordkeeping system implementation demonstrates that such systems need to be made up of much more than software. They must comprise a range of elements including:

- people
- policies
- procedures
- business rules
- tools
- technology
- training

All of these elements work together to make sure that the records that should be kept will be kept. Importantly, a system must allow recordkeeping to be as integrated into the normal operations of the organisation as possible, so that there is little additional burden on the people doing the business. Properly designed and implemented recordkeeping systems are a rich resource of reliable, useable information and evidence that serve as a vital part of an organisation's overall information assets.

It is important to note that recordkeeping systems for capturing and managing digital records are not restricted to the familiar business forms of emails, documents and the like. Business systems that produce records in forms other than these are common to most organisations. Recordkeeping professionals also need to determine the best means of capturing and keeping evidence of business conducted using these systems. This may mean building functional links between the business systems and a records management software application, or it may mean ensuring that information kept within a business system meets recordkeeping requirements (for example, tamper-proofing, contextuality and linkages to other records of the business).

Designing and implementing recordkeeping systems

In order to build systems for recordkeeping that take account of the complexities of modern organisations and the business they perform, a methodology originally drawn from analysis and design of information technology systems was developed. This methodology, for designing and implementing recordkeeping systems, or 'DIRKS' for short, is capable of dealing with complex and highly technical recordkeeping solutions but is equally appropriate for a modest implementation in a low-tech environment. The value of 'DIRKS' is that it requires solutions to be designed based on an understanding of the requirements they must meet and the environment they will be deployed in. The objective of seamless, integrated digital recordkeeping requires an approach of this sort, based on recognition that there are many variables that will affect the type of solution put in place, and that recordkeeping is most effective when it is an integral part of business process.

The 'DIRKS' methodology comprises eight steps:

Step A: preliminary investigation

Step B: analysis of business activity

Step C: identification of recordkeeping requirements

Step D: assessment of existing systems

Step E: identification of strategies for recordkeeping

Step F: design of a recordkeeping system

Step G: implementation of a recordkeeping system

Step H: post-implementation review

While for some projects the methodology may seem overly complex, it is designed for scalability. Many organisations conduct steps concurrently or combine aspects of steps to suit their purpose. It depends on the nature of the project and the resources allocated to it.

The 'DIRKS' approach can be employed to produce many different outcomes. For example:

- The business analysis steps (A-C) are a means to do the necessary analysis to develop a tool for records disposal – that is, a document that indicates appropriate retention periods and ultimate disposal decisions for records, based on an understanding of legal obligations, business requirements and community expectations.
- The system design steps (D-F) can be employed to ensure that a new piece of software to be used for recordkeeping meets identified gaps in the current system/s, and that recordkeeping is properly integrated with business processes.
- Talking to stakeholders and referring to documentary sources as indicated in Steps A-C can result in the identification of recordkeeping requirements not specifically about retention and disposal, for example, vital records, access restrictions or accessibility requirements.

Some organisations choose to adopt a DIRKS approach for a specific part of their organisation's activities, for example, personnel management, while others conduct a holistic review of recordkeeping across all functions.

A case study of a 'DIRKS' project is included below.

List of abbreviations, acronyms and glossary

DIRKS: Stands for 'designing and implementing recordkeeping systems'; an eight-step methodology to achieve a range of recordkeeping outcomes.

OAIS: An archive, consisting of people and systems, that has accepted the responsibility to preserve information and make it available for a designated community (Consultative Committee for Space Data Systems, *Reference model for an open archival information system (OAIS)*, Section 1.7.2, 'Terminology').

ODF: Open Document Format (ODF) is an ISO standard. An open-file format enables users of varying office suites to exchange documents, such as text-based documents, spreadsheets, charts, or databases, freely with one another. Any software maker can ensure its own application can read and write this format. (*Webopedia*, viewed 10 March 2008, <http://www.webopedia.com/TERM/O/OpenDocument_Format.html>)

XML: Short for Extensible Markup Language, a specification developed by the W3C (World Wide Web Consortium). XML is a pared-down version of SGML (Standard Generalised Markup Language), designed especially for Web documents. It allows designers to create their own customised tags, enabling the definition, transmission, validation, and interpretation of data between applications and between organisations. (*Webopedia*, viewed 10 March 2008, <http://www.webopedia.com/TERM/X/XML.html>)

Checksum: A simple error-detection scheme in which each transmitted message is accompanied by a numerical value, based on the number of set bits in the message. The receiving station then applies the same formula to the message and checks to make sure the accompanying numerical value is the same. If not, the receiver can assume that the message has been garbled. (*Webopedia*, viewed 10 March 2008, <http://www.webopedia.com/TERM/c/checksum.html>)

Recordkeeping metadata

Any digital recordkeeping project, whether conducted using a 'DIRKS' approach or not, will involve consideration of recordkeeping metadata. Such metadata is information that describes, manages and makes records accessible. It has always been around – in the registers, file systems and other control tools that records managers and archivists have always used. The advent of digital systems and the exponential growth in digital records simply meant that it became even more important to define and use metadata effectively to achieve recordkeeping goals. Some simple examples of recordkeeping metadata elements are 'Title', 'Date created' and 'Current location'. The metadata is not only information about records. It is about groups of records, people and organisations, business processes and functions.

Recordkeeping metadata derives from the tools we use to create records, from business processes, business systems, from tools such as classification schemes and disposal schedules, from archival management systems and from the records themselves. Harnessing and using all of these attributes of a record, as well as considering its purposes, helps us with its management and use over time.

The role of recordkeeping metadata

Recordkeeping metadata is essential for giving records the context which defines them, but it is important to note that the metadata takes a more active role than simply profiling or describing records. A well-designed and implemented recordkeeping system should be able to exploit the information contained within or linked to records to activate recordkeeping and other business processes. For example, in an organisation where personnel forms are digital, a staff member's 'date of separation' information can be used to communicate to a records-management application the start date for calculating that record's retention.

How is recordkeeping metadata maintained?

One of the challenges of digital recordkeeping today is how to fully exploit the power of metadata. As noted above, the metadata that gives records their meaning has much potential to play an active role in business processes. While traditionally the metadata has resided in the software we use to keep records, like electronic records and document management systems, and archival control systems, this usually involves duplication of data. The risk of inaccurate data being entered as a result of errors in manual input is high. When records move into archival systems, much data is once again duplicated and the full contextual picture of a record is not captured. A more effective method of deploying metadata is to build architectures that are capable of identifying and using recordkeeping metadata in a range of systems, repurposing it as the record moves through different uses. The 'Clever Recordkeeping Metadata Project' by Monash University Records Continuum Research Group, has been exploring this problem and testing solutions to it (Monash University Records Continuum Research Group 2008).

Recordkeeping metadata standards

Recordkeeping metadata has been defined and standardised by many records and archives groups and standards organisations. Building on the archival tradition of descriptive standards – such as EAD (or Encoded Archival Description) and ISAD (the International Standard for Archival Description) – newer standards are firmly based in the continuum model by offering metadata for records at all stages of their existence. Work done at Monash University in the 1990s resulted in a model for recordkeeping metadata, known as the Australian Recordkeeping Metadata Schema (RKMS). This model establishes recordkeeping metadata to describe and manage records, the people or organisations that create, keep and use them and the business functions, transactions and activities that they document. Much of this information can be found in the systems used to manage digital records in organisations today and serves as a key tool for using and understanding records right throughout their existence, up to and including their retention and use as archives. The records management standard AS ISO 23081.1-2006: *Information and documentation – Records management processes – Metadata for records – Principles* contains underpinning principles for the creation, management and use of metadata for records and AS ISO 23081.2-2006: *Information and documentation – Records management processes – Metadata for records – Conceptual and implementation* issues provides a framework for defining metadata for records in line with these principles.

Designing a recordkeeping system: A case study

By applying a strategic approach to recordkeeping, using tools such as the 'DIRKS' methodology and recordkeeping metadata, recordkeeping professionals are able to design and implement systems that will not only keep evidence of business to meet legal and accountability obligations, but also enhance business efficiency.

Jenny, the archivist for The Independent School, is concerned that important information that was once found in the paper-based correspondence and registers she holds in the school archives is no longer being reliably saved, following the move to electronic systems. Improving this situation is a key concern for Jenny. While her primary interest is in capturing those records that will become part of the school's archives, she also realises that she will gain support for her project by overhauling recordkeeping generally, to improve the efficiency and quality of the school's enrolment and student management processes.

Step A: Preliminary investigation

> *Collect information from documentary sources and interviews; identify and document the role and purpose of the organisation, its structure, its legal, regulatory, business and political environment, critical factors and critical weaknesses associated with recordkeeping.*
>
> (AS ISO 15489.1, Clause 8.4)

Jenny starts to assemble some of the sources of information that she will need in order to develop an appropriate recordkeeping solution. These include: the school's annual report and strategic plan, procedures manual and a history of the school that was prepared for its recent centenary celebrations. She also identifies some of the people that she will need to talk to as part of her project: the headmistress, chief financial officer, the deputy headmistress and the office manager.

Another key source is the minutes of the school Board. These show her that two of the key risk areas for the school at present are the management of late enrolment fees and failure to adequately following up on parent complaints. In one case, this led to an embarrassing report in the local media.

The school's technological environment consists of a wide-area network for the headmistress's office, boarding and classroom building and the chief financial officer's office. This network includes the enrolments payment system, a specialised application, and the usual array of office tools, including email, which is increasingly used to correspond with parents and other members of the school community. There is also a new photocopier in the Headmistress's office that has the capability of scanning or imaging paper documents and saving these to the network (this capability is not used at present).

Physically, the school is spread out over a large area, with some staff working in the boarding house on the other side of the campus, and the chief financial officer in a separate building to the headmistress's office.

The main recordkeeping system relating to students is a paper file system, controlled by a spreadsheet, noting a student number and file location for each file. The files contain print-outs or copies of all correspondence with parents, forms submitted by students and copies of invoices for enrolment fees.

Jenny realises that it will be important to keep track of the sources she has used to gather this initial information, so she starts a simple register where she records the details of each source, including the names of staff members she interviews.

Jenny's preliminary investigation reveals several key weaknesses with recordkeeping in the school, which have a negative impact on its ability to effectively manage enrolments and student issues. In addition, a key concern for Jenny is that the spreadsheet used for managing the student files has taken the place of the kinds of registers which are held by the archives, containing valuable summary information about the students. The spreadsheet was developed without a full assessment of the type of summary information that future users of the archives will seek to access for personal, career and family history purposes.

Having completed this preliminary investigation, Jenny compiles a report for the headmistress proposing the acquisition of an electronic record and document management system that will be capable of capturing and keeping digital records. Jenny's report also notes that her project will include a redesign of the current processes for tracking late enrolments and managing parent complaints, which will ensure that significant archival records will be routinely captured. The report is essentially a business case, noting the costs but also the benefits of the proposed system.

Making a business case for a digital recordkeeping project

Projects that involve investments in information and communications and technology (ICT) can be costly and risky. Therefore, it is important that a case is made for decision-makers that outline the benefits, both tangible and intangible, that will be derived from the system. Some examples of benefits that can be attributed to improved digital recordkeeping in business cases are listed here.

Intangible benefits:	**Tangible benefits:**
Support for knowledge management initiatives	Staff time savings in: • searching for records • retrieving records • filing • analysing records • re-working information
More effective decision-making	Reduced onsite storage costs
Better customer service	Reduced offsite storage costs
More accurate analysis of business activity for planning purposes	Avoided litigation
Better integration with online services	
More opportunities for collaborative work	

Table 15.1: Making a case for a digital recordkeeping project

Step B: Analysis of business activity

Collect information from documentary sources and through interviews; identify and document each business function, activity and transaction and establish a hierarchy of them, that is, a business classification system, and identify and document the flow of business processes and the transactions which comprise them.

(AS ISO 15489.1, Clause 8.4)

In order to implement a system that will properly support the activities of the headmistress's office, it is necessary to analyse the business that is carried out in the office.

The 'DIRKS' methodology recommends two methods of analysis:

- functional analysis, in which the business is broken down from broad functions into activities and then transactions, resulting in a business classification scheme
- sequential or process analysis, which is about tracking the steps of a business process from start to finish

Jenny already has a recently developed classification scheme for the school, and as her project is about the redesign of specific processes, she decides to concentrate her effort on the sequential or process analysis. She assembles the resources that she will need to do this analysis:

- the current procedure manual
- interviews with the office manager and the chief financial officer

The information that she gathers using these sources shows her that the process for managing late enrolment fees involves many steps, with no linkage between the enrolment payments system and the paper-based student file system. The process for dealing with parent complaints involves the staff member printing out the email or copying the letter, attaching it to the student file and then placing the student file in the appropriate staff member's or teacher's pigeon hole.

Step C: Analysis of recordkeeping requirements

Collect information from documentary sources and through interviews; identify the requirements for evidence of and information about each business function, activity and transaction which should be satisfied through records. The requirements can be derived from an analysis of the organisation's regulatory environment and the risk of not creating and maintaining the records. Determine how each requirement may be satisfied through records management processes, and articulate and document the requirements for records. Choose the appropriate records structure which best satisfies each business function, activity or transaction.

(AS ISO 15489.1, Clause 8.4)

When interviewing members of staff about processes, Jenny also began to gather information about the requirements that they and the school have for keeping evidence of late enrolments and parent complaints. She compiles this information along with other requirements that she identified when reviewing the documentary sources, such as the school's charter and audit requirements. She also refers to the Australian Society of Archivists' *Records retention schedule for non-government schools* (Eberhard & Fawbert 2007) and the school archives' own Appraisal Policy, to determine the records' disposal requirements, including the identification of archives. She identifies a number of requirements including those listed in Table 15.2.

	Source	**Requirement**
1	Interview with headmistress (Source 1)	There is a need for a committee of staff and teachers to simultaneously review student complaints as soon as they come in.
2	The Independent School audit requirements (Source 6)	Enrolment fee invoices must be linked with payment records.
3	Interview with deputy headmistress (Source 4)	Parent complaints need to be linked to the students to whom they relate. Sometimes this is more than one.
4	The Independent School Archives' appraisal policy	A policy objective to keep summary records documenting individual students' school experience.

Table 15.2: Register of recordkeeping requirements

Step D: Assessment of existing systems

Identify and analyse existing recordkeeping systems and other information systems to measure their performance against the requirements for records.

(AS ISO 15489.1, Clause 8.4)

Jenny reviews the recordkeeping requirements that she has gathered against the current systems, including the student file system, the enrolment payments system and the office network including the email application.

What she finds is that there are several gaps between how the records are managed now and the requirements she identified. These include:

- access to parent complaints by staff and teachers is slow, and sometimes not all parties receive the file

- not all enrolment fee invoices are printed off and attached to the file, making payments difficult to track
- the method of linking enrolment invoices to payment records is merely a physical attachment to the same file, making it a cumbersome process to cross check them. The spreadsheet controlling the student files is missing some key summary information relating to the student's progress in the school that would be beneficial for secondary users of the records in the school's archives.

Step E: Identification of strategies for recordkeeping

> *Identify strategies for satisfying recordkeeping requirements, which may include adopting policies, procedures and practices, designing new systems, implementing systems in a way which satisfies a recordkeeping requirement, or adopting standards. Strategies may be applied to each recordkeeping requirement separately or in combination. Strategies should be selected on the basis of the degree of risk involved in failure to satisfy a requirement within the business function which the recordkeeping system is intended to support, the existing systems environment and the corporate culture in which the strategy should succeed.*
>
> (AS ISO 15489.1, Clause 8.4)

Jenny realises that, in order to improve recordkeeping in these two key areas of the school's business, she will need to adopt a mix of strategies that will suit the school environment. The strategies she chooses are:

- the introduction of an electronic record and document management system (EDRMS) that will be integrated with the office applications, such as email, and the enrolment payments system as well as with the existing paper files on students, thus allowing access by staff in all parts of the school to the information they need, when they need it
- configuring the EDRMS so that it contains more comprehensive summary information linked to each student file, to assist with faster responses to parent enquiries and better reporting
- rewriting the school's records management policy to confirm that the capture and management of digital records includes email as authorised practice
- updating procedures for dealing with parent complaints and managing enrolment payments, in consultation with the relevant staff
- employing the scanning capabilities of the office photocopier to scan parent correspondence for capturing into the EDRMS
- running a series of training sessions for relevant staff on the new processes and using the EDRMS

Using policy to implement digital recordkeeping

Policies, procedures and business rules of all types can be powerful tools for influencing behaviour and ensuring that recordkeeping requirements are met in the digital environment. Some examples of effective uses of the 'policy' strategy are:

- criteria for staff on which emails should be captured into the recordkeeping system
- document titling conventions
- record-capture steps in operating procedures for common business processes
- reminders in codes of conduct about using templates for official emails
- quality control procedures for digitising of paper-based records

Step F: Design of a recordkeeping system

Design a recordkeeping system which incorporates the strategies, processes and practices endorsed by AS ISO 15489; ensure that the system supports, and does not hinder, business processes; assess and, if necessary, redesign business processes and operational business and communication systems to incorporate recordkeeping.

(AS ISO 15489.1, Clause 8.4)

Having reported on her proposed course of action and gained approval to proceed, Jenny commences the work to bring all of the desired elements together.

The first task is the choice of an EDRMS to provide the core functionality of their recordkeeping system. To ensure that she puts forward the best proposal for this purchase, Jenny conducts a thorough evaluation of the main players in the marketplace, in consultation with the school's ICT manager.

Screenshot of the Serco website featuring MoReq2: Model Requirements Specification for the Management of Electronic Records.

Selecting records management software

There are many considerations in choosing a software application to form the 'backbone' of a recordkeeping system, such as:

- Whether approved suppliers exist for your organisation; for example, this is often the case in government jurisdictions. The advantage of these arrangements is that some evaluation of the required functionality will already have taken place.
- Alternatively, some jurisdictions issue sets of functional requirements or specifications that indicate the required functionality. These also exist internationally, and can provide a useful benchmark. Examples of these include MoReq and the DoD 5015 sets of requirements.
- The level of technical support your organisation will be able to provide. Options for organisations without internal ICT support include sharing networked software with other organisations or hosted solutions, where the software is accessed via the internet.
- Whether the application being considered will be compatible with existing business applications.
- Whether the application will be capable of managing all the record types your organisation generates.

Having chosen the product that she will use, Jenny and the school's ICT manager must configure it to their requirements. In doing this, they address matters including:

- what information needs to be captured upon registration of student files and individual documents, both automatically added and user-defined (recordkeeping metadata)
- what levels of access to give to staff; for example: view records only, adding records or 'administrator'
- integration of the application with office tools such as email with the photocopier, in order to capture scanned paper records, and with the enrolments payment system
- the addition of a field to the student file profile in the EDRMS to link the legacy paper-based student records to the electronically kept records.

To implement the technical strategies she has identified, Jenny knows that it is critical that she work in partnership with the school's ICT manager. Archivists are usually not technology experts, nor do they have the same in-depth understanding of the technical environment that ICT staff have. She ensures that the manager is involved in the project from the start, and works collaboratively with him on the system design.

Building partnerships with ICT professionals

- Involve ICT staff from the earliest stages of the project. They can advise on practical matters including whether the organisation's technological infrastructure will support certain applications
- Set up a steering committee for the project which includes ICT staff
- Ensure the assessment of existing systems gathers information that will be useful for ICT, for example, security or data storage issues
- Include ICT staff in the preparation of system specifications and the evaluation of software applications
- Learn from ICT staff about the organisation's enterprise architecture and discuss how the proposed system will fit within it
- Be clear about boundaries of responsibility within the project

Step G: Implementation of a recordkeeping system

> *Implementing a recordkeeping system should be undertaken systematically using project planning methodologies appropriate to the situation and with a view to integrating the operation of the recordkeeping systems with business processes and related systems.*
>
> (AS ISO 15489.1, Clause 8.4)

The first thing Jenny did when considering the implementation of the new system was to consult with the staff and teachers on the implementation plan. Together they determined that the implementation would involve:

- a pilot of the new system for a period of four weeks to test it and iron out any bugs with the software or the revised procedures
- training sessions in small groups
- publishing the revised procedures on the school's intranet
- Jenny and the IT manager acting as a 'help desk' to answer questions that might come up in the early days of its operation.

"It's going great, boss ... In fact, I've already got all those files on the hard drive."

Common barriers to successful digital recordkeeping implementations

Projects to implement better digital recordkeeping or to introduce digital recordkeeping can be impeded for a number of reasons. Here, some barriers to successful implementations are noted, along with strategies to combat these.

Barrier:	Strategy:
Staff are reluctant to change from 'print and file'	The roll-out of the system should include a well-publicised 'cut-off date' from which no further paper documents may be registered, or only certain approved classes. Monitor this and discuss staff concerns as they arise.
Confusion about how to use the system leads to staff reverting to personal record stores	Any new system rollout should be accompanied by training for all users, ideally in front of the computer using examples of business processes relevant to their business area.
Fear that registration of digital records into the system will take too long	The design of the registration process should aim to use the least number of user entry fields possible. Fields can also be set up to inherit data from applications or parent records.
Specialist staff see themselves as outside of the system	This can often occur with professionals with special information management requirements such as engineers, lawyers or medical staff. Special care should be taken to ensure the system accommodates their requirements and training and communications should include specific examples of how the system will make their lives easier.

Jenny also put a simple form on the school's intranet for system users to submit questions or comments about the system so its implementation could be tracked over time. They all agreed that the system's operation would be reviewed after three months so that any major issues could be resolved.

Step H: Post-implementation review

> *Gather information about the performance of the records system as an integral and ongoing process. This may be undertaken by interviewing members of management and key employees, using the questionnaires, observing the system in operation, examining procedure manuals, training materials and other documentation, and carrying out random checks on the quality of records and control measures. Review and assess the performance of the system, initiate and monitor corrective action and establish a regime of continuous monitoring and regular evaluation.*
>
> (AS ISO 15489.1, Clause 8.4)

Having put in place mechanisms for tracking the operation of the system over the first three months, Jenny also arranged to interview key users about how it was working. The information she gathered showed that:

- the extra work of registering electronic records to files had been problematic at first, but that now staff were finding that the ease of access to records of parent complaints made the process of responding to them much simpler
- the linking of the enrolments payment system to the student files also ensured that these were more easily tracked, but that
- there was some confusion among staff about how to deal with outgoing paper correspondence, and whether to register both an electronic and paper copy of these, considering they were required to be signed before being sent

Jenny realised she needed to add some information to the procedures about capturing records where signatures were involved.

Digital recordkeeping and signatures

Signatures are one of the main ways that we can authenticate ourselves in our personal and business dealings. However, in many circumstances, a signature on a piece of correspondence is a matter of convention rather than legality. Digital signatures are used to authenticate emails and other digital transmissions by using encryption to 'seal' the record, requiring a 'key' to 'unencrypt' it. Some people refer to scanned images of a signature on paper as 'digital signatures'. These are usually a means of authenticating bulk paper correspondence. In both cases, care should be taken to use the technique most appropriate to the business process and to capture the record of the transaction in a way that shows that it was authenticated and by whom, but, in the case of encryption, so that the content is accessible.

At the conclusion of the project, Jenny puts in place a procedure for the yearly transfer of a report from the EDRMS containing the updated summary information on the student files to the archives. She knows that these rich profiles of students' careers will be invaluable for former students and their families, as they use The Independent School archives for generations to come.

Dealing with digital records from uncontrolled environments

While a proactive approach, such as the one used in the case study, is preferable, archivists still have to cope with situations in which they must deal with records from uncontrolled environments. For example, in the collecting archives environment, it may be necessary to receive digital records in a range of formats and on a variety of media from a donor. Similarly, a small institutional archive may be presented with a box full of disks from a business unit, or have to go through the hard drive and email 'inbox' of a retired member of staff to find records that may be required by the archives.

Strategies for dealing with legacy records in these types of circumstances include:

- obtaining any control records (lists, indexes) for the records that may be available
- gathering as much information as possible on the context of the records' creation and management (who created them? for what purpose? when?)
- using the available information on the records to appraise the records
- converting archival and long-term value records to stable, non-proprietary formats (see Preservation, below)
- prioritising based on a risk assessment: where there is little likelihood of archival records existing within a collection there is little value in paying costly computer forensic services to recover information and rendering it in a readable form

Preserving digital records

The preservation of digital records is not only of interest to archivists. Businesses, government organisations and others need to keep digital records 'in house' over long periods of time to meet business and accountability requirements.

Just as paper-based records are vulnerable to threats such as mould or poor environmental conditions, digital records are vulnerable to threats which can compromise them or lead to their loss altogether. Broadly speaking, these are threats to the records' accessibility and authenticity.

One of the most talked-about aspects of digital records preservation is the challenge of maintaining accessibility to records. For digital records to be considered accessible, they must be able to be read and understood by any who has permission to do so, throughout their existence. Obvious threats to accessibility are:

- the rapid rate of technological change, meaning that records may not be readable if the software used to create them is lost
- the vulnerability of digital systems to accidental or intentional damage from power surges, viruses or hackers

Authenticity is an important concept in any kind of recordkeeping environment, but has proven to be a key concern for those responsible for preserving digital records over longer periods of time. Authenticity denotes that a record is what it purports to be. It can be relied upon as representing the meaning intended by the person or organisation that made it. Whenever a digital record is moved from system to system (for example, during a software upgrade) or from one medium to another (for example, if it is copied from a server to a CD), it is at risk of a loss of authenticity. In the paper world, this risk is greatly lessened by virtue of the fact that many markers of authenticity reside on the record medium. A letter has letterhead, addressee and other information within it that denotes its origin and purpose. In a digital record, many such elements are linked, but not persistently bound together, and certainly not always apparent to the viewer.

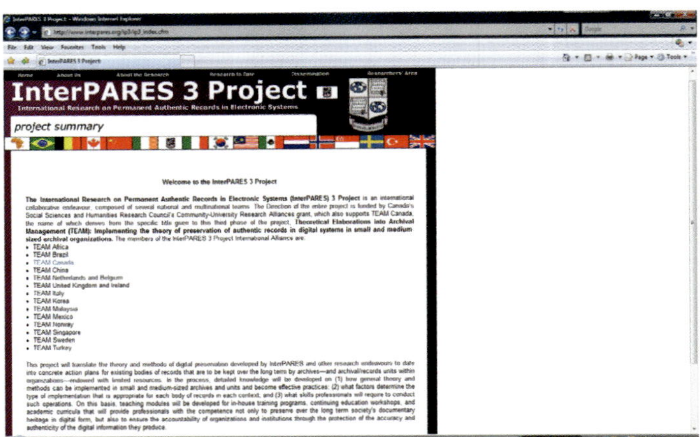

InterPARES: International Research on Permanent Authentic Records in Electronic Systems (<www.interpares.org/ip3/ip3_index.cfm>)

An important project concerned with the question of authenticity was the International Research on Permanent Records in Electronic Systems (InterPARES) project, coordinated by the University of British Columbia. To date, there have been three phases for this project. The first, InterPARES 1 from 1999 – 2001, InterPARES 2 from 2002 – 2006 and InterPARES 3 from 2007 – 2012. InterPARES 1 and 2 is about finding ways to define the elements that are needed to verify the authenticity of a digital record at any point in its existence. As with many questions in recordkeeping, the answer to this problem is largely contingent on the nature of the records that are being preserved, and on the legal and administrative environment in which the records were made. The findings of InterPARES 2 in 2006 indicated, amongst other things, the importance of an effective use of recordkeeping metadata to protect the accessibility and authenticity of records. The work of InterPARES 3 is concerned with building on the findings of InterPARES 1 and 2 and other digital preservation projects.

Recordkeeping metadata and the preservation of digital records

In addition to the basic recordkeeping metadata required to locate and use digital records, recordkeeping systems should also enable the capture and management of information about a record's physical format and technological dependencies, including storage requirements and migration, refreshment or conservation information. These details will be necessary to manage the threat of technological obsolescence. Capturing metadata as early as possible in a record's existence, preferably automatically, about documentary form and any special formatting or presentation requirements, will also allow later preservers or users to understand its original meaning. For example, it may be necessary to know that colours in a digital map or plan are essential to a full understanding of its contents. Recordkeeping metadata is also needed for proving authenticity. This can include information on the entities that have been responsible for the record, custodial arrangements for the record and authorisations given for disposal actions performed on the record.

Contemporary recordkeeping metadata schemas, such as those implemented by government archives for their jurisdictions, contain elements whose purpose is to preserve digital records by, for example, recording technological dependencies. In addition, there are sets specifically designed to support and document preservation processes for digital materials in libraries, archives and other environments, such as the PREMIS (PREservation Metadata Implementation Strategies) metadata set and data dictionary, jointly developed in 2005 by OCLC and the Research Libraries Group (RLG).

An active management regime

While digital records are in use, or are being retained for an organisation's own purposes, either prior to destruction or transfer to an archive, an active regime of management is required. This is equally true of digital records that are being maintained in an archive.

In the 2002 guideline *Future proof: Ensuring the accessibility of equipment/technology dependent records* by State Records NSW, a number of strategies are described which can support the accessibility of digital records. Depending on the context, a mix of these strategies can be adopted. It is important to note that not all strategies will be appropriate for all settings.

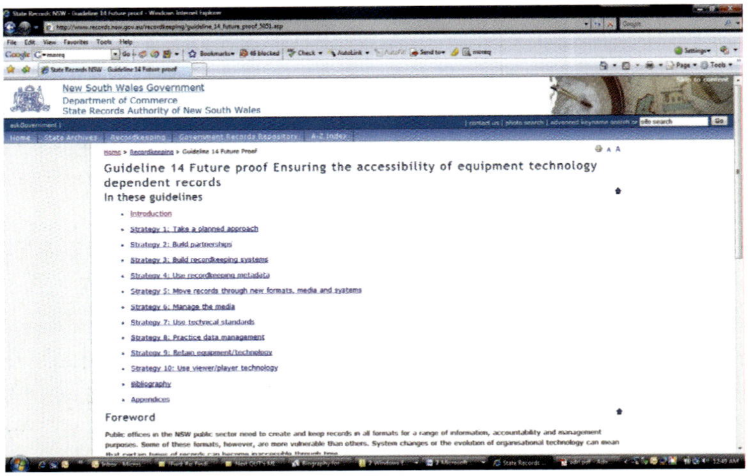

Future proof: Guideline 14 from State Records New South Wales is one of a number of resources to investigate in relation to digital records. (<www.records.nsw.gov.au/recordkeeping/guideline_14_future_proof_5051.asp>)

	Strategy	For example
1	Take a planned approach	• link preservation activities with records appraisal to ensure you are not wasting effort on records of short-term value • build preservation activities into normal planning of records/archives program • conduct regular monitoring of digital records
2	Build partnerships	With: • ICT staff, for technical expertise • management, for resource allocation • external experts, for example, archival authorities or digital preservation industry groups.
3	Keep records in recordkeeping systems	• records must be controlled and identified to allow for monitoring of accessibility • records not kept in recordkeeping systems lose authenticity

	Strategy	For example
4	Use recordkeeping metadata	Keep information linked to records on: • their technological dependencies • migration or conversion activities they have undergone • essential characteristics to preserve and ensure authenticity e.g. map must be preserved in colour.
5	Move records through new formats, media and systems	• keep records on up-to-date storage media e.g. CD, not 5 ¼ inch floppy • bring records forward as versions of EDRMS software changes • manage and document each migration.
6	Manage the media	• carry out routine checks of record media • regularly replace media to limit the risk of damage or loss of records • store media in appropriate conditions.
7	Use open/widely adopted/stable standard formats	• use non-proprietary, or very widely used, text and image formatting standards to make migration easier and to enable records to be reconstructed later if moved out of control systems. Examples of such formatting standards are OpenDocument Format (ODF) or PDF/A (see below).
8	Protect digital assets	• perform regular back-up for disaster recovery purposes • ensure records are protected from viruses and hackers • use password protection and other access controls.

Table 15.3: Strategies for ensuring the accessibility of digital records

Preserving digital records as archives

The archives/records and information technology communities have developed a range of techniques for keeping digital records accessible over long periods of time, including as archives. Digital preservation techniques, including migration, encapsulation and the use of long-term archival formats, may be used by organisations seeking to maintain authentic digital records for long periods, or by archives departments which need to preserve records as archives. In other words, the techniques described in this section can be used as part of a systematic approach to maintaining accessibility to digital records as previously described, or as part of a digital preservation program for an archival collection. Importantly, the technical aspects of digital preservation are only part of the picture. These must be supported by policy, procedures and other components.

Long-term archival formats

Using archival data formats is an approach which is usually implemented in conjunction with other approaches, such as encapsulation or migration, described below. Archival formats are data formats which are based on open standards or which have published codes allowing records to be reconstructed if applications are lost. Among archival institutions that employ archival formats as part of their preservation strategies, the use of the XML format is common. For example, the Public Record Office Victoria promotes the encapsulation of documents in PDF and other formats with an XML metadata 'wrapper'. PDF, while not a non-proprietary format, open, has published codes. PDF/A, now an international standard, is a version of PDF which contains fewer features than the original PDF, making it more suitable for long-term use.

The National Archives of Australia has adopted an approach that converts records to open standard formats such as Open Document Format (ODF), using their application XENA (XML Electronic Normalising of Archives). Open Document Format is '...an open, XML- based document file format for office applications that create and edit documents containing text, spreadsheets, charts and graphical elements' (OASIS ODF 2006). ODF is designed to be vendor- and implementation-neutral, making it possible for people to access, use and share documents regardless of applications or operating systems they are using, so they are not bound by the licences they may or may not hold, or the hardware they use.

In all cases of migration of digital records to new formats, care must be taken when using archival formats to ensure that the conversion does not cause the record to lose authenticity if its essential characteristics are affected.

Migration

As noted above, migration to a long-term archival format is a common preservation strategy. However, migration can be used to better preserve records at all stages of their existence. A simple example of migration in a current records environment is the process of moving a group of digital records from one version of an Electronic Document and Records Management System (EDRMS) to the next, or changing Word documents into PDF documents. This type of migration is a valid approach for maintaining accessibility and authenticity of records over time, while those records are required for current business or are being retained for short to medium periods of time, as described in the previous section.

Migration can be an effective strategy for organisations migrating records forward, as systems change can be made a routine part of the normal ICT upgrade of a public office. The migration must, however, be carefully planned to avoid the risk of loss or alteration. For an archives seeking to implement a long-term strategy for the preservation of digital records, migration is feasible only when the migration activity is strictly limited, for example, to a single migration into an archival format (see below), rather than a continuous cycle of migration for an ever-expanding quantity of records.

Encapsulation

Encapsulation has been described as '...the concept of packaging records with enough information so that someone in the future can obtain or build a viewer to display the records' (Heazelwood, in Ellis 2000). The leading example of the encapsulation approach in Australia is the Victorian Electronic Records Strategy (VERS), implemented by the Public Record Office Victoria. In the encapsulation approach, records are packaged with metadata enabling a user in the future to display them. Each record that is encapsulated can contain multiple documents that together form a record. Other preservation approaches link records and their metadata but store them separately.

Other components of a digital records preservation program

There are a number of other components which must be in place for a successful digital preservation program. These include:

- a policy statement on the digital preservation approach selected by the archive, and the reasons for selecting that approach
- procedures for digital records preservation processes.

Digital records preservation policy statement

In the evolving world of digital records preservation, a policy is an important public way of communicating to the archives' stakeholders what will happen to digital records being retained as archives, and how the approach that will be used was decided on. It is an overarching statement from which more detailed information in things like procedures, position statements and training materials will flow.

Topics to address as part of a digital preservation policy statement include:

- **Purpose:** what function does the policy statement serve for the community of stakeholders with an interest in how the digital records will be preserved?
- **Requirements:** what are the high-level requirements of the archives and/or its host organisation or jurisdiction for digital archives? This might include legislative requirements, business requirements or access requirements. Consultation with stakeholders is a necessary part of defining these.
- **Technique being used:** a description of the technical approach that will be adopted, in plain language, for readers with varying levels of technological literacy. This might also include a brief evaluation of the options available.
- **Responsibilities:** who will do what in the preservation of digital records as archives, who is accountable for the program?
- **Identification of procedures:** a pointer to the authorised procedures to be followed for digital preservation, perhaps in a separate document such as the archives' procedure manual.

The OAIS model for digital archiving processes

In order to establish operating procedures for a digital archive, it helps to have an established framework within which to operate. A commonly adopted standard for digital archiving amongst Australian Government archives is the OAIS (Reference Model for an Open Archival Information System) framework. At its simplest, this international standard describes the components and processes that are required for any trusted repository of digital information, including a digital archive.

The OAIS model is made up of six 'functional entities' that must be in place and interact for a repository to operate. The functional entities from the OAIS model are:

- **Ingest:** transfer of digital records into the archive and the safe receipt of the records
- **Archival storage:** storing, maintaining, locating and retrieving the records
- **Data management:** keeping up-to-date, descriptive information about the records and information needed to manage them
- **Administration:** the elements necessary to deal with depositors, requests for access, overall configuration of the archives and other aspects requiring standards and policies
- **Preservation planning:** ensuring that the contents of the digital archive are not compromised by changes in the nature of the depositing community, through monitoring and adoption of standards
- **Access:** services to allow use of the contents of the digital archive

(OAIS 2006)

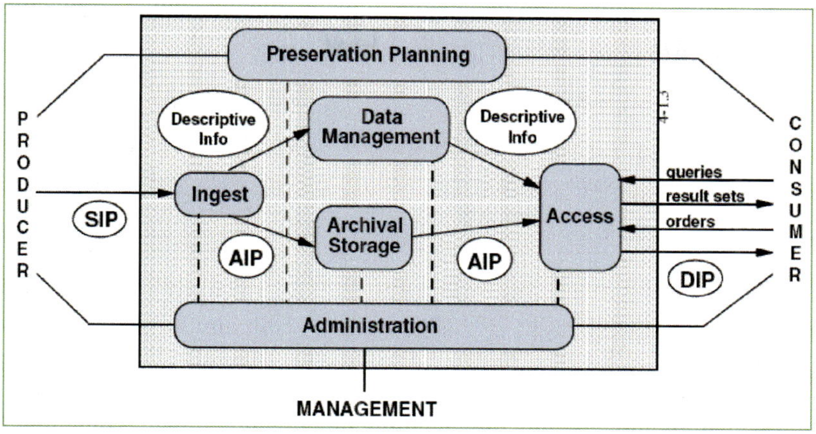

Figure 15.1: OAIS functional entities ((Figure 4-1 from page 4-1 of Reference Model for an Open Archival Information System (OAIS) CCSDS 650.0-B-1 Blue Book)

Each of these entities indicates a need for certain infrastructure, personnel, policies, procedures, standards and services. Some examples of these that might exist in a digital archive are presented below. (Note that this is not a definitive list. The examples of elements provided are drawn from the Australasian Digital Recordkeeping Initiative (ADRI 2007)).

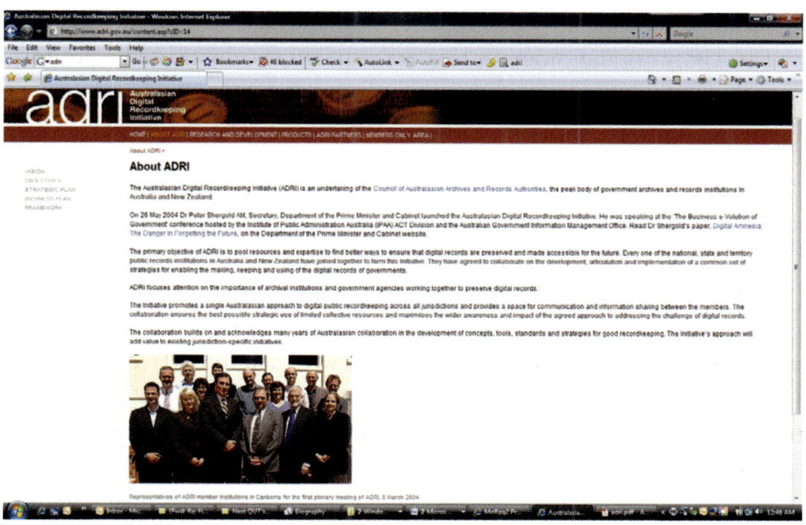

ADRI: Australasian Digital Recordkeeping Initiative is an undertaking of the Council of Australasian Archives and Records Authorities. For more information see <www.adri.gov.au>

OAIS functional entity	Examples of elements in an operational digital archive
Ingest	• procedures on the transfer of digital records to the archives • processes for checking the validity of the transfer, for example by running a 'checksum' on each consignment and comparing it to the manifest • personnel to receive and process transfers • requirements for acceptable methods of transfer, for example on media, online • virus checking software
Archival management	• storage devices for digital archives • software capable of retrieving items on demand • back-up processes • disaster recovery plan • policy on hardware replacement cycles
Data management	• metadata standards • software for checking referential integrity between archives and their descriptive information • database administrator
Administration	• security policy • 'help desk' facility for transferring organisations • routine monitoring of operation of the digital archive • transfer booking system • contractual arrangements with hardware/software suppliers
Preservation planning	• preservation standards • monitoring of record-creating technologies in use in jurisdiction • formulation of a policy for digital records preservation • facilities for testing digital preservation techniques on new and emerging formats and technologies • advice and tools for jurisdiction on preserving digital records
Access	• interface between users and the digital archive, web based or local network • software for the authentication of users • access policy • audit trails tracking access • use statistics

Table 15.4: Examples of elements of a digital archive arranged according to the OAIS model

Implementing digital records preservation

For an archivist working independently in a small archive setting, the prospect of a digital records preservation program can seem daunting. However, there are some simple approaches which can be effective in protecting records against technological obsolescence and loss of authenticity. These include:

- developing a digital records preservation policy, outlining your preferred approach and gaining senior level endorsement
- encouraging the adoption of an open standard for document creation, such as ODF
- ensuring that ICT staff consult with you prior to the decommissioning of any business system
- taking advantage of open source software, made available on the internet for converting digital records into long-term preservation formats (see below)
- ensuring that locations where digital archives are stored are backed up and included in business continuity planning

Digital preservation and repository management software

There is an increasing movement in the digital repositories world towards open-source repository and preservation software. For example, the National Archives of Australia has made its applications Xena (for converting digital content to a 'normalised' long-term format), DPR (digital preservation recorder) and Quest (for accessing digital archives) available for download from the open source development website SourceForge (<http://sourceforge.net/>). Other freely available tools currently include DSpace and Fedora (both for managing digital repositories), the Australian Partnership for Sustainable Repositories/National Library of Australia's AONS (an automated obsolescence notification application), and the New Zealand Library's Metadata Extraction Tool. In 2007, the UNESCO Memory of the World program released an international survey of open-source repository and preservation software, which found a plethora of technologies available to build robust digital preservation systems that comply with the OAIS model. Archivists responsible for preserving digital records should again seek to work with ICT professionals to adapt such tools to their own environments.

Conclusion

Digital recordkeeping is about making choices. This is not simply a choice about paper or digital – in fact, usually it still remains a matter of dealing with both – but rather choices about the best ways to create and keep digital evidence. These choices must be made on the basis of a clear understanding of the business we do, the risks we face and the technologies that we use. By making well-informed choices, systems can be deployed that not only ensure accountability but which actively contribute to business outcomes. In keeping digital archives, we can make choices about preservation in collaboration with a growing international community of groups with an interest in sustainable digital repositories. Digital recordkeeping has evolved tremendously in recent years, as it has moved from the theoretical to the practical, but it must continue to remain responsive to its environment if we are to continue making the right choices.

CHAPTER 16

plans, photographs & objects

KIM EBERHARD &
STEVE STEFANOPOULOS

CHAPTER ABSTRACT

Many archives hold photos, maps and plans in addition to textual records. Many small archives in particular act as the de facto museum for their parent institution and hold many objects in their collection. It can be challenging to apply the archival principles outlined elsewhere in this book to these 'other' records.

This chapter will give you an understanding of how to ensure your maps, plans, photos and objects are managed as a meaningful part of the whole archival collection, rather than as separate, format-based groups. Advice on the appropriate storage to ensure the protection and preservation of these different formats is also included.

Introduction

A great deal has been written elsewhere in this book about the principles which underpin archival practice, particularly provenance, and the need to maintain contextual information about the records in your care. More has been written about arrangement and description of archives, about preservation and storage, mainly with paper records, or their digital counter-parts, in mind. Objects – non-paper items in a collection – are traditionally regarded as being museum items, that is, the items are managed and cared for separately to archives.

Larger archival institutions, such as national or state archives and records authorities, tend not to include objects in their collections, and some of the collecting archives have collecting or acquisition policies which, for many sensible reasons, generally exclude 'objects' from the collection. Some archives, such as the National Film and Sound Archive, focus solely on format, while others exist to house specific collections, such as the photograph archives of professional photographers.

Large archives and those established specifically to care for photographic collections fall outside of what will be discussed in this chapter. Specialist information about the history of photography, the evolution of photographic processes and the differences in photographic media is not included. Please refer to Further Reading for some ideas about where to start researching this fascinating area. Likewise, details of the composition of fabrics, metals, timbers and paper are beyond the scope of this chapter. Advice about the best methods for handling and storing of textiles, maps, plans and objects is also provided in Chapter 4: *Preservation.*

"Apparently we get *this* guy along with Dr Frankenstein's records ..."

This chapter will focus on how to manage non-paper objects which find their way into small or in-house archives. While objects in archives exist in many different formats, they usually do not form a large proportion of the overall collection. However, they are significant nonetheless for the information they hold, the event they captured, or the 'story' they tell of a certain aspect of an organisation's history. Therefore, they need to be managed and cared for in a manner which is consistent with the care and attention given to the paper records in the archive. This chapter will set out some ideas on how to achieve this within resource limits – time, space and budget.

Why are objects part of the archives?

Objects such as textiles, furniture, shields and banners can stretch the conventional understanding of a 'record' but those who work in in-house or collecting archives know that these items form an intrinsic part of the overall 'record' of the organisation or institution. Further, small archives tend to have a museum component which assists or enhances the outreach and public relations functions of the archives.

Most small or in-house archives exist, by circumstance, as both archives and museum, becoming the de facto repository and custodian for a range of items that relate in some way to the organisation or people associated with the organisation. These can include (but are certainly not limited to):

- maps, plans
- textiles: uniforms, religious vestments, banners, flags etc.
- objects: trophies, shields, sporting equipment, old technology etc.
- photographs

Different formats have different storage needs

Different media or formats require different storage conditions, so it may not be possible, nor is it desirable, to maintain all the items of a mixed collection together, even though this may seem to go against the principle of maintaining original order. Order and context can be maintained through the intellectual control of records. Keeping detailed records of the provenance and context of the items in a collection will be far more beneficial to the overall collection than physically keeping them together. This is explained in further detail under each different format within this chapter.

Storage dilemma: an example

You have been given a donation containing a variety of formats: a diary, some minute books, several photographs, an audio tape of an opening address, a woollen blazer, a felt sporting pennant, a straw boater hat, and a small silver commemorative napkin ring. What to do with them?

The entire donation should be documented as a distinct 'collection', carefully noting the donor's name and contact details (for future reference, and to send a thank-you letter of acknowledgement). Any special details about the items should be recorded, answering these questions, and more:

Do they all belong to the same person? What was the pennant for? Details of the opening ceremony on the tape – did the donor participate in an official capacity? Are the speakers identified? The photographs: can the subjects be identified? Are the photos dated? Did the donor form part of the committee whose actions are recorded in the minute books?

Identify each item as belonging to the same donation. This can be achieved by attaching small archival-quality museum labels to each item, or marking each item with a soft pencil (in the case of the photos, diary and the minute books). The paper-based items should be stored in appropriate archival quality boxes; perhaps the minute books form part of a series which already exists? If so, also note their existence in the intellectual control system for that series, noting the specific donation or accession number. The audio tape should be stored with similar media, in a separate box (which is possibly in a separate section of the storage facility). The hat, pennant and blazer should be brushed clean of dust, and/or professionally cleaned, wrapped in acid-free tissue, and preferably stored flat in archival quality textiles boxes, which are large enough to take the blazer without folding it up too much. The collection may not be physically together, but intellectual control of the disparate items enables the collection to be re-assembled in its entirety, should the need arise.

Items of a typical donation to a school archives. Here a straw boater and school case complement some old items used for instruction. A diary, some photos and two books were donated by the same family.

Conservation and preservation – general notes

The chemical composition of most materials is such that they are unstable and change with time. Most objects begin to deteriorate from the moment they are made, and this is true of most of the material which forms any archival collection. The rate and degree of deterioration depends on the environmental conditions in which your items are, or have been, stored. While Chapter 4: *Preservation* covers conservation and preservation in detail, it is worth noting again the factors of which you need to be aware when caring for objects in the collection:

- temperature and relative humidity
- pests: insects, birds, rodents
- pollutants: dust and grime
- mould
- human influences

You may not be able to create ideal or state-of-the-art conditions for each type of object in your collection. You should, however aim to maintain a clean repository which has a stable temperature and relatively low humidity. Fluctuations in temperature and humidity will inflict more damage than stable levels, even if they are higher or lower than the recommended range.

Table 16.1 provides a summary of the types of threats which may adversely affect the collection, and some preventative measures you can put in place to remove or limit the threat.

Threat	Examples	Preventative measures
Physical forces	• Breakages • Shock • Vibration • Gravity	• Limit access to and use of collection items where possible • Ensure items are appropriately packed and stored • Do not over stack boxes and shelves
Thieves or vandals	• Theft • Damage • Graffiti • Tearing	• Limit access to and use of collection items where possible • Security measures in place in storage and display areas • Ensure display cases are lockable • Supervise research or 'public' areas
Disasters	• Fire • Flood	• Undertake a risk assessment • Develop a disaster plan • Introduce measures to reduce risks as outlined in the disaster plan • Install smoke detectors and fire suppressants • Ensure storage shelving is elevated (flood) and covered (leaks)
Inherent weakness	When an object is made from materials which are inherently weak, or made in a way that makes its structure inherently weak, they are more susceptible to damage, through no custodial fault	
Use	An object can be weakened or may have been weakened due to the way it has been used or handled	• Ensure careful handling measures such as using gloves • Use supports such as book pillows and boards for display or when moving the items
Environment	Factors of the environment can cause deterioration of objects: • Light • Relative Humidity (RH) • Temperature (especially fluctuations) • Pollutants (particles and gases)	• Install blinds over all windows • Install UV filters over all light fittings • Environment control to stabilise humidity and temperature fluctuations, e.g. dehumidifiers, fans, air-conditioning

Threat	Examples	Preventative measures
Biological attack	• Insects • Pests	• Good housekeeping: keep storage and display areas as clean as possible • Regular professional pest controls • Inspect collection regularly to gauge signs of deterioration
Incorrect storage or display	• Poor quality materials • Inappropriate techniques • Inadequate support • Inadequate protection	• Ensure all items are stored in appropriate materials and conditions • Ensure all items are adequately supported when stored and on display • Monitor materials and supports for effectiveness and change when necessary • Limit time material is on display • Rotate items between display and storage

Table 16.1: A summary of threats and preventative measures to consider when caring for objects

Table 16.2 provides an outline of signs of deterioration for various media. A program of regular inspections will help minimise damage, as the sooner it is discovered, the sooner steps can be taken either to limit further damage, and/or repair items already affected. If you are uncertain about any signs of deterioration, seek professional advice by consulting a conservator. Remember that signs of deterioration may be obvious by smell as well as by sight.

Taking images of the objects in the collection before they are stored away provides a ready reference to the holdings (as an element of the overall control and management system) and serves as a benchmark against which to measure deterioration, if any, over time.

Damaging factor	Signs of deterioration
Acids	Yellowing, discolouration, distortion of plastics, corrosion of metals, embrittlement
Mould	Visible spores, mildew, spotting, colourful bloom (foxing)
Pollutants	Build up of grime/dirt/dust on surfaces; surface colour change; corrosion of metals
Corrosion	Changes in surface texture or colour; crystalline buildup
Excess handling	Finger marks, impressions, hand oil, grime

Damaging factor	Signs of deterioration
Incorrect cleaning techniques	Surface agitation, build up of cleaning products, removal of decoration, removal of silver (or other) finishes
Inherent weakness	Deterioration related to natural ageing; no other obviously identifiable external factor
Use	Abrasion, wear and tear marks, staining, fading, cracking, creases, folds
UV Light	Fading of dyes, paints and inks; yellowing, patchy colour changes, fragility, weak or brittle fibres; discolouration of wood
Moisture	Damp, cold to touch, presence of water, mould growth, water staining; dye shift
Changes in temperature and relative humidity (RH)	Cracks, splits, tears; surface changes or distortion
Insects	Holes, cocoons, live or dead bodies, droppings, debris from burrowing
Incorrect storage materials	Discolouration, breaks, abrasions (to areas in contact with storage materials)

Table 16.2: Identifying deterioration in collection

Context, relationships and description

Certain contextual information about an item, such as provenance and its relationship to other items in the collection, should be recorded about each item in the collection. This augments basic descriptive information, such as the physical attributes of the item, and its condition. This information about the item, or metadata, can be roughly divided into a number of categories. How you list them or arrange them in your database is not set in stone; most databases and management tools have pre-determined headings and tables. If you are devising your own, or using a less automated system (e.g. handwritten lists, or tables developed on a word processor) you should aim to include information under the following broad headings.

Registration

This is the process of capturing the item or objects into the archival control system.

Registration usually involves allocation of an identification number, and recording, at the very least, some basic details about the item's provenance and some information about context. This latter process is known as accessioning, and has been fully described in Chapter 7: *Accessioning*.

Item number

Each item in the collection, whether it is a hat, blazer, trophy, map, plan, or photographic print, should have a unique identification number. This can be assigned automatically by the database, or can take the form of a meaningful combination of numbers, based on a previous classification scheme, or one you have devised. Combinations might include digits signifying year, donation, collection, accession or series details. This can become quite complex, so think this through fully before implementing.

Identity

This section is where you record information about the identity of the item as part of the archives collection, and establish the relationship between it and other items. The data you record should answer the following questions, at the very least: Does it have a title or a name? If so, record it. Is it part of a larger accession of material? If so, record the accession number. Does it form part of an existing series? If so, note the series number. Storage location? Make note of where it is for retrieval purposes.

Description

This section deals with the physical nature of the item: what it looks like and what it is made of. Note any distinguishing figures or marks, and transcribe, if possible, any inscriptions or notes on the item.

Physical condition

You need to record details about the condition of the item. Is it in good condition? Clean? Damaged? Has a condition report been written? Is one required? This latter information should be able to be manipulated into a conservation report, i.e. to identify items in the collection which may need conservation treatment. This in turn feeds into your budget and forward planning.

If it is a photograph, make notes about its size, whether it is black and white, or colour, and whether any copies or duplicates exist. Again, make notes about its condition, and whether it needs the attention of a conservator.

Context

This is information about the history and provenance of the item. Make notes about when and where it was made, when it was used, any information about the maker or photographer, as well as any technical or maker's details which are relevant to the specific item.

Acquisition

Record details of how the item came to archives: by donation, on loan, by purchase, or routine transfer? Names and addresses of donors or sources should be recorded. Note also any copyright restrictions, reproduction clauses or privacy issues.

Indexing

This is information which will be used to assist retrieval and searching. Make note of any subject headings, names, places, or dates by which the item can be searched.

Other information

Record information about the person who registered or described the item. Note whether there are any access restrictions, and any other information which may be of use or interest about the item

Maps and plans

Maps and plans outline proposed changes to places over time. They not only record physical works undertaken, but also proposed works that were thought of, but never executed. We all live in places that have changed over time, and maps and plans provide the evidence of this change, together with accompanying documentation such as specifications, details and other common paper-based collections.

Types

There are a number of different maps and plans in archives:

- architectural drawings
- elevations and sections of buildings
- maps of streets, places or areas
- sketches of buildings

The size of the object will also vary from A4 to A0 and larger, and the format or type of material will include generic paper, card, blue prints, translucent papers and many others.

Appropriate materials for handling

- use archival quality materials such as archival quality paper and card.
- encapsulate if necessary using a polyester such as Mylar ® or similar.
- hold flat with soft leather weights.

"They've archived their entire planet to Google Earth ... That'll make it easy to plan our invasion."

Inappropriate materials for handling

- any acid plastic, such as PVC (Polyvinyl Chloride)
- metal fasteners: staples, paper clips, pins
- self-adhesive papers or tape

Specialist storage

Flat or vertical cabinets?

Maps and plans come in a number of sizes and formats

Maps and plans should be stored in large format plan drawers or large archival quality boxes. It is best to avoid over-filling any drawer or box, as accessing the maps or plans at the bottom may be difficult and may exert vertical pressure on the object, thereby crushing it. Shallow drawers and boxes are best, so that they cannot be over-filled, and to facilitate easy access. Large format objects, such as maps and plans, should always be well supported and stored flat where ever possible.

Although it has been common practice to store maps and plans in vertical cabinets, this should be avoided where at all possible. Plastic strips and the glue used to fix them onto maps and plans can be highly acidic. Over time, this will damage the map or plan to which it is attached. Some hanging systems use large plastic envelopes rather than glue-on strips. Although the envelopes may be made of an inert plastic, hanging a large map or plan inside what is effectively a loose bag will eventually cause serious damage: the map or plan has no effective support, and might, over time, slip to the bottom of the envelope, effectively crushing itself. The stress placed on the map or plan by suspending it should be avoided, as some papers are very fragile and can fall apart if left hanging for too long.

It is recommended that maps and plans should, where possible, be stored flat with minimal, if any, folds and creases. Large format maps and plans should always be well supported when handled, as paper becomes fragile over time.

Some suggestions for protecting and storing maps and plans

Rolled maps and plans

Many maps and plans come to archives as tightly wound rolls. This is not adequate for long-term storage, and steps should be taken to flatten the maps and plans if they are of a size which will fit into map or plan drawers or large format archival quality boxes.

Gently unravel the roll onto a large, flat, clean surface, and allow the map or plan to relax over time by applying gentle pressure at appropriate places and intervals using soft leather weights. Ensure that sufficient numbers of weights are used to prevent tearing.

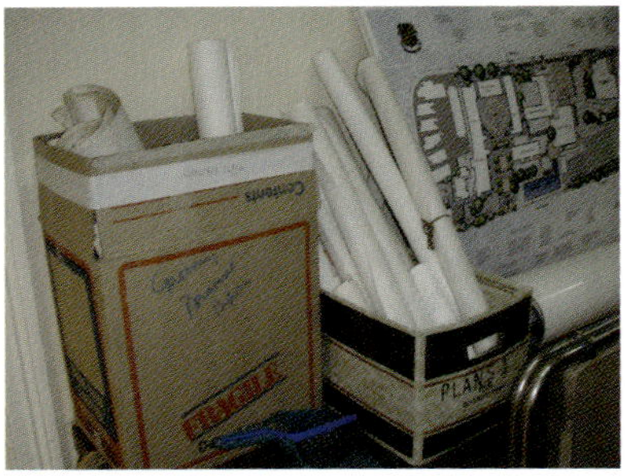

Rolled maps and other plans awaiting treatment

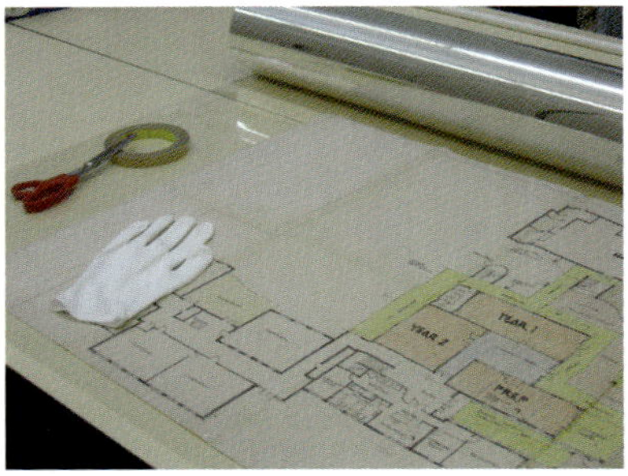

Plans ready for encapsulation

Alternatively, cover with a sheet of paper and a large board that covers the whole sheet and allow the map or plan to flatten gently.

Encapsulation

For more valuable objects, or those that are well used, encapsulation maybe appropriate. Not only does encapsulation provide support for the object when handled and stored, it also allows the object to be viewed and handled without direct interference. Encapsulation involves 'sandwiching' a document between two sheets of stable see-through material, such as Mylar. Two separate pieces, or one piece folded over a document, are held together using strips of double-sided tape. It is essential that the resulting 'envelope' is large enough to prevent the document coming into contact with the double-sided tape. This process allows a degree of air flow across the original document, and is entirely reversible if desired or necessary at any stage.

Note: **Encapsulation should not be confused with lamination!** Lamination involves heat and glue, and causes irreversible damage to the item within. NEVER laminate an original document.

Description

When describing a map or plan, the detail shown should be recorded in the registration process. It is important to identify the type of map or plan it is, i.e. indicate whether it is a map, and if so, of what area, what scale, what date.

If it is a plan, or series of plans, indicate whether it is architectural drawings, specifications or elevations. If possible, differentiate between specifications: electrical, hydraulic, engineering etc. It is also important to note details such as location (street and suburb), and record details such as the property owner, architect's name, the name of the builder or engineer involved, date the plans were drawn, date the plans were passed by local Council (if this is noted), and whether the plans are part of a larger sequence. Many have specific individual numbers assigned by the architect or architectural firm. Make a note of these. It is also important to note whether the plans form part of a contract and if they do, there should be accompanying specifications, and the contract itself. The relationships between all of these documents should be noted.

Identification

It is important to be able to differentiate between all of the information provided on the map or plan. Important elements such as the owner's, builder's or architect's details may vary from plan to plan and they may also not be recorded. If this is the case, additional research may be required to supplement the entry in the finding aids. Providing as much detail will assist in easy retrieval in the future.

Some maps and plans have their own numbering system. Although this may have been applied by the maker, this detail should also be recorded, as there may be reference to these numbers in other series, such as building or planning reports, permits, correspondence files, working papers or other documentation. Cross references to other series that may provide additional information is very useful.

Storage

Maps and plans should be stored in sequential number order based on the registration number or accession number (whichever is appropriate) so that they can be easily retrieved. You may also wish to store similar sized plans together, to maximise space. Although the registration numbers may not be sequential, they should still be in numerical order. Remember to note the location in the control system.

Photographs

'A picture tells a thousand words' and this is particularly true for archival collections! Photographs have become an indispensable part of most archives. Photos are records in themselves, evidence of a moment in time, often documenting more than the intended subject: streetscapes in the background of portraits or, collectively, snapshots of changes in fashion, transport, buildings, and families over time. Photographs are also evidence of technological and social change. A relatively new medium, photography has undergone a number of transformations, the most recent being the digital revolution, which leaves many wondering about the future. An image taken in 1899 is a physical object; it can be picked up and seen without a computer. How will generations

"I've just archived our entire photo collection to Flickr ..."

to come view the digital images of today? Both images, one from 1899 and another from 2008, present an archivist with implicit preservation and storage challenges.

It is important not to be distracted by the variety of formats which are present. The big-picture goal is to manage, or bring under some level of control, the whole image collection. It is true that each format has specific needs; however, the overall process of capturing contextual information in a consistent manner is the main aim. Ensuring that the information, and the images themselves, are useful for research and outreach is essential.

Slides and negatives on different media may form part of the overall photographic collection. Sizes, types and physical condition can vary dramatically.

Types

Most archives will have a range of image types in the collection, each with its own preservation and storage needs. Over time, photographs have been produced using different media and different processing methods. It is beyond the scope of this chapter to describe in detail these differences; it is enough, when starting out, to be aware of the various types you will be most likely to encounter, and to have some basic knowledge of how to handle them. Further specific advice can be obtained from other sources, some of which are listed under Further Reading. Chapter 13: *Digitisation & Imaging* provides details of the types and formats of digital images.

- photographic prints: contact prints, colour, black and white, mounted, framed
- negatives: glass negatives, polyester negatives of different sizes
- slides: colour, and black and white
- digital images: jpg, tiff etc

Remember that photographic prints are created as a result of chemical reactions and interactions. The chemicals are not always stable and some environmental conditions will exacerbate inherent instabilities. The resulting changes to the surface of the print, the image you can see, may not be immediately visible to the naked eye, but deterioration may occur over time. This instability is the main reason we recommend that a buffer such as a sheet of archival quality paper is placed between images, and that archival quality materials are used whenever possible.

Materials to use when handling images

- plastic gloves when handling photo negatives and prints
- archival quality materials such as polypropylene, or album covers and sleeves
- archival quality paper as buffers between prints
- archival quality board
- calico, cotton, linen
- soft pencils for marking, such as 2B
- polyester photo-corners

A photographic collection may be made up of many different types: framed images, loose prints, black & white, sepia or colour - these are just some of the variables to contend with! Different sizes and states of deterioration add another layer of complexity.

Test for Polyvinyl Chloride plastics (PVC)

Materials and equipment needed:

Copper wire (such as used for electrical wiring)
Flame source – high heat, blue flame

Technique:

Heat the copper wire in the flame
Collect a small sample of the plastic to be tested on the hot copper wire
Place the copper wire with the sample back into the flame

Positive result for PVC – flame will turn bright green
Negative result for PVC – flame will remain unchanged

Please note – this test is ONLY to be done on storage enclosures – never on actual archives or objects

Materials to avoid when handling images

- any acid plastic, such as PVC
- self-adhesive albums
- metal fasteners: staples, paper clips, pins

Environmental conditions for images on various media

Different media require different storage conditions to achieve optimal long-term preservation. Following are a number of tables which outline the different conditions required for different photographic media.

For most in-house archives, the best that is usually achieved is a balance between optimal conditions across a number of different media types, budget and other resources, and the practicalities of providing so many different conditions for what could amount to only a small portion of an entire collection.

In general, the best way to maintain a photograph collection is to ensure that the storage facility is clean and dry, that the images or prints are protected from direct contact with environmental threats such as light, water and pests, and that steps are undertaken to minimise big *fluctuations* in temperature and humidity over short periods of time.

Temperature ranges are often quoted by experts, and in standards such as ISO 18911 and ISO 18923. A rough guide to general conditions is:

Room temperature	Temperatures in the range of 16 °C to 24 °C
Cool storage	Temperatures in the range of 8 °C to 16 °C
Cold storage	Temperatures in the range of 0 °C to 8 °C
Frozen storage	Temperatures in the range of -18 °C to 0 °C

NB. Normal operating temperatures of domestic freezers is -18 °C

Recommended storage environments for still images

Glass plate negatives	Benefit from lower temperature storage but there is concern that frozen storage could result in separation of the gelatine emulsion from the glass plate.
Photographic prints	Should be kept in cold storage if possible. This will reduce colour fade and distortion.
Ink-jet prints	Should be kept in cold storage if possible, to slow image and colour fade. Contemporary ink-jet printers use pigments inks that can offer greater permanence than prints incorporating dye-based colours.
CDs and DVDs	Should be kept in cool to cold storage if possible. There is a concern that frozen storage could result in the separation of layers. Surface scratches and flexing of the disc can cause premature failure.

Access, use and preservation: is digitisation the answer?

The potential research value of photographs, and how and by whom they are likely to be used, are factors to be considered. Repeated handling, such as physical touching, and exposure to light and heat, will significantly affect the condition of a negative or a print. It may be advisable to devise a digitisation program for the older or more heavily used images in a collection. A digital copy will make access to, and therefore use of, the image(s) much easier for researchers. It will also reduce the amount of wear and tear an original is likely to be exposed to, especially if it is an iconic image, or one which is in high demand. Digitising the image may increase the effectiveness and usefulness of the archives, a significant point to consider, especially for an in-house archive. More information can be found in Chapter 11: *Access & Reference Services* and Chapter 13: *Digitisation & Imaging.*

This image has been created from a glass negative which was scanned using a flatbed scanner; accompanying software inverted the negative so it is now a 'positive' image. Such results are a powerful argument for digitisation of selected parts of a collection. Remember that this process will yield results when the original negative is in good condition, and you will need to weigh up all the associated pros and cons: available resources, likely use, potential harm to the negative etc.

Managing the bulk of the collection is a slightly different matter: not all archives are able to digitise their entire photographic collection. Digitisation is not yet a realistic solution for the long-term management of *thousands* of photographs. Digitisation is a resource-intensive exercise: just as man-hours, albums, folders, boxes and shelves are required to arrange and house a physical collection, man-hours, scanning equipment, hard-disc space or other forms of digital storage are required for digital counterparts. You need to weigh up the potential benefits against the effort and resources required, in order to make an informed decision about whether digitisation is right for the collection, or parts of the collection.

Access and use will certainly inform which parts of a collection should receive priority attention. A high demand for certain images or an upcoming anniversary may focus your efforts on certain parts of a collection. As with all activities in the archives, gaining control of the photograph collection will benefit from some careful planning and goal setting.

Contextual information and relationships

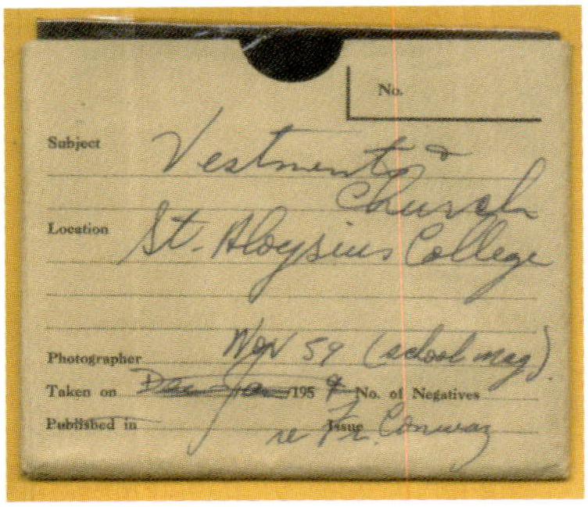

Inscriptions on the outside of a packet of negatives or prints can often contain vital descriptive information about the contents.

Although individual photographs are important, a group of photographs and the interrelationships between individual items within this group take on additional significance. Groups of photographs encourage comparisons, document changes over time and allow interpretations of both the photographers' or collector's intentions or points of view. Groups of photographs may have come from one photographer, and thus document the work of an artist as much as documenting the subjects of the images. Photographs taken annually at a school may have different students in them from year to year, but collectively record part of the history of the school. Recording information *about* a photo is recording information about its context: this gives the image veracity and authenticity, which strengthens its value as a record to the organisation, and to researchers.

Which arrangement and description system?

The system selected for the arrangement and description of photographs depends on a variety of factors. The scope of a repository's holdings is a major consideration. Ideally, the management system or database used to control the paper records can also be used for the management of the photograph collection. Remember that the quantity of images as a percentage of the entire archive collection may affect the decision. Some archives still use a separate system to control the photograph collection, although this practice is diminishing as databases become increasingly sophisticated. Users are also expecting one database to search across all facets of a collection, so a combined system is ultimately preferable. An archive concentrating on a particular subject area, such as a specific area of science or social welfare, or a particular institution, such as a business or religious order, may contain fewer and perhaps more narrowly focussed collections of photographs than will a general historical collection in a university or historical society.

A system needs to be in place to manage all images, whether hard-copy old originals, or the digital images taken toady. You need to be clear about what sort of management tool you will use, and what sort of information you are gathering about the photographs, *before* you start. Regardless of the format of the image, basic information needs to be recorded which is accessible at the same time as the image itself, and which can be used to assist in search and retrieval: i.e. you will need to establish what metadata you will capture, protocols for identifying an image, and a systematic approach to storage, which underpins retrieval. Simply scanning an image, and putting it onto the organisation's intranet for use (using the code assigned by the scanning system) is not managing the collection. Basic metadata about the image must be captured, and this is explained through the description process.

The management system used can take the form of basic information listed on individual forms, which can be entered into a database. There are several available commercially, and some available as free or 'shareware'. (Tabularium is available for free, and contains a component which can be used to manage images. Others, such as InMagic, are available commercially. See Chapter 10: *Using Computers* for more information). At a minimum, you should record enough detail to clearly and easily identify each photograph individually by including a description of the image as a physical object, of what the image shows, notes about its history, its relationship to other items in the collection, details of how it came to be in the archives and, importantly, its location. A unique identifying number or code is also essential.

Description

What is this image of? When was it taken? Who is in it? Who took it? How many copies do we have? How big is it? Is it available for use? How did we get it?

It is vital that information is recorded which answers these questions, and more, when the image is captured into the collection management system. This is commonly referred to as 'metadata' about the image. The provenance of the photograph and the context in which it was created is possibly as important as the subject matter of the image itself.

See Table 16.3 for the range of information which could be recorded into a database about an image.

Contextual and descriptive information: Photographs		
Item number	**This should be unique for each photograph**	
Identity	**Information about the photograph as part of the archives collection**	
	Title	Name of the photo
	Part of a series?	Relate to other items in a series
	Part of an accession?	Relate to accession details
	Previous ID details	Previous numbering or identifying marks
	Storage location	Album no., file no., box no., shelf no., room no.

Content/ description	Information about what the photograph looks like	
	Date range	Date taken or approximation
	Image description	What is the photo of?
	Inscriptions / markings	Note any inscriptions, or markings, including signatures
	Frame details	Is the photo framed? Mounted? Does this add significance?
Physical	**Information about the physical attributes of the photograph**	
	Format	Print, negative, slide, digital etc
	Photographic process	Information about how the item was made
	Black and White or Colour?	
	Original order	Was this photo once part of an album, or part of a larger collection in an album?
	Size	Record dimensions in centimetres (for individual photos)
	Description	Physical condition: good, faded, marked, torn, etc
	Date of condition report	Has one been made? Is one required?
	Copies?	Details of copies made for reference purposes?
	Duplicates	Details of duplicates in the collection

Context	Information about the history and provenance of the photograph	
	Photographer	Name of individual or studio
	Contributor	Details of who sold, gave or transferred the photo(s) to archives
	Original order	Was the photo once part of an album?
Acquisition	**Details of how the photograph came to the archives**	
	Method	Donation, purchase, collection, other
	Name of source	Details such as name, address, etc
	Date acquired	Date the archives took ownership of the photo
	Acknowledgments	Correspondence to donor/ seller
Indexing	**Information to assist retrieval of and research about the photograph**	
	Subject headings	E.g. people, buildings, sports, events etc
	Names	Names of people, groups or bodies in the image
	Place names	Place photo was taken/ background
Other	**Any other information about this photograph**	
	Restrictions	Copyright? Display? Access?
	Registration	Details of the staff member who registered this item, including date.

Table 16.3: Descriptive information for registration of photographs in the collection

Suggestions for managing different types of photograph collections

General comments

Whether you *physically* arrange images according to format, date, by subject, by provenance or by photographer is a decision you alone can make – though format may be the best way to physically arrange your collection. . The physical arrangement should be one which provides the optimum environment for long-term storage, protects the image regardless of its size or shape, and which facilitates retrieval and use of the image as a research object. The *intellectual* arrangement, i.e. the information which has been recorded through the description process, will enable disparate parts of a collection to be reassembled by subject, date or provenance should the individual items have been stored in separate locations. The contextual information will also make note of the relationships between individual images, other items and other images in the collection, enriching the informational value of the items and the collection.

Individual images

In general, the quantity of older images extant in a collection diminishes the further back you go. For example, the sum total of all images for the period 1901–1969 will usually be smaller than the total quantity for the 1980s and 1990s. This reflects the growth in photography as a hobby in the latter part of the 20th century, the rarity of photographs in the early part of the century, and the fact that many images simply have not survived over time.

Images processed into polypropylene albums and sleeves.

The quantity of the older images in an archives may be such that it is possible to describe each and every one individually. This is a luxury you may never achieve for the more recent holdings. A dedicated group of volunteers and/or extra staff may be able to do this for the entire collection if the photographs are a priority for the collection overall.

The decision regarding which images will be fully described must be made in the context of the overall value to the collection, the likely use to which the images will be put, and the resources available. It is important to consider options such as describing all, some, certain groups of images, images about specific subjects, or it may come down to an artificial line in the sand, i.e. all images pre-1969 are described individually, all images post-1969 are described at collection or subject level only.

Once a commitment has been made to describe each one individually, the description and process for description must be consistent for every photograph. It is possible to store the images in an album, or in a box, or in a filing cabinet. The important thing to remember is to protect each image from its neighbour.

You will need:

Nitrile gloves

Appropriate-sized album OR box OR filing cabinet

Sufficient quantity of sleeves/inserts OR archival quality file covers

Archival quality paper cut to size, to fill the sleeve pockets OR interleave between images in files

2B pencils

Pens – permanent pigment-based

Database or information recording sheet.

Method

- Clean the image if required (see Chapter 4: *Preservation*)
- Record all metadata available into management system
- Assign individual identification number
- Using 2B or similar soft pencil, write ID number on the back of each image, selecting a place which will not affect the front of the image, and which is, if possible, consistent for every photo, e.g. very top left hand corner

Albums

- Slip image into sleeve, having noted the image number on the archival quality paper insert
- Note album number on management system
- Repeat for next images and so on

Box or fling cabinet (suitable for larger or rigid images)

- Slip image into archival quality file cover
- Note the image number on the top flap of the file cover
- Insert sheet of archival quality paper between this image, and the next
- When file contains sufficient images, move on to next file (do not over-fill)

Albums containing photo prints. This archives has arranged the collection sequentially.

Images in albums

Many archives will have photographs which are in albums, some dating back many years. Many of those albums will not meet archival standards, for example, the cardboard will be highly acidic, or the album self-adhesive. In order to support long-term preservation, the photographs may need to be removed from those albums. A closer inspection will assist you when making some decisions. Before making a decision to disassemble the album, you MUST ascertain the provenance of the album and its context to the photographs – perhaps the photographer compiled it, in which case it may be very important.

For older albums, such as those which were produced in the first half of the 20th century, you may need to weigh up the pros and cons of removal. Many of these albums contain a sheet of glassine paper in between each leaf which forms a protective barrier (even though glassine is not of archival quality and may increase deterioration rates). If this is the case, do not remove the images without seeking further advice from a conservator. Have a close look at the images and the album; their overall condition will guide you. Have the photographs deteriorated much, given their age? Will removing them damage the photo more than leaving them as is? Is the album itself of intrinsic value?

In general, albums produced from the 1960s–1990s are the least able to support images for the longer term. Most of those albums were cheaply made, and usually include some form of sticky ('magnetic') backing, covered by a PVC plastic sheet. Compounding these issues are the photos themselves. Photographs taken in the 1970s have a distinctive look and colour about them. This is due to certain chemicals used in processing, and the types of paper used for prints. Acidic self-adhesive albums are far from ideal environments for prints or negatives: remove them as soon as possible, even if that means the photos are temporarily stored in an archive box before their final resting place is determined. Time is critical when it comes to acid, harmful plastics and the preservation of photos. Some of the glue will have perished to the point where it is easy to remove the photos – you can use dental floss under the photograph to lever or slide it off. In other cases, you may need to apply gentle heat (e.g. from a hair dryer on very low heat) to remove the glue and unstick the photos. Sticky residue from the glue can be removed using crepe rubber (see Chapter 4: *Preservation*). If it is impossible to remove the photos from the album, it is best to consult a professional conservator, or make high-quality copies of the originals to store appropriately.

Types of albums and enclosures used for photo prints, many of which are not archival quality.

If you have made the decision to remove the images from an old album, you must take care to preserve as much of the original order and contextual information as possible. Ideally, you will simply be moving the 'collection' from one housing or casing to another which is much more stable. It is important to retain the images in the same order as existed in the original album, if indeed some sort of order was evident. (This may have been as simple as a rough chronological order). If this not possible due to the varying size of photos, record the original order into the control system to preserve that piece of contextual information. When describing the images, you will need to make some sort of note indicating that these images were originally together in one album, possibly in a particular order. This might be a specific numerical or alphabetical system. You will also need to record any information which was present in the album, such as captions indicating date, subject matter, names, dates, places etc.

NB: Capturing the inscriptions

This image has an inscription on the front added by the photographic studio. The reverse contains even more information – a newscutting which includes a notice of the performance.

Some images contain a wealth of information on the back. This may take the form of handwritten notes, signatures, or, in some cases, news cuttings which have been attached with glue. It is important to capture the information included as inscription: this is contextual information. That said, it is also important to remember that the information may not be precise: often the names of people are inscribed after the event, and errors can easily occur.

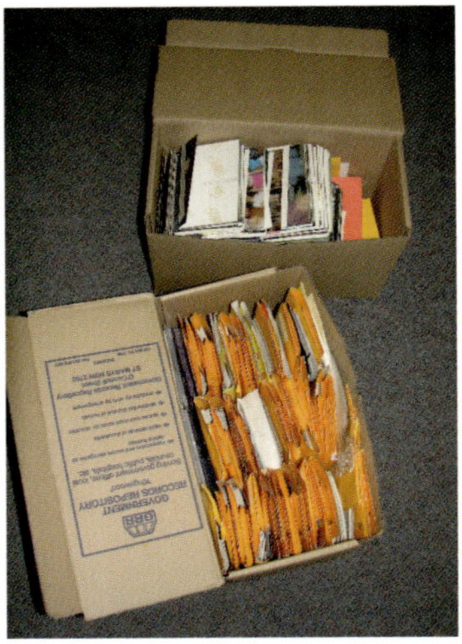

Boxes of unprocessed images – usually 6" x 4" prints – are a normal sight in many small archives.

Masses of 'happy snaps'

In general, most photograph collections contain large quantities of 6" x 4" prints (usually colour), common from 1980s or 1990s onwards. This reflects the increased availability of inexpensive or disposable photographic equipment and processing options. Arranging all of them into archival-quality albums may be prohibitive, due to the time and expense involved. However, there is a need to know, in general terms, what's there, for reference enquiries and general information, and to gain an overview of the entire collection.

Due to the quantity, it may not be immediately possible to identify and number each print uniquely. It is possible, however, to arrange these 'candids' or 'happy snaps' into annual lots, and identify them according to subject, date and/or photographer. This method facilitates a quick arrangement of large quantities of images into smaller 'chunks' which can later be fully arranged and described. This is an ideal task for a volunteer, or groups of volunteers.

This is the result of processing masses of 'happy snaps' using the method described overleaf.

You will need:

Archival quality boxes
Archival quality card
Archival quality paper
Group of volunteers (optional)
2B pencils
Pens – permanent, pigment-based
Guillotine or scissors

Method:

- use boxes designed originally for index cards (or similar), but which hold 6" x 4" prints very well.
- Make dividers from acid-free card, to stand approximately 1cm higher than the top of the prints.
- Make dividers from acid-free paper, cut to the same size as the prints.
- Cull the photographs. (See tips)
- Pre-sort images into annual lots, if this is possible. If not, use decades as a guide. Features such as clothes, cars or even the quality of the images can assist you in determining this.
- Work on one year or decade at a time.
- Remove photos from the envelopes or bundles in which they came, carefully noting any information contained on those envelopes, such as date, subject matter, or who they came from.
- Transfer this information to one of the dividers, ensuring that this is visible over the top of the print.
- Make corresponding entries into your database, or photographic indexes/lists.
- Place each photo on its edge, not stacked on top of one another.
- Interleave one sheet of pre-cut archival quality paper between each photo for protection.
- Continue in this manner until all photos for one year have been sorted into subject matter.

NB: If photos exist which are outside standard 6" x 4" format, use a different sized box.

A larger box has been used to hold larger prints. Unfortunately, the photographic studio has laminated the prints given to the archives. This is irreversible, and is likely to adversely affect the images over time.

Check list for culling

There will probably be too many images documenting one event, especially if it occurred in recent times. There is no point in keeping hundreds of images of the same subject. Resources are too scarce. Culling the images is a sensible exercise, but it must be applied consistently. Here are some tips for selecting images:

1. Can you see faces?
   If yes, then keep. If no, then check against point 3.
2. Is it blurry?
   If yes, throw it out.
3. Does it show buildings/grounds/district?
   If yes, keep.
4. Is it a bad photo, but one that is unique, i.e. no other even close in terms of 'historical' detail?
   If yes, keep it.

The photographs to be destroyed should be done so in a sensitive manner. Secure shredding is the best option.

If you are culling duplicates, an option may be to store the duplicates in a separate container (not necessarily archival quality). These can be used for displays, reference, or can be given away to people associated with the organisation.

Framed or oversized images

Many older images, or those which are considered to be significant to an organisation, are framed. The frame itself can be of value, or can hold clues or information about the provenance of the images. Many older images have been well protected over time by the fact of their framing, and this alone could be a good reason to retain the frame.

Alternatively, the frames can be generic in style and type, may be causing damage to the image, and contribute no value to the image whatsoever. Research into these aspects will be required to determine this. If the latter is the case, and space is an issue, it may be advisable to remove the image from its frame, and store the image as just that, an image. However, if the framing is of value (archival, monetary, sentimental etc), you will need to make provision to store the image as an object, which will take up considerably more room, and require slightly different treatment, than the images you have in albums, boxes or filing cabinets.

Ideally, you will be able to install banks of sliding racks upon which to hang framed images. The racks can also be used to hang and store works of art; indeed the idea of the racks was 'borrowed' from specialist gallery and museum storage systems. The racks are usually made of heavy gauge wire, and should be of sufficient size to hold several frames securely, each without touching its neighbour.

Alternatively, you may need to use wall space in the archives office or store to hang the frames, which would be done in the same way as a traditional wall hanging. The most common, although definitely not ideal, method is to store the frames on the floor in a little-used area, leaning against the wall or cupboard, with the image facing inwards, i.e. so that it is protected. It is best to wrap framed items stored this way with polyethylene foam or some other flexible, inert plastic. Use a palette or some other raised plinth to keep the frames off the floor in case of flooding.

Record contextual information about the image in the same way you would for a standard individual image. Note location as being the hanging racks – you might assign a rack number for each sliding unit, or the wall upon which it is hanging, for example, Room 3, southern wall.

Annual series of images

Some organisations, such as schools, or sporting teams, have annual photographs taken. It is reasonably certain that the subject matter will remain consistent over the years: prefects, First Fifteen football team, graduating class etc. Questions arise as to how these should be arranged. As these images form part of the official record of the organisation, we think it's important to record the information about them as a collection, but on an individual level. The images will most likely have been taken by a professional photographer, will have been taken on one day, or sequence of dates, and will have been presented to the organisation as a complete package. This is significant contextual information in itself: added to the previous years' worth of official photographs, the images form an outstanding record of change and growth for the organisation.

As mentioned in the general comments, the physical arrangement of images is not critical (as long as they are protected for long-term preservation). However, when thinking about arrangement in terms of these annual images, some pros and cons should be considered. The physical location of images will begin to matter less as images increasingly become virtual objects. Should they be arranged according to date, or by subject?

Arranged by date – annual series	Arranged by subject
All of one year together	Need to search through several files/ locations for the whole of one year
Need to search through several files for historical overview of one team	All for one team together, e.g. First XI over many years
Certain of date, if not included as part of the image	Not certain of the date: must rely on anecdotal evidence if date not included as part of the image
Know what was taken, what was not	Unsure of which images were taken: need to look through many files to ascertain

Table 16.4: Pros and cons of annual or subject arrangement of photos

Digital images

This section will not go into detail about the technicalities of digital images and their various formats. That is beyond the scope of this chapter. However, some simple tips for managing the images are offered.

The key to managing digital images is to use the same principles as you would all other images. The main difference between digital images, and those of earlier print formats, is the need to use a computer or intermediary device to view digital images. It is important to capture contextual information about the images, such as date, photographer, subject matter; some of this will have been embedded in the metadata surrounding each image. It is important to develop, impose or maintain some order for these images, simply because there are potentially so many. Further, digital images in an archives collection will have come from a variety of sources, in a variety of ways: as direct downloads from the camera itself, as attachments to an email, or as files stored on CD, DVD, or USB device. Older prints which have been scanned will also form part of the digital collection.

Increasingly, images come to archives as digital files on CD, DVD or stored on the computer network of the parent organisation. Suggestions for managing these images are provided below and overleaf.

Regardless of how the images come to archives, each individual image will have an intrinsic, unique file title. This will have been 'assigned' by the device that 'took' the image i.e. the camera or the scanner. This file title usually consists of numbers or letters, or most commonly, a combination of both. This file 'title' usually does not contain any easily discernible descriptive information. An example is: PCO 00567.jpg. Alternatively, the person who took the image, or scanned it, may have assigned a file title to each image or group of images, which is slightly more descriptive, e.g. Building_Opening_Feb_2008_001.jpg. In either case, you will need to develop a system which facilitates easy identification of images.

Most basic computer software now includes some form of image viewing and management option or application. Most commonly, images will be saved into that application, which also offers several ways for you to see the image files when opening the application. File titles can be shown as lists, or as thumbnails or filmstrips of the images, among a number of options.

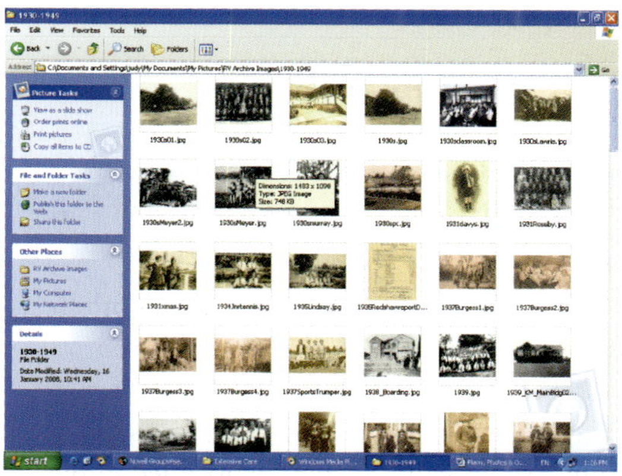

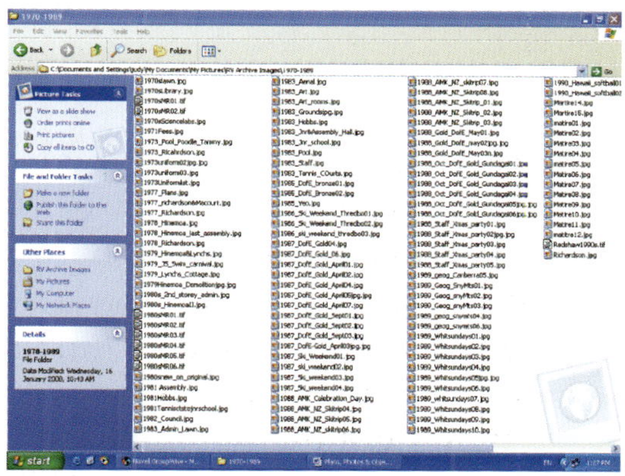

While 'thumbnails', i.e. small versions of the full image, are a useful way to visually recognise the image you are looking for, it is not enough to rely on this as the only form of retrieval, or indeed, description. Further context needs to be given to the images to provide a greater level of detail, to distinguish subjects and to provide a level of authenticity for future users. A database specifically designed for the management of images can achieve this. If such software is beyond the archives budget, there are simple ways to temporarily manage digital images by applying some simple, consistent classifications. As with prints, the exact way digital images are arranged is up to you: by subject, in annual groupings etc. Given that it should be possible to manage images as they are created, or to develop a simple schema which can be followed by many users at *the time of creation*, arranging in annual groups, with subjects as sub-groups, seems to be a sensible start. One example is as follows, which is based on a scheme developed for an independent school:

Set up a series of files on the hard drive of the computer, starting with a 'master' file called **Photographs**. Within that file, set up annual files, e.g. **2006**, **2007**, **2008** etc. Within each of those files, set up subject files, such as Debating, Creative Arts, Opening Celebrations 29 Feb, Surfing Yr 9, Year 11 Camp etc. Within this system a file can also be established for the official annual images. Once these annual files are established, images can be transferred into the relevant sub-files. It is not absolutely necessary to amend the file title of every image within the subject file; the original unique file title can be retained. However, remember that you are managing an archival collection, i.e. images which have been selected for permanent retention, and as such the ultimate aim is to describe each archival image as fully as possible.

This system is far from perfect, although it does allow simple storage and retrieval using common sense principles, while working some way to incorporating archival description. It works on the same principle as that applied to managing thousands of 6" x 4" prints. Obviously there are drawbacks. For instance, there may be a number of photographers for any given subject. It is very difficult to record this information for each set of files or images without some sort of database.

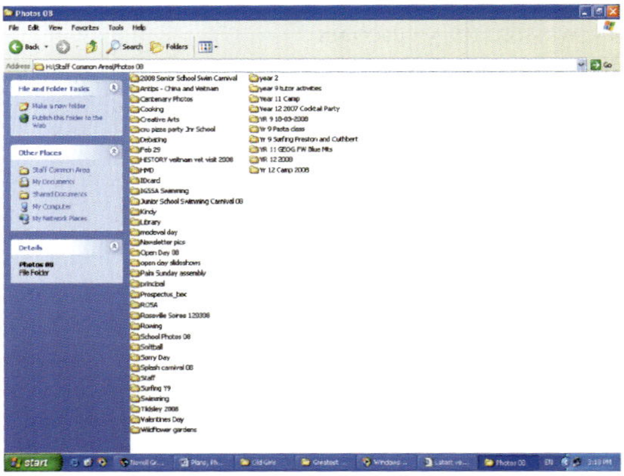

Culling these images is also recommended. Use the same criteria as you would with prints. There is no need to keep multiples of the same images simply because they exist.

What of preservation, for the long term? Conventional practice has for some years been to burn images to CD or DVD, and use that medium as long-term storage. As the exact longevity of such media has yet to be *proven*, some archivists prefer to print a selection of the best images for a subject or year, and store these as one would traditional prints. It is advisable to be very selective about the type of paper, ink and printer used. Professional materials will yield professional results. It is also important to remember that the files of images on CD must be migrated onto new storage media and to new versions of the same software over time to avoid redundancy and media failure. As new methods for the capture and preservation of digital records are being developed, it is hoped that digital images will also be able to be managed in a more streamlined manner in the future.

Objects

Many different items may form part of the archive collection. Following is a sample list of the different objects found in a typical in-house archive:

Textiles

- uniforms and special clothing: blazers, dresses, skirts, trousers, shirts, aprons, pullovers and vests, waistcoats, overcoats, socks and stockings, undergarments
- ecclesiastical vestments, robes, habits
- military uniform and equipment
- domestic textiles, decorative pieces, hand work: embroidery, stitching, quilts, knitting, weaving, etc
- ribbons, pennants, banners and flags
- sporting equipment: uniforms, costumes, bathers

Headwear

- caps, boaters, top hats, dress hats (ceremonial), helmets

Metal objects

- trophies, shields
- medals, badges, brooches, pins
- plaques
- silverware (tea services, cutlery etc.)
- weapons (guns, knives, swords etc.)

Hatbands and pockets are typical textiles held in a school archive. The items can be made of silk and felted wool, and are as fragile as they are precious. The emblems on such items form part of the overall 'corporate' identity of the school.

Honour cap, made of velvet, felt, hessian and metallic thread.

Other 'special' items

- sporting equipment: rowing boats, rugby balls, cricket stumps and bats. Olympic or Commonwealth Games memorabilia etc
- medical equipment: stretchers, surgical instruments, anatomical dummies
- scientific equipment: microscopes, Bunsen burners, charts etc.
- artworks
- research collections: flora and fauna, anthropological, geological, etc.

Cabinet with silverware and pennants.

Materials to use when handling objects

- archival quality paper (text)
- archival quality board: boxes, supports, dividers
- polyethylene or polypropylene products: 'Coreflute', 'Mylar ® Type D, 'Melinex ® 516'
- rag board (100 percent cotton rag) buffered or unbuffered
- washed cotton, linen or poly-cotton products e.g. calico, Parsilk, washed unbleached Japara
- padding and wadding e.g. cotton (quilting) wadding, Dacron ®, Polyethylene padding
- wrappings: Tyvek ® , Sontara ®, archival quality tissue paper
- cotton tape (flat, broad, white)
- supports, e.g. mesh mannequins, covered in polypropylene
- acrylic (e.g. Perspex)

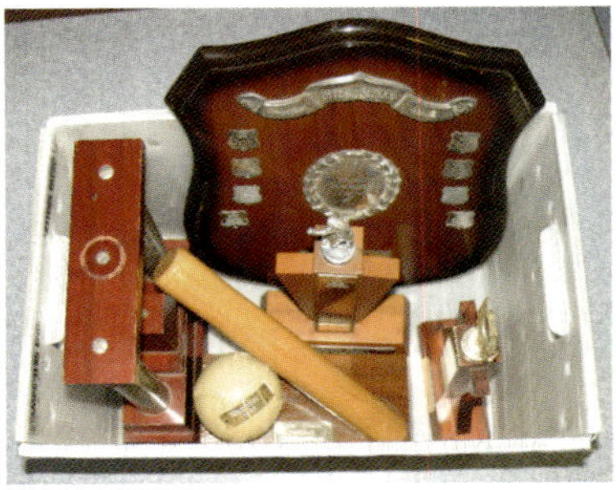

Trophies and shields in a variety of sizes and shapes. They have been boxed together for ease of storage, but should ideally be individually wrapped for further protection.

Materials to avoid when handling objects

- metal fasteners: nails, staples, pins and wire (remove where possible)
- chipboard, masonite, Medium Density Fibreboard (MDF), plywood, craftwood (unless sealed)
- glues, adhesives, tapes (unless archival quality)
- plastics: high PVC content (highly acidic), expanded polystyrene foams, cellophane

Specialist storage containers

Containers and boxes should be:

- archival quality
- of appropriate size for the object
- strong enough to support the object
- not air tight, but dust 'tight'
- fitted lids which fit over the base
- of ample height.

Rolls

- archival quality, or cover with material as a barrier, such as polyester film (Mylar®) or aluminium foil and then archival quality tissue paper
- large diameter
- longer than the textile to be rolled by at least a hand width each end.

Description

It is important to record information about the provenance of your item, and the context in which it was created. This can take the form of basic information listed on individual forms, or you can enter the information into a database. At a minimum, you should record enough detail to clearly and easily identify the object, a description of it, notes about its history, its relationship to other items in the collection, details of how it came to be in the archives and its location. A unique identifying number or code is also recommended.

See Table 16.5 for further details of the information needed to register the item fully.

Unusual objects which can form part of an archives.

Contextual and descriptive information: Objects		
Item Number	**This should be unique for each item.**	
Identity	**Information about the object's identity**	
	Title	Name of the object
	Part of a series?	Relate to other items in a series
	Separated from the series?	Is it physically separate from other items of the series?
	Storage location	Box no., shelf no., room no.
Description	**Information about what the object looks like, and what it is made of**	
	Classification	Type, e.g. textile, ceramic, metal etc
	Brief description	Distinguishing features
	Inscriptions/markings	Note any inscriptions etc
Physical	**Information about the physical attributes of the object**	
	Condition	Good, damaged, fragile etc
	Details of condition	Tears, pests, faded etc
	Material	Details of the fabric, metal, ceramic etc
	Production method	Hand, machine etc
	Assessed?	Date, who by etc
	Conservation report	Has one been made? Is one required?
Context	**Information about the history and provenance of the object**	
	When made	Date, or date range
	When used	Date or date range
	Where made	Location details (if known)
	Maker's details	
	History of object	Technical details, personal information, chain of custody etc

Acquisition	**Details of how the object came to the archives**	
	Method	Donation, purchase, collection, other
	Name of source	Details, name, address, etc.
	Date acquired	Date the archives took ownership of the object
	Acknowledgments	Correspondence to donor/seller
Indexing	**Information to assist retrieval and research about the object**	
	Subject headings	E.g. people, buildings, sports, events etc.
	Names	Names of people, groups or bodies in the image
	Place names	Place photo was taken/background
Other	**Any other information about this object**	
	Restrictions	Copyright? Display? Access?
	Registration	Details of the staff member who registered this item, including date

Table 16.5: Descriptive information for the objects in the archives collection.

> **Tip**: Take a digital photo of each object to add into your database. This avoids unnecessary handling, provides a useful visual index to the collection, and is a snap shot of the condition of the item to gauge changes or deterioration over time.

Some suggestions for protecting and storing objects

General:

- every object must be clean before being put into storage
- objects should not be over-handled when being packed
- pack so that the object doesn't move around inside the box
- do not over-pack the box
- do not over-stack the boxes

- storage materials must be safe (long term)
- stored objects should be clearly labelled and identifiable from the outside to avoid unnecessary handling

Most small archives will not have the resources to establish specific storage areas, with appropriate environmental conditions, for the various media in the collection.

The quantity of the objects as a proportion of the total collection, as well as the proportion of types of objects, (for example the percentage of metal objects against the percentage of textiles), will also be factors in deciding how you devote your resources in terms of buying storage furniture. Depending on your circumstances, it may be more practical to invest in specialist storage furniture designed to hold textiles, or it may be better to invest in a cabinet for medals, trophies and shields. It is most likely that you'll have a collection which has a 'bit of everything', and specialist furniture is out of reach, at least initially. Therefore, you'll have to compromise, all the while aiming for 'best practice', with the aim being to store the various items in order to maintain them in as good a condition for as long as possible. Investing in good quality storage materials such as archival quality boxes, tissue and other wrapping materials is a wise first step.

The following are some suggestions on how to store typical objects in a small archives collection.

Hanging uniforms wrapped in calico bags has been a relatively common practice in small archives. However, hanging is not recommended as a long-term storage solution.

Textiles – hanging

The main objective when storing textiles is to reduce or eliminate stress on any part of the item. Therefore hanging is not encouraged, as over time gravity and weight of the fabric will pull on the seams and joints, such as the shoulders, causing distortion or tearing. If you have to hang, ensure that the hangers used are well padded and are moulded or shaped to fit each individual garment. It is also advisable to encase each item in a separate cover, such as one made of washed unbleached calico. This provides a buffer between one item and the next, and to some extent, protects the item from dust, light and other particles. Calico covers will not protect the items within from pests, or completely from dust or mould. Plastic sleeves provided by drycleaners should be removed as soon as possible and never used to store an object. The plastic sleeve may cause the object to sweat and thus provide an ideal breeding ground for mould.

> **Essential tips for objects:**
>
> Everything you do must be reversible, and leave no trace whatsoever if it is removed.
>
> Ensure objects are clean before they are stored away.
>
> You will need plenty of room to wrap textiles, such as a large work bench, or a board table.
>
> Take a photo of the object before you wrap it away for ease of identification, for research purposes and for condition comparison purposes later.
>
> Identify each item by sewing on a small label, or attaching a tag (make your own by cutting out pieces of archival quality card, punching a hole with a hole punch. Attach with a length of cotton tape).
>
> Identify the outside of the storage container or roll.

Textiles – folding

Folds in any textile should be kept to a minimum, as creases form weak points which over time will split or break. If folding is necessary, it is advisable to insert a pad or support made of archival quality tissue under or inside the fold, to reduce the sharpness of the fold. It is best to use unbuffered tissues with all textiles, as some fibres react adversely with the calcium carbonate buffering.

Most textiles will not fit into a box without some folding, even if it is a textile box. The sleeves of a blazer, parts of a skirt and pant legs will need to be folded so that the item fits within the box. The aim is to keep the number of folds to a minimum, and to pad them out where possible. Sleeves are usually padded out with tissue, or with pads of wadding covered in calico made especially to fit. Similar pads can be used for supporting collars, padding shoulder seams, or to support folds in a full skirt.

Large boxes, especially designed to hold textiles and other large objects, are placed on shelves spaced to allow good air circulation. Labels on the boxes replicate information captured into the control system, and aid in identification and retrieval.

Ensure that each item is wrapped in archival quality tissue, or that a layer of tissue is placed between each different item in the box. Keep the layers to a minimum – the weight of other objects above will crush the textile on the bottom. As a rule of thumb, it is better to have many shallow textile boxes rather than one deep one. This is true for the items within, and in relation to OH&S issues for the archivist – a large textiles box, when full, can be very awkward and heavy.

When wrapping costumes for storage:

- wrapping is preferable to hanging; if hanging, use custom-made padded support hangers, and cover with fabric cover sewn to size
- ensure textile is clean
- pad out the form of the costume with scrunched archival quality tissue, or insert specially made padded forms into the garments
- wrap the garment in archival quality tissue
- store in appropriately-sized archival quality storage box.

A blazer is padded with scrunched archival-quality tissue prior to folding for storage in a large textiles box.

Ecclesiastical vestments have been stored flat in converted furniture which also allows display. The items rest on archival-quality tissue.

Textiles – rolling

Large, flat textiles such as banners or flags store well if they are rolled. The inner tube should be strong and rigid, able to support the weight of the item rolled around it. Mailing tubes (from most post offices) make good cores once they have been wrapped in a protective buffer of archival quality tissue and/or calico. (This is to prevent leaching from the cardboard, which will not be archival quality). Tubes from inside rolls of fabric or carpet are excellent for large textiles, such as banners, or flags, although they may be difficult to source, and then to store, as they may be quite long.

Ensure that the textile you are rolling is clean before you begin. On a clean, large surface, lay out a piece or pieces of archival quality tissue which is slightly bigger than the banner. Lay the banner flat on top of the tissue, and place a layer of wadding (if you can) and tissue on top of the banner. Place the inner tube (which has itself been padded with wadding and/or tissue) at one end of the banner, and begin to roll, ensuring that there are no wrinkles or creases forming as you roll. Do not roll too tightly, as you will place stress on the fabric; do not roll it too loosely, or else the fabric will not be supported. Once completed, you should have a large 'sausage' which can be tied with linen or cotton tape at each end, and also at a number of places along its length. Remember to label the outside of the roll with a tag which includes all relevant identifying information.

Rolling flat textiles for storage:

- ensure textile is clean
- interleave with archival quality tissue
- roll onto archival quality storage roll (or one which has been covered in archival quality tissue)
- wrap with clean tissue or fabric (depending on size of the piece)
- tie the ends with flat cotton tape. Do not tie too tight.
- NB: never roll a folded textile

Textiles – hats and caps

Hat and caps are difficult to store because they vary in size and shape, and are made of a variety of materials, some of which are extremely delicate, or have become so due to wear or age. Hats and caps should never be stored on their brims. If storing in a box, always pad the crown with wadding covered in archival quality tissue, or just archival quality tissue. Ensure the hat does not rest on its brim by using enough padding to keep the hat raised. Each item should be wrapped individually in order to reduce friction and damage. Ideally, specially sized archival-standard boxes should be used. If the budget doesn't quite stretch that far, boxes which hold A4 or A3 reams of paper can be used temporarily, provided that they have been lined with archival quality tissue to form a buffer between the hat and the acidic cardboard of the box. Wire hat stands are a better option, although time consuming to make: a timber base and core, topped with a padded section which fits into the crown is ideal. These can be placed inside fixed shelves or cupboards; the same stands can be used for display purposes. Remember to label the hat with relevant identifying information. This can be sewn inside the crown, or attached with a length of cotton tape.

Here hats are stored on specially-made padded stands.

Hats can be stored in large archival-quality boxes. Be sure to pad the crown with scrunched archival-quality tissue or similar.

Top: Shields – a combination of timber and metal.

Above left: Typical trophy which is silver, or more commonly, silver plate.

Above right: Badges and pins have been arranged for display and storage. Be careful when choosing backing and support material. Always aim for archival quality to ensure the long-term condition of the items.

Metal objects – trophies and shields

Large metal objects such as trophies and shields seem to be quite robust. However, they, like everything else, will degrade over time if not enough attention is given to their care. They always look at their best when shiny and bright, however polishing is a form of abrasion and/or chemical reaction, and should only be undertaken when absolutely necessary.

Remember to take note of any information included on the trophy or shield, and also note its maker. See Table 16.5 for further information about contextual and descriptive information.

Trophies come in an array of sizes, and are made of various materials. More modern ones can be made of moulded plastic, others are brass, glass, silver plate or sterling silver, or a combination of materials. Damage occurs through wear, which occurs mainly through polishing, or if the trophy is or was a perpetual trophy, through the festivities which surrounding its annual presentation. Shields will usually have a backing made of timber. It's not necessary to polish the trophy or shield before you put it away, although it is advisable to clean it, gently removing dust, grime and other accumulations. You can wrap each item in archival quality tissue, and then protect it with a layer of bubble wrap, although this isn't absolutely necessary if you have stable environmental conditions. The main aim is to reduce further wear or damage through bumps and knocks, or from one item rubbing up against another. Ensure that each item is clearly marked or labelled with a tag containing identifying information, and record its location in the archives management system or database. Trophies and shields can be stored in archive boxes (usually with the lid removed to allow for size), or on open shelves. Remember that objects will move if the items are not secured in place on the shelves of mobile shelving units as they are moved.

Wrapping metal objects for storage:

- always use nitrile gloves to handle metals
- wrap in archival quality, non-buffered tissue
- store in archival quality, non-buffered storage box

Wrapping delicate objects for storage:

- ensure delicate surfaces are fully covered
- ensure no movement can occur in the storage box

Metal objects – medals, badges, brooches and pins

Medals, badges, brooches and pins can form very valuable and meaningful parts of an archive collection. Signifying belonging, or reward, they are often highly sought-after items for display; their relative strength and durability also make them ideal for display purposes. Identifying and storing them can present a challenge as each item, although small in size, can have a great deal of contextual information.

Each item should be tagged, to hold identification information. Use small museum tags, or make your own by cutting out pieces of archival quality card, punch a hole with a hole-punch, and attach with a length of cotton tape. The options for storage are many; the choice made will depend on how many there are, how regularly they will need to be accessed, and the inherent value of each one.

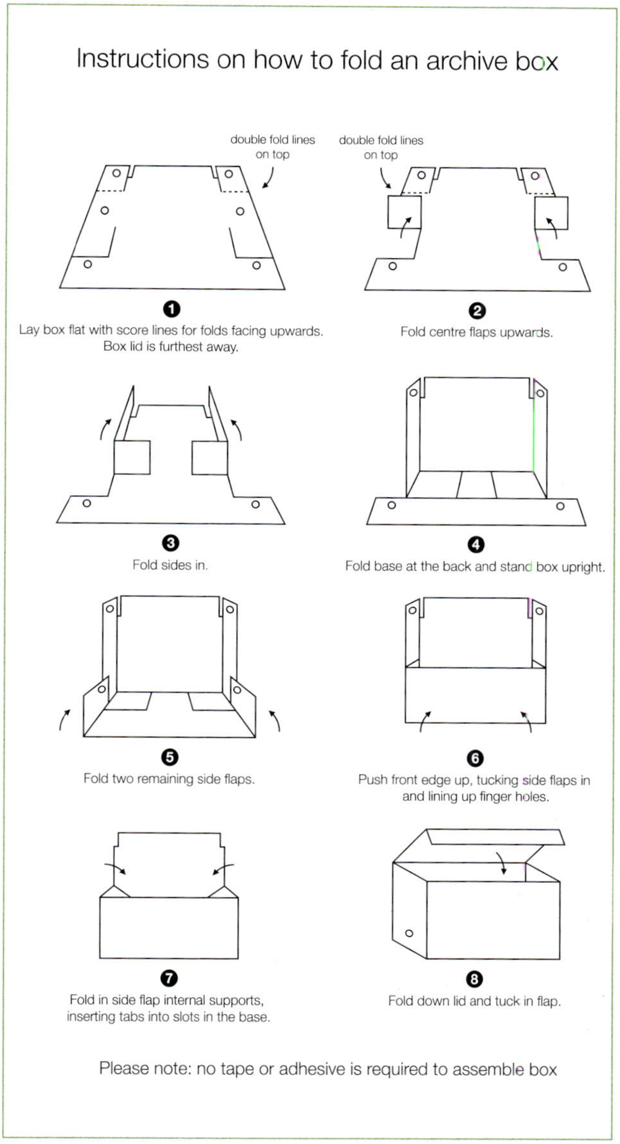

Figure 16.1: Instructions on how to fold an archive box.

- Individually wrap in archival quality non-buffered tissue, mark with identification information, and insert into small clip-lock plastic bag (food grade), and put these bags into a small box such as a clam shell box.
- Purchase specialist storage/display boxes specially made for small items.
- Use dense foam or polystyrene covered with aluminium foil or polyester film and archival quality tissue and/or washed calico (or similar) and 'attach' each badge by sticking the pin into the foam. Place these into display cases or on top of one another in archival quality card boxes.

Medals and ribbons have been professionally mounted into a piece of furniture converted into a display unit.

Conclusion

Managing the various other 'things' which find their way into archives can present some challenges, especially in relation to the provision of adequate protection and storage. This chapter has provided some tips and examples of how to overcome some of the issues more commonly faced by small or in-house archives. The range of 'stuff' which finds its way into such an archives can be interesting, to say the least! It is important to remember that ideal conditions may not always be feasible for every item in your collection: aim for a clean and stable environment, and do your best to protect each item from dust, pests, and other causes of damage. If the items are of great value, and have deteriorated despite your best efforts, it is time to call on expert conservators, who will repair the item and advise on storage solutions for the future.

As for managing the 'stuff' in an intellectual way? The guiding principle is to approach items as you would paper records. Make note of provenance, relationships and other contextual information such as maker, user and date ranges. That way the items will form part of the archive, and will come to be viewed and used as such by the people for whom your archives exists.

CHAPTER 17

sound recordings

ROBYN GAMBLE &
LOUISE CURHAM

CHAPTER ABSTRACT

The ability to record and retain both moving images and sound recordings has existed for over a century. The inclusion and growth of audiovisual formats within the archival environment is reflective of modern patterns and forms of communication. Today, potentially more information is conveyed to the public via audiovisual media, than by reading or writing. However, while most archives now consist of more than just textual records, dealing with audiovisual archives is still often seen to be unusual, and 'out of the norm'. Therefore audiovisual formats within the archival environment continue to be approached with caution. These formats need to be managed along with more conventional textual formats.

In this and the next chapter, Chapter 18: *Moving Images,* we will look at sound and moving image records in archives. These formats share many features, so we will start by considering them together under the umbrella of audiovisual records. We then discuss how to identify, preserve and enable access to sound recordings. Chapter 18 focuses on the identification, preservation and access to moving images.

Together, these chapters give you the tools to know what kinds of sound recordings and moving image recordings you have, their significance, and how to manage them for the long term. In Chapter 18: *Moving Images* we also work through how to set up an audiovisual archiving project. Further resources for both chapters are included on the accompanying CD.

How do audiovisual records differ?

For many archivists, despite best intentions, audiovisual records languish on the shelf. The formats are unfamiliar, and equipment to replay them is not to hand or not maintained. Often there are few clues to their content. Accurate or meaningful listings may not have been supplied, and labels are obscure or technical. This makes it difficult to prioritise the processes involved in investigating them further.

Audiovisual records are as diverse as all record groups in their content and formats. For instance, an archive may receive video footage documenting failed building repairs, 16mm film of product testing, 8mm home movies, recordings of speeches and events, surveillance footage, recordings from television and radio relevant to a particular entity. While many will be on older outdated formats, there are also likely to be recent recordings on contemporary formats: digital sound recordings on CD, moving images on DVDs, modern copies of obsolete formats and documentation of business activities that may come straight to the archives as soon as they are made.

A selection of audiovisual records likely to be found in a typical small archives

So what's different about audiovisual records? As cultural artefacts, they operate very differently from text. Their ability to bring to life a particular time and place contributes a unique cultural and evidential perspective that makes their potential value high, historically, culturally and even economically.

Technically, audiovisual records can present challenges for the archivist. Lack of familiarity is a big factor. While audiovisual materials are increasingly part of the daily lives of all of us, most archivists are unfamiliar with the professional formats and the language they employ.

Instability of the media

Audiovisual records are generally less robust than traditional format records. They are vulnerable to benign neglect. Unlike some paper records, which can survive long periods of time in less-than-ideal conditions, many audiovisual records can deteriorate rapidly without active preservation treatment and optimal storage conditions. Warmth and moisture will radically degrade them, and mishandling can damage them drastically. Some formats have employed materials that can deteriorate even in stable, dry conditions. 'Vinegar syndrome' in acetate film bases, including motion picture film, is a classic example. The technical developments for these formats occur in the commercial sector, and these are rarely influenced by archival requirements. We will cover the preservation issues of audiovisual formats later in this and the following chapter. Preservation issues as they relate to all formats are also covered in Chapter 4: *Preservation.*

Dependence on technology

All audiovisual records require equipment on which to listen, view and gain access to the content. As such, audiovisual records can only convey information if they are in good condition. Even minor damage can seriously affect the quality and usefulness of recordings. Thus audiovisual records require handling and storage provisions which actively work to impede deterioration and damage. However, good storage alone will not ensure the survival of the record. The second aspect of this dependence on technology is the requirement for the equipment used for playing and copying audiovisual records to be maintained in good working order. This can mean that an archives must keep an array of equipment for every format within the collection. A collection containing phonographic records, compact audio cassettes, 8mm film and VHS would require access to equipment for each of these different formats.

Technology that becomes obsolete

With the rate of technological change affecting these formats, rapid obsolescence is a fact. Even if the records are in good condition, they may outlive the actual technology required to play them. This relationship to technology means that copying in some form is an inevitable part of their long-term management, either as the technology becomes unavailable, or the records become too badly deteriorated to withstand replay. This brings with it the need to make choices about maintaining the records and the technology required for preserving and accessing them, or moving the content to the next generation of audiovisual formats.

Resource-intensive records

Working with audiovisual materials can be time consuming. Often they will need to be played to undertake basic archival activities, such as documenting content, undertaking appraisal or copying for preservation. Providing the records are in a condition to be played, they will generally require replay or copying in real time. This means a 20-minute tape will require 20 minutes of replay time plus administrative time. Because the content can appear across multiple items, it may be necessary to compare items to determine both their similarities and differences. All of this handling, research and checking can impact on the resource requirements for archival work such as appraisal, selection, description, preservation, copying and access by users.

Audiovisual archiving as a discipline

In general, audiovisual archiving embraces the same range of activities as those undertaken for traditional or standard record formats. The primary role of guardianship is just as applicable to audiovisual records as for textual records, and includes activities such as building, organising, documenting, maintaining, preserving and accessing the collection.

Audiovisual archiving is an emerging and evolving discipline in its own right. It was only in 1980 that the General Assembly of UNESCO passed the *Recommendation for the safeguarding and conservation of moving images.* This was the first time moving images were declared to be part of the world's cultural heritage.

There are subtle differences in the ways different institutions collect and organise audiovisual records. They can exist in the broader context of libraries, archives and museums, or in institutions with a specific mandate to collect audiovisual records. It is helpful to be aware of the differences in philosophy and practices adopted by these institutions.

Specialist audiovisual archives usually focus on the cultural value or re-use potential of their collections. Put broadly, they collect works made specifically as products for the film, recording and broadcast industries, aesthetic works on these media, amateur productions and works to show the technical history of the media. In this type of archive, the format of the records, such as film or sound recordings, are placed at the centre of the collecting policy. Other records, such as files, scripts and photographs, may be limited in scope and have the status of supporting related documentation. Within Australia, 'The National Film and Sound Archives collects, preserves and aims to ensure the permanent availability of the nations audiovisual heritage' (NFSA 2006).

There are tensions in managing audiovisual records and other formats, such as those discussed in Chapter 16: *Plans, Photographs & Objects* as objects separated from other archival records or adopting an integrative approach.

The total archives approach recognises that audiovisual records may be created as part of the business activities of a wide variety of government, businesses and other bodies, while carrying out many different functions including training, promotional activities and scientific and technical research. Since these chapters are concerned with the overall management of audiovisual records as archives, we will generally follow the total archives approach. In this instance, the key to their management as archives is to apply traditional methods of intellectual control, while attending to their specific format needs to ensure their long-term preservation and availability to users of the archives.

Ethics in audiovisual archiving

On most points, ethical practice for audiovisual archiving parallels that of archival practice in general. Ethics play an important role in managing and safeguarding all audiovisual materials. It is the areas of preservation and collection development that make particular ethical demands on the archivist. In moving image preservation in particular, it can be difficult to achieve the quality proposed in ethics statements. It is in these situations that guidelines on ethical practice become a useful tool to support a course of action.

It is interesting that high individual professional standards make a special mention in the ethics of the audiovisual archivist. This points to an often-passionate engagement by donors, creators and users in documents 'that move and speak', which can impact on collection managers. Audiovisual records capture real events in progress, and can therefore clearly express two types of information that textual records do not, time and emotion. This can create an emotional link to the records which may translate into conflicts of interest. Often, acquiring audiovisual material involves building a strong rapport with the creator or custodian. The creators often expect to be fully involved in the ongoing management of the records. The continuing engagement by creators and donors in these works can therefore put pressure on ethical behaviour. For instance, there can be a temptation to prioritise their access requests or proposals for preservation.

For those who work in managing audiovisual collections, they may develop specialist expertise in particular collecting areas or particular formats. Despite the best appraisal and preservation intentions, this can result in the over-development of that collecting area or format within the organisation. The acquisition and preservation of these records may be prioritised because the person understands it better, has networks to acquire it and treat it for conservation. This problem is not the sole domain of audiovisual formats, but it can be emphasised in this context.

Ethics in preservation

Preservation treatments introduce a host of ethical issues. Some of these will be dealt with later in the section on preservation. However, the issues raised are applicable to all audiovisual recordings and it is worthwhile examining them in some detail here.

Documenting the processes of restoration is important for all archival records. For audiovisual records, detection of the restoration processes can be difficult, if not impossible, without documentation. In tape and film formats, the extent of the material means it can be difficult to detect what has been done. For example, in winding through 100 metres of film with many existing splices, it can be very difficult to detect a new splice and when it may have been carried out.

Documentation is particularly significant where the delivery format is entirely different from the original. When provided with streamed QuickTime clip or VHS of *Storm Boy*, the viewer should be informed that the copy they are watching originated on 35mm in a 90-minute cinema release.

Within audiovisual archives, ethical practice requires making copies faithful to the original. Put from a conservation perspective, the aim is to preserve the quality of the original. For some audiovisual formats, there is no avoiding a reduction in quality when copying occurs. Here we are thinking specifically of motion picture film and other analogue media. It is well documented that during copying, each generation of analogue format sees a reduction in quality. A photocopy of a photocopy of a photocopy gives a good example of the inherent degradation in analogue-to-analogue copying. For an explanation of analogue media, see Appendix 17.2.

A second significant factor in making copies faithful to the original is avoiding the temptation to use new technologies to 'improve' the recording by contemporary standards. In the realm of digital preservation, the ability to make changes can bring ethical considerations about the appropriateness of the treatment, and how to document the decisions made during digitisation. It is easy to blur the line between conservation and restoration, and so needs to be carefully documented.

The language of audiovisual records

The audiovisual production industry and archiving disciplines each have their own terminologies, glossaries and concepts. The words used to describe these records can have different meanings and connotations, depending on the context and the country. As yet, there there are no international standards or consensus on the terminology and, as a result, the meaning and interpretation of words is not always clear. Add to these technical terms a seemingly endless array of letters, numbers and acronyms (for example: A and B Rolls, VHS, CD, DA88, Hi8, LTO, IASA, FIAF) and this technical jargon can begin to appear overwhelming and confusing to archivists unschooled in this technical speciality. It is important to remember that audiovisual archiving is a growing industry which therefore has an evolving vocabulary.

Words used in audiovisual archiving can have a meaning which varies from accepted archival terminology. Even seemingly simple terms such as 'audiovisual' and 'document' can have complex definitions. For example, the word audiovisual has been used to encompass a variety of definitions such as: moving images or recorded sound in various formats; radio and television; audio slide presentations; multimedia presentations; still film photography; video games or anything projected onto a screen.

While there may be a desire to avoid the jargon, sometimes this is not always possible. The terminology will appear in a variety of contexts for the archivist, in reference texts, related documentation, within listings of the records, on labels, or included in the specifications for copying. For the archivist dealing with audiovisual records, acquainting themselves with the general terminology will go a long way towards demystifying the media. Defining and building a controlled or standardised vocabulary for your collection will be helpful. This will involve analysing the common terms and applying them in the context of your collection.

Common terms used in these two chapters:

Audiovisual: moving images and/or sound recorded in any medium now known or yet to be invented. Audiovisual includes, but is not limited to, the formats of film, video and audio tape, digital files and machine-readable or encoded data, embodying moving images and/or sound.

Carrier: the physical medium on which the audiovisual content is recorded. This may be a reel of tape, an audio cassette, a roll of film or a disc.

Medium: the type of material used to create or carry the information. This may be a video tape, a negative film, a phonographic disk. This term is often used interchangeably with *format*.

Component: a group of related, technically identical carriers which form a cohesive whole. For example, the three reels of film which make up the duplicate negative. These components may also be called *elements*.

Appraising audiovisual recordings

The appraisal of audiovisual records is still a challenging task for many organisations. The criteria used for most archival records are a good starting point. The identification of selection criteria is most effective when it links back to and supports the overall selection policies of the organisation. Do the records add relevant or significant materials to the archives now and for the future? Traditionally, the aesthetic, informational and cultural content of audiovisual formats has been their perceived source of value. However, as portable recording equipment has developed, audiovisual formats have become more widely used as evidence gathering tools, for example field recordings, royal commission submissions, and scientific data. Thus evidential value is likely to become a more prominent consideration in the appraisal of audiovisual records.

Once an organisation decides that selection is necessary, then it must define the criteria for that selection process. It is not enough to simply define the criteria, it must be supported with practical information on how to implement it. Many specialised archives and associations have developed methods and criteria for selecting audiovisual material for retention.

Generally, the appraisal approach taken with records in traditional textual formats is relevant for audiovisual recordings. A simple and productive approach is to consider three broad categories: sociological value, cultural value and historical value. To prepare yourself, you need to understand the broad provenance of the records, have a sense of user needs and a basic knowledge of the history of the medium.

However, while archivists in the text-based world primarily make their appraisal decisions on the basis of content, context and how well the records fit within the collection or acquisition policy, it is difficult and often not practical to ignore technology factors when dealing with audiovisual records. Technological changes are motivated by primarily commercial considerations, and typically do not consider the longevity of media or their reliability from a recordkeeping or archival perspective. As new types of technology emerge, there is usually a period in which various commercial products compete to become the industry standard (e.g. Beta vs VHS video tapes). For the archivist, the results of this phenomenon are:

- a collection of standard and non-standardised formats, many of which do not have the supporting technology, expertise or reliability to manage them as archives
- the overwhelming challenge of trying to keep up to date and to understand the complexity and diversity of technology formats and versions available

The appraisal of all audiovisual records can seem more complex because of the nature of the media on which it is recorded. Identifying which components to keep, from a host of items that all the bear the same title, can be a daunting task. There can be a variety of formats in the collection. There may be multiple copies or components with the same content, or different versions of records. How do you identify the original record? How do you know if they are worthy of retention as an archival record? Archivists will need to decide whether they are trying to preserve and provide access to the full experience of the record its content and form, or to the information, look and feel of the audiovisual record?

This adds an extra level of technical selection to the appraisal process. As a result, criteria can be considered in terms of:

- **content-based criteria:** selection based on the content or evidential and informational value of the material
- **technical selection criteria** (selection according to technical aspects)**:** format, media, quality of recording, production process, condition, obsolescence

Audiovisual media have other characteristics which can affect their appraisal:

- **Do the records fall within the collecting policy of the archive?** Audiovisual records may be retained if they provide context to enhance the usefulness of similar or other recordings. Are they sufficiently useful to justify the costs involved in keeping them? They often have artistic or cultural value seldom found in textual records and a case may be made for their retention on these grounds.

- **Are the records published, unpublished or broadcast?**
  - Published, or commercial material, is likely to be preserved elsewhere. Can you verify where it may be held? Given the resource implications in managing and preserving these formats, is it worth referring the records to another institution? Unless they are master components – for example matrices from which phonographic records are pressed, or master recording tapes – they may not be strictly be relevant to your collection.
  - Unpublished material is less likely to exist elsewhere. Unedited materials may contain more information than was distributed or broadcast. For example, the complete recording of an oral history may contain much more information than was included in the final production. Some archives look at the re-use factor of this type of material.
  - Broadcast recordings may also be preserved elsewhere, such as the archives for the broadcasting station.
- **Unique content: are there several versions or interpretations of the records?** Are they originals or copies?
- **Format and media: what are the qualities of the format?** Is it of sufficient quality to warrant retention? Is it likely to become obsolete, or deteriorated?
- **Unique format (or rarity)**: it may be possible that a format you can't identify has intrinsic significance as a unique type of audiovisual record, even if the content of the recording is of low value. For some formats, the fragility of the medium may mean the archivist is dealing simply with what has survived up to this point of time. A specialist in the relevant media may assist in identifying such formats and recommending an appropriate action to take.

Other criteria recommended by some audiovisual organisations include:

- **Degree of completeness:** completeness can be considered to be the extent to which the whole or complete version is retained, all the appropriate components are retained, or the complete set of a series is retained. Completeness as a criterion can also be linked to metadata, and the information surrounding the record. Audiovisual records are rarely created in isolation. If it is proposed that the records be retained, consideration should also be given to the supporting documentation. If these related records are not kept, the audiovisual records will lose much of their context, and therefore their value.
- **Availability: do the records exist elsewhere?** If you chose not to retain the records based on their existence elsewhere, are they accessible through the other organisation? Are you able to make the records available if you do retain them?
- **Quantity:** the volume of material may be a matter for consideration. Not only should consideration be given to what is sitting on shelves, but also to what is yet to be produced. As creating audiovisual formats becomes easier and equipment

more available, more people will have the ability to produce these records in greater quantities. It is likely that far more material will be produced than can be retained or made accessible. Selection at the point of origin will become a necessary process for many archives in the future.

In addition to the standard archival appraisal considerations, archivists dealing with audiovisual records will also need to take into account the:

- **long-term resources** associated with managing, storing and preserving (including migration) audiovisual records
- **long-term capability** associated with managing, storing and preserving (including migration) audiovisual records
- continued **accessibility** of records
- **availability of supporting text-based material** to contextualise and ensure a full and accurate record is kept and used

We have mentioned the difficulty of browsing audiovisual media and the fact that they are likely to be fragile. There will be instances where playing them back to assess their value may damage them. If you have a sense that you hold valuable but deteriorated material, it may warrant fast-tracked preservation work before other activities such as arrangement and description work is carried out.

Acquiring audiovisual records

Generally, archival collections are created in response to administrative or cultural needs. In acquiring audiovisual material, these records should support and contribute to the collection or acquisition policy of the organisation. In theory, appraisal and selection of material should occur prior to acquisition. However, all too often the archivist will not have been able to control the acquisition of the audiovisual formats in their collection. They may simply appear on the desk or the shelves, possibly with a note asking: 'Can we put these somewhere?' They may have already been in the collection for years, but never been touched or evaluated.

In a world of finite resources, deciding whether to keep and maintain records which will require on-going investment of resources can be a difficult one to make. There is little doubt that retaining audiovisual formats within a collection can bring added pressure on the resources of an archive, in the provision of staff, specialised equipment, handling and a never-ending cycle of copying and migration. By their nature, audiovisual records can be costly to maintain.

However, advances in technology can mean that, not only will the use of audiovisual records become more prevalent in business transactions, but these same advances in technology will improve the cost-effectiveness of production, storage, preservation and the provision of access to these formats. As the availability and costs of digital technologies come within the reach of the average archives, the need for restrictive selection and acquisition policies (based on the needs of different media) may not be necessary.

Factors to consider in the acquisition of audiovisual records:

- **What are the ongoing needs of the record?**
  - Facilities: will they require specialised storage (cold storage, static storage, digital storage)? If you cannot provide the necessary storage, do you have alternative solutions?
  - Equipment to handle, view, hear or copy the records. Will you be able to maintain the equipment required? Do you know where to access the equipment easily or locally, if it is not held onsite?
  - If the records are data files, does the archive have the ability to recognise, read and copy these files? What is the archives' approach to digital preservation?
  - Do the archives' staff members know how to recognise and handle these formats?
- **Are these records in *preferred* archival formats?** The practicalities of managing the formats may require limiting the number and types of formats coming into the collection.
  - Can organisations and donors be encouraged to create audiovisual records on formats more suitable for ensuring preservation and providing access? Can you supply advice about the preferred formats for archiving in your collection?
- **What is the age of the record?** Given ongoing issues with obsolescence and deterioration of audiovisual formats, it may be necessary for these records to be taken into custody sooner rather than later. Can you proactively seek to acquire these records from your agencies or donors?
- **What is the condition of the records?** What levels of deterioration can be observed? Are they already obsolete? Will you have the resources to ensure their preservation (both in terms of staff time, equipment, storage, repackaging and ongoing funding for copying and migration)
- **Is this the best surviving source material?** Is it unique or do copies exist elsewhere, perhaps in your own collection? Can this record replace a deteriorated copy in your collection?
- **What documentation is being provided – identification of the record, supporting documents – notes, log-books, indexes, labels, production files?** You may wish to supply forms to the organisation creating the material while it is being made to ensure accuracy and consistency of the information being provided.
- **How do you verify and support the integrity of the records?** Given the ease with which some audiovisual formats may be modified with little or no discernible evidence, can you always ensure their authenticity?

Clearly establish the terms of deposit

Rights and restrictions

It is important to clarify the rights and use of the material at the point of acquisition. Audiovisual records can have restrictions imposed on their use, as in the case of recordings which contain confidential, controversial or personal references, or ethnographic recordings. For example, unpublished recordings such as an oral history may be restricted at the request of the interviewee. Rights can cover recording rights, performing rights, and moral rights. Special restrictions may apply to recordings from Indigenous or ethnic communities. These may not be covered by copyright but the archive is ethically obliged to acknowledge, document and observe such rights and restrictions. Further discussion on audiovisual records relating to indigenous and ethnic communities is provided in Chapter 18: *Moving Images.*

You must determine and document:

- What rights for access and use of the material will the archives have?
- To whom do the restrictions apply?
- What is the period of the restriction?
- Who else is delegated to grant access if the original donor cannot be contacted?
- Are there special conditions for handling the records?

Copyright

It is not possible to discuss rights and use of material for audiovisual records without also discussing copyright. Copyright provisions for these records can be complex. More than one copyright can exist side-by-side in the one recording; for example, a radio broadcast may include copyright provisions for the script, the performers and background music. Copyright is dealt with more closely in Chapter 11: *Access & Reference Services.*

Briefly, in terms of audiovisual records: Copyright is a property right which grants the owner exclusive rights to their works. Copyright can cover such audiovisual records as dramatic artistic works, sound tracks in films, and radio broadcasts.

For audiovisual works, these rights cover:

- reproduction
- distribution
- public performance
- the right to make derivative works
- the right of public display

Where possible, identify who owns these rights. Deposit of the audiovisual formats in an archive does not mean an automatic transfer of rights to the archives. Copyright owners will normally want an assurance that copies of their records will not be made or supplied without their consent. It is important that employees within the archives or institution understand the legal rights and responsibilities for the audiovisual records in their care. The unauthorised use of audiovisual records by staff or researchers can lead to breaches of the donor agreements or copyright liability. This can leave the institution vulnerable to civil action or fines. Developing policies on the use of material for access, exhibition, internet use, and preservation will be beneficial. The next step is to educate staff on how to implement those policies.

Copyright gives the copyright owner an exclusive right to copy an original work. Copyright owners are also entitled to demand payment for granting others permission to copy the work. While this may appear to place archives in a difficult situation, and leave the archivist wondering whether they will be able to do anything with the record, the copyright act does recognise the important role non-profit and public institutions play in saving audiovisual heritage. There are provisions in the Australian *Copyright Act 1968,* which specifically covers circumstances of copying for reference and preservation within libraries and archives.

Arranging and describing audiovisual records

In describing audiovisual records, the task is the same as for all archival description – to inform the researcher of the nature of the individual record and its relationship with other records.

Specifically, the description of audiovisual records needs:

- to alert the archivist and researchers to the informational content of the recording
- to provide a description which supplies the archivist with enough technical information about the recording for preservation and access work (information the researcher may also benefit from)
- to differentiate between similar items, e.g. reel 1 of 2, reel 2 of 2, uncut version, edited version.

As with all other archival arrangement and description work, the first task is identifying the provenance and original order of the material. Generally, most series will consist of items in the same recording format, but it is, of course, possible that different formats have been employed during the active life of a series (for example, a series of oral history records might have begun using reel-to-reel tapes and later used audio cassettes). The description should reflect this continuation within the one series and maintain original order. Where you can discern no original order, creating a format-specific series may best serve practical arrangement considerations and preservation needs.

While the intellectual arrangement and description reflects the original order of the records, the specific preservation needs of audiovisual material is likely to mean that physical arrangement is quite different from their intellectual arrangement. When it comes to physically arranging the material, practical management issues like storage space and the material well-being of the records may mean the recordings are best served by storage with other audiovisual records of similar format. In this instance, ensuring that the description reflects their original order is important.

If the decision is made to send original materials to a specialist archives, keeping only publicly-accessible copies in house, intellectual control that reflects provenance and original order means the value of the record is retained while its material needs are also adequately served. There are potential pitfalls in this arrangement. The terms of the deposit need to be worked out very clearly with the specialist archives, specifically the parameters for their use of the records and their preservation responsibilities.

Describing audiovisual records – series or item level?

You will need to consider what level of description the recordings warrant. Where there is uniformity to the physical carriers, their modes of recording and their content, series-level description may suffice. However, to make the richness of the recordings accessible, item-level description is likely to be required. Detailed item-level description is most useful for moving images, especially in productions with multiple components where content information repeats for every item, with the only point of differentiation being the physical description of the type of moving image component.

Specialist film archives get around the problem of similarity among records by creating an over-arching title entry that deals with the content information of the production with the physical descriptions of the various components nested inside this 'cover' title. This approach represents the structural divergence between the film archives and general archives. The bulk of records in film archives are stand-alone film productions, where arrangement and description by title is the most relevant form of control. The concept of provenance, with its focus on the context of the creation of the records, is not their primary method of arrangement. Contextual information is still important to film archivists, for example production files, paper forms of scripts, files related to directors and producers and others, but it does not govern their systems of arrangement.

Another consideration is that most of the formats are fragile in different ways. Some are fragile to the extent that they may withstand only a single playback. This makes their management difficult – in playing the recording to assess its value, it may be damaged in the process. Records in other formats that accompany sound recordings are thus very important.

Paper records, and catalogues about the production of the audiovisual records, can assist in the description process. These paper files are also useful in the appraisal process as they can reduce the handling of the recordings. The carriers of audiovisual records are likely to bear at least some information about the recording, either on their packaging or their face labels. Thus information on the leaders or the cans or cassette cases may be critical. If repackaging work is undertaken, documenting this information is essential. A potential problem is that the nature of the information or its meaning may not be clear at the time of the repackaging, as the traces of information may be very subtle. Copying the original packaging with a photocopy or scan is the surest method. Documenting the nature of the original container may also be important. In some instances, the original packaging may itself have value.

Descriptions for audiovisual records can become very technical. The most useful rule of thumb is that, where technical information is available, include it in the description. The most basic information required will be the item's title and the fact that it is an audiovisual record. If the date of recording and duration is known, this also falls into the category of useful basic information. The audiovisual cataloguing rules focus on describing the identifiers of the recording, for example information about the creation of its content, followed by its physical characteristics. In the small archives context, it may be feasible to add specific content information that will enhance the accessibility of the recordings to users of the archives. Where the information is available, useful information for the description includes:

- **Identifiers**
  - **Title**: e.g. program title, segment title, episode title, interview title
  - **Date**: date of recording, date of broadcast and date of production
  - **Unique identifier**: e.g. item number, barcode, UMID (unique material identifier).
  - **Creator information**
  - **Credits**: principal credits, i.e. key individuals who made the work, in commercial productions, the producer and director, production company or producing agency
  - **Personnel**: e.g. presenter/interviewer/interviewee
- **Content information**
  - **Genre or style** of recording: e.g. interview, report, live-to-air, field recording, oral history
  - **Content note**: e.g. topics in recording, people recorded, summary or synopsis
- **Physical or technical characteristics**
  - **Quantity**: e.g. audio cassette 2 of 2; CD 1 of 3
  - **Duration**: may be in length (e.g. 'feet' for moving images) or time
  - **General class of audiovisual material**: e.g. film reel, magnetic tape, optical disc

- **Specific type of component**: e.g. BWF file on Hi 8 tape, original negative; interpositive, digital beta
- **Physical dimensions of carrier**: e.g. 12" vinyl disc, 7" magnetic reel-to-reel tape
- **Gauge** (for motion picture film): this is the dimensions of the films 8mm, 16mm, 35mm
- **Colour characteristics**: colour or black and white
- **Sound characteristics**: silent, mute, playback speed, (e.g. 33 1/3 rpm); number of tracks, (e.g. 4 track audio cassette recording); encoding (e.g. Dolby, stereo, mono).

In terms of general metadata standards, in Australia, Australian Standard 5044: AGLS covers metadata (descriptive data about data including sound or moving image records). This is a resource-discovery metadata standard that specifically enables people and computers to find and identify published material. Five metadata elements must be present for compliance with this standard. The mandatory elements are: creator, title, date, subject or function, identifier or availability. The audiovisual cataloguing rules conform to this in general with their three-part structure: title information, creator information including date, physical information.

Documenting preservation activities, such as copying, is essential. It is vital that the archives documentation can clearly link the originals to the copies. An easy way to achieve this is to retain the items in the same series. In this way, all the copies of the same information are linked intellectually. However, care will need to be taken to clearly differentiate between items created by the agency and items created by the archives. Alternatively, where preservation copying has occurred, there are benefits to creating series for the copies that separates them from the originals. Intellectually, it ensures there is no confusion with the originals. It enables the copy series to be stored separately from the originals, wise in the event of a disaster in the archives. It also means a version of the original control symbol (item number) can be applied to the copy item.

Describing data files of audiovisual records

Describing digital records can add another layer of information to the descriptive requirements. In a mass storage system of any kind, identifying one set of data from another is a key issue. The concept of metadata has been created to address this issue. It is often described as being 'data about data'. This concept is discussed in further detail in Chapter 8: *Arrangement & Description* and Chapter 15: *Digital Recordkeeping.*

For digital audiovisual files, as with all digital formats, metadata is not simply the descriptive and contextual information. It is structured to enable identification of the file for preservation, management and access. A file which cannot be found cannot be preserved or made accessible.

Metadata for audiovisual data files should include the following:

- identification information (including unique identifier, title, checksum – the digital signature that allows authentication of the file)
- the provenance and content of the file (including identification of the original carrier, its format and level of preservation)
- the technical information that enables recognition and replaying of the file (including file format, digital resolution, sampling rate)
- the preservation metadata that records the preservation process applied to the file (including equipment used, any processing applied to the file, such as de-hissing, de-clicking etc).

Comprehensive metadata will be required to maintain, preserve and access the digital files. Metadata can be integrated with the digital file, or maintained separately. Some metadata will be required for identification, control and management of the file, and this should be integrated for the file. Other metadata assists in discovery and access of the records. In this instance, not all metadata need be integrated with the file. For example, descriptive information can be kept separate to allow updating of this information as it becomes available. However, it is important to establish clear links between the file and metadata. Maintaining information about all aspects of the file assists in building a history of the item, and helps to ensure its integrity. Further information about metadata for digital records is provided in Chapter 15: *Digital Recordkeeping.*

Metadata standards for audiovisual records

As yet, there is no agreed authoritative practice for what constitutes minimum or complete metadata for digital audiovisual records in the library, archive and museum sectors. There are, however, many metadata standards available which could be used or adapted for the purpose of capturing audiovisual metadata. Some key websites for audiovisual and preservation metadata include:

- Dublin Core Metadata Initiative, <http://www.dublincore.org>
- Metadata Encoding and Transmission (METS) Standard, <http://www.loc.gov/standards/mets>
- Synchronised Multimedia Integration Language (SMIL), <http://www.w3.org/AudioVideo>
- PREMIS (PREservation Metadata: Implementation Strategies), <http://www.oclc.org/research/projects/pmwg>
- Authority Tools for Audio-Visual Cataloguers, <http://ublib.buffalo.edu/libraries/units/cts/olac/capc/authtools.html#g>
- Authority Resources for cataloguing Popular Music, <http://library.music.indiana.edu/tech_s/mla/wgpms/wgpms.htm>

Sound recording formats

We have discussed many of the archival activities which relate to all audiovisual formats, including sound recordings. We will now examine sound recording formats in greater detail, including their history, how to identify them in your collection, factors which affect their preservation and access. The specifics of moving images, their identification, preservation and access are discussed in Chapter 18: *Moving Images.*

Before undertaking any archival activity, it is necessary to understand the characteristics, and be able to identify different formats in your collection.

The word 'format' can refer to a number of characteristics for sound recording media. It can refer to the physical shape and dimensions of the item, for example, 12" vinyl disc, 1/4" reel to reel tape, Compact Disc (CD). The word can also be used to refer to the method by which the recording is made, for example, digital audio tape (DAT), WAVE data file (*.wav). Sometimes these two characteristics, the physical object and the recording method, are intrinsically linked (as is the case for phonographic discs). These formats are called *media-dependant formats* (or tangible formats).

However, sometimes the two characteristics can be considered separately. In this instance, the record is generally a digital file format which is independent of the medium on which it is stored. These formats are called media-independent formats (or intangible formats). A digital *.wav file may be held on a compact disc. In this case, the disc is simply the storage mechanism for the data file. The file can easily be copied to another medium without changing its format or essence.

In the future, archives will increasingly contain both media-dependant and media-independent formats.

Within an archive, the most common sound recording formats that can be found sitting on the shelf will reflect three predominant recording systems:

- **Phonographic recordings:** acetate, shellac, and vinyl discs as well as their predecessor, the wax cylinder
- **Magnetic tape recordings:** 1/4" reel-to-reel tapes, compact cassettes, micro-cassettes and digital audio tapes (DATs), as well as their predecessor, the magnetic wire recording
- **Optical digital recordings:** Compact Discs (CDs), Digital Versatile Discs (also known as Digital Video Discs or DVDs).

The most likely scenario for archives will be that sound recordings in their collections will date predominately from the magnetic tape era onwards. In Australia, these would date from the early 1950s. The most common physical formats to appear in archival collections will be 1/4" reel-to-reel magnetic tape and audio cassette tape. More recent material is likely to be on optical disc: CD, DVD or minidisc. However, given the range of formats available, there may be more than a single type of sound recording format within the overall collection.

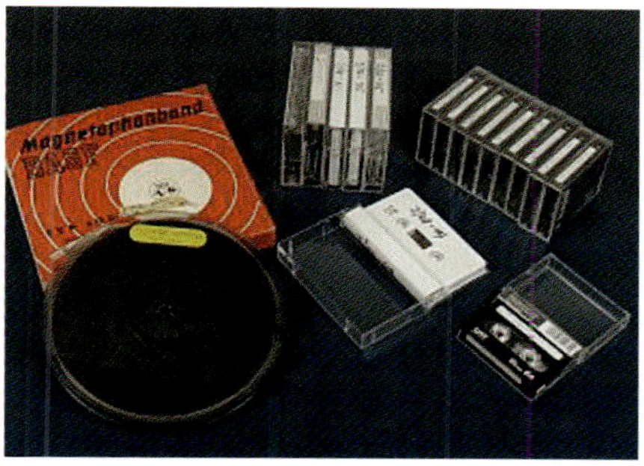

Common sound recording formats

When identifying sound recording formats, remember, the sound recording industry has a proliferation of proprietary formats. Companies developing new formats seek to gain a competitive advantage through the application of new technologies. As a result, these formats can be tied to both the operating system and the technology required for playback.

Grooved recording technology – Phonographic recordings

Phonographic formats are the oldest commonly used technology for sound recording and reproduction.

Gramophone discs

The flat, grooved disc developed in tandem with the cylinder but took some time to gain ascendency over the cylinder. The precursor to the 'record' or gramophone disc as we know it (the grooved vinyl 12") is in American Emile Berliner's 1887 patent. He designed a recording system using a glass disc coated with lamp black which was later fixed with lacquer. The grooves were arranged as a spiral on the surface of the flat disc. From this development, early discs were predominantly laminates or lacquers of acetate, or cellulose nitrate over a solid core, such as metal or glass. The grooves were cut by a stylus into the lacquer coating. Some of the earliest discs were direct or instantaneous recordings, so called because they could be played back straight after they were recorded, without the need for any further processing. These instantaneous discs gained wide spread use, particularly in radio stations. They were used prior to the advent of magnetic tape sound recordings. Due to their common use in radio broadcast, they can appear within archival collections. In Australia, they can appear under the term of transcription discs.

Developments in phonographic discs meant they had the advantage of being able to be replicated. This made them a popular choice for commercial use in sound recordings. As plastic technology developed, it was incorporated into mass-production record pressing. However, it was not until the 1950s that record companies had adapted the grooved disc technology to create discs from flexible, 'unbreakable' materials. These are the long-playing 10" and 12" vinyl pressings we are now familiar with. Gramophone discs were eventually superseded by the optical disc in the 1980s. They are now generally considered to be an

Phonographic disc

obsolete format. The optical or laser disc continued the groove system in principle, but will be dealt with in this chapter as a separate format.

Magnetic tape recordings

Magnetic tape recordings have been readily available for the last half a century or so. Until a few years ago, this would have been the most common sound recording format found within an archive. The first magnetic recordings were on a steel tape, and were used for dictation and telegraphy. However, it was not long before a cheaper alternative was devised. This was based on a flexible tape coated with magnetic powder.

Originally released as 1/4" wide tape on *open reels*, the progression of magnetic tape format was towards enclosure of the tape in *cassette cases* of various kinds, for example, audio cassettes, micro cassettes, digital audio tapes (DATs).

The magnetic tape used in sound recordings is made up of two layers of material, a clear flexible film base and the magnetic layer. Magnetic tape recording has had widespread use in the broadcasting industry (both radio and television). Originally, recorders were bulky and heavy, but advances in the tape and recording technology gradually lead to the development of portable recording machines. While initially used in the professional market, it was not long before manufacturers started aiming at the domestic or amateur markets. Eventually, the development of the cassette format saw a growth in home audio recorders. The compact audio cassette quickly dominated the domestic market, and was still in high use until recently.

Magnetic sound recording formats – microcassette, compact cassette

For many years, the professional 1/4" reel-to-reel tape was the preferred preservation format for sound recordings in archives. This format will appear as both original and preservation copies within archival collections. As a preservation format, they are now being superseded by digital audio formats. No audio cassette format has been recommended for long-term storage of sound recordings. However, they regularly appear in archives as original records. They were often the format of choice for field and oral history recordings.

Most sound recording tape formats are now considered to be obsolete. So, while many magnetic sound recordings can be found in collections, the technology is becoming unavailable, and the means for playing and reproducing them will eventually disappear. Although magnetic tape for video recording, particularly in the home video market, is still in use, it can be expected that these technologies will gradually become absorbed as part of the information and communications technology (ICT) world. It is here in the computer and ICT world that magnetic media and magnetic tape still play a predominant role, where they are used for computer backup and storage. Many digital audio and video recordings found with archives are now being stored on data magnetic storage such as LTO tapes, and hard drives.

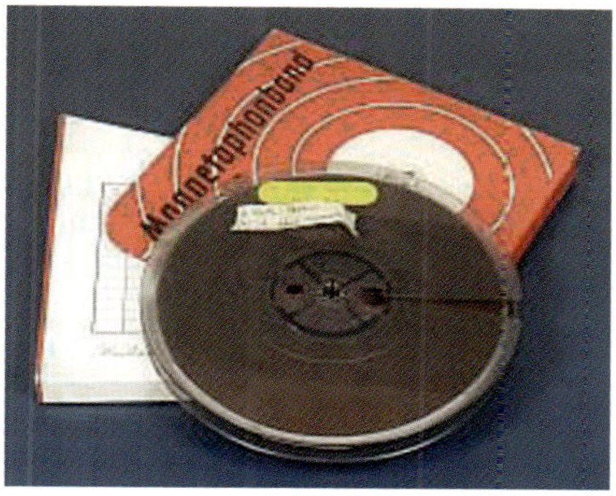

Magnetic sound recording formats – 1/4" reel-to-reel tape

Optical discs

Optical discs have commonly been used as a recording medium for sound documents since the late 1980s. Optical discs, or laser discs as they are also known, occur as CDs, DVDs, video discs, and minidiscs.

Compact Discs (CDs) have become one of the dominant technologies for recording and disseminating information. The compact disc was initially developed for the storage and replay of digitally encoded audio. However, it soon became apparent that the format was an ideal medium for the dissemination of general data. CDs, like DVDs, are now a common format for recording and storing documents such as sound recordings within archives. Part of their popularity is related to their ease of use, affordability and common familiarity.

The content of an optical disc is etched into the reflective layer on the disc as depressions on the surface – holes or pits. In order to obtain the information, a laser light is focused on the disc as it revolves. Where the laser finds depressions in the disc, the light beam is reflected back into the playback apparatus, which converts the reflection into the playback signal. The DVD is a high-density development of the CD, and has the information-carrying layer sandwiched between two laminated layers. It has the same physical dimensions as a CD but stores far more information than a CD by using a shorter wavelength laser which is able to interpret more information.

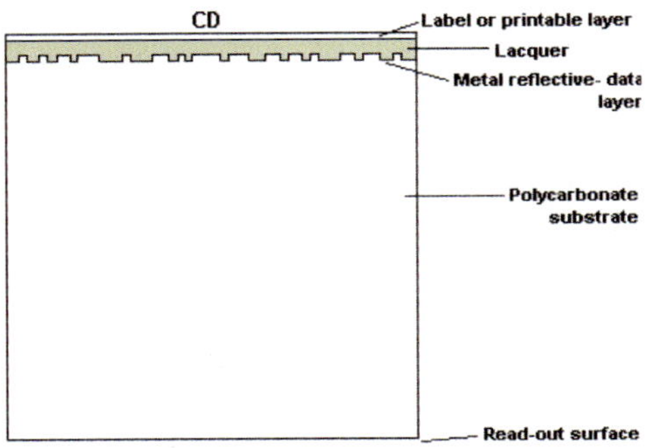

Diagram of layered structure for compact disc

Compact discs stored in archival-quality boxes

Optical discs are created as a laminated structure:

- **The body:** they all consist of a transparent body of polycarbonate.
- **The information layer:** in CD-ROMs, the upper surface of the polycarbonate layer is the information layer. It consists of a track of 'pits' (holes) and 'lands' (non-holes) of different lengths, embossed into the surface of the polycarbonate. In recordable discs (CD-R) the information layer sits on the upper surface of the polycarbonate layer and consists of an organic dye. It is this dye layer that gives the CDs their distinctive look, with the colour depending on which metal is used in the reflective layer. For rewritable discs (CD-RW) the information layer is a film of metal alloy.
- **The reflective layer:** in all CDs, the body and information layer is covered with a reflective layer, usually a metal or metal alloy, such as aluminium, gold or silver.
- **The protective lacquer:** the reflective layer is covered with a protective lacquer. The lacquer is also used to carry the label or content information (Schuller 2008).

There are three main types of optical disc:

- **Read-only discs**, which contain pre-recorded information that cannot be changed or added to by the user. They are more correctly termed CD-ROMs (ROM stands for 'read-only memory'). These CDs are also known as replicated CDs, and are the types of discs that would be purchased as commercial recordings. There have been a number of sizes of this format including the obsolete laser disc, a 30cm picture disc. Read-only discs are similar to grooved records in that they are physically stamped out from a master into a plastic layer.

- **Recordable (write once) optical discs** are blank discs that can be recorded only once. They can't be rewritten. Blank CD-Rs and DVD-R are recordable optical discs. Recordable optical discs have a dye layer just above the reflective surface, under the main polycarbonate surface. The laser recording beam ablates short sections of the dye layer to form transmissive and non-transmissive strips which either allow the reading laser through to reflect off the metal layer, or to absorb the light, creating a similar signal to the pits on a moulded disc.
- **Rewritable optical discs** allow information to be recorded onto the disc, erased and replaced. Re-writable CD-RW, CD+RW and DVD+RW are examples. Re-writables heat a metal alloy that eventually produces two phase states that can be interpreted by the laser. This change of phase is what registers the digital signal. Recording on to rewritable discs requires dedicated hardware (Bradley 2006; Schuller 2008).

Data files

There is another sound recording format which needs to be discussed. This is the audio data file. In this kind of system, the sound recording is created and stored as a data file with no intrinsic carrier. An archive may receive audio data files from two sources – they may be 'born digital', created by the agency, or they may be digitised copies of original records.

The data file is a digital signal that translates the sound waves into a string of on/off signals, where the characteristics of the sound wave are recorded by their different positions on the string. A variety of specific computer applications are used to perform this encoding. The encoded data can be output to any physical carrier, for example CD or magnetic tape format. Increasingly, access to sound recordings is likely to be directly from its encoded data format, for example, MP3 audio files available on the internet and Wave files in mass storage systems. Given the international trends in this direction, audio data files and mass storage will increasingly become the reality, even in small archives.

Examples of audio data file formats include:

- WAVE - WAV (*.wav) or BWF (BWF.wav)
- MP3 – MPEG -1/2, Layer 3 (*.mp3)
- RealMedia - "RealAudio" (*.ra, *.rm, *.ram)
- AIFF - Audio Interchange File Format(*.aif, *.aiff)
- FLAC - Free Lossless Audio Codec (*.flac)
- Windows Media Audio- WMA(*.wma)
- SUN Audio (Uncompressed) (*.au)
- Standard MIDI (*.mid, *.midi)
- Ogg File Format – Ogg (*.ogg).

The first three file formats on this list are those most likely to be in common use and therefore may appear in archival collections. However, it is useful to know what file formats exist, and what purpose they most often serve. This will allow an archive to effectively describe, manage and preserve these records so they can be identified when they are either acquired or created. For example, AIFF was developed by Apple for storing high-quality music, and RealMedia is a compressed format commonly used for web distribution.

This is not an exhaustive list of audio file formats. For a more comprehensive list see The Library of Congress site (http://www.digitalpreservation.gov/formats/fdd/sound_fdd.shtml) and the NINCH guide (http://www.nyu.edu/its/humanities/ninchguide/index.html).

Many digital formats used for disseminating content and access purposes employ encryption or compression. These include files used for dissemination over the web.

A note of caution when trying to identify audiovisual formats – digital recordings are not solely the domain of the data file. Many of the physical carriers such as magnetic tape can deliver either a digital audio signal or a data file. A cassette or CD in your collection may be recorded simply as a digital audio 'stream' (signal) or alternatively as a data file. This highlights the need to provide correct metadata and labelling wherever possible. The decision to select or create these formats for audiovisual records must also be taken carefully, as they can affect the preservation and access options in the future. For example, an audio CD (a CD with a digital audio stream) can limit the possibility of online access, and may create migration difficulties in the future.

Preserving sound recordings

Preventive conservation: pro-active, macro strategies such as environmental control that provide care to the greatest number of records

Conservation treatment: intervention to repair or stabilise individual records

Restoration: conservation treatments that return an archive to as close to original condition as possible. These are usually aesthetic treatments that are time consuming and costly, and not often applied to archival records.

Preservation is not a discrete process, but a never-ending management task. It is easy to believe that placing an item in good storage or making a new copy is the end of the process. But sound recording formats will require continual assessment, survey and migration. The rate at which recording formats become out of date and unusable can be frustrating for any archive dealing with audiovisual media. Preserving the medium may not ensure the item can be played, as hardware and software rapidly change.

While the overall aims of preservation have been covered in Chapter 4: *Preservation*, the specific preservation principles for sound recording collections are:

- acquire or capture the best attainable copy and format.
- retain originals in safe, secure and sustainable storage environments. This includes ensuring digital records are stored in sustainable digital repositories.
- maintain the integrity of original items.
- aim to copy items without loss of quality or alteration of content where possible. All treatment and copying actions for an item will be documented.
- stabilise the content. Do no harm to the original item
- record and retain all necessary descriptive information, provenance, supporting documentation and metadata.
- ensure safe access to collection and its content into the future. No access or duplication should be undertaken without first ensuring the stability and safety of the original.

A primary aim of the archivist with sound recordings is to increase the useful life of these formats under their care. While it is not possible to extend the life of most sound recording formats indefinitely, every effort must be taken to maintain the carriers in a usable condition for as long as possible.

For most materials, we know that certain actions taken to preserve them at a given stage will ensure that they remain in a **useable state for a defined time**. This is the basis for determining the life expectancies of the various media.

Determining the life expectancy of materials must take into account a number of factors. These include:

- the quality of the materials used in the creation of the items
- the technology used in the creation of the record, and continuing technological needs
- the level of handling and use the records have received
- the physical arrangement and environmental conditions in which the records have been stored.

A dependency on machinery and technology, combined with their complex layered structures and the use of materials prone to rapid deterioration, means sound recordings generally have a shorter life expectancy than traditional media such as paper files. For an example in how similar media can vary significantly in their life expectancies, compare the gramophone discs created in 1970s, which are generally physically and chemically stable formats and are likely to still be playable, with optical discs created only 5-10 years ago, which may well have deteriorated or be incompatible with new technology, rendering them unplayable.

When dealing with sound recordings, the words preservation, conservation and restoration take on subtly different meanings than those which apply when dealing with textual records.

For many archives with sound recording collections, the word **preservation** has often been closely associated with copying. When asking 'has the item been preserved?', they most often meant, 'has the item been copied?' or in recent times 'has the item been digitised'? However, the preservation of sound recordings must take on a broader definition to cover a range of activities, from storage and handling, to duplication and access.

The term **conservation** can mean the treatment and protection of the original item. This means the original item has been given value as an object. This may be applicable for historical analogue formats, such as phonographic discs. But, as has been noted before, keeping an item in good condition will not guarantee the long-term survival of the content.

Where original recordings are damaged or deteriorated, the first step in their preservation is to obtain a satisfactory sound signal as close to the original as possible. This may involve inspection, treatment and manual repair of the original item, but otherwise involves copying and the use of electronic processing to remove artefacts introduced into the signal by the damage or deterioration. The aim of the application of 'clean up' technology is clear cut here. The intention is to recreate the quality of the original signal. Of course, assessing the quality of the original signal is a subjective business and it is here that this process of repair, or reclamation as it is known, crosses over with audio restoration work.

In audio **restoration**, contemporary technologies are applied to create what is considered, by the standards of the day, to be the best available result from the original. Technology makes 'cleaning up' audio an easy and invisible process. However, such 'clean up' work can impact on the integrity of the original recording. There is the danger of trying to *improve* on the original recording. The unwanted noise removed in restoration may be the result of damage and deterioration over the years, but it may also partly reflect techniques and equipment used to make the original recordings, and therefore be very much a part of the original record. Archivists and conservators working in this area must clarify what they are trying to achieve with these techniques. A policy decision must be made about the purpose of the copying, and this will inform whether to clean up or enhance recordings (for example, is it a preservation master, is the recording required for access, or is it required for re-broadcast or exhibition). Many institutions will create two copies, an unaltered/unprocessed preservation master, and a restored copy which can be used for access or business purposes.

Therefore, in summary:

- The 'conservation' approach aims to avoid adding more unwanted noise during copying, without seeking to remove existing problems. The aim is to produce an unaltered version of the original.

- The 'restoration' approach seeks to remove or reduce the faults resulting from the original recording process, and any later deterioration, to produce a signal as close as possible to the sounds heard during the original recording.

The 'conservation' approach is regarded as appropriate for archives work. This is especially so when the very act of copying, and thus preserving the signal, will result in damage or even destruction for the original recording. Standard practice in specialist sound archives is to ensure a flat, unrestored copy is made. The desired amount of processing for listening can then be done on another copy without changing the signal irreversibly.

As is the case with other archives conservation work, audio preservation and restoration work must be carefully documented, particularly because it cannot necessarily be detected otherwise.

Deterioration of sound recordings

Three primary types of damage can occur to sound recordings:

- **Physical**: types of physical damage include, warping, planar distortion, delamination, shrinking, stretching, cracking, breakages, scratching and gouges, the effects of contaminants such as dust.
- **Chemical**: the various parts of a carrier may break down over time as a result of chemical interactions with the environment or packaging, or because of reactions between internal constituents. In some carriers one layer may decompose faster than other layers.
- **Biological**: biological attack means living organisms such as mould, insects, rodents and bacteria can harm the media.

As indicated earlier, currently the formats most likely to be encountered as sound recordings in an archive are 1/4" reel-to-reel, audio cassette and CD. However, a basic familiarity with the predominant recording systems and their preservation issues is useful. Before progressing further, let's revisit the four recording systems for sound recordings and examine the factors which influence their preservation.

Grooved recordings: Cylinders and phonographic discs

The composition of grooved recordings can vary depending on the actual format. All of the materials used in the creation of grooved recordings are vulnerable to mechanical damage. There are two primary hazards for grooved recordings: physical damage through handling and playback, and delamination.

Physical damage can take the form of dirt, scratches, or wear and tear on the grooves (for example, heavy styli on old record players wore the grooves down). The playing surfaces should never be touched, and staff handling the discs should wear soft cotton gloves. The discs should be placed in protective boxes and sleeves for storage. In the case

Packaging for phonographic discs

Damaged phonographic disc

of phonographic records, the kinds of base materials may mean they will become increasingly brittle with age. It is possible for the coatings to shrink and flake off the support. The discs are fragile and will shatter or break if dropped.

Delamination can occur as most phonographic records and CDs are layers of different materials whose deterioration can cause their binders to pull apart. A simple measure to ensure the survival of these recordings is to store them on static shelving to reduce the risk of items falling off the shelves. When storing discs, they should be stored upright, with adequate support. Vinyl discs can warp if stored horizontally, leaning at an angle, or stored vertically without support. Boxes provide extra protection and make it easier and safer to move the recordings.

Handling and copying techniques are also of prime importance. Given they can be easily damaged during play-back, the discs must be played on equipment that is correctly adjusted to the original recording. It is recommended that an experienced specialist duplicate recordings such as cylinders, early shellacs and instantaneous discs.

The storage environment is another consideration. High temperatures in particular are of concern. Almost all the thermoplastics, for example, vinyl discs, are prone to heat damage which causes warping (Ward 1990). Controlling temperature and humidity is also important for phonographic and cylinder recordings. In particular, the wax on early cylinders is highly susceptible to fungal growth, and as such should be placed in cool dry storage to minimise the risk of fungal growth.

Tape recordings

As discussed before, the magnetic tape used in sound recordings is composed primarily of two layers – the base film and the magnetic layer. The hazards magnetic tape face include physical damage, such as creasing or tearing of the tape, chemical deterioration of the materials, and interference with the magnetic signal.

Let's look at the materials which make up magnetic tapes.

The base layer

The kinds of base plastics used to make the tape include cellulose acetate, Poly Vinyl Chloride (PVC) and polyester. Cellulose Acetate was used from the 1930s to the 1960s. This material is very susceptible to deterioration in high temperatures and relative humidity. The deterioration gives off a distinctive smell, hence it being referred to as 'vinegar syndrome' (see also the preservation of film in Chapter 18: *Moving Images*). As the tape deteriorates, it becomes brittle and shrinks, thus leading to difficulties in replaying the tapes.

PVC was used as a tape base between 1944 and 1972. Then, from the 1950s, polyester tape bases gradually replaced the cellulose acetate and PVC tapes. It has been the most common base for magnetic tapes since the 1960s. It is used for all contemporary audio, video and data magnetic tape formats. Polyester is chemically stable and mechanically robust, making it an ideal medium for sound recordings. The primary drawback of polyester is that it is prone to stretching. This ability to be stretched and deformed can result in play-back difficulties. Correct tension in play-back equipment and ensuring even winds in the reel of tape will reduce this risk.

Repeated use of magnetic tape can cause wear and tear that shortens the effective life of the tape. The ability to play the tapes safely depends on functional and well-maintained equipment. Another potential harm for tape is poor winds. A loose or uneven winding tension on the spool can expose ridges of tape, making them vulnerable to damage. An even, flat wind can be achieved by winding the tape properly after use, so that it receives a complete wind in one go. (If the tape is in a condition which allows it to be played, play or forward the tape to the end, and then rewind without stopping the tape).

The magnetic layer

The magnetic layer generally consists of a powder of magnetic pigments or magnetic particles bonded together and onto the tape. The binders used to hold this layer together are at the greatest risk of chemical deterioration. The binders for some tapes can absorb moisture from the atmosphere. This moisture can react with the chemicals in the binders, causing a change in the chemical and physical properties of the molecular structure. This effect is known as hydrolysis. As a result of this reaction, the tapes become sticky. They often squeal during replay and shed sticky magnetic powder deposits on the audio (and video) heads. This clogs the heads and leads to a significant loss of high frequencies. High temperatures and relative humidity (RH) can initiate and accelerate this reaction. Some treatments can slow down or counteract this deterioration but these generally require a skilled audio technician trained in audio preservation. It is recommended that tapes be stored in a cool, dry environment to

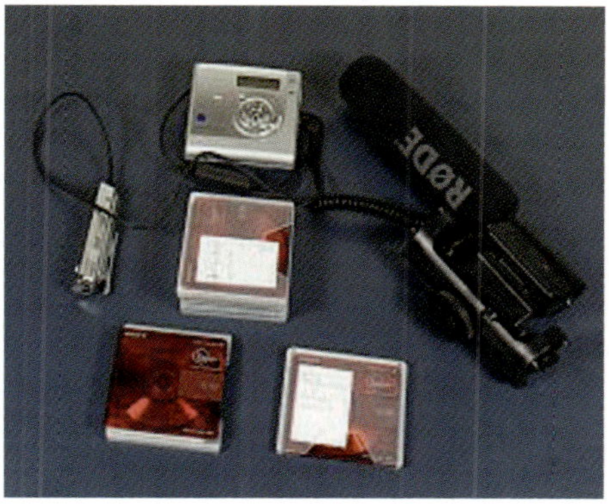

Range of sound recording devices. Digital recordings are increasingly common.

reduce the risk of hydrolysis occurring in the binder. Tapes suffering from hydrolysis will require treatment and copying to ensure the preservation of the information.

'Print through' is another potential problem with poor-quality stocks. The audio information prints through from one magnetic layer to the next (Eilers 1993; van Bogart 1995). This will produce a notable audio effect when the tape is played, where a 'pre-echo' occurs during quiet periods on the recording. There have been various methods employed over the years to remove print through. Most of these will require treatment by a specialised technician.

Demagnetisation – is it a risk?

Contrary to popular belief, demagnetisation of a tape recording is an infrequent occurrence. While it is recommended that tapes do not come in contact with strong magnetic fields, it is unlikely that the magnetic information will completely vanish with time. A very large magnetic field would be required to erase the recording. (Equipment such as dynamic headphones, microphones and loudspeakers can produce magnetic fields, and tapes should not be stored near these items. However, these are unlikely to be strong enough to completely erase a recording). The most likely cause of erasure of tapes will be when the record button is pressed during play-back. For this reason, it is recommended that tapes should be played only under supervision, or on a machine that has had the record function disabled to prevent accidental erasure of archival tapes. Provided tapes are properly produced, handled, stored, and accessed they will not lose their magnetic qualities.

Biological damage, specifically mould growth, can affect all sound recording carriers. In conditions of high relative humidity, mould can grow on the surface of the magnetic tape layer, and in some instances can penetrate the magnetic layer. Mould can make the tapes difficult, and sometimes impossible, to play. Items affected with mould should be handled carefully (and staff should be protected from inhaling or coming into contact with the mould). Mould-affected items should be isolated, away from the rest of the collection. The storage environment should be cool and dry, avoiding conditions of high relative humidity.

Optical discs

The life expectancy of optical discs is still a matter of debate. The life expectancy of various optical discs have been quoted to be anywhere from 5 to 100 years. Optical discs were primarily developed for the consumer market. While some manufacturers will claim a longer life for their product, stability of the individual materials used is not the only factor affecting their expected lifespan. The variability between the methods of manufacture, the types of materials used, recording processes and storage can greatly affect the longevity of the formats.

As a result, CDs are not considered to be archival formats suitable for the long-term storage of records. This does not discount their use as an interim solution, while more reliable digital storage system is implemented. However, if used as a storage medium, adhering to a strict regime of testing, analysis and survey of the collection will be required. If this is not possible (including the purchase of a reliable CD tester) then you should choose an alternative storage medium.

As a general rule, it is recommended that only reliable and well-tested brands of CD be used. The quality of the CD and its ability to survive will depend on three factors: the choice of blank stock, the recording drive and the selected speed of recording. The only way to produce optimum results is to test all three parameters.

The compatibility (or incompatibility) of discs and machines is also an issue. There are many points where this incompatibility can occur: the blank disc, the computer, the software, the disc burner, the disc reader. The interaction of the blank discs with the CD writers, and later the interaction of recorded discs with CD readers can create a number of situations which produce either poor performance of the discs, or inability to retrieve the information. An example of this at its most basic is for rewritable discs. These discs cannot be written and sometimes cannot be read in recordable disc drives.

Identify the recording format, and what equipment will be required for replay. For example, older CD players may only play CD audio recordings and may not be able to play digital files (MP3).

The factors that may affect the long-term usability of CDs are:

- **Physical damage**: Optical discs are prone to physical damage. It is important to avoid damage to the disc surface. Scratches on the polycarbonate layer can obstruct the laser beam, and scratches on the protective layer may allow damage to occur to the reflective layer, or increase the chance of oxidation.
- **Oxidation**: All of the reflective layers except gold are prone to oxidation. This occurs when they are exposed to moisture. The protective lacquer layer therefore plays an important role in protecting the disc from penetration of moisture. Oxidised layers can render a disc unreadable.
- **Stability of the dyes**: There are three different dyes used in recordable CDs, cyanine, phthalo-cyanine and azo. Whilst the phthalo-cyanine is considered the most stable, all dyes are susceptible to damage by light. Tests have shown that exposure to sunlight can render recordable discs unreadable within weeks. They should therefore be stored away from direct light.

Generally, the polycarbonate layer is stable, and rarely shows signs of deterioration.

Data files

Data files require the right combination of hardware and software to access the record. Accessibility of the format is highly vulnerable to changes in technology. Both hardware and software can be superseded over time. Market-driven innovations mean that manufacturers will release new systems, software applications and technology at a rapid rate.

General requirements for archival data files for preservation purposes are:

- **Open standard formats**: data files for which the technical specification have been made public domain are desirable
- **Well-established format**: popular file formats which have widespread use are likely to have broader and longer lasting support
- **File format should be relatively stable** and not subject to constant change (new versions should be backwardly compatible)
- **No data reduction**: preferably uncompressed or, if necessary, lossless compression
- **High sampling rate** (IASA TC-04 recommends a minimum of 48 kHz, though 96 kHz is preferable)
- **High bit rate** (IASA TC-04 recommends 24 bit rate)
- Accompanying **metadata** support
- **Verification** of the file
- **Quality checking** of file (be free of 'uncorrectable' errors and lowest possible number of correctable errors)

Once a recording becomes a digital file, whether it's born digital or created during the copying process, to all intents and purposes, it's a digital record and requires the same management approaches as digital records in general. There are extra description elements to make sure all of the necessary context travels with it over its life, and the file sizes can be very substantial, but essentially their management issues in this form are those of digital records. Many issues relating to digital records are covered in Chapter 15: *Digital Recordkeeping*.

Data files which have not been checked for their data integrity should be considered to be endangered.

An issue in digital archiving is the trend towards increasingly dense information storage. This is a particular risk with migrated material, where a single data DVD may hold the individual data files for 10 audio tapes. Any damage to that DVD has a greater impact than would occur to the original individual tapes. Data files and their carriers may fail at any time. It is therefore imperative to have at least one copy as a back-up, preferably stored in an alternative location.

Preservation measures for sound recordings

The major preservation treatments for sound recordings are providing optimum storage conditions, rehousing recordings in appropriate packaging, and copying deteriorated or obsolete formats to current or more stable formats.

Factors that may influence prioritisation of items for preservation include financial resources, limitations of staff, facilities, equipment, and availability of treatment options. The archivist must evaluate what is the probable cost of preserving the collection over time. Factors which slow deterioration are generally far more cost-effective in the long run than any process to treat or restore an item.

- Handling: all equipment must be in good working order. Have equipment serviced regularly. Limit the use of original materials in play back equipment. Originals should only be used to produce a master copy from which additional copies can be made.
- Provide cool dry storage wherever possible.
- Store originals and copies in different locations. This is a risk management process. It ensures that all records will not be lost in the event of a disaster.
- Repackaging into archival quality containers, and labelling so they can be clearly identified.
- Maintenance of the collection: conduct periodic inspections. Some damage may not be visible when surveyed but will only become apparent when tape is played. The only way of knowing the condition of these items is constant and comprehensive surveys and inspection.
- Migration of formats to fresh media and contemporary well-supported formats
- Disaster preparedness: be prepared for something that may happen. Even an uncontrolled storage environment, leaking pipe or box damaged during transit can be a disaster.

Environmental conditions

As has been noted, the storage environment in an archive can affect the long term stability of physical sound recording formats. The conditions in which the records are used and stored are crucial to their preservation.

Temperature and moisture are two key factors which directly affect the deterioration of sound recording formats. Moisture from the air (relative humidity, or RH) can trigger chemical reactions such as hydrolysis or oxidation in some materials. Temperature, or changes in temperature, can cause dimensional changes such as warping, shrinking or swelling of materials. High temperatures can also increase the rate of chemical reactions in the materials. Storage areas which have high temperatures and relative humidity can promote the growth of mould. This has been known to occur at RH levels of 70 percent or higher. Mould can grow on nearly all types of sound recordings, and render them unplayable.

For these reasons, it is recognised that controlling the storage environment is of paramount importance. Improving storage conditions is possibly the single most important step an archivist can take to ensure the preservation of their collection. Studies have shown that storing audiovisual formats in conditions of low temperatures and relative humidity effectively slows down the rates of deterioration. Ideally, the records will be stored in good conditions from the point of creation. Items in poor condition, such as magnetic tapes affected with hydrolysis, will require more stringent climate conditions than magnetic tapes in better preservation condition to achieve a similar lifespan.

In general, cool, dry storage is recommended for sound recording formats. The environment should aim to be stable, where fluctuations in temperature and humidity are kept to a minimum. This type of storage will win a measure of control for your collection, and will buy you time for other preservation processes such as copying. Sudden climatic change should be avoided, particularly between the storage, handling and access areas of the archival building. It is often not practical to use the sound recording items in the storage environment. Records being moved from cool, dry to warm, moist conditions should be allowed to acclimatise slowly to their new environment before being played. This may require they be left in an isolated controlled room or, in the absence of such facilities, within an insulated container (such as an 'esky'). Although the time required for acclimatisation can vary depending on the weight of the material, a good rule of thumb is to allow 24 hours before using them.

The Image Permanence Institute (IPI), International Standards Organisation (ISO), Audio Engineering Society (AES) and International Association of Sound Archives (IASA) all provide good overviews and standards for accepted storage conditions for sound recordings. In particular, The IPI Media Storage Quick Reference (MSQR) recognises that many repositories must house their media together. They have therefore developed charts that assist in choosing storage solutions to suit a range of materials in the collection. If cool, dry conditions cannot be achieved, then good storage conditions as used for paper records that minimise fluctuations in temperature and humidity will be adequate for sound materials.

Direct sunlight or direct heat will harm sound recordings, particularly optical discs and phonograph records. These factors should be avoided wherever possible.

Storage dos and don'ts

Good housekeeping is a necessary component of preservation. It takes time and discipline, but saves unnecessary loss and double handling.

Maintain a dust-free environment. Sound recordings are very prone to damage by contaminants, especially particulate dust. Even the smallest particles can result in damage to the recording surface and lead to play-back errors. They are also prone to damage from other contaminants, such as fingerprints, mould and pollutants. Cleanliness of storage and work areas is important, including play-back equipment.

Correct storage extends beyond the provision of appropriate conditions. Storage equipment and packaging is as important, as the correct environmental conditions in prolonging the life of the collection.

The shelving should be designed to minimise unnecessary handling and retrieval times. It should also promote maximum airflow and stability for materials, as well as utilising space to its maximum capabilities in order to accommodate a mix of container types and dimensions. As a rule of thumb, sound recordings should be stored vertically, side-by-side on the shelves, rather than stacked.

Example of shelving containing sound recordings

The storage enclosures used for records will aid in the protection, organisation and identification of items. The primary function of enclosures is to protect items from environmental hazards such as light, dust and physical damage. In some instances they can also act as a buffer against rapid environmental changes. Containers should be chemically and physically stable, preferably constructed of acid-free materials. Items should be correctly and clearly labelled to assist in identification and retrieval. Keep the sound recordings within their protective cases or packaging wherever possible.

Digital storage

The issue of storage does not relate simply to the physical storage of the carriers. The storage requirements of digital file formats also need to be considered. Digital storage encounters the same level of complexity as physical storage. It must factor in a wide range of technologies and processes, including storage format, capacity, file sizes, application requirements, storage time, access time, work flow processes and identification of the items.

When computer technology was first introduced, the lifecycle was approximately 10 years. Now the characteristics of the hardware and software change every two years. An archives will be obliged to update and make changes to the system as an ongoing process every two, four, or six years due to lack of industry support for the old systems and equipment.

Copying

A preservation strategy aimed at minimising the risk of loss of information will include the creation of duplicate components and copies. Where an item becomes deteriorated, damaged or obsolete, all efforts should be made to facilitate accurate duplication, thus ensuring the information is preserved. The copies should resemble the original as closely as possible, with no avoidable loss, or degradation of the audiovisual content. The other advantage is that it can also provide a convenient means of providing access to the content that will not damage or endanger the original medium.

The priority for copying should be:

- those items at immediate risk
- those items that are obsolete or no longer supported within the archives
- those items in regular demand

For copying to be most effective in ensuring the survival of the record, it should not be delayed until the format is deteriorated. The most effective copying, both in terms of quality and economics, occurs when records are still in good condition. Records which are damaged or deteriorated may require intensive treatment, thus increasing the cost of preparing the item and handling during the copying process.

As in the case of photographs and moving images, an audio copying program involves making three kinds of copies:

- **A preservation copy** – The preservation copy is kept in storage, acts as a security copy, and is not played at all, unless absolutely essential. The preservation copy must contain the most authentic and highest-quality representation of the original or source recording. For this reason, their production and use must be specifically defined and tightly controlled. If the preservation copy is a digital file, this must be supported with a sustainable digital repository – including the need to back-up the files in an off-site location.
- **A duplicating/working copy** – The duplication copy is similarly made on a high quality archival medium. This copy should be as high qualityas possible to prevent any need to return to the preservation or original materials. It is expected to have a longer lifespan than an access format and high enough resolution and quality to serve most business purposes. When copying to digital formats, these can be created as required rather than at the actual point of transfer (provided the preservation file has a back up file).
- **An access copy** – The reference or access copy is best supplied on the most convenient format for your reading room, (for example, audio CD or MP3 files).

Depending on the play-back machinery available to the archives, there are still many ways in which a collection can be copied. However, current copying technology for sound recordings focuses on the digital signal. While copying to 1/4" reel-to-reel tapes was previously the preferred format for preservation copying, converting analogue recordings to digital formats is now the accepted preservation practice. The IASA publication IASA-TC 04 *Guidelines on the production and preservation of digital audio objects,* provides a comprehensive overview of the requirements for conversion of analogue to digital formats. We recommend reading this publication if undertaking preservation copying of sound recordings for preservation purposes.

Copying from one analogue format to another analogue format (such as copying from gramophone disc to ¼" magnetic tape) is no longer considered suitable to ensure the preservation of sound recordings. This is for two primary reasons:

1. Most analogue formats are now considered to be obsolete, or at the very least endangered. Therefore, a copying program that incorporates analogue technology will have to be undertaken again in the very near future. The exception to this may be in the production of access copies. Some archives may wish to provide access via a cassette format. However, given the prevalence of computers and CDs, these are most likely to be the preferred format for access.

2. Deterioration of the analogue signal. Whereas digital migration can permit an unlimited number of copies to be produced without change to the quality of the recording, every generation of analogue copying will cause deterioration of the sound signal.

Many of the processes and theory outlined in Chapter 13: *Digitisation & Imaging* are applicable to the digitisation of sound recordings. Despite differences in formats and standards, the fundamental issues of capture, storage and management are very similar.

Consideration should be given to the advantages of outsourcing digitisation. In general, sound recordings will require specialised equipment and trained staff to undertake the copying. There are a number of copying bureaus within Australia which have the equipment to undertake the digital copying of sound recordings. However, given the fragility of some sound formats, and the types of deterioration, it will be necessary to ensure these bureaus are able to deal professionally with archival sound recordings.

Copying 1/4" magnetic tape

It is worth noting that copying for audio faces the perennial problem of obsolescence. No sooner is one format selected than it becomes obsolete. However, preserving recordings as encoded data files is a widely accepted current practice (IASA; NFSA; NLA; NAA). At present, there is general agreement that the digital file format preferred for preservation is the Broadcast Wave File (BWF). This is a version of the Wave file format (.wav) which was introduced by the European Broadcasting Union (EBU).

Digital audio preservation is not possible without metadata. There are several kinds of metadata, including descriptive (e.g. track listings), administrative, and technical (e.g. a description of audio hardware used in digital transfer, hardware settings, and data compression used) which can accompany a digital recording.

As with moving images, it is important to bear in mind that advances in technology may make a currently unplayable recording accessible in the future. Digital technologies can bring challenges, but also new tools and opportunities. Technologies may advance, giving future benefits in copying, time and cost savings. It is unlikely that a single copying project will ensure the survival of sound recording formats. Rather, an archives will have to ensure that the information is continuously copied and migrated well into the future. Do not discard originals after copying. Preserve original medium and equipment for as long as possible. Disposal of originals should not be taken lightly. Many archives have regretted disposing of originals only to find the copies produced are inferior or prone to greater preservation problems than the original format.

Providing access to sound recordings

There are many different kinds of access the archives should consider and plan for. Firstly, there is reactive access: responding to enquiries, research and retrieval. The second type of access is proactive: provision on-line, publication, exhibition, and broadcasting.

While access may seem to be the end of the line for archival materials, it should be a consideration from the start. It is not an effective use of archival resources to acquire, describe store and preserve sound recordings if they cannot be made accessible. All of these activities are closely linked. In particular, access and preservation are two sides of the same coin. The ability to keep the records usable and accessible is the primary aim of preservation.

Access to sound recordings can be a problem for archives, as playing original recordings can damage them. The creation and provision of access copies in most cases will act as a surrogate for the originals. They should generally be replaceable if lost or damaged. While the temptation to provide short-term access may be high, it should not be allowed to put the long-term preservation of sound recordings at risk. Generally, explaining the situation to the researcher is a better strategy than exposing a fragile recording to irreversible damage.

Where and how to provide access

Generally, access to sound recordings is provided in the form of a reference copy for play-back in the reading room, usually on a portable format such as CD or audio cassette. While physical on-site access is possible and affordable, technological advances will bring the potential for greater access, regardless of geography. As multi- and interactive media permeates all aspects of society, access expectations will expand and clients will expect more from sound recording collections and how they are delivered.

Archives are increasingly turning to digital technology to assist in the provision of access to their collection. The creation and use of data files such as MP3 files to provide access is becoming more prevalent in the archive community. As data communication networks such as the Internet offer greater opportunities to make archival collections accessible, so it can be expected that there will be increasing demands on archives to provide their sound recordings on-line. The provision of access via digital copies can be more efficient, flexible and cost effective and this can lead to increased opportunities for access. However, it cannot be assumed that converting analogue audiovisual records to digital file formats is quicker, cheaper and easier. Experience demonstrates that the costs of digitisation are high and the process is time consuming. A program to produce digital copies mustbe well planned, resourced with skilled staff, include good quality data capture and have sufficient lead time for the specialised work that needs to occur prior to digitisation.

It is still possible that some researchers may wish to look at the carriers of original sound recordings, for example, to examine the labels of phonographic recordings. Particular care will be required here to ensure that the recording is handled correctly. A policy that allows only staff members to handle and play original materials will reduce the risk of damage if access to originals must be considered.

Like moving images and photographs, sound material is often sought for use in productions of many kinds, such as films, television and radio programs and advertisements. Quality copying at the preservation stage enables you to provide your duplicating copy in a standard that is suitable for this kind of use. Staff members will also be invaluable in assisting access. Through activities such as appraisal, describing and preserving the collection, they will develop a depth of knowledge of the collection that no database or catalogue can replace.

Copyright and rights protection have been dealt with earlier in this chapter and Chapter 11: *Access & Reference Services*. But it is important to note that these factors need to be considered when determining delivery options. Generally, provision of access of sound recordings within a reading room will be less problematic. The provision of on-line delivery must allow for the protection of the content from potential misuse. This may mean researchers are able to listen to the recording, but are unable to download or copy the record.

Summary

Audiovisual records are a distinctive part of modern culture. Modern technology has made low-cost, high-quality recording available to everyone. Music, public performance, oral histories and documentation of events can be recorded at a quality never before accessible to the professional and amateur alike. The purpose of this chapter has been to assist archivists to extend their knowledge of the archival principles associated with audiovisual records, including sound recordings. The principles of appraising, acquiring, describing, preserving and making these records accessible are closely related to those of textual records. Nevertheless, the nature of the media means there are other imperatives that will impact on their management. The key factors to consider are the reliance on specific equipment to gain access to the record content, the format obsolescence caused by technological advances and the potential for rapid deterioration of the media. By becoming familiar with the characteristics of these media, the archivist can begin to effectively incorporate, and enhance, their sound recordings within the context of their collections.

"This is a tape of the minister yodelling ... I say we file it under 'lost' or 'damaged' ..."

CHAPTER 18

moving images

LOUISE CURHAM &
ROBYN GAMBLE

CHAPTER ABSTRACT

Moving images are often some of the treasures of an archival collection yet, like sound recordings, are often regarded as unusual and difficult to manage. They exist on fragile physical carriers and in a range of formats unfamiliar to the non-specialist.

This chapter will help you identify and understand the types of moving images you may have in your collection, and specific issues regarding appraisal, control, preservation and storage.

This chapter should be read in conjunction with Chapter17: *Sound Recordings,* which provides an overview on the general principles that apply to all audiovisual records.

Introduction

Collecting moving images began in Australia with the National Historical Films and Speaking Record Library. This was established in 1937 as part of the National Library (Jeffrey 1973), concurrent with the first film archives in Europe and the US (Slide 1992). The aim of the National Library's new endeavour was to collect 'films of the past and contemporary events of historic interest, or which might throw light on our social development; a limited number of scientific and industrial films, including anthropological films; and films illustrating the development of film-making in Australia' (Jeffrey 1973). As a reflection of society and culture, and increasingly as evidence of it, moving images form part of our documentary heritage.

As time-based records that exist on physically fragile carriers, moving images share much with sound recordings. In the first instance, they often share the same recording media. Chapter 17: *Sound Recordings,* covers much ground relevant for moving images, starting with a general introduction to audiovisual records. To gain a comprehensive overview of the issues for managing these media as archives, the chapters are intended to be read together.

How do moving images differ from other types of records?

Like digital records, the principles for managing moving images are the same as those for archives in more traditional forms. Their formats add a layer of complexity to the archival kit bag but the same key task of setting them in their original context is the focus of working with these formats as archival records.

Before we discuss how moving images differ, it is useful to draw parallels with the now more familiar world of digital records, parallels beginning to draw attention (de Lusenet 2006).

Properties that moving images share with digital records include:

- a dependence on technology for capture and replay
- a dependence on metadata to provide a useable record
- format obsolescence
- an essence that can be separated from a carrier (often controversial for motion picture film).

Unwittingly, Kevin stumbles onto the simplest method of archiving the moving image.

The introduction to audiovisual records provided in Chapter 17: *Sound Recordings* works through the differences common to sound and moving image in detail. To recap on some pertinent points, the formats tend to be unfamiliar to non-specialists. Production methods vary widely, using a huge range of formats. Typically, many parts come together to make up one production. Both film and video are dependent on technology to capture and replay the information.

Audiovisual records have potentially significant cultural and monetary value, often amplified for moving image records. There is an added intangible value in the ability of moving images to convey a sense that the past moves and speaks. This tends to bring out passionate responses from key stakeholders about how they should be managed. This is also part of the great satisfaction in learning to manage them as archives – the tendency for a diverse audience to care deeply about them.

Changes in technology

In the broadest sense, all moving images find their foundation in photography, in its relationship between light-sensitive surfaces and time. There is a strange paradox in moving image technology – while technical change is a characteristic of electronic moving images, motion picture film has barely changed since it was introduced in 1896. It remains in essence a purely mechanical, photographic process.

On the other hand, video technology changes increasingly fast. Obsolescence is a particularly significant problem for video. (Marlow & Secunda 1991).

Audiovisual records are rarely one for one

Film and video production in the pre-digital era involved a chain of duplication to create the final production, so often numerous parts make up the whole. Similar iterative processes occur in the digital production chain, but often these versions or 'stems' exist as files rather than physical entities. In most instances, moving image productions are made with sound, which adds to the volume of material that forms the final work.

Volume of material to make up one work.

Often there are numerous final versions produced from the same source material

In advertising, there are typically three or four commercials of different lengths made, often with changes for different target audiences. In education and training films, it is not uncommon to find different edits for different language groups or audiences. There can be complete re-edits for political reasons, not infrequently the case with government films portraying community groups.

Working your way through these variations takes time

To distinguish between duplication and subtle but significant differences can involve time-consuming examination. Although we can see the individual film frames on the reel with our naked eye, 'performing' it, like video, is a real time process.

Ways to think about your moving image collections

The history of moving images is intrinsically linked to popular culture and mass production. Moving image technology continues to develop in response to the commercial industries. However, like all forms of communication technology, the use of moving images in society has always been broader than the commercial imperative that developed it.

This helps us to conceive of moving images in two broad categories. There are productions created for the film and television industries. Intended for a ticket-buying or advertising-watching public, these are products made by an industry. As we have acknowledged, the movies and programs we watch have become important cultural, sociological and social history texts in their own right. As archives, these are usually collected by specialist audiovisual archives. While there is no agreed terminology to describe this broad category, we will refer to them as industry productions.

The second broad category of moving image records are those where the technology of moving images has been used to capture or transmit information that is best conveyed in a document that moves and speaks. Military training films, films of scientific experiments, surveillance footage, documentation of speeches and events, home movies, documentation of cultural practices – these are all examples where the intrinsic ability to make a visual record in real time and space tells us information and provides evidence we could never gather from the written word. These types of moving image records are referred to as 'informational moving images'.

What's on your shelf?

Most archives are likely to receive records from the second category, informational moving image records. They are likely to be documentation of events, people or locations, for example, home movies of a notable person. In a general archives they are likely to include off-air recordings or purchased copies of broadcast media that have significance in their context, like video compilations of television coverage relevant to an organisation or an individual. They may be copies of productions or footage owned by another entity, used as source material for new works, i.e. stock footage.

Where archives find completed productions on motion picture film, they are likely to be for education or promotional purposes, such as with 16mm film prints of education films or corporate videos promoting activities and achievements.

Unless proactive appraisal and acquisition strategies are in place, it is unlikely that all the physical components or the all-important originals of a moving image production will be retained as archives. However, it is not impossible.

What is a component?

Completed productions can consist of many pieces of moving image material, known as elements or components. For instance, in a video production there may be motion picture film camera negatives, video copies of the negative or 'rushes', sound location recording tapes, a video sub-master of the final edit, and a final master video tape (we unpack the jargon of these terms as the chapter progresses). These all played a role in the production of the final work. In a motion picture film production in particular, these pieces that make up the whole are important in preserving the final work. Each was produced to reflect a new layer of decision-making, or as 'insurance' to keep the final version safe.

Knowing when to call the specialists

There are going to be times when you need a specialist. You may find works that seem to be unique and of obvious value or suffering from advanced deterioration. For these works, identifying an audiovisual archives that can either provide advice or preserve the properties of the original carrier is likely to be the best solution. Knowing when to make this judgement call is important. For some works that are truly unique and of obvious value, obtaining professional help or transferring custody of your originals is a realistic solution.

Working with audiovisual archives

While the movement to establish film archives began in the 1930s (Slide 1992), the discipline of audiovisual archiving is young. In Australia, there is one specialist archive, the National Film and Sound Archive and many specialist collections within archives and libraries. The Register of Audiovisual Collections (NFSA 2007) demonstrates how widespread audiovisual holdings are in all manner of collections in Australia.

Many film archives place a premium on the value of films as objects, applying museum practices to their collections. They seek to preserve the original artefacts and to replicate the original experience of them as closely as possible (Usai 2006; NFSA 2006). Practice in these archives does not exclude making these works available on other media, but the focus is on presenting the work in a form as close as possible to the original experience. This is an altogether different goal from a total archives dealing with collections of informational film records.

A note on ethics and moving images

There are ethical issues specific to moving images. If access material is different from the way the record was originally created or presented, it is important to make information about the original available to researchers and audiences.

Preservation introduces significant ethical issues. Treatments and interventions may be very difficult to detect without documentation. Accountability and the compatibility of future treatments depend on this trail of documentation.

'Improvements' by contemporary standards are easily performed with digital technologies. These may not be readily identified or understood without documentation. Preservation principles require that a clear distinction is made between deteriorated originals and 'restored' versions that attempt to return the deteriorated record to its original state. An unaltered version of the original must be kept where restoration occurs.

Regarding communities

Where records document cultural practices and traditional cultural expression, they require policies that recognise sensitivities for particular communities. This is true for records depicting many social groups and communities. In an Australian context, it is of particular relevance to Indigenous communities – moving image records that relate to Indigenous communities form a relatively small but very significant part of our film history.

Since the 1990s, there has been a conscious push in Australia to address the impact of the culture in libraries and archives on Indigenous communities. In 1995, protocols were published, specifically the *Aboriginal and Torres Strait Islander protocols for libraries, archives and information services* (Byrne et al. 1994). The protocols addressed the way in which libraries and archives interact with Indigenous communities, both in how collections are managed and the access process (Nakata 2005).

The World Intellectual Property Organisation (WIPO) defined some of the problems communities face when their traditional cultural expression is used by others. Problems arise from unauthorised, inappropriate use, appropriation and failure to acknowledge tradition-based creation or innovation (Wendlend 2006). There is a link here to the moral rights aspect to copyright, where the creator has an inalienable stake in their authorship.

The importance of moral rights is echoed by Canadian archivist Kristina Laszlo (2006). Where legal possession resides outside the community, there is still a right to the moral ownership of the content. Laszlo crystalises some other issues for culturally sensitive records. She proposes that archives regard culturally sensitive material on an equal footing with personal privacy and confidentiality. She proposes that restricting materials because they contain outdated ideas of ethnicity and racial representation is not appropriate. Where material depicts sacred and ritual expression, these are legitimate grounds for restriction.

Laszlo points out that there are implications attached to material made in circumstances not ethical by today's standards. She identifies the need to balance the archival mandate to make materials available to as many people as possible with an awareness of their impact on those communities to which those records relate.

Understanding your formats

We now look more closely at the different physical formats of the records to start to build the tools to identify the different types of moving image records, both different physical and intellectual entities. We will work through each format with a general description of it, followed by more information on the technical processes that surround it and the language used to discuss and describe it. The purpose of these extended sections is to familiarise you with the technical language and format-specific issues that will help you manage these records.

There are several phases in industry production which means the final work is made up of many components, all related to one another and all serving a purpose in the long-term usefulness of the work. What's most important is to keep all the related components together and to understand that parts related to particular production steps are more valuable than others.

Since the mid 1990s, production methods have been increasingly digital. High-end technology developed for the film and television industries is quickly adapted for the domestic market. The last 5-10 years has seen a proliferation of domestic digital moving image tools, from the digital camera, to the mobile phone to the portable MP4 player.

There are four main types of physical media that carry moving images:

- motion picture film
- magnetic media: video tape, hard disk drives
- optical discs: DVDs, CDs
- flash and solid state computer media.

Film

As we've said, in most instances, you are likely to be dealing with single films like home movies or film prints like education films or newsreel diaries. Sometimes, an entire production may come into your collection. Even for the single print films, understanding the fundamentals of the commercial production process will assist you in identifying what you've got and how to appraise it.

In essence, film production is a copying process aimed at producing a seamless print for film projection, where the editing and printing processes that the production has undergone are invisible. The film-making process creates an abundance of parts, known as components, in the steps from shooting the film to its final exhibition prints. The relationship between these components establishes the form of the finished product and its ongoing preservation.

The types of film components include:

- the original camera materials (original negative, original reversal)
- duplicating components (internegative, duplicate negative, interdupe, fine grain, interpositive)
- prints for editing (workprint, slash dupe)
- sound components (location tapes, field tapes, mixing or dubbing tracks, final mix, music and effects, optical sound negative, optical sound positive)
- prints of the production which were used in distribution (release print, low-contrast print for television)
- out-takes, off-cuts, trims which were not used in the final version.

The basic film production process works along these lines. The original material is filmed in the camera. Traditionally, a print copy of this original material is edited resulting in a workprint. Contemporary practices now involve computer editing at this phase. The camera original material is cut to match this edited workprint or its contemporary equivalent. In order to prolong the life of the camera-original material, it is duplicated by the use of what is known as 'film intermediates'. These are called 'intermediates' because they are produced at the stage between the camera originals and final prints. Often there are two intermediate steps, positive duplication, which results in components called 'fine grain positives' and 'interpositives', followed by negative duplication which results in 'interdupes', 'duplicate negatives' and 'internegatives'. The prints are then made from these negative intermediates. See the NFSA *Film Preservation Handbook,* and *Film Duplication and Generations* for further guidance.

While manufactured to withstand demanding mechanical processes, motion picture film is a physically organic medium, prone to damage from poor storage and poor handling. Its physical composition has its foundation in photography. It is particularly sensitive to temperature and humidity. The film strip consists of a series of layers: a base or support layer, a gelatin emulsion layer that carries the image, a protective top coating, or supercoat and anti curl layers on either side. We look at the physical properties in detail later in the chapter in the section on preservation.

The technical process and the language of film

As we've said above, the detail that follows is to assist the archivist in identifying what they have before them. Within the family of motion picture film, there is a wide variety. That variation can reveal significant information about the content and context of the record and how it should be cared for. Learning to interpret that information is part of the business of managing motion picture film as records.

While the technology of motion picture film has been very stable when compared to the obsolescence-prone video, there have been developments in the way that technology is applied. The three main variations are different sized systems, the development of colour and the development in plastics used in film bases.

There are variations in all these aspects:

- the size of the film itself, known as the film gauge
- the aspect ratio (produced by the frame, the gate which determines the area of the frame through which light is projected, and the projector lens which determines the ultimate size on the screen)
- the presence of sprockets on both or one side of the frame
- the frame rate.

Film gauge

The film gauge refers to the width of the film from edge to edge, expressed in millimetres. Identifying the gauge of the film is often the first step in identifying the type of film and its original function. Equally important as the gauge is the type of sprockets on the film. On most sizes of film, or gauges, there are two sets of holes on the side of the film, one on each side of the image area. These are known as sprocket holes or perforations. These interlace with a claw on the camera to transport the film over the gate. In the later production stages, they interlace with cogs on the printer.

Professional gauges

These are used to produce 'industry' moving image records:

- 70mm
- Vistavision (35mm, landscape image orientation)
- 35 mm
- Super 35mm (single perforation, image extends to edge of film)
- Super 16mm (single perforation, image extends to edge of film).

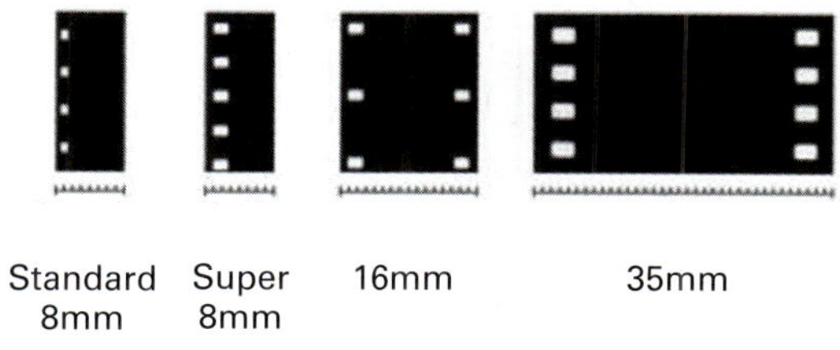

Typical film gauges, the sizes of which are expressed in millimetres.

Amateur gauges

These were used to produce 'informational' moving image records:

- 16mm has also been widely used for industry production in the television era.
- Super 8 mm (single sprocket, image extends to edge of film)
- 16mm

Obsolete amateur gauges

- 9.5mm
- standard 8mm (superseded by Super 8 in 1968)

Film Generations

First generation	• camera negative • edited camera negative. In 16mm, likely to be compiled into two rolls with 'chequer-boarded' black spacer, known as A and B rolls • trims from edited camera negative • out-takes or unused shots from camera negative.
Second generation	• edited workprint. The early edit is known as the 'rough cut'. The final edit is the 'fine cut'. • interpositive, printed from the fine cut negative. Interpositive is colour, printed from colour negative, contains few or no splices. • duplicate negative, printed from fine cut negative. Duplicate negative is B&W, printed from B&W negative.
Third generation	• In Australia, colour at this generation is referred to as the internegative. B&W at this generation is referred to as the duplicate or dupe negative. Also known as interdupe.
Fourth generation	• Projection print. First print struck is to test printing settings. This print is known as the trial print or answer print. When printing parameters are correct, prints thereafter called release prints. For television, may have low contrast print.

Table 18.1: Film generations

Colour systems – colour or black and white

The first film systems were black and white, producing a positive image from the original shot in the camera. When projected over and over for incredulous audiences, these shoot-and-show originals deteriorated rapidly, part of the reason for the paucity of existing material from the earliest days of cinema. This problem was corrected as the use of negatives in the camera became the standard. This meant many copy prints could be generated from one original negative.

There have been numerous systems for colour film. Most relevant for archives in Australia is colour negative, characterised by an orange colour caste we are familiar with from our minilab negatives for our home photo snaps. In Australia, these stocks will date from the mid 1950s, as Kodak released this stock in 1950.

Reversal film was the other prevalent colour system in Australia. This produced a positive image from the camera. The colour Kodachromes and Agfachromes and later Ektachromes were widely used in news gathering for early colour television and in the amateur gauges. In Australia, films on these stocks date from the late 1930s, as Kodachrome was released in 1935. As reversal produced a positive image from the camera, it was not usable in the usual negative positive film duplication process. This restricted its use to 16mm and non-professional production (Enticknap 2005).

Reversal film was also produced in black and white, the dominant form in Australian television archives. It was the source material for broadcasting from 1956 to 1973, until the introduction of colour television in 1975. If you have reversal film in your collection it may well be unique.

The other key technical variation in motion picture film is the kind of plastic used in the film base. We mentioned that the physical make-up of film consists of a supporting plastic base coated in a photographic emulsion. The plastic used in the base has evolved with 20th century plastics technology. It began with the notoriously flammable cellulose nitrate base, used for 35mm production until the 1950s, when it moved to the less dangerous but still chemically unstable cellulose acetate base. Acetate was used for the smaller gauges from the 1920s (Enticknap 2005). In the early 1990s in Australia, polyester was used for projection prints and duplicating intermediates, promoted as the preservation panacea with its predicted 500 year life span. It's worth noting that acetate is still produced. Camera negatives continue to be acetate as the tear-resistent polyester is hazardous to the delicate precision mechanics of film cameras (McKeown 2008).

World wide, concerted effort by audiovisual specialists has seen most of the cellulose nitrate motion picture film identified and brought into specialist care. It is found almost exclusively on 35mm in Australia. Deteriorating acetate is a real problem for those caring for film collections. This is compounded by the fact that this is the most widespread base in Australian collections. You'll find acetate bases for 16mm from the 1920s, for 35mm from c. 1950. As we have already noted, camera original material continues to be produced on acetate. Polyester has been adopted for all steps after the camera original since the early 1990s.

A note on deterioration of reversal film, also on acetate base: anecdotally, the deterioration of the acetate base for reversal films appears to be radically slower than for acetate used in a negative production path.

Video

Video sits within the family of magnetic media. Chapter 17: *Sound Recordings* describes the early development of magnetic media. Its application to video began in earnest with the release of 2" video tape in 1956 (Enticknap 2005). Also in the magnetic media family, alongside audio and video, are the floppy disk formats and computer hard disk drives.

The history of video is one of constant technical change. The problems for video as archives stem from the fragility of magnetic media and this fast pace of change.

What's on your shelf

On your shelf, you are likely to find domestic formats. Among them may be some that are truly obsolete, like Betamax, some no longer manufactured but still available to purchase, like Hi8 and those still used like VHS and miniDV. These formats are likely to have been used in domestic video cameras or to tape off-air recordings.

You may find professional formats, used to create industry productions. These may be both analogue and digital. The professional formats used for broadcast started with 2", literally a two-inch-wide ribbon of tape. This was so expensive at its inception that the same set of tapes were constantly recorded over at station.

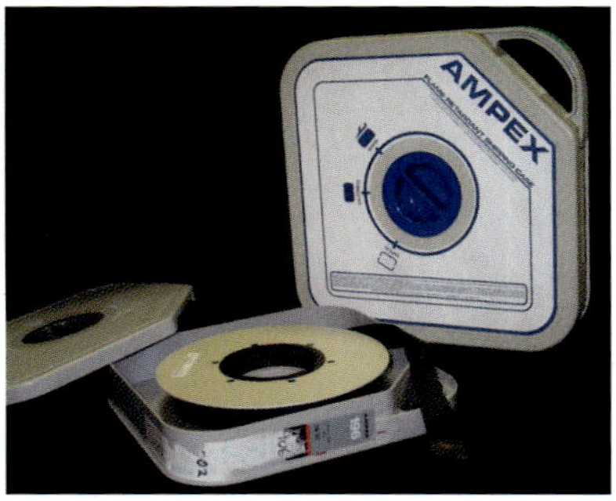

Open reel video (1")

This progressed through U-Matic, a 3/4" wide tape in cassette housing to 1" video by the early 1990s in Australia. Both 1" and 2" are open-reel tapes with no protective cassette enclosure.

The first portable video recording system, the reel-to-reel Portapak, enabled location recording on 1" and 1/2" video tape. In the main, the open-reel formats were used with studio cameras in very controlled environments, or were created by editors for broadcast. 1" was a default standard for broadcast until the mid 1990s, when it started to be replaced by Digital Betacam.

Decoding video tape names and acronyms

Betamax, Betacam SP, Digital Betacam: proprietry name, often referred to as beta

U-matic:	proprietry name, high band, low band, SP (superior performance)
VHS:	Video Home System
SVHS:	super VHS with an extra 'track' used for timecode
Hi8:	first of the small format tapes
DV, miniDV:	mini digital video tape, many manufacturers
DVCam:	proprietary format, small format
DVCPro:	proprietary format, small format.

Videocassettes

Video formats showing similar appearance in different tape types

The difference between digital video tape and digitisation

It's easy to think that once we've copied all our VHS and U-matic tapes to Digital Betacam or DVCam, we are part of the world of data, ready to make our records available on line, to store in our digital mass store. Not so. While the signal on the tape is a digital signal, it is not a data file. The signal on a video tape is dependent on tape recorders and players to play it back. It can't be accessed as a piece of computer data. There is another step to digitise the signal to a data file, making the content independent of the video tape.

Digital video tape works with an initial analogue signal received in the camera. It presumes that not all the initial signal information is necessary. It plots points across the signal where it takes snapshots, discarding the information in between. It stores these snapshots as a string of digitally encoded numbers, i.e. as a digital signal. Each digital video tape format encodes the signal in a different way. The encoding tools are built into the cameras, recorders and players. To play back the signal requires the same system that recorded it (or one in the same family. There is some compatibility, for instance DVCPro will replay DVCam and MiniDV).

Data files no longer depend on the encodings of a particular camera, recorder or player. Their encodings are independent of recorders and players. Instead, the files are now dependent upon a particular piece of computer software for replay. A familiar example of this is capturing movies using mobile phones or still cameras. These are data files that replay independently of the phone or camera that recorded them.

Digital video tapes can of course be subject to this next step and turned into data, or 'digitised'. Here the video tape signal goes through the encoding process, sampling the signal to create a data file. Typically, encoding is followed by a compression process which uses rules or algorithms to discard what is deemed unnecessary information in the signal.

Between professional and consumer

Digital technology and the ever-increasing power of desktop computers has blurred the boundary between professional and domestic production with the expansion of the 'prosumer' sector. The term is derived from a contraction of the words 'professional' and 'consumer'. Prosumer technology emulates expensive systems targeted at professionals at prices affordable to upper-end consumers. Prosumer equipment makes professional production paths available to the low budget sector – training and education films, corporate videos and independent film making.

Prosumer analogue formats like Hi8, and SVHS opened the door initially. Prosumer digital formats like miniDV, DVCPro and DVCam reflect an increasing democratisation in video production, away from the artisanal specialists of the film industry, and technical specialists of the television industry. This new-found accessibility draws on digital's ability to duplicate without loss of picture quality, combined with affordable desktop post-production. Many of these prosumer formats take advantage of the development of metal particle and metal evaporated magnetic tapes. These capture a large volume of information on a small surface area, hence the comparatively small size of DVCPro and the other formats. This technology is also used in computer data tapes.

To summarise, video tape appears in a number of formats. Since its introduction as a commercial format in 1956, it has been a continually evolving technology. Thus, there are a number of video formats that are no longer in use.

Video and film working together

Video and film production are often interwoven. A typical industry production path, still in use, is to shoot on film and transfer to video, a process known as telecine. The video tapes produced by the telecine are then treated on par with the camera tapes or 'rushes'. They are copied, or 'dubbed' with the timecode carried over from the camera tape or ingested into a digital editing system with the timecode attached. This process results in multiple generations. You may find material marked rushes, sub-master, master, or dub.

Once the film has been telecined to video (or theoretically, straight to data files), from there, all the decision-making happens on video (or electronically). In film, the digital intermediate process means the whole production is completed to video. The very last step is to scan out to motion picture film for cinema projection. Where cinemas are equipped with digital projectors, the scan-out step can be skipped. This is the model of digital cinema, a distribution model much discussed in the past five years (Watson 2007).

The amateur production path

As noted before, the amateur production path is a scaled-down version of this process. The footage will be shot in a camera. Typically the formats most likely to be used are VHS, Hi8, MiniDV, DVD, or increasingly, hard disc. The film may then be put to use or sent straight to the archives. Alternatively, it may be migrated to a computer and edited. It will typically then be output to another carrier such as DVD or miniDV for screening or access or published on line.

What is a generation?

This describes how far away from the camera original material a particular component is. For instance, a VHS of a betacam SP tape may be three generations away from the original. In film and video the term 'generation' reflects the use of duplication and copying in the production process.

First generation	• camera tapes • telecine transfer tapes (where film is transferred to video).
Second generation	• off-line edit (used in era before digital editing) • on-line edit sub-master • on-line edit final master if no sub-master.
Third generation	• on-line edit final master if sub-master • dub (copy of final master).
Fourth generation	• dub if sub-master used (copy of final master).

Table 18.2: Duplication and copying in the production process

Recap of video variables

Formats

- Open reel tape formats: 2", 1" and 1/2" (rare)
- Cassette formats: analogue Betacam SP, 3/4" U-matic (hi-band, low band) , VHS, SVHS, Hi8, Digital Betacam, Betamax.
- Small cassette formats: mini DV, DVCam, DVCPro.

Generations

- rushes
- off-line edit
- on-line edit
- sub-master
- master
- dub

Open reel video tape

Sound variables

Video carries sound as well as image. It can carry several tracks of sound.

These multiple tracks are used for several purposes. One is to carry stereo or surround sound to accompany the image. Video tape labels may carry information about these tracks:

- mono (single track)
- stereo (two tracks)
- 5.1, surround (five tracks and low-frequency track)
- Video can also carry components for the final sound track: the dialogue tracks, the music tracks, the music and effects mixed together and the final mix itself. These tapes may be labelled:
  - 2 track, 4 track
  - final mix, music and effects (M&E).

Aspect ratio

This describes the dimensions of the image. A familiar example of this is found in recent developments in television screens, where before we watched television in 4:3, with the images slightly wider than they were high. Now we are replacing these with wide-screen television sets where the screen dimension is almost twice as wide as it is high at 16:9.

Regional television standards

- PAL 25 frames per second, 50 Hz, established in UK, used in Australia and most Commonwealth countries, Europe.
- NTSC 30 frames per second (precisely 29.7), 60 Hz, established in USA, also used in Japan
- SECAM 25 frames per second, established and used in France

Optical discs

Optical discs are described in the previous chapter, so we will not repeat that information here. However, we do need to note that while DVD appears to be an improvement on VHS quality, the lifespan of this optical media is relatively short. The risks to it from delamination, oxidation of the recording layer and scratching and marks on the surface are high (Byers 2003).

Data formats

A fourth area of consideration for moving image records is the data file. Moving images and sound are increasingly created as or copied to data files. These are electronic records, dependent on the correct mix of hardware and software to 'perform' them, with the same problem of obsolescence and requirements for persistent metadata as other digital records.

Mobile phones, digital stills cameras, and some video cameras record data. The data itself is stored on a wide range of portable media – CD, DVD, USBs (memory sticks, flash drives), portable hard drives, compact flash cards (CF cards) and Secure Digital flash memory cards (SD cards). The latter card types are used in digital cameras, digital audio recorders and mobile phones. This list demonstrates the breadth of formats. Four technologies are employed in this list alone – optical disc recording, flash and solid state memory (two different storage systems with no moving parts) and magnetic media in the coated spinning disks of the hard drive.

This points to another important distinction introduced by data, the separation between the capture system and the storage system at the moment of capture.

The point of difference for data files from film and video is that there is no intrinsic carrier to the data file. As we've seen, they can be recorded to a wide range of media. With appropriate software, they can also be played out to a wide variety of formats, including motion picture film and video. A typical Hollywood process is to scan motion picture film to data to add computer animation, scanning it back out to film on completion. A typical big-budget television production process is to telecine film to video, digitise the video to data, add computer animation and play back out to video.

The key challenge with moving images as data is the large file sizes and the high computing speed required to 'perform' the recording. The finer the quality, the bigger the file. File sizes that seek to replicate motion picture film or high-end video tape are very large as these formats capture vast amounts of picture information.

The solution to the problem of too much data is compression. Essentially, compression is the re-encoding of data to decrease its volume. Compression is applied to both data files and almost all video formats to varying degrees.

For moving images on DVD and on the internet, compression is pivotal. There is little consistency in the compression systems employed, although in professional production the MPEG-2 system is a default standard. MPEG is an acronym for Moving Picture Experts Group, whose work is involved with setting standards for the creation and distribution of media in digital environments. MPEG-4 is used in portable video players and on the internet, MPEG-21 for multi media. Further reading points to some MPEG resources.

In essence, the compression process involves analysing the picture information that makes up each frame, looking for inessential or repeating information. It culls this information which reduces the overall size of the file, resulting in a moving image that aims to have little perceptible difference from its uncompressed state. The great leap forward presented by DVDs for movie fans is that the storage capacity is big enough to hold a file that keeps its compression for the most part undetectable.

There are two types of compression, 'lossless' and 'lossy'. Lossless compression reduces picture information for storage but is able to re-perform all of that information when the file is retrieved. This is a concept we are familiar with from zipped files used in still image production and in design and publishing applications. In lossy compression, a significant amount of unrecoverable information is lost. It trades off better quality for smaller file size.

The data can be output to a range of formats. CDs and DVDs are common carriers. Small-gauge magnetic tapes have been used widely for holding data , for example in Hi8 tapes and DA-88 tapes. Magnetic tape has been widely used for data capture. For individual productions, Hi8 and DA-88 are two formats that have been used to capture sound for moving image productions.

Data files are playing a significant role in the area of access to moving images in archives. From an access perspective, the great advantage of the data file is the ability to modify it for different uses with relative ease and economy, for instance to make small, heavily compressed files for web publication. This malleability is also part of the risks of data, as changes can be imperceptible, raising ethical issues for preservation and custodianship of the record in general.

Lossless, lossy video compression

- Motion JPEG — Lossy
- JPEG 2000 — Either lossy or lossless
- MPEG-1 — Lossy
- MPEG-2 — Lossy
- MPEG-4 — Lossy
- H.264 (MPEG-4 AVC) — Lossy

Common moving image media containers or file types

- .avi — Audio Video Interleave File
- .mov — Apple QuickTime Movie
- .mp4 — MPEG-4 Video File
- .mpg — MPEG Video File
- .qt — Apple QuickTime Movie
- .rma — RealMedia
- .swf — Macromedia Flash Movie
- .wma — Windows Media Video
- .dv — Digital Video Encoding (DV, DVCAM, DVCPRO)
- .vob — DVD Video Object

The information for this table is sourced from the Library of Congress Digital Formats website (2004) and the *NINCH guide to good practice in the digital representation and management of cultural heritage materials.*

Preservation

Moving image preservation and access are intertwined

For all records, preservation and access are interdependent. We preserve in order to use, we use and appreciate records and therefore we wish to preserve them. The ways in which you plan to give access need to be considered as part of the decisions around preservation. This is of particular significance with moving images for two reasons: records may be too fragile to withstand more than one preservation treatment; and the preservation treatments are resource intensive.

The mindsets of the two activities are different. In access, we want to make the material available as swiftly and efficiently as possible; in preservation, we want to make the content stable for long term use. As we have said, we preserve to show.

Considering access alone can lead to complications. For instance, you may copy to VHS to give access to the content, only to find researchers then request a higher quality format for use in a new production. It is likely that the higher quality formats would also meet your preservation requirements of capturing the properties of the original on a more stable format.

Likewise, considering preservation alone can lead to complications. Faced with an unused, deteriorating collection, it is easy for the preservation needs to overshadow access requirements. Once that preservation work is done, overlooking access presents as a major oversight. For example, preservation principles may lead to a decision to copy to a professional video tape format, to which you can't feasibly supply access.

Like all preservation work, there is no one-size-fits-all solution or quick fixes. Decisions are on a case-by-case basis and require thinking through all the implications. For instance, let's take a scenario that focuses on the re-use potential of the records. A decision evolves to copy to a quality that attempts to meet all future uses, so a professional broadcast format is selected. However, the originals are low-quality VHS. This inherent poor quality is faithfully duplicated on the high-quality dub, of little re-use value to the end users wanting to incorporate it into a new production.

From this scenario, we start to form a picture of the benefits of applying preservation principles to decisions about how to give access. In our VHS scenario, preservation principles would guide us to select a format that maintains the properties of the original. We may choose to preserve straight to digital files with access over the web as copying our VHS originals to Digital Betacam does not have benefits for either preservation or access.

We also start to form a picture of the benefits of understanding your formats – how and why they were created along with their physical characteristics.

Key principles in preservation

There are some important first principles in preservation, asserted in Chapter 4: *Preservation* and Chapter 17: *Sound Recordings*:

- first do no harm
- apply treatments that can be reversed

First 'do no harm' is at the heart of the access-preservation relationship – where access compromises long-term usability it is difficult to characterise access as reasonable and responsible. The do-no-harm principle also raises an ethical dimension. In some instances, to do nothing is to ensure the loss of the content. However, duplication may mean the original object is damaged or lost in the process. For example, it may be possible to transfer extremely brittle film just once, as during transfer it becomes damaged beyond further use. The content survives and becomes accessible however.

From a materials conservation perspective, a first principle of 'do no harm' often relates to storage. In general, the cooler and drier the environment, the better for long-term preservation, however there are limitations in the combination of cool and dry for photographic materials. The gelatin emulsion can become stressed under the wrong combination (McCormick-Goodhart 1996).

Ethics are another crucial aspect to preservation:

- treatments must be documented
- the distinction between restoration and preservation must be observed

The preservation principles laid out in Chapter 17: *Sound Recordings* are a useful snapshot:

- acquire or capture the best attainable copy and format
- retain originals in safe, secure and sustainable storage environments. This includes ensuring digital records are stored in sustainable digital repositories.
- maintain the integrity of original items
- copy items without loss or alteration of content
- do no harm
- record and retain all necessary descriptive information, provenance, supporting documentation and metadata
- ensure safe access to collection and its content into the future

A note on long-term storage

Standards issued by the International Standards Organisation (ISO) in the past decade talk about storage conditions in the language of short-term, medium-term and long-term. They are defined as 5-10 years, 10-25 years and greater than 25 years. A key research centre for photographic conservation, therefore motion picture film, is the Image Permanence Institute in Rochester, New York. Research scientists there have extensively investigated impacts of cold and dry conditions on various aspects of photographic deterioration, and impacts of time out of these conditions. For an overview of the storage requirements of various moving image media, both film-base and magnetic-base, we suggest you refer to the Further Reading.

Preservation treatments are interdependent

While preservation and access are interdependent, preservation treatments themselves often depend on other treatments or workflow steps. For instance, the good work of setting up best practice conditions to store video in a reliable 8 °C and 30% relative humidity (RH) can be drastically undone by moisture condensing on the tape if the videos are taken straight out of these conditions into an office environment at 22 °C, 50% RH. As a second example, the benefits of cool and dry conditions can become superfluous if workflows mean items are constantly recalled for access.

Obsolesence and the digital panacea

As the convergence between moving image technology and the IT sector matures, more moving image will be produced as data and the content from existing carriers will be transferred over to data formats.

Standards for files for digital preservation are starting to be established. As yet, files for moving image are still not standardised, although the industry has adopted some files as default standards. For example, JPEG 2000 has been adopted for digital cinema distribution.

Once standards are fixed, and meet end-user needs, the migration merry-go-round is likely to become less frequent. It is worth noting that many of the standards relate only to the structure of the data file or to its compression specifications not to file essence, as in the case of the MPEG standards, and the MXF, AAF wrappers. The VERS standard has parallels with the wrapper systems adopted by moving image production in the past 10 years, a wrapper with metadata and various essences.

As previously stated, when it comes to preservation problems, you may need to draw upon the skills and resources of specialist film archives. However, regardless of who does the work to preserve the records, it's important to have a general understanding of the issues involved in preserving moving images.

Storage

Preservation focuses on actions that benefit collections as whole rather than individual items. Storage is a cornerstone to good preservation.

Best practice steps for storage are to:

- Focus on providing storage with controlled temperature, humidity and air quality, aiming for cool and dry. Remember that once active deterioration is occurring, controlled storage will slow deterioration but can't halt it.

- Package the items in containers that maximise the benefits of the storage environment – for example, where airflows extract vapours that result from deterioration like vinegar syndrome, use purpose-designed vented film cans.
- Store items on the shelves to minimise harm – for example, stack film cans flat (horizontally), no higher than 6-8 reels, with smooth even winds at a tension that allows some 'play' in the film pack – not loose, but not tight. For video tapes, store upright (book style) on the shelves, with an even pack wound completely to the head or tail.
- Understand the impacts of your storage arrangements on workflows. For instance, if you decide to use low tension winds on your films, moving them in this state exposes them to risk of 'cinching', where the layers of the film rub together causing irreversible marks and scratches on the film emulsion. Moving them requires special handling.

Motion picture films in rusted cans in temperature-controlled storage awaiting processing.

Surveying

Information about the condition of your collection is critical to managing it for preservation. Survey the collection to assess its condition. Typical surveys gather information about base deterioration (so for film information on colour fade, vinegar syndrome, condition of the film in the can e.g. are films on reels or cores? Are they held down with end tapes?), numbers of items per can, types of formats per can (e.g. magnetic sound tracks canned with image reels). Continue to monitor the collection to assess how conditions like vinegar syndrome and colour fade are changing. To reduce the workload for monitoring and surveying, consider using sampling techniques.

Preservation copying

Copying is an inevitable step in moving image preservation. Where ever possible, keep the original material. At the time you copy, technical or resourcing limitations may mean the copies are not able to maintain the properties of the original material. The ability to return to the originals can be significant. For example, BetacamSP dubs of original U-matics were state-of-the-art in 1992. By 1996, Digital Betacam copies captured that original signal without the loss inherent in the analogue duplication to Betacam-SP. Another classic example of the significance of retaining originals is illustrated by the mass throw-out of nitrate film that occurred after it was duplicated to 'safety' film. That safety film was acetate based and is now itself deteriorating from vinegar syndrome. Where original nitrates have been kept in good storage, they are often still able to undergo duplication and can give better results than the deteriorated acetates.

Duplication and copying of collections is time-consuming. To transfer one hour of original audio material takes three person-hours, video at least twice that (Schuller 2005, p.31), and when the administration time is taken into account, the time demands of the task become evident.

For some records, it is possible to replicate the record by duplicating the format – motion picture film for instance – although cost would rule this out in many instances. For most records however, preservation copying involves migrating the record to a new format.

Copying for preservation has three main purposes:

- to preserve the image and sound on a more stable long-term medium than that of the original material
- to provide a security copy in case of loss or damage to the original
- to provide reference and duplicating copies so that the original material is handled as little as possible.

A copying program for moving image records involves making the following kinds of copies:

- **A preservation copy**, which also serves as a security copy. The preservation copy is stored with the same care as the original material and is not used for any purpose unless absolutely necessary. With motion picture film, film-to-film duplication may be required for records considered to be of particular value, for which only a single component exists. Film duplication can create new film intermediates and prints, a costly exercise, but considered to be the most certain in terms of long-term preservation of the material. With stand-alone film productions with multiple component parts, because of the interdependency of the components, there may be a need to plug gaps in the set of components by making new film components. When copying film to video and migrating video formats, the copy should be made to the highest practicable quality.
- **A duplicating or duping copy**. This copy is used to make reference copies or to make copies for clients.
- **A reference or access copy**. This is the copy viewed by researchers. Currently, the simplest format is VHS or DVD. However, if you have equipment and sufficient excess of film prints, some researchers will welcome the option to view film-originated records on film.

If you are in a position to undertake moving image copying, think through the process carefully. Not only is it costly, but as we've said, the originals may not withstand more than a single pass. The better quality the copy, the better for the long-term preservation of the record as it is less likely to require re-copying in the event of a client wanting to incorporate the material into a new production. Also consider future requirements, i.e. high definition and/or widescreen. Furthermore, the users of the archives are unlikely to ever have the privilege of seeing the original – its values should be as accurately portrayed as possible in the copy.

Having made these different copies, it is essential to ensure that each is easily identifiable from the others. Separate copy series is one method. A colour coding system to differentiate between copies has been adopted by the principal cultural institutions in Australia. This employs red for preservation copies, green for duplicating copies, and blue for reference copies.

Damage from handling

Incorrect handling and damage during use are the other perils that moving image records face. All three formats of film, magnetic and optical media will suffer from poor or improper handling. Dropping them can cause irreversible harm. For video tapes, this can damage cassettes, in turn damaging the tape itself and potentially, replay equipment. It can also cause damage, such as creasing, to the tape itself. In motion picture film, the film is likely to rub against itself, causing scratch or cinch marks. Optical discs are sensitive to any kinds of scratching on their reflective surface, making them skip or repeat information where the scratch or mark appears. Delamination of DVDs can also be caused by dropping or other physical shock. Videos and films in particular need to be correctly packaged for transit to minimise the amount of movement within their packaging.

Apart from deterioration over time, the greatest danger both to film and video tape lies in the risk of damage during use. Both the manual handling of film and running it through equipment such as a projector or even a film viewing machine can result in scratches on the emulsion layer, damaging the image. Dirt and grease from hands can also lodge on magnetic tape, producing scratches on the oxide layer and damaging the heads of playback equipment.

Moving image carrier deterioration

This section considers the causes and effects of deterioration to the carrier of various moving image formats. Specifically it considers:

- motion picture film
- video tape
- optical discs

Motion picture film

Motion picture film consists of a plastic base substance which forms the ribbon of transparent film, either cellulose nitrate, cellulose acetate or polyester. A layer of gelatin binds the emulsion layers to the base. The emulsion layers contain the photosensitive materials where the image is physically created. All motion picture film is subject to gradual deterioration.

A key factor that determines deterioration is the make-up of the material base.
In Australia, 35mm negative film made before 1950 used a base of nitrocellulose

Vinegar syndrome deterioration

Testing for vinegar syndrome

Removing a film from a can safely

which is inherently flammable. When this trait came to prominence in the 1980s, archives adopted mass duplication of nitrate based film to a more stable base and the originals were destroyed. Since then appropriate storage strategies for this material have been developed, and, in line with our preservation principles of keeping the originals, the film should not be destroyed. However, it most certainly should not remain in its decomposing state in your collection. It is worth noting that the push in the 1980s to duplicate nitrate means it is now infrequently found in collections. It was used in Australia almost exclusively on 35mm. Usually it can be identified by the words 'Kodak Nitrate Film' printed in the side area of the film. Of course, this mark can be duplicated through from the original film to acetate duplicates. There are further tests that can be conducted to ascertain if the film is nitrate. This is a situation where the best course of action is to consult an audiovisual specialist.

Acetate film, or 'safety' film as it is also known, was developed as a response to the flammable danger of nitrate film. There are two key preservation issues with acetate film, colour fade and vinegar syndrome.

Vinegar syndrome involves the production and evaporation of acetic acid as the acetate base decomposes, causing a characteristic vinegar odour. The base softens and the layers on the film reel often adhere. This is known as blocking. The chemical reaction that causes vinegar syndrome is autocatalytic – the volatile acids the breakdown releases cause the reaction to accelerate, in other words it feeds on itself. This means it can spread in collections, speeding up decomposition in other acetate components. Separating unaffected components is an important step. Build-up of these volatile acids is considered to be a key contributor to film deterioration, so the use of loose winds on the film pack and vented film cans is recommended to promote air flow to encourage the acid vapour to disperse. This is predicated on acid scavenging filters in the air-conditioning system and sufficient air exchange to continue the dispersal out of the storage environment. Chemical reactions slow in cold temperatures, so cold conditions are considered the best way of slowing the affect of vinegar syndrome. Temperatures at 2 °C or below, with relative humidity of 30–35% percent are the current recommendation.

Testing for vinegar syndrome is a realistic undertaking for archives of all sizes. The Image Permanence Institute has developed easy-to-use acid detecting strips (A-D strips) that can be placed in film cans, with readings taken 24 hours later. These strips can provide an indicator about the level of vinegar syndrome that may be affecting acetate based items.

Prioritising copying of vinegar-affected material is the only option for long-term preservation. Pronounced shrinkage is one the major side effects it causes. The perforations in the film can become too shrunk to permit duplication that relies on sprockets. There are digital imaging options, but they come at a price.

What is a preservation wind?

In a preservation wind, the film is wound around a large sized film core (3"), just tightly enough to hold its shape on the film core, loose enough to allow some 'play' in the film pack, not a totally solid mass. This helps the acetic acid trapped in the film roll to diffuse while still providing enough support to the film to stop it from buckling (Newnham & Garvie 2003).This helps air flow around the film while still providing enough support to the film to stop it from buckling. If the film is wound onto a core, it is important that it is always supported by its can. If it must be handled out of the can, it needs to be held upright in a vertical position to avoid it falling off the core.

Polyester base now used by the film manufacturers has a far greater predicted life span than an acetate safety film base, if stored in optimal conditions. Polyester is used for duplicating and print stocks. As discussed earlier, polyester is not used in film cameras, as the delicate mechanisms are endangered by polyester's ability to tear under strain.

Motion Picture film deterioration

Chemical breakdown

Description of deterioration

- Early plastics are prone to chemical breakdown
- Nitrate film reacts with moisture, forming nitric acid, leading to eventual total decay
- Vinegar syndrome – acetate film reacts with moisture forming acetic acid. Autocatalytic process occurs – the more acetic vapour, the faster the decay, leading to eventual total decay
- Vinegar syndrome results in drastic colour fade and drastic shrinkage

What to do about it

- Chemical breakdown is active decay. Benign neglect will lead to total deterioration
- Survey using acid testing strips to find out how advanced the deterioration is. Monitor how fast it is progressing
- During examination, measure shrinkage, monitor shrinkage as this will drastically affect the ability to copy the material and the quality achievable from copies.
- Storage. Buy time with the best storage conditions you can achieve.
- Maximise the benefits of storage with good preparation of items. Wind the films with a looser wind 'preservation wind'. Use vented film cans. Where possible, use carbon scavenging filters in air conditioning to reduce build-up of acetic acid vapour.
- Prioritise for copying. Amongst the records, establish copying priorities that take into account content and state of deterioration.
- Take preventive measures for material not yet affected. Separate them from affected material. Survey their condition. If possible, copy before decay occurs as copying is easier from good condition items.
- Occupational Health and Safety – when handing vinegar-syndrome affected material, be extremely cautious. Open film cans away from the body. If possible allow the items to 'off gas' or vent before handling them. While there is no confirmed literature on health impacts from vinegar syndrome-affected material, anecdotally some people experience headaches, air passage irritation (coughing, sneezing).

Mechanical breakdown

Description of damage

- Damage from equipment
- Damage in handling, marks and scratches, adds 'blobs' in the image
- Tears require repair which can lead to loss of focus on replay and/or inability to replay
- Poor winds that leave strands of film vulnerable from the reel (popped strands)
- Poor transit handling – dropped items result in scratches, marks.

What to do about it

- This is inactive decay but irreversible. Once the mark is there it can be minimised but not removed.
- Training in safe handling – do not touch image area, always support films on cores with film cans to avoid film falling off core.
- Maintain equipment, training in proper use of equipment.
- Establishing and following good work processes is the best way to minimise the occurrence of mechanical damage

Photographic deterioration

Description of deterioration

- Colour fade
- Silver deterioration
- Reaction of coatings applied to film with other treatments
- Mould (also known as biological decay)

What to do about it

- Photographic deterioration is active, benign neglect will result in eventual catastrophic loss
- Colour fade – colour film goes from magenta colour caste to monochrome. Usually accompanies vinegar syndrome. Coldest feasible storage down to sub-zero temperatures are the best treatment.
- Silver deterioration leads to changes in density in the image, fading of the image which means it will no longer reproduce as intended. Pollutants in the environment are a known contributor so controlled air quality in storage environment assists.
- Unknown coatings and lubricants applied to film prints, like the coating Permanew, are not visible to the eye but can cause irreversible damage through contact with solvents like ultra-sonic film cleaning liquid. These can cause active decay by speeding up other deterioration processes. Test all film.

- Mould can permanently deform the emulsion. Inspect films. Handle with extreme caution as some moulds pose OH&S risks. Vacuum with special filter, clean with solvents (ethanol, perchloroethylene), preferably under a fume hood. This requires specialist advice and intervention.

Obsolete technology

Description of deterioration

- This is an issue with some early gauges e.g. 9.5mm, standard 8mm. Technology to replay becomes difficult to source, impacting on viewing and copying options.

What to do about it

- Plan to copy. As technological development in motion picture film has been limited compared with video, suppliers can be sourced for most formats. Both 9.5 and standard 8 can currently be copied in Australia.

Table 18.3: Motion Picture film deterioration

Video tape

Video is made up of a base support layer, binder and a signal layer.

A key deterioration problem for video is in the binder between the signal and base layers. In some formulations, the binder layer reacts with moisture in the air, a reaction known as hydrolysis. This causes the binder to break down and exude moisture into the tape pack making the tape stick over the replay heads, a problem known as sticky shed.

The polyester base layer has a magnetic metal coating that carries the signal. In some formats, the coating is incorporated into a binder, in others the metal particles sit directly on the base. As video deteriorates, the coating begins to shed, resulting in interference or loss of information in the signal. The condition known as shedding occurs when the binder begins to deteriorate, flaking off.

The polyester base can be damaged by uneven winding, creases in the tape or stretching the tape. Strong magnetic fields in close range can damage tapes by interfering with the magnetic signal. Apart from damage and deterioration, the most important consideration for video is format obsolescence. Generally, the evolution of video has been towards products of improved quality, although some formats like metal evaporative tape were notoriously unstable in their early developments (Gilmour 1998).

Video tape deterioration

Sticky shed syndrome

Description of deterioration

- Binder layer deterioration. Magnetic tape is made up of plastic base and binder layer that holds the metal particles. Polyester urethane was used extensively as a binder from the mid 1960s. It is particularly prone to hydrolysis where it reacts with moisture in the air causing it to break down. This results in a gummy substance that clogs playback machines. It can result in a tape pack that is completely 'blocked', where the tape pack has formed one solid entity.

What to do about it

- This is active decay, once detected tapes should be copied as soon as possible
- Store tapes in cool and dry conditions as warm temperatures and high humidity encourages hydrolysis
- If playback machines clog, clean the tape heads immediately with isopropyl alcohol on cotton buds
- If the tapes are blocked, there is little that can be done. In Australia, the NFSA has an experimental de-blocking technique that relied on specially modified equipment.
- Specialist treatments can be performed by or in conjunction with AV specialists. These include cleaning the tape with a tape cleaning machine. 'Baking' or drying out the tapes by exposing them to a low humidity environment over an extended period.

Shedding magnetic coating

Description of deterioration

- Magnetic layer of tape shedding. A brown dust the colour of the oxide layer is evident on the tape housing or case. This has been observed on U-Matic tapes, sprocketed magnetic tracks and occasionally on 1/4" tapes. Sprocketed magnetic tracks on acetate base are particularly prone, where it is found where vinegar syndrome is occurring.

What to do about it

- This is active decay, once detected tapes should be copied as soon as possible
- If playback machines clog, seek specialist advice on how to clean the tape heads. This should be done as soon as practicable.
- Observe careful OH&S practice, wear gloves, goggles
- Copy as soon as possible.

Poor playback signal

Description of deterioration

- Video signal is very low quality, image is not sharp, colour is not true
- Image moves around on screen

What to do about it

- Clean tape guides/heads
- Check formats for compatibility, e.g. SVHS played back in VHS player
- Seek specialist advice. They may be able to adjust playback tension on machines or use a time-base corrector or other video processor may correct the problem

Demagnetisation

Description of deterioration

- Erasure of signal on tape

What to do about it

- This is a rare problem. It requires a very strong magnetic field to interfere with the signal for instance a transformer in an elevator motor. However, accidental erasure by pressing record on playback machines is a factor. Disabling the record function on access equipment is recommended.

Edge damage or warped tape

Description of deterioration

- Warping or stretching of tape

What to do about it

- Store tapes upright on shelves supported by cases with hubs.
- Ensure there are no 'popped strands' in the tape wind (exposed pieces of tape sticking up out of the tape pack)
- Avoid touching the tape
- Rewind tapes completely to head (start of tape) or tail (end of tape)

Table 18.4: Video tape deterioration

Optical discs

Physically, optical discs are a moulded plastic base that carries information as a series of tiny depressions, covered by a thin layer of reflective metal, usually aluminium. The preservation problems with optical discs arise from scratches, marks or grease on the reflective surface and from problems with the final plastic coating pulling away from the metal layers. Optical discs benefit from storage in temperatures between 18–20 °C with relative humidities between 45–50%.

The status of DVDs as an archival medium is in question. Certainly, industry is attempting to set standards to create DVDs with an anticipated life span of 30 to 50 years.

Optical disc deterioration

CDs, DVDs deterioration

Description of deterioration

- Oxidisation of metal layer. Optical discs are a reflective metal layer sandwiched between plastic layers. If the metal layer oxidises, this affects the ability to replay. Oxidisation can occur if the plastic layers delaminate or become porous. The metal layer sits beneath the top label so the use of soft pens and inks that do not affect the plastic are recommended to protect the metal layer.
- Scratches and marks on the base. Optical discs have a certain error correction ability which enables them to compensate for some loss of information. Usually visible scratches and marks exceed this.

What to do about it

- Avoid exposing the metal layer by reducing the chance of delamination by cool and dry storage
- Use only purpose designed soft pens with non-permeable ink on labels
- Keep out of direct sunlight, as this can contribute to delamination and can affect the dye layer in record-once media.
- Avoid scratches and marks on base.

Table 18.5: Optical disc deterioration

Access to moving images

As is the case with most archival media, providing access to moving images means providing a service at two fundamental levels: enabling the researcher to view the material and enabling the client to use selected material in a film, video or broadcast production.

VHS video or DVD are efficient forms of access to moving image records that can be easily accommodated in the reading room. Be aware that the trend in access to moving images is over the internet. If a researcher wants to use your moving images as stock footage for inclusion in a film or television production, your access copies probably won't be suitable quality. It's at this point that the value of high quality copying becomes apparent. Ideally the quality of the duping copy is sufficient to meet your clients' needs and there is no need for access to the preservation or original materials.

The archivist needs to be familiar with the application of the *Copyright Act 1968* as it applies to moving images. A rule of thumb is that intellectual property remains under copyright for 70 years after the death of the copyright holder. In the case of moving image productions, they are under copyright for 70 years from their first date of broadcast or the year in which they were made (IP Australia 2008). Bear in mind that there may well be several copyright holders for the single production, i.e. copyright for the production as a whole and separately for the script and the music. Furthermore, new contracts or at least permission may be required to use the images of people or places depicted. Actors are likely to be covered by contracts. We discussed cultural sensitivity earlier in the chapter – moral rights are an important factor here. Often re-use of archival moving images puts them to a purpose entirely different from that for which they were created. The moral rights aspects to copyright are significant here. The creators of the original work can continue to have a legal moral right in how that work is used in the future. Chapter 11: *Access & Reference Services* provides more information on copyright.

Summary

This chapter provides archivists with some of the technical and practical tools required to appraise, describe, preserve and make film and video formats accessible. With the increasing use of moving image technologies in business processes and daily communication, they are now found in all kinds of archival collections. This chapter aims to make the archivist and cultural institution practitioner familiar with the technical standards, production paths, deterioration mechanisms, format obsolescence and the language of film and video. An understanding of these issues gives confidence in the appraisal, intellectual control and preservation of these records. Knowing the characteristics of this media facilitates strategic preservation and access strategies. Like other audiovisual media, video formats are vulnerable to physical and chemical damage and subject to format obsolescence. An understanding of digital formats and file standards is necessary to allow informed preservation, intellectual control and migration.

biographies

Jackie Bettington

Chapters 1 & 5

Jackie Bettington is Principal Consultant with Corporate Information Management Services and has over 15 years experience working in various records and archives related roles in NSW, the ACT and Queensland. Her experience has included working in all archival areas in business archives, government agency archives and Queensland State Archives. She has a particular interest in strategic recordkeeping issues, appraisal and disposal, recordkeeping metadata, public history and archival education. Since the early 1990s, Jackie has been an active member of the ASA within the NSW and Queensland Branches, and at a national level as a member of ASA Council, from 2002–2006. Jackie is currently Vice President of the ASA. She holds a Post-graduate Diploma in Information Management (Archives Administration), Diploma of Education, a Master of Letters (Public History) and Masters Degree in Business Administration with concentrations in strategy and corporate governance. Jackie is a professional member of the Australian Society of Archivists, Records Management Association of Australasia and the Australian Library and Information Association.

Peter Crush

Chapter 6

Peter Crush began working with the Commonwealth Archives Office in January 1970. In July 1978 he became the first full-time professional archivist employed by the Adelaide City Council, where he established the Adelaide City Archives, administered the City of Adelaide Oral History Project and developed the City of Adelaide Civic Collection and an internal technical/special library for the Corporation. In 1989 he also became responsible for the Corporation's current records management. In June 2000 he left the Council to begin his existing consulting business in Archives and Recordkeeping. He was recently appointed to the State Records Council of South Australia.

As an active member of the Australian Society of Archivists since its establishment in 1975, Peter has served as a member and President of the ASA Council and is currently Treasurer of the SA Branch of the ASA, member of the ASA Education and Professional Development Committee and Convenor of the Accreditation Sub-committee. Peter holds the Library Association of Australia Registration Certificate in Librarianship specialising in archives administration, a Bachelor of Arts degree and a Masters Degree in Management Information Systems.

Louise Curham

Chapters 17 & 18

Louise Curham trained as a film maker (Swinburne, VCA School of Film and Television 1991–1993). During the 1990s, she undertook commissions from the AFC and the ABC and directed several award-winning dance films. Other early professional experience was as a television commercials producer.

Louise became involved in archives in 2001 when she began working with Sydney archivist Dr. Peter Orlovich to complete a study in managing local government archives. From 2002 until 2007, Louise worked in film preservation at the National Archives of Australia. During this time, she undertook the preservation of significant ABC TV productions and early Commonwealth Film Unit films.

In Sydney, Louise presents film events and screenings as the co-curator of the Teaching and Learning Cinema. Louise maintains her involvement in audiovisual preservation through Media Archaeology, media archiving for the arts and humanities. Currently, Louise works as the records manager at the Australian National Maritime Museum.

Louise holds a Masters Degree in Fine Arts for a research project on Expanded Cinema and a Graduate Certificate in Audiovisual Archiving through Charles Sturt University.

Lisa Darnell

Chapter 12

Lisa Darnell works for BHP Billiton Archives as a Senior Archivist. She has an interest in e-permanence and the impact and opportunities of advancing technologies for archives and access. Lisa holds a Bachelor of Arts/Bachelor of Information Management and Graduate Diploma in Information Services and Systems.

Kim Eberhard

Chapters 1, 2 & 16

Kim Eberhard has worked in the private sector for most of her archival career, with wide experience in recordkeeping and archival administration in 'small archives', especially those of business, independent schools and community organisations. She has also worked in local government and at State Records NSW. She is the co-author of the Records Retention Schedule for Non-Government Schools. Kim has developed and delivered a number of seminars and workshops on archival issues and practicalities, many aimed at helping those just starting out or establishing archives for the first time. Kim has been a member of the ASA Council since 2004, and President from 2006–2008. She holds a bachelor degree in Communications (Journalism and Public Relations) and a Master of Information Management (Archives / Records).

Cassandra Findlay

Chapter 15

Cassandra Findlay works for State Records NSW, where she has been responsible for recordkeeping guidance and training programs and for digital records strategy. She has been the Secretary of the International Council on Archives' Committee on Appraisal, Convenor of the Australian Society of Archivists' Electronic Records Special Interest Group and Secretary of the Mander Jones Awards Judging Committee. Cassandra was the guest editor of the May 2003 issue of the Australian Society of Archivists' journal, Archives and Manuscripts. Cassandra holds a Bachelor of Arts Degree and a Master of Information Management – Archives / Records.

Robyn Gamble

Chapters 17 & 18

Robyn Gamble is an Assistant Director of Audiovisual Preservation at the National Archives of Australia. She has worked in the Preservation Section since 1989. Based primarily in the Sydney office, she has been responsible for managing the preservation of the paper, photographic and audiovisual collection. Since 2001, Robyn has worked predominately in audiovisual preservation. She is currently responsible for writing and implementing an overall strategy for audiovisual records held by the Archives. Robyn holds a Bachelor of Applied Science in the Conservation of Cultural Materials (specialising in Paper Conservation) and a Postgraduate Certificate in Photographic Conservation.

Elizabeth Hadlow

Chapter 4

Elizabeth Hadlow is currently Senior Conservator with the State Records NSW. Since commencing work with State Records, she has developed a good working knowledge of both large archives and the particular problems facing archivists and record managers within smaller organisations and agencies. Previously she worked with the National Archives of Australia, the Powerhouse Museum and International Conservation Services (ICS). While working with ICS, Elizabeth gained a great deal of experience with working on an enormous variety of collection types, including wallpapers and painted surfaces in heritage buildings. In 1994 Elizabeth was appointed Paper Conservator at the Australian National Maritime Museum. While in this role, she acquired expertise in exhibition conservation, as well as further extending her knowledge of paper conservation. She was later appointed Senior Paper and Photographic conservator with the Museum.

Elizabeth was awarded a Churchill Fellowship in 2003 to study at the Centre for Photographic Conservation in London, as well as visit numerous collecting institutions throughout the United Kingdom, including the National Archives of Scotland, the National Archives Kew and the National Screen and Sound Archive of Wales. Elizabeth is President of the NSW Division of the Australian Institute for the Conservation of Cultural Materials. Elizabeth holds a Bachelor of Applied Science in Conservation of Cultural Materials.

Jenni Jeremy

Chapter 11

Jenni Jeremy is the Foundation Librarian and Manager of the Bob Hawke Prime Ministerial Library at the University of South Australia. In this role, she has developed a significant national collection of resources in all formats relating to former Prime Minister Bob Hawke and to the Hawke era of government, including a reference and access service and the delivery of public programs. As the Bob Hawke Prime Ministerial Librarian, Jenni has convened four national conferences relating to issues associated with person-specific and gender-based archival and library collections. Jenni also lectures part time to TAFE Library Studies students in acquisitions, preservation, selection, and access and collection development.

Previously, Jenni was the Serials Librarian at the University of South Australia, managing an acquisitions budget and ten staff providing journal resources to the University Library. Jenni maintains a professional interest in political history, archives and acquisitions in libraries and archives. She holds an Advance Diploma in Library Tech, a Bachelor's Degree in Library and Information Management and Certificate IV in Workplace Training. Jenni is a professional member of the Australian Society of Archivists and an associate of the Australian Library and Information Association.

Lyall Kupke

Chapter 11

Lyall Kupke is the archivist at the Lutheran Archives in Adelaide, where he manages the historical records of the Lutheran Church of Australia and the earlier Lutheran churches in Australia. He is a member of the committee of the Friends of South Australia's Archives, and the convenor of the Religious Archives Group in South Australia. Lyall holds a Graduate Diploma in Archives and Records Management.

Ted Ling

Chapter 3

Ted Ling formerly worked for the National Archives of Australia, and was with the Archives for 31 years, working in a number of national and state programs, including six years with the Archives' Facilities Program, which is where he acquired his interest in archive buildings—how they are designed, built and managed. He has written a number of books and journal articles on the subject including: Guidelines for Mobile Shelving for Archives, Libraries and Museums (1997); and Solid, Safe, Secure: Building Archives Repositories in Australia (1998).

Ted was also a member of the ICA's committee on Buildings and Equipment in Temperate Climates from 2000 to 2004. He has undertaken several projects on behalf of the ICA, mostly involving low cost storage facilities, including the use of shipping containers as alternative records repositories, and shelving.

Ted retired from the National Archives in June 2006 and is now a full-time student, undertaking a PhD into the pastoral industry of the Northern Territory.

In recent years, Ted has also presented a number of workshops on archive buildings at conferences in the USA and Singapore, and has most recently presented a paper as part of a conference organised by the National Archives of Korea to commemorate its new archive building at Seong-nam. He holds a BA (Hons) from the University of New South Wales, and an MA from Macquarie University.

Rowena Loo

Chapter 1

Rowena Loo works for Queensland State Archives, where she has been responsible for developing policy in many aspects of recordkeeping. She has worked in a number of government archives during her career, focusing on appraisal and recordkeeping policy, with brief stints in arrangement and description and reference. She also has a keen interest in digital recordkeeping and digital preservation. Rowena is an active member of the Queensland Branch of the Australian Society of Archivists and also represented the Society on the Standards Australia committee to develop a Knowledge Management standard. She holds an honours degree in modern history, Graduate Certificate in Records and Archives Management and Master of Arts in Information.

Lyn Milton

Chapter 8

Lyn Milton was a foundation member of The Australian Society of Archivists Inc. She was long associated with Westpac Archives, commencing in 1972 as Assistant Archivist to Pat Quinn at the then Bank of New South Wales archives, when she gained experience in both reader services and arrangement and description. When Clive Smith was appointed Chief Archivist in 1983, she came to know and love the series system. After Clive's accession to the World Bank in 1991, she became Chief Archivist. In 1994 she had a brief foray into the small archives world at Burnside (Uniting Church child and family services). Later that same year, she joined the Archives Authority of New South Wales (later State Records NSW), by far the major part of that time as Senior Archivist, Context and Documentation, where she was responsible for the implementation of the series system of archives control. After retirement in 2006, she became Company Archivist at Fairfax Media, responsible for the revival of the archives that had lain dormant for a decade (including of course the introduction of the series system.)

Ann Pederson

Chapters 9 & 14

Ann Pederson is a retired Senior Lecturer in Recordkeeping Studies at the School of Information Systems, Technology & Management (SISTM) at the University of New South Wales (1981-2000). Ann is best known for her co-authorship of the SAA manual *Archives and Manuscripts: Public Programs* (1982), the first edition of *Keeping Archives* (1987), the CD-ROM *Documenting Society* (1998-2000) and the award winning website: *Understanding Society through Its Records* <http://john.curtin.edu.au/society>. She is a fellow of the Society of American Archivists (SAA), a Distinguished Achievement Awardee of the Australian Society of Archivists (ASA) and represented Australia on the Steering Committee of the Section on Archival Education of the International Council on Archives(ICA/SAE) from 1996–2002. Now an archival consultant and educator based in Sydney, she maintains an active interest in archival education and advocacy.

David Roberts

Chapters 10 & 13

David Roberts was Director of the State Records Authority of New South Wales, the NSW Government's archives and records management authority, from 1998 to 2008. In this role, among other things, he led the development and implementation of a series system-based cataloguing, access and management system for the State archives, oversaw a major expansion of online archival services and products, and established a digitisation program. David has a long-standing interest in the application of technology to the management of archives and is the developer of Tabularium, a freeware collection management system for small archives. He has spoken and published widely on aspects of archives and records management, has served on a range of industry and professional bodies and is a Fellow of the Australian Society of Archivists. David holds a Bachelor's Degree in Arts and a Graduate Diploma in Information Management (Archives Administration).

Maggie Shapley

Chapter 7

Maggie Shapley is the University Archivist at the Australian National University in Canberra with responsibility for the University Archives, the Noel Butlin Archives Centre and the Pacific Research Archives. She previously worked at the National Archives of Australia. Her roles in the Australian Society of Archivists have included Treasurer and Council member, Convenor, Secretary and Treasurer of the ACT Branch and Editor of *Archives and Manuscripts.* She is currently a member of the management committee of the Australian Women's Archives Project and the assessment committee of the Australian Memory of the World Register. Maggie holds a Master of Arts (Honours) degree and a Postgraduate Diploma in Information Management (Archives Administration).

Clive Smith

Clive Smith has worked for the Australian Archives in Canberra, Westpac Banking Corporation in Sydney and the World Bank in Washington DC. A founding member of the Australian Society of Archivists, he has served as President and as Managing Editor. He has also been active in the ACT and NSW Branches of the Society, and in the Business Archives Special Interest Group. Now retired, he has been honorary Treasurer of the Society since 2001. He compiled the Glossary for the first edition of *Keeping Archives.* Clive holds a Bachelor of Arts Degree in Asian Studies.

Steve Stefanopoulos

Chapter 16

Steve Stefanopoulos is the Heritage Collection and Records Manager, Loreto Mandeville Hall, Toorak. Prior to this appointment he held archival positions with the Blessed Sacrament Congregation and St Francis' Church, Melbourne, De La Salle College, Malvern, and Mentone Girls' Grammar School.

He often provides professional advice to a number of schools, churches, hospitals and religious orders regarding their heritage (archive and museum) collections. He is a former Committee Member of the Victorian Branch of the ASA and currently a Committee Member of the Vic School Archives Special Interest Group of the ASA. Steve is currently Chair of the Stonnington History Committee and has been a Councillor for the City of Stonnington since 2004. Previously, he held the positions of President, Treasurer, Committee Member and Magazine Editor for the Association of Catholic Archivists (Victoria). Steve holds a Bachelors Degree in Teaching (Primary), a Graduate Diploma in Archives and Records Management, a Graduate Diploma in Planning and Design (Architectural History & Conservation) and a Graduate Diploma in Museum Studies.

Enid Woodley

Chapter 11

Enid Woodley is Assistant Director of Access and Communication in the Adelaide office of the National Archives of Australia. In this role, she manages local reference and access services for researchers, widely promoting the National Archives and the use of records in its custody. Previously, Enid worked for 12 years with the Education Department of South Australia as a teacher-librarian and community librarian in country and city schools.

glossary

Term	Definition
Access	The right, opportunity, means of finding, using, or retrieving information.
Accession	A group of records transferred at one time from the same source. May contain part of a series, or may contain one or more series.
Accessioning	1. To take legal and physical custody of a group of records or other materials and to formally document their receipt. 2. To document the transfer of records or materials in a register, database, or other log of the archive's holdings.
Acquisition	1. The terms of agreement, procedures and documentation used by archival repositories to obtain physical and legal ownership of archival material from depositors. 2. A unit of archival material that has recently been collected or acquired.
Appraisal	The process of evaluating business activities to determine which records need to be captured and how long the records need to be kept, to meet business needs, the requirements of organisational accountability and community expectations.
Archival Quality	Archival media should have certain attributes to be considered 'archival'. A high-quality archival record should display the following attributes: • Permanence, or the ability to last as long as possible • Strength and durability, or the ability to withstand use • Inherent stability, or to be relatively chemically inert and not adversely react with other materials • Continued accessibility, or the ability to be readable in future years
Archives	1. records of organisations and individuals that have been selected for indefinite retention on the basis of their continuing value for legal, administrative, financial or historical research purposes. 2. The name given to the repository in which an archival collection resides. 3. An organisation (or part of an organisation) whose main function is to select, manage, preserve and make archival records available for use. (The context of the term will usually indicate which meaning is relevant.)

Archivist A person professionally responsible for the management of archival records.

Arrangement and description The process of organising materials with respect to their provenance and original order, to protect their context and to achieve physical or intellectual control over the materials, and the process of analysing, organising, and recording details about the formal elements of a record or collection of records, such as creator, title, dates, extent, and contents, to facilitate the work's identification, management, and understanding.

Authenticity Authenticity denotes that a record is what it purports to be – it can be relied upon as representing the meaning intended by the person or organisation that made it.

Chain of custody The sequence of organisations and individuals that have had possession and/or control of an archival record.
The chain of custody of records must be proven and verified in order to satisfy any doubt about the authenticity of records.

Collecting archives An archives that collects materials from individuals, families, and organisations other than the parent organisation.

Collection management system Software that allows archives (and other collecting institutions) to manage data about the items in their collection.
Archival collection management systems are designed to capture information about the provenance of records, in addition to item information.

Conservation Restorative action to treat damaged and at risk records.
One aspect of *Preservation.*

Context The knowledge necessary to sustain a record's meaning or evidential value. Context describes the 'who, what, when, where and why' of records creation and management.

Creator The creator of the records is the person or organisation who gathered together records into a system, such as receiving correspondence and placing it on a file.
Within 'their' records there will be letters written by other people that they have received and filed, as well as drafts or copies of letters they have written and sent to others.

Custody The responsibility for the care and management of archives, based upon their physical possession. Custody does not always include legal ownership, or the right to control access to records.

Deaccessioning The process by which an archives, museum, or library permanently removes accessioned materials from its holdings.

Depositor The person or organisation transferring records to a repository. Includes 'donors'.

Digital records Records created, communicated and maintained by means of electronic or computer equipment

Disposal A range of processes associated with implementing appraisal decisions. These include the retention, deletion or destruction of records in or from recordkeeping systems. They may also include the migration or transmission of records between recordkeeping systems, and the transfer of custody or ownership of records.

Documentation Programs Documentation programs are activities to assemble documents or to capture information of historical interest for future research, to fill gaps in an archival collection or to complement the archival record.

Finding Aids Tools to guide users to the information they are seeking from or about archives, to aid access. They provide additional access points to the archival collection. Types of finding aids include registers, guides, inventories and indexes and may be in hard copy or electronic form.

Fonds See *Record group*

In-house archives An archives that holds records created or received by its parent institution.

Metadata Data describing context, content and structure of records and their management through time.
See also *recordkeeping metadata*

Original order The sequence or grouping in which archival records were originally accumulated or kept by their creator.
Maintaining the original order preserves the context of their creation and the authenticity of records. It also provides valuable evidence about the organisation and/or person who created the records.

Preservation All actions taken to retard deterioration of or prevent damage to cultural material. It involves controlling the environment and conditions of use, and may include treatment in order to maintain an object as nearly as possible in an unchanging state.
See also *Conservation.*

Processing The arrangement, description, and housing of archival materials for storage and use by patrons.

Provenance The relationships between records and the agencies or individuals that created, accumulated and/or maintained those records in the conduct of personal or corporate activities

Public Programs A formal structure and planning approach to create a coordinated body of activities that enhance all archival functions.

Record group A record group represents all the records created by a specific agency or function. It is a hierarchical arrangement that describes the creating organisation, followed by a description of the series, items and documents created and managed within this environment.

Record series A group of records which result from the same business or recordkeeping activity, have a common system of control or relate to a particular subject or function, have a similar format, or have another relationship arising out of their creation, receipt and use.

Recordkeeping Making and maintaining complete, accurate and reliable evidence of business transactions in the form of recorded information. Recordkeeping includes the following:

(a) the creation of records in the course of business activity and the means to ensure the creation of adequate records;
(b) the design, establishment and operation of recordkeeping systems; and
(c) the management of records used in business (traditionally regarded as the domain of records management) and as archives (traditionally regarded as the domain of archives administration).

Recordkeeping Metadata Data describing the context, content and structure of records and their management through time.
Structured or semi-structured information that enables the creation, management and use of records through time and across domains. Recordkeeping metadata can be used to identify, authenticate and contextualise records; and the people, processes and systems that create, manage, maintain and use them.

Recordkeeping systems Information systems that are specifically designed to capture, protect, store and manage data or documents as reliable records for as long as they are needed to satisfy business, legal, fiscal and historical requirements.

Records Information created, received and maintained as evidence and information by an organization or person in pursuance of legal obligations or in the transaction of business.

Records continuum model The whole extent of a record's existence. Refers to a consistent and coherent regime of management processes from the time of creation of records (and before creation, in the design of recordkeeping systems) through to the preservation and use of records as archives.

Records management The field of management responsible for the efficient and systematic control of the creation, receipt, maintenance, use and disposition of records, including processes for capturing and maintaining evidence of and information about business activities and transactions in the form of records.

Series See *Record series.*

Series system The series system is a method of describing records and their contexts of creation and management over time.
The key feature of the series system, and that which distinguishes it from other methods of descriptive control, its separation of record and contextual description. In practice this means that:

- Records
- The persons or organisations that create and management them, and/or
- The business they describe are each individually described as separate entities. Each of these individual descriptions is then linked to enable a full and informative representation of records, their context and their administration through time.

Acknowledgements

Australian Council of Archives. Acland, Glenda, Compiler, Glossary of Australian Usage of Archival Terminology. Discussion Edition. 1993. Canberra: Australian Council of Archives, 1994.

Australian Society of Archivists Committee on Descriptive Standards 2007, *Describing archives in context: A guide to Australian practice,* Australian Society of Archivists.

Standards Australia, AS 4390 – 1996 *Records Management*

Standards Australia, AS ISO 15489 – 2003 *Records Management*

Pearce-Moses R 2005, *A glossary of archival and records terminology,* Society of American Archivists, Chicago.

Pederson, Ann 2004 Understanding Society through its Records http://john.curtin.edu.au/society/index.html

State Records NSW 2003 *Glossary of Recordkeeping Terms.* http://www.records.nsw.gov.au/recordkeeping/glossary_of_recordkeeping_terms_4297.asp

index

Page references in bold type indicate definitions; page references in italics indicate illustrations.

A

B

C

D

E

F

R

U

V

W

X